MW01630581

GREAT ~~WOMEN~~ PAINTERS

GREAT WOMEN PAINTERS

Φ

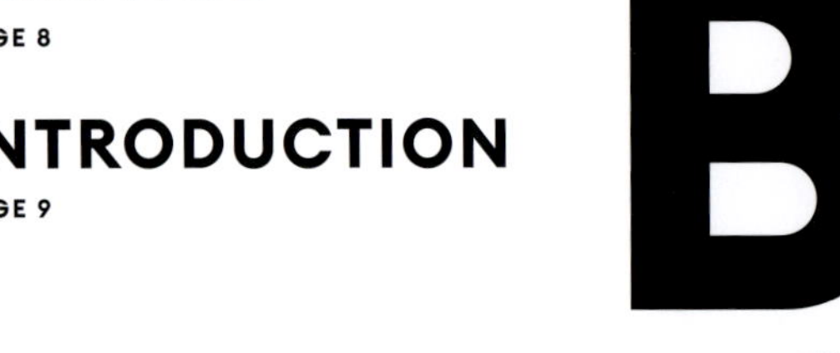

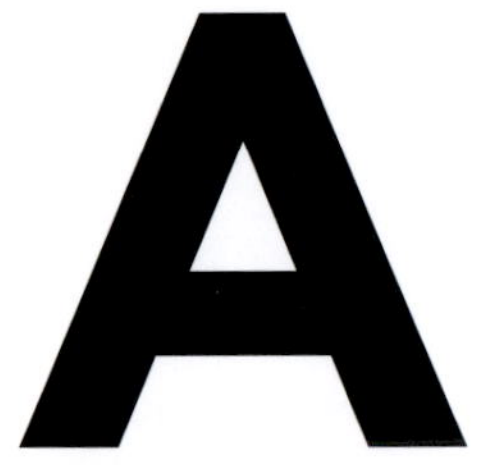

B

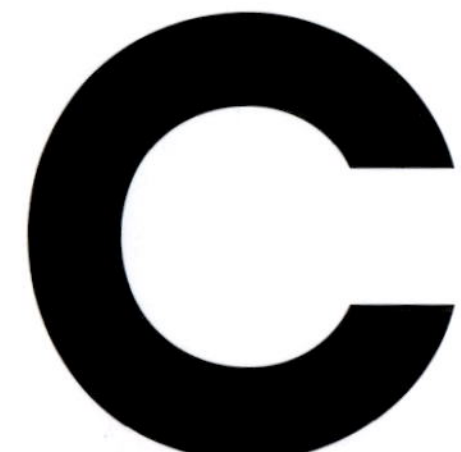

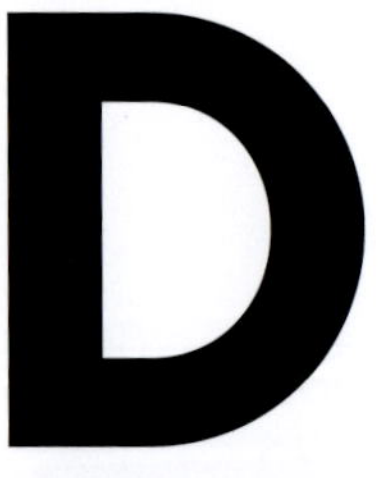

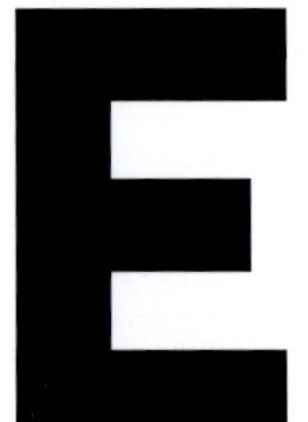

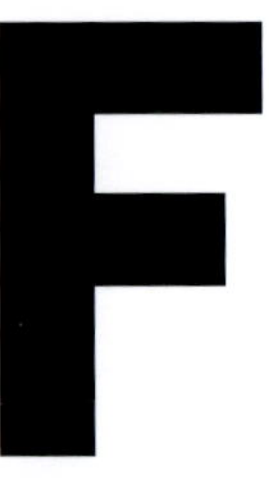

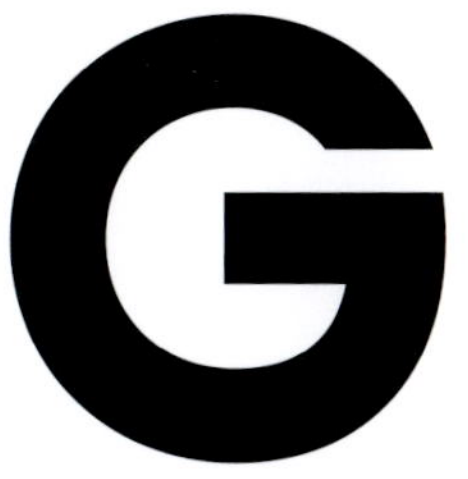

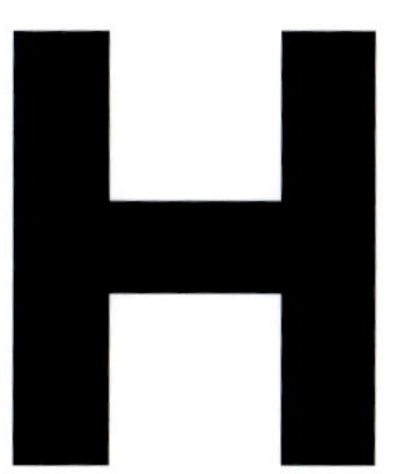

I

J

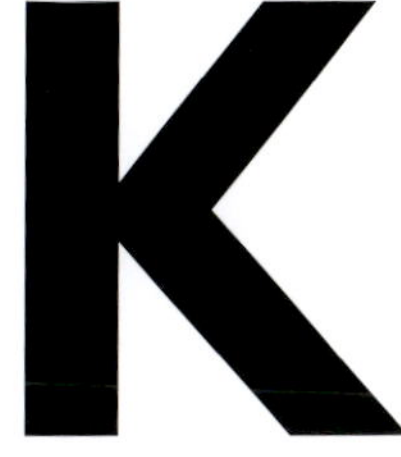

L

M

N

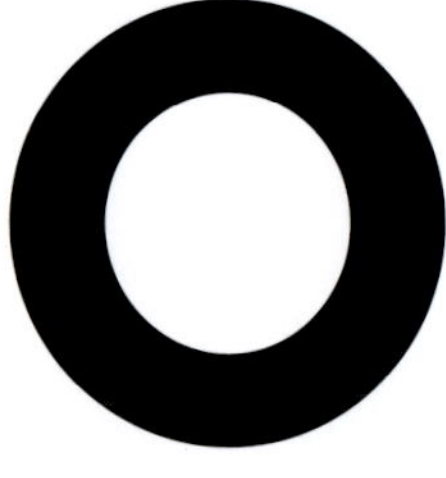

P

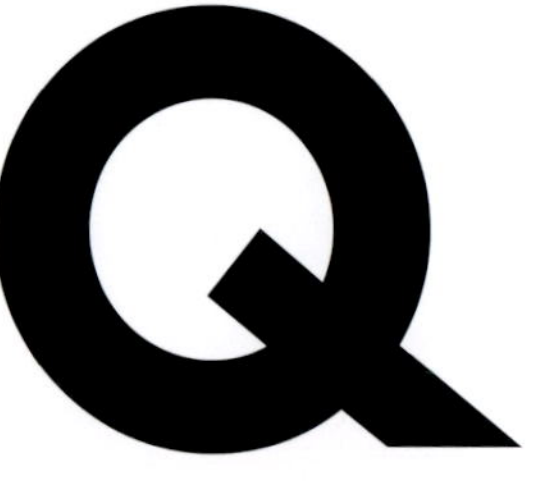

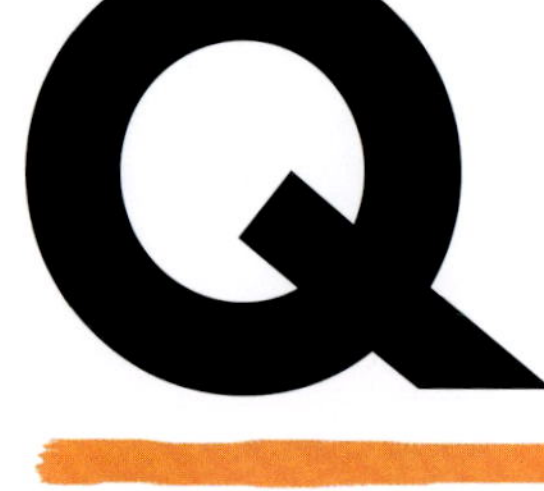

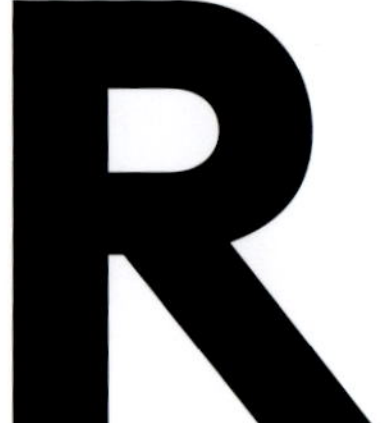

PREFACE

For their tongue-in-cheek update of Raymond Williams's seminal dictionary of culture, *Keywords* (1976), for *frieze* magazine in September 2011, Dan Fox and Jennifer Higgie defined painting as follows: 'Alive and well. Involves paint on a surface. Surprisingly straightforward, really.' In many senses, they were right. In an age where art can be anything and anything can be art, painting remains fundamentally simple and direct. It is the medium most people think of when hearing the word 'art'.

It is also the oldest art form we know. Images made in ochre pigments on cave walls in Spain have been dated as over 64,000 years old – probably made by Neanderthal hands. Yet the notion of 'painters' as named producers of specific works of art is a much more recent concept, going back only a few hundred years in those cultures where such attributions have become increasingly important markers of value.

For women artists, in particular, being a painter has long been a complicated proposition due to numerous obstacles, both practical and ideological. As Alison M. Gingeras explains in her introduction to this volume, even overcoming such challenges and achieving success and acclaim in their lifetimes did not prevent many women painters from later being written out of scholars' accounts of the history of art. And yet, despite gender-specific hurdles, throughout every era, style and movement, women have existed as experts and pioneers of painting, alongside their male counterparts.

Great ~~Women~~ Painters is a testament to these individuals. It reveals the stories of over three hundred women born in sixty different countries, working across five centuries, who have made paintings of every imaginable subject and vision. This book does not position them as the great*est* women painters – any such selection is inevitably subjective and the long list of potential names could have filled these pages many times over – but rather seeks to demonstrate a diversity of biographies, approaches and techniques of practitioners across time and geography.

Each is represented by one key work, which is intended to function as a catalyst to spark the reader's curiosity and interest. Organized alphabetically by surname, it follows the structure of Phaidon's ground-breaking 'The Art Book' series, creating juxtapositions and connections that transcend chronological limitations and offer opportunities to see artworks anew. It is also the sister volume to Phaidon's *Great ~~Women~~ Artists* (2019), with some overlap of names but a wholly different choice of artworks. Above all, *Great ~~Women~~ Painters* celebrates the persistent endurance of painting by repositioning the place of women in its history.

REBECCA MORRILL, SIMON HUNEGS AND MAIA MURPHY, EDITORS

INTRODUCTION

ALISON M. GINGERAS

LA CITÉ DES DAMES: THE NEVER-ENDING PROJECT OF FEMINIST ART HISTORY

A CALL TO HISTORY: BUILDING BLOCKS OF KNOWLEDGE AND POWER

How can the lives of women be known if men write all the books? This is the central question asked by the medieval writer Christine de Pizan (1364–*c.*1430) – the first woman to earn a living as a professional writer. Her proto-feminist manuscript *Le Livre de la Cité des Dames* (*The Book of the City of Ladies*, 1405) was the first historical account of great women throughout time. Pizan's historicizing impulse was a response to the systemic misogyny that she and other women experienced as well as the slandering of women in the literature of the French court. She proposed building an allegorical 'Cité des Dames' to house heroines and noble women whose nobility was not defined in terms of their class but by their moral character. Pizan was the first thinker who asserted the vital role of history as a means to protect and enshrine the legacies of women of the past, present *and* future.

Pizan's urgent feminist call to historiography was answered in the twentieth century by art historian Linda Nochlin. Her essay – 'Why Have There Been No Great Women Artists?' (1971) – singlehandedly launched the discipline of feminist art history. Not only did Nochlin enumerate, for the first time, the multiple systemic reasons why it was 'institutionally made impossible for women to achieve artistic "excellence"',[1] but she underscored how the very construct of greatness is rife with gender bias. In the spirit of her medieval forebear, Nochlin shone a light on the impact of generations of exclusively male tastemakers and gatekeepers who solely dictated which artists were acknowledged, sold and collected, let alone anointed as 'great'. She meticulously deconstructed the biases inherent in her titular question while underscoring the centuries' worth of misogyny inherent in received ideas around the myth of genius. By revealing the 'erroneous intellectual substructure' upon which the question of greatness is based, namely the assumption of the non-existence of women artists before the nineteenth century (ensured by the categorical denial of arts training for women in previous centuries; the revolutionary admission of women artists to art schools such as Paris's Académie Julian was poignantly immortalized in Marie Bashkirtseff's 1881 genre scene) and the dearth of women artists as a 'natural condition',[2] Nochlin paved the way for the emergence of revisionist art histories – denouncing the discipline's foundational investment celebrating the masculinist cult of individual genius. Nochlin made explicit the submerged premise of Pizan's *Cité des Dames* – the very historical construct of 'greatness' is gendered and must be countered by new histories, new research, new vocabularies, new methodologies. Passing Pizan's torch to the next generation, Nochlin created the foundational arguments for why we needed (and continue to need) books and exhibitions devoted uniquely to 'housing' our knowledge of women's achievements.

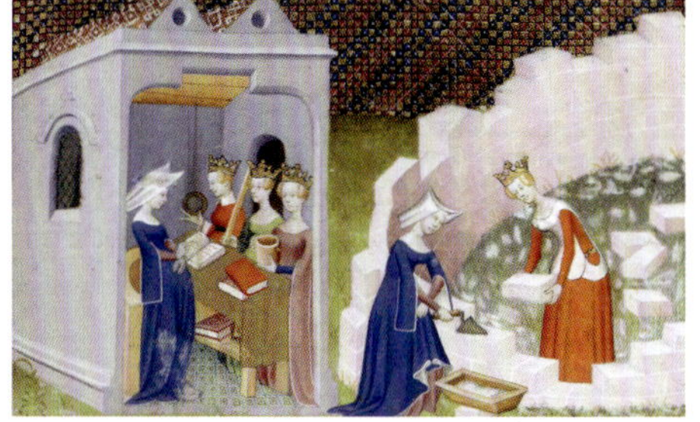

Master of the Cité des Dames, *Christine before the personifications of Reason, Rectitude and Justice and Christine with Reason building the Cité des Dames*, detail from Christine de Pizan's *Le Livre de la Cité des Dames* (*The Book of the City of Ladies*), *c.*1410–*c.*1414, vellum, British Library, London, UK

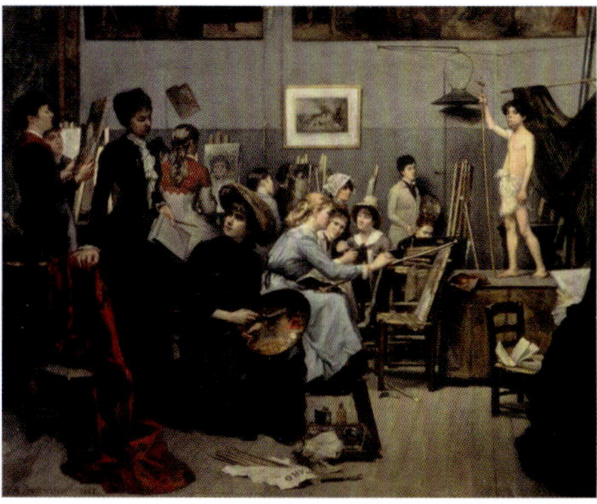

Marie Bashkirtseff, *In the Académie Julian, Paris*, 1881, oil on canvas, 154 × 188 cm (60⅝ × 74 in), Dnipropetrovsk State Art Museum, Dnipro, Ukraine

Despite these solid foundations, this art-historical wing of the *Cité des Dames* is an unfinished project; its construction must continue brick by brick, uncovering new understandings of the obscured achievements of women artists of the past while scaffolding the way for new generations. In the five decades since publishing her essay, Nochlin's now infamous question has catalysed scholarship that has cast a bright light upon female artists who have been obscured, neglected or repressed. And in recent decades, her work has inspired a younger generation to study artists beyond the traditional geopolitical confines of Europe and North America. Calling out the gender-based gaslighting at the heart of her field, Nochlin redefined the very criteria of judgement used to shape the art-historical canon – itself no longer a fixed monolith of art stars but an ever-shifting, global work in progress.

The medium of painting has dominated these renegotiations of the canon over other disciplines. Despite the heterogeneity of the arts and all the calls for abolishing old cultural hierarchies from progressive academic circles, why does painting continue to retain such primacy? In 1976, Nochlin followed up her epoch-defining essay with an exhibition that should have been entitled 'Women Painters: 1550–1950'.[3] Co-curated with Ann Sutherland Harris at the Los Angeles County Museum of Art (and then touring to the University Art Museum, Austin, Texas; Carnegie Museum of Art, Pittsburgh; and Brooklyn Museum, New York), this first-ever survey of European and North American women artists sketched out a continuum of creative power on canvas, from the Flemish portraitist Levina Teerlinc (*c.* 1520–76) to the American Surrealist Dorothea Tanning (1910–2012, p.296). In their curatorial introduction, Nochlin and Harris acknowledged their decision to limit the five-century survey to only painters, explaining that it was a methodological choice. For the sake of subject-matter consistency, their focus on a single medium allowed them to underscore the extraordinary conditions necessary to become a female painter before the mid-nineteenth century – other practices like sculpture and photography had radically different histories that would have diluted their project. Yet what their curatorial rationale left unsaid was that painting has almost always occupied the pinnacle of social cachet, economic power and cerebral heft, above other art forms in Western culture. Since the Middle Ages, painting's elitist aura has enabled its enduring commercial dominance of the art market. Oil on canvas has proved to be an easily transportable, surprisingly durable, yet precious medium, allowing for long-term conservation as well as enabling relative ease of global transactions. 'At the apex of the hierarchy of forms,' historian Isabelle Graw potently argues in her book *The Love of Painting*, 'the high status of painting is above all explained by its intellectual prestige. More than any other art form, it has a long history of theoretical exaltation.'[4] Painting, so it can be reasoned, is above all a vehicle for knowledge and power. And both knowledge and power are the very substances that we must use to fortify our *Cité des Dames*.

1 Linda Nochlin, 'Why Have There Been No Great Women Artists?', in Maura Reilly (ed.), *Women Artists: The Linda Nochlin Reader* (New York: Thames & Hudson, 2015), p.67.

2 ibid., p.65.

3 The exhibition was titled 'Women Artists: 1550–1950'.

4 Isabelle Graw, *The Love of Painting: Genealogy of a Success Medium* (Berlin: Sternberg Press, 2018), p.11.

5 Paul Chrystal, *Women in Ancient Greece* (Stroud, UK: Fonthill Media, 2017), p.115.

6 'The very term "Old Mistresses", first used by Elizabeth Broun and Ann Gabhart for an exhibition of women artists of the past in 1972, also exposed the ideological, that is to say interested, partial and exclusionary, underpinnings of language in general. There is no equivalent term of respect such as "Old Master" to designate the artist-women who made Renaissance, Baroque and subsequent art in the West. Mistress has very different overtly sexual connotations.' Griselda Pollock, 'Preface to the Bloomsbury Revelations Edition', in Rozsika Parker & Griselda Pollock, *Old Mistresses: Women, Art and Ideology* (London: Bloomsbury Academic, 2020), p.xxix.

7 Germaine Greer, *The Obstacle Race: The Fortunes of Women Painters and Their Work* (New York: Farrar Straus & Giroux, 1979), pp.14–15.

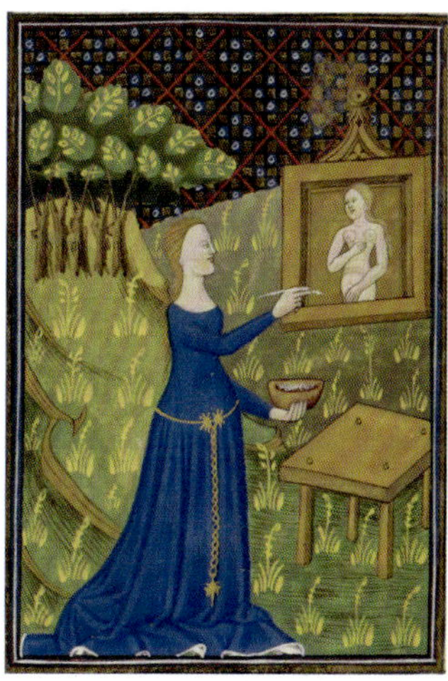

Talbot Master, *Thamyris Painting the Goddess Diana*, detail from Giovanni Boccaccio's *De Claris Mulieribus* (*Concerning Famous Women*), illuminated manuscript in an anonymous French translation, *c.*1440, vellum, British Library, London, UK

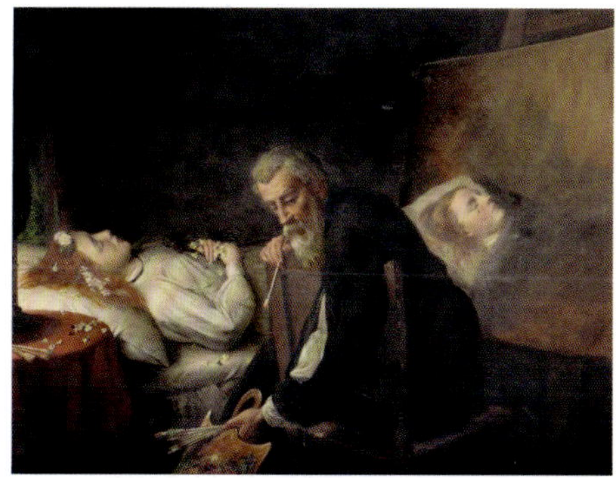

Henry Nelson O'Neil, *Tintoretto Painting His Dead Daughter*, 1873, oil on canvas, 86.5 × 110 cm (34 × 33¼ in), Wolverhampton Art Gallery, UK

IN SEARCH OF OLD MISTRESSES

So, if we accept that greatness in painting can no longer be defined in relationship to fame, fortune or perceived exceptional skill, new art histories – and volumes such as *Great ~~Women~~ Painters* – must place the medium's intellectual value as the core of its accounting of the past. As such, the urgency of creating and deepening our knowledge about women artists trumps the traditional metrics of greatness. Looking back through six centuries of visual culture, pre-modern women painters had to work against the odds, persevering despite denial of formal artistic training and membership in artistic guilds, as well as surmounting restrictions associated with their socio-economic class. The sheer triumph of being both a woman *and* an artist is an exceptional fact to be celebrated when seen through the lens of these historical and social realities. And yet, in many cases, this proof of existence is elusive, especially for the women artists of antiquity. The material record is devoid of actual examples of the work of Greco-Roman painters such as Eirene, Marcia, Aristarete, Helena of Egypt, Calypso, Iaia and Thamyris – first names only known to us by their mention in ancient accounts by Pliny and Plutarch. An illuminated miniature depicting the fifth-century BCE Thamyris from Boccaccio's book *De Claris Mulieribus* (*Concerning Famous Women*, 1361–2) is a meagre but vital emblem to remind us of the unknown number of women painters of the ancient world condemned to obscurity.

Becoming an artist was often completely dependent on the circumstance of a woman's birth. Like Thamyris, who in the words of Pliny 'scorned the duties of women, and practised her father's art',[5] most pre-modern women painters were the daughters of established artists or artisans. Many of the Italian 'Old Mistresses'[6] – an imperfect coinage adopted to avoid the 'disqualifying' term 'female old master' – trained in their fathers' studios: Lavinia Fontana (1552–1614, p.111), Artemisia Gentileschi (1593–*c.*1653, p.117) and Elisabetta Sirani (1638–65, p.277) to name a few of the most well-known examples. One of the most romanticized representations of this rare father-daughter artistic transmission is enshrined in several Victorian paintings, including by Henry Nelson O'Neil (1817–80), depicting Tintoretto (Jacopo Robusti, *c.*1518–94) painting his dead daughter's portrait. Marietta Robusti (*c.*1550/60–90, p.251), known in Venice under the feminized moniker 'Tintoretta', died during childbirth at the age of thirty. Various accounts from her lifetime report that Marietta followed her father everywhere, often dressed as a boy. His love for his daughter was so great, he did not want her taken from his sight. Despite all this lore, nearly her entire oeuvre is lost. One of the few surviving works – a self-portrait in the collection of the Uffizi Gallery in Florence – is thought to be by her hand (though its attribution is hotly debated). As Germaine Greer noted in her aptly titled meditation on women painters, *The Obstacle Race* (1979), 'Modern scholars attribute none of the work in the Tintoretto *bottega* to her, although she worked there more or less full time for fifteen years.'[7] Sadly, without attributable paintings, Tintoretta is relegated to the footnotes, forever trapped in her father's shadow.

Unlike Tintoretta, several Italian women painters from the early Renaissance through to the Baroque period achieved 'professionalization' – defined by their obtaining technical knowledge under a master artist, having their own workshop with specialized tools, acceptance into a guild and achieving legal autonomy, as well as receiving patronage or access to the art market to earn a living from their work.[8] Other Europeans like the Dutch artists Judith Leyster (1609–60, p.180) and Rachel Ruysch (1664–1750, p.254), the French painter Louise Moillon (1610–96, p.206) and the Englishwoman Mary Beale (1633–99, p.47) join their Italian counterparts as a small class of professionalized women painters in this era. In addition to these establishment figures who were relatively well documented in their time, recent scholarship turned its attention to a host of 'unprofessionalized' artists in the same period – what scholar Sheila Barker has dubbed 'an alternative scene' of nuns and noblewomen. The Florentine Sister Plautilla Nelli (1524–88, p.220) and Countess Lucrezia Quistelli (1541–94) were both mentioned in the second edition of Giorgio Vasari's *Lives of the Most Excellent Painters, Sculptors and Architects* (1568) yet records of their works barely survived for posterity. For Quistelli, the 'debasing associations with a manual profession'[9] caused her not to sign her work nor to sell it, therefore condemning all but one surviving work to the dustbin. Her family repressed her talents and omitted any mention of her art practice from official records and monuments. In Nelli's case, even though she was able to run a large studio within the Santa Caterina da Siena Convent, much of her work has been lost, neglected or destroyed. Her magnus opus – a seven-metre (twenty-three-foot) wide depiction of the Last Supper (pp.220–1) – survived wars, geopolitical turmoil and floods. It was rolled up in storage and only finally restored and displayed at the Museo di Santa Maria Novella in 2019. 'Orate pro pictora' (Pray for the paintress) is how Nelli signed her masterpiece. It seems those prayers were answered centuries later in this miraculous recovery of her work. Such an emblematic tale begs the question: how many lost works are yet to be rediscovered from this historical 'alternative scene'? Herein lies the deep value of revising our understandings of the past, to build art-historical knowledge to empower the future.

At the extreme opposite of these 'alternative' forebears stands the now legendary Artemisia Gentileschi (p.117). Emerging from the Italian humanist firmament, Gentileschi not only achieved notoriety in her own lifetime, surpassing her father's renown, she has also surfaced as the premiere Old Mistress superstar. She and the French court portraitist Élisabeth Vigée-Lebrun (1755–1842, p.310) have arisen as newly minted blockbuster artists. Their survey exhibitions at public institutions including the National Gallery in London (Gentileschi in 2020) and the Metropolitan Museum of Art in New York (Vigée-Lebrun in 2016) have attracted broad audiences, crossing over into the popular consciousness and breaking out of the stuffy confines of specialized feminist scholarship. Not only can their posthumous success be attributed to their larger-sized, well-conserved oeuvres, their ambitious

8 For a deeper discussion, see Sheila Barker, 'Art as Women's Work: The Professionalization of Women Artists in Italy, 1350–1800', in Eve Straussman-Pflanzer and Oliver Tostmann (eds.), *By Her Hand: Artemisia Gentileschi and Women Artists in Italy, 1500–1800* (New Haven and London: Yale University Press, 2021), pp.43–51.

9 ibid., p.49.

10 Julia Jacobs, 'Female Artists Made Little Progress in Museums Since 2008, Survey Finds', *The New York Times*, 19 September 2019, www.nytimes.com/2019/09/19/arts/design/female-art-agency-partners-sothebys-artists-auction.html. Accessed 13 March 2022.

11 'Artist Micol Hebron, who has tracked the representation of women on gallery rosters since 2013, points out that many galleries that profess to promote equality still fall short: "A 65–35 ratio is repeated over and over – that's still almost twice as many men as women."' Julia Halperin & Charlotte Burns, 'Female Artists Represent Just 2 Percent of the Market. Here's Why – and How That Can Change', *Artnet News*, 19 September 2019, news.artnet.com/womens-place-in-the-art-world/female-artists-represent-just-2-percent-market-heres-can-change-1654954. Accessed 13 March 2022.

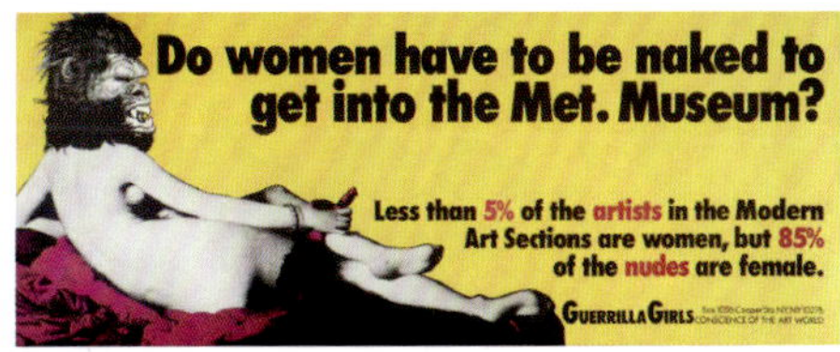

Guerrilla Girls, *Do women have to be naked to get into the Met. Museum?*, 1989, screenprint on paper, 28 × 71 cm (11 × 28 in)

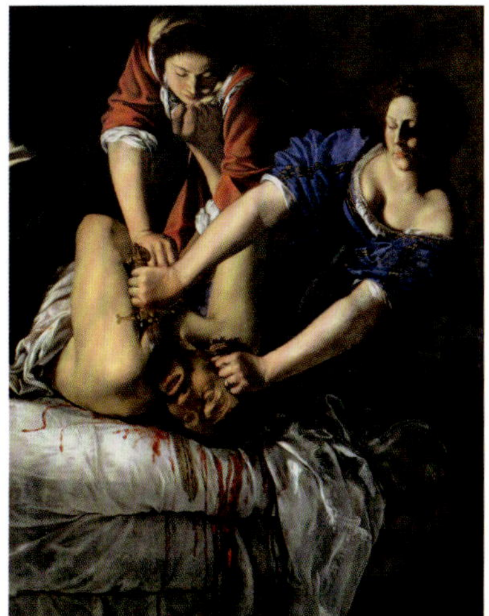

Artemisia Gentileschi, *Judith Beheading Holofernes*, *c.*1612–13, oil on canvas, 158.8 × 125.5 cm (62 ½ × 49 ⅜ in), Museo di Capodimonte, Naples, Italy

compositions and the overall quality of their work, both are also compelling figures whose stories have been amplified by the impact of decades of feminist activism. Thanks to feminist campaigns such as the Guerrilla Girls' infamous *Do women have to be naked to get into the Met. Museum?* (1989), museum directors and curators have been shamed and cajoled into enacting a sea change that has engendered these first-ever Old Mistress blockbusters. Since the turn of the twenty-first century, mega museums like the Centre Pompidou in Paris – whose 2009 all-female artist takeover of the permanent collection entitled 'Elles' was a deeply influential revisionist gesture – have attempted to redress their past neglect of women artists. In the commercial sphere, there has been slow but steady affirmation coming from rising auction prices for Old Mistress works – Vigée-Lebrun holds the Old Mistress record at $7.2 million as of 2022 (a pittance compared to the $27.9 million price tag of her Rococo peer Jean-Honoré Fragonard in 2013). While prices at auction for 'blue chip' twentieth-century painters like Georgia O'Keeffe (p.227), Frida Kahlo (p.152), Tamara de Lempicka (p.178) and Joan Mitchell (p.203) are more robust and financially eye popping, there is still a huge price gap between these artists and their male peers. The only bracket where there is price and gender parity is on the secondary market's speculation on the youngest painters – for example, an expressionist figurative canvas by Dana Schutz (b. 1976, p.261) fetched $6.4 million in 2021 at Christie's whereas an artwork by her generational peer Nicolas Party (b. 1980) sold for $3.2 million in the same sale. Wildly popular podcasts and Instagram accounts have transformed the complex biographies of artists like Vigée-Lebrun and Gentileschi into more accessible stories that have generated fangirl devotion. Like a celebrity only known by her mononym, 'Artemisia' has joined the pantheon of populist feminist heroes, with her real-life tale of survival of sexual violence making her story timelier than ever. As such, her *Judith Beheading Holofernes* (*c.*1612–13), has transcended its rarefied Baroque origins to become an instantly recognized banner for the #MeToo movement. These are all important affirmations that cannot be quantified.

But the Artemisia success story has not moved the needle much when it comes to the overall statistics that the Guerrilla Girls have highlighted in their consciousness-raising posters. 'Less than 5% of the artists in the Modern Art Sections are women,' their admonishing Met Museum poster read, 'but 85% of the nudes are female.' A rigorous study of American museums published in 2019 showed 'that between 2008 and 2018, only 11% of art acquired by the country's top museums for their permanent collections was by women. And contrary to any hope that acquisitions of artworks by women are inching upward, the percentage remained relatively stagnant.'[10] In the same period, only 14% of special museum exhibitions were devoted to solo shows or majority group shows of women artists. Gender parity in the art market is similarly skewed. On the primary market, most gallery stables favour men over women at 'a 65–35 ratio'.[11] Exercises that quantify the persistent gender inequality in museums do not tell the whole story of course – scholarly victories and breakthroughs cannot be measured numerically, and these figures obscuring bold corrective initiatives are not reflected in aggregated national data pools. Institutions including the San Francisco Museum of Modern Art and Baltimore Museum of Art have adopted 'deaccessioning to diversify' programmes, selling works by 'canonized white men' like the twentieth-century painters Kenneth Noland, Franz Kline and Mark Rothko to enable them to thoughtfully acquire works by women and artists of colour in order to reshape the canon, while they critically amend their collections.[12] Change to achieve total gender parity remains incremental. Naysayers baulk at institutional gender quotas and right-wing culture warriors decry curatorial affirmative action, but these empirical data points objectively make the case that the struggle for knowledge, visibility and critical recognition for women artists is still persistent, necessary and urgent.

'THE VALUE TEST' VERSUS 'DIFFERENCING THE CANON'

'Oh God! Women simply don't pass the test,' proclaimed 1980s art star Georg Baselitz (b. 1938) in his now infamous 2013 interview with *Der Spiegel*.[13] The journalist retorted, 'What test?' Baselitz continued, 'The market test, the value test.' The Neo-Expressionist maestro went further, delivering his oft-repeated zinger: 'Women don't paint very well. It's a fact.' Whenever Baselitz's unflinching misogyny is trotted out, his essentializing one-liner could easily be thwarted with Nochlin's 1971 toolbox. Baselitz provides just another example of an alpha-male gatekeeper making sweeping, unsubstantiated claims about *all* women painters' skills – a pathetic attempt to reaffirm his perceived place as a 'great artist' and assert himself as an authoritative arbitrator of painting mastery.

He continues the interview, dangling the keys to the Big Boys' Brush Club, 'There are, of course, exceptions. Agnes Martin or, from the past, Paula Modersohn-Becker. I feel happy whenever I see one of her paintings. But she is no Picasso, no Modigliani, and no Gauguin.'[14] Is it even necessary to counter such cartoonish, macho bloviations today? Why do we even give passing consideration to Baselitz's chauvinism, if just to confirm the continuity to the centuries of sexism that women painters have endured?

Beyond its tabloid shock value, the full text of Baselitz's diatribe contains an important point that requires radical revision. His hegemonic 'value test' is a core mechanism of art-historical gatekeeping that must be dismantled and replaced. If we again remind ourselves that the traditional metrics of greatness are gendered, that markets are slow to monetize shifting tides of gender politics and revisionist art history, we must instate a new 'value test' that reinforces our expanded canon, that supports our new and still expanding knowledge base. Casting aside the yardstick of auction prices and the subjective categories of aesthetic beauty, technical mastery and 'wall power', the feminist measure of art-historical value is not a pass/fail assessment.

12 Julia Halperin & Charlotte Burns, 'Case Studies: How Four Museums Are Taking Dramatic Measures to Admit More Women Artists into the Art Historical Canon', *Artnet News*, 19 September 2019, news.artnet.com/womens-place-in-the-art-world/case-studies-how-four-museums-are-taking-radical-measures-to-admit-more-women-artists-into-the-art-historical-canon-1654717. Accessed 24 March 2022.

13 Susanne Beyer & Ulrike Knöfel, 'My Paintings Are Battles', *Spiegel International*, 25 January 2013, www.spiegel.de/international/germany/spiegel-interview-with-german-painter-georg-baselitz-a-879397.html. Accessed 29 March 2022.

14 ibid.

15 Griselda Pollock, 'Preface to the Bloomsbury Revelations Edition', in Rozsika Parker & Griselda Pollock, *Old Mistresses: Women, Art and Ideology* (London: Bloomsbury Academic, 2020), p.xxii.

16 Marie Darrieussecq, *Being Here Is Everything: The Life of Paula Modersohn-Becker* (trans. Penny Hueston) (South Pasadena, California: Semiotext(e), 2017), p.137.

17 Isabelle Graw, *The Love of Painting: Genealogy of a Success Medium* (Berlin: Sternberg Press, 2018), p.12.

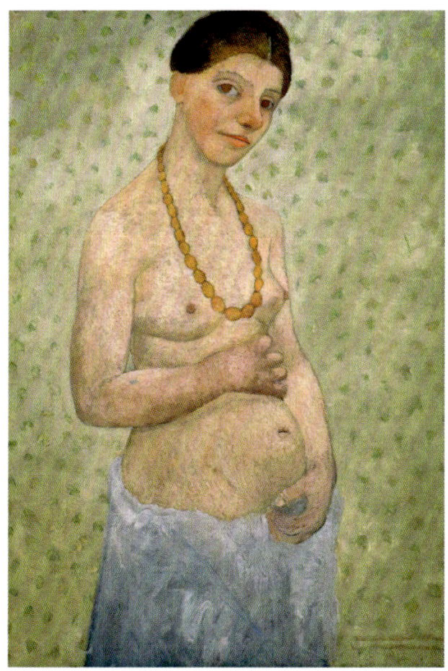

Paula Modersohn-Becker, *Self-Portrait on Sixth Wedding Anniversary*, 1906, oil on card, 101.8 × 70.2 cm (40 ⅛ × 27 ⅝ in), Paula Modersohn-Becker Museum, Bremen, Germany

Instead, the calculus of valuation must encompass the works' historical context, intellectual content and, above all, must adopt language that stresses 'the singularity and difference' of women artists, as opposed to making them conform to masculinist litmus tests of so-called greatness. Art historian Griselda Pollock called this process 'differencing the canon', arguing that:

> As a woman viewer, I desire difference. I want to know about ways of seeing the world produced from situations I might recognize through some commonality such as being a woman… [differentiating the canon] not only seeks to understand the work of each artist in her singularity that includes gender and sexuality, class and race as it [is] lived and represented by each person. It also counters all universalizing, colonizing and selective misrepresentations of the complexity of the worlds artists dare to represent to and for us.[15]

Liberated from traditional barometers of importance, works can be evaluated according to the 'differentiated canon' – wherein paintings are understood as vehicles to preserve and transmit testimonials of each artist's experience, vision, intellect. Take for instance Paula Modersohn-Becker (1876–1907, p.205); she may win 'greatness' points from Baselitz for the dexterity of her hand, her astonishing textured brushwork and sense of colour, but the singularity and difference of her painting lies in her radical self-representation. *Self-Portrait on Sixth Wedding Anniversary* (1906) is a watershed depiction of a pregnant woman by a woman artist – and the first time a Western woman painted herself nude.[16] Modersohn-Becker's pictorial and emotional agency upended conventions of representation of the female nude. Made in defiance of social mores in the early twentieth century, capturing the sensations of her lived experience, her unabashed pride in her changing body has been transformed into an icon of female experience. Baselitz was right – she is no Picasso! Countering centuries of objectification, Modersohn-Becker has enshrined her female gaze onto the canvas. Her independent vision is the furthest thing from Picasso's libidinous, exploitative eye – and it is *that* radical divergence that elevates the status of her painting into an enduring cultural treasure.

This book, *Great ~~Women~~ Painters*, documents the work of over three hundred artists, spanning five centuries, six continents and just as many genres. Each artist has harnessed their medium's inherent power: 'the singularity, preciousness, and longevity of the painted picture',[17] in part to contribute to the continuity of our visual culture. Transhistorical projects such as this publication make the case for the continued need, *à la* Pizan, to expand the canon of feminist art histories, to topple gendered value tests and continue to build up the *Cité des Dames* as a means of enforcing and preserving women's agency in our global culture for future generations.

PACITA ABAD

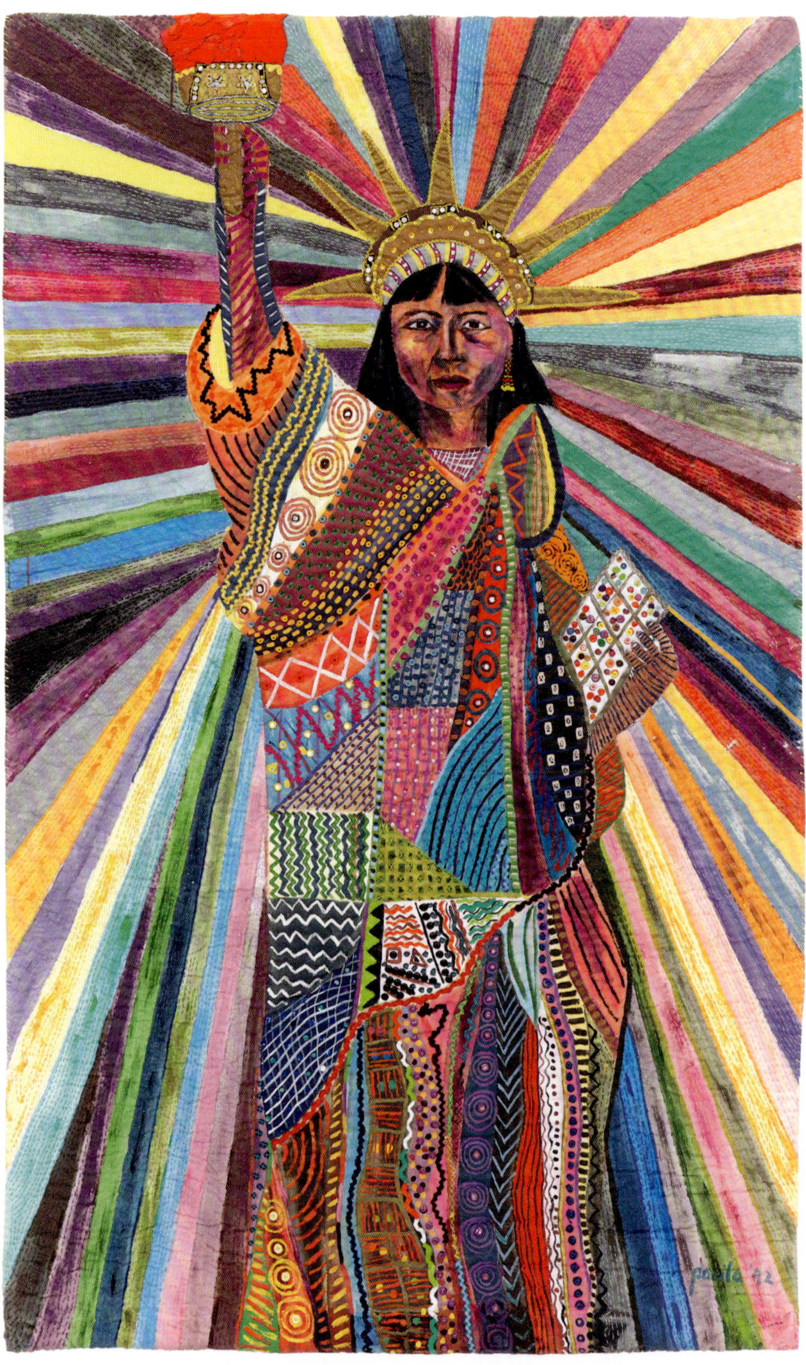

L.A. LIBERTY
1992, acrylic, cotton yarn, plastic buttons, mirrors, gold thread and painted cloth on stitched and padded canvas, 239 × 147 cm (94 × 58 in), Pacita Abad Art Estate

Pacita Abad, born 1946, Batanes, Philippines. Died 2004, Singapore.

Born into a political family on a small island in the Philippines, Abad initially studied law, but due to her political activism was forced to continue her studies abroad. Abad then lived for nearly a decade in the United States, where she committed herself to painting and studied art. She would live and travel throughout Asia, Africa and Latin America in the years that followed, painting everyday people and absorbing the palette and textures of the artistic traditions she encountered. While she worked in both figurative and abstract modes, her series are unified in their radiating waves of vibrant colour, which she described in a 1996 article by Ian Findlay-Brown as, like her personality, 'bold, strong, and crude'. With its intricate textures and unexpected materials, this representation of New York's Statue of Liberty (sometimes referred to as 'Lady Liberty') exemplifies Abad's mature style, which seamlessly blends rich source material gathered over a lifetime. It also reflects the social commitment that animated her life; long sympathetic to the plight of refugees, this reimagining of an American icon – and a classic metaphor for immigration – resonates anew in an era of migration crises and xenophobia the world over.

MARY ABBOTT

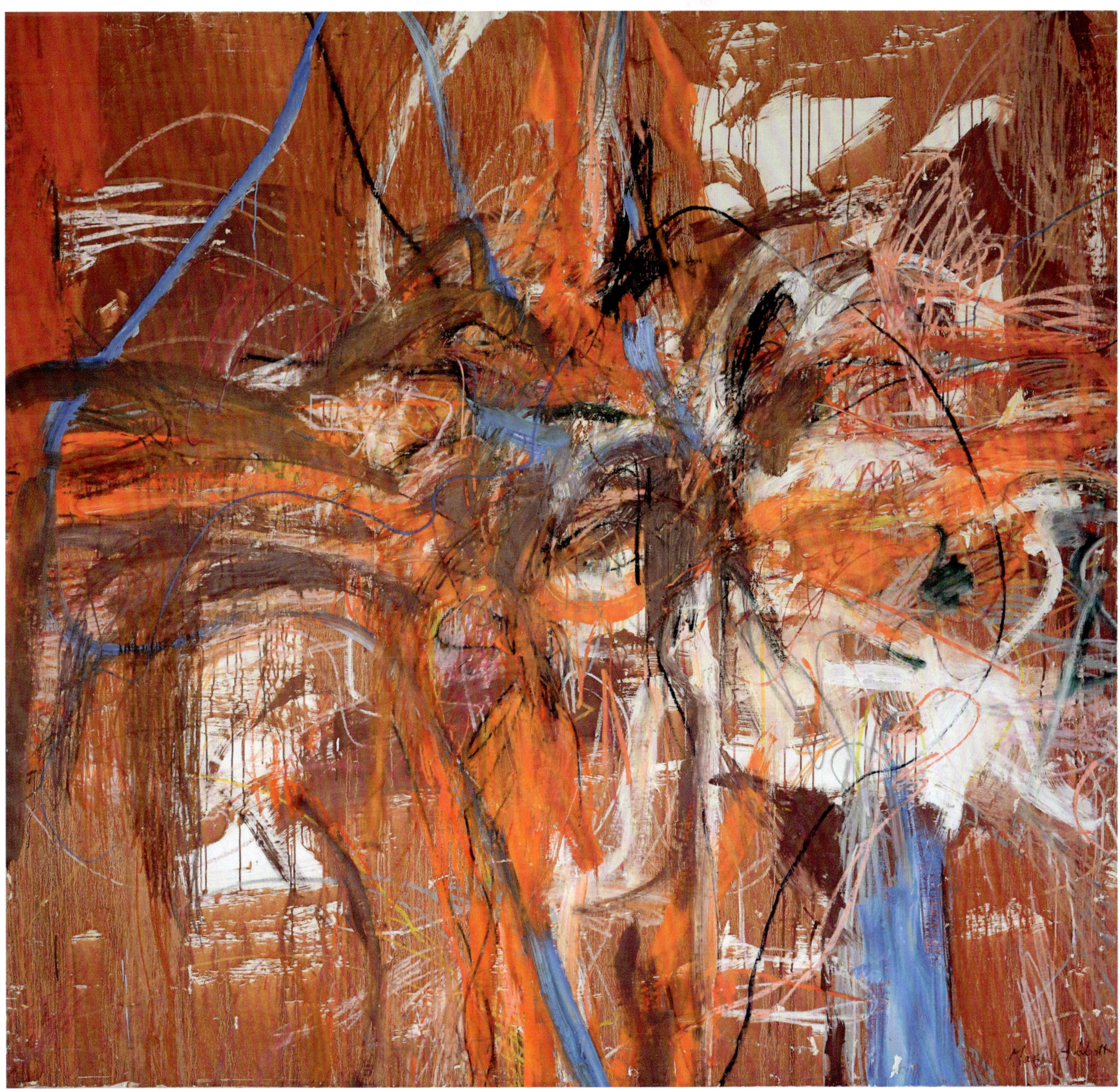

IMRIE
1952, oil and mixed media on canvas, 180.4 × 193 cm (71 × 76 in), private collection, Chicago, USA

Mary Abbott, born 1921, New York, USA. Died 2019, Southampton, New York, USA.

An early exponent of Abstract Expressionism, Abbott created bold, gestural paintings that translated the wildness and beauty of nature to canvas. At the age of seventeen, Abbott enrolled at the Art Students League, where she studied with German painter George Grosz (1893–1959), later attending the Corcoran Museum School in Washington DC. In the late 1940s she studied at the Subjects of the Artist school, which practised an alternative teaching method of working directly with artists, including co-founders Barnett Newman (1905–70), Mark Rothko (1903–70) and Willem de Kooning (1904–97), who invited her to join as one of three members of his artist circle known as 'The Club'. Exemplary of Abbott's early painting style is the large-scale *Imrie*, dominated by slashes of red, orange and blue paint. In the 1950s and 1960s, Abbott travelled frequently to the Caribbean, resulting in vivid paintings inspired by the region's vegetation and culture. She continued to paint well into her nineties. Her late work depicted her garden in Southampton, New York, a continuation of her lifelong interest in nature.

SOUAD ABDELRASOUL

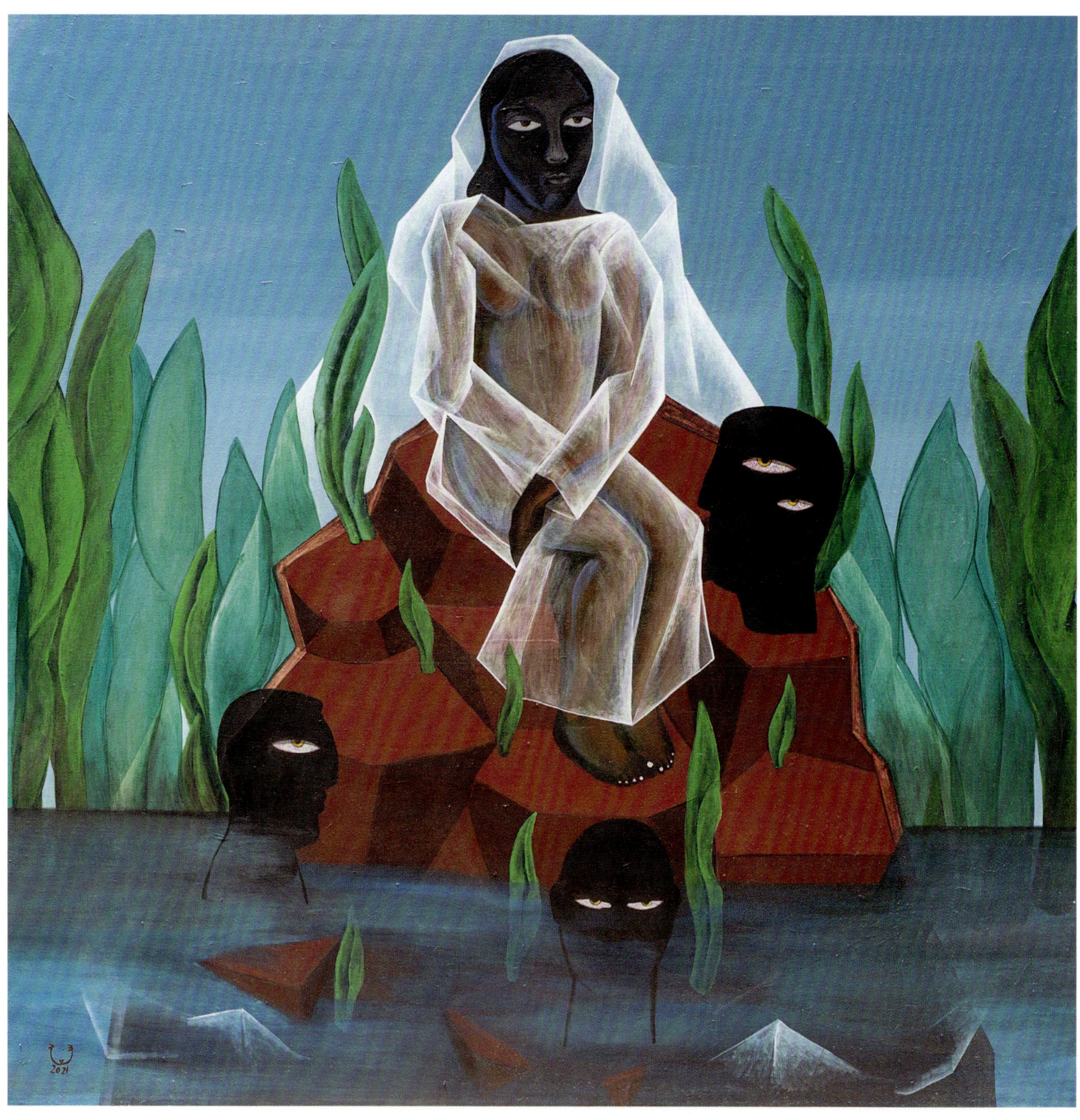

NILE CROCODILES
2021, acrylic on canvas, 187 × 185 cm
(73 5/8 × 72 7/8 in)

Souad Abdelrasoul, born 1974, Cairo, Egypt.

Alongside painting, Abdelrasoul's multifaceted artistic practice has spanned collage, drawing, sculpture and graphic design, in addition to illustrating children's books. She often populates her work with metamorphosized characters, fusing human figures with animals and botanical elements. Human life is shown as deeply connected to the environment, particularly through the growth of trees, vines and leaves to convey the emotional connection between feminine spirituality and the natural world. She often uses anatomical drawings as source material, and has sometimes painted her images over old maps. In *Nile Crocodiles*, the figure perched on a rock is dressed in a white translucent dress and veil, items of clothing that recur in Abdelrasoul's paintings. The sheerness of the fabric indicates that although the female form is shrouded, its implicit nakedness is still visible to others, symbolized by the bright eyes of the disembodied male heads approaching and swimming below her. Equating lurking crocodiles with the behaviour of predatory men, Abdelrasoul constructs a metaphor for the vulnerability of women in a patriarchal society.

GERTRUDE ABERCROMBIE

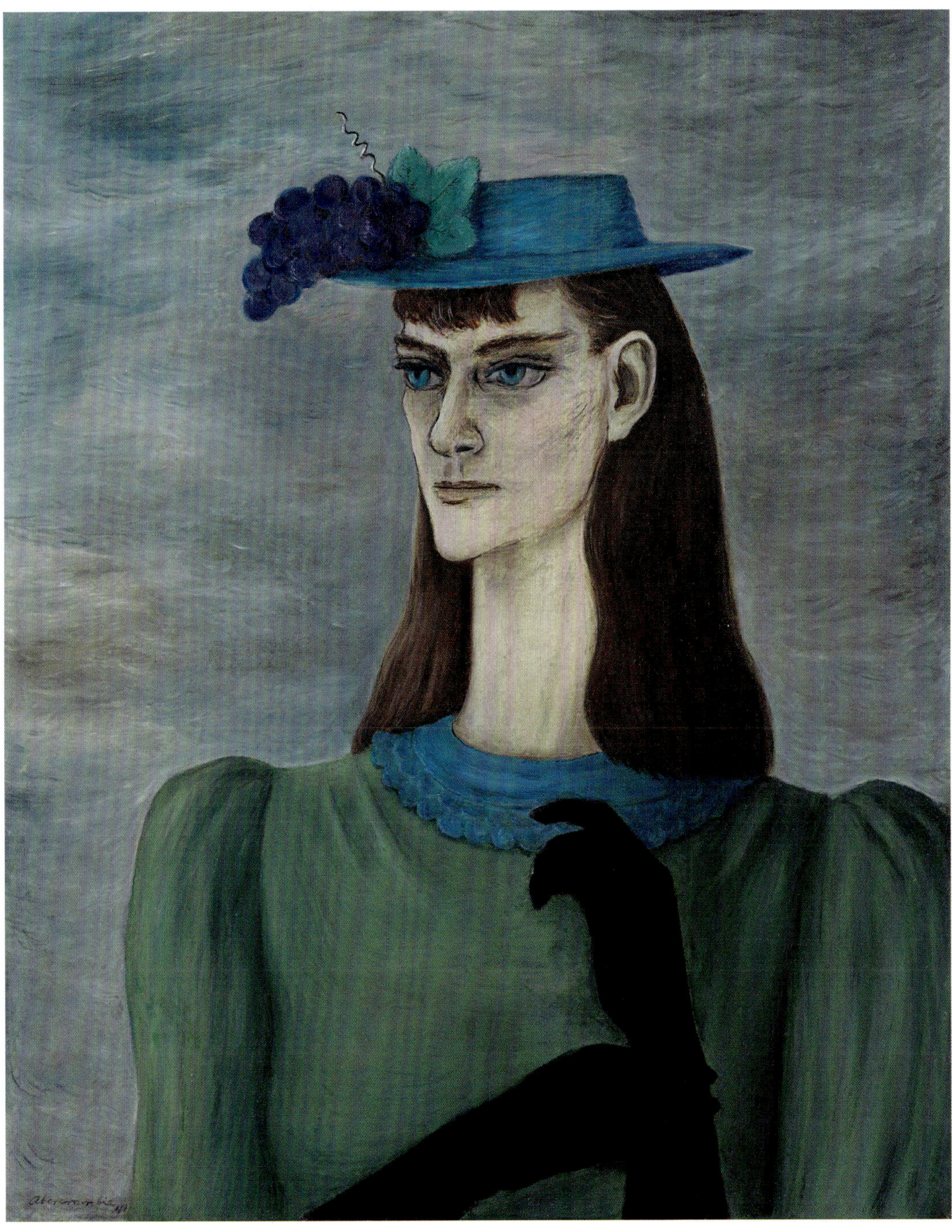

SELF-PORTRAIT OF MY SISTER
1941, oil on canvas, 68.6 × 55.9 cm (27 × 22 in), Art Institute of Chicago, USA

Gertrude Abercrombie, born 1909, Austin, Texas, USA. Died 1977, Chicago, USA.

After an itinerant childhood tagging along with her opera singer parents, Abercrombie made Chicago her home and became a fixture of the city's vibrant mid-century arts scene. The Saturday salons and Sunday jam sessions she hosted at her apartment became legendary gathering places for jazz musicians like Dizzy Gillespie and Charlie Parker, as well as writers like Thornton Wilder. Abercrombie's Surrealist, sparsely composed paintings continually reinterpret a repertoire of motifs: the moon, a barren tree, a lone cat. The flat, unsettling landscapes that fill these compositions evoke the Illinois flatlands of the artist's youth, but her work aims to represent the psyche rather than exterior reality. As Abercrombie put it in a 1977 radio interview with the writer Studs Terkel: 'It's always myself that I paint.' *Self-Portrait of My Sister* exemplifies Abercrombie's persistent interest in exploring the nature of selfhood. But, as the contradictory title implies, this is not a straightforward subject. Abercrombie was, in fact, an only child – with the figure shown here, she realizes in visual form an alternate, fictitious self.

NINA CHANEL ABNEY

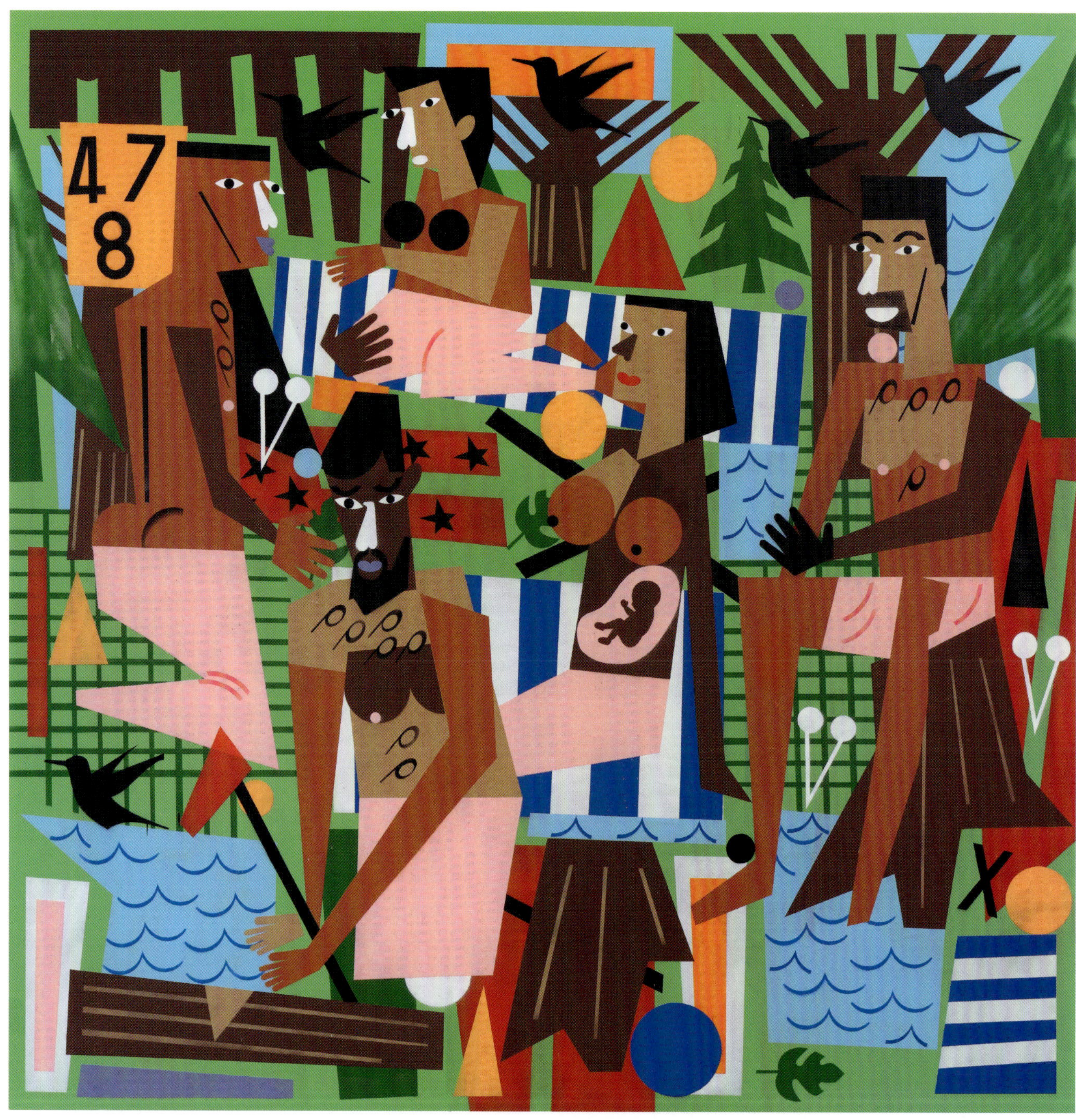

FEMME GAMES
2020, acrylic and spray paint on canvas,
243.8 × 243.8 × 4.1 cm (96 × 96 × 1 ⅝ in)

Nina Chanel Abney, born 1982, Chicago, USA.

Abney's vibrant canvases pulse with life as they explore themes like race, celebrity, religion, politics, sex and the history of art. The artist works with materials including acrylic and spray paints and techniques like collage to achieve her graphic, flat and hard-edged geometric style, sometimes translating her works into large-scale public murals. Though Abney turned away from her early portraiture of famous Black figures and towards scenes that evoke history painting and landscape, figuration remains at the forefront of her practice. Abney's scenes are composed with a candy-coloured palette that belies the nuances contained within, drawing on references from sources including her own biography, current events, oral history traditions, tabloid magazines, hip-hop culture, video games, cartoons, Renaissance memento mori, and the collages of Romare Bearden (1911–88) and cut-outs of Henri Matisse (1869–1954). In her body of paintings begun during the COVID-19 pandemic, of which *Femme Games* is a part, Abney imagines the possibility of Black queer social life, liberated from patriarchal, heteronormative and white urban spaces.

TOMMA ABTS

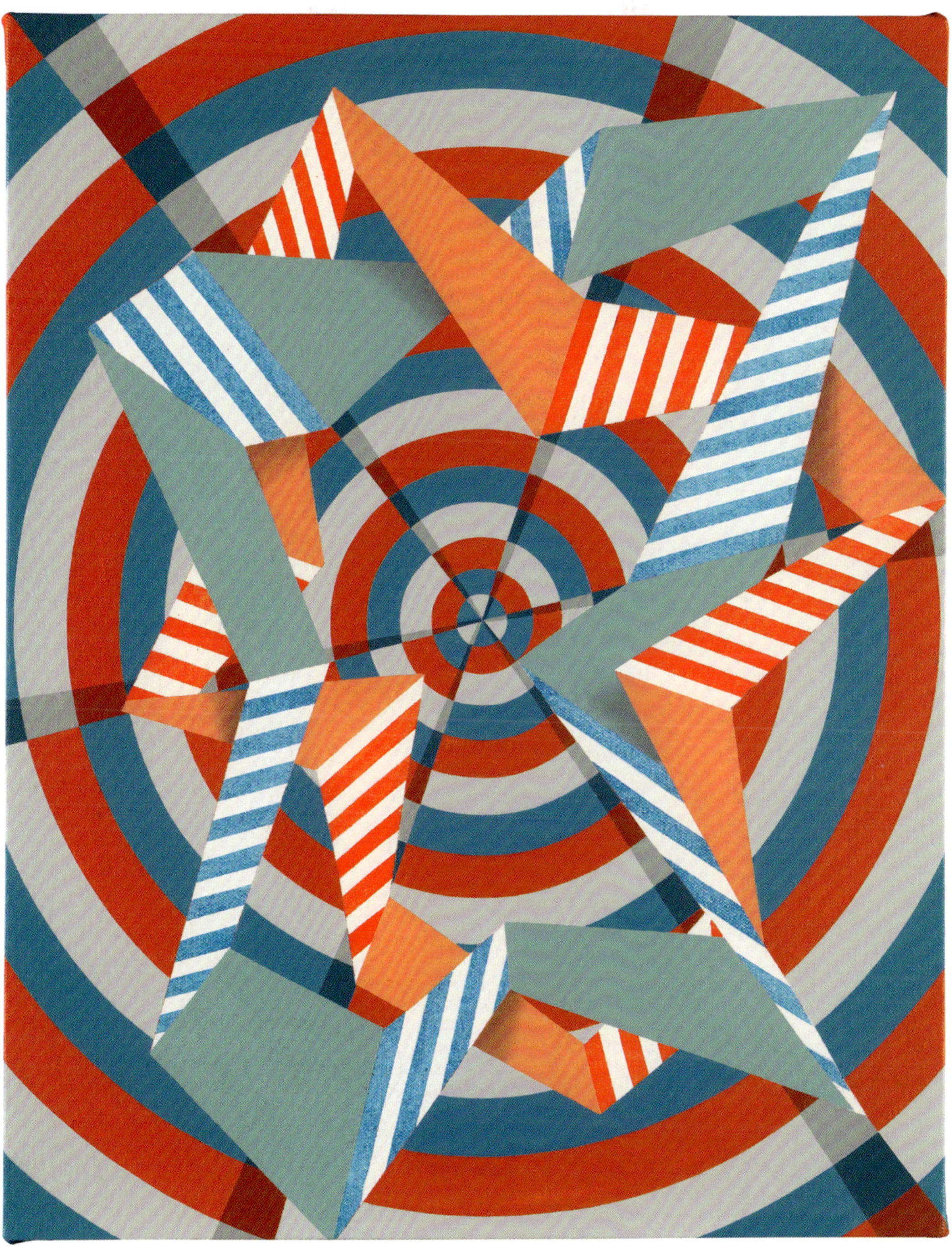

FIMME
2013, acrylic and oil on canvas, 48 × 38 cm (18 ⅞ × 15 in), collection of Sascha S. Bauer, Chicago, USA, and London, UK

Tomma Abts, born 1967, Kiel, Germany.

After studying structuralist film at art school in Berlin, Abts moved to London in 1995 and, in 2006, was the first woman painter to win the Turner Prize. Apart from a few exceptions, her paintings are always the same dimensions: 48 × 38 centimetres (18 ⅞ × 15 inches), a format that fits in the crook of her elbow so she can cradle the canvas as she paints. Her intricate and exacting works are both complex and coherent, as though mapped out from the start. However, this impression belies the spontaneous process of their making, since Abts never creates sketches in advance and paints successive layers without a plan, slowly laying down an image as it appears in her mind's eye, until the work comes alive. In *Fimme*, a target rendered in complementary hues of blue and red erupts into an interlocking pair of star-shaped garlands made even more optically stimulating with strobing white stripes. With apparently contradictory shadow effects and the illusion of depth and fragmentation, it is a symphony of movement and direction that both attracts and baffles the eye.

CARLA ACCARDI

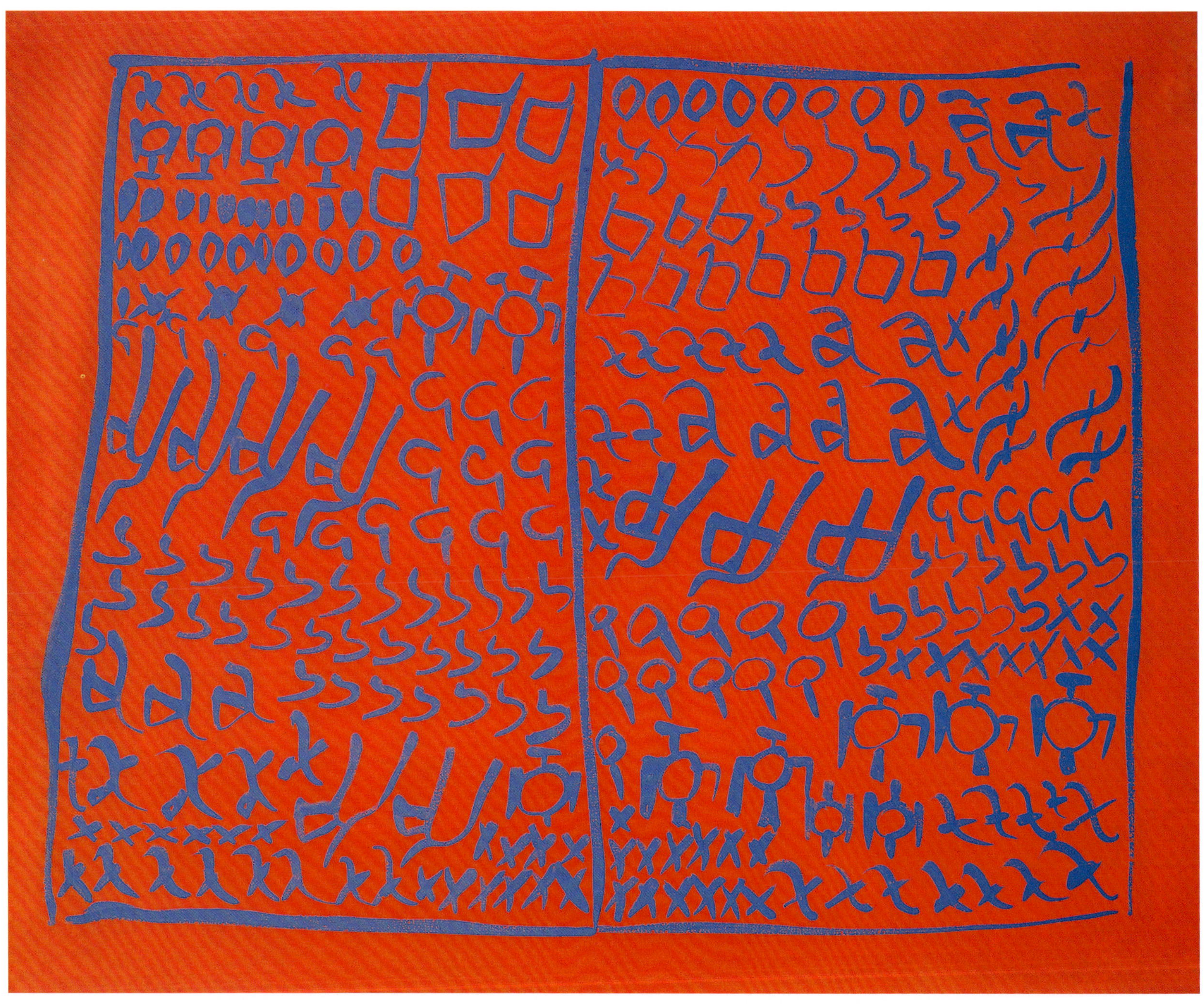

BLUROSSO (BLUE-RED)
1963, casein on canvas, 73 × 92 cm (28 ¾ × 36 ¼ in), Galleria Civica d'Arte Moderna e Contemporanea di Torino, Turin, Italy

Carla Accardi, born 1924, Trapani, Italy. Died 2014, Rome, Italy.

An abstract painter, Accardi spent most of her career in Rome, where she moved in 1946. There she met a group of fellow artists, including her husband, Antonio Sanfilippo (1923–80), with whom she founded Forma 1 in 1947. The group's members declared themselves both 'formalists and Marxists', in stylistic opposition to Socialist Realism. Accardi was the only woman in Forma 1, which disbanded in 1951. In the early 1950s Accardi began to develop the visual vocabulary of quasi-calligraphic marks for which she is best known, although initially she painted only in monochrome; it was not until the following decade that she introduced the bold, contrasting colours of paintings such as *Blue-Red*. Some of the hand-drawn, repeated symbols on this canvas resemble letters or shapes, but Accardi insisted – as quoted in a 1998 exhibition catalogue – that in her work 'a symbol does not have a meaning on its own but merely exists in relation to other symbols'. In the 1970s Accardi became heavily involved in feminist activism, as part of the Rivolta Femminile (Women's Revolt) group in Rome. She continued to work – making paintings, ceramics and sculptural installations – until her death.

ETEL ADNAN

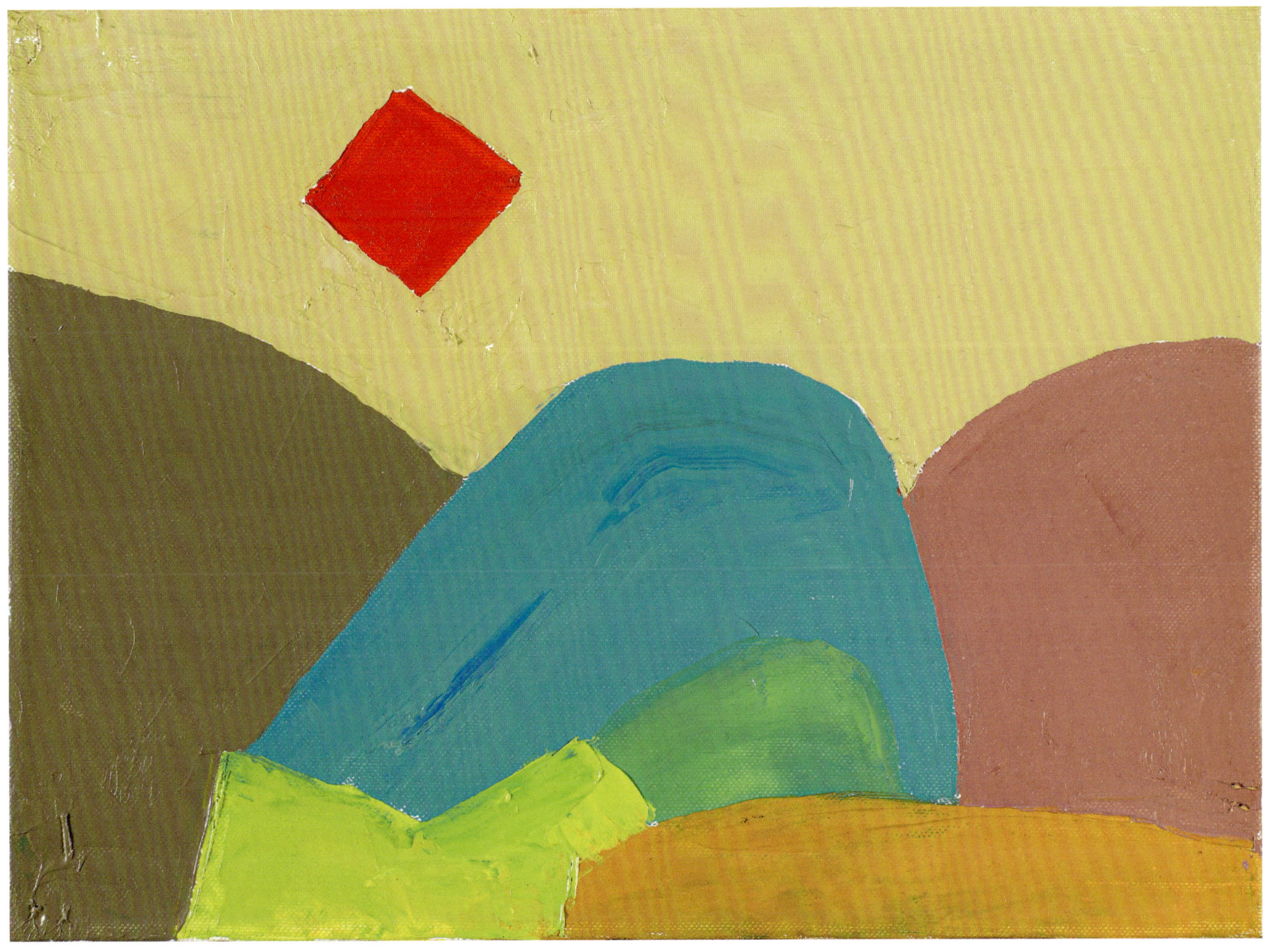

UNTITLED
2010, oil on canvas, 28.2 × 37.6 × 3.5 cm
(11 ⅛ × 14 ¾ × 1 ⅜ in)

Etel Adnan, born 1925, Beirut, Lebanon.
Died 2021, Paris, France.

An internationally renowned novelist, poet and journalist, Adnan maintained a painting practice that expressed the beauty of the natural world and her belief in the strength of the human spirit. Raised in a multilingual family in Beirut, Adnan studied philosophy at the Sorbonne in Paris and the University of California, Berkeley, beginning to paint in the late 1950s. Dispensing paint directly from the tube and manoeuvring it across her canvases with a palette knife instead of a paintbrush, Adnan employed radiant mauves, blues and other fields of colour in her paintings to capture the effects of sunlight on her surroundings. Enchanted by the view of Mount Tamalpais from her home in Sausalito, California, she created many literary and visual odes to the landscape, including a series of small-scale, colour-blocked paintings of the point at which land, ocean and sky meet. In this work, an abstracted blue mountain rises to meet a diamond-shaped sun that is rendered in a shock of red. Adnan's meditative work – which also includes artist books, tapestries and leporellos (accordion-style booklets) – hums with an emotional and spiritual valence that reflected her experience of life.

HILMA AF KLINT

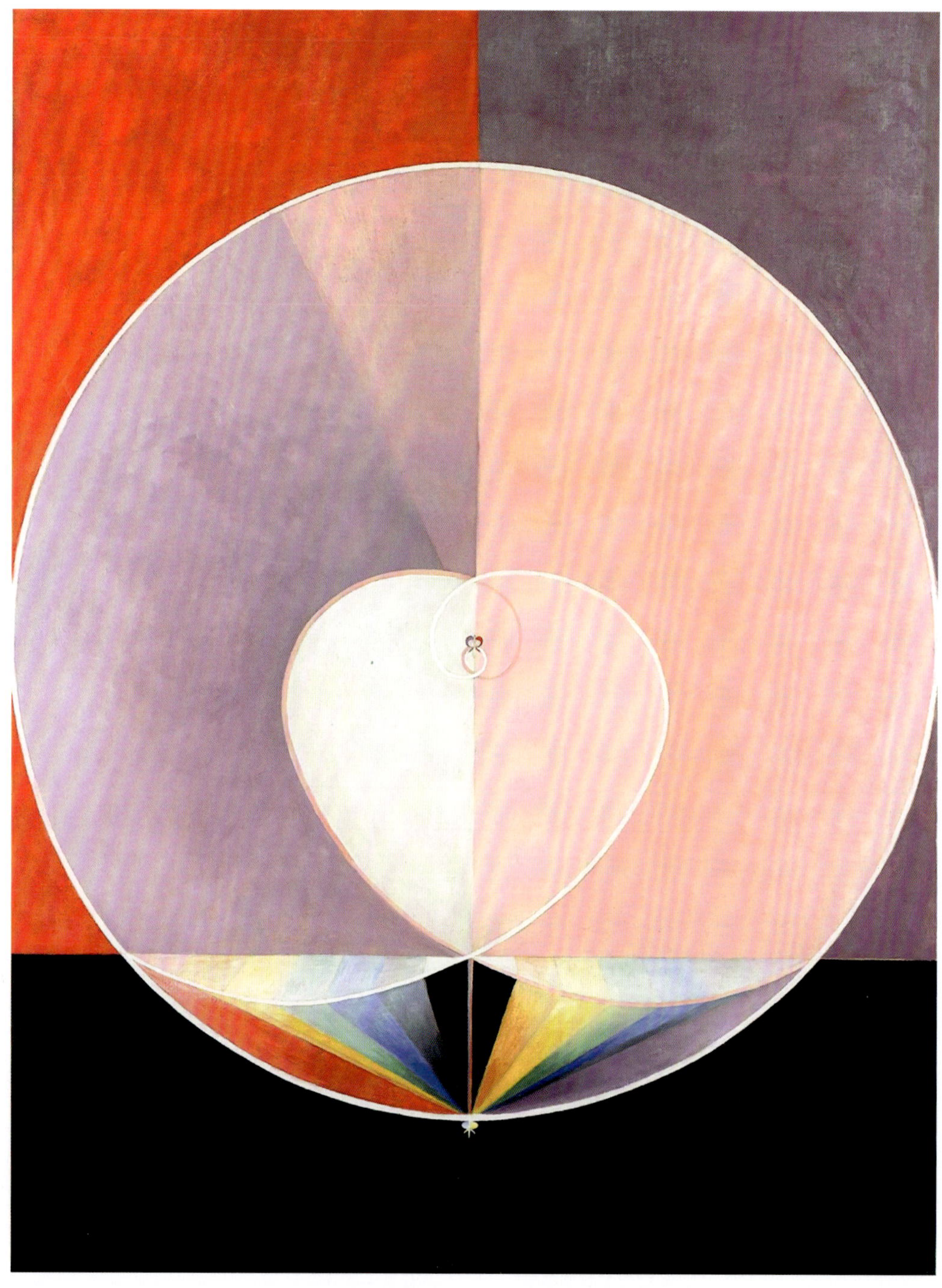

DUVAN NR. 2 (THE DOVE NO. 2), GROUP IX, SERIES SUW
1915, oil on canvas, 152 × 115 cm (59 7/8 × 45 1/4 in), The Hilma af Klint Foundation

Hilma af Klint, born 1862, Solna, Sweden. Died 1944, Djursholm, Sweden.

The artist and mystic af Klint is known for her large-scale and colourful paintings in which she departed from realistic representation, with some dubbing her the first abstract artist. She kept her practice very private and her work was never exhibited in her lifetime, writing in her will that it could not be shown until at least twenty years after her death. Using geometric shapes and biomorphic forms, af Klint's paintings represent the invisible forces that she believed connected the world with the spiritual realm. She perceived that a higher consciousness was speaking through her, and stated that she painted on the instruction of this spirit. The series of paintings she produced between 1906 and 1915, including *The Dove No. 2* with its striking hues of mauve, salmon pink and red, reflect the artist's interest in religious and sacred symbols, from cosmology to the zodiac. The dove, associated with peace, is considered a messenger for the divine. These reverent associations are enhanced by the sense of compositional harmony and pictorial serenity.

EILEEN AGAR

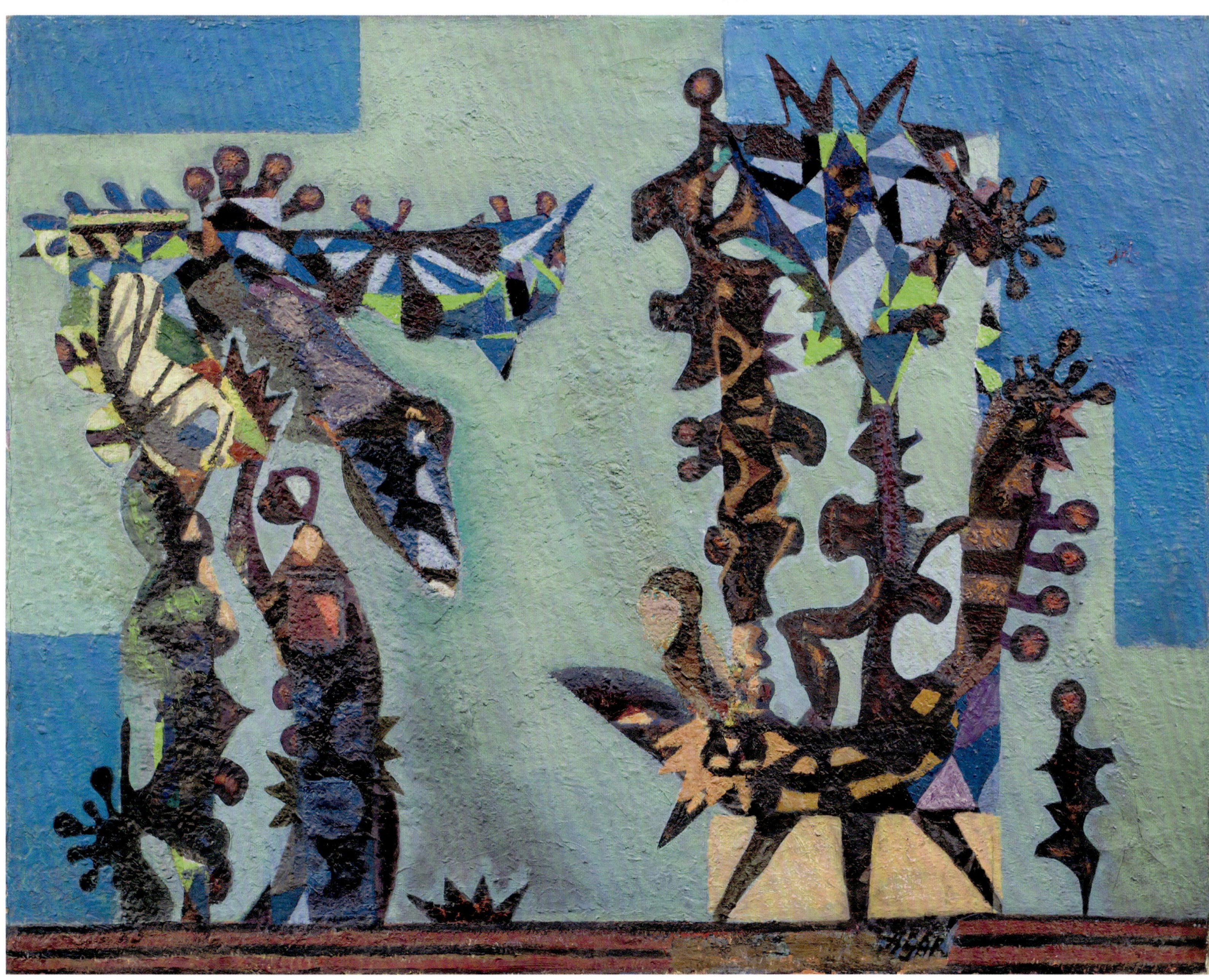

MUSICAL GARDEN (SPIKY)
1952, acrylic on canvas, 28 × 36 cm (11 × 14 ⅛ in)

Eileen Agar, born 1899, Buenos Aires, Argentina. Died 1991, London, UK.

As one of the few women included in the International Surrealist Exhibition of 1936, Agar is closely associated with the movement spearheaded by André Breton (1896–1966) – although over her seven-decade career she forged her own distinct path. Born to a wealthy family in Buenos Aires, she was sent to school in Britain, where her artistic talent was discovered. She studied art in London in the 1920s before moving to Paris, where she first encountered Breton and took painting lessons with the Cubist artist František Foltýn (1891–1976). Upon her return to Britain in the early 1930s she joined the London Group. Throughout her lifetime she produced many paintings – as well as collages, photographs and found-object assemblages – that fused Surrealist ideas about the unconscious mind and abstract concerns about form and texture with her own personal passion for the natural world. *Musical Garden (Spiky)* is one of several garden-themed compositions by Agar, although the objects in the painting are not easy to decode. Rather, a series of organic shapes hints at the presence of flora and fauna, such as a tuft of grass and a snail's head. With its patterned forms and plain background, the canvas has the feel of a collage – one of the Surrealists' favoured mediums.

SHIVA AHMADI

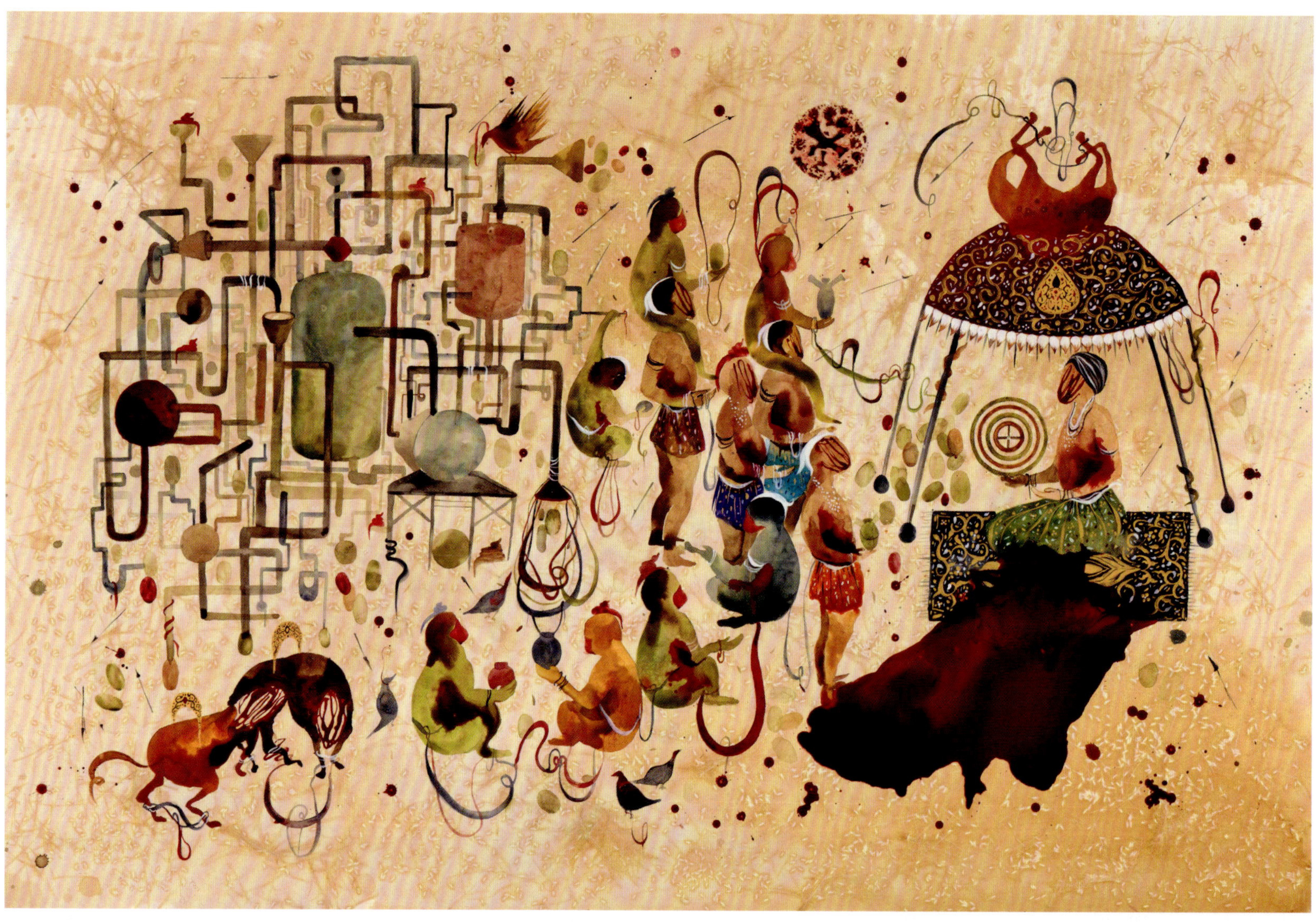

PIPES
2013, watercolour, ink and acrylic on Aquabord, 101.6 × 152.4 cm (40 × 60 in), Metropolitan Museum of Art, New York, USA

Shiva Ahmadi, born 1975, Tehran, Iran.

Growing up in Tehran, Ahmadi's early life was marked by the Iranian Revolution of 1979 and the subsequent Iran–Iraq War (1980–8). After studying painting at Azad University, she moved to the United States in 1998 to pursue graduate studies. Working primarily in watercolour and video animation, Ahmadi weaves the ornate patterning seen in Persian, Indian and Middle Eastern art into narrative scenes that refer to current social and political issues. The uncertainty and instability of the region is symbolized by her use of water-based or fluid media, as she stated in a 2020 interview with *BOMB*: 'Water (including watercolour, ink or acrylic) runs and is out of control. It is transparent, temperamental and honest.' In *Pipes*, Ahmadi borrows a subject from medieval Iranian book painting in which a prince sits atop a throne, depicting him with concentric rings hovering above his open palm and surrounded by exotic animals based on characters from the Hindu epic poem, the *Ramayana*. Ahmadi created the work's textured background by scattering hair, rice and salt across the painting's surface and allowing watercolour to dry over it. As is typical of her work, Ahmadi tethers the scene to the contemporary with elements such as a tangle of pipes.

NJIDEKA AKUNYILI CROSBY

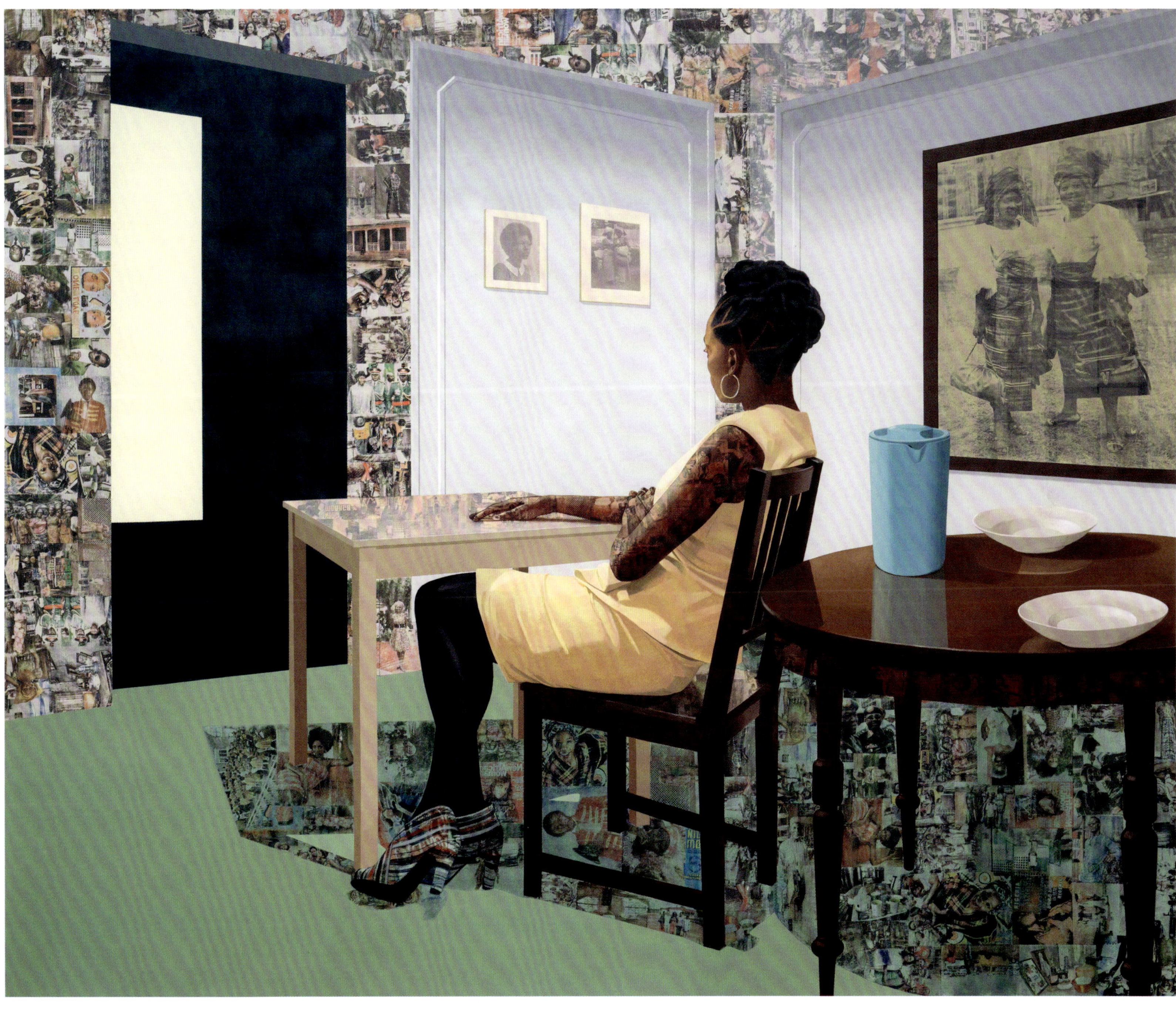

IN THE LAVENDER ROOM
2019, acrylic, transfers, coloured pencil, pastel and collage on paper, 243.8 × 292.1 cm (96 × 115 in), Statens Museum for Kunst, Copenhagen, Denmark

Njideka Akunyili Crosby, born 1983, Enugu, Nigeria.

In 1999, at the age of sixteen, Akunyili Crosby moved from Nigeria to the United States with her older sister, an experience that deeply informed her painting practice. 'I felt an urgency to tell my story as a Nigerian in the diaspora,' she said in a 2016 *BOMB* interview. She studied art and biology at Swarthmore College and painting at the Pennsylvania Academy of the Fine Arts before earning an MFA at Yale School of Art. This rigorous academic training is reflected in her work, which depicts Black figures in imagined domestic interiors that offer a postcolonial perspective on similar scenes from the traditions of European painting. She takes a similarly hybridizing approach to the materials in her work, applying acrylic paint not to canvas but to paper and combining it with elements of collage, drawing and printmaking. Most notably, as demonstrated in *In the Lavender Room*, Akunyili Crosby uses the technique of photo-transfer to incorporate pre-existing images – a mix of intimate family snaps and pictures referencing Nigerian culture and history more widely – into her paintings. Here, the photographs, ranging from fashion spreads to political coverage, are densely layered across the walls and on the seated figure's skin and clothing, acting as a map of her interior landscape.

ELLEN ALTFEST

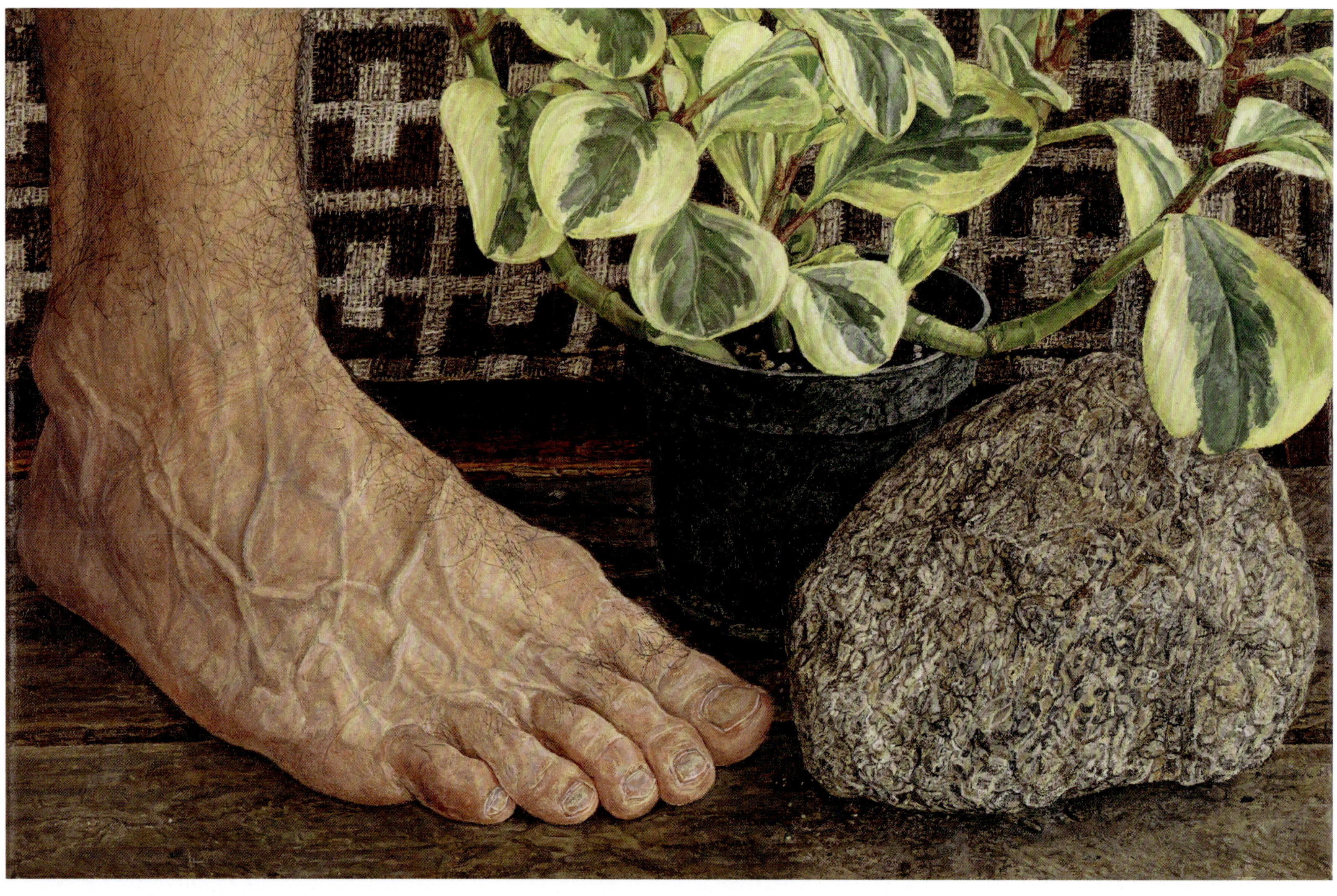

ROCK, FOOT, PLANT
2009, oil on canvas, 22.9 × 35.6 cm (9 × 14 in)

Ellen Altfest, born 1970, New York, USA.

In a hyperreal style developed while studying for her MFA at Yale School of Art in the mid-1990s, Altfest works strictly from observation, meticulously teasing out details that reveal more about a subject than an observer could perceive in real life. Working on a small scale, her process is painstakingly labour intensive, described in a 2013 *New York Times* article as 'an exercise in obsessiveness and physical stamina that brings to mind not so much endurance performance art as religious asceticism'. Altfest depicts unclothed figures, still lifes and landscapes with a parity of approach, focusing in particular on surfaces: textured skin (both human and vegetable), coarse rock, rough bark and botanical markings. What is included within the composition is chosen with such precision that what is omitted becomes equally significant. Many of her images of the (usually identifiably male) body are truncated or obstructed to show only specific parts, rendering the sitter as much an anonymous object as the gourds or trees that also recur as subjects. In this work, the model is reduced to a single right foot, equal in status with the plant and rock, yet compelling in its brutal realism, a tangle of prominent veins resembling a network of tree roots.

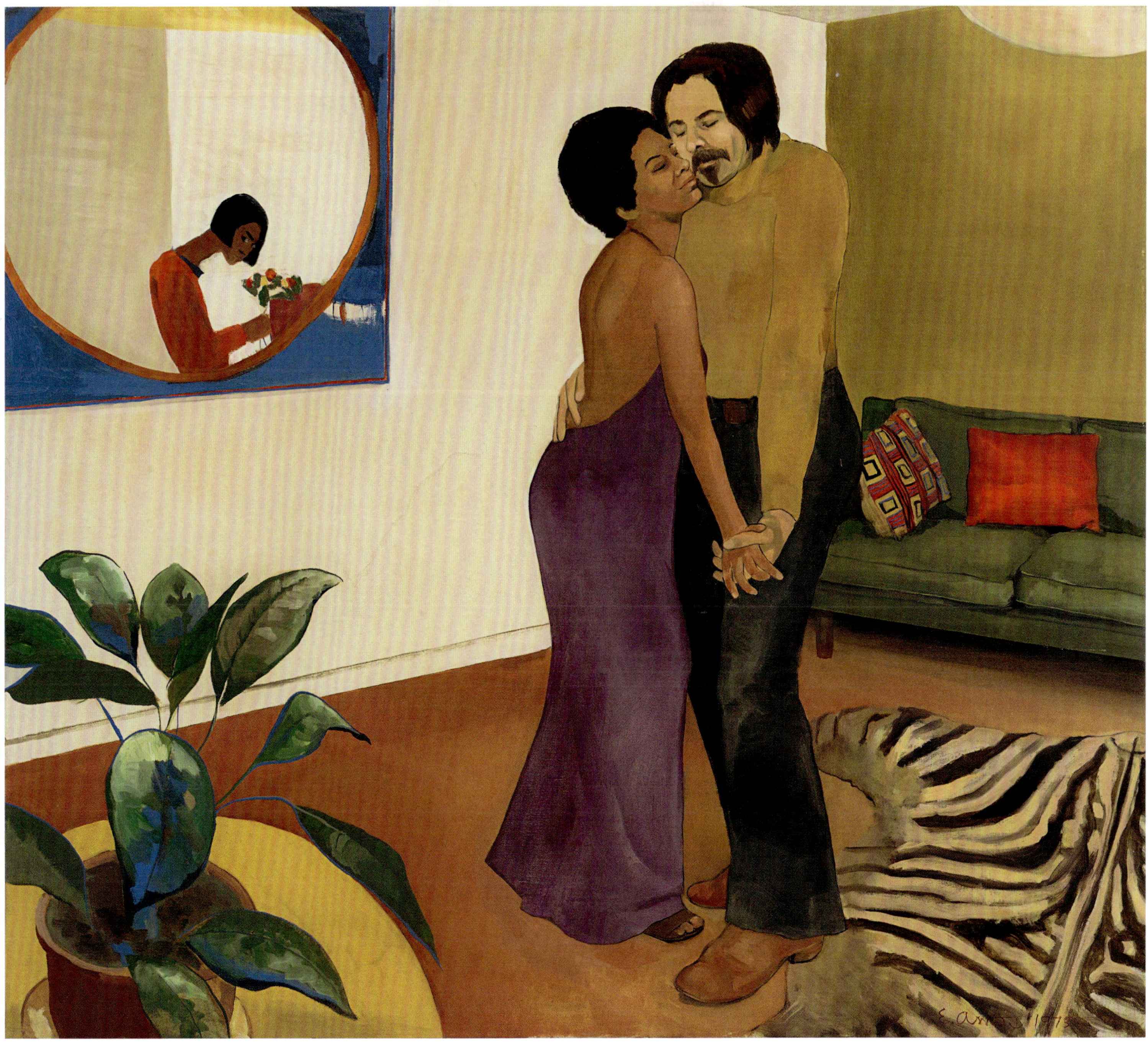

SANDY AND HER HUSBAND
1973, oil on canvas, 112.4 × 127.6 cm (44 ¼ × 50 ¼ in), Cleveland Museum of Art, Ohio, USA

Emma Amos, born 1937, Atlanta, USA. Died 2020, Bedford, New Hampshire, USA.

Amos's art incorporates multiple media often employed in inventive combinations, along with a bold use of colour and a wry repurposing of motifs from the art-historical canon. Amos grew up in Atlanta, the child of a family whose social circle included W.E.B. Du Bois, Zora Neale Hurston and painter Hale Woodruff (1900–80), who would later invite Amos to join the Black art collective, Spiral. At sixteen, she left Georgia to attend the countercultural Antioch College in Ohio before pursuing degrees at London's Central School of Art and New York University. In New York, Amos would become Spiral's only woman member, alongside artists including Romare Bearden (1911–88) and Norman Lewis (1909–79). Later, in the 1980s and 1990s, she participated in feminist collectives such as Heresies and the Guerrilla Girls. Amos's political and artistic commitments were deeply entangled; as she put it in a 1998 exhibition catalogue, 'For me, a Black woman artist, to walk into the studio is a political act.' In *Sandy and her Husband*, Amos depicts a vibrant, intimate scene between two lovers, inserting herself into the image with an earlier self-portrait, which hangs on the wall of their living room.

MAMMA ANDERSSON

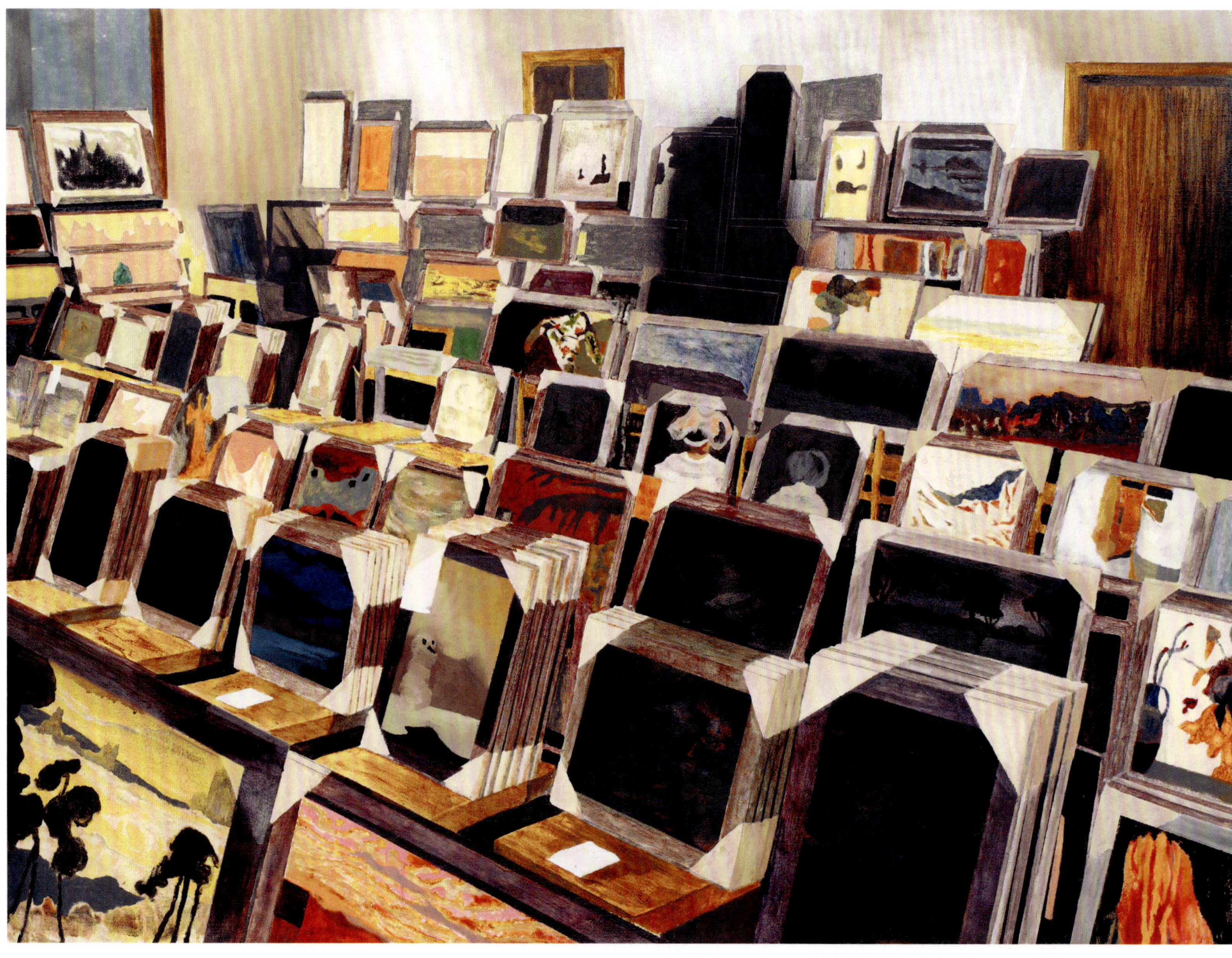

SAMLA TANKARNA (COLLECT ONE'S THOUGHTS)
2005, acrylic and oil on canvas, 110 × 150 cm (43 ¼ × 59 ⅛ in)

Mamma Andersson, born 1962, Luleå, Sweden.

A sense of mystery pervades Andersson's beguiling paintings, which are populated with familiar elements yet withhold explanation. The artist is known for her unsettling landscapes and domestic interiors, unbound from specific time or place, which hint at a fragmentary narrative that the viewer is left to piece together. Taking inspiration from stage sets, interior design and the sparse Swedish landscape where she was raised, Andersson constructs complex psychological compositions that call to mind Nordic folk art and late-nineteenth-century Romantic painting traditions. *Collect One's Thoughts* is a characteristically ambiguous work, presenting a room packed with neatly stacked canvases with protective corners, some facing the front featuring landscapes, portraits and abstractions, others shown from behind. Is this a storage space, or have these works been selected for an exhibition? Implicit in the title is a state of perturbation and the need for solace; the lack of space to move within the room evokes a sense of claustrophobia. And what is one to make of the foreboding black shadow in the background? In Andersson's paintings, questions are left hanging, evoking moods rather than providing answers.

SOFONISBA ANGUISSOLA

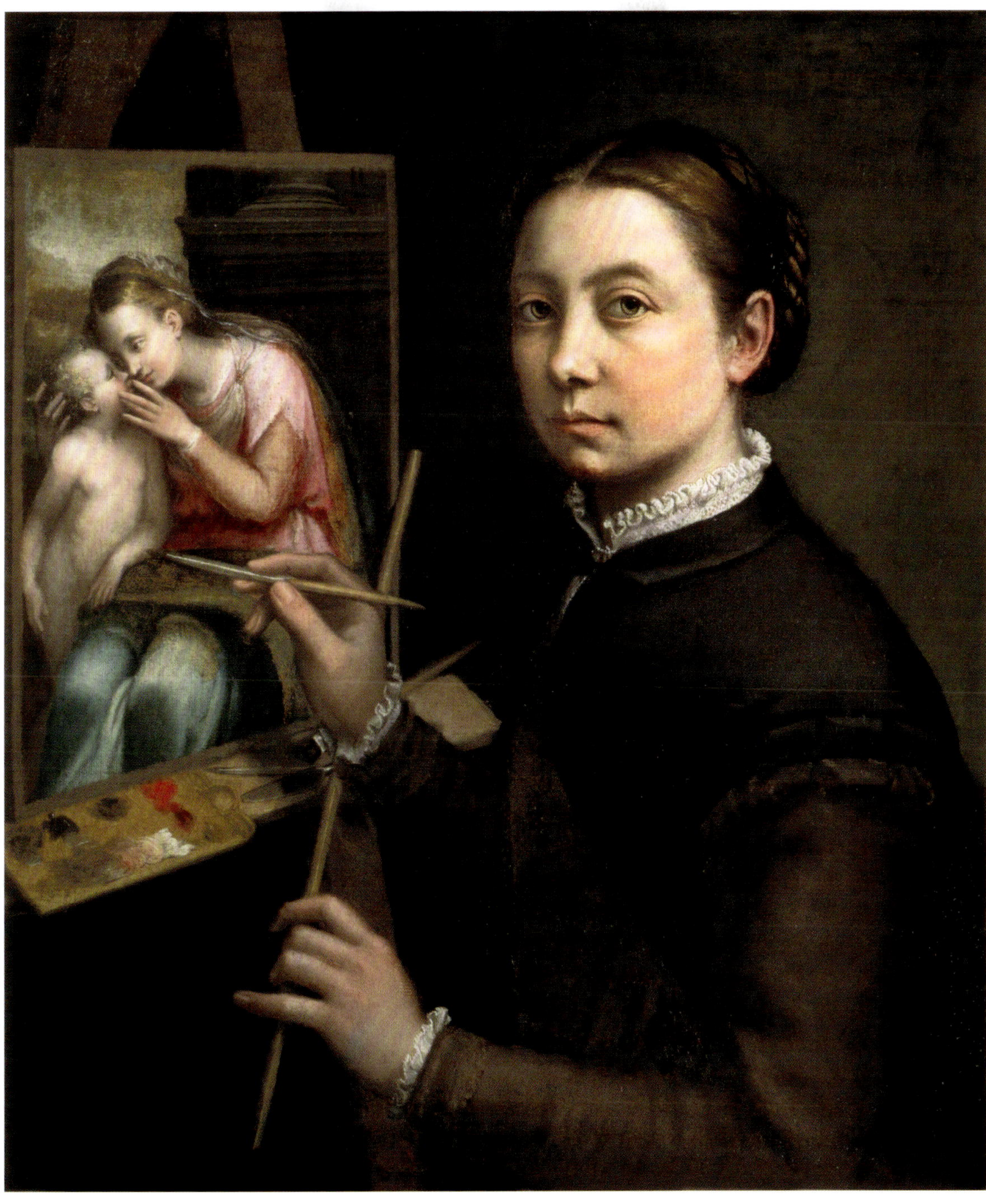

SELF-PORTRAIT AT THE EASEL
1556, oil on canvas, 66 × 57 cm (26 × 22 ⅜ in), Castle Museum, Łańcut, Poland

Sofonisba Anguissola, born *c.* 1532, Cremona, Italy. Died 1625, Palermo, Italy.

Both as a woman and as an aristocrat, Anguissola broke with convention when she undertook to become a painter. Aged eleven, she began her training under a professional male artist, Bernardino Campi (1522–91). Her youthful works were praised by Italy's most respected experts, including Michelangelo (1475–1564). This fame prompted an invitation to become a lady-in-waiting to the queen of Spain, Elisabeth of Valois, in 1559. Here, at the Spanish court, Anguissola made portraits of the royal family and taught the queen to paint. Married twice but childless, she spent her final years in Palermo, Italy, where Anthony van Dyck (1599–1641) visited her in 1624. She died the following year, amid a plague. In this self-portrait, Anguissola poses with tools in hand, following Catharina van Hemessen's (p.133) important precedent. Visible on Anguissola's small canvas is a devotional scene of Mary and the Christ Child. Mary's tender movement, effusive expression and vibrant silks contrast sharply with Anguissola's own sober dress, rigid posture and impassive demeanour. This look of moral rectitude shielded Anguissola from criticism while she carried out her transgressive, trailblazing profession.

RITA ANGUS

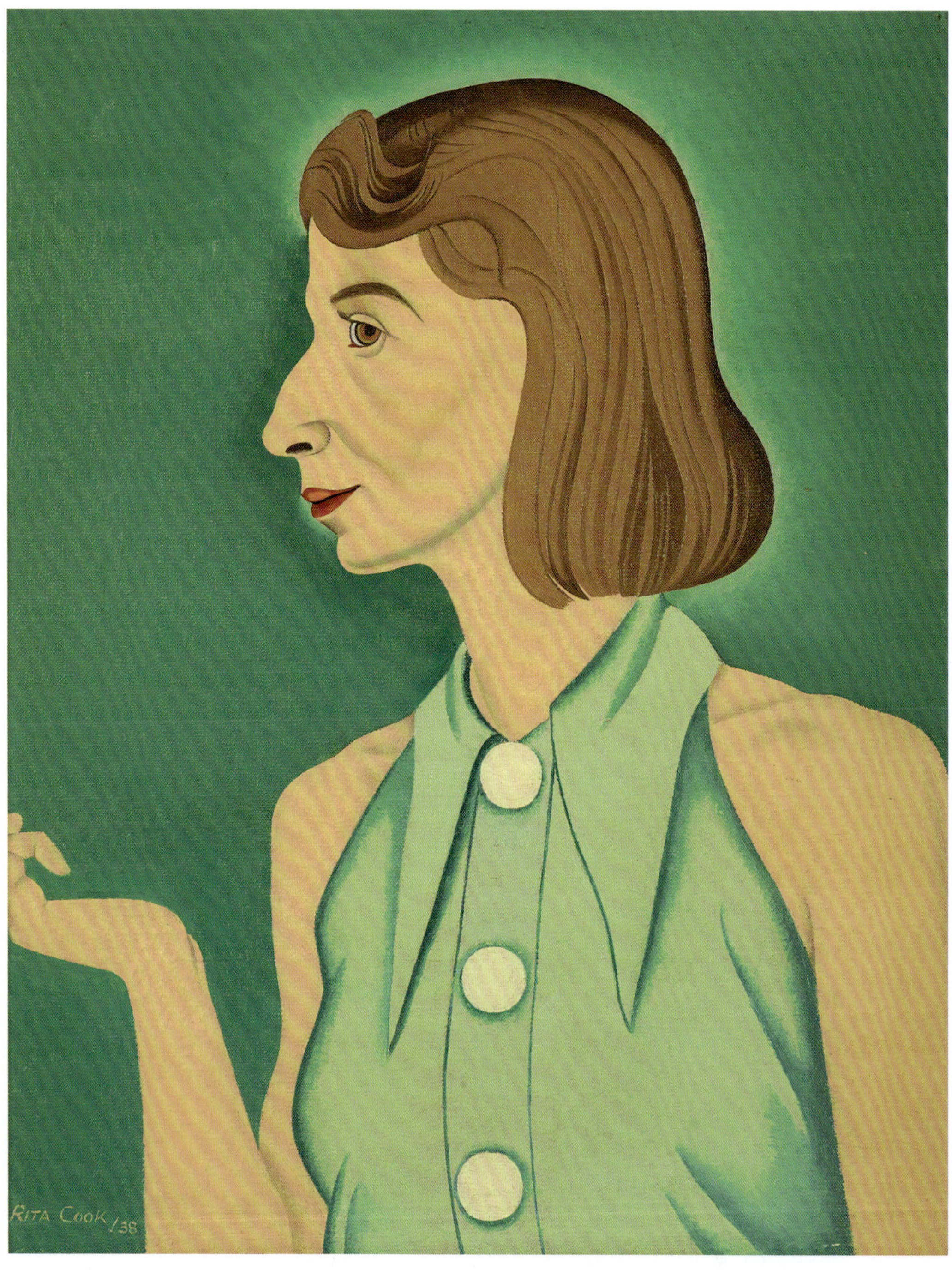

CLEOPATRA
1938, oil on canvas, 46.4 × 37.6 cm (18 ¼ × 14 ¾ in), Museum of New Zealand Te Papa Tongarewa, Wellington

Rita Angus, born 1908, Hastings, New Zealand. Died 1970, Wellington, New Zealand.

A committed feminist and pacifist, Angus was a pioneer of modern painting in New Zealand and is best known for her crisply defined portraits and landscapes painted in a flat, graphic style. From 1927 she attended Canterbury College School of Art in Christchurch, New Zealand, where she was influenced by Renaissance and medieval European art, as well as the compositions of Johannes Vermeer (1632–75) and Paul Cézanne (1839–1906). She remained committed to painting despite choosing not to complete her diploma. Separating from her artist husband Alfred Cook (1907–70) in 1934, Angus continued to sign her paintings as Rita Cook for many years, including this striking self-portrait as the ancient Egyptian queen Cleopatra. Employing a stylistic convention common in ancient Near Eastern art, her head and neck are shown in profile, while her body, dressed in contemporary clothing, is depicted frontally. In addition to her many carefully observed portraits and self-portraits, Angus painted numerous landscapes, particularly in Wellington and the rural Hawke's Bay areas of New Zealand's North Island.

HELENE APPEL

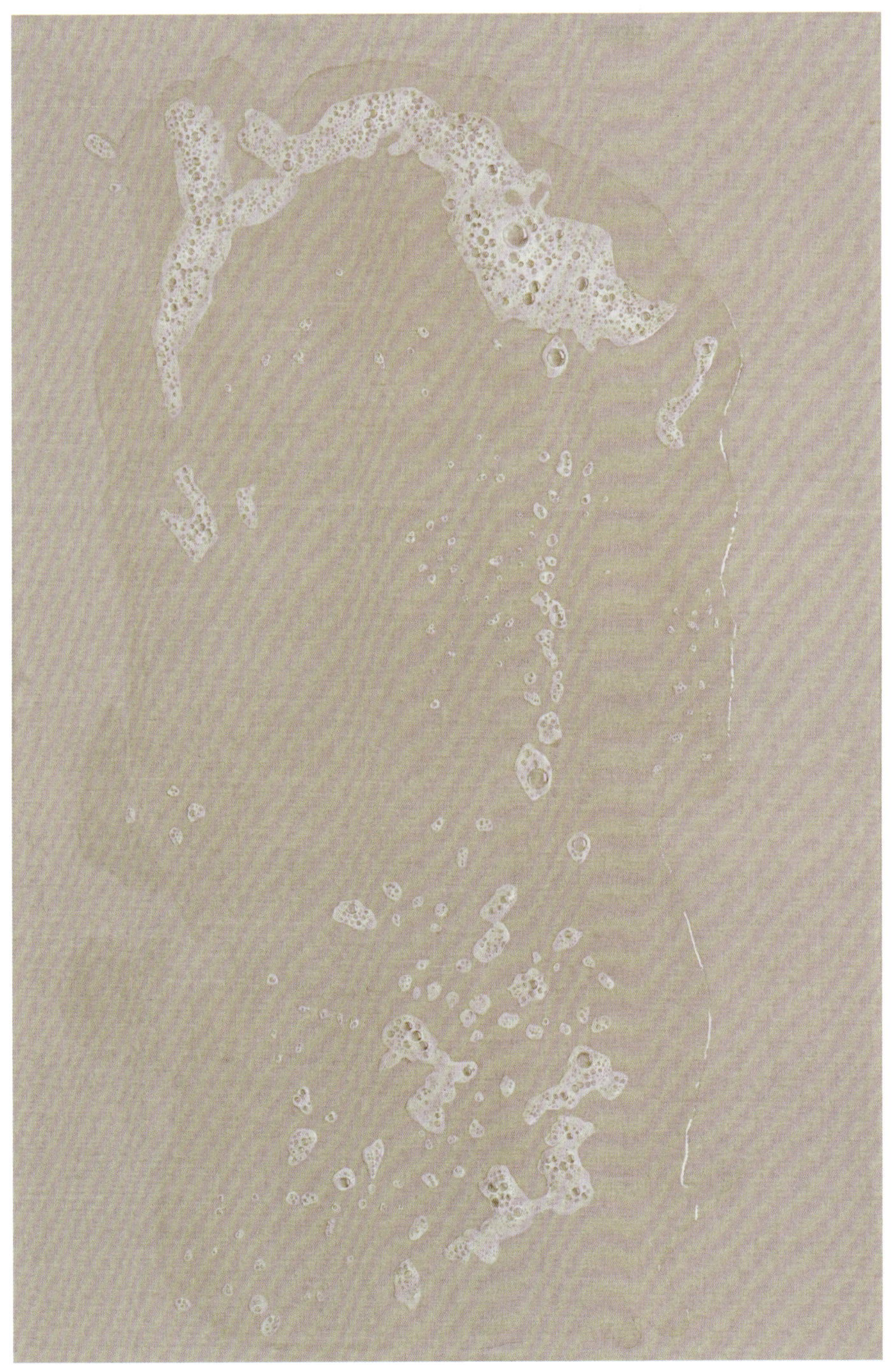

WASHING LIQUID
2018, acrylic, watercolour and oil on linen,
120 × 80 cm (47 ⅛ × 31 ⅜ in)

Helene Appel, born 1976, Karlsruhe, Germany.

At once unassuming and startlingly life-like, Appel's trompe l'oeil paintings on linen and burlap depict everyday objects often found in domestic spaces, such as slabs of meat, grains of rice, lettuce leaves, accumulated dust and debris, and netting, all depicted from an aerial view with textural precision and complete with intricate shadows. Appel attended the Hochschule für Bildende Künste in Hamburg before receiving her master's degree in painting from the Royal College of Art in London in 2006. Her work, simultaneously abstract in its spare design and hyperrealist in technique, has been compared both to Minimalism and the Photorealist painters of the late 1960s and early 1970s. In *Washing Liquid*, made using watercolour as well as acrylic and oil, a puddle with soapy foam appears to pool on the painting's surface, the surface tension of its edges exactingly rendered with subtle reflections of light. Finding beauty in the mundane, Appel devotes an extreme level of attention and care to sights and objects that are often overlooked, and in the process trains her viewers to reconsider what they might otherwise take for granted.

FARAH ATASSI

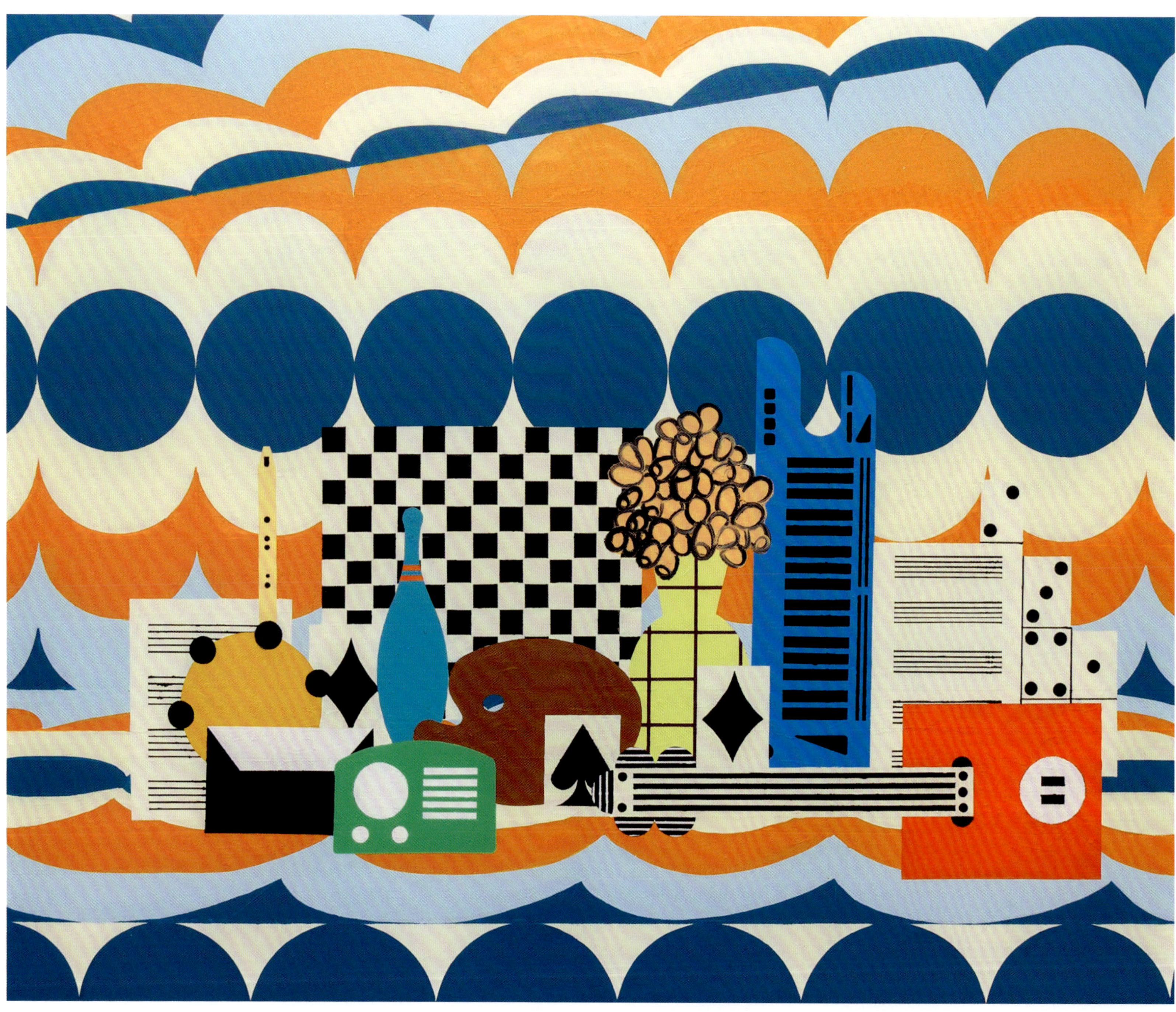

STILL LIFE WITH PALETTE AND ROSES
2018, oil and enamel on canvas, 180 × 220 × 2.5 cm (70 ⅞ × 86 ⅝ × 1 in), private collection

Farah Atassi, born 1981, Brussels, Belgium.

In her boldly chromatic and eclectic renderings of still-life tableaux and studio scenes, Atassi offers a new dialogue with the history of modern art. Across her paintings, the artist smartly quotes and displays motifs connected to the work of Pablo Picasso, Piet Mondrian, Kazimir Malevich or Henri Matisse, as well as elements borrowed from classical art and textiles. Simplified depictions of bottles, artistic implements, musical instruments and the occasional model are often nestled within kaleidoscopic arrays of concentric patterns and repeated abstract shapes, which lend a sense of optical rhythm to the surfaces of Atassi's canvases. *Still Life with Palette and Roses* features an arrangement of Cubist archetypes – guitars, sheet music, bottles, a flower vase and playing cards. These fill the painting's lower half and are surrounded by a field of pulsating circles and waves, inspired by the psychedelic aesthetic. Using clean contours and flatly applied colour, Atassi creates a characteristically dynamic matrix of anachronistic shapes and subjects waiting to be discovered.

SYBIL ATTECK

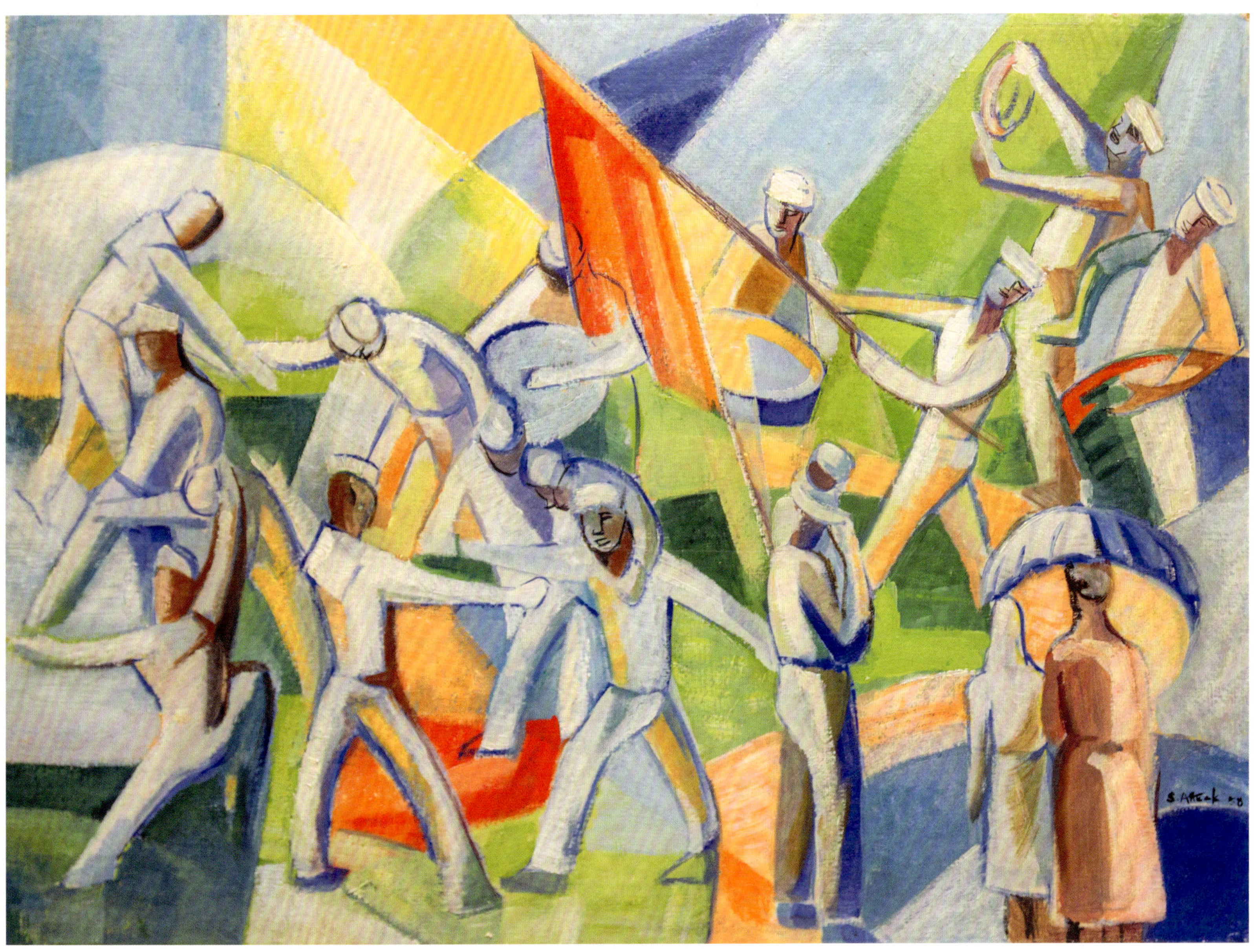

FLAG WAVERS
1958, oil on canvas board, 26.7 × 39.4 cm (10½ × 15½ in)

Sybil Atteck, born 1911, Tableland, Trinidad and Tobago. Died 1975, Valsayn, Trinidad and Tobago.

Born to a Chinese family who nurtured her passion for drawing and painting, Atteck was a pioneering figure in the art history of Trinidad and Tobago, celebrated for her dynamic depictions of the islands and their people. Atteck first worked as a botanical illustrator for the Ministry of Agriculture before studying internationally in London, Lima and St. Louis, USA. In the 1950s she stoked national pride with paintings such as *Flag Wavers*, which captures the exuberant carnival celebrations in Port of Spain, showing sailor figures – one waving a flag – dancing energetically against a variegated background of overlapping geometric shapes. Atteck's landscapes and scenes of everyday life represent an anthropological commentary on the environment, people and culture of Trinidad and Tobago. The lively, expressionistic style she developed was foundational to the country's first recognizable school of painting, which emerged as it edged towards independence in 1962. As the first contemporary woman painter from Trinidad to find international acclaim, Atteck was appointed to the government committee that designed the country's new national flag and the symbols for its coat of arms.

DOTTY ATTIE

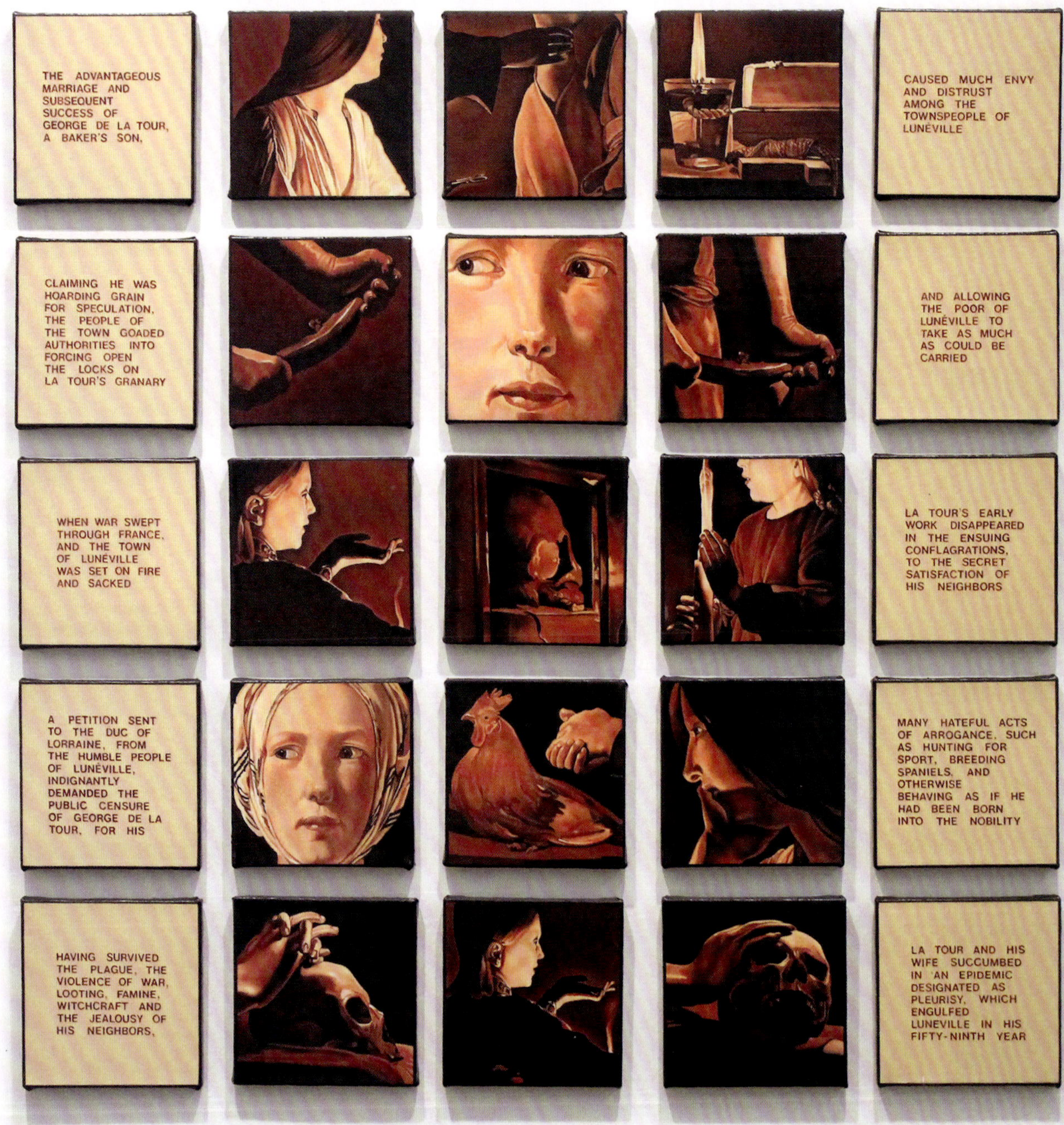

LUNEVILLE
1991, oil on linen, 25 panels, each: 15.2 × 15.2 cm (6 × 6 in)

Dotty Attie, born 1938, Pennsauken Township, New Jersey, USA.

Encouraged by her father to pursue painting, Attie graduated from Philadelphia College of Art in 1959. Since the 1970s she has worked with a distinctive figurative approach, reproducing and recontextualizing fragments of paintings by historic artists – such as Johannes Vermeer (1632–75) and Jean-Auguste-Dominique Ingres (1780–1867) – as well as Hollywood film stills and stock photography. A staunch feminist, Attie was a founding member of A.I.R. Gallery (see p.279), a New York cooperative dedicated to showing the work of women artists, where her 1972 solo show won her wide recognition. Her multi-panel paintings combine images with short texts that together form narrative sequences, often offering subtle critiques of gender bias and the male gaze in representations of women. The twenty-five square panels of *Luneville* are arranged into a grid format and reference the life and work of painter Georges de la Tour (1593–1652), who lived and worked in the French town of Lunéville. Fifteen central images reproducing details from the Baroque painter's works are flanked by ten text panels presenting a less than flattering account of his life, their proximity charging the isolated portions of his famous paintings with new resonances.

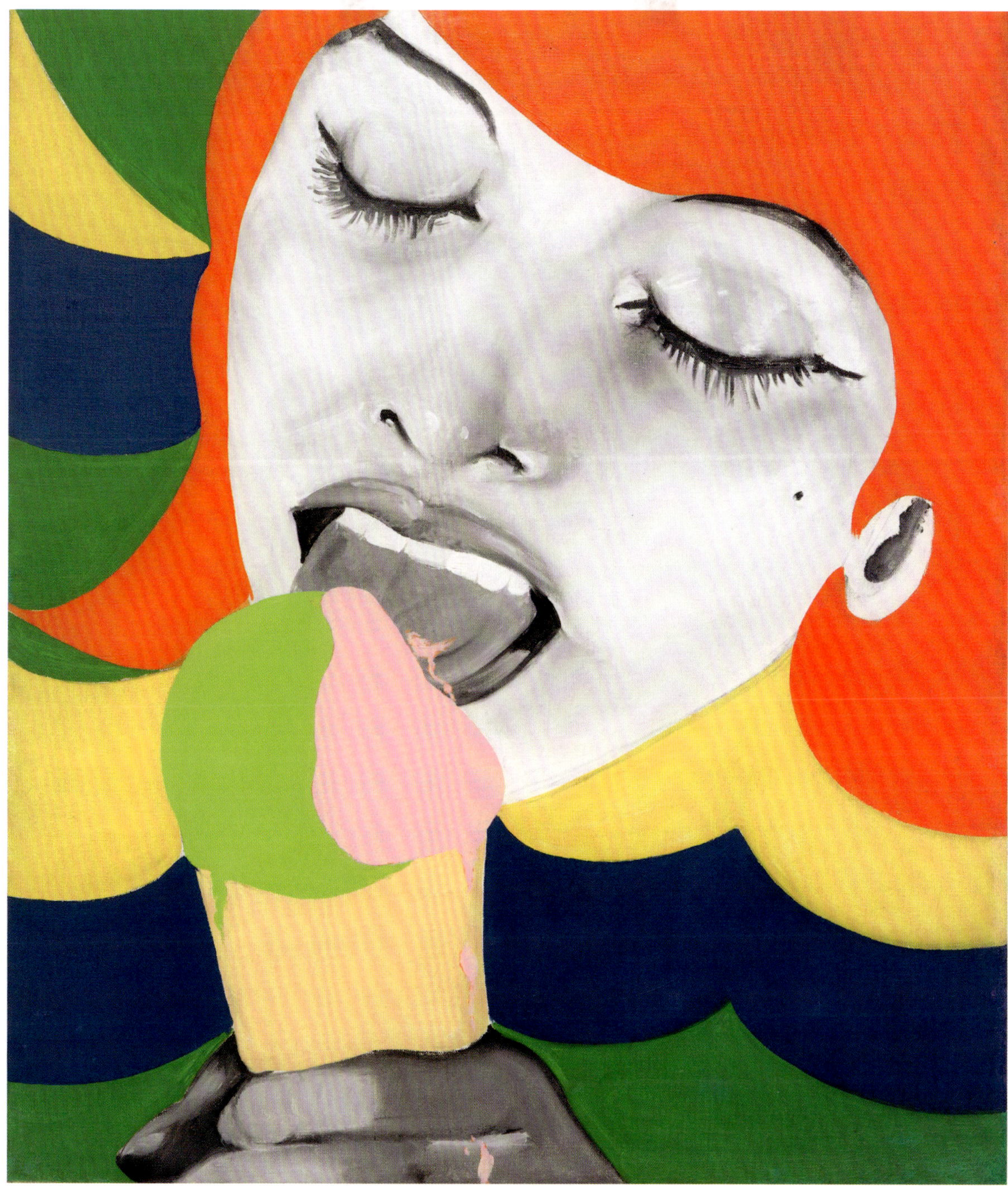

ICE CREAM 1
1964, oil on canvas, 80 × 70 cm (31½ × 27½ in)

Evelyne Axell, born 1935, Namur, Belgium.
Died 1972, Zwijnaarde, Ghent, Belgium.

One of the few European women artists to fully embrace the global Pop art movement, Axell took art lessons from Surrealist artist René Magritte (1898–1967), who was a family friend. Having been introduced to British Pop artists Pauline Boty (p.60), Allen Jones (b.1937) and Patrick Caulfield (1936–2005) by her husband, who was directing a film about them, Axell set about merging Surrealist iconography with the Pop predilection for common culture. She created her own style by cutting female silhouettes from vinyl sheeting and subsequently painting the resulting shapes, often in vivid enamel colours. *Ice Cream 1* audaciously depicts an elegant woman licking a two-toned ice cream cone. Alluding to advertising aesthetics, wavy multi-coloured stripes surround her black-and-white face and tomato-red hair, while a splash of pink paint dripped onto her fingers suggests melting ice cream. Suggestive, ironically objectified images of women were common in Pop art. In this painting, however, Axell reclaims femininity for her own painterly pleasure – the image radiates emancipation and coolness, granting permission for other women to do the same.

NADIA AYARI

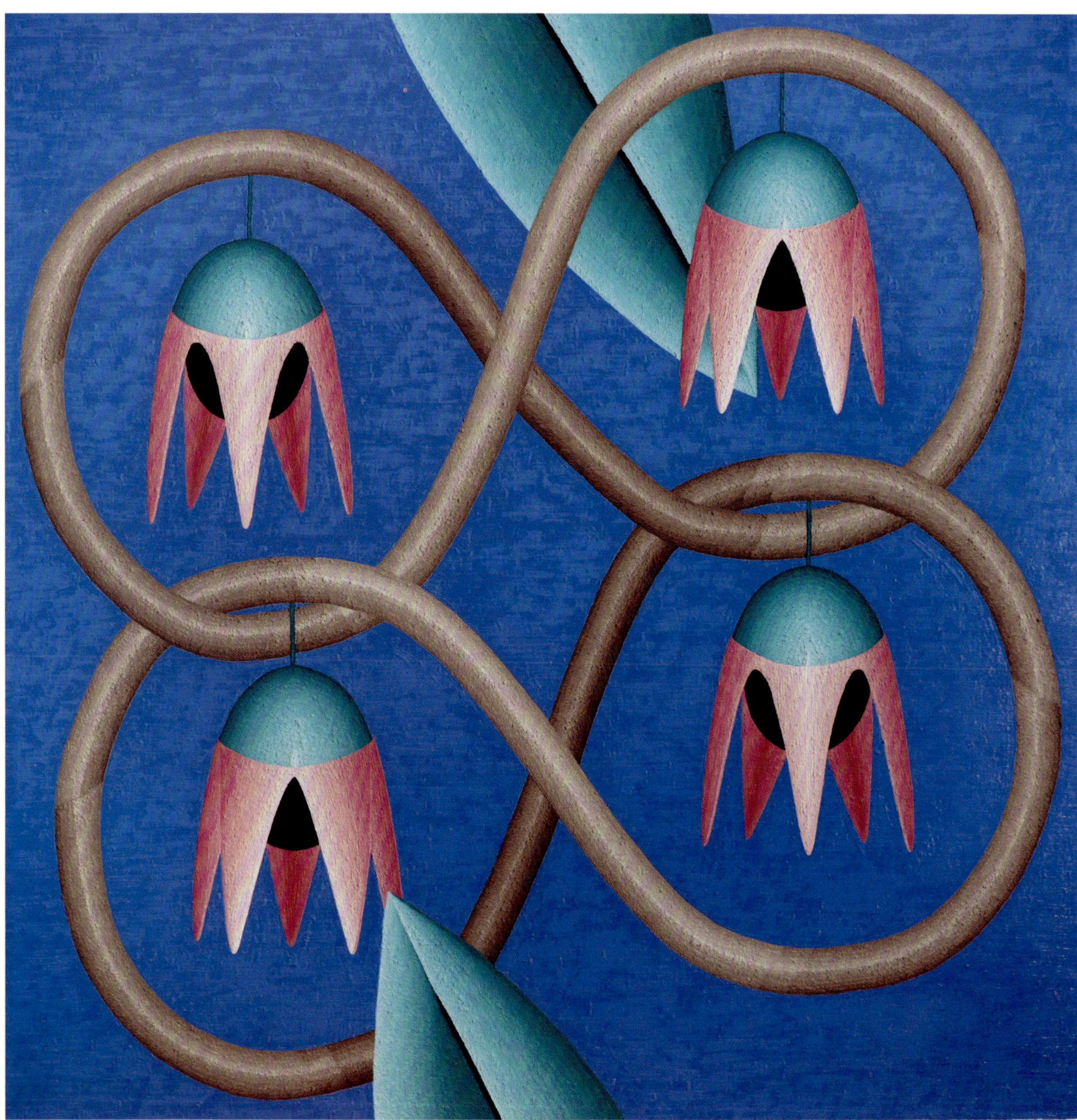

LOOP III
2021, oil on linen, 152.4 × 152.4 cm (60 × 60 in), collection of Lisa Schiff, New York, USA

Nadia Ayari, born 1981, Tunis, Tunisia.

Raised in Tunisia, Ayari moved to the United States in 2000, where she attended Boston University, the Rhode Island School of Design and Brandeis University before settling in New York, where she lives and works. In serial paintings that feature a tight selection of recurring motifs – among them flower blossoms, leaves, eyes and figs – Ayari explores the mystical and personal symbolism to be found in nature. The artist draws inspiration from the landscape and native flora of North Africa as well as poetry, language, science fiction and spiritual practice, often distilling visionary narratives and botanical forms into stylized, esoteric compositions that are executed in a limited palette of jewel-toned purples, blues, greens and pinks. Her recent paintings, whose surfaces are built up slowly from layers of thick impasto, render familiar subjects wholly enigmatic through visual devices such as cropping and repetition. In *Loop III*, for instance, abstracted flowers hang from crossing infinity-looped stems, their pointed pink petals concealing their dark cores. Framed by giant leaves rendered with similarly applied gradations in colour, they float together within a dreamy, lapis-lazuli field.

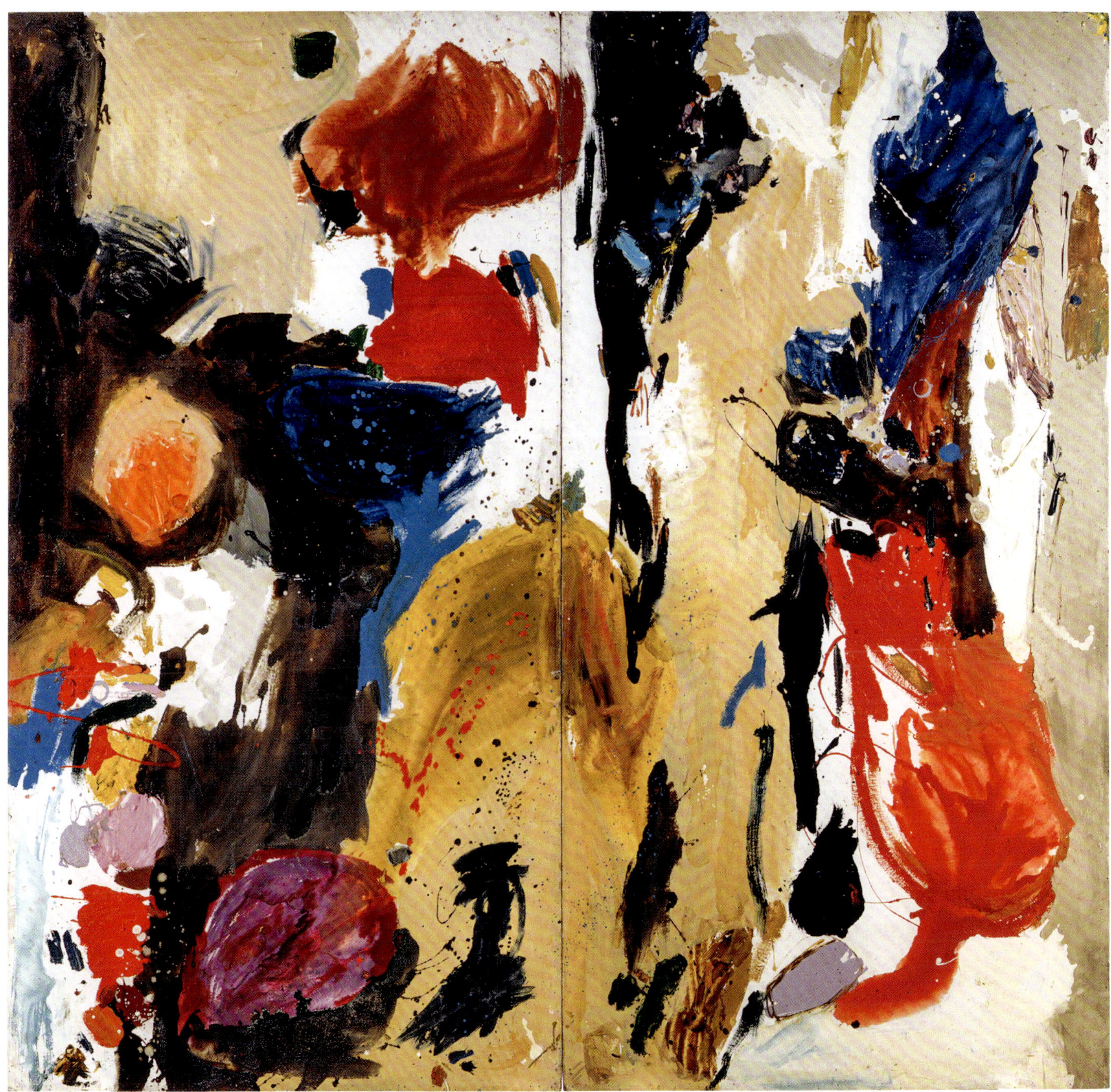

CUMULI
1959, oil and Ripolin on board, diptych, overall: 305 × 320 cm (120 ⅛ × 126 in)

Gillian Ayres, born 1930, London, UK. Died 2018, North Devon, UK.

In a prolific career spanning almost seventy years, Ayres was one of the leading proponents of abstract painting in post-war Britain, remaining firmly committed to the medium, about which she described herself as 'obsessed'. Her inaugural solo exhibition at Gallery One, London, in 1956 was later followed by prestigious presentations at public institutions in London including the Serpentine Gallery (1983), Tate Gallery (1995) and Royal Academy of Arts (1997), and she was nominated for the Turner Prize in 1989. Ayres also taught throughout the 1960s and 1970s, becoming the first female head of painting at a British art school (Winchester) in 1978. She was renowned for her large-scale works, which she initially painted on the floor and later using ladders. Flowing across two abutting boards, *Cumuli* is typical of Ayres's colourful, gestural Tachist compositions of the late 1950s. It was exhibited in the landmark 'Situation' exhibition of 1960 at the Royal Society of British Artists (RBA) Galleries, London, in which she was the only woman artist – as highlighted in a portrait of the Situation Group by Sylvia Sleigh (p.279) painted the following year.

CHRISTINE AY TJOE

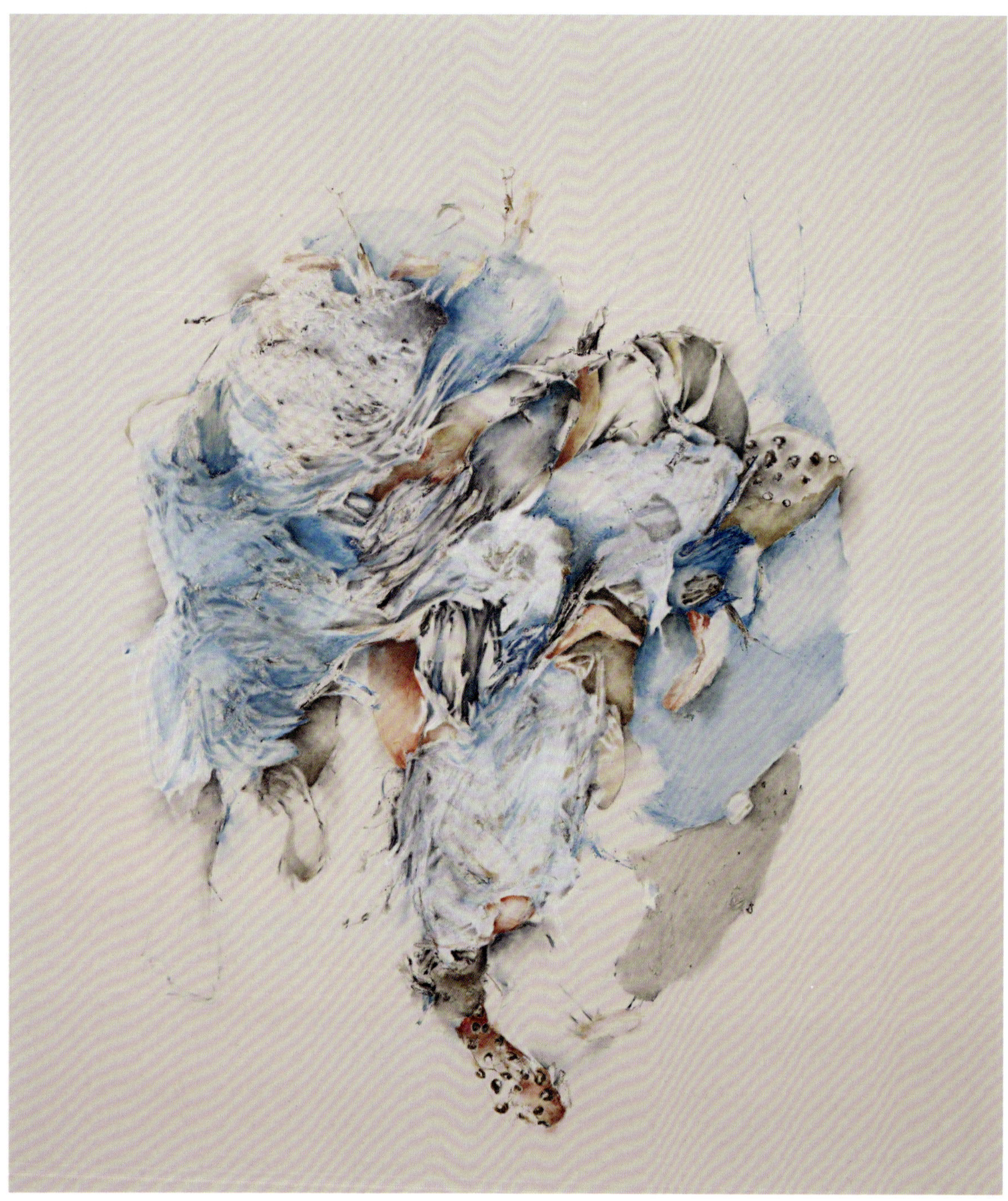

BLUE CRYPTOBIOSIS #04
2020–1, oil on canvas, 230 × 200 cm
(90 ½ × 78 ¾ in)

Christine Ay Tjoe, born 1973, Bandung, Indonesia.

Unlike other post-war Indonesian artists addressing the country's colonial past through art, Ay Tjoe references the familiar flora and fauna from her native Bandung to convey existential themes and psychological complexities. Her painting practice is rooted in an early interest in drawing, resulting in her gravitating towards drypoint etching on metal plates and preferring oil stick over paintbrush. In her expansive canvases, layers of colours and textures juxtapose controlled lines with spontaneous finger smudges. Using natural surroundings as inspiration – tangles of tree roots, for example, or clumps of moss and fungi growing out of walls – Ay Tjoe abstracts and intuitively assembles them, often leaving large expanses of raw, untreated canvas in her finished compositions. This work comes from 'Blue Cryptobiosis', a series she developed during the COVID-19 pandemic, whose title refers to the physiological state when metabolic activity reduces to an undetectable level, allowing certain organisms to survive an extreme period of duress. Different hues of blue, presented here as feathery waves and puddles that resemble the shape of a human heart, dominate this series and symbolize hope for the artist, amid a standstill moment throughout the world.

HARRIET BACKER

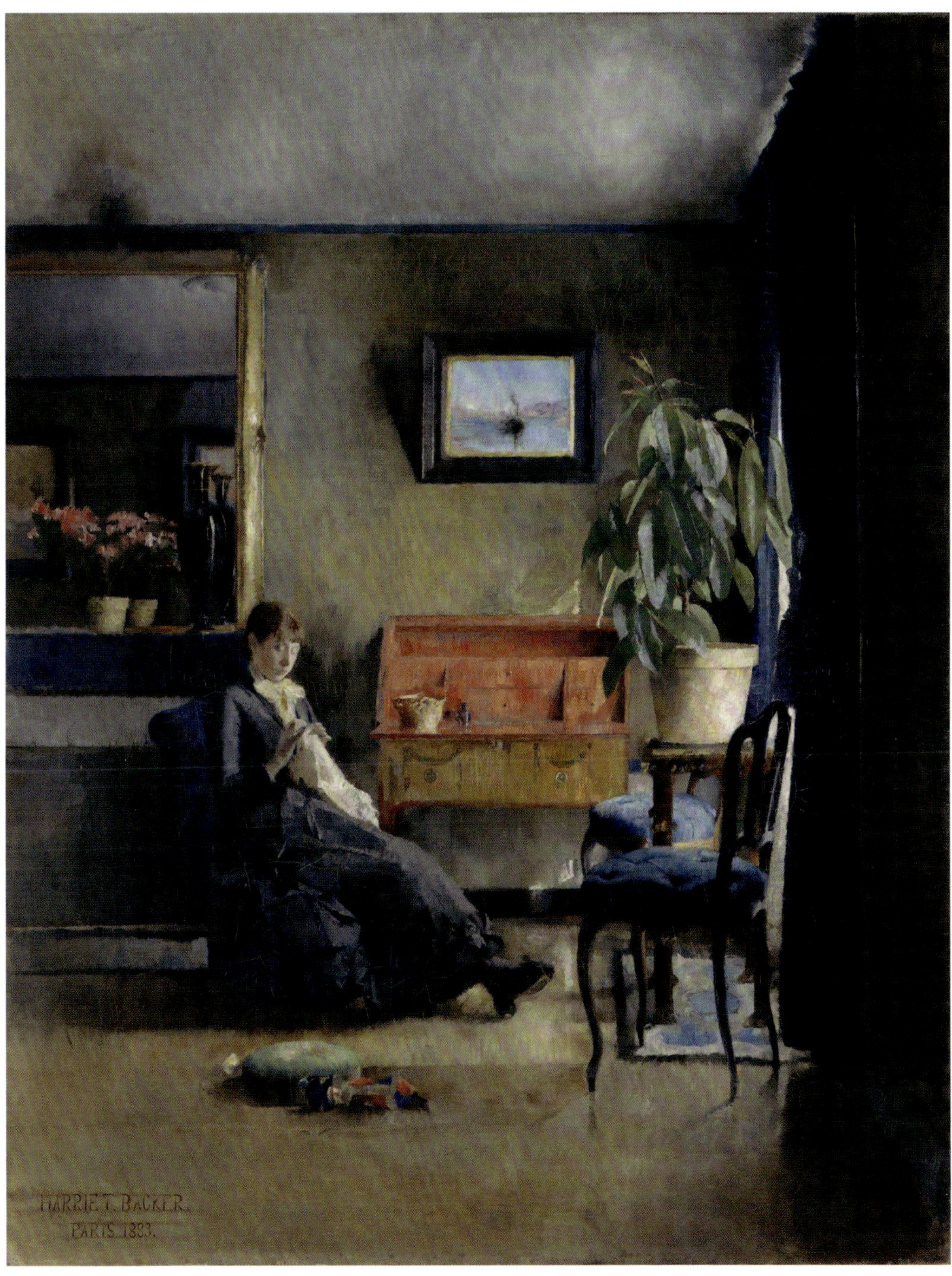

BLÅTT INTERIØR (BLUE INTERIOR)
1883, oil on canvas, 84 × 66 cm (33 ⅛ × 26 in), National Museum, Oslo, Norway

Harriet Backer, born 1845, Holmestrand, Norway. Died 1932, Oslo, Norway.

Between 1865 and 1878, Backer was travel companion to her older sister, the composer-pianist Agathe Backer Grøndahl, which afforded her the opportunity to visit many of Europe's major art museums. After completing private art studies in Berlin, Oslo and Munich, in 1878 she moved to Paris to attend Madame Trélat de Vigny's art school for women, where her cohorts included Hélène Schjerfbeck (p.260). In 1880, Backer's painting of a contemplative woman in a stark interior entitled *Solitude* was accepted (with honourable mention) into the annual Salon exhibition at the Académie des Beaux-Arts in Paris, alongside works by Claude Monet (1840–1926) and Édouard Manet (1832–83). Figures in domestic settings became a principal subject for Backer, who also moved towards the looser brushstroke favoured by Impressionist painters of the day. *Blue Interior* exemplifies this approach and demonstrates a sophisticated handling of light across the composition from an unseen window. Returning to Oslo in 1888, Backer established a school for painters, which she ran until 1910. In 2022 the National Museum of Norway honoured the artist with her own room in its permanent collection, a belated and fitting tribute to an artist who continued to win awards and exhibit internationally until her death.

JO BAER

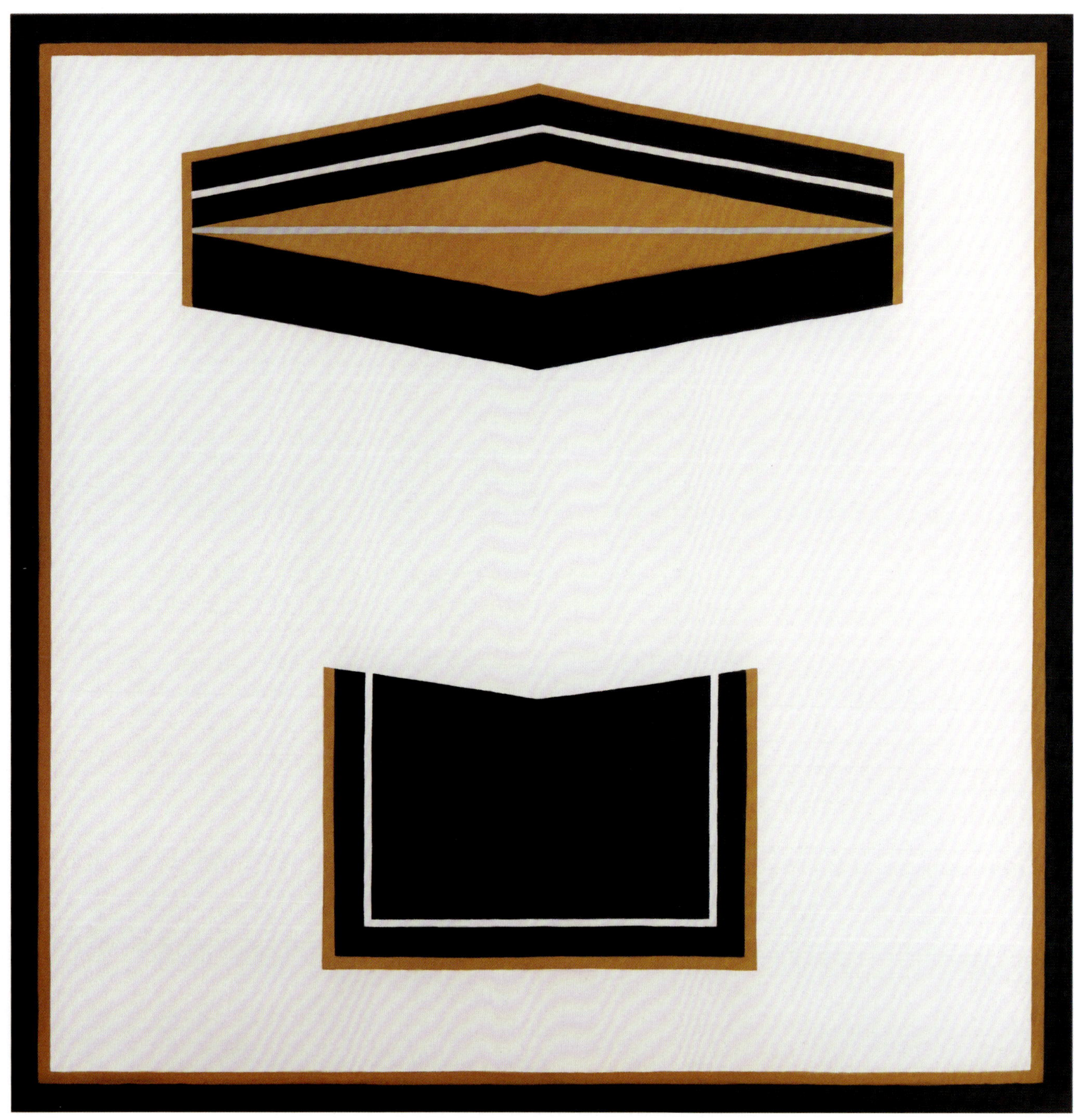

THE RISEN (WINK)
1960–1/2019, oil on canvas, 183.8 × 183.8 cm
(72 ⅜ × 72 ⅜ in)

Jo Baer, born 1929, Seattle, USA.

With a career spanning more than fifty years, Baer was part of the Minimalist movement in 1960s New York, making hard-edged, geometric abstract paintings. These monumental works explored relationships between lines, shapes and contrasting colours in space. By the end of the decade, she became critical of the Minimalist conceit and the self-declared leaders of the movement's rejection of the medium of painting. Following an exhibition of her work at the Whitney Museum of American Art in 1975, she relocated to the Irish countryside, London and, finally, Amsterdam, in search of a language outside the mainstream. Her subsequent works have included figurative references to nature, such as rocks, mountains and rivers, as well as symbols and signs of human civilization. This painting comes from 'The Risen', a 2019 series of five large-scale abstract canvases modelled on works Baer made in 1960 and 1961 that she subsequently destroyed – but not before taking photographs of herself posing defiantly next to them. In recreating these works, Baer draws connections between her earlier ideals and her more recent approaches to the medium, delineating a trajectory that demonstrates the artist's fundamental commitment to painting.

ALICE BAILLY

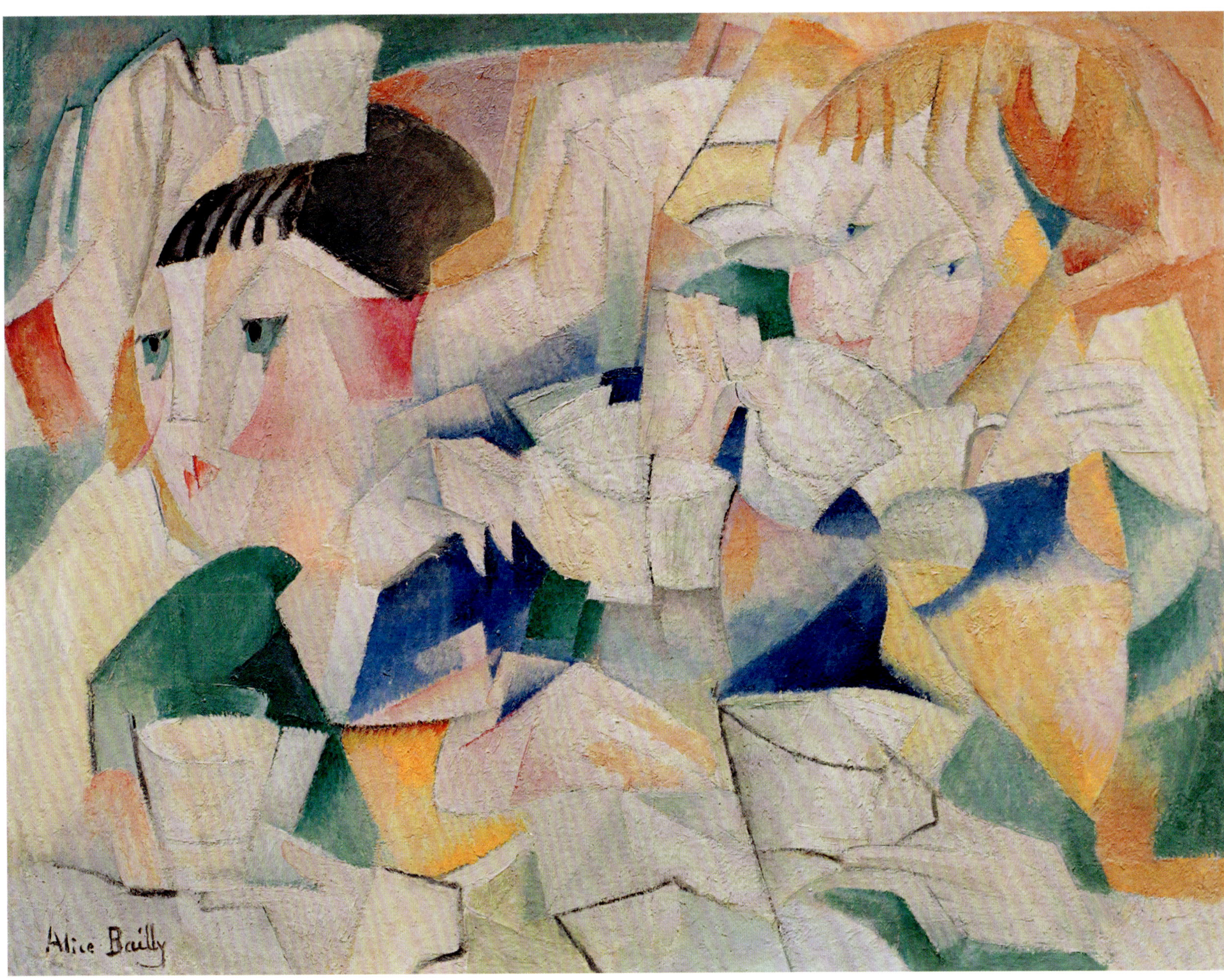

LE THÉ (TEA TIME)
1914, oil on canvas, 49 × 65 cm (19 ¼ × 25 ⅝ in), Aargauer Kunsthaus, Aarau, Switzerland

Alice Bailly, born 1872, Geneva, Switzerland. Died 1938, Lausanne, Switzerland.

Having studied drawing in her native Switzerland, Bailly moved to Paris in 1904 when the city was on the cusp of an artistic revolution. There she fell in with avant-garde painters such as Juan Gris (1887–1927), Francis Picabia (1879–1953) and Marie Laurencin (p.175) and encountered diverse influences including Fauvism, Cubism and Futurism. Bailly took inspiration from these approaches and in 1908 exhibited her canvases at the Salon d'Automne alongside several Fauve painters. She returned to Switzerland after the outbreak of the First World War and was briefly involved in the Dada movement. She later developed her signature 'wool paintings', employing yarn to simulate brushstrokes. In this early work depicting two women taking tea, Bailly has divided the composition into a vibrant mass of colourful overlapping facets. Multiple disjointed cups and hands can be discerned, conveying the impression of successive movements from several perspectives simultaneously. There seems to be a disconnect between the two women, who look away from each other, absorbed by their own thoughts as they sip their drinks. Their countenances betray a sense of malaise that stands in tension with her vibrant colour rendering of this social ritual.

BARBARA

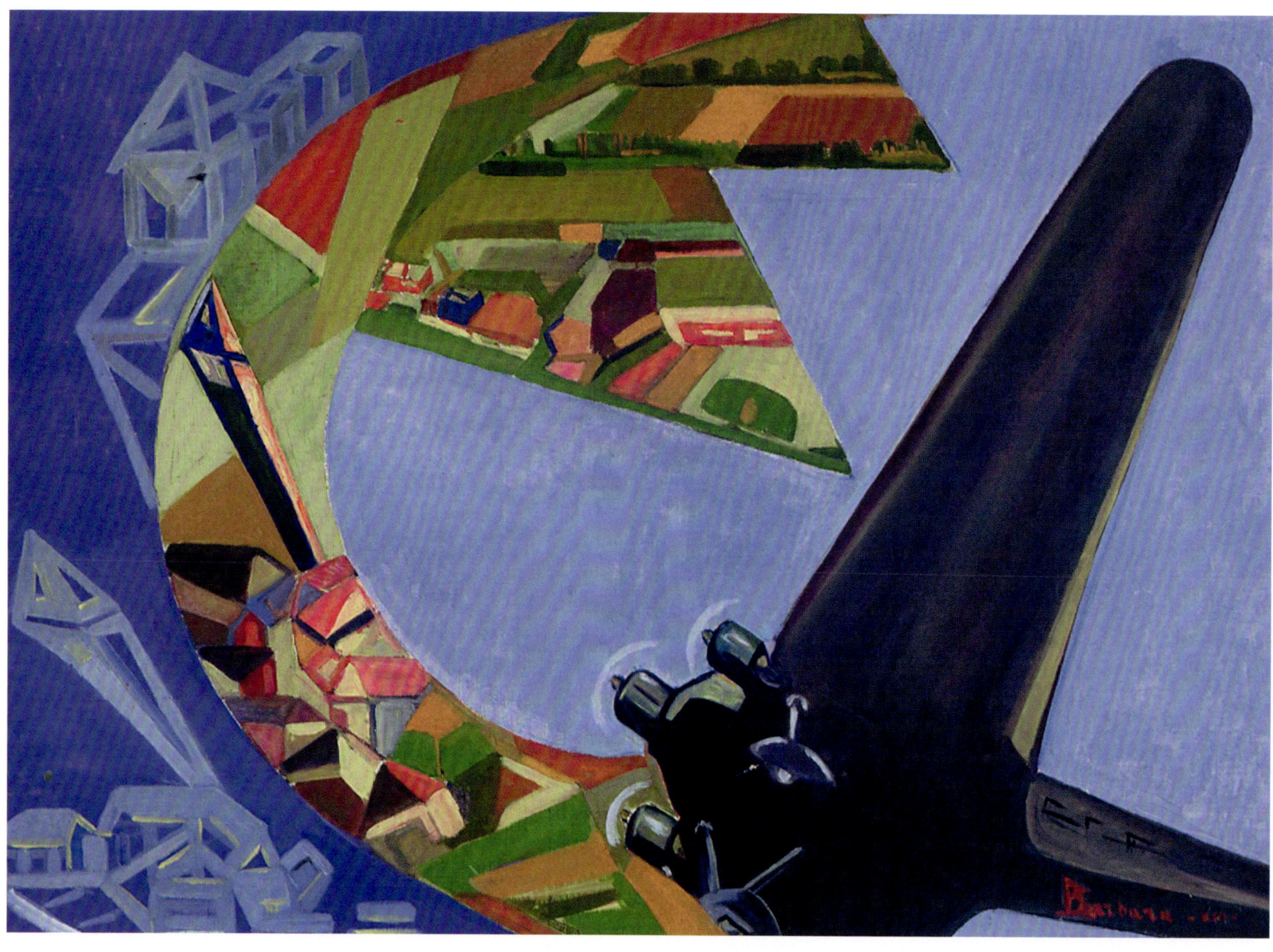

AEROPITTURA (AERIAL PAINTING)
1938, oil on prepared canvas, 49.5 × 69.5 cm
(19 ½ × 27 ⅜ in)

Barbara, born 1915, Mortara, Italy. Died 2002, Rome, Italy.

Having taken art lessons from the age of eleven, Barbara (born Olga Biglieri) secretly studied to become a pilot, securing a full licence aged eighteen. This achievement afforded the teenager a unique aerial view on the world, which inspired her work in drawing while she was a student at the Brera Academy in Milan. In 1935 the artist began associating with the second generation of Italian Futurists, changing her name to Barbara to channel attributes of the barbaric and strong. The hallmarks outlined in the 1929 'Manifesto of Aeropittura' codified the genre of Aeropittura (aerial painting) as seen in this 1938 work, where the wing of a plane in flight cuts a swathe through a landscape of fields and buildings. Contrasting perspectives, forms and colours capture the dynamism and speed of a futuristic machine age, soaring free from a terrestrial and fixed-perspective past. One of few women painters associated with Futurism (Benedetta, p.51, was another), Barbara separated from the movement at the outset of the Second World War, uncomfortable with its close ties with fascism. Abandoning art for a number of years, she later founded a fashion press agency and became a vocal pacifist, receiving a Nobel Peace Prize nomination in 2000.

BISERKA BARETIĆ

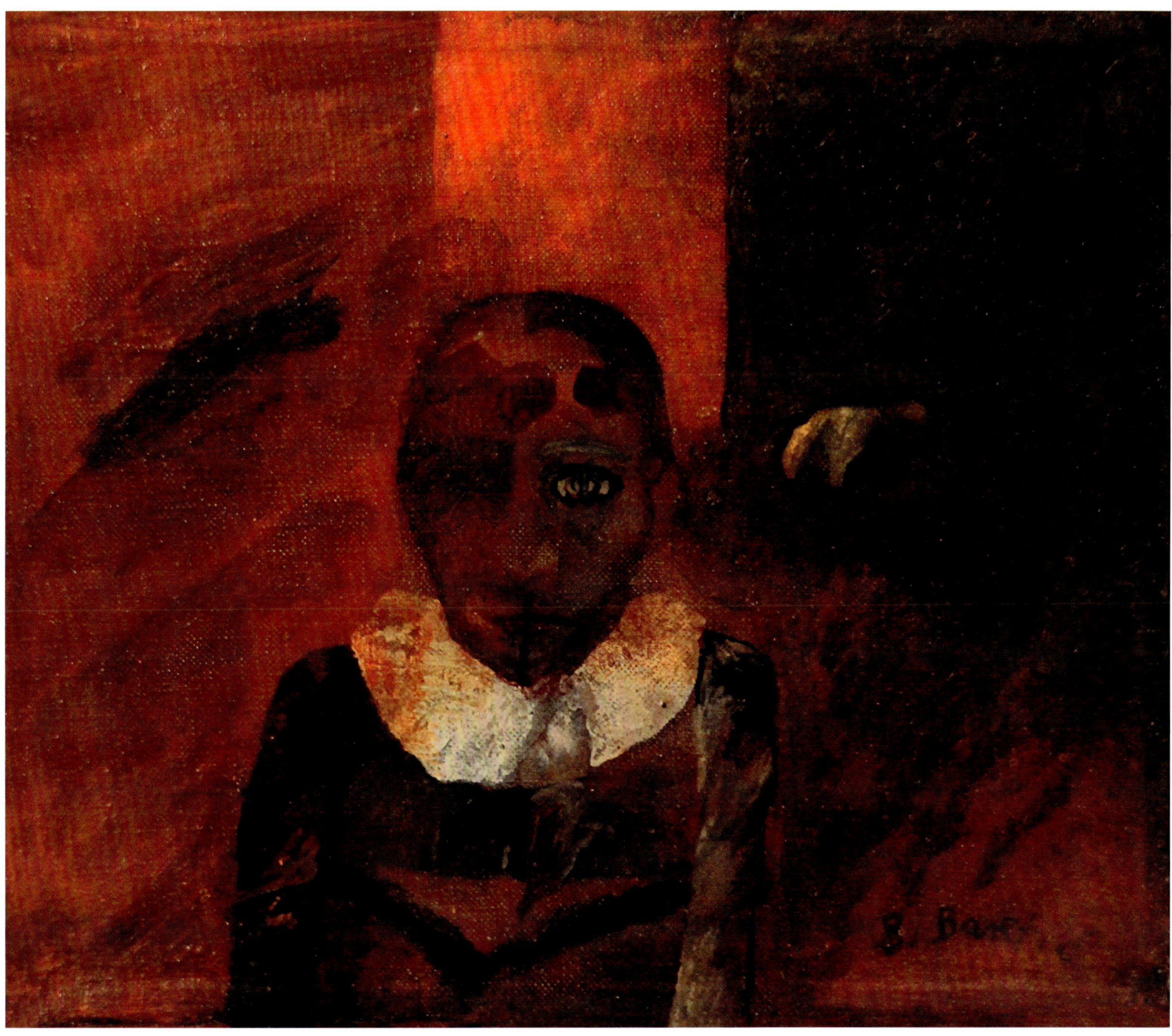

ŠUTNJA (SILENCE)
1958, oil on canvas, 22.5 × 30 cm (8 ⅞ × 11 ¾ in), private collection

Biserka Baretić, born 1933, Zagreb, Croatia.

Trained as a painter and a graphic artist, Baretić studied painting at the Academy of Fine Arts in Zagreb from 1951 to 1953. She then moved to the port city of Rovinj, where she began showing Surrealist-inspired paintings. In these haunting works, of which *Silence* is an example, lingering limbs emerge from darkness, faces blur, threatening to either disappear or emerge in total clarity, and creaturely forms dance across the canvas. By the early 1960s, the artist's style became more abstract, and she often abandoned the figure completely. Her paintings, drawings and prints feature evocative colours and uncanny imagery that stir a sense of unease in the viewer. Interested in chaos and entropy, Baretić's scenes explore the possibility of beauty in the wake of despair, sometimes appearing as apocryphal landscapes and at others wholly abstract. Dramatic colouration and disjointed imagery result in spaces that appear untenable and uninhabitable, too discordant to sustain life. Yet in the murkiest patches of colour and form, there are bright lines that breathe through, seeming to insist that something will emerge out of the darkness. In Baretić's world, horror and hope are symbiotic.

JENNIFER BARTLETT

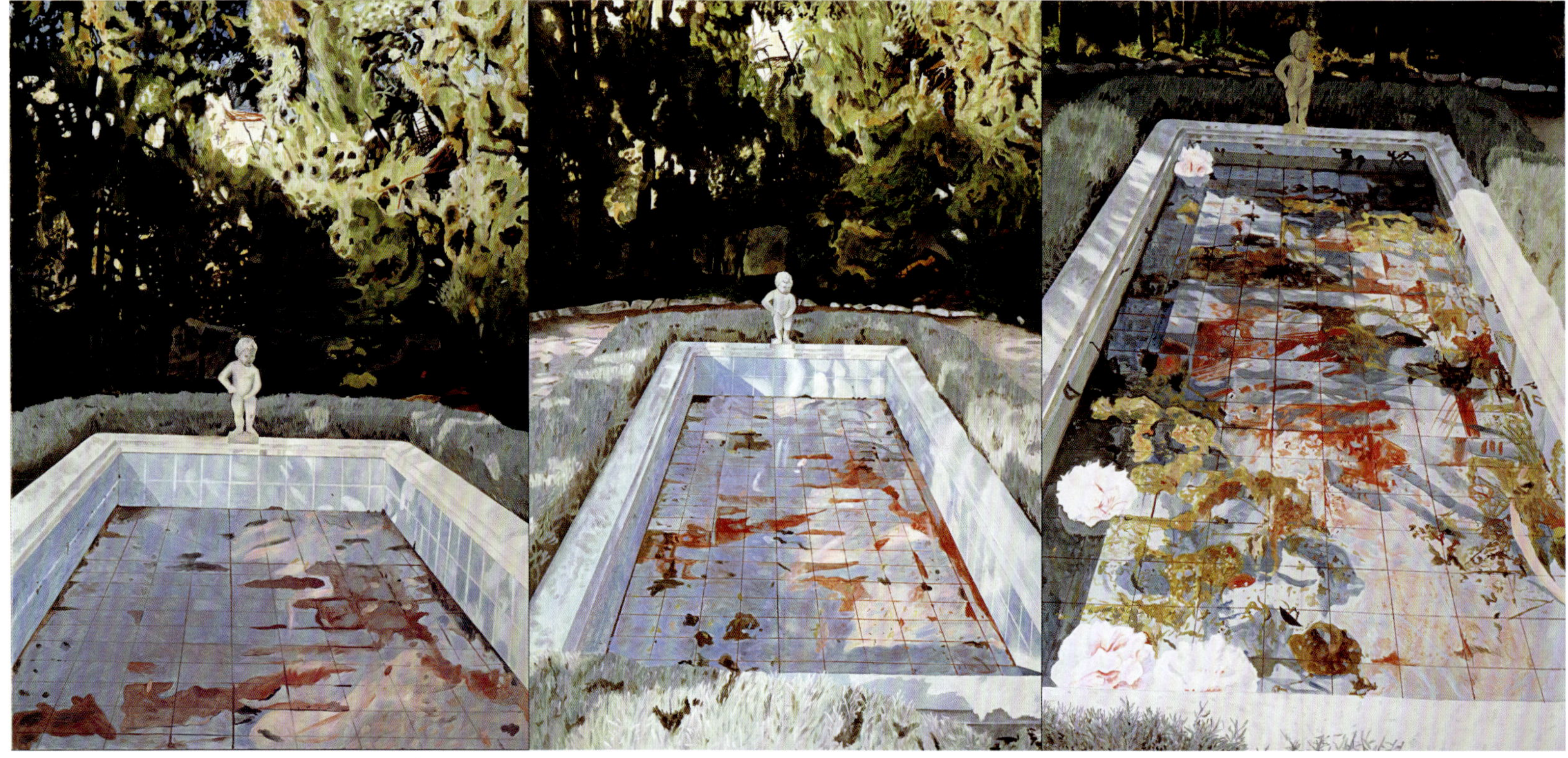

POOL
1983, oil on canvas, triptych, 213.4 × 457.2 cm (84 × 180 in)

Jennifer Bartlett, born 1941, Long Beach, California, USA.

Postmodernism is a term often applied to painting in the 1980s, suggesting the freedom and decadence on the far side of abstraction – a return to spectacle and swagger during a decade of American excess. The three panels of *Pool*, together measuring over four-and-a-half metres (fifteen feet) in length, are certainly colossal in scale, but they also plumb the deeper possibilities of a moment when painting and photography were drawn from their respective corners and into productive relation. In this work, a desolated basin takes on a cinematic cast, growing more enigmatically beautiful as the viewer is drawn closer, frame by frame. This scene recurs throughout Bartlett's oeuvre, both the pool and surrounding garden, as well as the grid of tiles at the centre of the composition. From humble roof shingling to the bounding line of graph paper, these rectilinear meshes create pictorial zones that distort perspective or conjure the austerity of Conceptual art. In other series, Bartlett commingles lines and dots, creating diaphanous waves in which figure and ground are irrevocably blurred. Here, painting returns to its more traditional work of representation, but newly imbued with a visual grammar deftly purloined from mathematical theorems and traditions of Minimalist art.

MARY BEALE

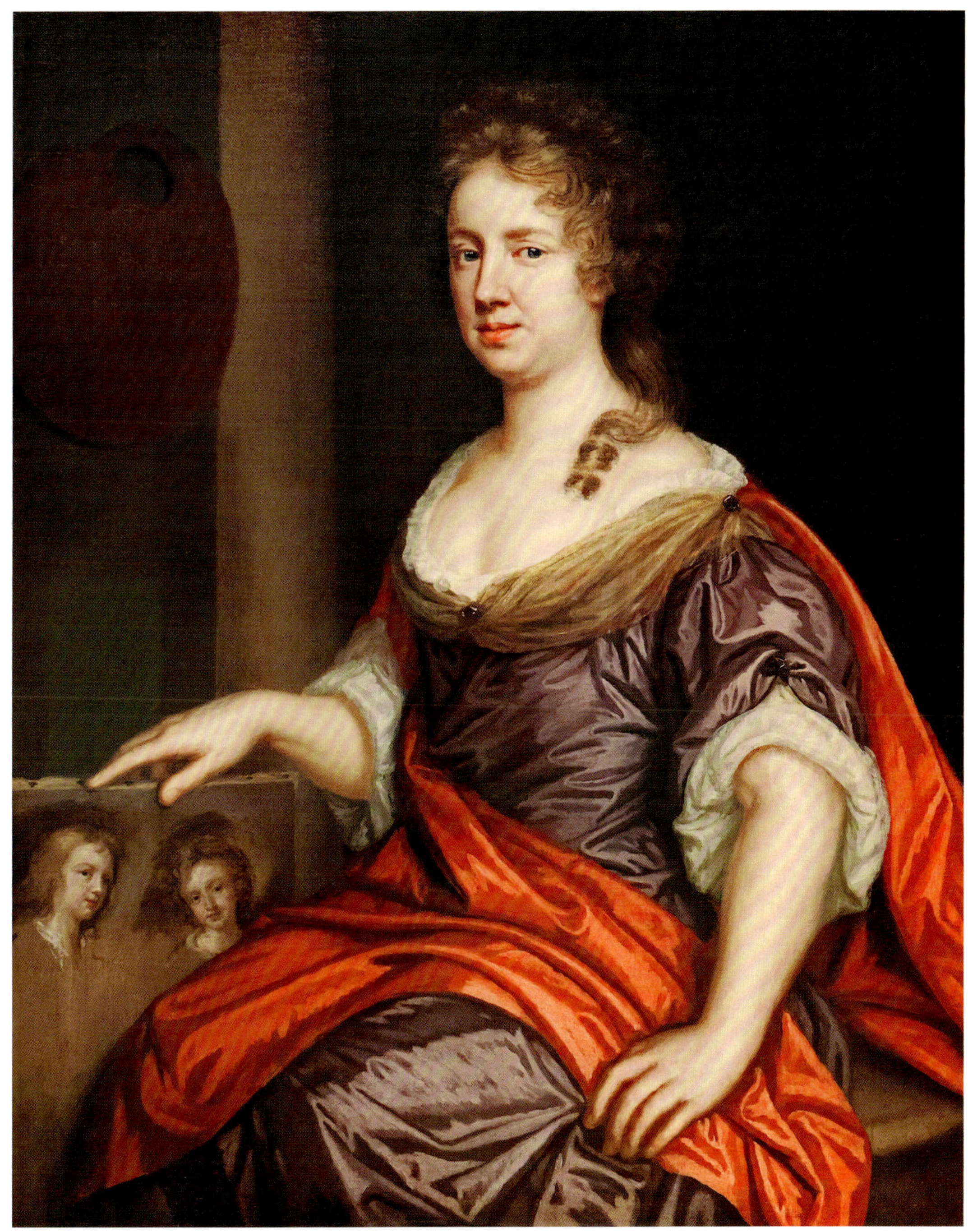

MARY BEALE
*c.*1666, oil on canvas, 109.2 × 87.6 cm (43 × 34½ in), National Portrait Gallery, London, UK

Mary Beale, born 1633, Barrow, Suffolk, UK. Died 1699, London, UK.

One of the few women artists acknowledged in seventeenth-century British art history, Beale is today represented by a substantial selection of attributed paintings. These works offer intimate insight into Beale's commercial studio, the first set up by a woman painter in England. Though without formal art education or guild affiliation, she enjoyed twenty years as a successful society painter, her sitters numbering esteemed politicians, aristocrats, clergymen and intellectuals among them. Beale's training, guided by the imitation of works she admired – particularly those of court artist Sir Peter Lely (1618–80), with whom she was acquainted – was one of determined self-improvement. Her text *Observations by MB* (1663), an instruction on painting apricots, is among the first such texts on painting by an English artist and reveals Beale's commitment to careful observation in pursuit of verisimilitude. In a quietly subversive allusion to her role as maker of images and maker of flesh, this self-portrait offers a likeness of Beale as both artist and mother – with an unfinished study of her two children set beneath a painter's palette.

GINA BEAVERS

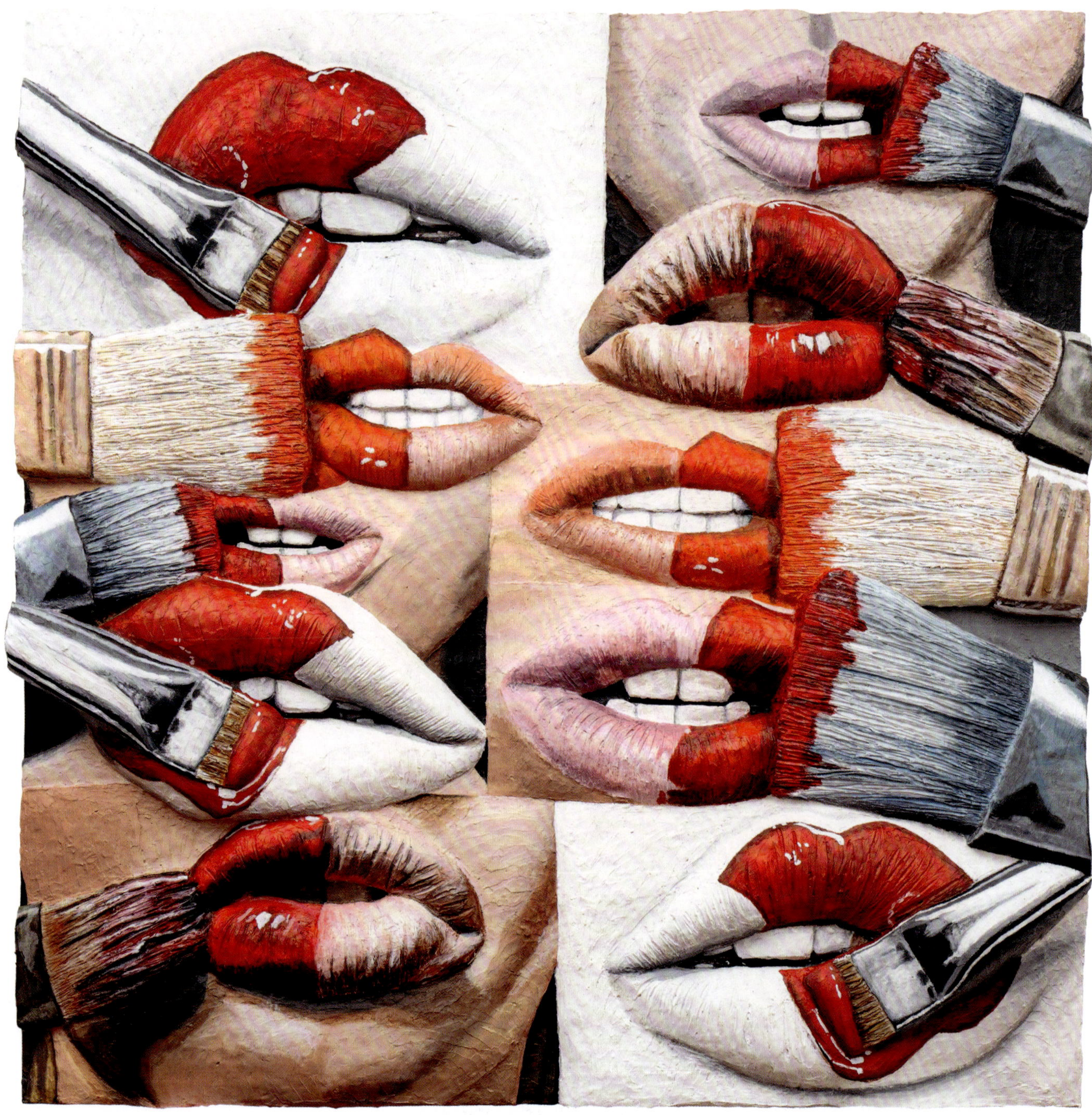

PAINTER'S LIPS
2019, acrylic and foam on linen and panel, 182.9 × 182.9 × 25.4 cm (72 × 72 × 10 in)

Gina Beavers, born 1974, Athens, Greece.

In a 2019 conversation with *MoMA Magazine*, Beavers remarked: 'How do I put something new into painting when everything has been done?' By embracing low-culture subject matters that saturate the internet, whether stock photos of make-up tutorials or social media posts under the hashtag #foodporn, the artist revamps Pop art, while commenting on the artifice of today's consumer culture. In works such as *Painter's Lips*, her compositions protrude into the viewing space, as red-stained brushes smear lipstick-paint onto puckered, plumped lips that echo the aesthetics of plastic surgery and the seductive yet grotesque paintings of Marilyn Minter (p.202). Beavers's work is a tactile synthesis of corporeal object and glossy Instagram image that refuses to conform neatly to any traditional medium. From her studio in New Jersey, the artist moulds and contours her three-dimensional works using layers of unpigmented acrylic and foam before applying a topcoat of colour. Both alluring and repulsive, Beavers's paintings transform once marketable and desirable images into comically crass works, calling into question the pervasive glorification of a narcissistic consumer culture.

RANA BEGUM

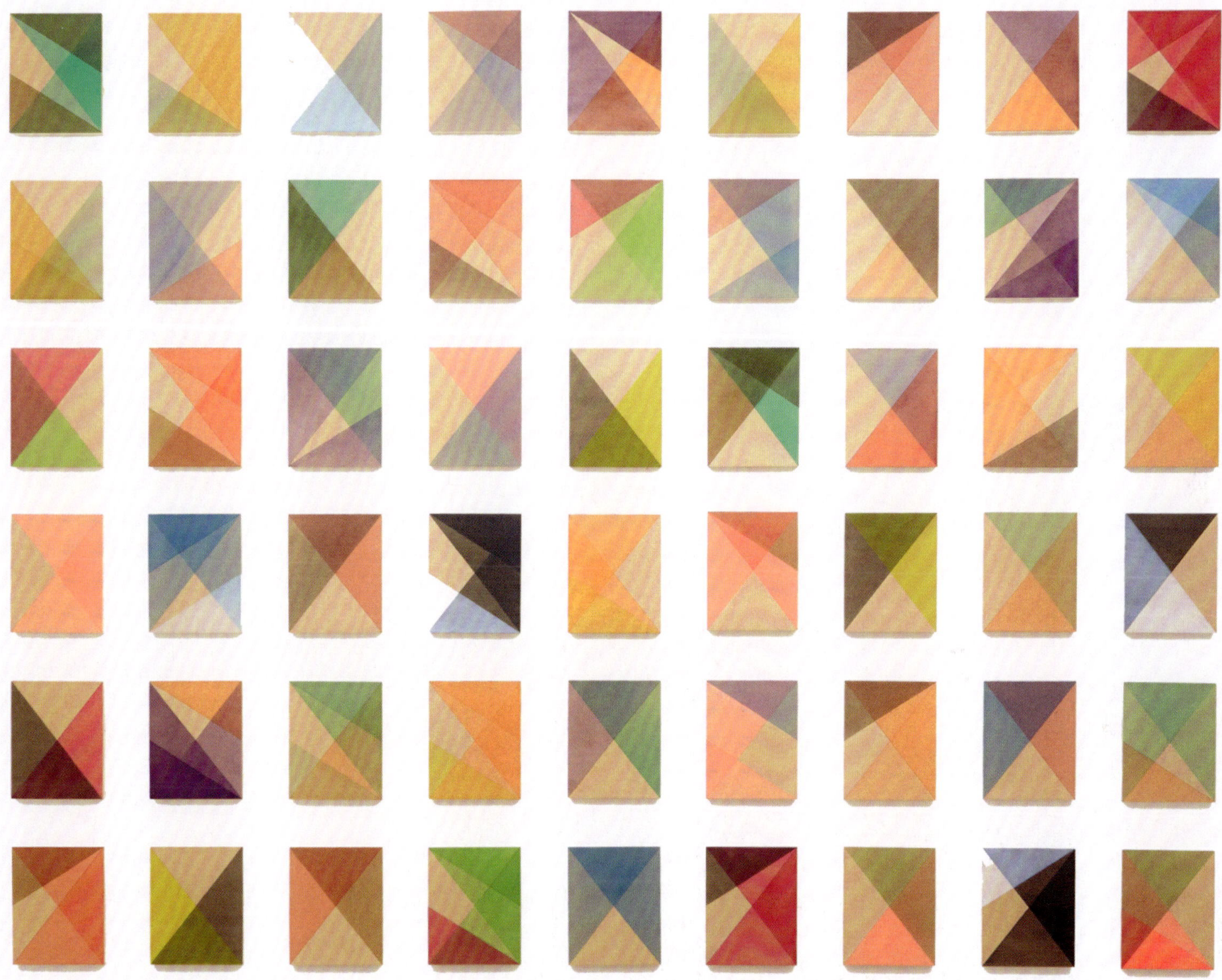

NO. 680 PAINTING
2016, acrylic on MDF, 54 panels, overall:
200 × 258 × 4 cm (78 ¾ × 101 ⅝ × 1 ⅝ in)

Rana Begum, born 1977, Sylhet, Bangladesh.

A graduate of the Chelsea College of Art and Design and Slade School of Fine Art in London, Begum's practice pivots on considerations of light, space and colour. Through geometric forms, often informed by Islamic and urban architectural design, she explores the relationship and sensorial effects that can be achieved through interplays of these three foundational elements. This experimentation has given rise to a practice that moves between sculpture, installation and painting and is underpinned by traditions of Minimalism and Op art. With bright pigment, Begum creates work that, while appearing simple and concise, has perplexing perceptual effects; her works are shaped to interact with light, with colours often changing intensity when viewed from different perspectives. In *No. 680 Painting*, a multi-panel painting on wooden blocks, she brings together a striking palette of colours that, although refined into triangular sections aligned in a grid formation, bleed together. Reliant on the viewer's movement as well as changes in the light, the work shifts in appearance and can be perceived as both fifty-four individual pieces and one whole. For Begum, this morphing reflects life's constant motion and the changing of the world.

VANESSA BELL

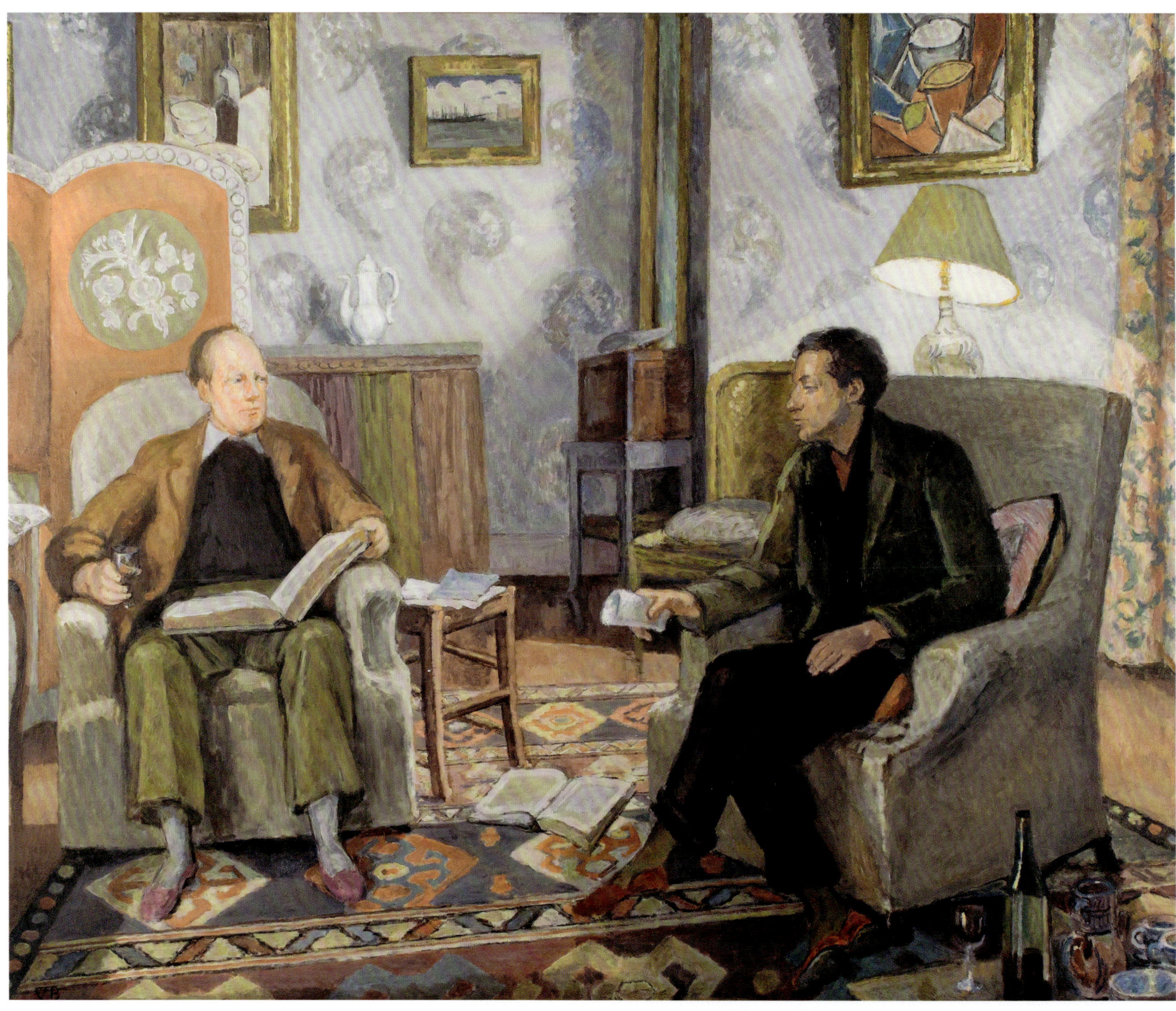

INTERIOR SCENE, WITH CLIVE BELL AND DUNCAN GRANT DRINKING WINE
*c.*1920–5, oil on canvas, 122 × 152 cm (48 × 59⅞ in), Birkbeck, University of London, UK

Vanessa Bell, born 1879, London, UK. Died 1961, Firle, East Sussex, UK.

Bell was a founding member of the Bloomsbury Group – one of Britain's most significant avant-garde circles of the first half of the twentieth century, named after the West London district that brought together its informal and largely bohemian community of artists, writers and intellectuals. Bell, who had studied under John Singer Sargent (1856–1925) at the Royal Academy Schools, was the sister of writer Virginia Woolf, who was also a member of the group. Bloomsbury attitudes to relationships were unusual for the time, reflected in Bell's own living arrangements: she was married to art critic Clive Bell, but in 1916 moved to Charleston house in the Sussex countryside with the artist and designer Duncan Grant (1885–1978). In this painting Bell depicts Clive – who would regularly visit at weekends – and Duncan Grant, chatting and drinking wine in the sitting room at Charleston. Bell's painting, which demonstrates an understanding of Impressionism and Post-Impressionism, captures the cosy yet unconventional spirit of both Charleston and the circle; the stencilled paisley wall, patterned rug and decorative screen can all still be found at Charleston, now open to the public.

BENEDETTA

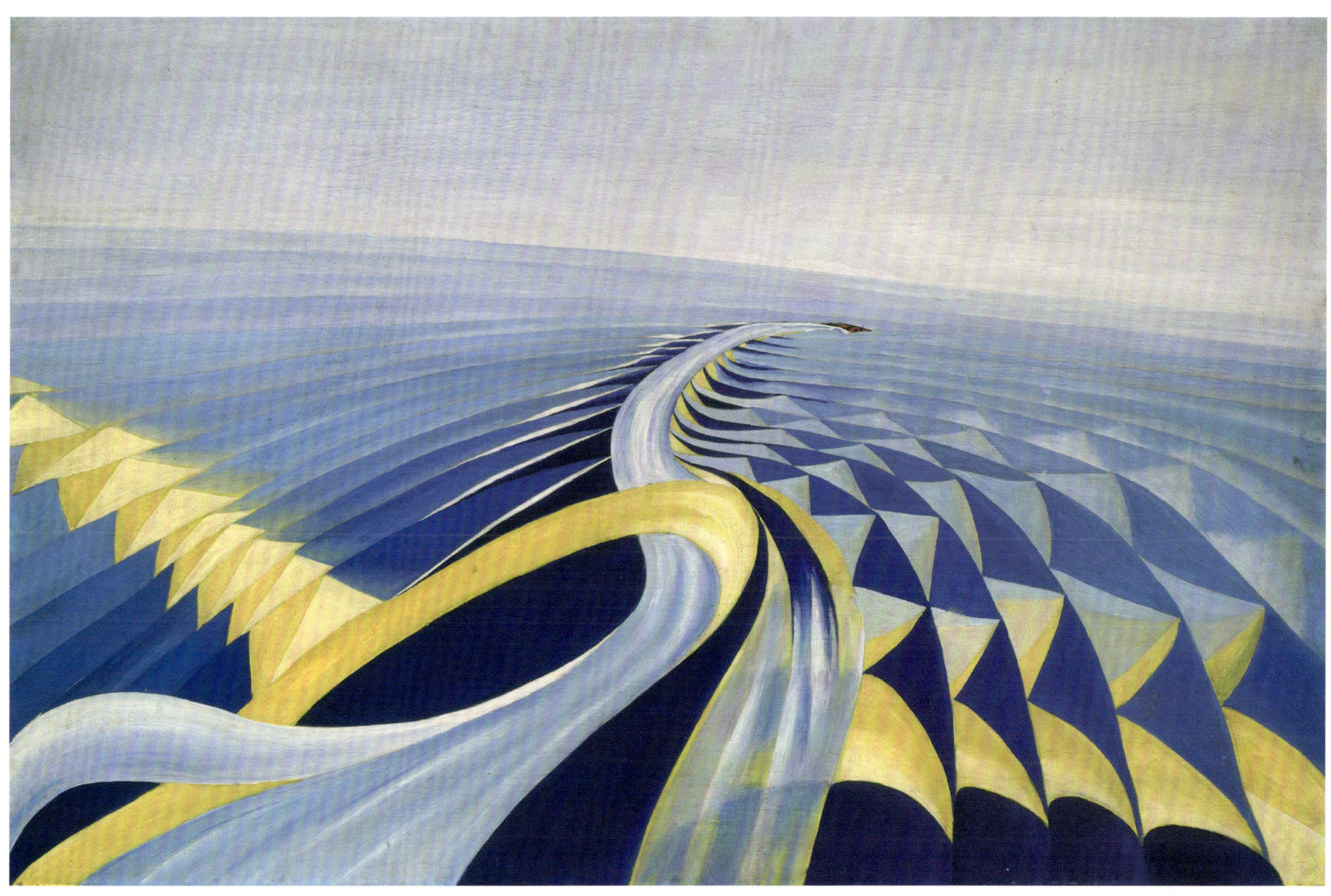

VELOCITÀ DI MOTOSCAFO (SPEEDING MOTORBOAT)
1923–4, oil on canvas, 70 × 100 cm (27 ½ × 39 ⅜ in), Galleria d'Arte Moderna, Rome, Italy

Benedetta, born 1897, Rome, Italy. Died 1977, Venice, Italy.

Born Benedetta Cappa but referring to herself as 'Benedetta', the artist was one of a number of women painters in the Italian Futurist movement, along with Barbara (p.44) and Marisa Mori (1900–85). After receiving a degree in education, in 1917 Benedetta began training as a painter in the studio of Giacomo Balla (1871–1958) and through him met Filippo Tommaso Marinetti, the author of the first 'Manifesto of Futurism' (1909), whom she would later marry. As a Futurist interested by innovations in technology, transport and communications, during the 1930s Benedetta was commissioned to create a series of five tempera and encaustic canvases for the director's conference room in the central post office in Palermo, Sicily. Her fascination with speed and motion is evident in *Speeding Motorboat*, in which the boat itself is just an arrow-like speck as it approaches the distant horizon, leaving both the viewer and a sinuous trail of rhythmic, angular, sunlight-catching waves in its wake. Benedetta was closely associated with Aeropittura – painting from an aerial point of view – adding to the vertiginous dynamics of the image and contributing to early pictorial representations of the age of the aeroplane.

ANNA-EVA BERGMAN

N°5-1970 PAYSAGE VERT ET BLEU (N°5-1970 GREEN AND BLUE COUNTRYSIDE)
1970, acrylic and metal leaf on paper mounted on canvas, 80 × 60 cm (31 ½ × 23 ⅝ in)

Anna-Eva Bergman, born 1909, Stockholm, Sweden. Died 1987, Grasse, France.

Frequently inspired by Scandinavian landscapes and myth, Bergman explored the lines and volumes of nature, seeking harmony between material and form in her paintings. She was raised in Norway, studying art there before moving to France in 1929 where she spent much of the rest of her life. An established though overlooked member of the international avant-garde, she rejected the term 'abstract art', preferring to instead speak about the 'art of abstracting'. By the late 1940s, her figurative painting had become minimal, elemental and, by the 1950s, guided by a vocabulary of archetypal motifs such as stones, planets, boats, mountains and the horizon. The vibrant yet austere bands of colour in this work are set off by a luminescent strip of metal leaf, a material the artist often used. The shimmery presence of gold, silver or copper leaf in the work is like light itself, bringing vivid depth to the composition and transforming the perception of neighbouring colours. The artist did not paint from nature, nor did she represent it realistically, but instead sought to convey the sublime experience of sensing a landscape rather than simply seeing it.

KATHERINE BERNHARDT

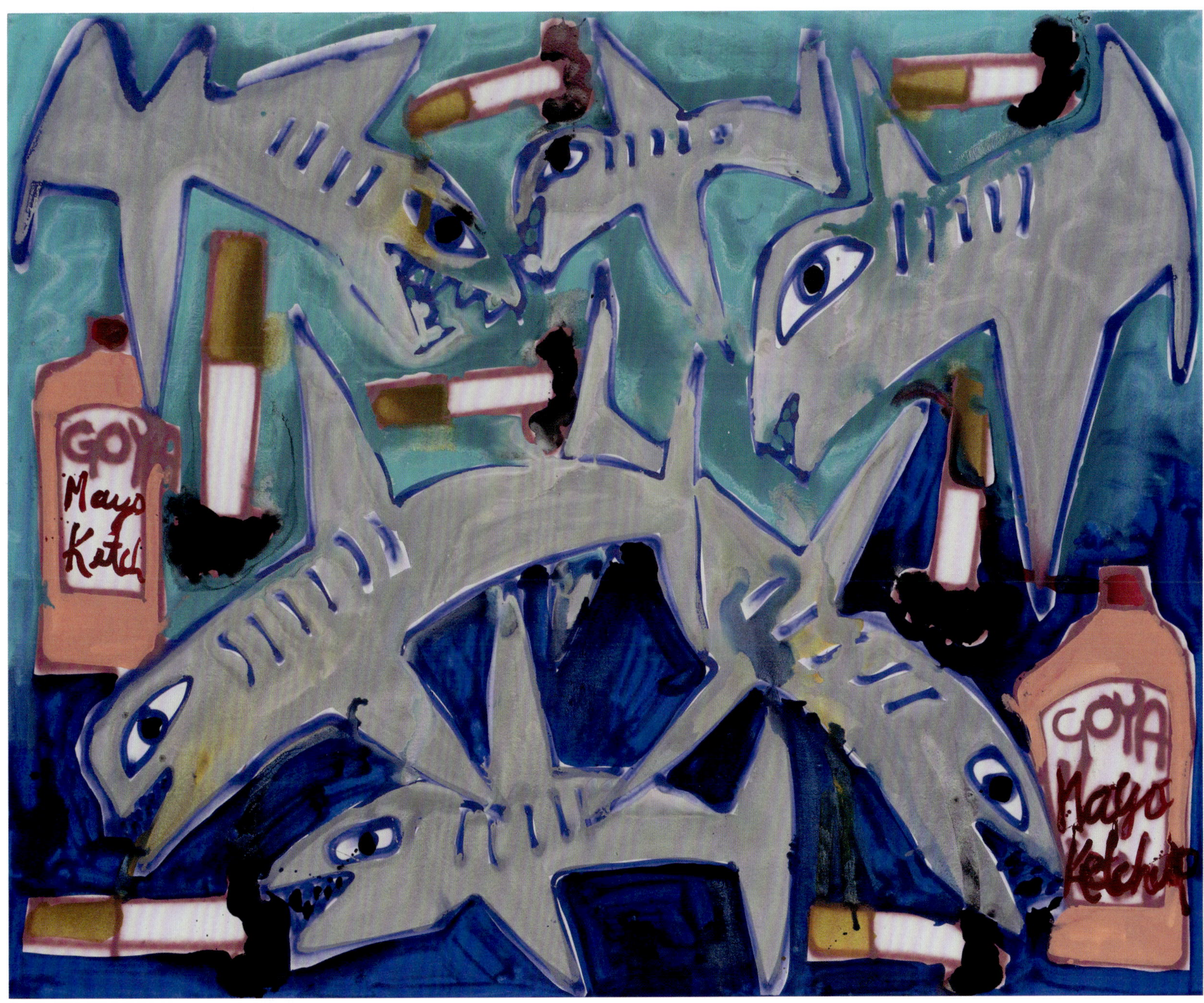

SOLO DE MI
2020, acrylic and spray paint on canvas,
243.8 × 304.8 cm (96 × 120 in)

Katherine Bernhardt, born 1975, St. Louis, USA.

Brash, loud and cartoonish, Bernhardt's paintings evoke a complicated politics of material culture that is both humorous and critical. The artist is best known for her spray paint and acrylic canvases that depict familiar consumer goods and symbols, such as emojis and the iconic Nike swoosh, alongside quotidian objects including cigarettes, Windex and Goya Mayo-Ketchup bottles, and beloved animated characters like Garfield, the Pink Panther and the Smurfs. Often repeating so that they create raucous patterns, Bernhardt's icons float like spectres of capitalism's ubiquitous stronghold amid flat, amorphous painterly spaces, mirroring the artist's own process of improvisation – translating free associations of her mind onto canvas in a style that simultaneously recalls Colour Field painting and street graffiti. In a body of work begun in the early 2010s, from which this painting comes, Bernhardt, who regularly visits and works in Puerto Rico, incorporates tropical motifs such as sharks, fruits, turtles and toucans into her large-scale patterns. The artist purposefully smashes together discordant icons, resulting in a critical rupture in what the discipline of art history has deemed acceptable referents.

JUDITH BERNSTEIN

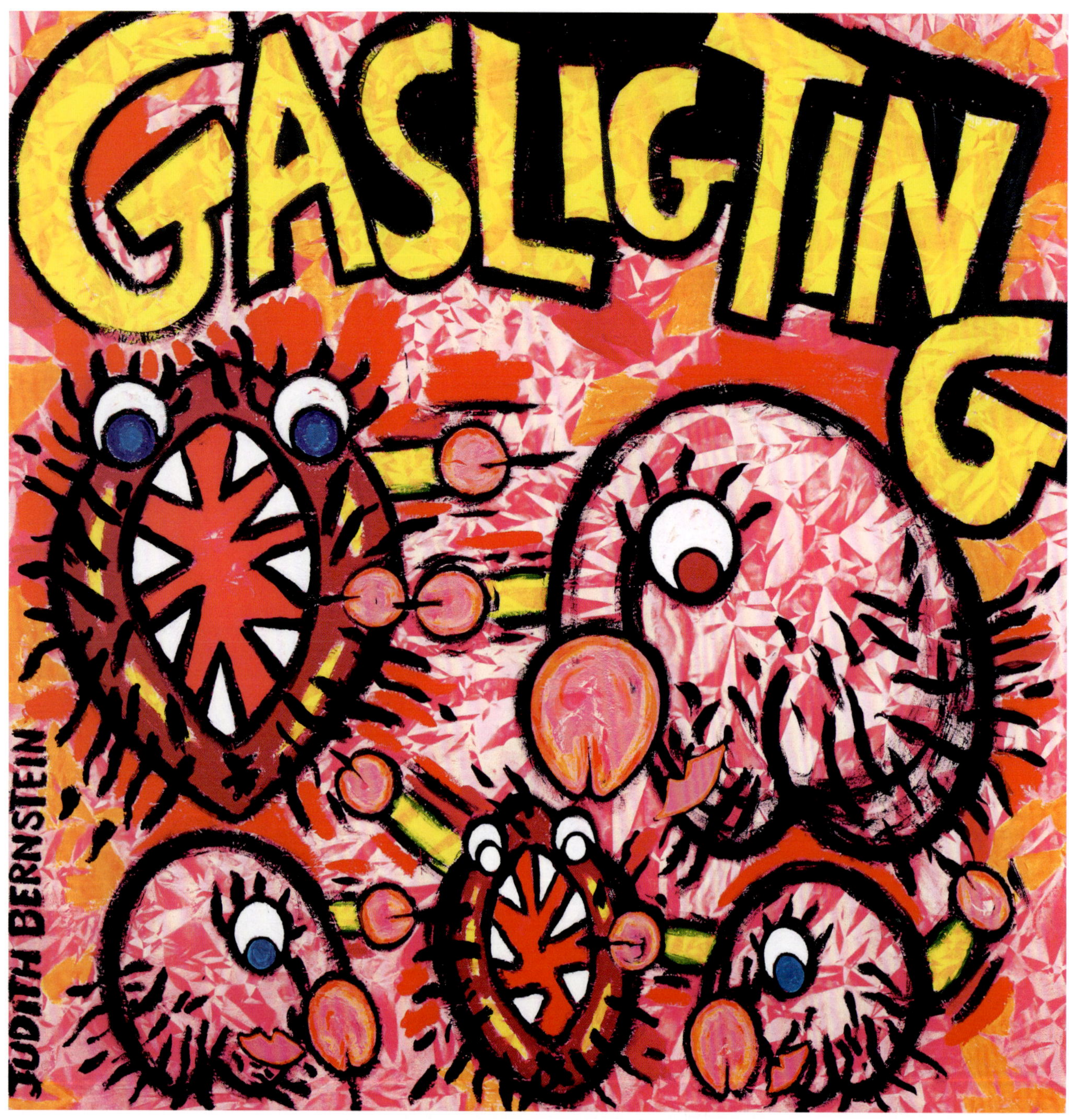

GASLIGHTING (RED)
2019, acrylic and oil on canvas, 227.3 × 224.8 cm (89 ½ × 88 ½ in), Burger Collection, Hong Kong, China.

Judith Bernstein, born 1942, Newark, New Jersey, USA.

Since the mid-1960s when she was a graduate student at Yale School of Art, Bernstein has produced provocative, unabashedly political and feminist work. Coming to prominence with charcoal drawings that protested against the Vietnam War, she is often inspired by public toilet graffiti, combining text and image and using acidic, raunchy humour and depictions of genitalia to unflinchingly critique the United States government and patriarchal culture. As Bernstein explained in a 2020 video interview for *Artforum*, 'I'm very much into images that assault you, that are right in your face. They have an enormous amount of message. They have an enormous amount of impact.' After working with phallic imagery throughout her career, in the 2010s the artist introduced the motif of what she calls the 'active cunt' into her paintings. In *Gaslighting (Red)*, Bernstein renders these ferocious *vagina dentata* in battle against three impotent penile forms that she terms 'Schlong Faces'. These characters rage beneath a banner of text that reads 'gasligting', intentionally misspelled so that viewers, according to Bernstein, 'momentarily question their own sanity' – an effect that mirrors the fallout of phallocentric culture and the psychic effect of Donald Trump's presidency in particular.

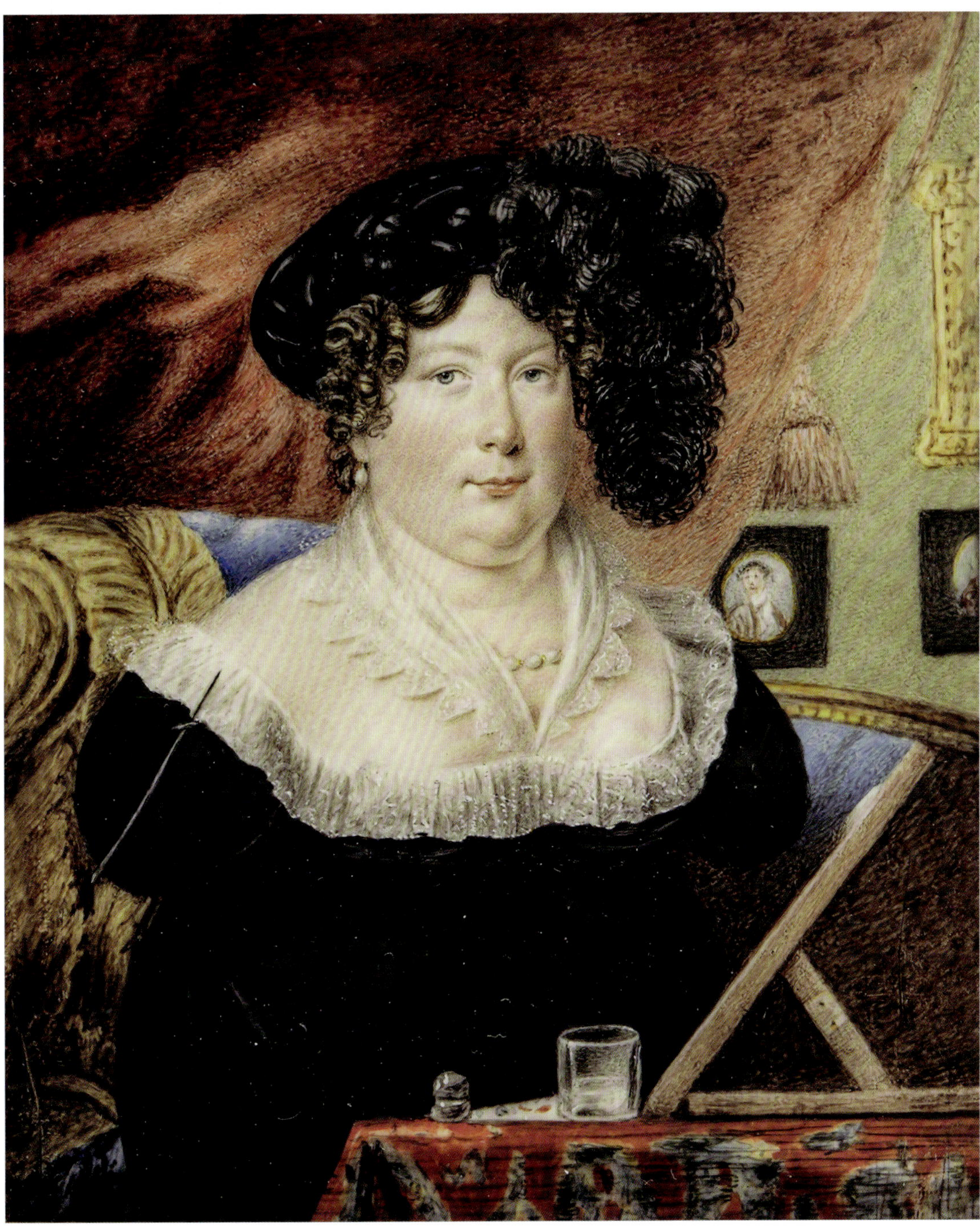

SELF-PORTRAIT BEFORE HER EASEL
*c.*1821, watercolour and body colour on ivory, gilt-wood frame (not pictured), 12.4 × 10.3 cm (4 ⅞ × 4 in)

Sarah Biffin, born 1784, East Quantoxhead, Somerset, UK. Died 1850, Liverpool, UK.

Born without arms, hands or feet, Biffin overcame adversity and prejudice to become a highly successful miniaturist who painted portraits of the British royal family and aristocracy. She learnt to paint as a child by holding a paintbrush in her mouth, yet her artistic talent was overshadowed by her congenital disability and in the late 1790s she was exhibited as a sideshow attraction. By chance, George Douglas, the Earl of Morton, spotted her talent in 1808 and sponsored her to study under the English painter William Marshall Craig (before 1787–1827), whose connections led to royal commissions, including portraits of George IV and his companion Maria Fitzherbert. Her 1839 portrait of Edward the Duke of Kent was bought by his daughter, Queen Victoria, and she exhibited her work at the Royal Academy of Arts in London. She also painted several self-portraits; this one, made at the height of her fame, shows her as a dignified and resilient woman artist. Posed on a sofa, she is surrounded by her paintings and tools, including her brush pinned to a sleeve.

MARÍA BLANCHARD

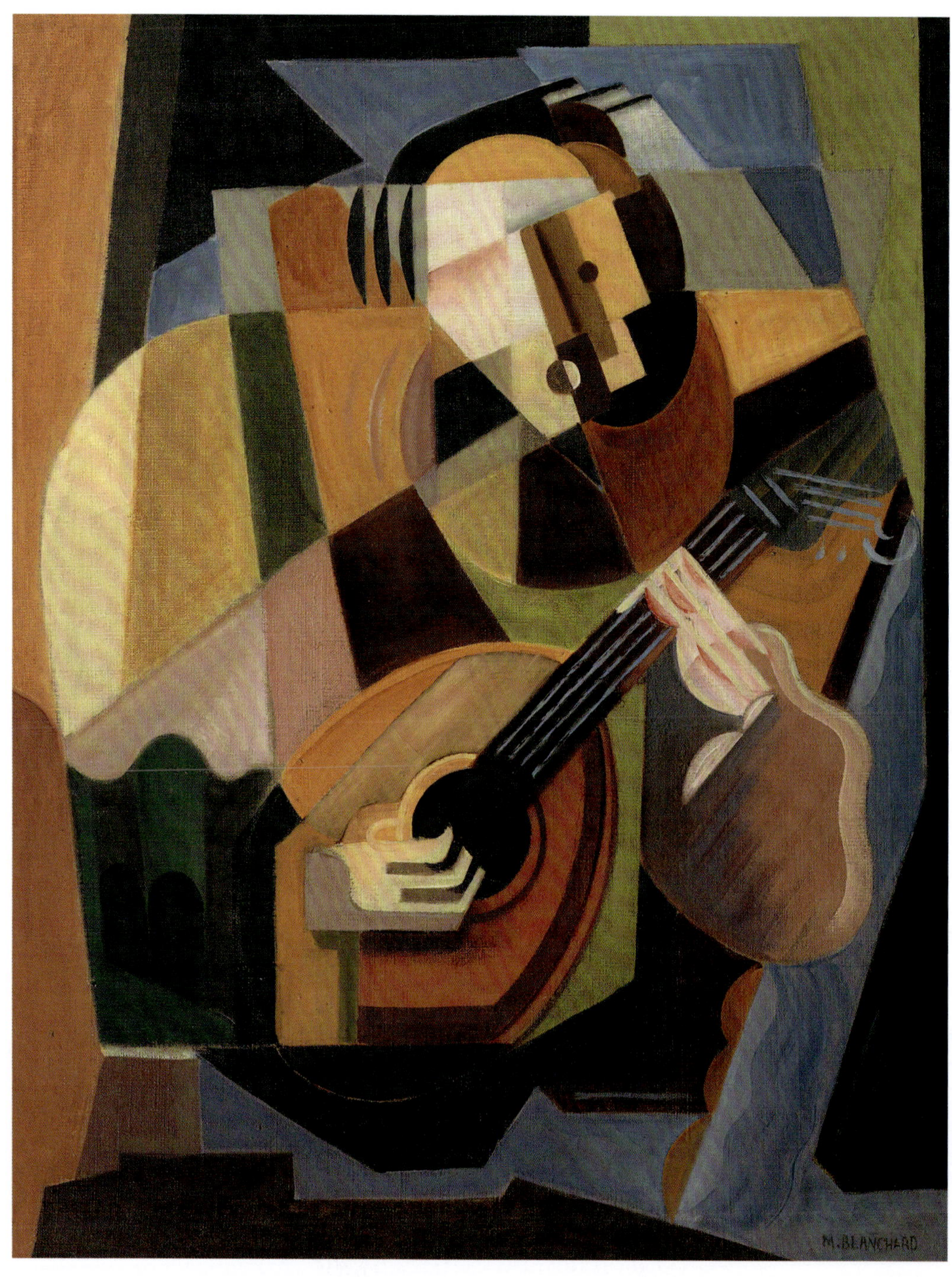

LE JOUEUR DE LUTH (THE LUTE PLAYER)
1917–18, oil on canvas, 92 × 73 cm (36¼ × 28¾ in), private collection

María Blanchard, born 1881, Santander, Spain. Died 1932, Paris, France.

Blanchard was a central, if historically overlooked, member of the early twentieth-century avant-garde. She moved to Madrid to study art in 1903 and there befriended Mexican artist Diego Rivera (1886–1957) who became a lifelong champion of her work. After winning a government grant to continue her education at the Académie Vitti in Paris, she connected with fellow Spanish painter Juan Gris (1887–1927) and the Lithuanian-born sculptor Jacques Lipchitz (1891–1973), who were working in the radical new style of Cubism. The First World War saw Blanchard return to Madrid, where she taught and painted in an austere, academic fashion, but by 1916 she had permanently moved back to Paris, becoming a member of the artist group Section d'Or (Golden Section). She soon began developing the fractured compositional style for which she became best known. This dynamic painting of a singing lute player exemplifies her work of this period, with intersecting angular planes and sections of bold, bright colour. Blanchard suffered with her physical and mental health, facts reflected in the sombre themes and palette of her oeuvre, eventually contracting tuberculosis, which left her unable to paint.

IRMA BLANK

RADICAL WRITINGS, SCHRIFT-ATEM-BILD, 4-8-1992 (RADICAL WRITINGS, WRITING-BREATH-PICTURE, 4-8-1992)
1992, oil on canvas, diptych, each: 200 × 100 cm (78 ¾ × 39 ⅜ in)

Irma Blank, born 1934, Celle, Lower Saxony, Germany.

Originally from Germany, Blank relocated to Sicily in 1955, a cultural and linguistic uprooting that would become the foundation of her art practice. With no knowledge of Italian, she became preoccupied with detaching the written word from meaning and language as a way to explore the visual and spiritual aspects of writing. Her 'Self-Writings' (1968–73) consist of script-like lines resembling writing, while in 'Transcriptions' (1973–9) she replicates the text layouts from newspapers, replacing the words with meaningless markings. In 'Radical Writings' (1983–96), she inscribes her canvases with long, uniform strokes of colour, often blue or pink, representing harmony and utopia. Each meditative mark translates to the length of a single breath as she moves the paintbrush from the centre to the canvas's edge before exhaling and beginning a new line. The title *Schrift-Atem-Bild* refers to these three essential elements: writing, breath, picture. Typically and ritualistically completed within the course of a day, each canvas resembles an open book, continuing Blank's exploration of the representational possibilities of the written word.

ROSA BONHEUR

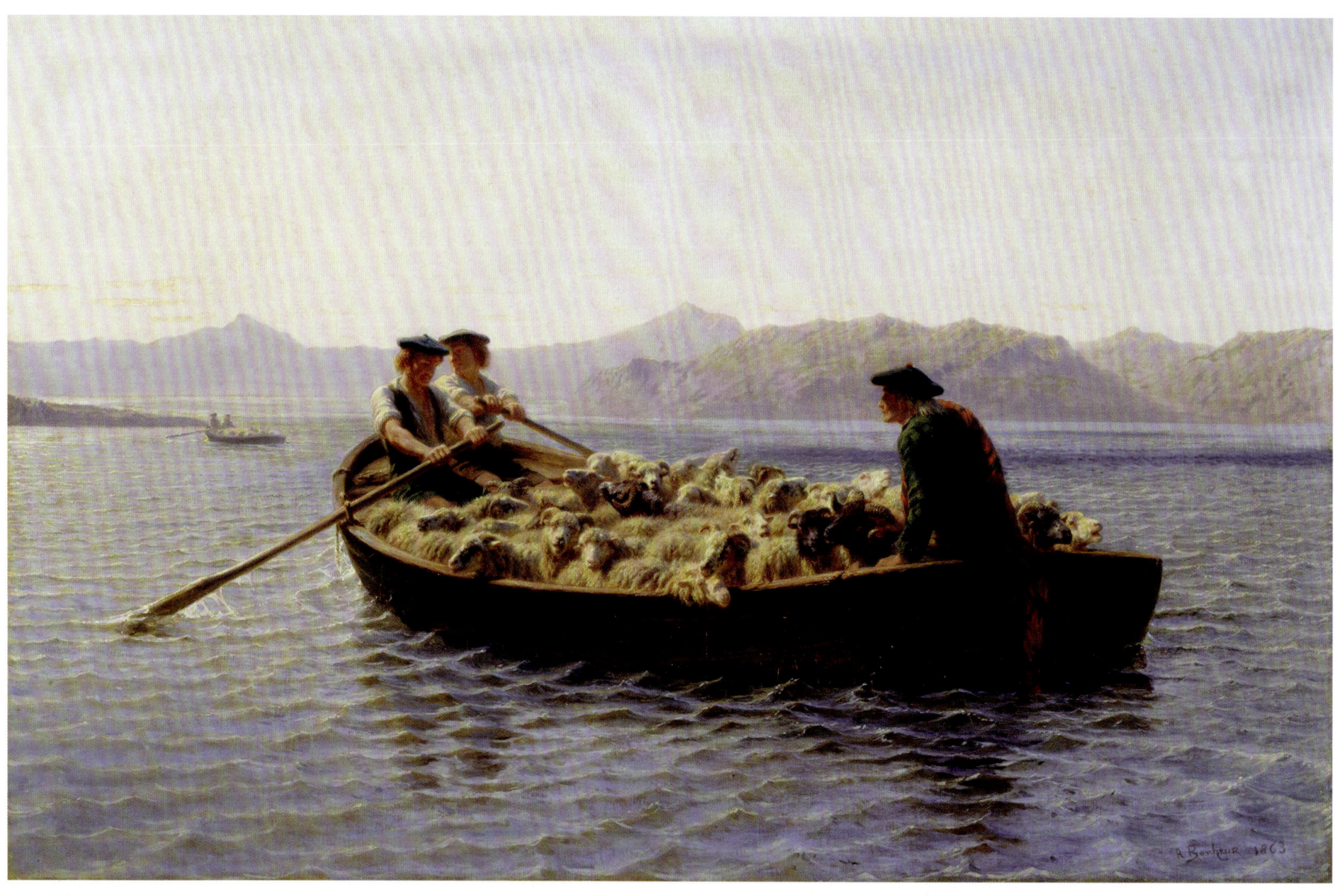

CHANGEMENT DE PÂTURAGES (CHANGING PASTURES)
1863, oil on canvas, 64 × 100 cm (25 ¼ × 39 ⅜ in), Hamburger Kunsthalle, Hamburg, Germany

Rosa Bonheur, born 1822, Bordeaux, France. Died 1899, Thomery, France.

Bonheur was taught to draw by her father, Raymond, who believed in gender equality and recognized her precocious talent: she first exhibited at the Paris Salon at the age of nineteen. Her status as a feminist icon derives from her financial independence, her openly lesbian attachments, and her insistence on smoking cigars and wearing masculine dress for work. Bonheur was an *animalier* – a painter of animals and landscapes – and she painted with academic precision in the style of Realism, often working *en plein air*, following the Barbizon School painters she admired. Her acute powers of observation, studying animal anatomy in abattoirs, stood alongside her strong belief that animals had souls. This painting of sheep being transferred across a loch to new pastures is one of Bonheur's Scottish works, created following an extended tour of the country. Bonheur enjoyed great success throughout her life; she was awarded France's Légion d'Honneur in 1865 and thirty years later became the first woman to be promoted to the rank of Officer.

JESSIE ARMS BOTKE

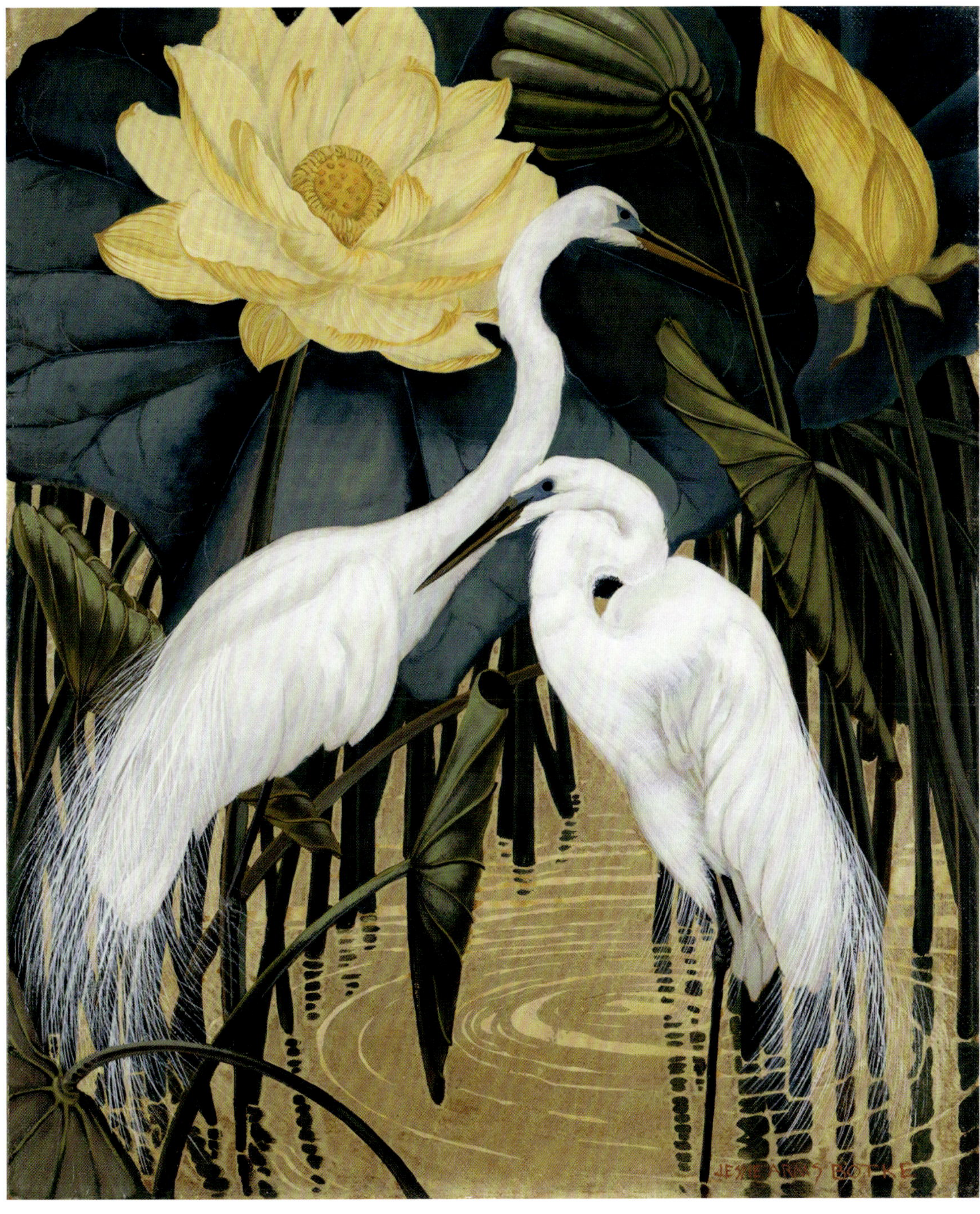

EGRETS AND LOTUS
date unknown, oil and gold leaf on Masonite,
61 × 50.8 cm (24 × 20 in)

Jessie Arms Botke, born 1883, Chicago, USA.
Died 1971, Santa Paula, California, USA.

A leading decorative painter of the twentieth century, Botke made lush and colourful paintings, watercolours and woodblock prints of scenes in nature. Born into an artistic family whose business was interior design and furnishings, Botke designed woven tapestries and book illustrations and worked as a muralist in New York, Chicago and San Francisco in the early 1910s. During this time, she was also politically engaged and marched with fellow suffragists in New York for women's right to vote. By the late 1910s, Botke had relocated to California, where she became associated with California Impressionism and the practice of working *en plein air*. She became sought after for her paintings of birds that were often embellished with ornate materials including flat expanses of gold leaf. Botke, who exhibited frequently during her lifetime, painted sumptuous scenes of the avian world, including peacocks, cockatoos, ducks, geese, swans, toucans and – as seen here – egrets, set against scenes of water and flora that were inspired by the art of Japanese screens. Though in her later decades Botke turned to still lifes, her bird paintings have remained her most celebrated works.

PAULINE BOTY

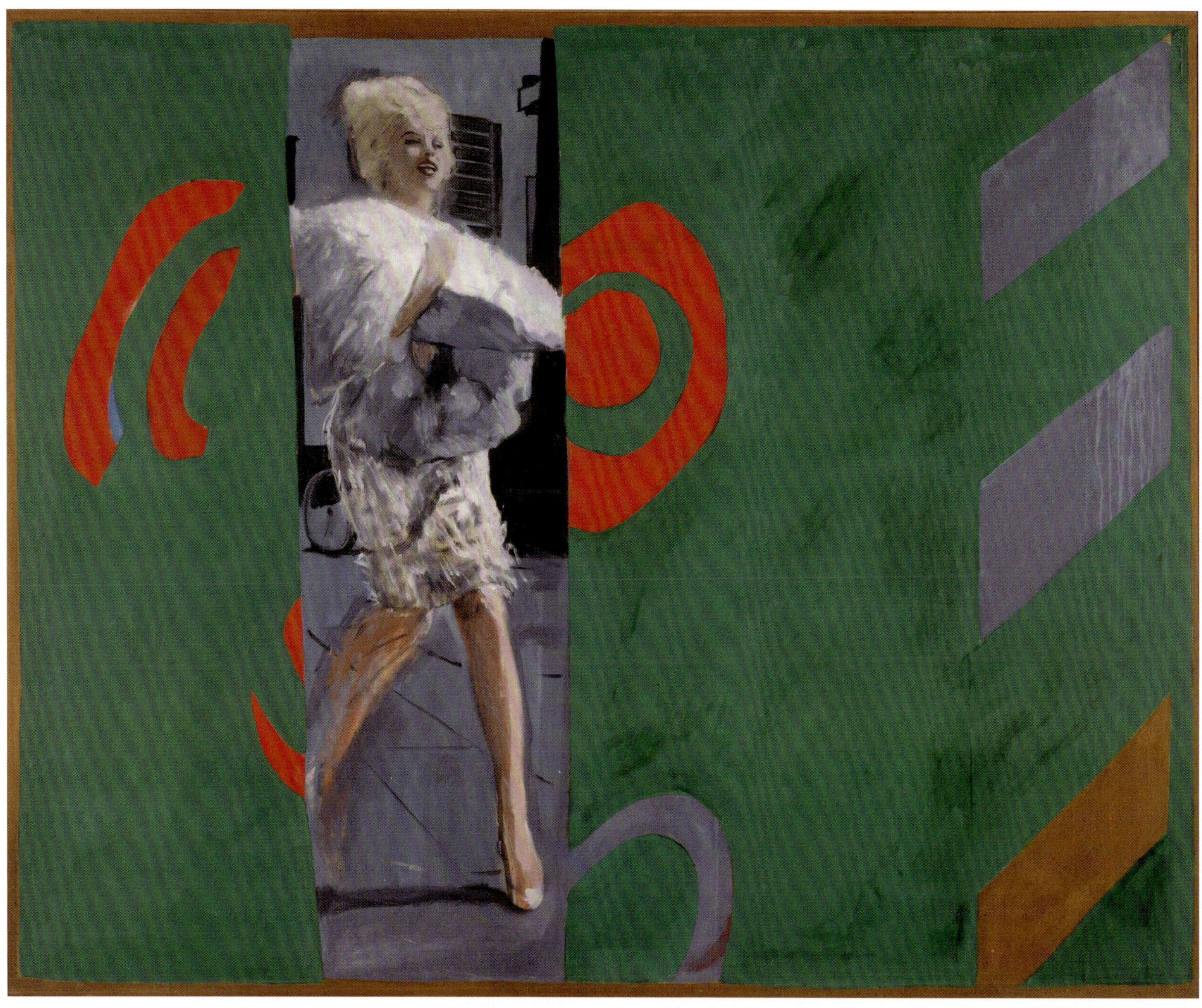

THE ONLY BLONDE IN THE WORLD
1963, oil on canvas, 122.4 × 153 × 2.5 cm (48 ¼ × 60 ¼ × 1 in), Tate, London, UK

Pauline Boty, born 1938, London, UK. Died 1966, London.

The sole British woman painter associated with the Pop art movement of the 1960s, Boty consistently defied convention in both her spirit and her art. She attended the Royal College of Art in London, working as a radio presenter, actor and dancer as well as making pioneering, politically punchy, photorealist paintings. Like her Pop peers she was influenced by mass-media imagery, but unlike the men who dominated the movement, Boty explored ideas of image and representation specifically through the prism of gender and sexuality – often employing cheerful colours while serving up sharp criticisms of a society that favoured men. *The Only Blonde in the World* depicts Pop art muse Marilyn Monroe in a confident pose – not as Marilyn herself, but as one of her best-known characters, Sugar Kane, from the 1959 film *Some Like It Hot*. Boty suggests that the Monroe we want to see – like the swirling abstract forms that crowd her in the painting – is only an image, a mythology over which the real woman has little claim or control. The title contains a biting irony as well, given that Boty herself often felt valued for her appearance rather than her artistic achievements.

MARIE BRACQUEMOND

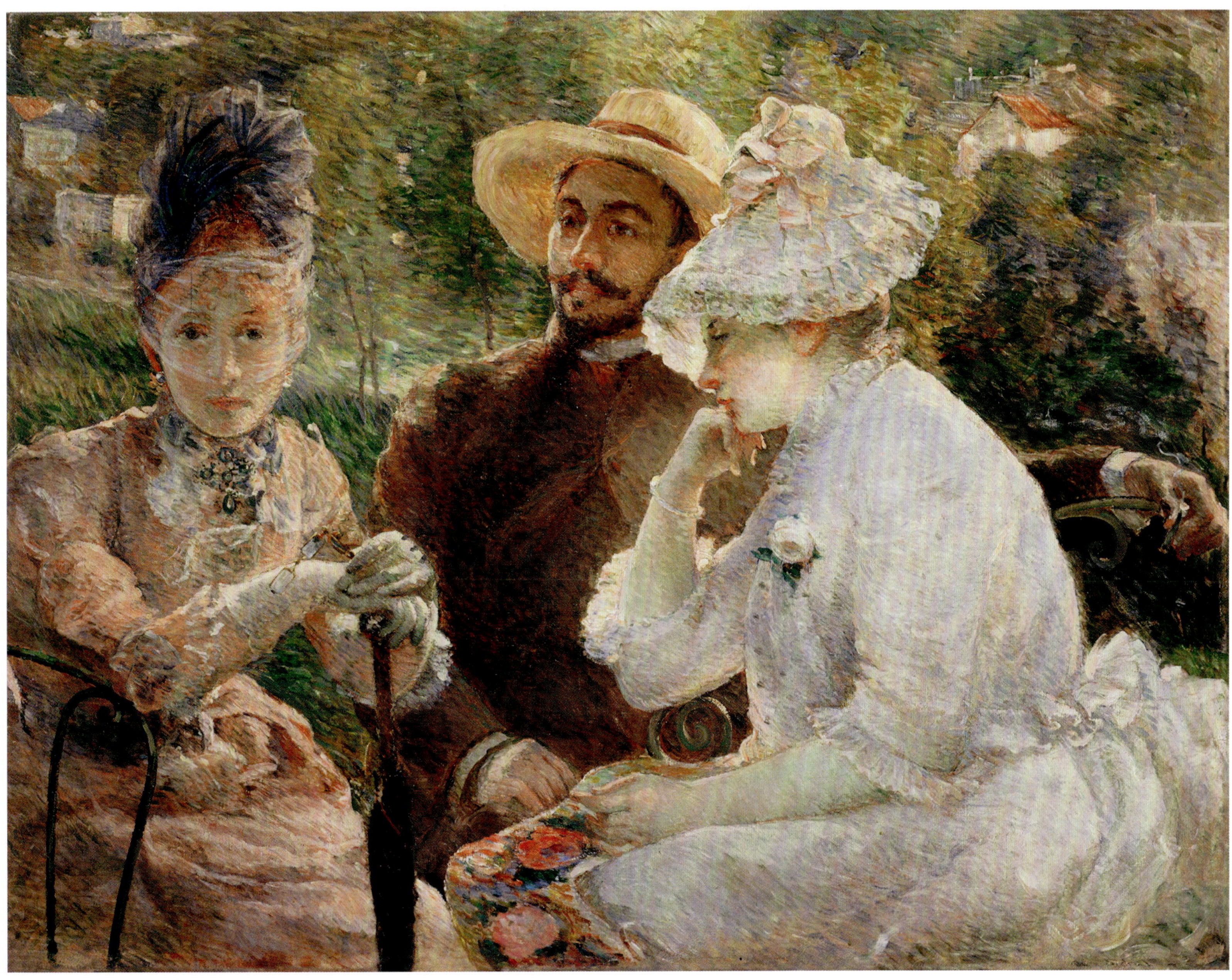

SUR LA TERRASSE À SÈVRES (ON THE TERRACE AT SÈVRES)
1880, oil on canvas, 88 × 115 cm (34 ⅝ × 45 in), Musée du Petit Palais, Geneva, Switzerland

Marie Bracquemond, born 1840, Landunvez, France. Died 1916, Sèvres, France.

Regarded by critic Gustave Geffroy in 1894 as one of the '*trois grandes dames*' of Impressionism, alongside Berthe Morisot (p.207) and Mary Cassatt (p.73), Bracquemond is remembered for her masterful treatment of light and colour. At the age of seventeen she had a painting accepted for the 1857 Salon, which led to an introduction to Jean-Auguste-Dominique Ingres (1780–1867), in whose studio she worked briefly. She met the painter and etcher Félix Bracquemond (1833–1914) while copying Old Masters at the Louvre and married him in 1869. Inspired by the Impressionist movement, and her friendships with Claude Monet (1840–1926) and Edgar Degas (1834–1917), Bracquemond's paintings grew larger and her palette more intense. She began to paint *en plein air*, though she still prepared using preliminary sketches. *On the Terrace at Sèvres*, in which she sits with her sister and the painter Henri Fantin-Latour (1836–1904), was painted in her garden. Unfortunately, Félix Bracquemond despised Impressionism and resented his wife's career, leading her to abandon painting. Nevertheless, she continued to defend the movement for the rest of her life.

SASCHA BRAUNIG

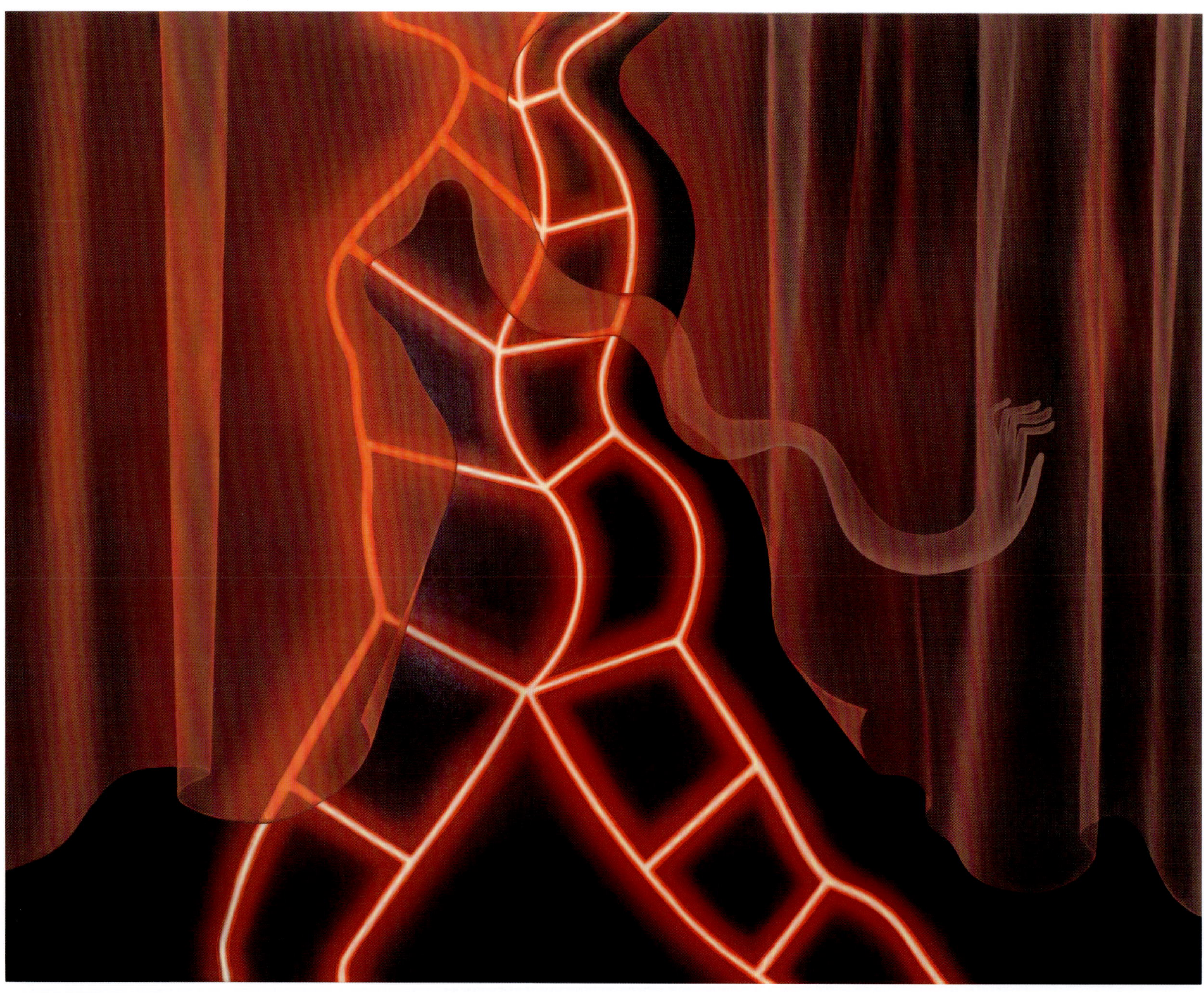

THE CURTAIN
2017, oil on linen over panel, 91.4 × 116.8 × 5.1 cm (36 × 46 × 2 ⅛ in)

Sascha Braunig, born 1983, Qualicum Beach, British Columbia, Canada.

Since completing an MFA at Yale School of Art in 2008, Braunig relocated to Portland, Maine, and developed a distinctive painting practice that has been presented in numerous exhibitions worldwide. Her fantastical, uncanny paintings appear suspended in time and place, as though in an imagined dimension, with shapeshifting, feminine figures disembodied or rendered as mechanical and cyborgian forms in phosphorescent, neon hues. Described by Roberta Smith of the *New York Times* in 2015 as 'an inspired reanimator of Surrealism', Braunig also pays homage to Op art and the visual vocabulary of sci-fi and internet culture. Adopting the high definition of digital imagery, the artist describes herself as a 'precisionist painter' and has coined the term 'superficial realism' to categorize her approach. Braunig's works are painted from three-dimensional clay models that she illuminates in her studio with bright, artificial lighting, contributing to the sculptural, voluminous quality and dramatic play of light in her paintings. The motif of the curtain often appears in her work, indicating how the very nature of vision – or at least its parameters – is constantly negotiated within the pictorial frame, through veiling and unveiling, performing and withdrawing.

LISA BRICE

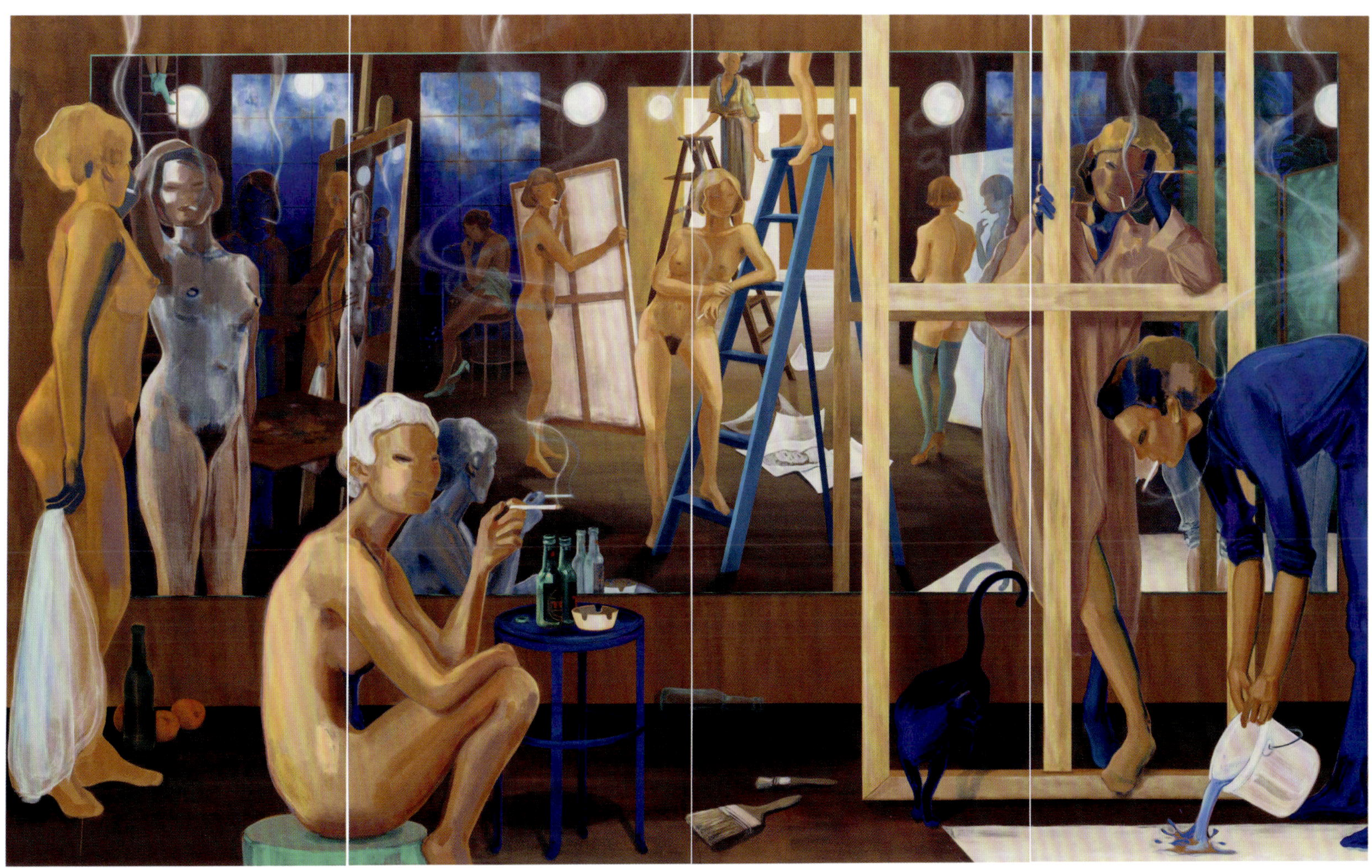

SMOKE AND MIRRORS
2020, ink, gesso, synthetic tempera, chalk, oil pastel and oil on canvas mounted on wooden panel, 200 × 330.9 cm (78 ¾ × 129 ⅞ in)

Lisa Brice, born 1968, Cape Town, South Africa.

Known for her ethereal paintings of nude and semi-clad women, Brice liberates her subjects from the male gaze of art history by reworking traditional portrayals of the female nude. She often depicts her subjects in group scenes or engaged in self-referential activities – painting themselves or looking at their own reflections in the mirror – positioning them not only as subjects and image-makers, but also as spectators. After studying at the Michaelis School of Fine Art in Cape Town, Brice moved to London in 1998, where she lives and works, also spending extended periods in Trinidad. Brice's striking incorporation of blue hues – in part a nod to the Trinidadian Carnival character the Blue Devil – along with her loose brushwork deliberately obscures the identity of her figures, their facial features reduced so that they appear anonymous and are kept at a distance from the viewer's consumption. This element of disguise also manifests across her work in motifs of cigarette smoke, mirrors and veils, as seen in this large-scale, elusive narrative tableau. Brice depicts women – who appear to be models, studio assistants and artists, including Helen Frankenthaler (p.112) at the far right – engrossed in their own activities and engaging in the process of forming their own image, not for the viewer but for themselves.

ROMAINE BROOKS

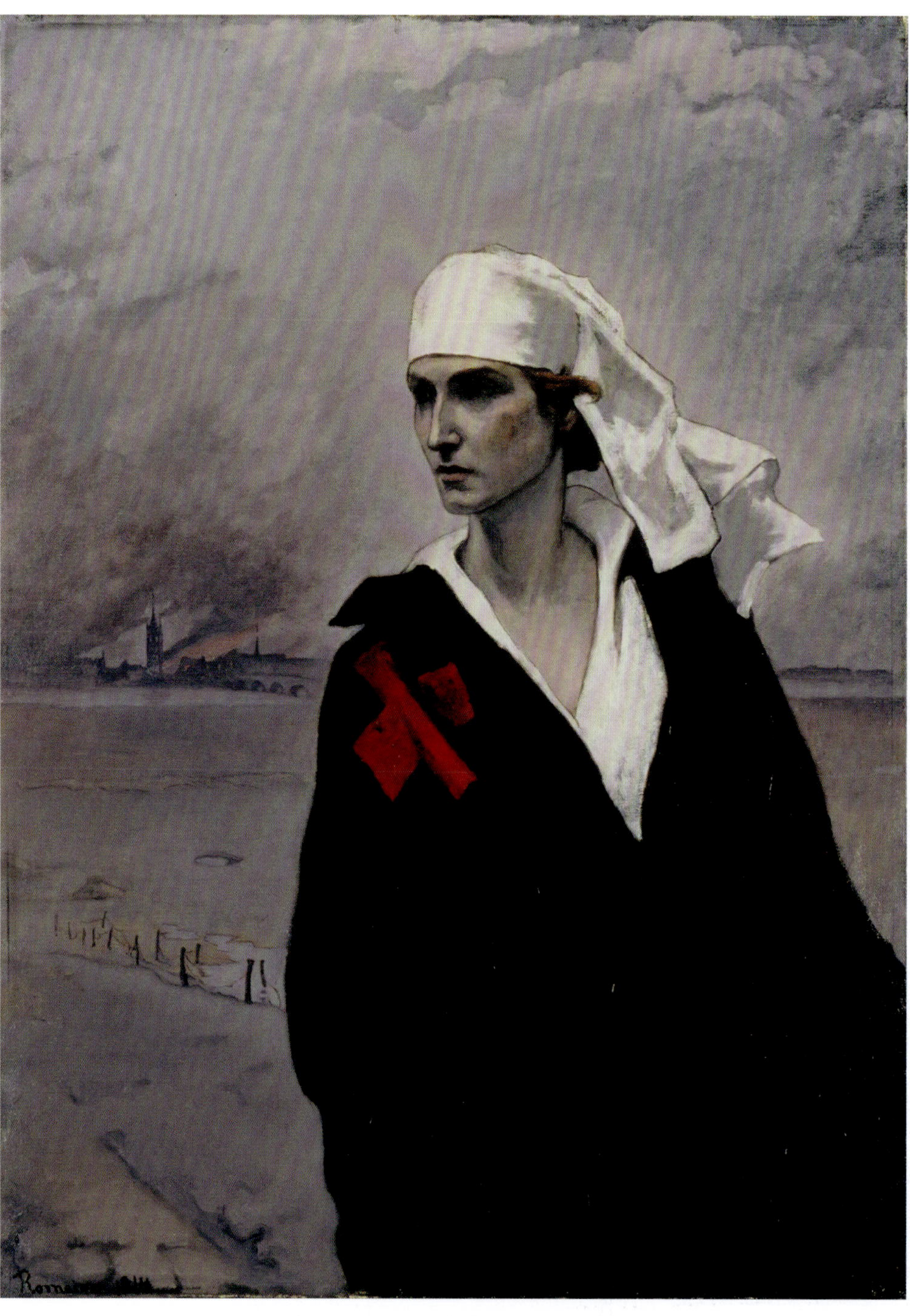

LA FRANCE CROISÉE (THE CROSS OF FRANCE)
1914, oil on canvas, 116.2 × 85 cm (45 ¾ × 33 ½ in), Smithsonian American Art Museum, Washington DC, USA

Romaine Brooks, born 1874, Rome, Italy. Died 1970, Nice, France.

An American born in Rome, Brooks was part of a Parisian bohemian circle of artists and intellectuals, many of whom were sexually liberated and financially independent expatriate women. Her portrayals of statuesque female nudes and androgynous tuxedoed women in muted palettes of black, white and grey celebrated her own vision of gender and sexuality. Brooks painted *The Cross of France* at the outbreak of the First World War. Her close friend and revolutionary poet Gabriele D'Annunzio wrote four sonnets that accompanied prints of the painting to raise funds for the Red Cross. France is personified as a female crusader, a valiant and determined nurse who stands in a flowing cap. An insignia of the Red Cross is emblazoned against her dark cloak, while the Belgian city of Ypres burns in the background. Brooks based the figure's strong, chiselled features on those of her romantic partner Ida Rubinstein, a famed Russian ballet dancer who frequently served as the artist's model from 1911 until their break-up in 1914. In 1920 Brooks was awarded the Cross of the Légion d'Honneur for her patriotic, allegorical canvases of the war years.

CECILY BROWN

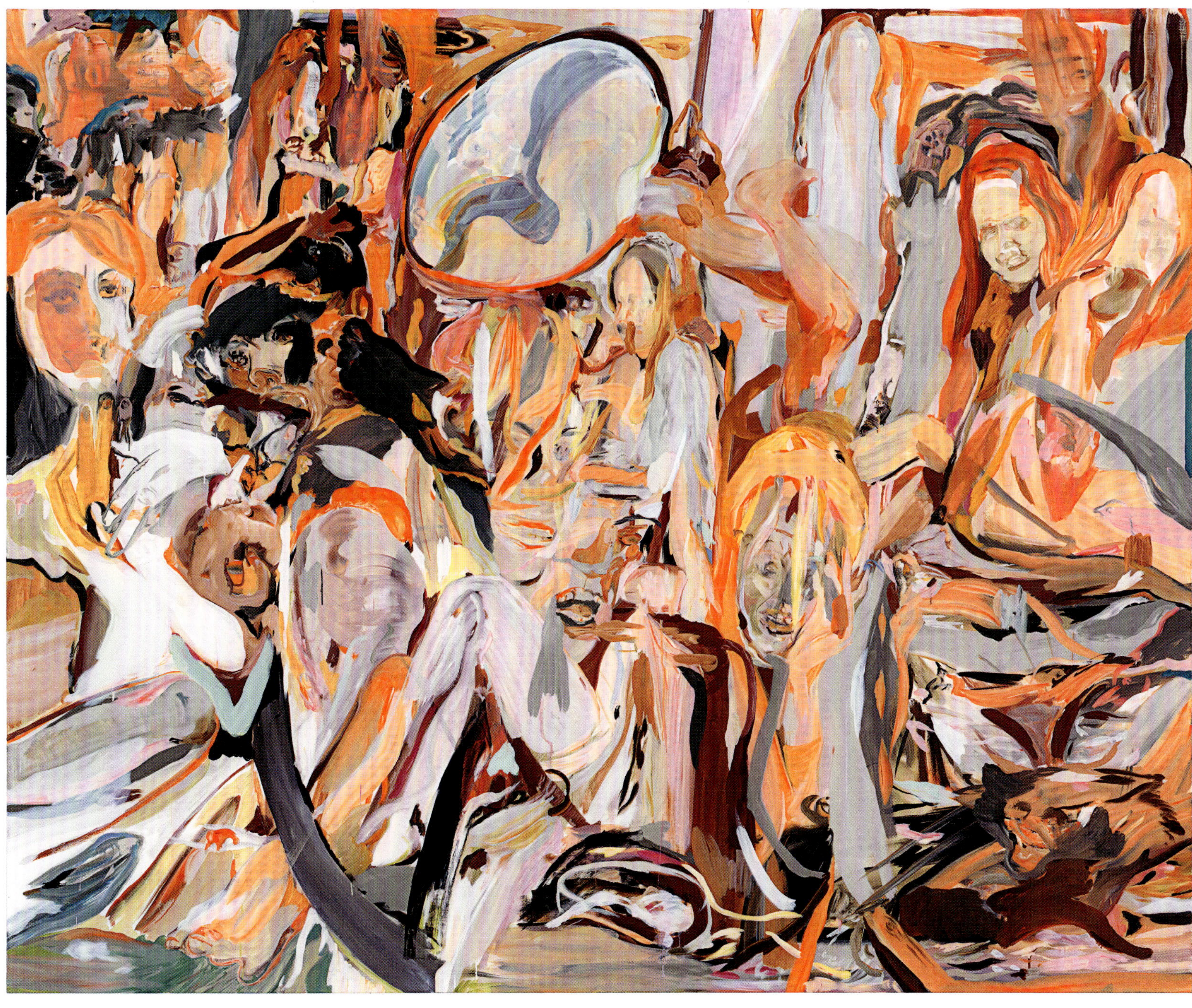

WHERE THEY ARE NOW
2013, oil on linen, 170.2 × 210.8 cm (67 × 83 in)

Cecily Brown, born 1969, London, UK.

Brown's monumental canvases teem with life: swirls of foliate green and swathes of fleshy pink that can sometimes be identified as bodies. After studying painting at the Slade School of Fine Art in London, Brown moved to New York in 1994, where she currently lives and works. At the time, her devotion to the medium of painting put her at odds with much of the contemporary art scene, especially in the United Kingdom, where the Young British Artists (YBAs) were attracting attention for their coolly ironic embrace of everyday media. Brown, instead, has participated in a rekindling of painterly expression, with a characteristic gestural style that merges a range of artistic influences, from Francis Bacon (1909–92) to Cy Twombly (1928–2011) to Edvard Munch (1863–1944). *Where They Are Now* belongs to a series of paintings that imaginatively rework a photograph taken by David Montgomery for the cover of the Jimi Hendrix Experience's 1968 album, *Electric Ladyland*. The original photograph depicts a dense cluster of nude women sprawled out across the floor, staring into the camera. In Brown's canvas, mouths, limbs and eye sockets dissolve into a morass of rich, sensual brushstrokes. Transgressing centuries of art-historical tradition, her paint conceals as much as it reveals.

MIRIAM CAHN

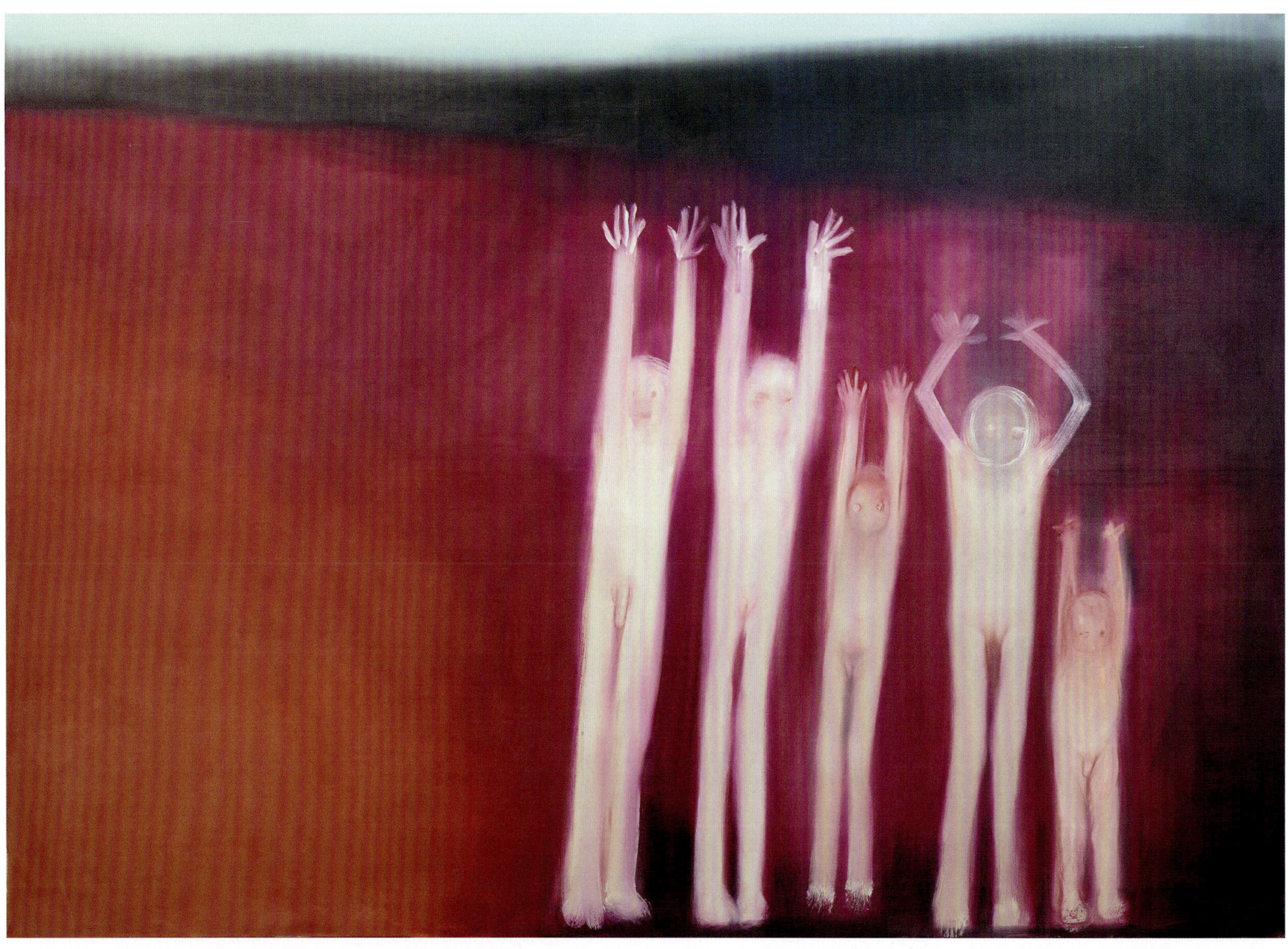

HÄNDE HOCH! (HANDS UP!)
2014, oil on canvas, 280 × 400 cm (110 ¼ × 157 ½ in), private collection, Vienna, Austria

Miriam Cahn, born 1949, Basel, Switzerland.

Reaching adulthood at the height of the women's liberation movements in the 1960s and 1970s, Cahn roots her practice in a commitment to social, political and environmental concerns. Like many of the women activists and artists of that period, Cahn has always acknowledged the central role of the body in her work, often exploring it as a site of abjection and vulnerability. Working across painting, drawing, writing, film, sculpture and photography, her works centre in particular on gender, violence, sex, power and family, and evoke experience as complex and interdependent. Cahn often challenges the conventions and prejudices that shape representation and ways of seeing, questioning binaries such as body and environment, male and female, pleasure and pain, human and more-than-human. The figures that fill many of her compositions are ambivalently pictured, glowing and merging with their surroundings, at once spectral and palpably corporeal, with body parts that are freighted with social meaning. In *HANDS UP!*, Cahn creates a feverish scene, investing emotional intensity into a universal gesture of fear and surrender.

HUGUETTE CALAND

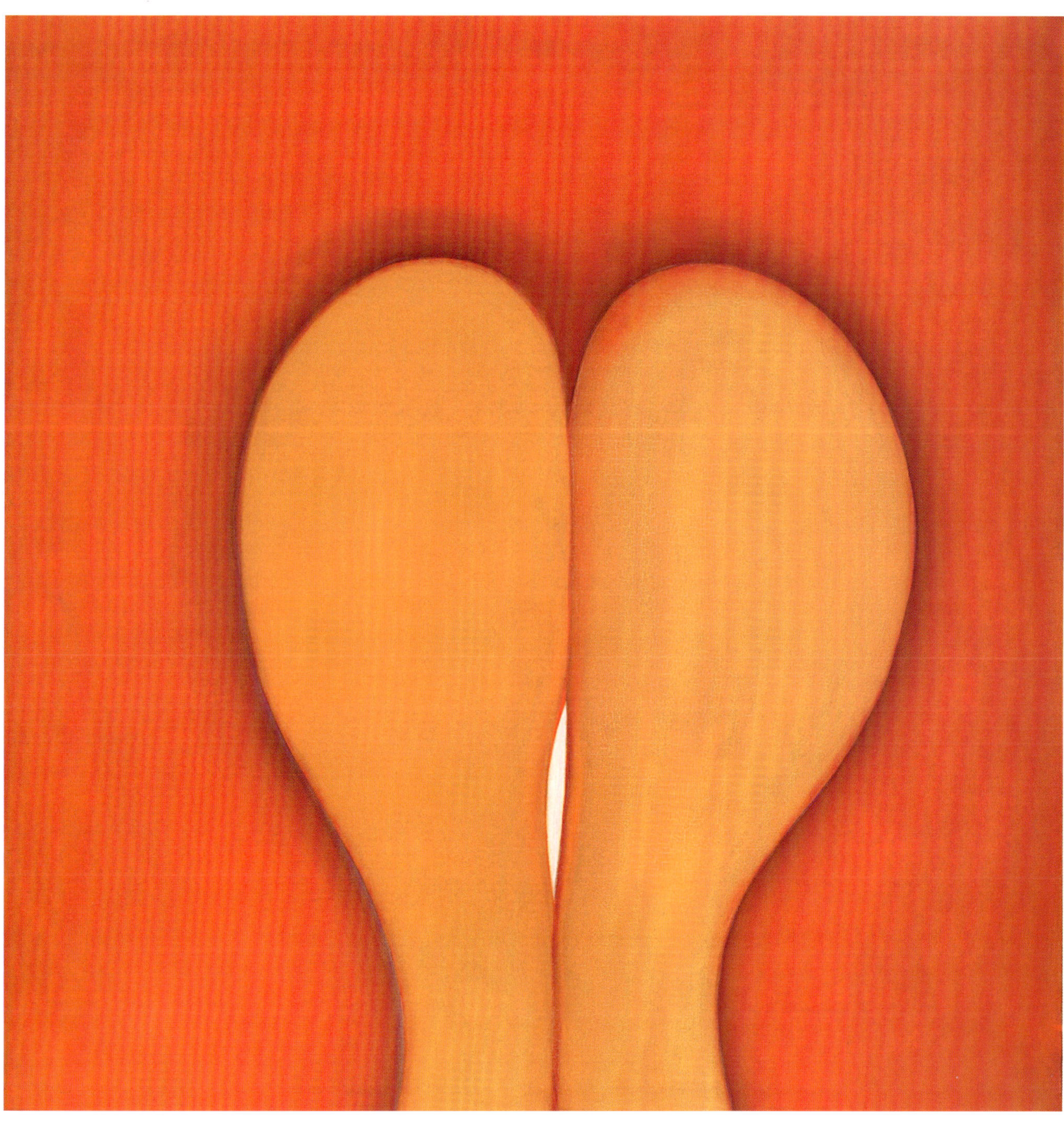

BRIBES DE CORPS #296 (BODY BITS #296)
1973–4, oil on canvas, 152.4 × 152.4 cm (60 × 60 in), Metropolitan Museum of Art, New York, USA

Huguette Caland, born 1931, Beirut, Lebanon. Died 2019, Beirut.

Speaking to sensual bodily experiences, eroticism and desire with paintings that emanate warmth and joie de vivre, Caland, in a 2013 interview with the *Los Angeles Times*, characteristically said, 'I love every minute of my life… I squeeze it like an orange and eat the peel.' Growing up in an elite environment of social expectations defined by her gender and social status – her father was independent Lebanon's first president – Caland studied at the American University of Beirut in the 1960s. Caland moved to Paris in 1970, and in 1973 began her best-known series, 'Bribes de corps' ('Body Bits'), which features sensual, abstracted images of body parts of her friends, lovers and herself – as seen in this painting resembling the backside of a figure bending over, rendered in succulent and swelling reds and oranges. Also working with textiles alongside painting, by 1978 Caland was designing garments for fashion designer Pierre Cardin, including caftans decorated with breasts and buttocks. Living in Los Angeles from 1987 to 2013 before then returning to Beirut, Caland was the subject of a 2016 exhibition at the Hammer Museum and was included in the 57th Venice Biennale a year later, bringing her long overdue recognition.

MARIE GABRIELLE CAPET

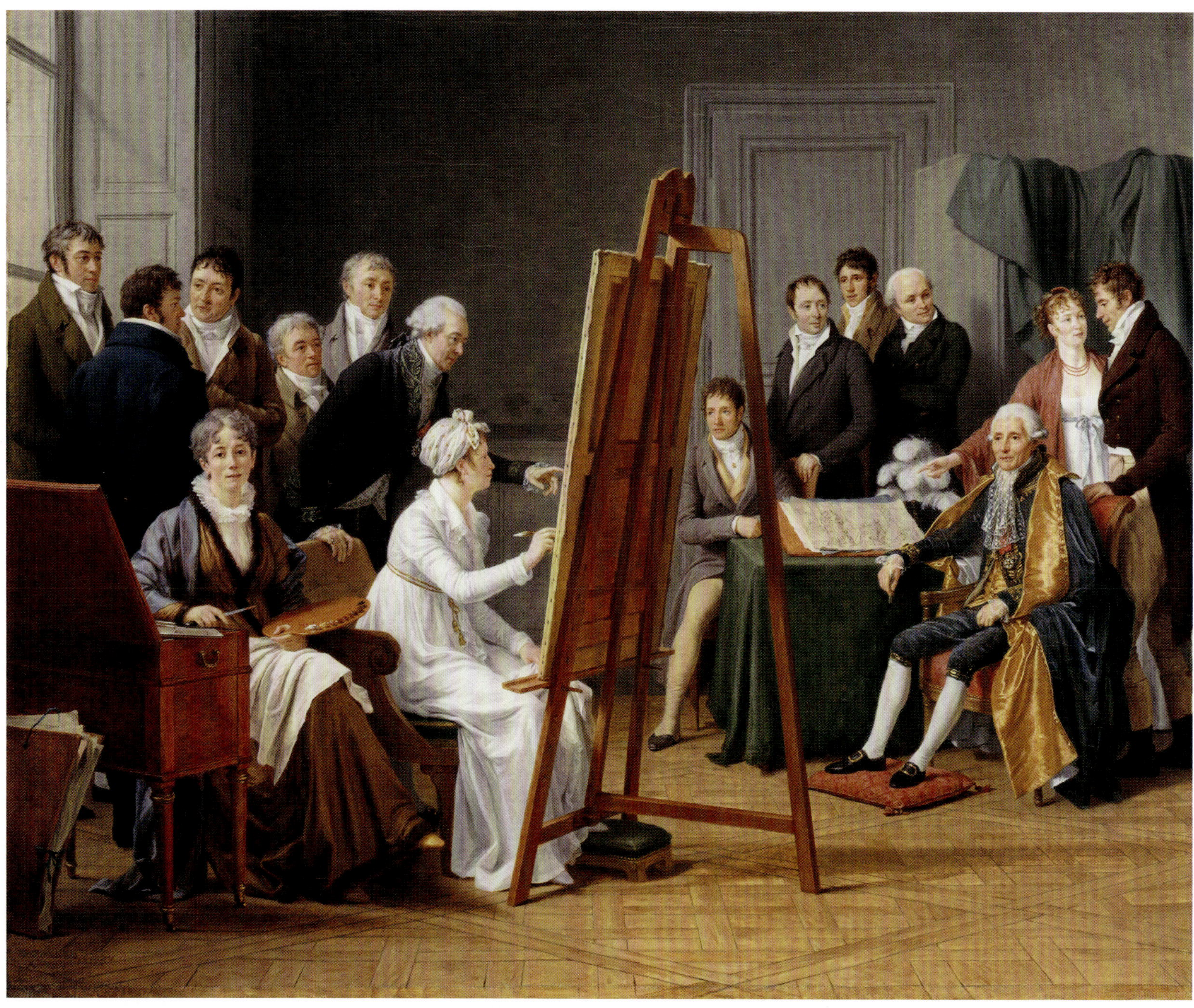

STUDIO SCENE (ADÉLAÏDE LABILLE-GUIARD PORTRAYS JOSEPH-MARIE VIEN)
1808, oil on canvas, 69 × 83.5 cm
(27 ⅛ × 32 ⅞ in), Neue Pinakothek, Bayerische Staatsgemäldesammlungen, Munich, Germany

Marie Gabrielle Capet, born 1761, Lyon, France. Died 1818, Paris, France.

A precocious talent for drawing took Capet to Paris in 1781, where she became the student of the eminent Neo-Classical painter Adélaïde Labille-Guiard (p.169). Capet established a considerable reputation as a portraitist in pastels and oils, and her canvases and miniatures were praised for their outstanding draughtsmanship and sensitive use of colour. With the support of Labille-Guiard, she secured commissions from the upper middle classes, nobility and royal family. After the French Revolution, Capet was one of the first female painters to participate in the Salon of the Académie Royale de Peinture et de Sculpture. Capet, who never married, formed a lifelong friendship with Labille-Guiard, living with her for many years, even after she married the painter François-André Vincent (1746–1816). In this large-scale history painting, Capet pays homage to her teacher, showing her working in the studio surrounded by pupils. Capet, looking directly at the viewer, portrays herself as an assistant, holding Labille-Guiard's palette as she paints her husband's own painting tutor, Joseph-Marie Vien (1716–1809).

JOAN CARLILE

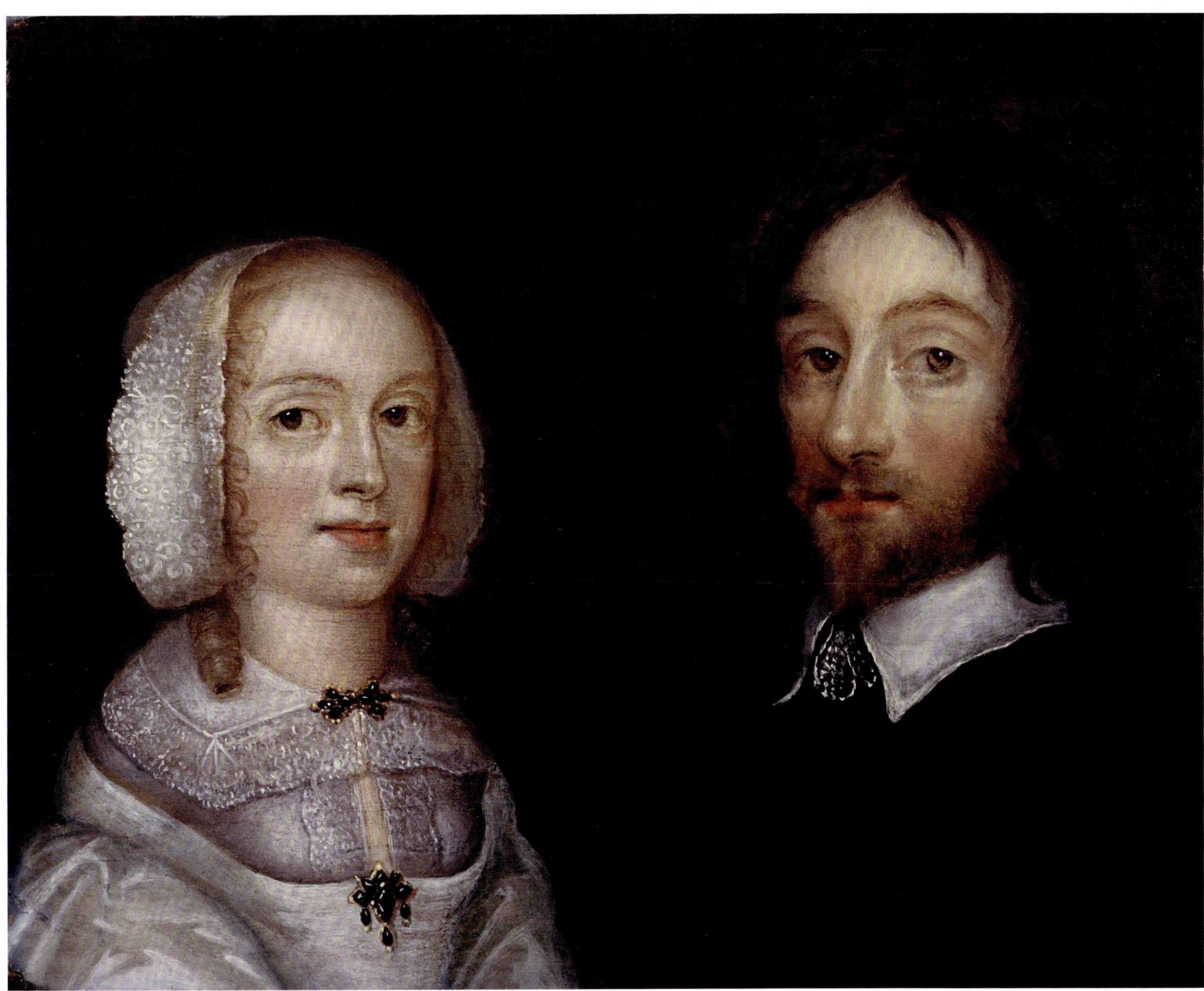

DOROTHY, LADY BROWNE (NÉE MILEHAM); SIR THOMAS BROWNE
*c.*1641–50, oil on panel, 18.4 × 22.9 cm (7 ¼ × 9 in), National Portrait Gallery, London, UK

Joan Carlile, born *c.*1603, London, UK. Died 1679, Petersham, Surrey, UK.

Carlile was one of Britain's first professional women portraitists, working during a turbulent period in the country's history. There are no records of formal artistic training, but her marriage in 1626 to Lodowick Carlile, a courtier to Charles I, gave her access to the Royal Collection. She is known to have copied a number of the king's paintings and was possibly mentored by the leading court painter Anthony van Dyck (1599–1641). The outbreak of civil war in 1642 meant a loss of income for Lodowick, making Joan the main breadwinner. Although she mainly worked in Richmond, during the 1650s Carlile briefly kept a studio in the bustling artistic hub of Covent Garden in London, where she took commissions such as this small portrait of the English polymath Thomas Browne and his wife, Dorothy. One of around ten known paintings by Carlile, the delicate portrait demonstrates her skill in depicting fabrics such as the lace collar and cap worn by Dorothy Browne. Dorothy's finely rendered curls and the silvery highlights are also typical features of Carlile's painting – although this is one of her only works to include a male figure.

GILLIAN CARNEGIE

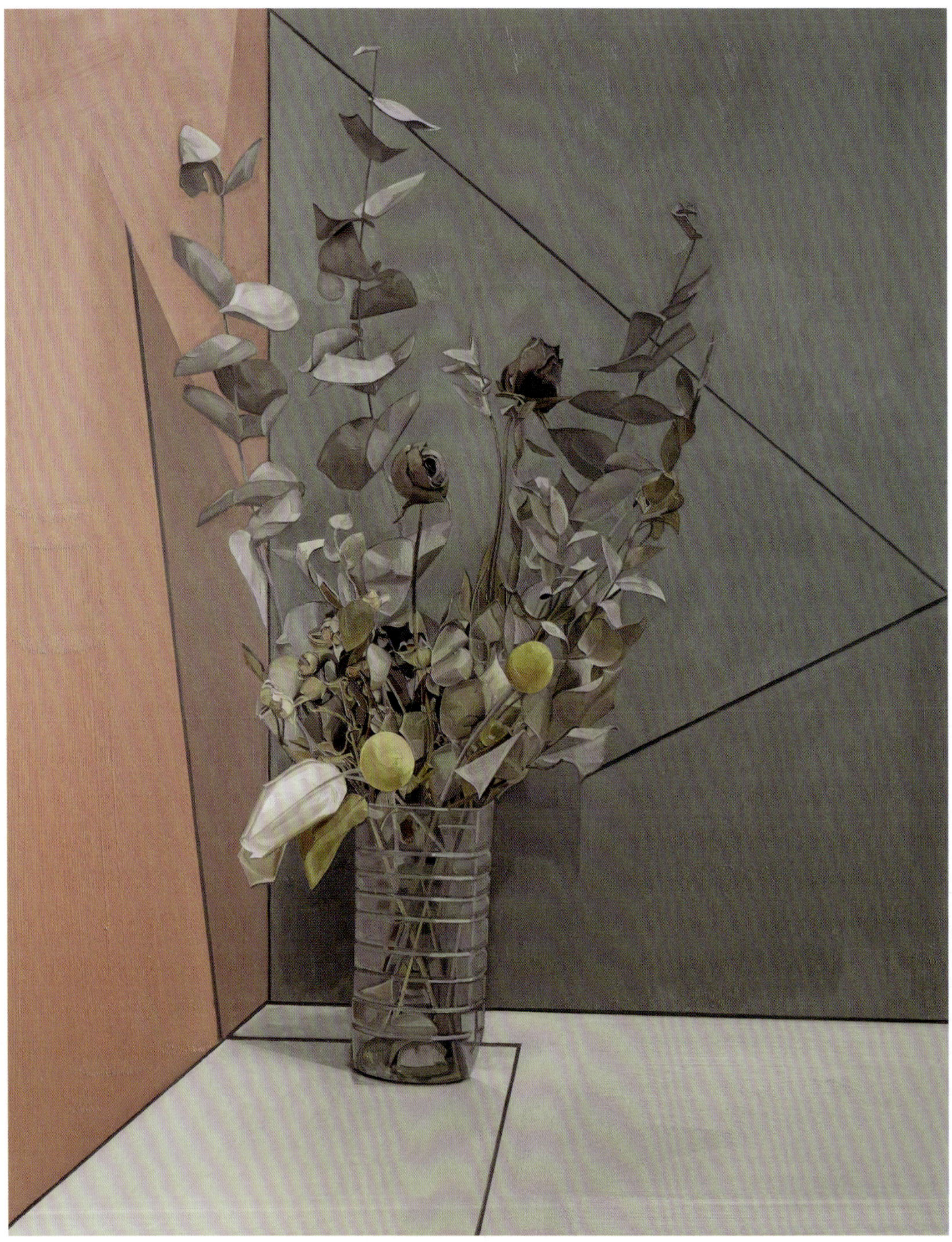

AMINADAB
2014, oil on board, 73.7 × 58.4 cm (29 × 23 in)

Gillian Carnegie, born 1971, Suffolk, UK.

Adopting painterly genres such as the still life, interiors and the female nude, Carnegie paints uncluttered domestic spaces, cats, flowers and, in an infamous series of 'bum paintings', her own backside. But Carnegie, who is a graduate of London's Royal College of Art and was nominated for the 2005 Turner Prize, is less interested in provoking than in satisfying a human urge to paint and exploring how paintings can convey a range of subtle feelings, ideas and information. She builds up precise planes of thick impasto with sharp edges that catch the light and keep the eye moving across the canvas. Her use of paint produces a psychological effect in which texture, colour and form evoke states of mind rather than exactly representing the world. Narrative interpretation is often halted in scenes that exude an aura of privacy and stillness. In *Aminadab* a bouquet placed in a cut-down plastic water bottle is rendered in muted tones, less to convey the exact qualities of the flowers than to enhance the emotions their fading might provoke.

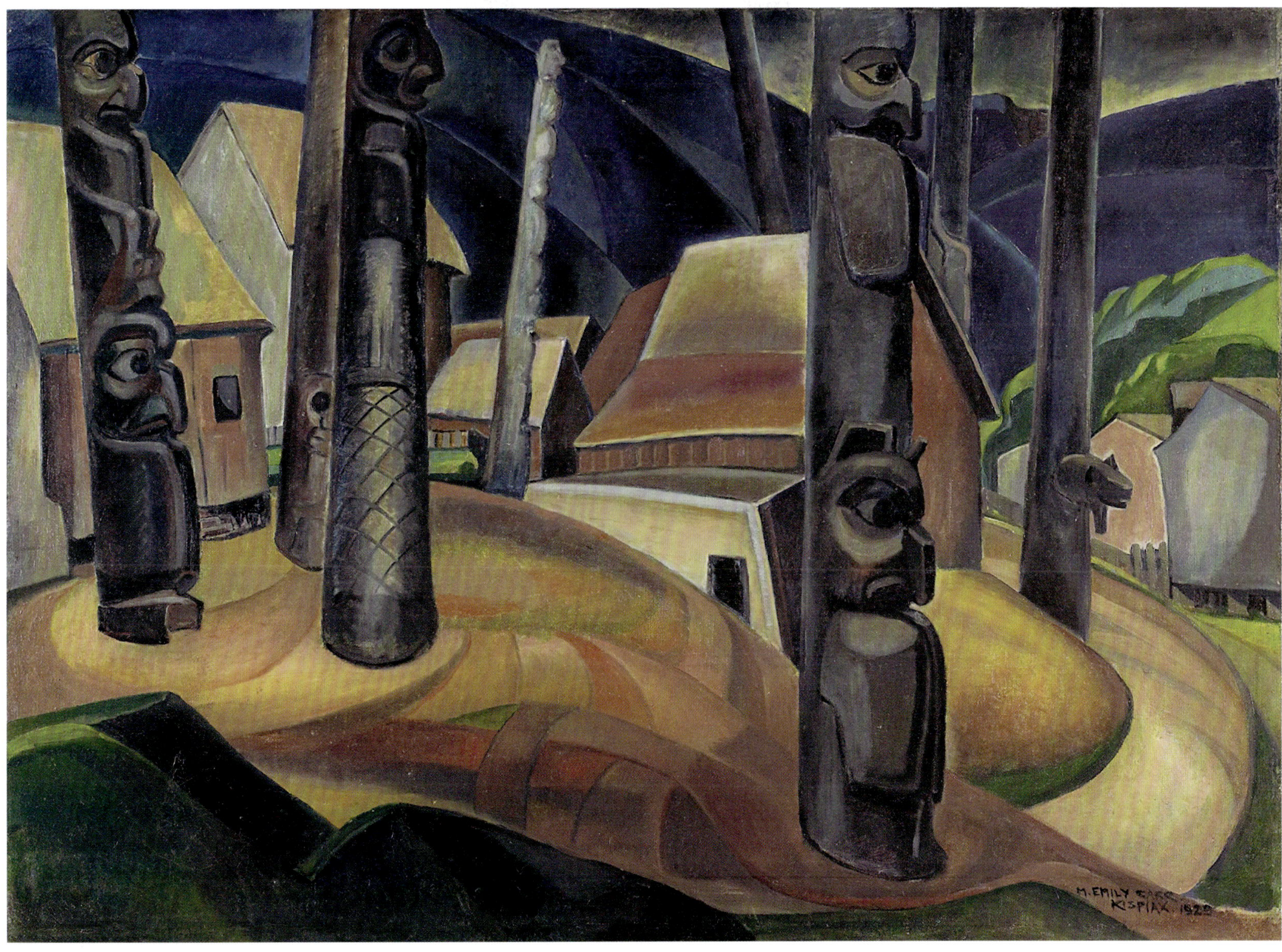

KISPIAX VILLAGE
1929, oil on canvas, 91.8 × 128.7 cm (36 ⅛ × 50 ⅝ in), Art Gallery of Ontario, Toronto, Canada

Emily Carr, born 1871, Victoria, British Columbia, Canada. Died 1945, Victoria.

The sweeping landscapes of her native British Columbia were a lifelong inspiration for Carr, whose paintings and writings reveal a love for the spiritual forces of nature and fascination with Indigenous cultures. She trained in San Francisco and London, and was particularly influenced by Fauvism during a two-year stay in Paris between 1910 and 1912, evidenced by her expressive canvases and bold use of colour. Carr frequented First Nations villages in Canada, where she became preoccupied with the powerful presence of totem poles. In *Kispiax Village* the undulating image is tightly framed around the soaring carved structures that extend beyond the edges of the painting. Such unusual compositions, as well as her daring palette and loose brushwork, earned her recognition from the Group of Seven (1920–33), Canada's leading modernists of the time. Carr rejected the genre scenes and pastoral views typically associated with women artists in favour of subjects with political and cultural significance, especially around issues of settlement and displacement of Indigenous populations. The artist has been posthumously celebrated for her pioneering visions of the Pacific Northwest, while more recently her work has been re-examined through a postcolonial lens attuned to the exoticizing effects of her documentation of Aboriginal customs.

LEONORA CARRINGTON

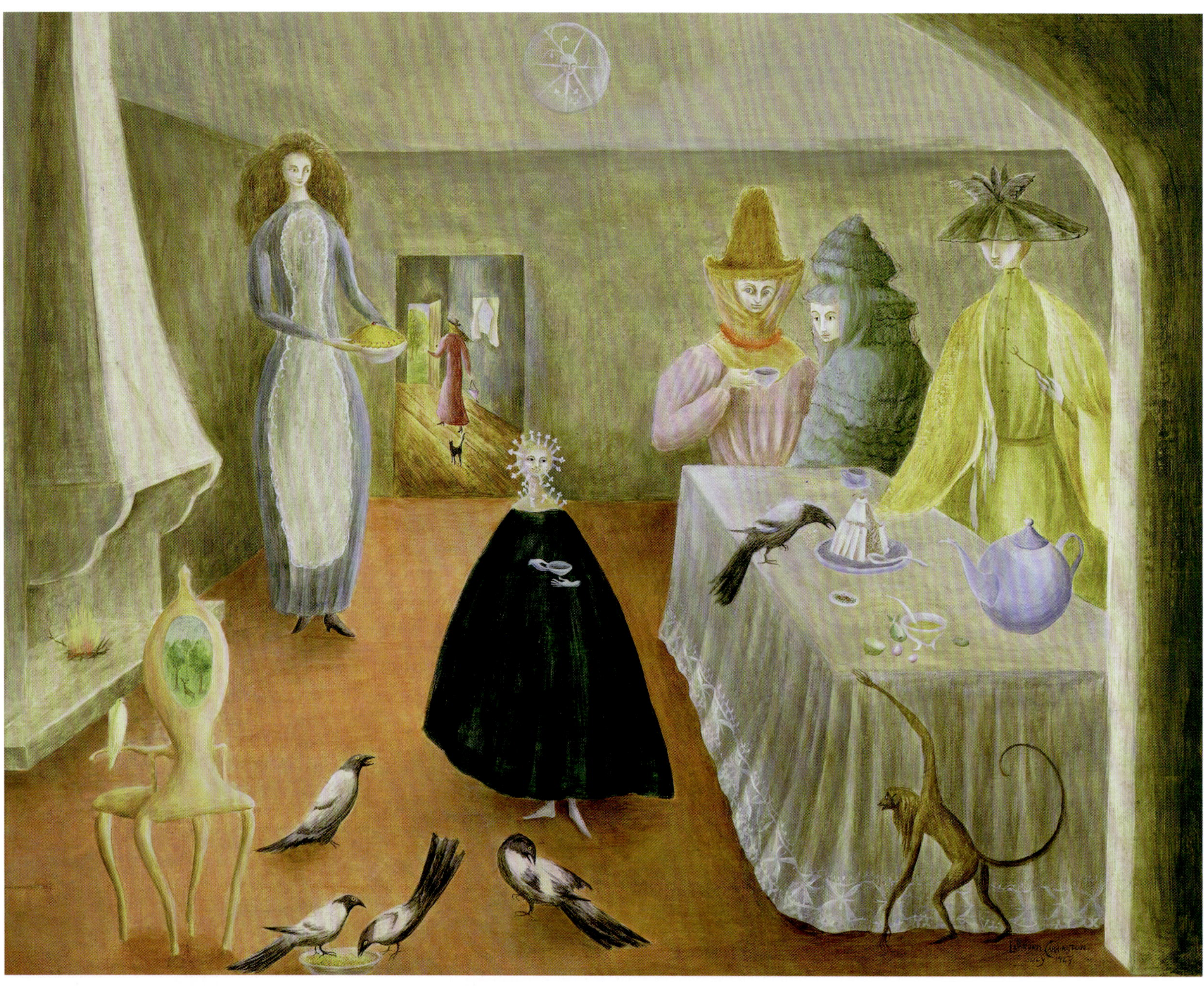

THE OLD MAIDS
1947, oil on board, 58.2 x 73.8 cm (22 7/8 x 29 in), Sainsbury Centre, University of East Anglia, Norwich, UK

Leonora Carrington, born 1917, Clayton-le-Woods, Lancashire, UK. Died 2011, Mexico City, Mexico.

Born into an upper-class Irish-Catholic family, Carrington spent her childhood captivated by fairy tales and later, as she matured, began to rebel against the expected life of a female socialite. In 1936 she met the artist Max Ernst (1891–1976), and shortly thereafter they moved to France, where she published her first short stories accompanied by his illustrations. Their mutually encouraged Surrealist expressions in both literature and visual art ended abruptly after his arrest in 1939 as an 'undesirable' as war gripped Europe. Carrington fled to Spain, the United States and eventually Mexico in 1942, where she joined a thriving arts scene that included Frida Kahlo (p.152) and Remedios Varo (p.308). Expressing her Surrealism with influences ranging from Celtic and Mayan mythology to witchcraft and the occult, Carrington created beguiling works on canvas in addition to designing stage sets and theatrical costumes and continuing to publish her writing. Representative of Carrington's singular Surrealist aesthetic, this painting's use of distorted proportions and perspective ushers the viewer into a curious tea party attended by mysterious, not-quite-human subjects and their familiars, including a flock of pigeons, a monkey and the archetypal witch's black cat.

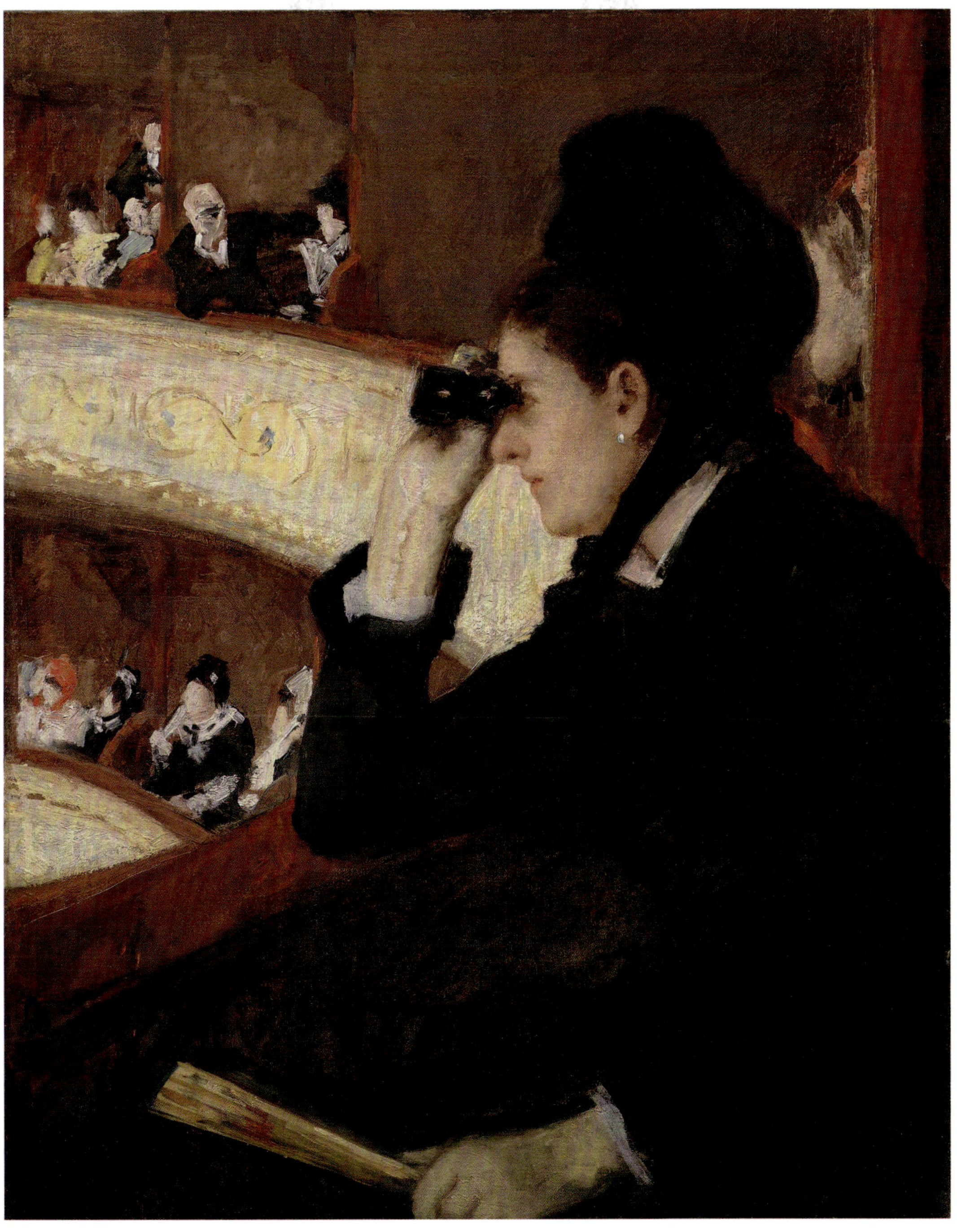

IN THE LOGE
1878, oil on canvas, 81.3 × 66 cm (32 × 26 in),
Museum of Fine Arts, Boston, USA

Mary Cassatt, born 1844, Allegheny City, Pennsylvania, USA. Died 1926, Le Mesnil-Théribus, France.

Having lived in Paris in the mid-1860s while studying art, Cassatt moved there permanently in 1873. After her work was rejected by the 1877 Salon, she was invited by Edgar Degas (1834–1917) to join the independent group of artists who painted scenes from everyday life in quick, loose brushstrokes, pejoratively labelled by a critic as the Impressionists. *In the Loge* is one of a number of Impressionist works that focused on the popular bourgeois cultural destination of the theatre. With matinée performances one of the few attractions that women could attend unchaperoned, these venues gave women agency within the public, urban environment. This work has often been discussed, particularly by feminist art historians of the 1970s onwards, in terms of the politics of looking. The fashionable though demurely dressed woman gazes intently through opera glasses at an unrevealed subject (generally agreed to be another spectator rather than a performer on stage) while she in turn captures the attention of a loosely rendered man leaning over the balcony beyond to observe her more closely through his lenses. An active viewer herself, rather than solely the object of the male gaze, the work complicates the traditional gender relations represented in art.

JORDAN CASTEEL

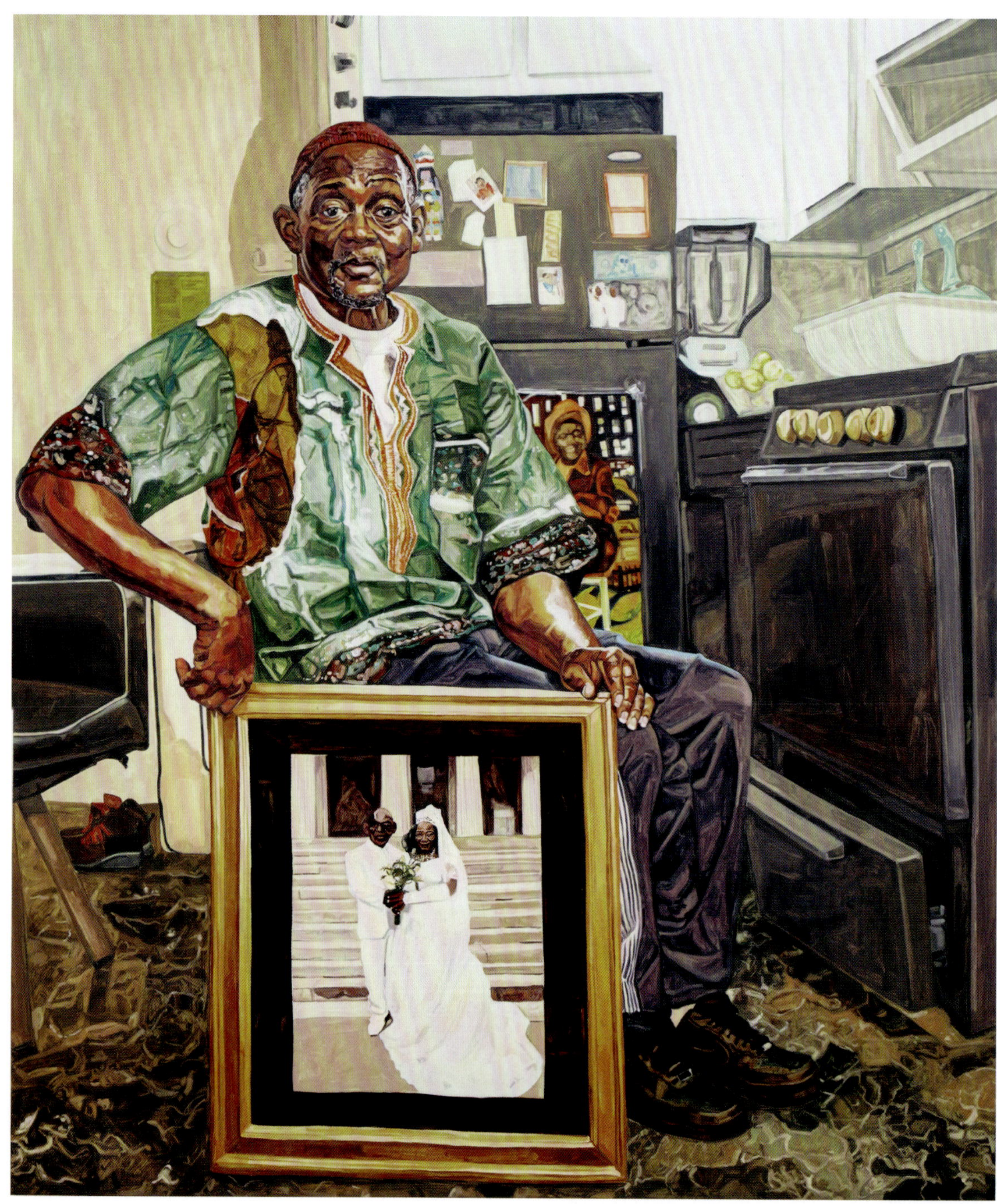

YVONNE AND JAMES II
2021, oil on canvas, 228.6 × 198.1 cm (90 × 78 in), Metropolitan Museum of Art, New York, USA

Jordan Casteel, born 1989, Denver, Colorado, USA.

Part of a dynamic new generation of figurative painters, Casteel is renowned for her large-scale, empathic portraits often depicting people of colour. Deeply committed to her subjects, Casteel gives them agency; they look directly at the viewer, comfortable in their skin, which she renders with a sensitive, varied colour palette. During a 2015–16 residency at the Studio Museum in Harlem, New York, Casteel photographed the neighbourhood's residents and local business owners for her portraits – among them, James Boyd and his wife, Yvonne, who became her close friends. In this image of quiet grief, made after his wife's passing, James is portrayed with dignity, seated in his modest kitchen holding a wedding picture. A fragment of Casteel's earlier portrait of James is visible on the refrigerator behind. This poignant composition showing the subject from three perspectives underscores the passage of time and James's loss.

GEORGETTE CHEN

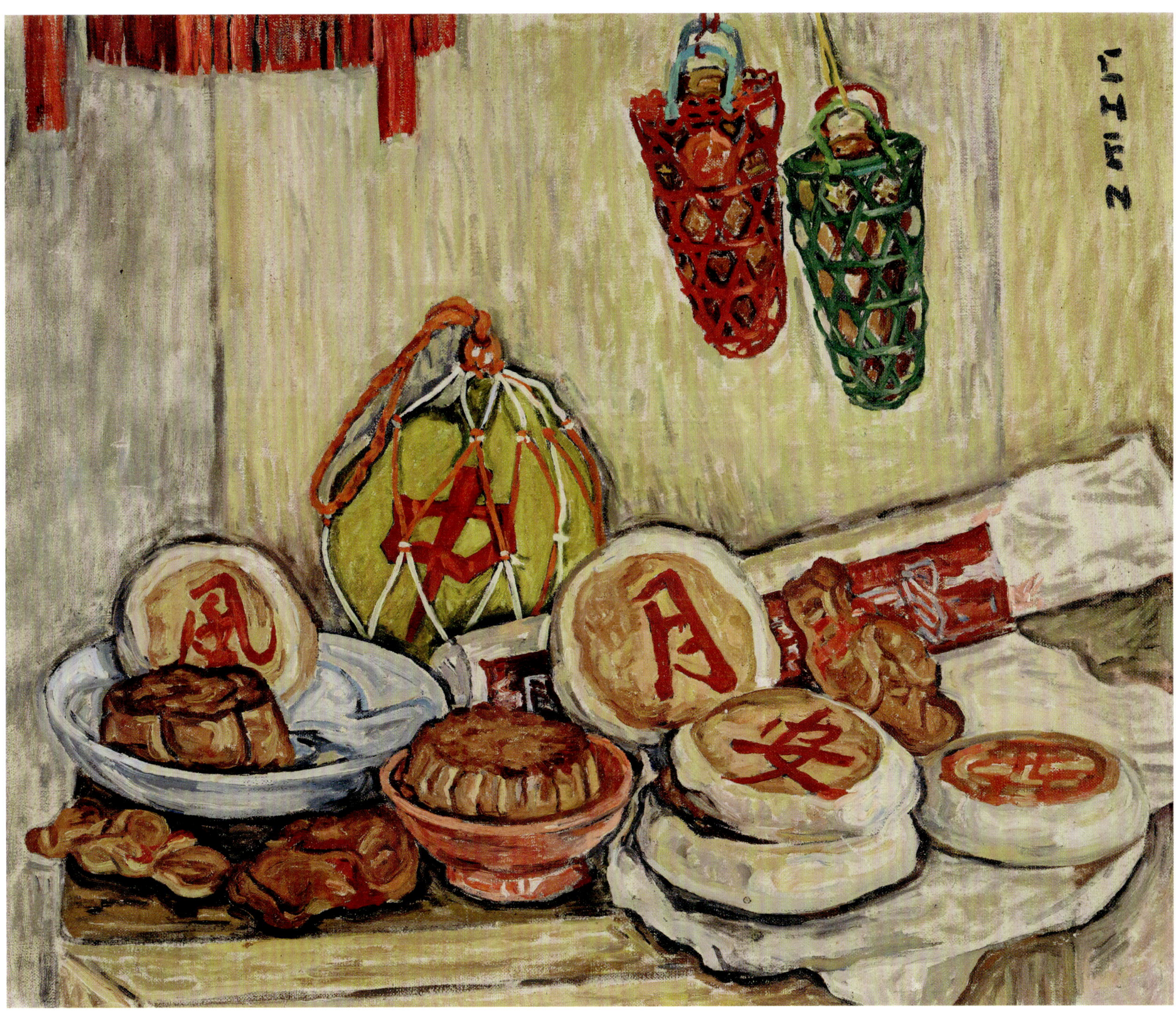

MOONCAKES WITH GOLDEN POMELO
1965, oil on canvas, 46 × 56 cm (18 ⅛ × 22 in),
National Gallery Singapore

Georgette Chen, born 1906, Zhejiang Province, China. Died 1993, Singapore.

The fourth of twelve children born to a wealthy Chinese merchant father, Chen had an international upbringing between Paris, New York and Shanghai. As a young adult, she studied for a year at the Art Students League in New York in 1926, and later in Paris, where she was influenced by nineteenth-century European movements such as the Barbizon School and Realism, producing works that were later selected for the prestigious Salon d'Automne in 1930. She later settled into a style inspired by Post-Impressionism and Fauvism, in particular the still lifes of Paul Cézanne (1839–1906). She settled in Singapore in 1953, teaching art part-time at the Nanyang Academy of Fine Arts from 1954 to 1980. Chen pioneered what came to be known as the Nanyang style, practised by Chinese artists in Singapore, in which Southeast Asian subjects and themes are rendered using European techniques. In this large-format still life, Chen's energetic brushstrokes bring to life the traditional items used to celebrate the Chinese Mid-Autumn Festival as it is celebrated in Southeast Asia.

CHEN KE

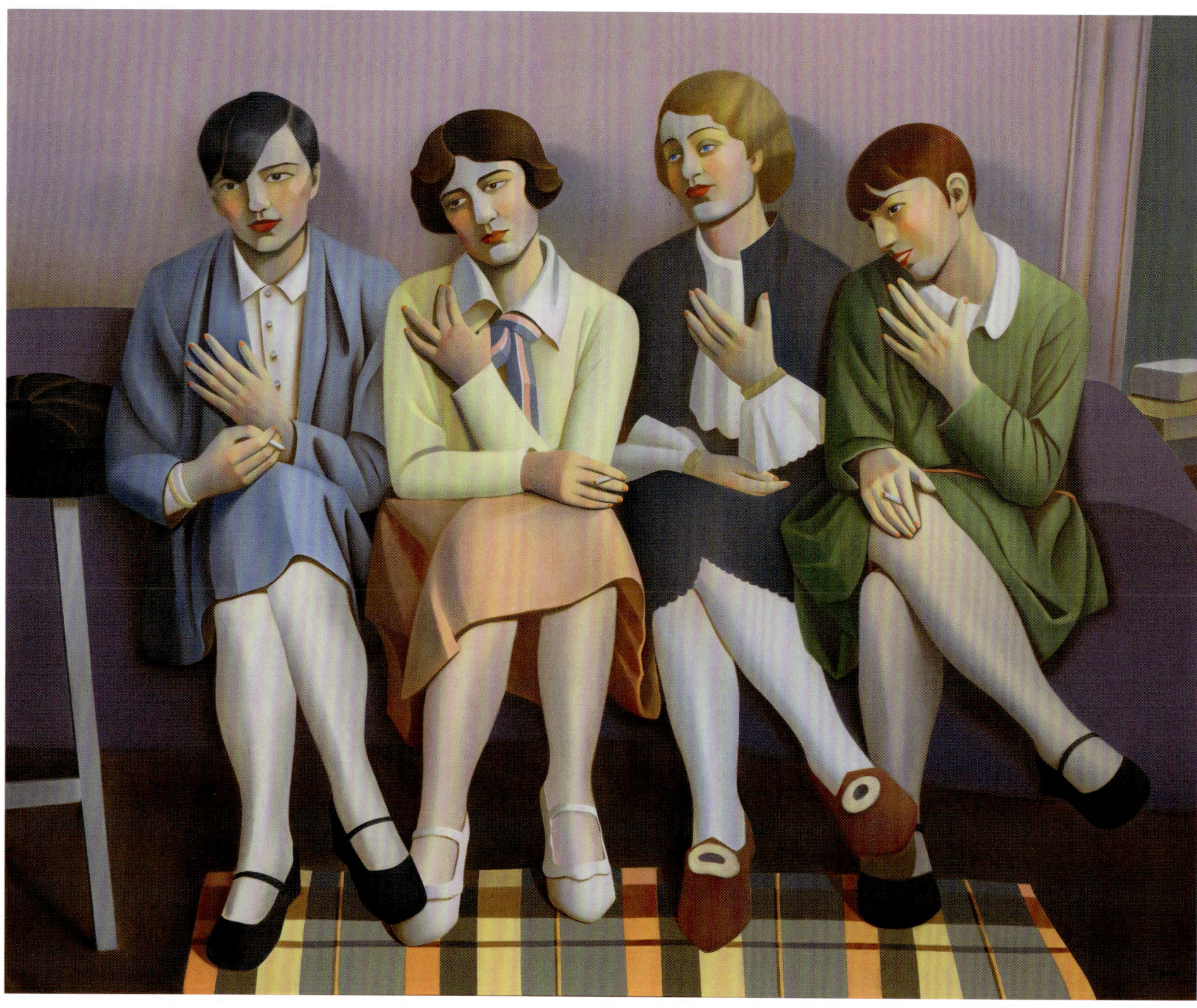

BAUHAUS GAL NO.12
2021, oil on canvas, 200 × 250 cm
(78 ¾ × 98 ⅜ in)

Chen Ke, born 1978, Tongjiang, Sichuan Province, China.

After completing a master's degree at the Sichuan Academy of Fine Arts in 2005, Chen moved to Beijing to launch her career as an artist. While her early works depicted anonymous figures rendered in an exaggerated cartoon style, she moved on to using historical images of well-known figures as source material, including Frida Kahlo (p.152), Marilyn Monroe or, as seen here, the young women of the Bauhaus School in Germany, who were famously not allowed to study painting (nor carpentry, metalwork or architecture), directed instead to the 'feminine' weaving workshop. Inspired by a book of archive photographs taken at the Bauhaus between 1919 and 1933, Chen perceived the young students as 'fresh, independent, confident, and full of expectation for the future,' as she explained in an artist's statement accompanying her 2021 exhibition 'Bauhaus Girls'. This show presented a series of works around the subject, which transform black-and-white imagery into brightly coloured, stylized paintings of varied sizes, including abstract motifs on shaped aluminium panels. Through these works, the artist articulates her feelings and thoughts about the conditions and place of women in society, explaining in a 2021 video interview for Perrotin gallery, 'We are all dancing with shackles to find a shelter for ourselves within limited freedom.'

JUDY CHICAGO

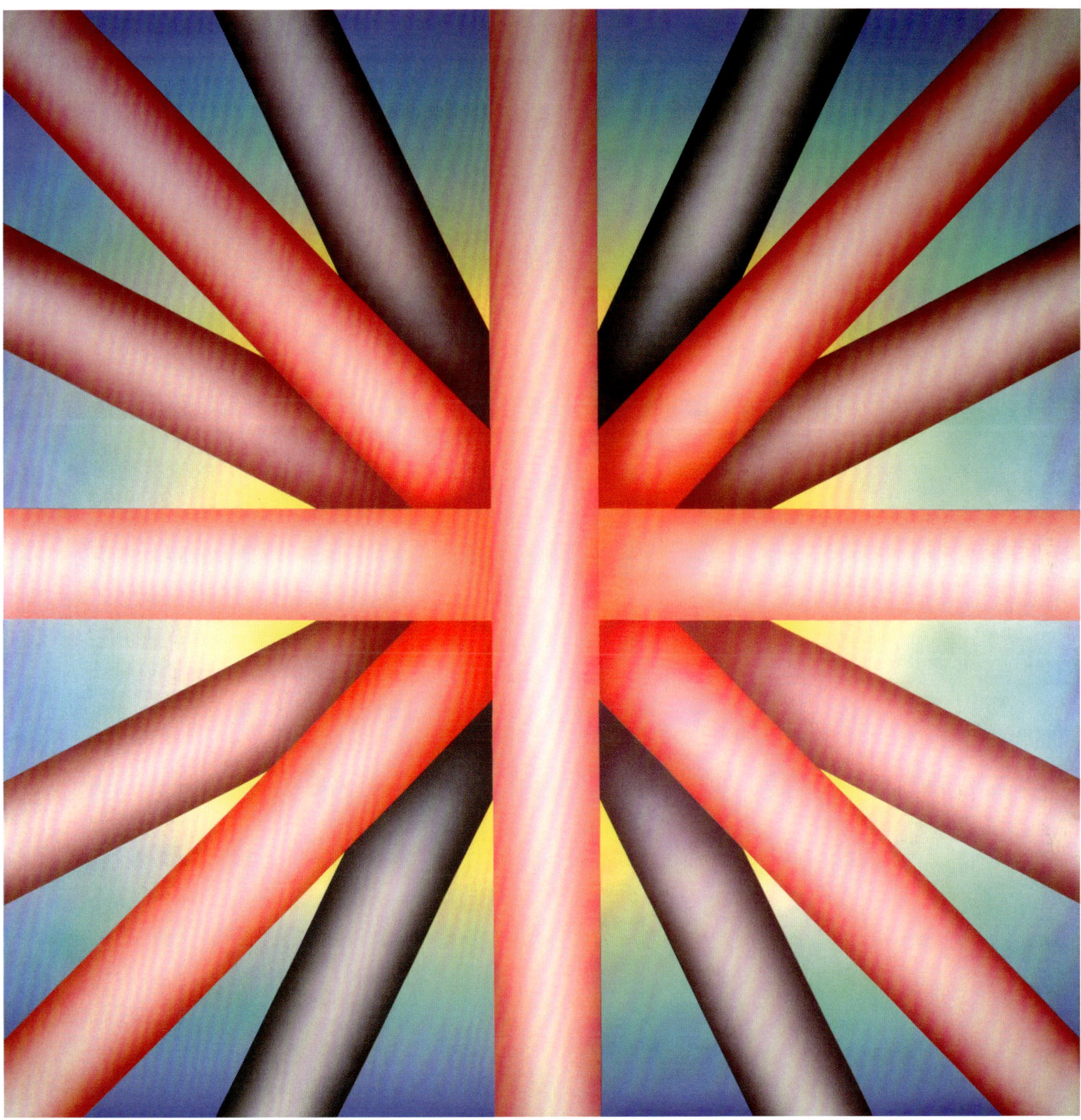

HEAVEN IS FOR WHITE MEN ONLY
1973, sprayed acrylic on canvas, 203.2 × 203.2 cm (80 × 80 in), New Orleans Museum of Art, USA

Judy Chicago, born 1939, Chicago, USA.

While most famous for her iconic feminist installation *The Dinner Party* (1974–9), Chicago has created art across many media, including painting, drawing, sculpture, textiles and pyrotechnics. She focused on painting while studying for her master's degree at the University of California, Los Angeles, from the late 1950s to early 1960s, but her biomorphic imagery and pastel colour palette were criticized by the male painting instructors, and she turned to making hard-edged Minimalist sculptures. Chicago's early works also included paintings on car hoods, having learnt spray-painting techniques at an auto-body school (the only woman among 250 students). At the end of the 1960s, after encountering the women's movement, she set out to create a distinctly feminist art practice – a pioneering concept at the time – and in 1970 took a new surname that was independent of any man, father or husband. In the early 1970s, Chicago made a series of square-format abstract paintings that featured a central, circular motif. With vivid, contrasting colours and forms modelled with graduating tones, these pulsating works demonstrate and celebrate female energy and creativity while offering critiques on patriarchal values with their punchy titles.

IRENE CHOU

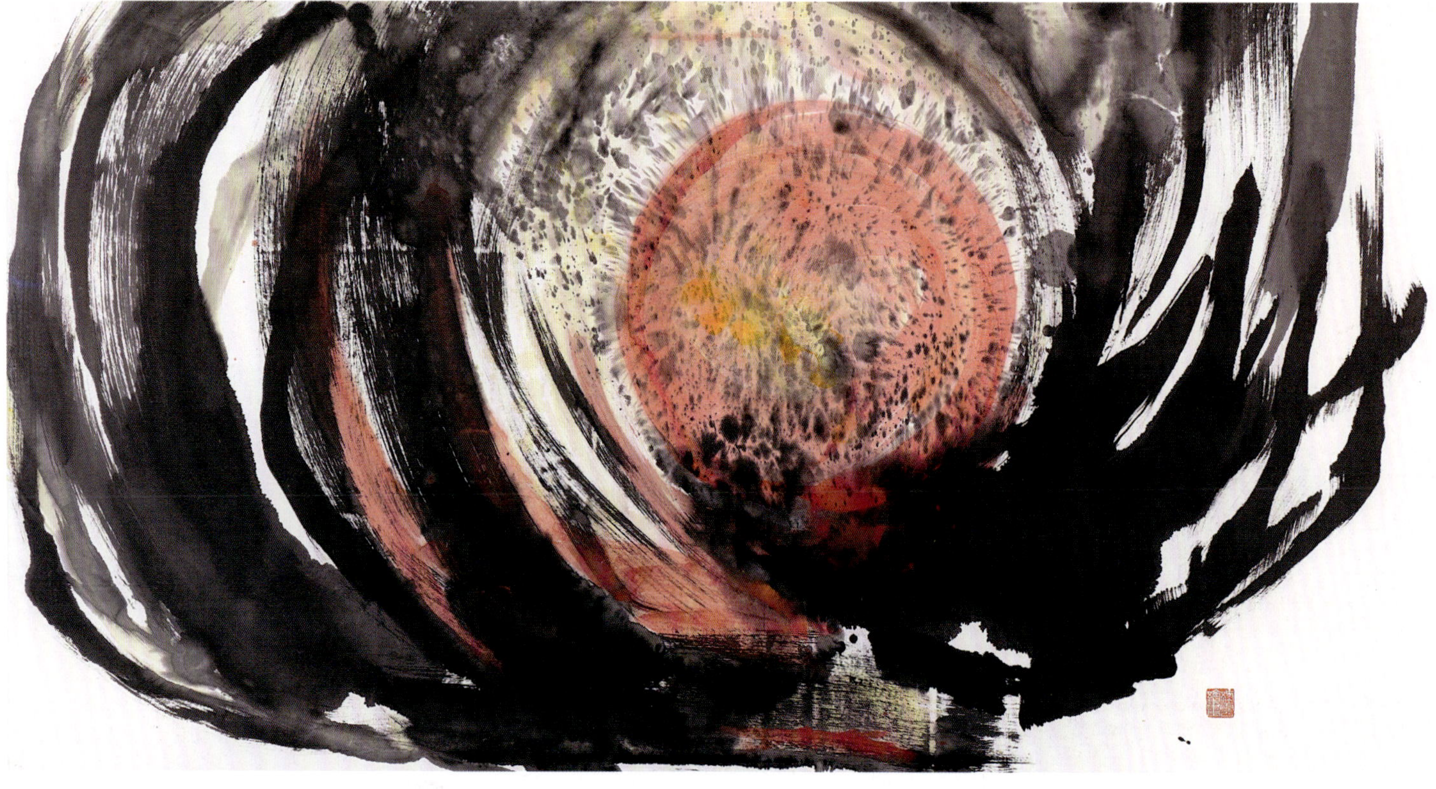

IMPACT II
1977, ink and colour on paper, 66 × 139 cm (26 × 54 ¾ in), M+, Hong Kong, China

Irene Chou, born 1924, Shanghai, China. Died 2011, Brisbane, Australia.

Chou studied economics at St John's University in Shanghai and worked as a journalist before formally training with Zhao Shao'ang (1905–98), a master of the Lingnan School of Painting. In the 1960s, despite her mastery of traditional calligraphy and ink painting, Chou began to experiment with new ideas and techniques, encouraged by the founder of Hong Kong's New Ink Painting movement, Lui Shou-Kwan (1919–75), and informed by Western art movements such as Abstract Expressionism. Chou explored an extensive vocabulary of mark-making methods such as 'splashed ink' – where the ink is applied in spatters – as well as bold 'one stroke' paintings and her own adaptation of the 'piled ink' technique, in which small, delicate strokes of ink are slowly built up to create a textural, sculptural effect. Chou is also known for her bold approach to subject matter, introducing themes and images related to harmony and healing, drawing analogies between the female body and the infinity of the cosmos. In *Impact II* – one of a series of works – a central, cell-like form with impactful, sweeping washes of dark ink surrounding it may allude to both the dark inner recesses of the womb and the expansiveness of the universe.

SALOUA RAOUDA CHOUCAIR

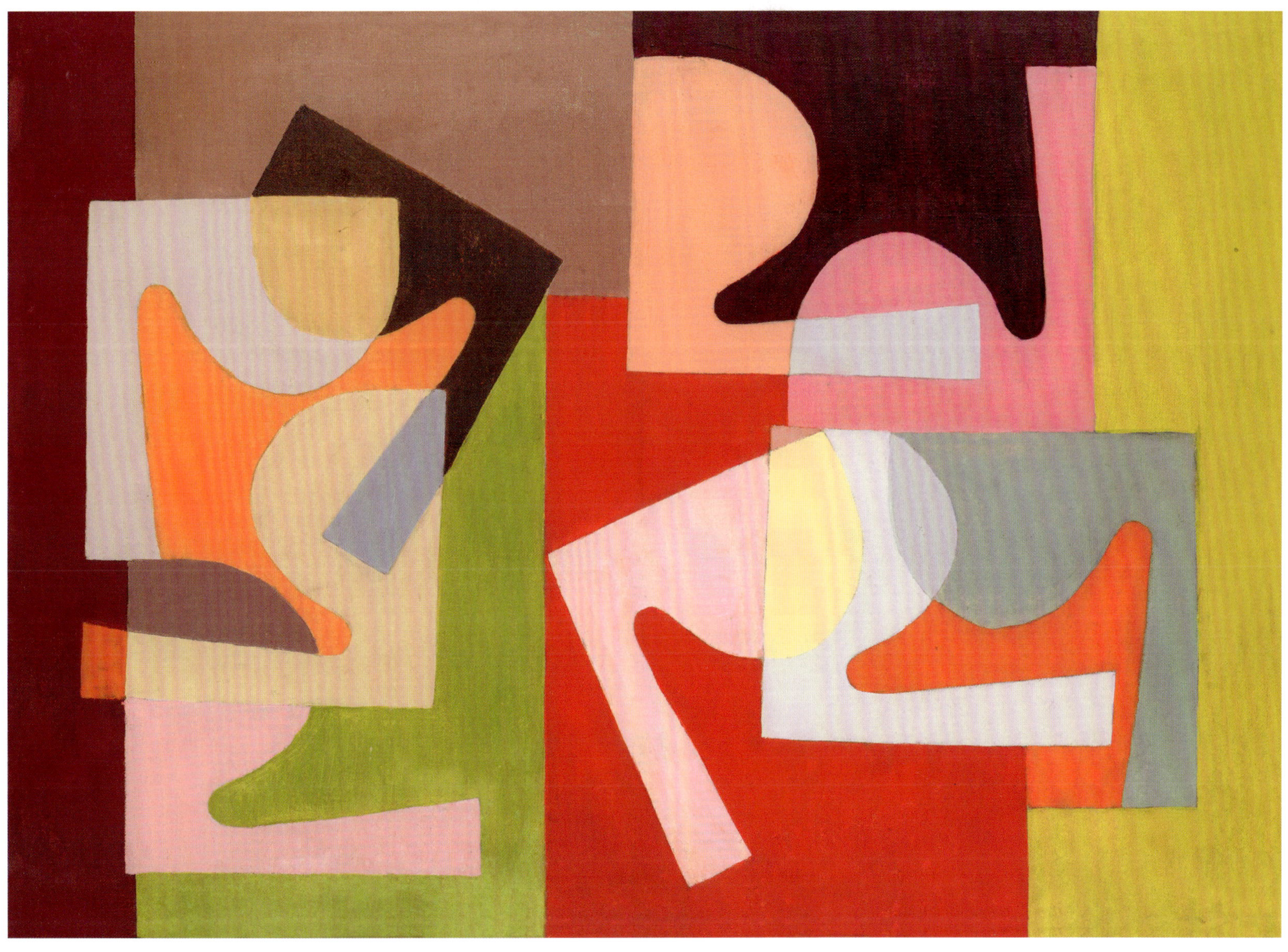

FRACTIONAL MODULE
1947–51, oil on canvas, 49 × 59.5 cm (19 ¼ × 23 ⅜ in)

Saloua Raouda Choucair, born 1916, Beirut, Lebanon. Died 2017, Beirut.

By the time of her centenary year, Choucair had come to be recognized as a leading modernist of the Arab world, yet she sold no work in her native Lebanon until her mid-forties and was little known outside her home country until her first international retrospective at Tate Modern, London, in 2013. A creative child who assisted her fellow pupils during art class, in 1942 she had three months of formal training with pioneering Lebanese Impressionist painter Omar Onsi (1901–69) and, in 1947, her work was included in a group exhibition at the Arab Cultural Gallery – considered to be one of the first abstract painting exhibitions in the Middle East. The following year she enrolled at the École Nationale Supérieure des Beaux-Arts, Paris, and began combining aspects of European abstraction with Islamic motifs, receiving acclaim from French critics for her bold forms. Returning to live in Lebanon, by the late 1950s she began making sculptures – in stone, wood, metal and fibreglass – and often in modular forms that echoed the shapes in her painted compositions. *Fractional Module* manifests a disorderly repetition of forms intertwined with a vibrant palette of colours.

PRUNELLA CLOUGH

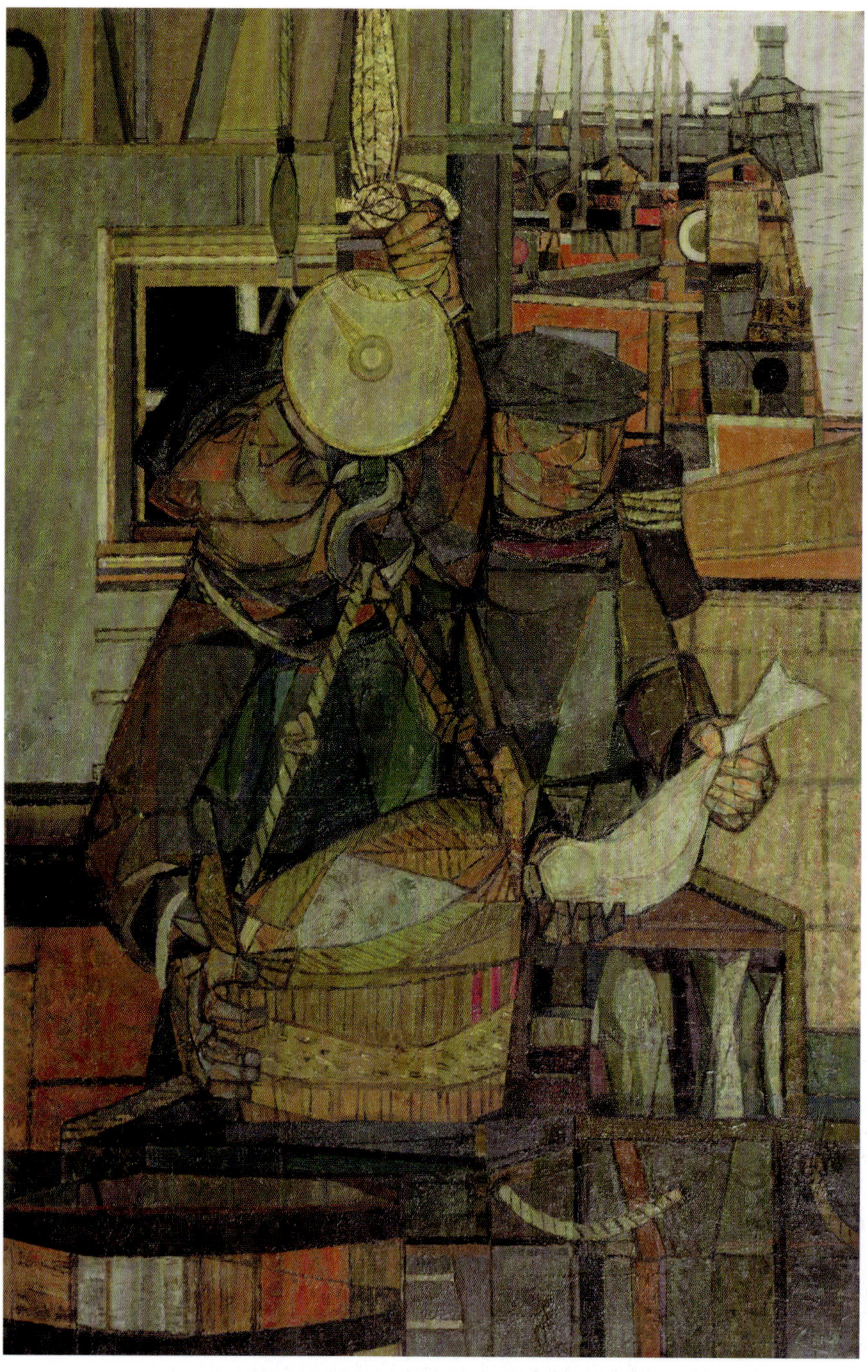

LOWESTOFT HARBOUR
1951, oil on canvas, 162.6 × 106.7 cm (64 × 42 in), Arts Council Collection, Southbank Centre, London, UK

Prunella Clough, born 1919, London, UK. Died 1999, London.

While she also made prints and created assemblages of collected objects, Clough is best known for her paintings. In 1938 she enrolled at the Chelsea School of Art, London, where she took classes with Henry Moore (1898–1986) until her studies were disrupted by the outbreak of the Second World War. During the war, she trained as an engineer's draughtsperson and cartographer, developing technical skills and a preoccupation with borders that would inform her painting practice. Though she hailed from an affluent, aristocratic family, Clough was drawn to depicting working men in industrial settings and was a frequent visitor to the docks along the Thames and the fishing harbours of Southwold and Lowestoft. In a 1982 interview, she stated: 'Living rooms are not exactly enough. I enjoyed the drama of the exotic, which was what factories or industrial areas offered me.' Clough painted *Lowestoft Harbour* for the 1951 Festival of Britain, a post-war fair organized to foster a sense of recovery and progress. Anticipating her later work, Clough's figures veer towards geometry and abstraction – her interest in shapes and subdued colours is given the same significance as the labour of the men portrayed.

ITHELL COLQUHOUN

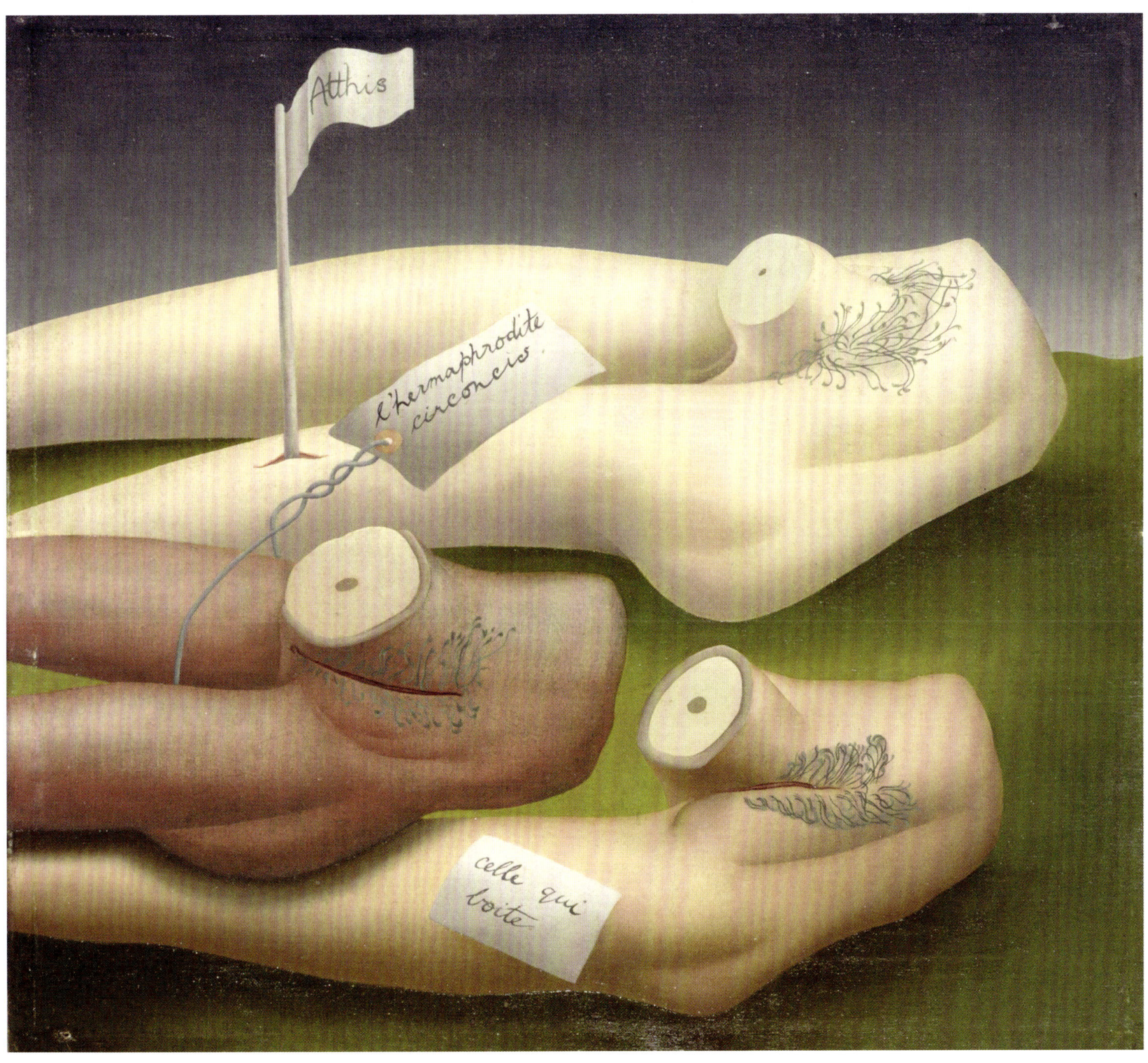

THE PINE FAMILY
1940, oil on canvas, 46 × 54 cm (18 ⅛ × 21 ¼ in), Israel Museum, Jerusalem

Ithell Colquhoun, born 1906, Shillong, Meghalaya, India. Died 1988, Lamorna, Cornwall, UK.

Born into a British family stationed in India, Colquhoun moved to England as a young child and later attended the Slade School of Fine Art in London, where she trained to paint large-scale classical and biblical scenes. In the early 1930s she moved to Paris, where she encountered Surrealism and the influential work of Salvador Dalí (1904–89) and René Magritte (1898–1967). She later joined the British Surrealists but broke with them to assert her creative independence. A lifelong interest in occult and esoteric traditions, along with her belief in the artist as a magician, guided her to create images charged with psychological and symbolic meaning, often employing Kabbalistic colour schemes and sacred geometry. She also wrote poems, travelogues and essays discussing Surrealist techniques, divination and the elements. In the late 1940s she moved to Cornwall, where she connected with the mystical qualities of the land. Erotic and violent undertones permeate this painting, in which male, female and intersexed bodies have been variously amputated. These ambiguous forms are realistic enough to be disturbing; when it was first displayed, some condemned the image as pornographic.

CAROLINE COON

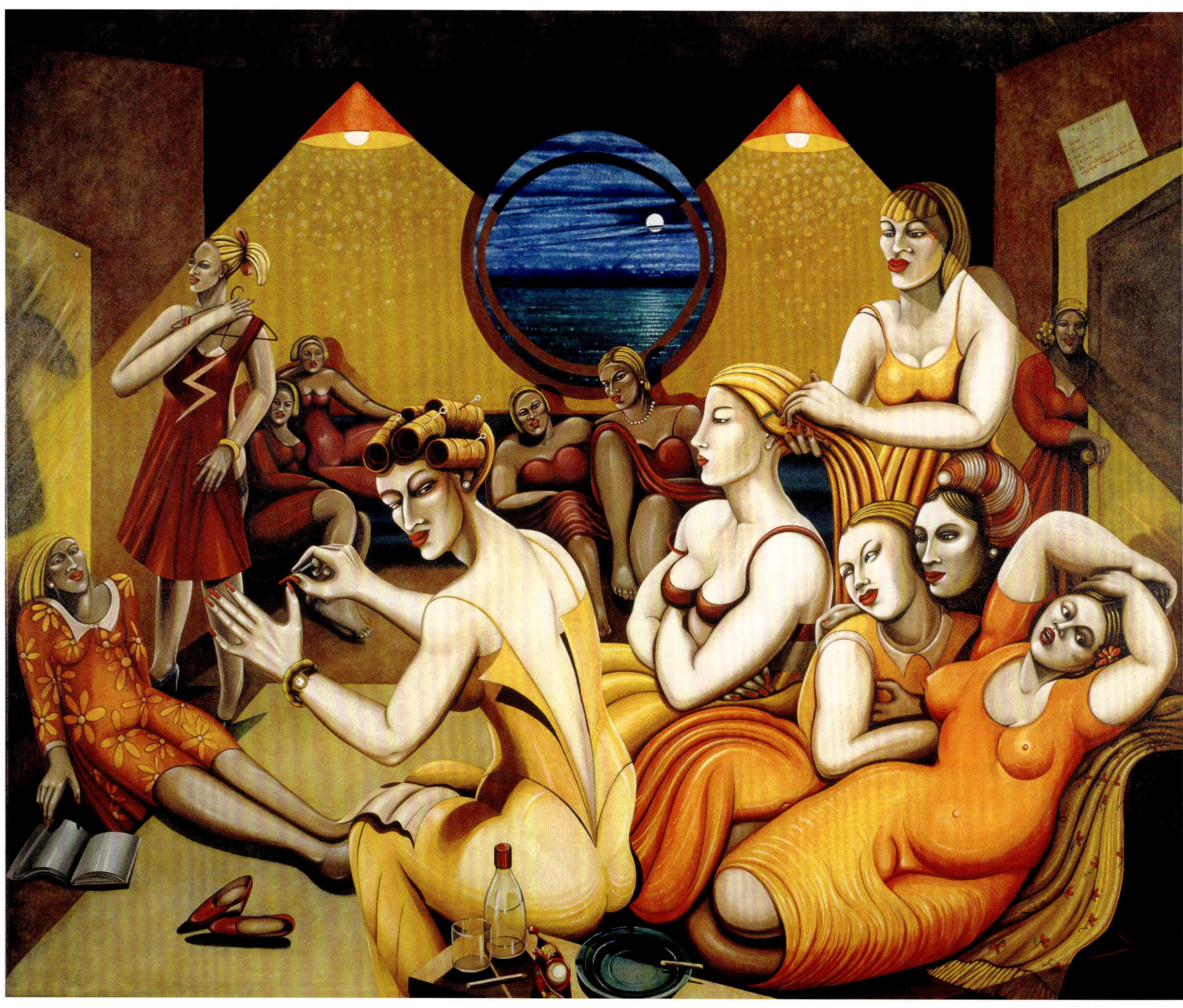

BETWEEN PARADES
1985, oil on canvas, 122 × 152 cm (48 × 59 ⅞ in)

Caroline Coon, born 1945, London, UK.

A central figure in the countercultural London scene, Coon has been making provocative, politically overt work since the 1960s. Coon is a devoted political activist who has consistently campaigned for women's rights and against the criminalization of sex work, and in 1967 co-founded Release, a UK legal advice agency for those arrested on drug charges. *Between Parades* comes from her 'Brothel Series' (1996–ongoing), narrative works depicting scenes of women sex workers through a feminist lens, reversing the dynamics of their depictions by male painters throughout art history. The women's muscular and curvaceous bodies, angular faces, broad features and red lips are quintessential elements of Coon's figurative style. Stripped to their undergarments, the backs of their dresses unzipped or high heels kicked off, the women smoke cigarettes, paint their nails and style their hair as they wait between clients. Set at dusk, the exuberant orange, yellow and red colour palette elicits a sense of warmth that is mirrored by the collective sense of intimacy and kinship. The figures in the work come from Coon's own experiences of sex work, which she cited in her 2016 memoir *Laid Bare*.

MARY CORSE

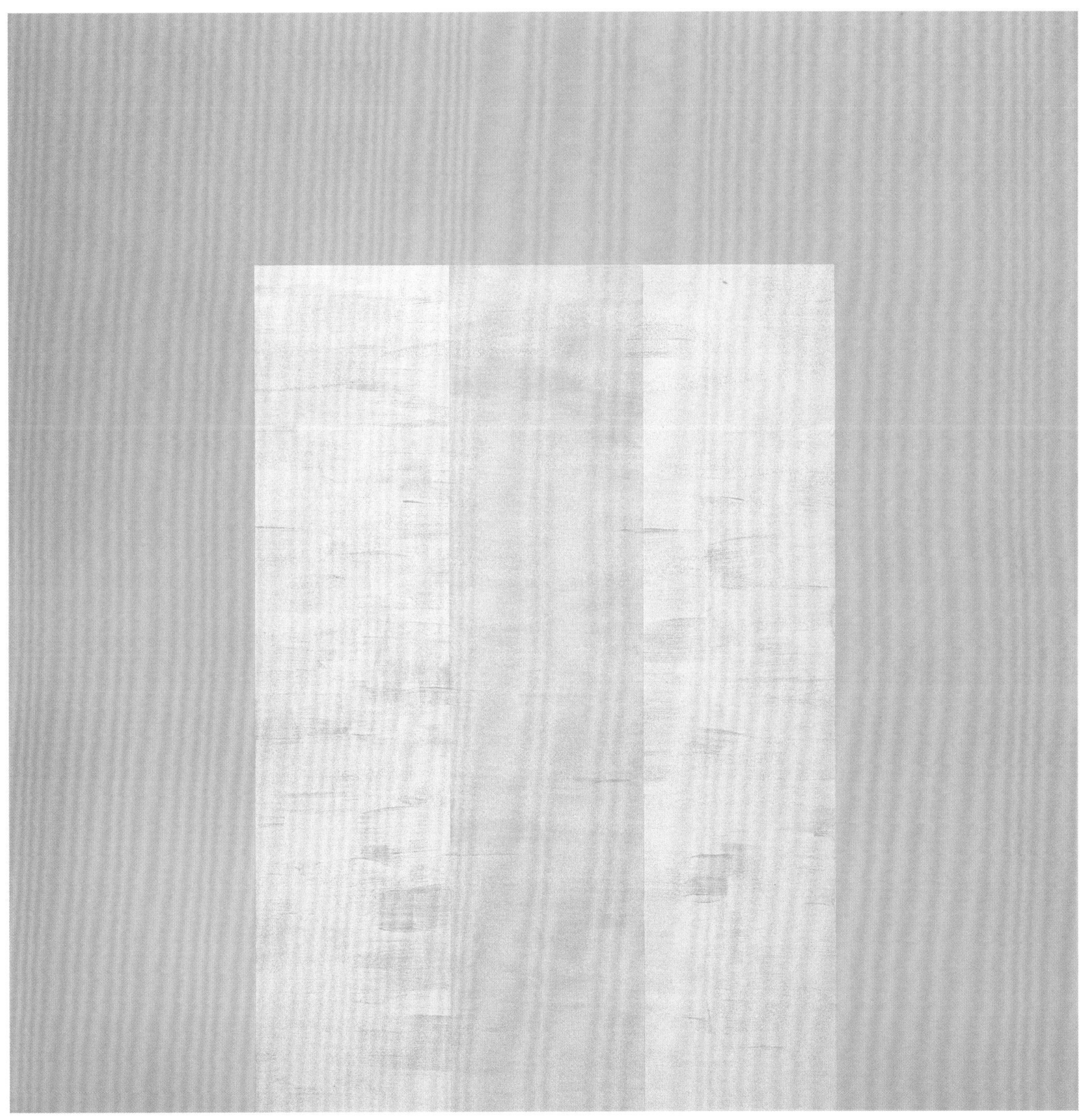

UNTITLED (WHITE ARCH INNER BAND SERIES)
1996, glass microspheres and acrylic on canvas,
245.1 × 243.8 × 6 cm (96 ½ × 96 × 2 ⅜ in),
Los Angeles County Museum of Art, USA

Mary Corse, born 1945, Berkeley, California, USA.

For more than fifty years, Corse has experimented with unconventional art-making materials such as metallic flakes, glass microspheres, fluorescent lights and plexiglass to consider perception and the possibilities of light as both subject and material. One of the few women connected with the Light and Space movement that originated in Southern California in the 1960s and 1970s, Corse devoted most of her practice to painting even as her contemporaries abandoned the medium in favour of environmental installations and sculpture. Corse began her iconic 'White Light' paintings in 1968, after investigating three-dimensionality in the mid-1960s in her shaped canvases and light-box installations. Products of scientific enquiries into quantum physics, these works physically embody light – made up largely of vertical bands of acrylic paint mixed with microspheres that refract and reflect light. While they evoke tenets of modernist painting such as the grid and the monochrome, the artist's hand is ever-present in her gestural brushwork. In this work, a rectilinear arch surrounds three vertical white strips, all painted with subtle differences that can only be detected as viewers shift their position, producing an oscillating effect that is at once destabilizing and mystical.

GRACE COSSINGTON SMITH

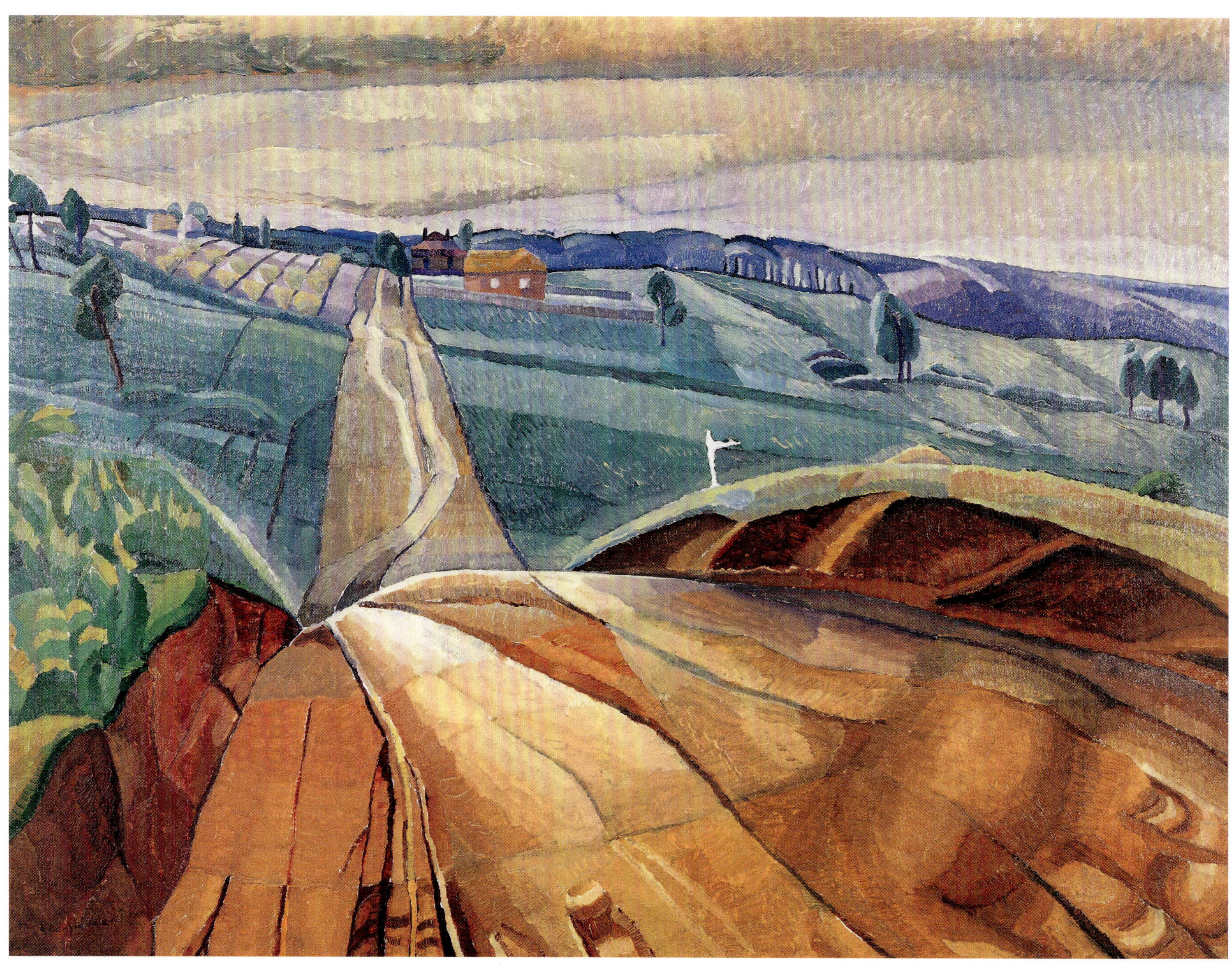

LANDSCAPE AT PENTECOST
1929, oil on paperboard, 83.7 × 111.8 cm (33 × 44 in), Art Gallery of South Australia, Adelaide, Australia

Grace Cossington Smith, born 1892, Sydney, Australia. Died 1984, Sydney.

Cossington Smith was instrumental in introducing European Post-Impressionism to Australia through her light-infused landscapes and depictions of city life. After studying art in England and Germany in the early 1910s, she began to exhibit in 1926 with the newly formed Contemporary Group, a collection of modernist painters in Sydney, and had her first solo exhibition in 1928 at Sydney's Grosvenor Galleries. Cossington Smith developed an individual technique of using rhythmic, broken brushwork in unmixed, high-key palettes. *Landscape at Pentecost* exemplifies her powers as a highly skilled colourist. The view is believed to be north of Bannockburn Road, just a few minutes' walk from the artist's residence and studio in Turramurra, New South Wales. Cossington Smith grounded this work in both a localized experience of a familiar place and a broader sense of transcendental nature and spirituality that stemmed from her Christian faith and upbringing. For her pioneering contributions to Australian modernism, in 1973 she was awarded the Order of the British Empire, followed by a major retrospective organized by the Art Gallery of New South Wales that toured the nation.

GRACE CROWLEY

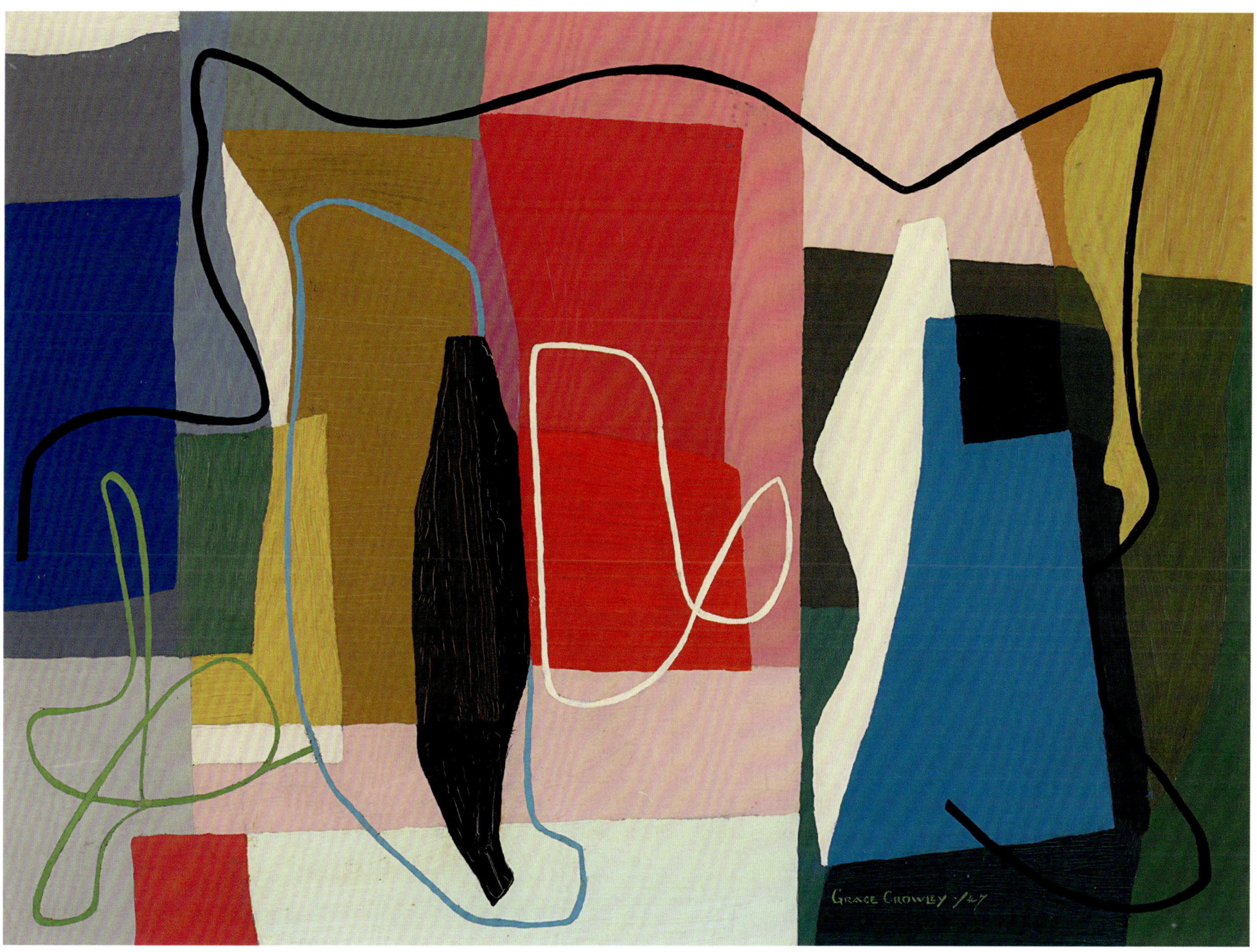

ABSTRACT PAINTING
1947, oil on cardboard, 60.7 × 83.3 cm (23 ⅞ × 32 ¾ in), National Gallery of Australia, Canberra

Grace Crowley, born 1890, Cobbadah, New South Wales, Australia. Died 1979, Sydney, Australia.

Counted among Australia's first abstract artists, Crowley was central to the move to non-objective art in mid-century Sydney. Having studied in Paris under leading Cubist artists André Lhote (1885–1962) and Albert Gleizes (1881–1953) in the early 1920s, she returned to an Australian art world hostile to her modernist preoccupations. Only in the late sixties, several decades after Crowley exhibited her earliest geometric abstractions, did the painter find belated recognition. In addition to her pursuits as an artist, Crowley taught at leading Sydney art schools and worked to further the career of her friend and former student Ralph Balson (1890–1964), to whom history has lent the moniker of 'father of Australian abstraction'. Crowley's oeuvre – represented in only a dozen drawings and twenty-five paintings – notates the trajectory of her formal language, from her early Impressionist scenes to Cubist canvases, first forays into abstraction and final poured paintings. Composed with the aid of paper cut-outs and string, *Abstract Painting* has about it a bright transparency despite the opacity of its pigment. The many forms, appearing layered one upon the other, offer at each intersecting plane discrete studies in colour mixing.

CUI JIE

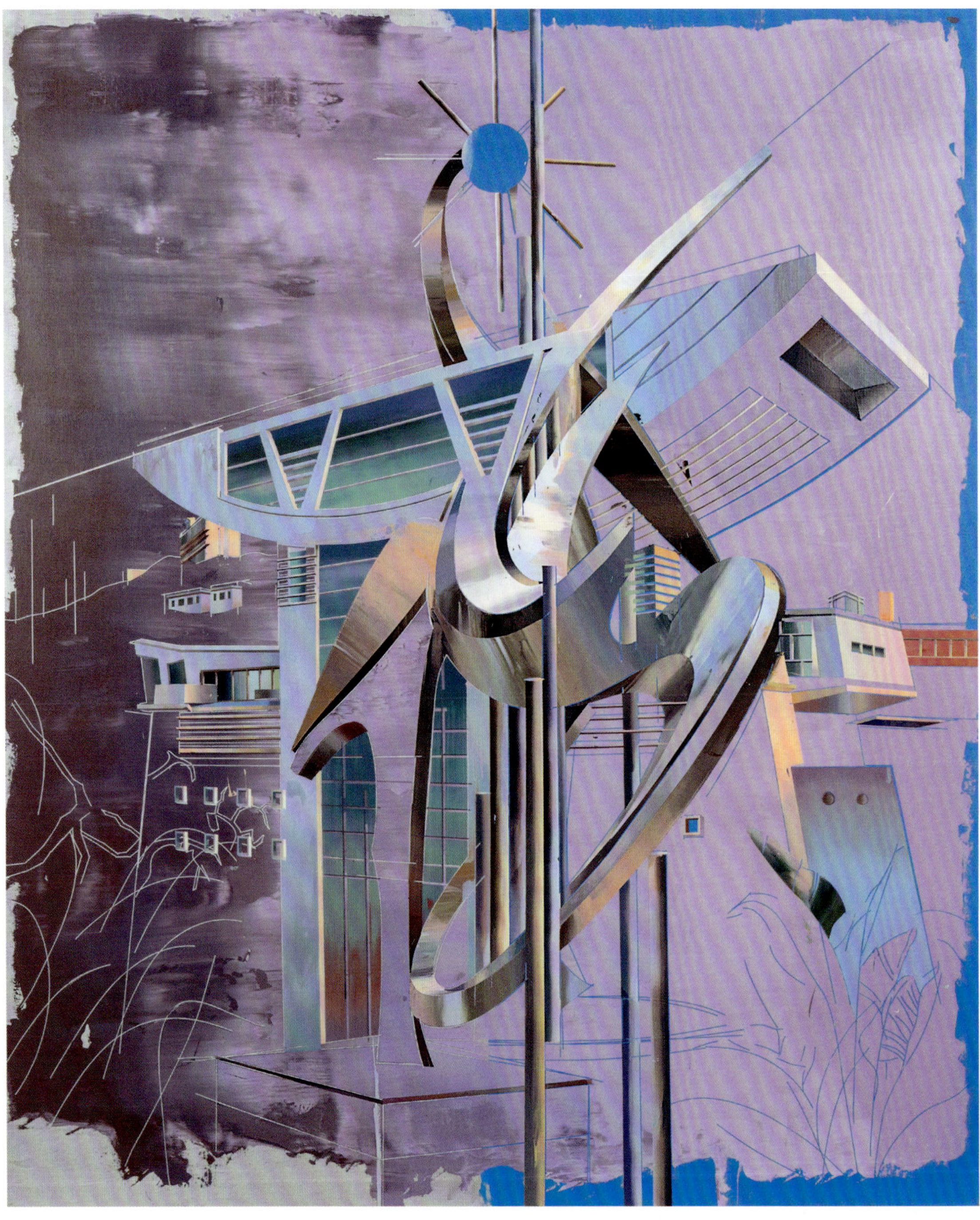

THE SECOND GENERATION OF PEAK TOWER
2019, acrylic on canvas, 250 × 210 cm
(98 ⅜ × 82 ⅝ in), collection of Alexander V. Petalas

Cui Jie, born 1983, Shanghai, China.

Decades of Chinese architectural history are condensed within Cui's monumental paintings of imagined skyscrapers and modernist towers, which float within vibrant fields of violet, turquoise and silver. While they do not always make reference to specific buildings or cityscapes, Cui's swirling compositions capture the sense of rapid change and modernization that have defined the landscapes of contemporary cities like Beijing and Shanghai over the course of her life, and each of her paintings appropriates and reconfigures a range of architectural styles seen there – from Bauhaus pavilions to socialist modernism and contemporary skyscrapers. In this work, Cui depicts the Peak Tower, a postmodern structure designed by British architect Terry Farrell, which sits near the summit of Victoria Peak in Hong Kong, China. The shining metal surface of a soaring steel sculpture in the foreground is framed by diagrammatic lines and fragmented botanical forms, which are layered across loosely defined fields of brushwork and impasto. It is as if Cui's artistic process – which arrests the image in a painterly state of emergence – mimics the continuous cycles of construction and destruction in the urban landscape.

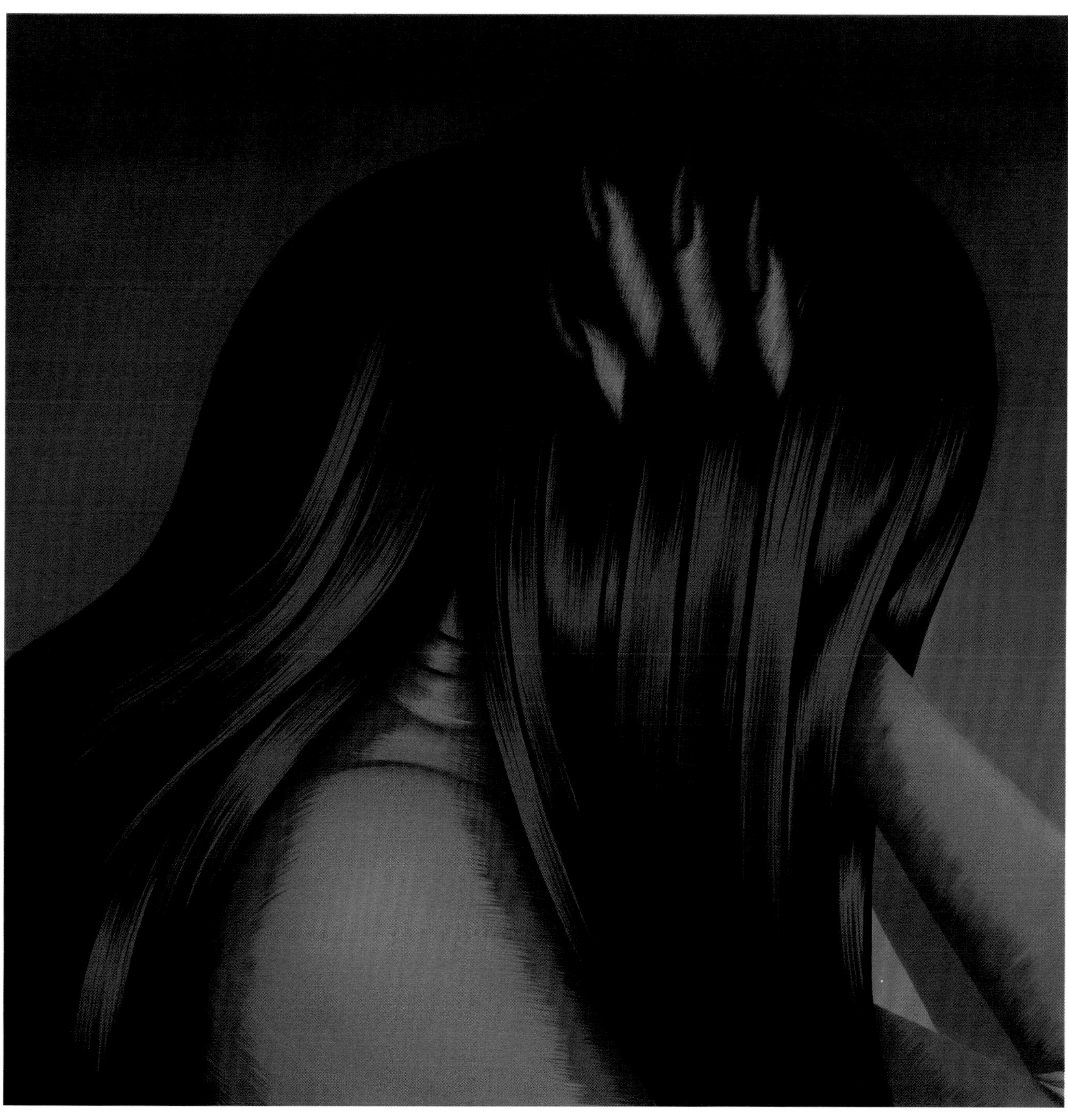

COMB THROUGH
2019, acrylic and oil on canvas, 76.2 × 76.2 cm (30 × 30 in)

Julie Curtiss, born 1982, Paris, France.

'Painting hair, for me, is kind of meditative, in the way that I focus on something and try to reveal its pattern,' Curtiss told *W Magazine* in 2019. Coiffed and coiled locks recur throughout her enigmatic practice, in which the artist transforms the female body, objects, accessories and foodstuffs into highly stylized, sometimes otherworldly images. With comparisons made between her work and the Surrealist deployment of the uncanny, as well as the graphic style of the Chicago Imagists – such as Christina Ramberg (p.243) – Curtiss's canvases declare a break with reality, exploiting the tension between humour and horror, beauty and repulsion. In *Comb Through*, Curtiss revels in the texture of hair, painstakingly rendered across every surface of the image, from straight, shiny locks to slick striated sweater down to the furry fingers and nails that perform the titular action. Is the figure pictured human, animal or somewhere in between? As with many of her works, the impact of the image is almost cinematic, with the seductive anonymity of the protagonist, rendered in dramatic lighting, suggestive of film noir.

JAY DEFEO

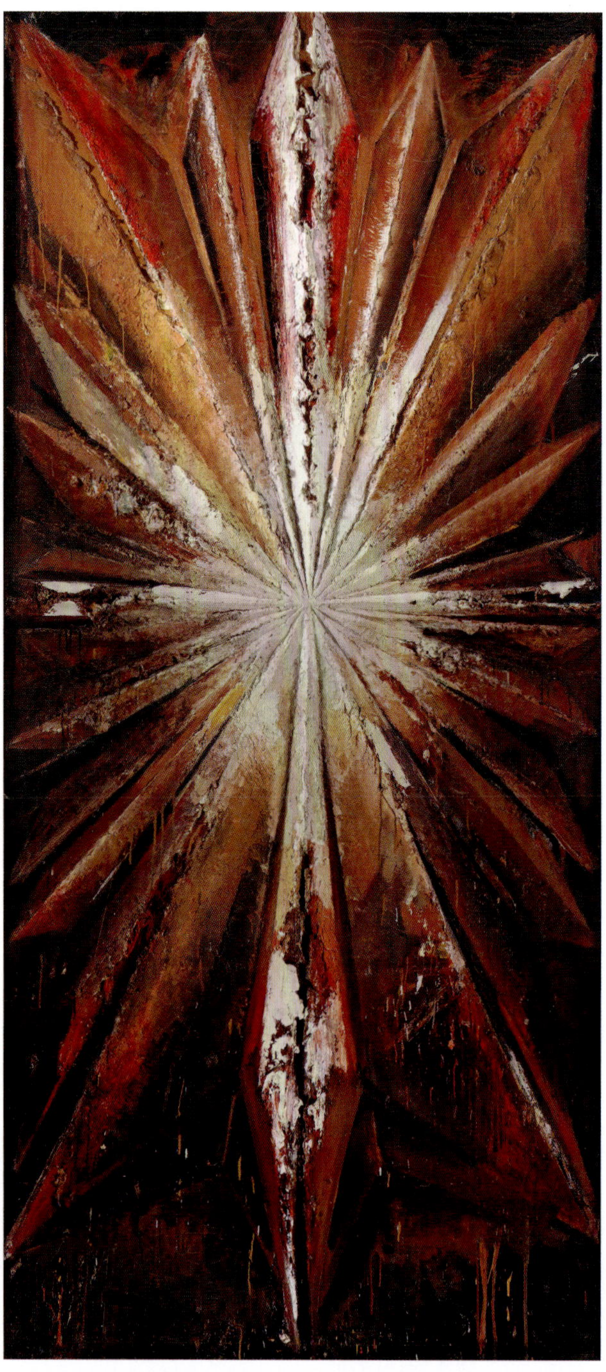

THE JEWEL
1959, oil on canvas, 304.8 × 146.1 × 7.6 cm (120 × 57½ × 3 in), Los Angeles County Museum of Art, USA

Jay DeFeo, born 1929, Hanover, New Hampshire, USA. Died 1989, Oakland, California, USA.

A tenacious experimenter, DeFeo pushed the conventions of painting throughout her career. After graduating from the University of California, Berkeley in 1951, she travelled in North Africa and Europe – a formative experience reflected by her first major paintings that combined influences from Abstract Expressionism, African and prehistoric art, and Classical architecture. In the late 1950s, she was a prominent figure in San Francisco's Beat generation of artists and writers, producing densely textured canvases exploring the interplay of geometric and representational forms. Following her first major solo show at the Dilexi Gallery in San Francisco in 1959, her work was included in the canonical exhibition 'Sixteen Americans' at New York's Museum of Modern Art (1959–60). Embodying DeFeo's singular approach to painting, *The Jewel* is composed of radiating shards of encrusted paint carved with a palette knife, with a thickness that adds almost sculptural dimensionality to the work. As with many of her paintings, the large-scale canvas carries celestial and transcendent connotations. Later explorations with materials saw her add plaster to her paint as well as elements of collage, including paper, plastic and small objects to achieve various surface effects.

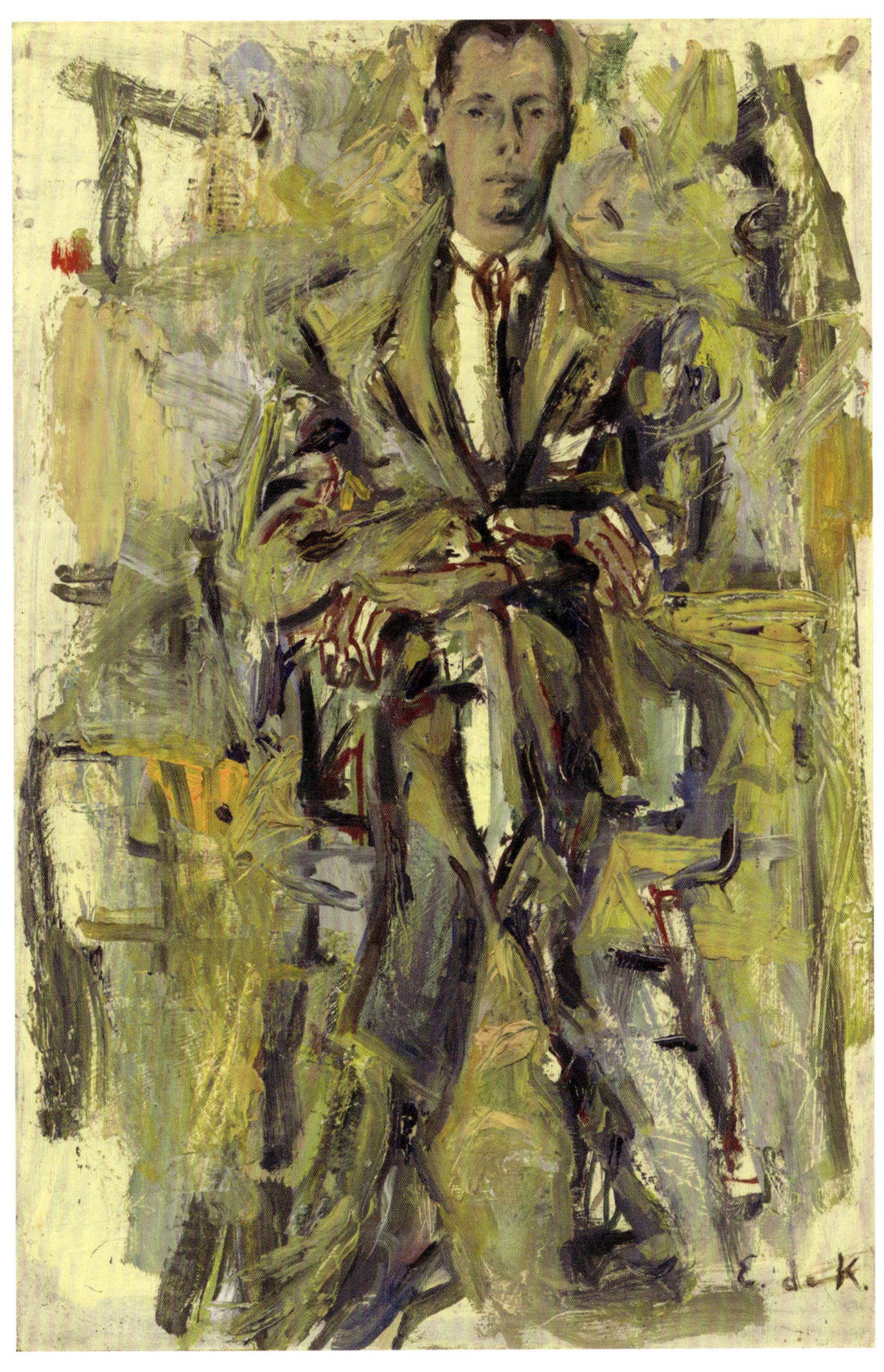

TOM HESS #1
1956, oil on Masonite, 58.1 × 40 cm (22 ⅞ × 15 ¾ in), National Portrait Gallery, Smithsonian Institution, Washington DC, USA

Elaine de Kooning, born 1918, Brooklyn, USA. Died 1989, Southampton, New York, USA.

Gifted as both a figurative and abstract painter, de Kooning was dedicated to the promotion of Abstract Expressionism and one of its earliest practitioners, her husband Willem de Kooning (1904–97). She was a respected writer and critic, a popular teacher and a fearless proto-feminist. De Kooning enrolled at New York's Leonardo da Vinci Art School in 1937, and shortly after began taking drawing lessons from the man who in 1943 would become her husband. While her early works were influenced by Cubism, by the 1940s she was painting abstractions. Though a fierce defender of Abstract Expressionism, she became best known for her portraits, particularly of men, and she is credited with having reinvented the modern portrait by combining figuration with an abstract vocabulary. In 1948 she began working at *ARTnews* under the editor Thomas B. Hess, writing essays on such painters as Franz Kline (1910–62) and Arshile Gorky (1904–48), and making Abstract Expressionism accessible to a wide audience. This portrait of Hess shows what he described as her ability to attach meticulously observed faces to bodies 'spun from bravura paint ribbons'.

ANGELA DE LA CRUZ

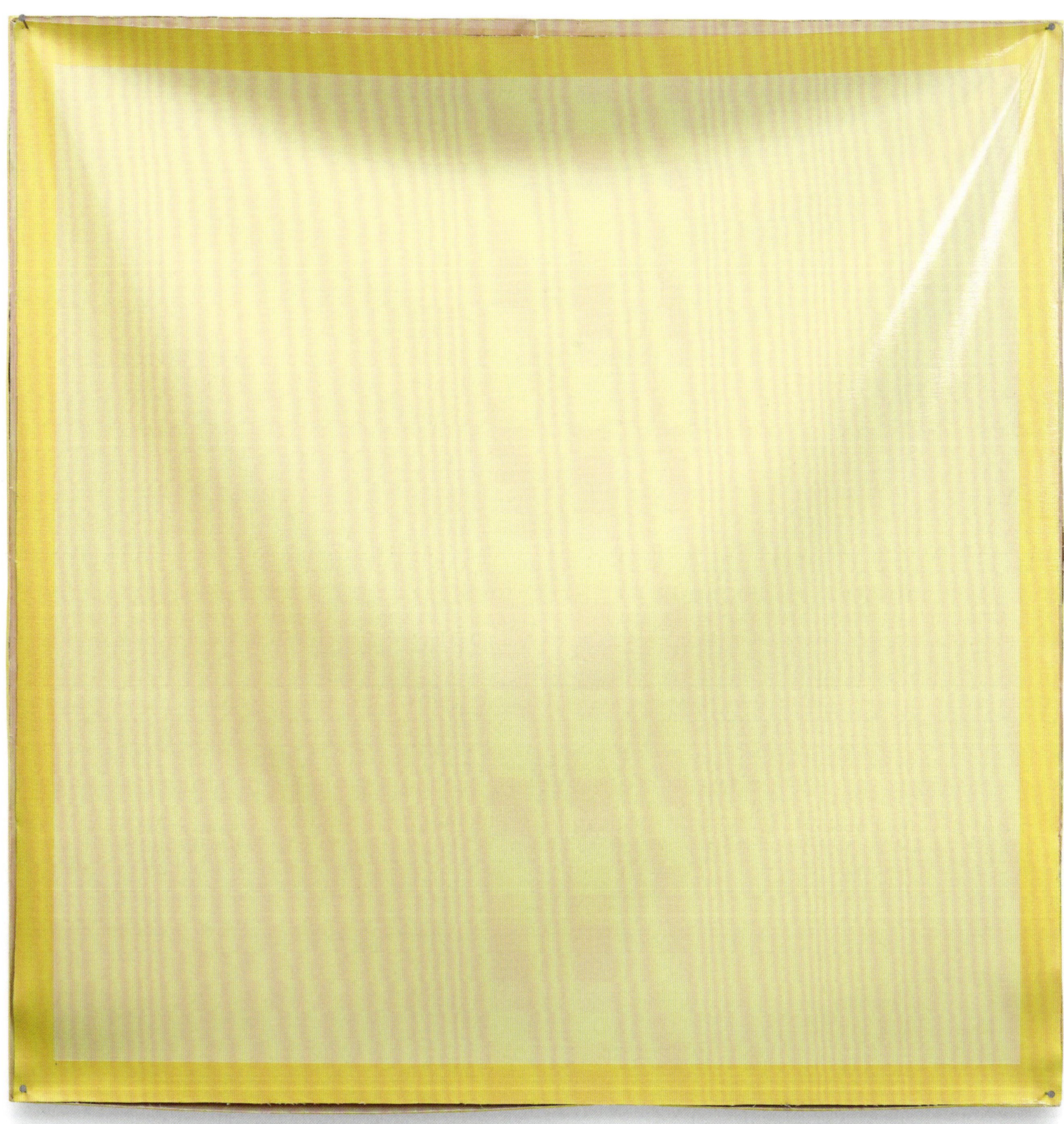

BARE (YELLOW)
2017, oil and acrylic on canvas, 153 × 153 × 7 cm
(60¼ × 60¼ × 2¾ in)

Angela de la Cruz, born 1965, La Coruña, Spain.

On the occasion of her first solo exhibition, held at the Camden Art Centre, London, in 2010, de la Cruz recounted how she developed her signature style, which is simultaneously both painting and sculpture. It was during her studies at the Slade School of Fine Art, London, in the mid-1990s that she removed a stretcher's crossbar and saw the previously taut canvas bend. 'From that moment on,' she explained, 'I looked at the painting as an object.' Citing influences ranging from the clay-soaked canvases of Piero Manzoni (1933–63) to Jacques Derrida's theory of deconstruction, de la Cruz continues to explore ways of deconstructing painting – both physically and conceptually. Although no longer able to produce work independently due to disabilities resulting from a stroke in 2005, de la Cruz – who was nominated for the Turner Prize in 2010 – directs studio assistants to realize her artworks. Thick horizontal brushstrokes of glossy monochromatic paint are applied to canvas, or other materials such as aluminium, which is then slashed, crushed or reshaped. Domestic furniture is also sometimes incorporated. *Bare (Yellow)* is part of a series of canvases painted in different shades, cut from their stretchers and then reattached. The gaps that remain expose the vulnerability of the illusion of a painted surface.

KATHERINE S. DREIER

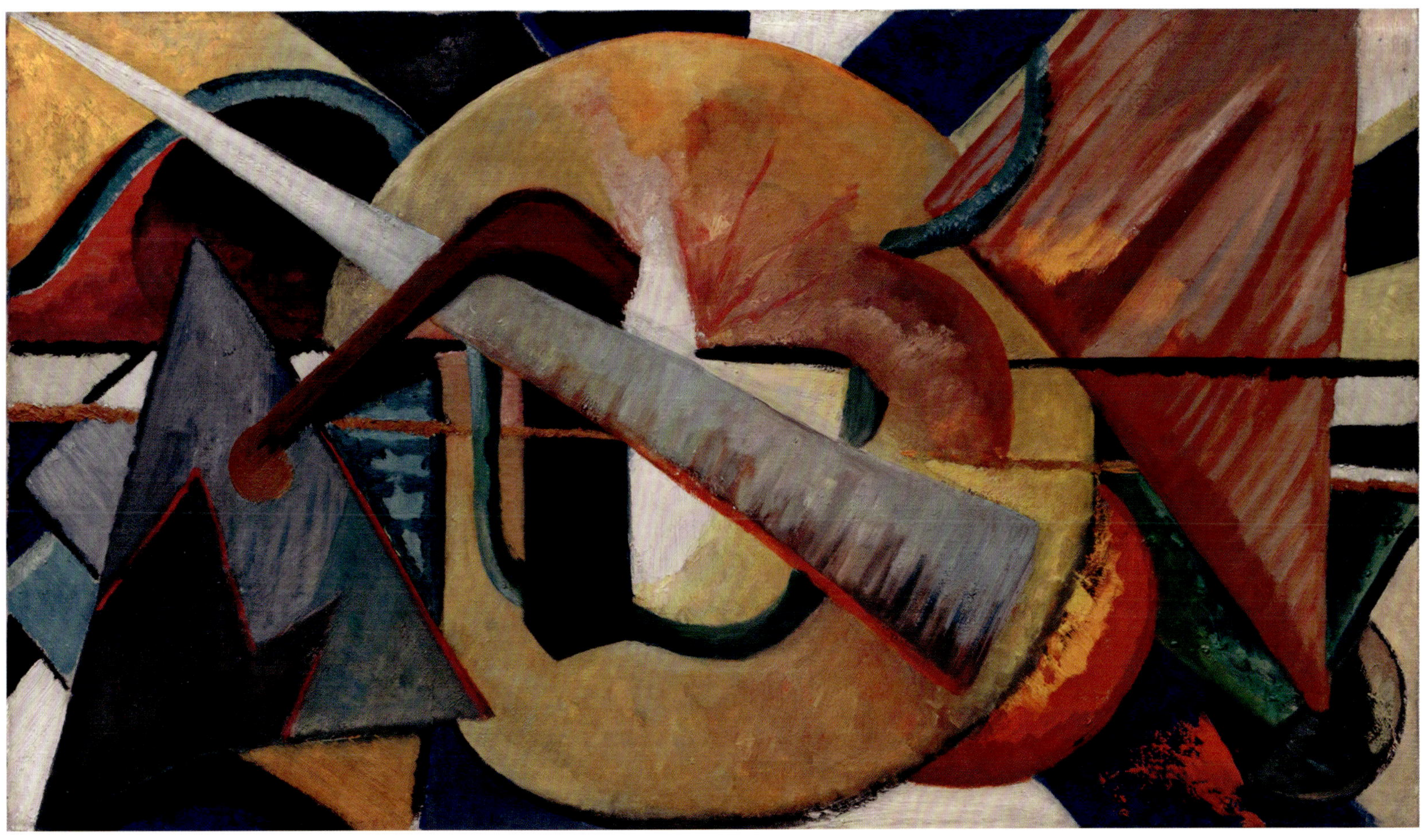

ABSTRACT PORTRAIT OF MARCEL DUCHAMP
1918, oil on canvas, 45.7 × 81.3 cm (18 × 32 in), Museum of Modern Art, New York, USA

Katherine S. Dreier, born 1877, Brooklyn, USA. Died 1952, Milford, Connecticut, USA.

Best remembered as a curator, collector and patron of the arts in the early twentieth century, Dreier was also a painter whose artistic legacy remains obscured in American art history. As a young woman Dreier studied at the Brooklyn Art Students League and Pratt Institute, both in New York, and was a staunch supporter of the suffrage and labour movements. Following her first solo exhibition in London in 1911, she exhibited at the historical New York Armory Show of 1913, and in 1920 merged art and activism by co-founding the Société Anonyme Inc.: Museum of Modern Art, to which she dedicated her energy and time for thirty years, organizing over eighty exhibitions, lectures, events and loans. In 1918, inspired by Theosophy and the work of Wassily Kandinsky (1866–1944), Dreier's painting style changed from realism to non-objective, albeit symbolic, abstraction. In this portrait, the best known of her works, Dreier chose each shape and colour to embody specific personality characteristics of her friend, the artist Marcel Duchamp (1887–1968). In Theosophy the triangle symbolizes the apex of spirituality and, for Kandinsky, represented the soul in movement. Dreier's repeated triangle, therefore, symbolizes the high esteem in which she held Duchamp.

ROSALYN DREXLER

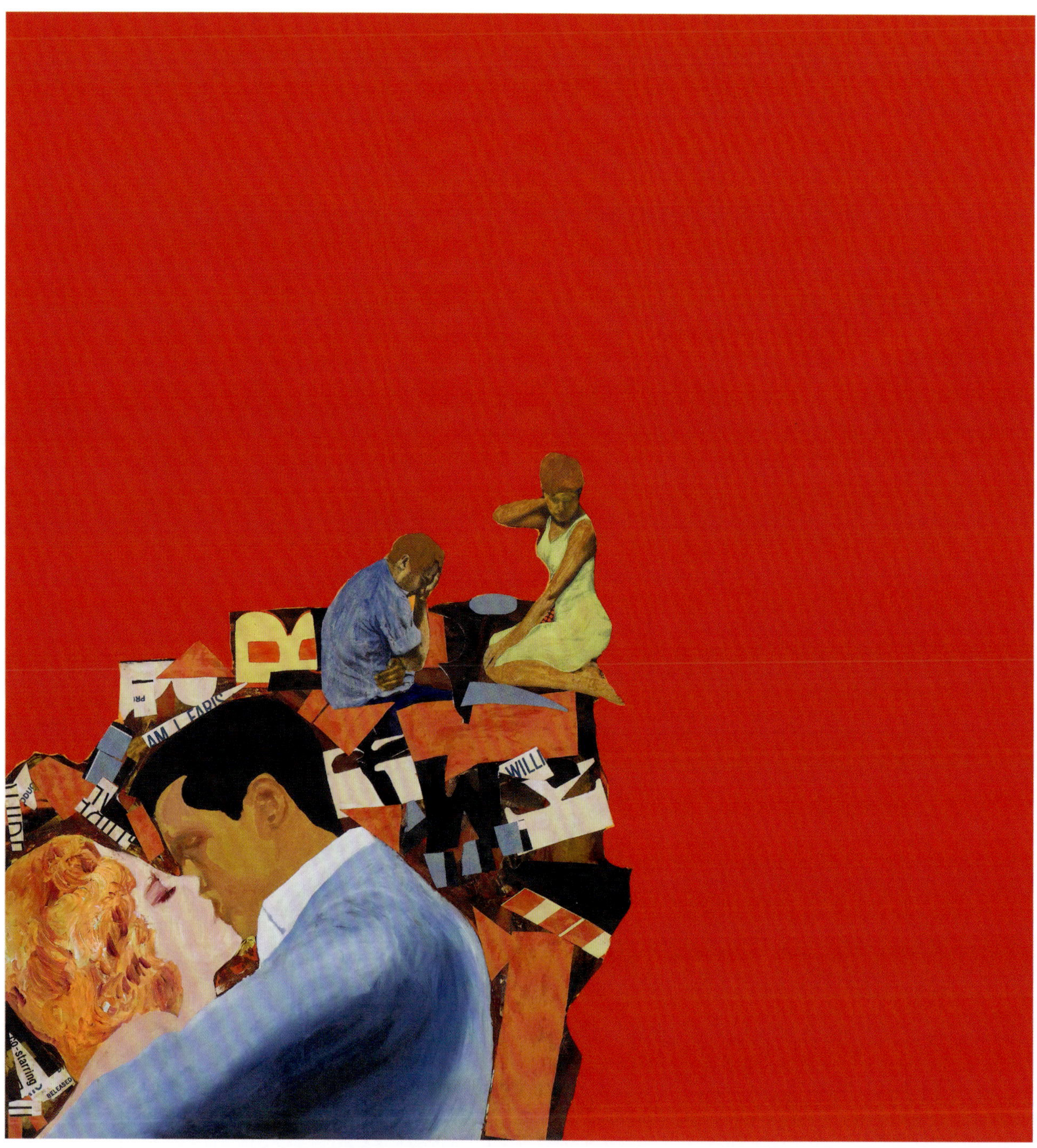

LOVERS
1963, acrylic and paper collage on canvas, 140.3 × 132.1 cm (55 ¼ × 52 in), Albright-Knox Art Gallery, Buffalo, New York, USA

Rosalyn Drexler, born 1926, New York, USA.

Drexler, who also works as a novelist and playwright, began her artistic career as a sculptor in the late 1950s but shifted to painting in 1961. Drawing on images taken from popular culture – particularly newspapers, magazines and movie posters – her work presents a sinister, feminist approach to Pop art that examines gender dynamics and power structures, and how the media reflects and creates them. To execute her paintings, Drexler enlarges and reprints her chosen images before collaging them onto canvas and painting over them, a step that renders the familiar slightly strange. *Lovers* depicts two scenes of couples on top of a mélange of geometric shapes and fragments of text against a flat red background. The figures in the foreground – Elvis Presley and Judy Tyler, taken from a promotional poster for their 1957 film *Jailhouse Rock* – kiss, while the smaller pair at the centre of the canvas are caught in an uncertain conflict. The composition leaves the viewer questioning whether the painting presents a continuous narrative of a single couple, adding an additional layer of ambiguity and ominousness to the picture.

ELSIE DRIGGS

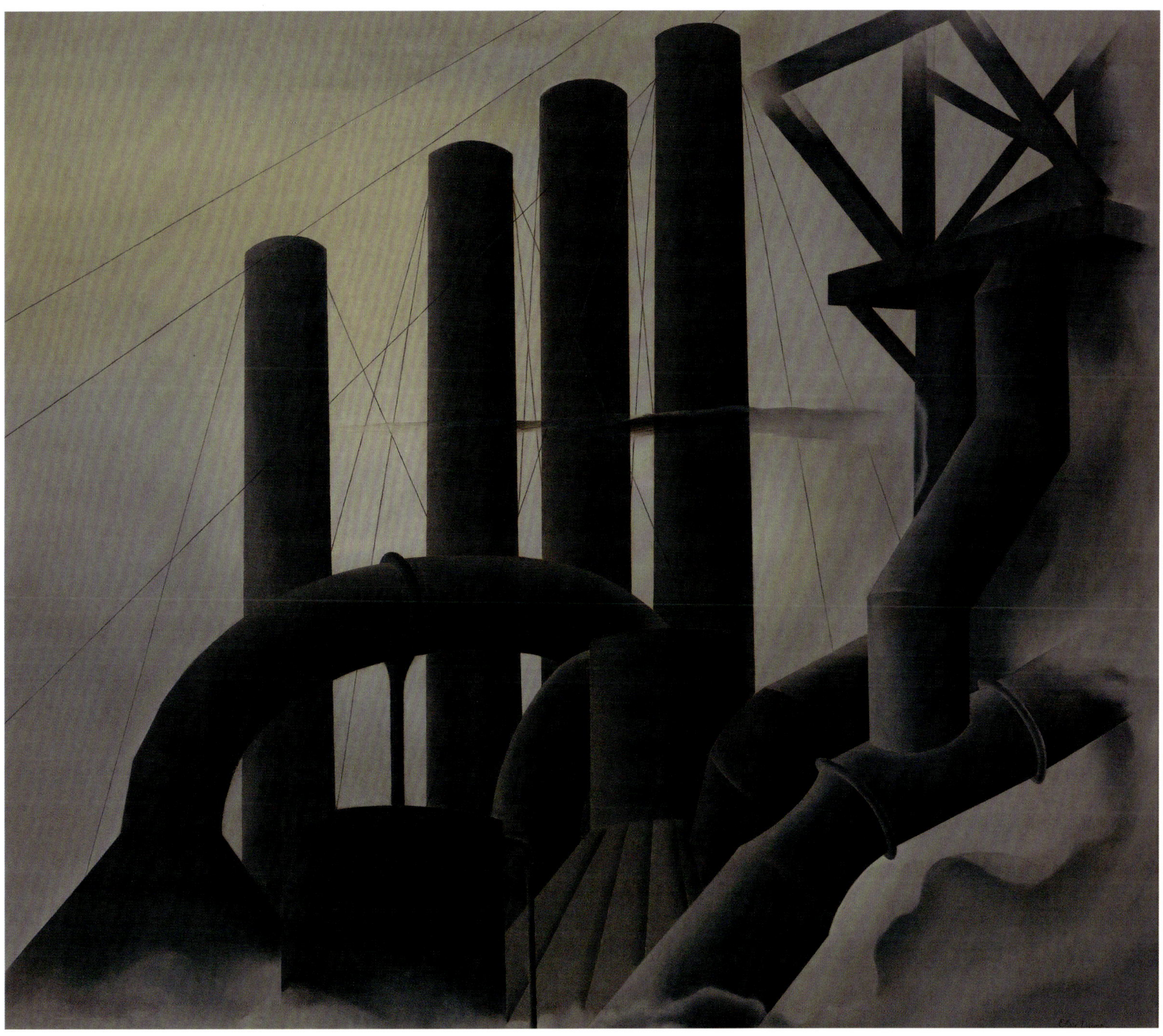

PITTSBURGH
1927, oil on canvas, 87 × 102.2 cm (34 ¼ × 40 ¼ in), Whitney Museum of American Art, New York, USA

Elsie Driggs, born 1898, Hartford, Connecticut, USA. Died 1992, New York, USA.

Driggs contributed to the first modern art movement developed in the United States, Precisionism, which filtered Cubism's focus on geometry and Futurism's attention to technology through quintessentially American imagery. Having studied in Rome, Driggs was inspired early on by the work of Florentine painter Piero della Francesca (*c.*1415–92) to flatten and simplify forms in order to structure a composition. While other Precisionists, such as Georgia O'Keeffe (p.227), Charles Demuth (1883–1935) and Joseph Stella (1877–1946), combined a similar classical order with a sense of geometry, Driggs employed unconventional subject matter to create bold statements. In *Pittsburgh*, for example, she monumentalizes blast furnaces, inspired by a childhood memory of travelling with her family by night train, viewing the factory where her father worked as an engineer. These structures can be seen as embodiments of the hubris and socio-political assertiveness of the Industrial Era. The crisp linear precision with which she articulates the support cables contrasts with the dark, almost velvety tones of the tubular smokestacks, all merging with a murky haze of toxic fumes, reflecting on the contradictions of a time of rapid social and technological transformation.

MARLENE DUMAS

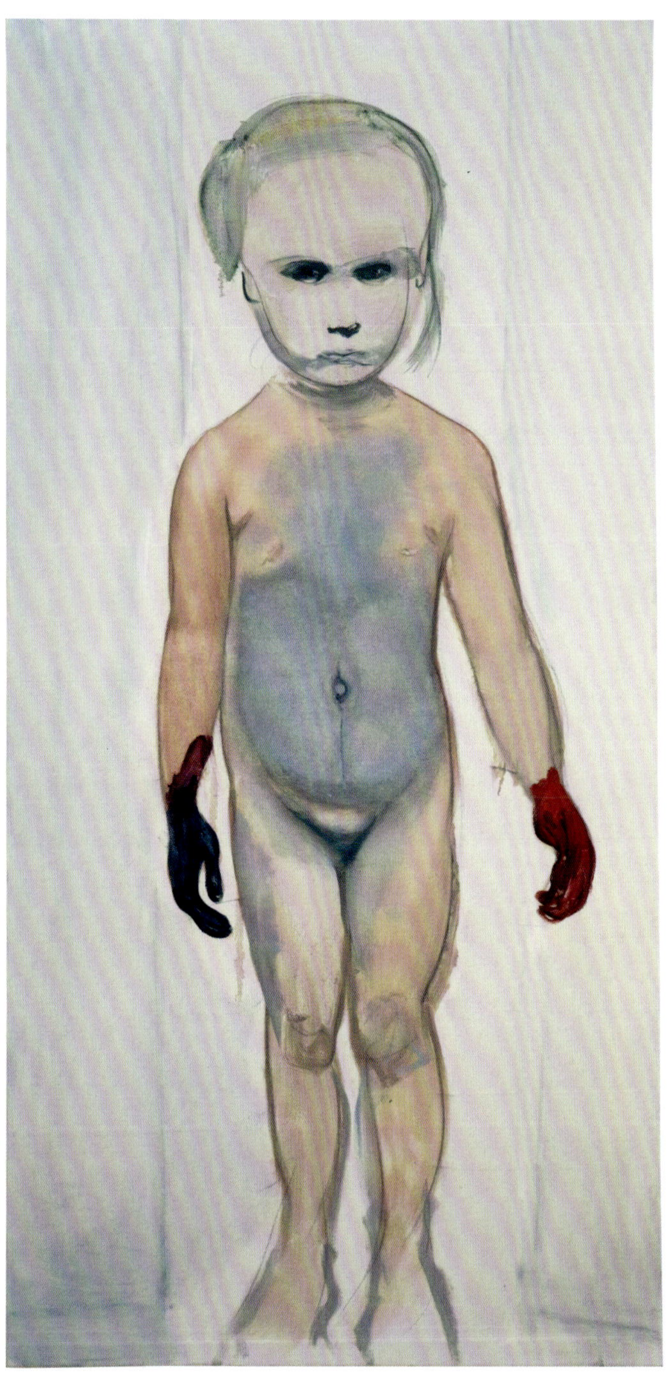

THE PAINTER
1994, oil on canvas, 200 × 100 cm (78 ¾ × 39 ⅜ in), Museum of Modern Art, New York, USA

Marlene Dumas, born 1953, Cape Town, South Africa.

After studying art at the University of Cape Town, in 1976 Dumas moved to the Netherlands – where she still lives and works – to continue her studies at Ateliers '63 in Amsterdam. She began studying psychology in 1979, intending to become an art therapist. Although Dumas did not eventually follow that trajectory, her artworks explore psychological themes like desire, violence and conflict. As inspiration for the portraits for which she is known, Dumas's source material includes images from print media or photographs of friends, family, fellow artists and strangers – but the artist never paints directly from life. Her paintings, with their spare brushstrokes and thin washes of paint, seem to embody how others can exist in one's memory. In *The Painter*, a young, naked child stares with a vacant expression, a strand of hair falling down one cheek. The child is the artist's daughter, Helena, and her hands are covered in red and blue, a self-reflexive gesture that signifies the paint used to create this very portrait. Dumas revels in the overlaps between reality, representation and interpretation, manifested in the ethereal greys and blues that conjure the haunting figure.

NATHALIE DU PASQUIER

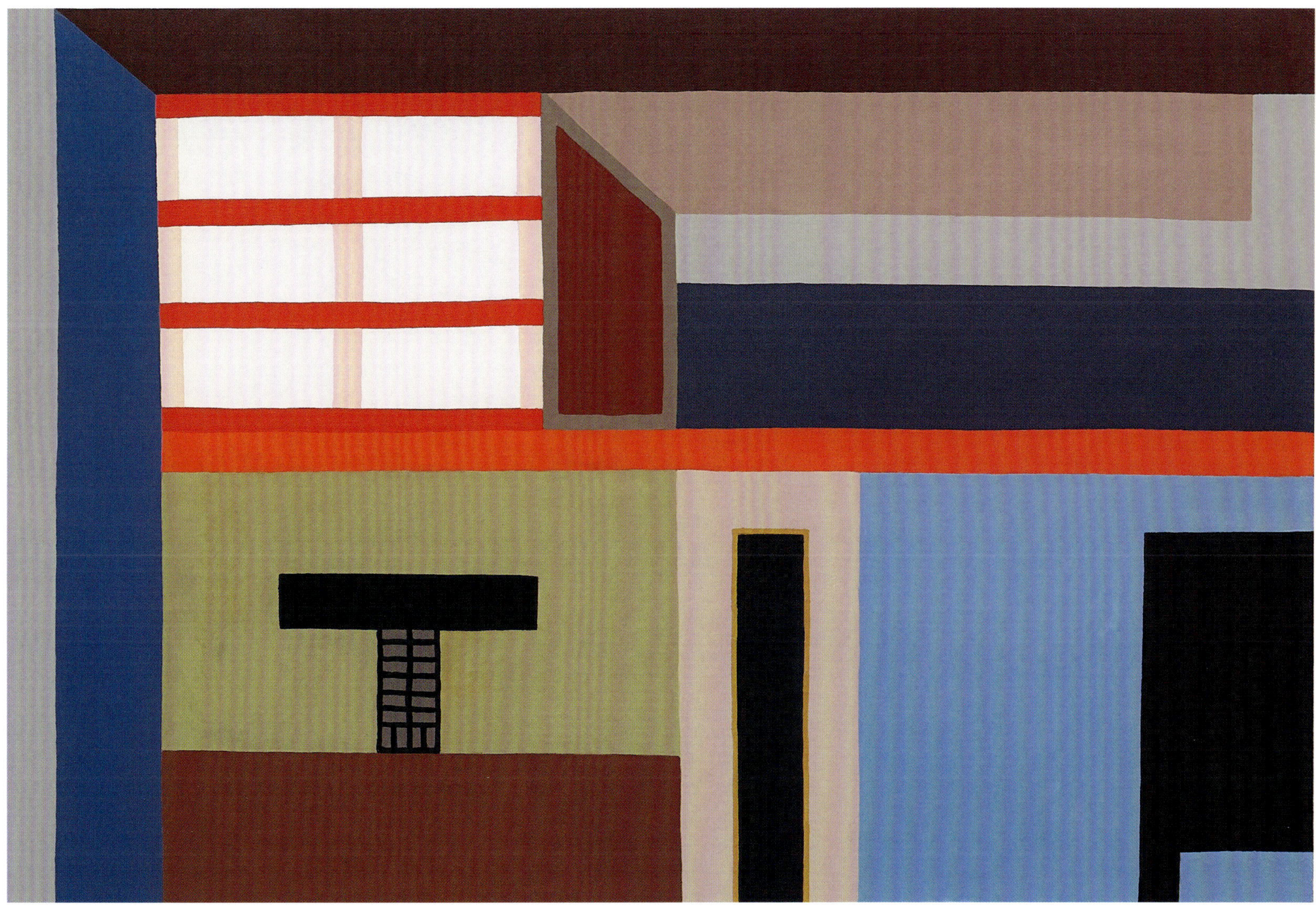

BOX
2018, oil on canvas, 100 × 150 cm (39 ⅜ × 59 in)

Nathalie Du Pasquier, born 1957, Bordeaux, France

Born in France, Du Pasquier has lived in Milan since 1979, where in 1981 she was a founding member – along with designers including Ettore Sottsass and Alessandro Mendini – of Memphis, the influential postmodern Italian design group. Designing patterns for decorated surfaces such as textiles, carpets and plastic laminates, as well as furniture and objects, Du Pasquier exemplified Memphis's ethos of bright, clashing colours as well as lusciously cacophonous and playfully opulent motifs. Since leaving Memphis in 1986, Du Pasquier has focused on painting, furthering her investigations into the spatial relationships between forms. While her early paintings mainly consisted of figural still lifes, she eventually shifted to a more abstracted mode that is nevertheless painted from direct observation, in the form of assemblages of geometric wooden blocks she constructs herself. These abstract compositions often recall interior spaces and are defined by flat colour, sharp contours and shifting geometric arrangements. Sometimes populated with furniture, lamps, floorplans or stairways, works such as *Box* embody the artist's lifelong interest in the total design environment.

JOAN EARDLEY

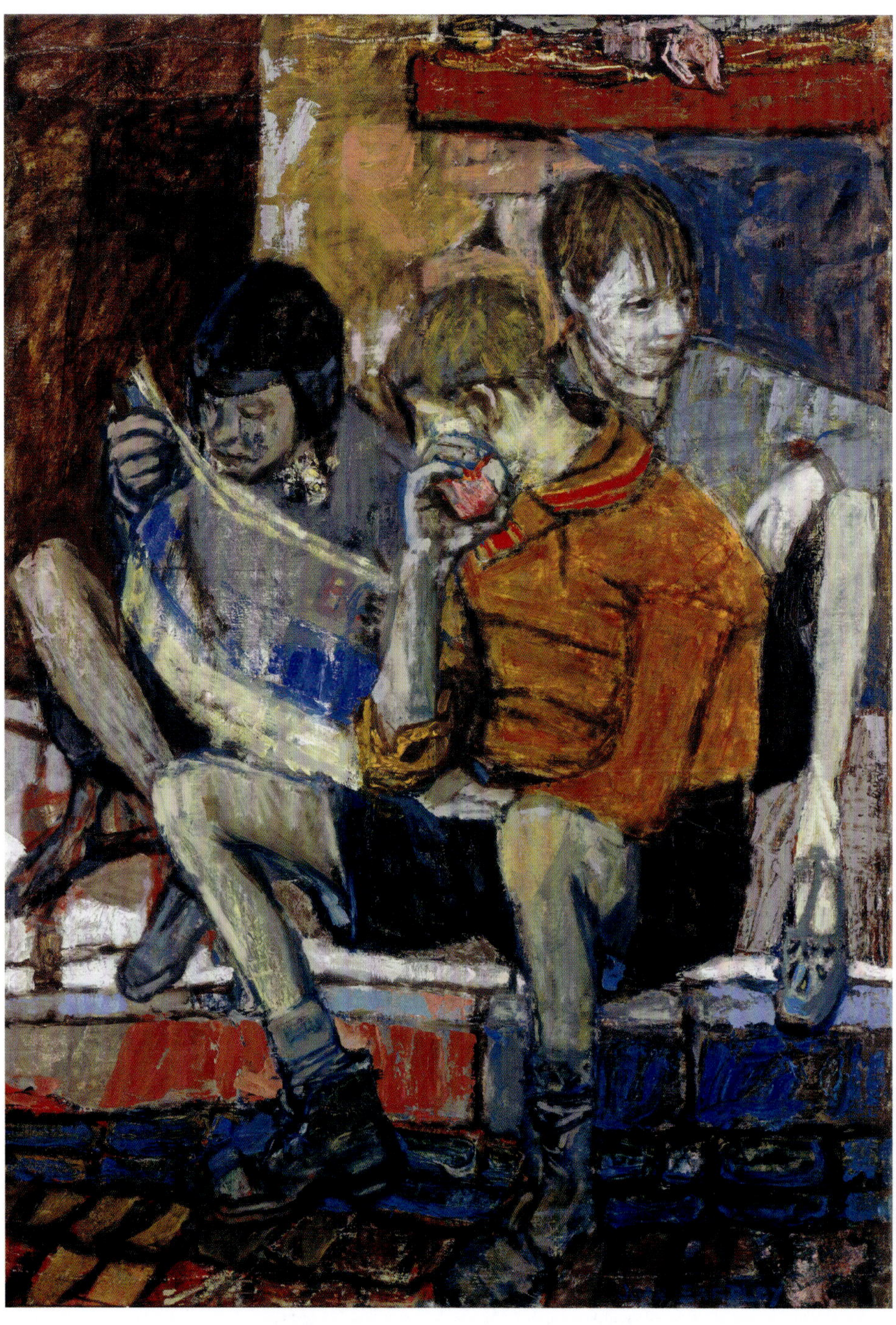

STREET KIDS
*c.*1949–51, oil on canvas, 102.9 × 73.7 cm (40½ × 29 in), National Galleries of Scotland, Edinburgh, UK

Joan Eardley, born 1921, Warnham, West Sussex, UK. Died 1963, Killearn, Scotland, UK.

In her short career, Eardley became an influential and much-loved painter of post-war Scotland – the country that became both her home and the persistent theme of the oil paintings she produced up until her untimely death from cancer at the age of forty-two. Eardley studied at Glasgow School of Art in the early 1940s and, by the end of the decade, began to portray the children of the disenfranchised district of Townhead, east Glasgow. The Townhead children continued to fascinate Eardley and remained a subject in her work well into the 1950s: she would sketch the children who visited her studio, or go out and draw them in the streets. This early example depicting street kids demonstrates Eardley's characteristic expressive style, conveying a sense of the raw vitality she observed in the community's working-class families. Eardley was also known for large-scale seascapes and landscapes of the dramatic terrains of Catterline, northeast Scotland, painted *en plein air* and often in extreme conditions. Though Eardley's emotive, realistic approach represented a bold break with the traditions and popular painterly modes of her day, she has gained little recognition to date outside Scotland.

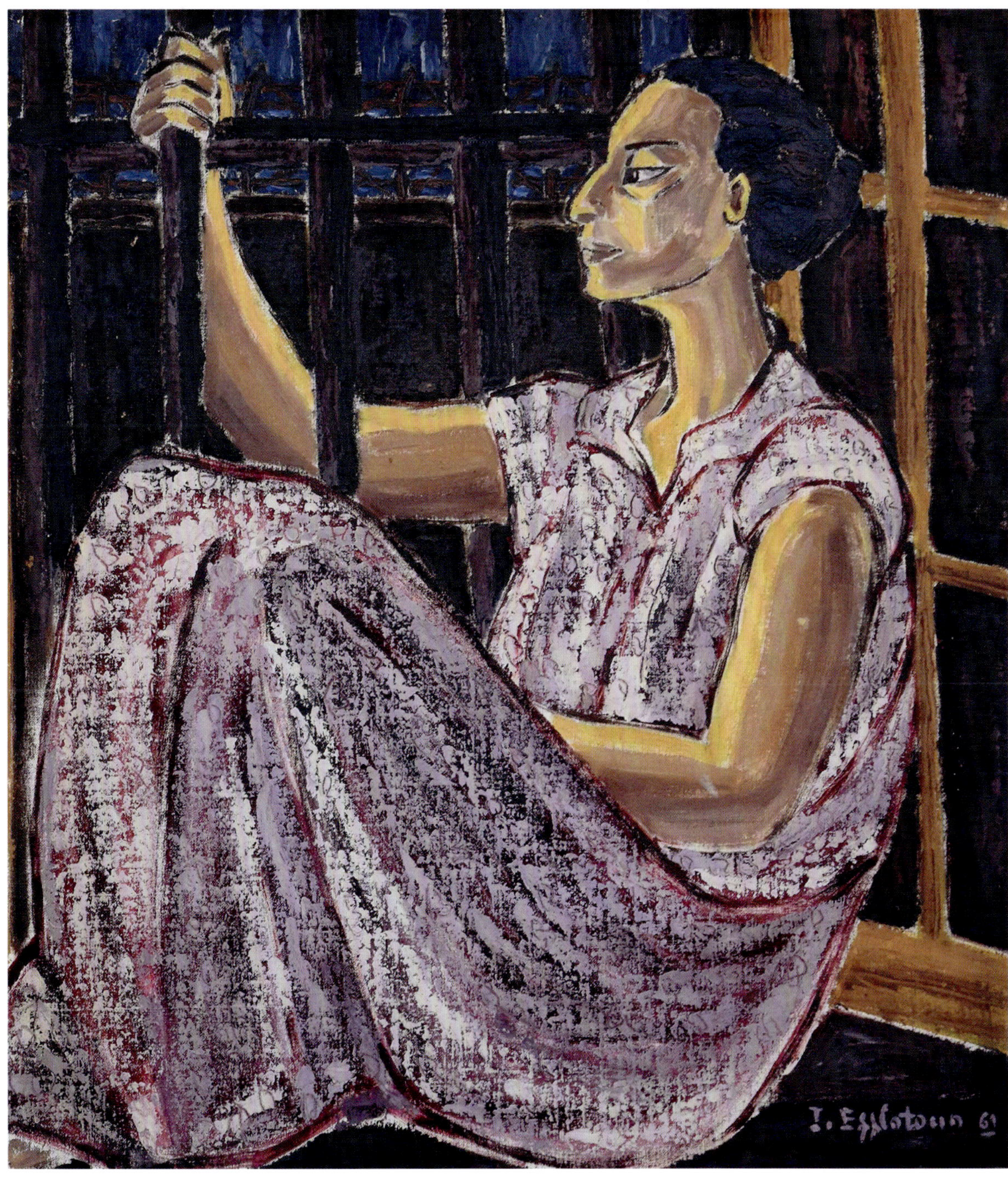

DREAMS OF THE DETAINEE
1961, oil on canvas, 50 × 40 cm (19 ¾ × 15 ¾ in), Barjeel Art Foundation, Sharjah, UAE

Inji Efflatoun, born 1924, Cairo, Egypt. Died 1989, Cairo.

Born into an upper-class family from Cairo's French-speaking aristocracy, at fifteen Efflatoun began studying art with the Egyptian Surrealist Kamel El-Telmissany (1915–72), a founding member of the Art and Liberty Group of artists who espoused anti-imperialist principles and embraced Surrealism. One of the first female art students at the University of Cairo, Efflatoun campaigned for gender equality and authored manifestos denouncing imperialism and class and gender oppression. During visits to Nubia and the Nile Delta, she began painting domestic scenes and portraits of working-class Egyptian *fellahin* (farm labourers). Her work gained international recognition at the 1952 Venice Biennale and the 1953 São Paulo Biennial. Meeting Mexican muralist David Alfaro Siqueiros (1896–1974) in 1956 steered Efflatoun towards Socialist Realism, and she painted violent scenes from the British occupation of Egypt. Her communist leanings led to her arrest in 1959 by the Egyptian government and she was detained for more than four years in a secret prison camp, where she painted portraits of fellow inmates and everyday Egyptians. In this work, a detainee reaches her arm through the prison bars towards freedom in what is also a gesture of strength and resistance.

EGUCHI AYANE

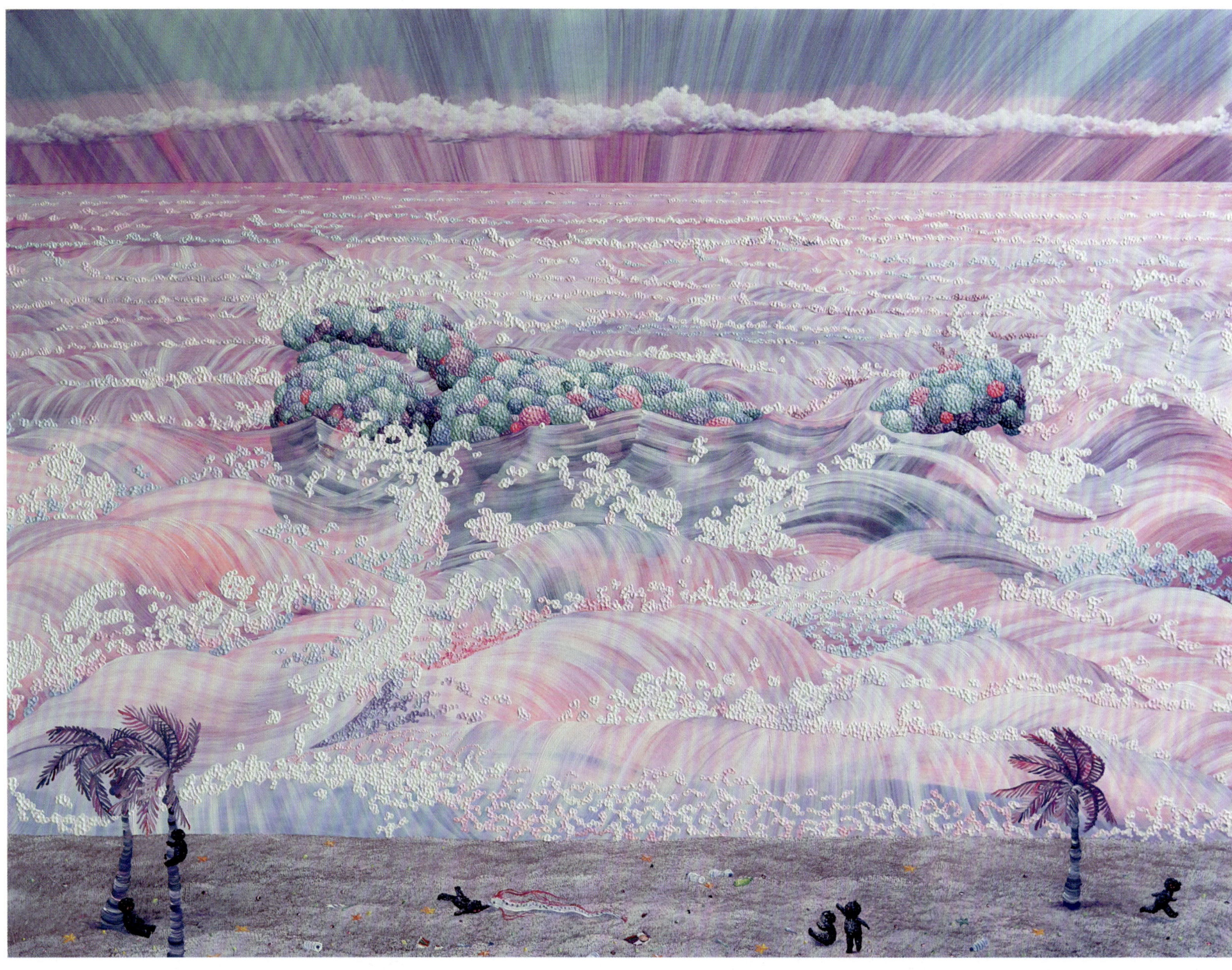

MARINE LIFE
2019, oil on canvas, 60 × 80 cm (23.6 × 31.5 in), private collection

Eguchi Ayane, born 1985, Hokkaido, Japan.

A 2011 graduate of Kanazawa College of Art, Japan, where she studied oil painting, Eguchi creates intricately painted scenes that often feature sublime, candy-coloured – and sometimes fantastical – scenes of the natural world teeming with life, from stormy seascapes and swamps to mountains and beaches. Her technique involves applying multiple layers of oil paint across the canvas before removing some areas and building up others to create a textured surface. Her typical palette of pastels lends such scenes an overall impression of innocuousness, but a closer look reveals unsettling episodes in which the natural world seems by turn threatening and strange. In these wonderlands seeded with terror, the body of a squid might open to reveal a tree trunk and a snake, or a teddy bear might be trapped in a giant spider's web rendered by countless globules of black paint. The recurring teddy bear character 'KUMA' – resembling the word for 'bear' in Japanese – exemplifies a primary theme in her work: how an apparently innocent exterior can conceal darker realities. In this work, anxiety and levity are finely balanced: it is unclear whether KUMA's gesture from a lush, roiling sea is a friendly hello or a call for help.

NICOLE EISENMAN

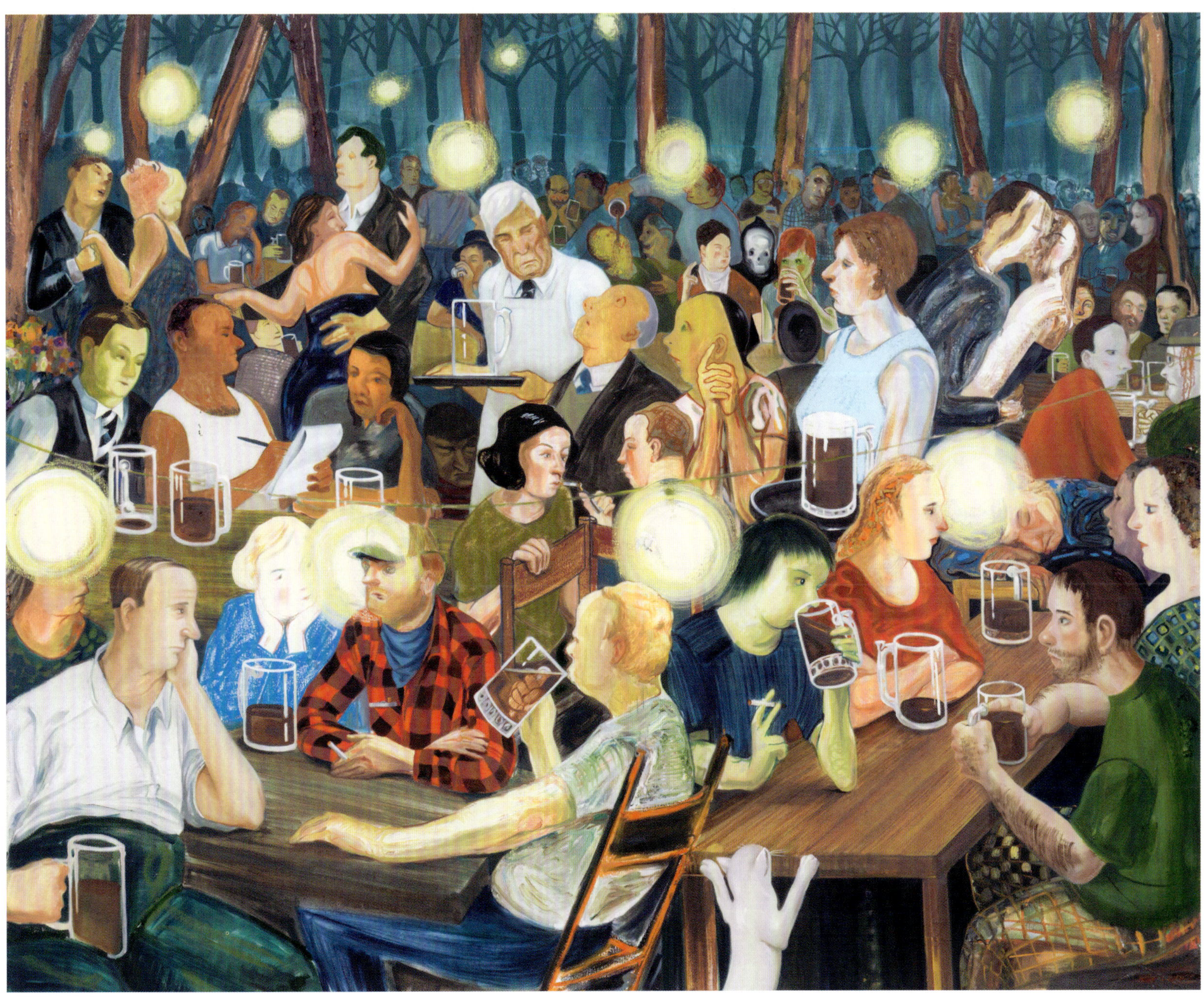

BROOKLYN BIERGARTEN II
2008, oil on canvas, 165.1 × 208.3 cm (65 × 82 in)

Nicole Eisenman, born 1965, Verdun, France.

In dense, wildly chromatic paintings, Eisenman blends art-historical reference with incisive commentary on identity and our contemporary social condition. Since emerging onto the New York art scene in the 1980s, the French-born artist has been recognized for their work's Neo-Expressionist edginess and cool conveyance of queer and gender politics, tackled with an imaginative sense of humour and encyclopedic references to the history of painting. *Brooklyn Biergarten II* – painted in a garish Expressionist palette – features a crowd of figures who mingle, dance and festively imbibe within a forested outdoor courtyard. Despite an implied ambience of conviviality reminiscent of Pierre-Auguste Renoir's (1841–1919) Impressionist homages to Parisians at leisure, there is an anxious undertone to Eisenman's setting, which is illuminated by an array of glowing string-lights that recall the pulsating nocturnal skies of Vincent van Gogh (1853–90) or Edvard Munch (1863–1944). Across each nuanced rendering of individuals, couples or groups of friends, the viewer can discover subtle moments of both intimacy and disconnection, flirtation and loneliness – attesting to the psychological pressures that often mark our relationships to one another and ourselves.

IDA EKBLAD

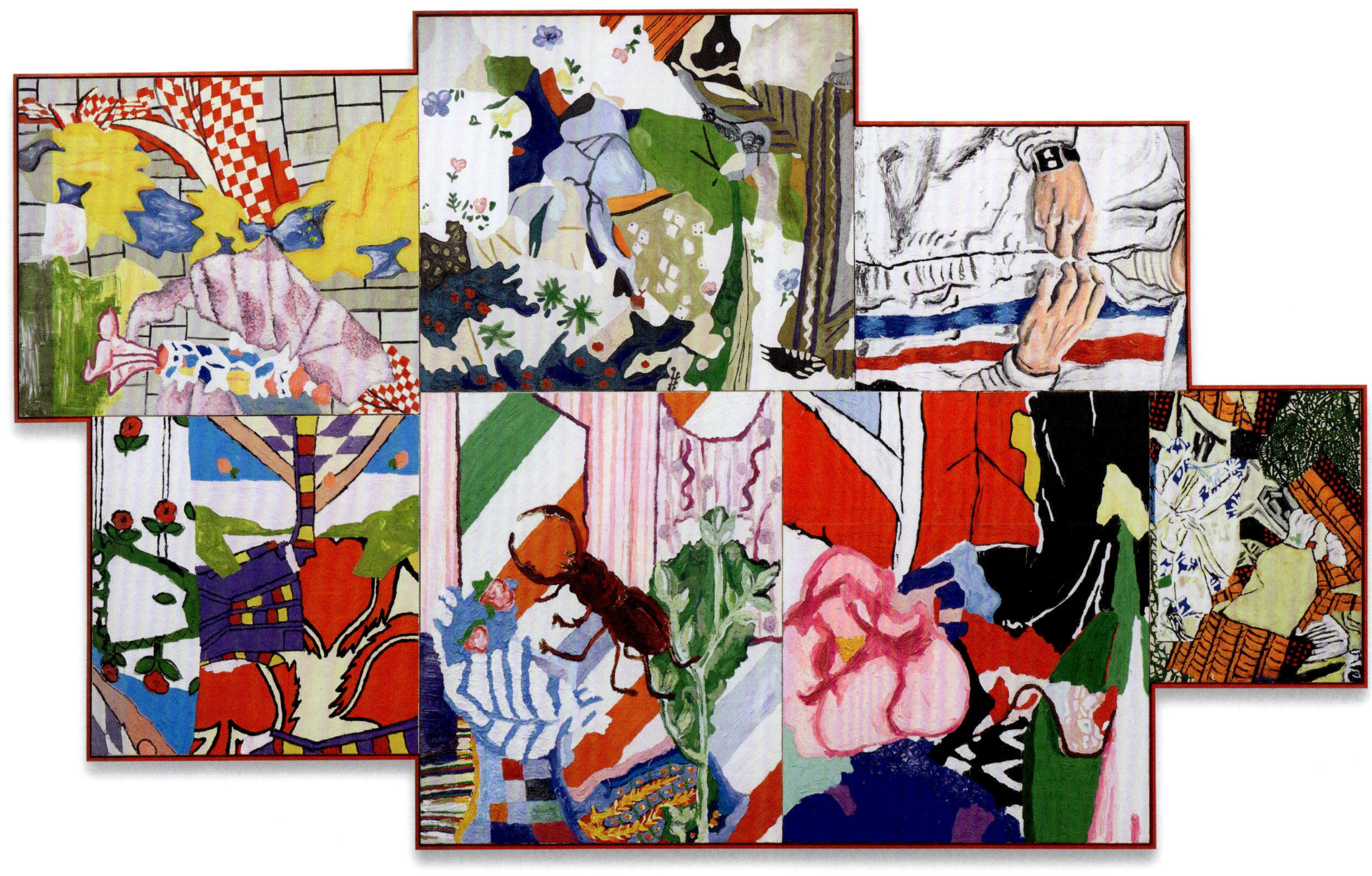

MONSTER'S BLOOD
2019, plastisol and puff paint on canvas, in artist's frame, 440 × 755 cm (173 ¼ × 297 ¼ in)

Ida Ekblad, born 1980, Oslo, Norway.

Ekblad's paintings contain a riotous energy. Influences ranging from twentieth-century art movements such as CoBrA and Abstract Expressionism to graffiti, memes and manga collide in rhythmic compositions in which everything jostles for attention. She employs a wide variety of techniques and materials, using brushes, airbrushing and inflating textile paint with heat to create puffy effects on flat surfaces. Her wider practice also includes sculpture, performance and poetry, and has been presented in numerous institutional solo exhibitions including at Bonniers Konsthall, Stockholm (2010); BALTIC Centre for Contemporary Art, Gateshead, UK (2015); and Museo Tamayo, Mexico City (2019). Ekblad's kaleidoscopic works do not create binaries between good and bad taste, nor do they distinguish high- from low-brow cultural value: everything from a Murano vase to a Scandinavian cast-iron stove, rats, crochet or barbed wire is included. *Monster's Blood* unites an eclectic and animated mix of images from the desultory to the poignant, the figurative to the abstract. A single frame composed of seven paintings welded together, it depicts zoomed-in views including someone buttoning their shirt, a crawling scorpion and various clutter and debris, but the perspectives are distorted and flipped so that the items themselves dissolve into uncertainty.

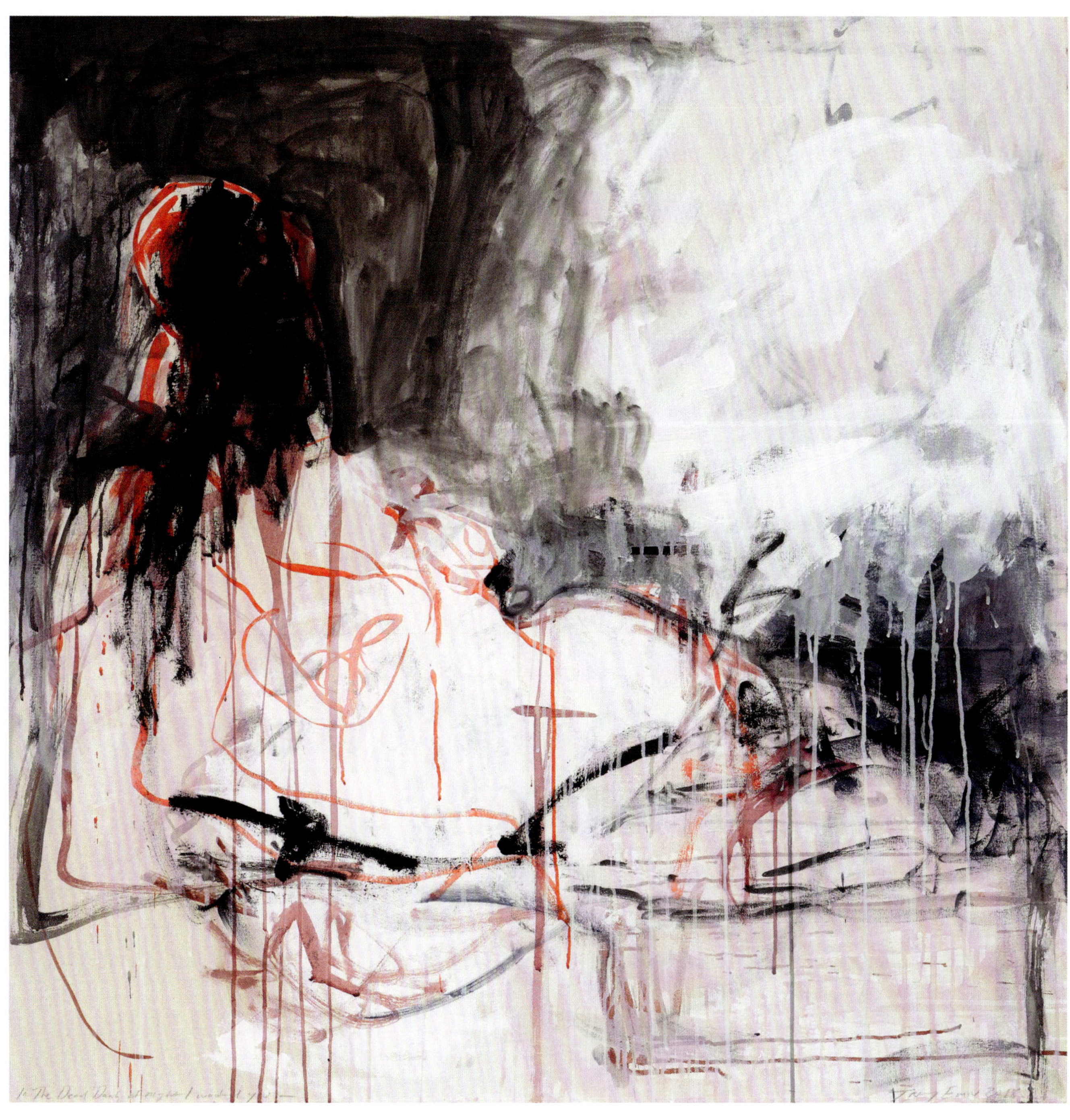

IN THE DEAD DARK OF NIGHT I WANTED YOU
2018, acrylic on canvas, 122 × 122 × 3.5 cm
(48 × 48 × 1 3/8 in)

Tracey Emin, born 1963, London, UK.

Profoundly intimate and personal, Emin's wide-ranging works draw on her experiences of trauma, love, sexual assault, sickness and loss. First coming to prominence in the 1990s, Emin has since represented Britain at the 52nd Venice Biennale in 2007 (only the second woman to do so after Rachel Whiteread, b. 1963, in 1997) and, together with Fiona Rae (p.241), in 2011 became one of the first female professors of the Royal Academy Schools, London. During her early career, Emin worked with drawing, photography, video, printmaking, textiles and neon, having abandoned painting and destroyed the works she made in the medium as a student. Returning to painting in middle age, it is now central to her practice. Over periods that can last years, Emin vigorously paints and repaints compositions that are often centred on the female body, using the process to work through thoughts and feelings. *In The Dead Dark of night I wanted you* was created after the death of her mother and periods of debilitating insomnia. With a palette suggestive of bruising and blood, Emin seems to suggest the dripping paint is as vulnerable as the body she has conjured up.

INKA ESSENHIGH

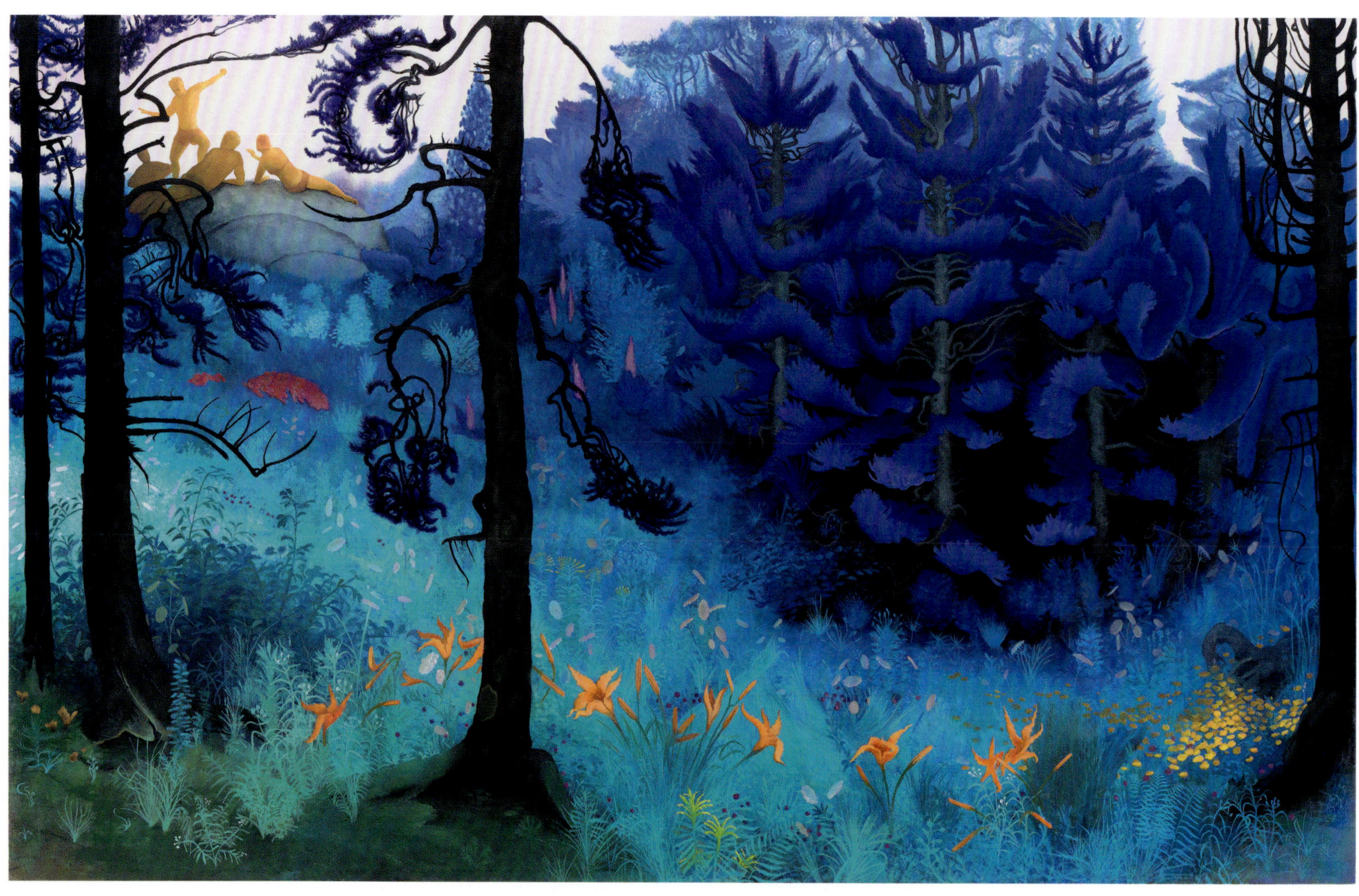

BLUE SPRUCE
2020, enamel on canvas, 127 × 203.2 cm (50 × 80 in)

Inka Essenhigh, born 1969, Bellefonte, Pennsylvania, USA.

Essenhigh creates dreamlike worlds in her paintings, often depicting natural landscapes and their cycles as a way to explore the fragility and transience of life. Graduating with an MFA from New York's School of Visual Arts in 1994, Essenhigh was initially associated with Pop Surrealism and, later, with Comic Abstraction -- featuring in the Museum of Modern Art's landmark exhibition on the movement in 2007. Essenhigh's works, however, are difficult to pin down – sublime natural environments contain an air of eerie familiarity but are inhabited by goddesses, spirits, nymph-like figures, sensual flowers and anthropomorphic fauna, alluding to folklore, myth and the mystical. The distinctive luminosity of her paintings (whose glossy surfaces are achieved with enamel paint) adds to the non-naturalistic effect of her works, while hypnagogic colour palettes and mysterious light heighten the drama of her paintings and evoke enigmatic, unseen energies. Her works often place the viewer in the realm of the unconscious: in *Blue Spruce* we enter an idyllic forest, bathed in blue, vibrant and scintillating with life, where four elfin figures – perhaps human, perhaps not – converse on a hilltop in the distance.

ALEXANDRA EXTER

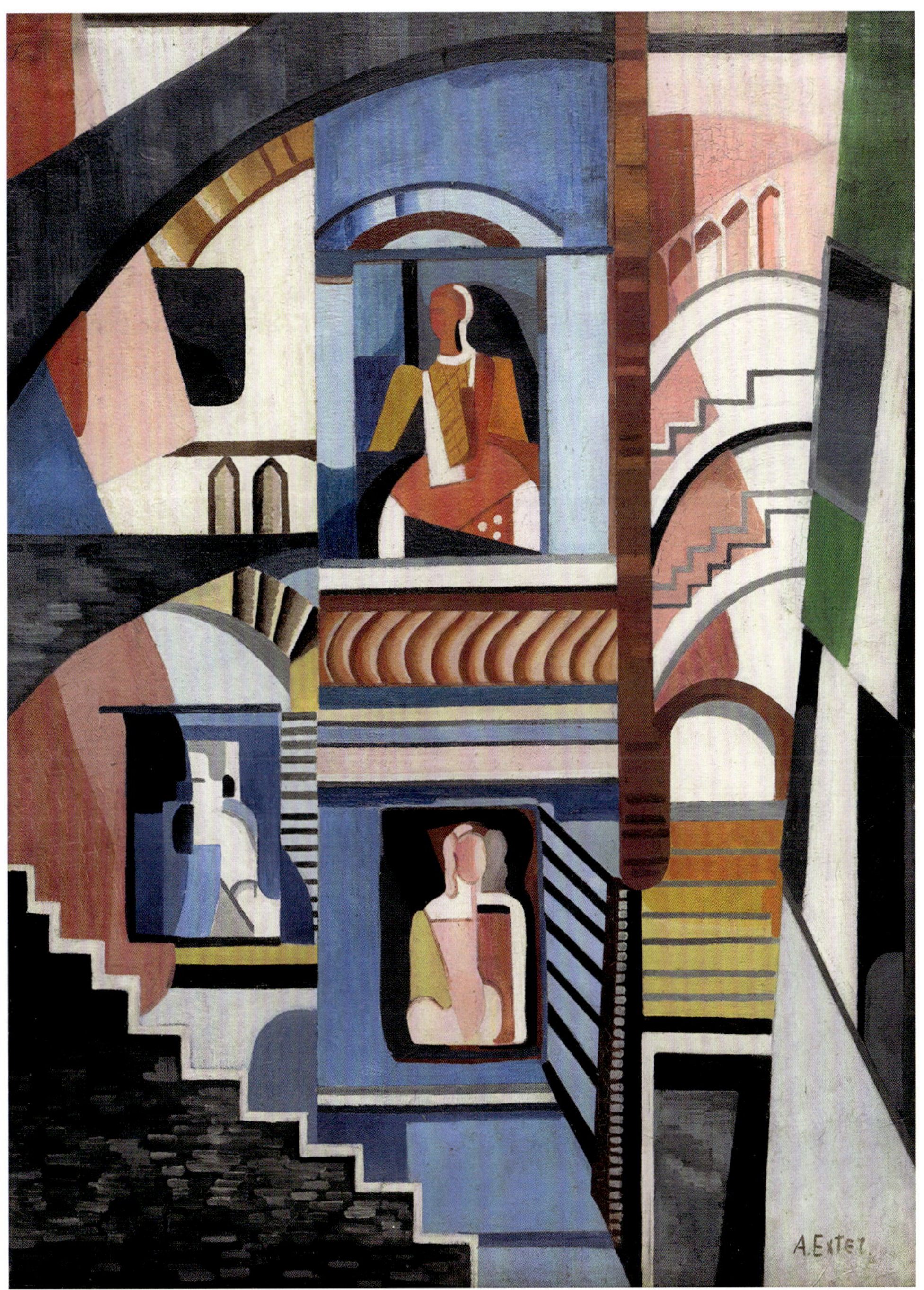

THEATRICAL COMPOSITION
*c.*1925, oil on canvas, 149 × 108.9 cm (58⅝ × 42⅞ in), Museum of Modern Art, New York, USA

Alexandra Exter, born 1882, Białystok, Poland. Died 1949, Fontenay-aux-Roses, Paris, France.

A true Renaissance woman of the early twentieth century, Exter made work encompassing abstract paintings, illustrations, and fashion and stage designs. After attending Kyiv Art School, she travelled in 1908 to Paris, where she continued her art training and encountered the city's flourishing vanguard culture. While she was inspired by the Cubist fracturing and flattening of spaces, and valued the sense of speed and rhythm in Italian Futurism, she combined the two into her own visual vocabulary that also incorporated Russian and Ukrainian aesthetic traditions. Not only has she been credited by some scholars with introducing 'Cubo-Futurism' into the Russian lexicon, but she also implemented the Constructivist focus on unobstructed built environments that would better facilitate performances in her set designs for the experimental Kamerny Theatre in Moscow. Exter's proclivity towards an architectural logic of structures is evident in *Theatrical Composition*. The space is fragmented into interlocking geometric planes of multiple floors, flights of stairs and platforms, like an extensive stage construction. Dynamic colour, movement and what appear to be costumed figures evoke the frenzied backstage of a theatre production in progress.

JADÉ FADOJUTIMI

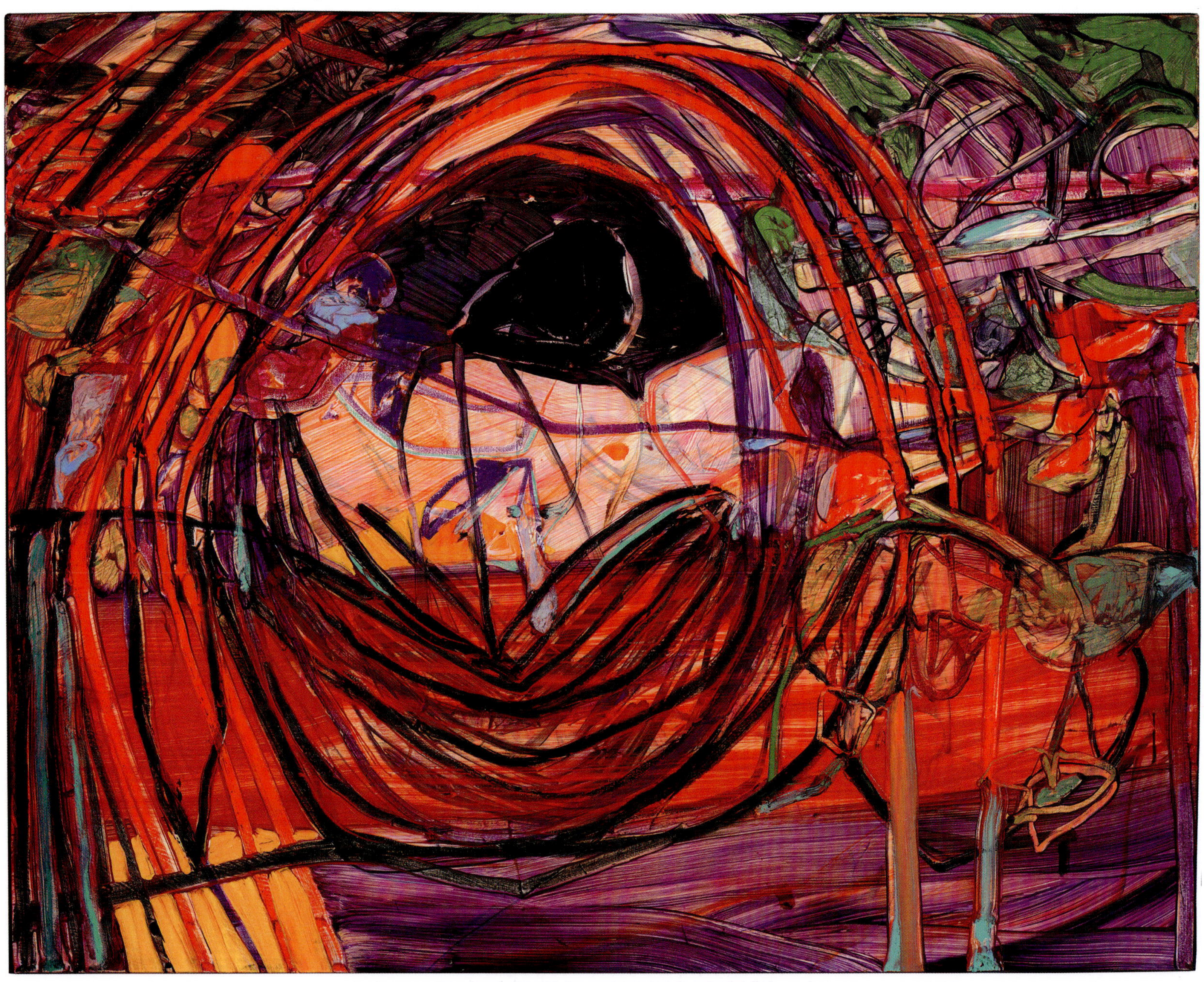

VITAL ABUNDANCE
2020, oil and oil stick on canvas, 109.9 × 140 cm (43 ¼ × 55 ⅛ in), Baltimore Museum of Art, USA

Jadé Fadojutimi, born 1993, London, UK.

Graduating with a master's degree from the Royal College of Art, London, in 2017, Fadojutimi's career has seen a meteoric rise, becoming the youngest artist in the Tate Collection following the acquisition of her work *I Present Your Royal Highness* (2018) in 2019. Each of Fadojutimi's paintings is a singular 'event' – a coincidence of self, place and perception. Impasto paint, gestural lines and luminescent hues shape her energetic, rhythmic works, which she paints intuitively. Often responding to the immediate surroundings of her studio – drawings tacked to the walls, music, patterned shirts and stockings, mementos from her travels in Japan – Fadojutimi manifests the emotions and memories these prompts conjure onto large-scale canvases. While she often weaves figurative elements into her compositions, they all but dissolve in expansive, kaleidoscopic scenes. 'I relish manipulating their malleability,' she said in an interview with *Studio International* in 2021, 'carrying them in and out of focus, making their recognition fragile.' Such representational fragility shapes *Vital Abundance*, a vibrant choreography of colour and movement that appears abstract regardless of its referents, left open to the viewer's idiosyncratic impression.

SYLVIA FEIN

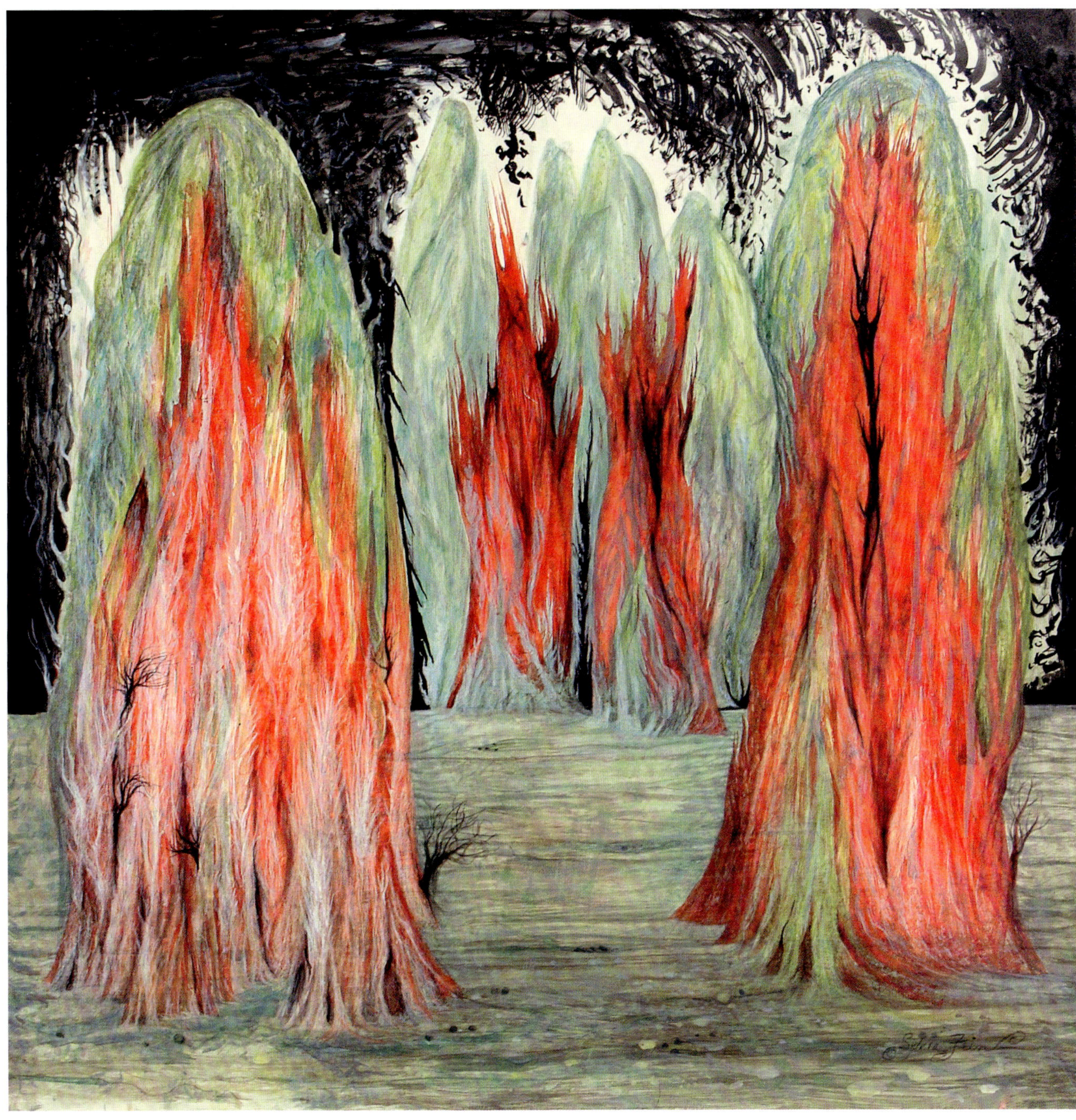

THE PAINTING TOLD ME WHAT TO DO
2012, egg tempera on gesso board, 61 × 61 cm (24 × 24 in)

Sylvia Fein, born 1919, Milwaukee, Wisconsin, USA.

A painter of magical realism employing motifs of cosmic eyes, trees and bewitching animals, Fein is often associated with Surrealism and her work draws parallels to such artists as Leonora Carrington (p.72), Remedios Varo (p.308) and Dorothea Tanning (p.296). Apart from a stint in Mexico in the early to mid-1940s, Fein has lived most of her long life in California. As a student at the University of Wisconsin, she belonged to a group dubbed 'the Midwest Surrealists' – which also included Gertrude Abercrombie (p.19) – and learnt the ancient technique of painting with egg tempera, which became her signature medium. She participated in the 1946 Annual Exhibition of Contemporary American Painting at the Whitney Museum of American Art alongside contemporaries of mid-century North American painting including Georgia O'Keeffe (p.227) and Doris Lee (p.176), before completing an MFA at the University of California, Berkeley, in 1951. In the 1970s Fein gave up painting to write books, only picking up her brush again in the early 2000s. This dreamlike work depicts a group of mysterious tree creatures that seem to burn from within. Cloaked in green, their flaming 'bodies' are a mass of arteries and roots. The title implies Fein has yielded control to her subconscious, a practice common among the Surrealists known as automatism.

RACHEL FEINSTEIN

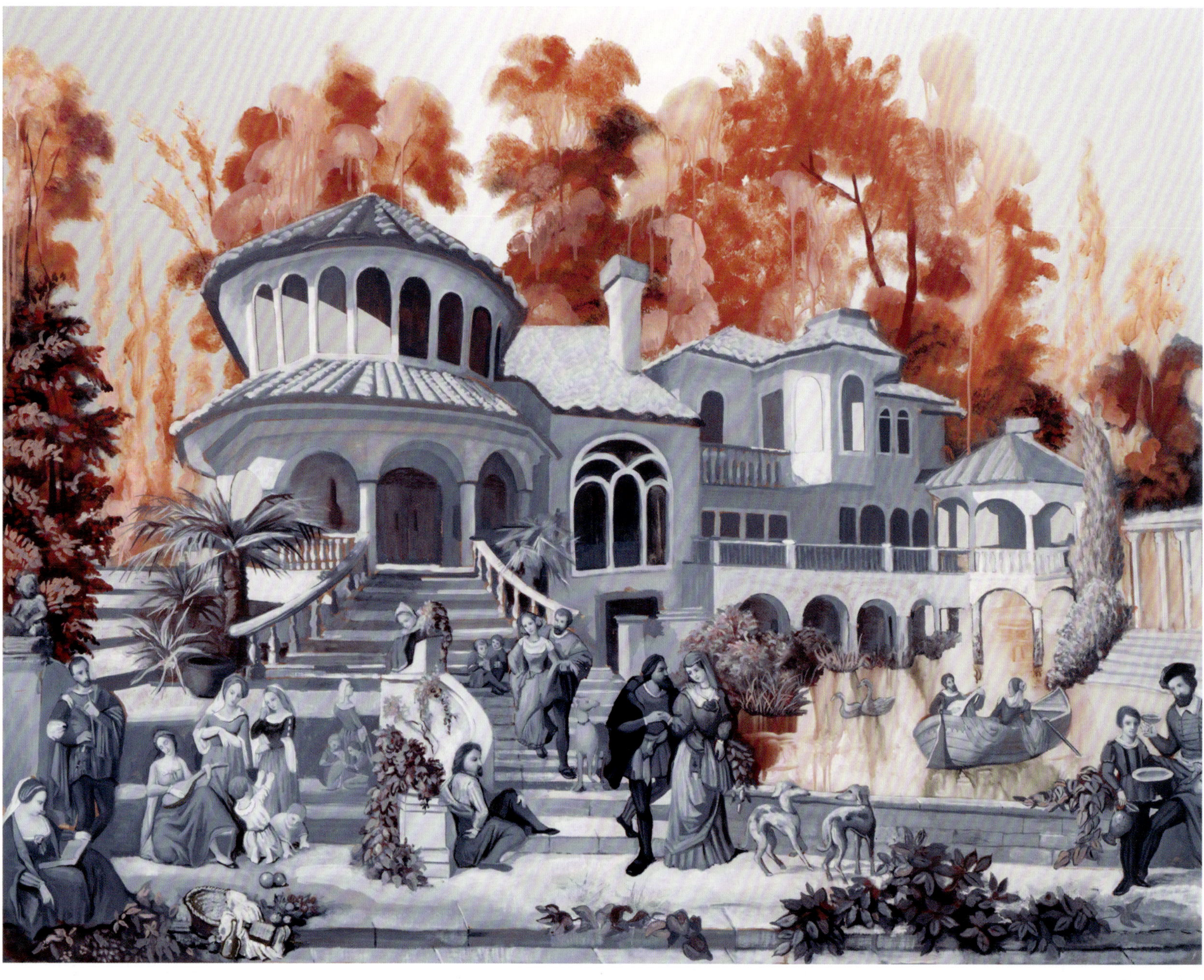

BRADBURY
2018, oil and enamel on mirror, 106.7 × 137.2 cm (42 × 54 in)

Rachel Feinstein, born 1971, Fort Defiance, Arizona, USA.

Feinstein's fantastical practice combines painting, sculpture and installation to create immersive, theatrical environments. Growing up in Florida, she frequently visited Disney World with her family, always stopping at Cinderella's Castle, whose distinctive spires echo Neuschwanstein Castle in Germany, itself a nineteenth-century ode to the Gothic architecture of yore. Feinstein's work explores these same themes of history and reinvention. 'I've always been interested in portraying some kind of fantasy, then showing that it's completely constructed,' Feinstein said in a 2018 *Wall Street International* interview. *Bradbury* belongs to a series of paintings on mirrors that situate modern luxury houses in frothy garden landscapes. These pleasure gardens are populated by figures in Baroque and Rococo dress who pose strumming lutes and sipping wine from chalices, motifs borrowed from eighteenth-century wallpaper designs. In a 2018 exhibition at Gagosian gallery in Los Angeles, Feinstein hung them on top of wallpaper compositions of her own devising that repeated the garden scenes at large scale. She also showed a group of sculptures in lurid candy colours portraying Victoria's Secret 'Angels', thus drawing a connection between the fantasies offered by lingerie, luxury real estate and interior decor.

GENIEVE FIGGIS

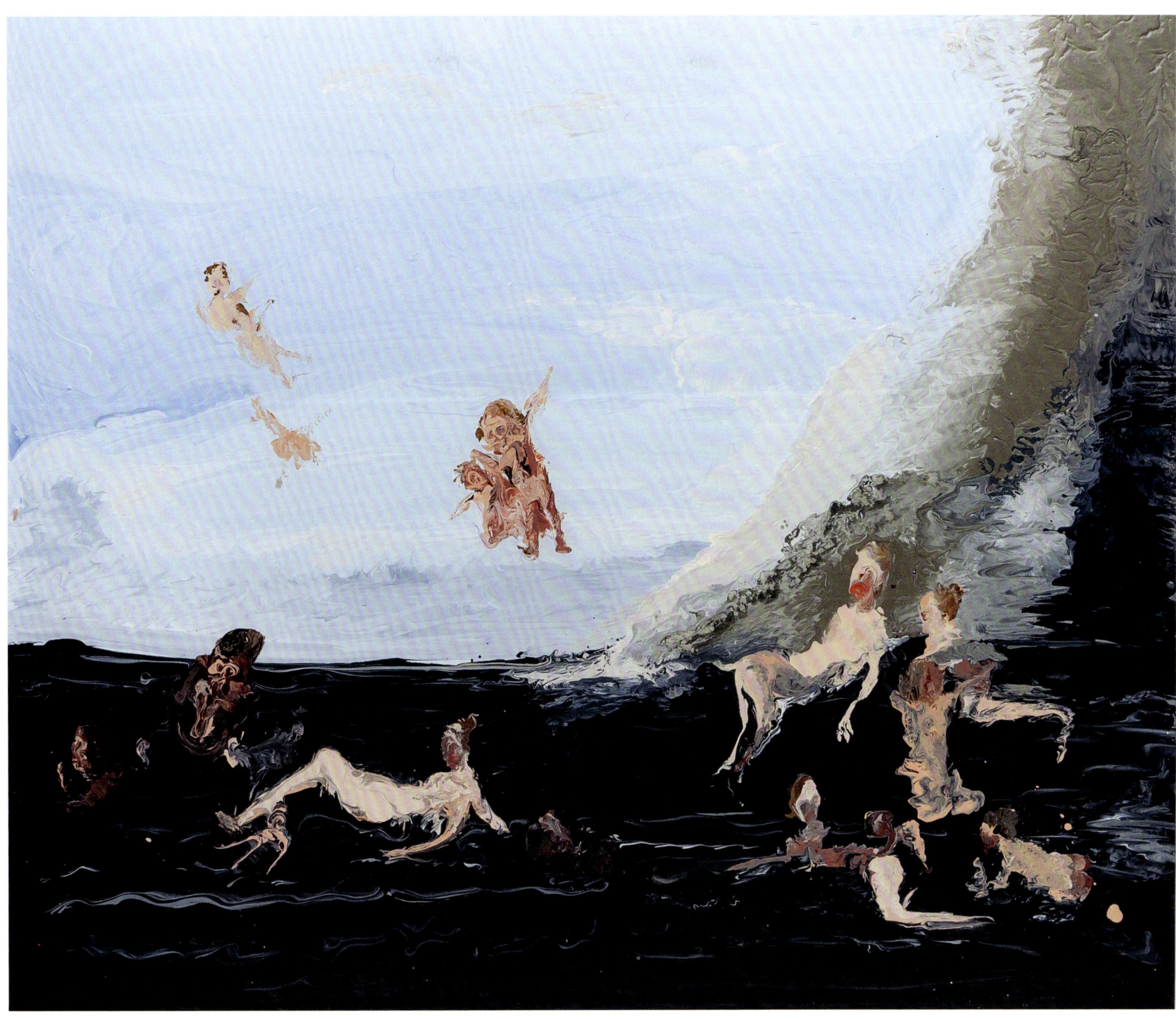

BIRTH OF VENUS AFTER BOUCHER
2016, acrylic on canvas, 99.1 × 119.4 cm (39 × 47 in)

Genieve Figgis, born 1972, Dublin, Ireland.

Figgis's works in acrylic and oil often remix canonical paintings by the likes of Goya, Velázquez, Fragonard and Gainsborough, though she also works with old photographs or images she encounters in her day-to-day life. Figgis is interested in the role of painting throughout history – in particular the medium's function as a status symbol and as a documentation of collective aspirations – and she satirizes its social mores with a trenchant sense of humour. Transgression and sex are prevalent in her works, a reaction in part to the artist's experiences growing up in 1970s Catholic Ireland. Figgis's paintings are distinctive for their densely layered surfaces, rendered in swirling brushwork that produces a dizzying and almost disturbing effect. In many of her works, a facade of luxury – resplendent Regency or Rococo interiors and elaborate costumery – is dissolved with thick impasto that erases details such as her subjects' faces. In this work Figgis pays homage to the French artist François Boucher's (1703–70) Rococo masterpiece of 1740, reinventing the mythical scene in rippling brushstrokes, the goddess and her entourage of nymphs and tritons transformed into garish, ghoulish characters who appear more sinister than serene.

LEONOR FINI

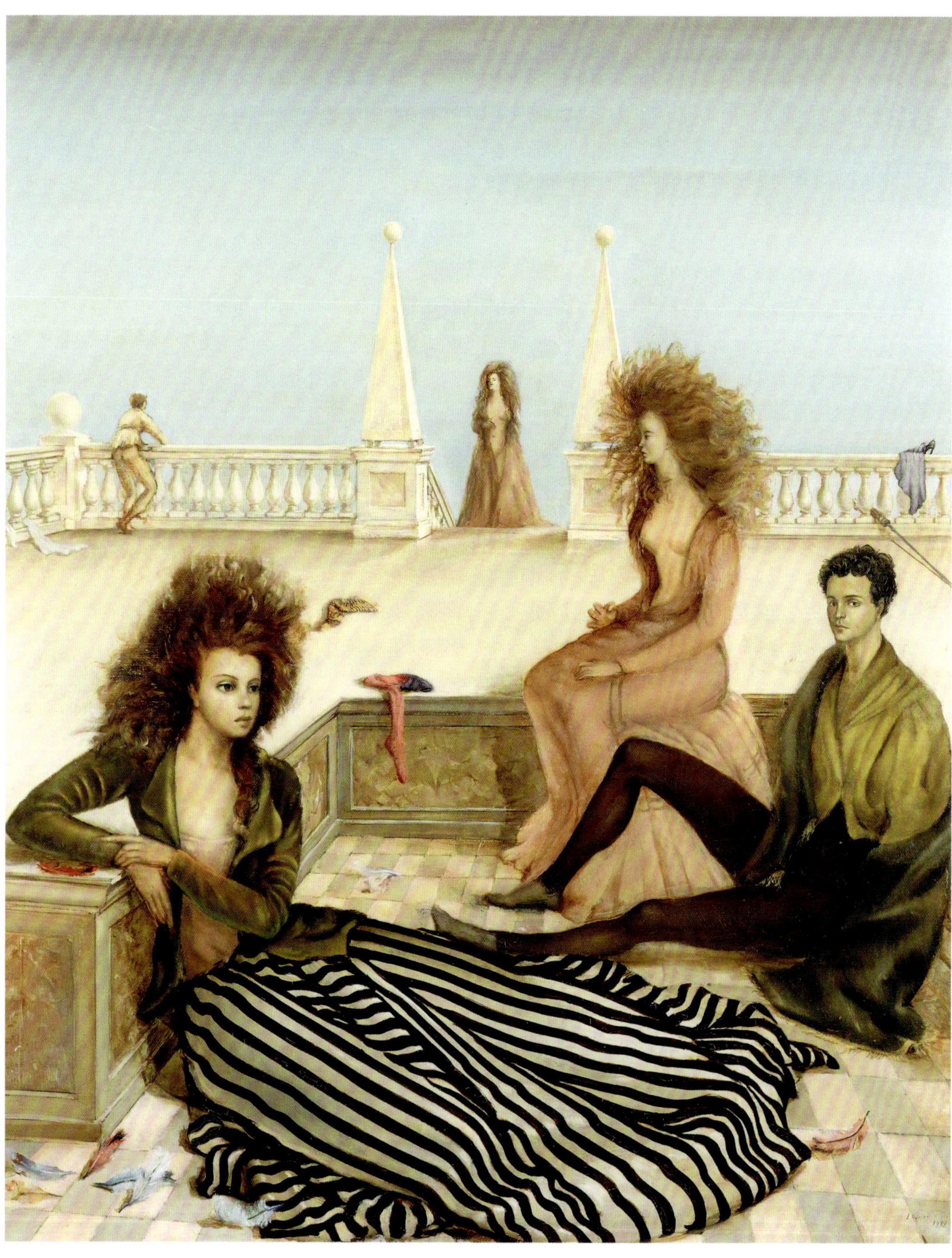

COMPOSITION WITH FIGURES ON A TERRACE
1938, oil on canvas, 100 × 81 cm (39 ⅜ × 32 in)

Leonor Fini, born 1907, Buenos Aires, Argentina. Died 1996, Paris, France.

Leaving Argentina for Italy as a young child, Fini moved to Paris in the early 1930s, where she absorbed the teachings and aesthetics of magical realism and Surrealism. Fini was an artist unto herself; she was uncompromising in her views and refused to be known as a 'woman artist' or be claimed by the Surrealists, although she considered many of them friends. Avoiding the dogma of artistic movements, she developed a singular practice that threw into the spotlight female sexuality and the many dimensions of desire, often playing off passive men with fierce women. Fascinated with morbidity from a young age, Fini visited morgues and collected animal skeletons that informed her characteristically supple figures, seen here on a terrace. Central to the image is Fini herself, dressed in a velvet jacket with a billowing skirt typical of her flamboyant style, caught in the midst of an erotic reverie among strewn clothes, a sword and feathers. With her libertine spirit, Fini was a celebrity in her time and enthralled such fashionable figures as Coco Chanel and Elsa Schiaparelli.

BEVERLY FISHMAN

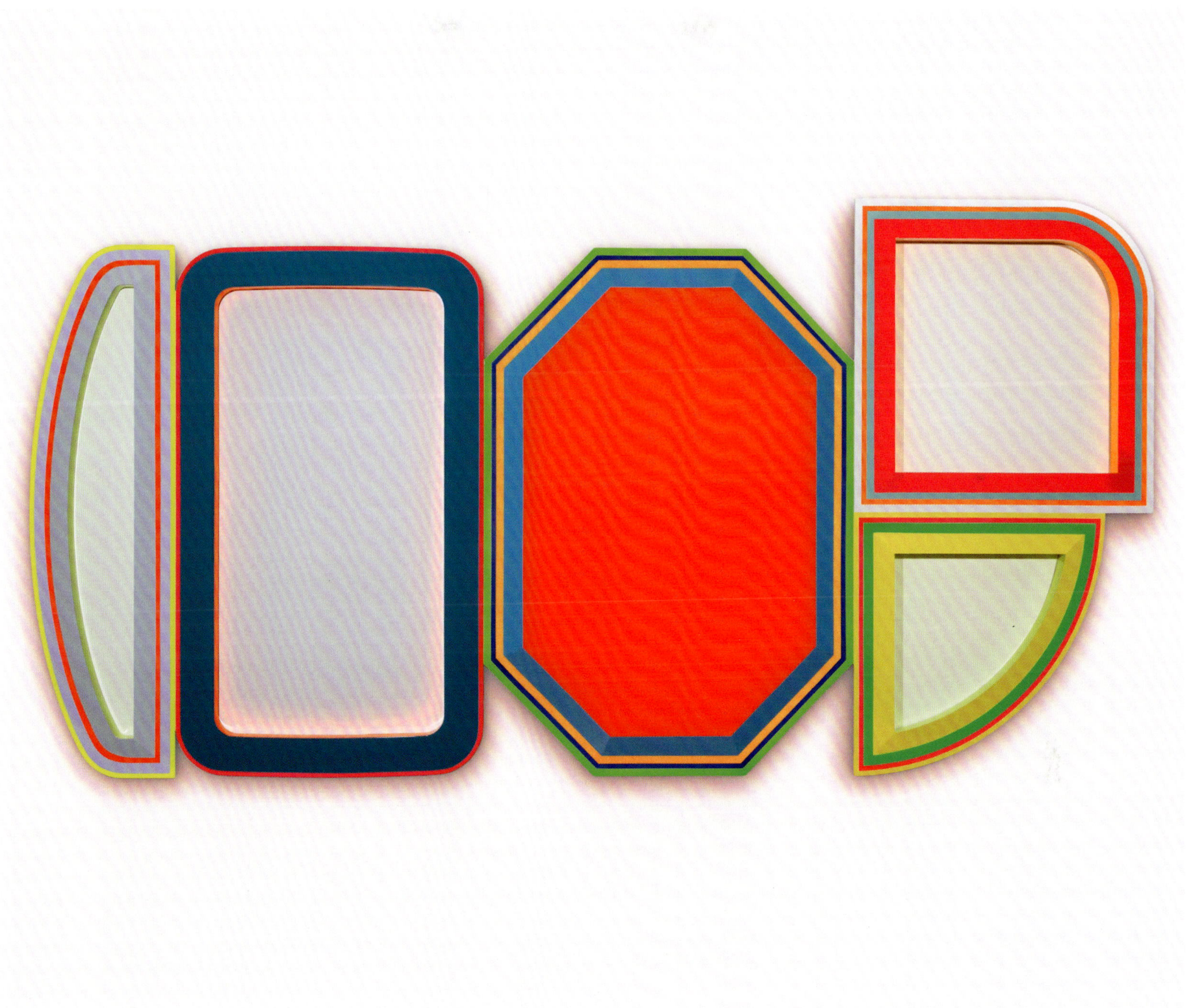

UNTITLED (BIPOLAR DISORDER, OSTEOPOROSIS, HIGH BLOOD PRESSURE, OPIOID ADDICTION, PAIN)
2020, urethane paint on wood, 144.8 × 289.6 cm (57 × 114 in)

Beverly Fishman, born 1955, Philadelphia, USA.

Soon after receiving her MFA from Yale School of Art in 1980, Fishman experienced serious illness in her family, prompting her long-standing interest in sickness and medicine. The unfolding AIDS crisis reinforced these concerns, sparking several series of works exploring the aesthetics of the medical–industrial complex. The best known are her hard-edged Minimalist pill paintings such as this one: precise geometric works that, despite appearing wholly abstract, are derived from the physical form of tablets and capsules. Employing similar strategies to pharmaceutical advertisements, Fishman's brightly coloured paintings seduce, using glowing neon automotive paint that belies the ailments listed in their titles. The shapes in this painted relief relate to 'polypharmacy', the condition of taking several medicines together to combat multiple conditions, including mental and physiological health problems. Though entirely handmade, its high-gloss finish is so slick as to appear machine-fabricated. In an increasingly medicated world, Fishman questions the extent to which such technology alters our perception of ourselves, alluding to its life-improving benefits at the same time as it points to the system's ultimate prioritization of profit over health.

AUDREY FLACK

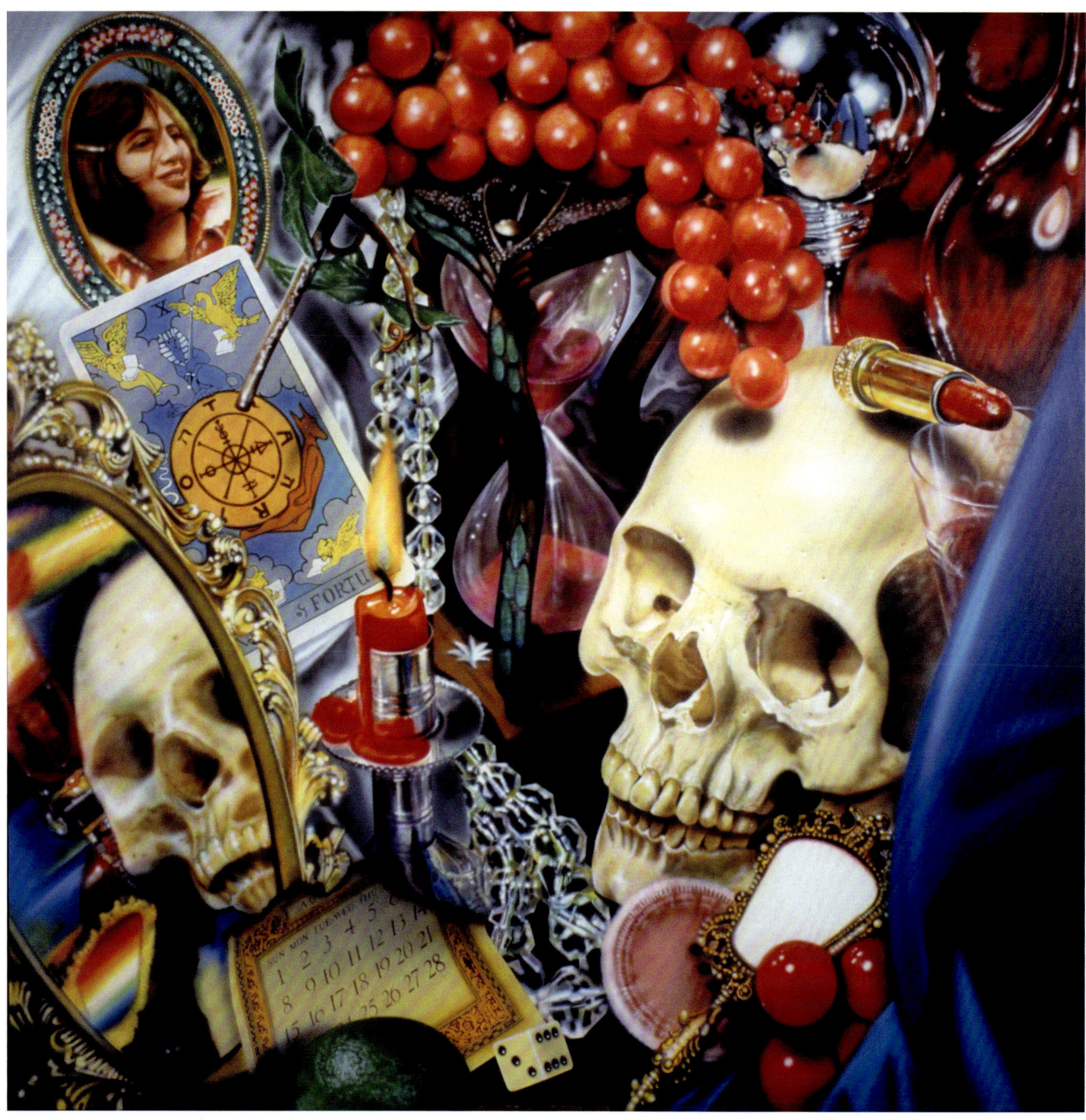

WHEEL OF FORTUNE (VANITAS)
1977–8, oil over acrylic on canvas, 243.8 × 243.8 cm (96 × 96 in), Parrish Art Museum, Water Mill, New York, USA

Audrey Flack, born 1931, Brooklyn, USA.

A pioneer – and one of the only women painters – of the Photorealism movement, Flack investigates art-historical tropes and the social construction of gender. Training under Josef Albers (1888–1976) at Yale University, Flack produced Abstract Expressionist work in the early 1950s and began creating her vibrant and fastidiously rendered Photorealist paintings during the late 1960s and 1970s. Her quintessential large-scale still lifes are based on photographs the artist took herself and are products of her use of an airbrush to layer paint, enhancing the works' flatness. While her male colleagues generally painted cool and unemotional Photorealist paintings, Flack's works often function socio-politically, incorporating signifiers associated with the beauty industry to interrogate the cultural construction of femininity. This painting is from a series of works in which Flack employs the classic genre of the *vanitas* still life, meticulously arranging a variety of symbolic objects, including a human skull, which together serve to remind the viewer of the fleeting nature of life. In *Wheel of Fortune (Vanitas)*, Flack includes symbols of chance – tarot cards, a die – along with a picture of her daughter, lending the painting an autobiographical dimension as well.

LAVINIA FONTANA

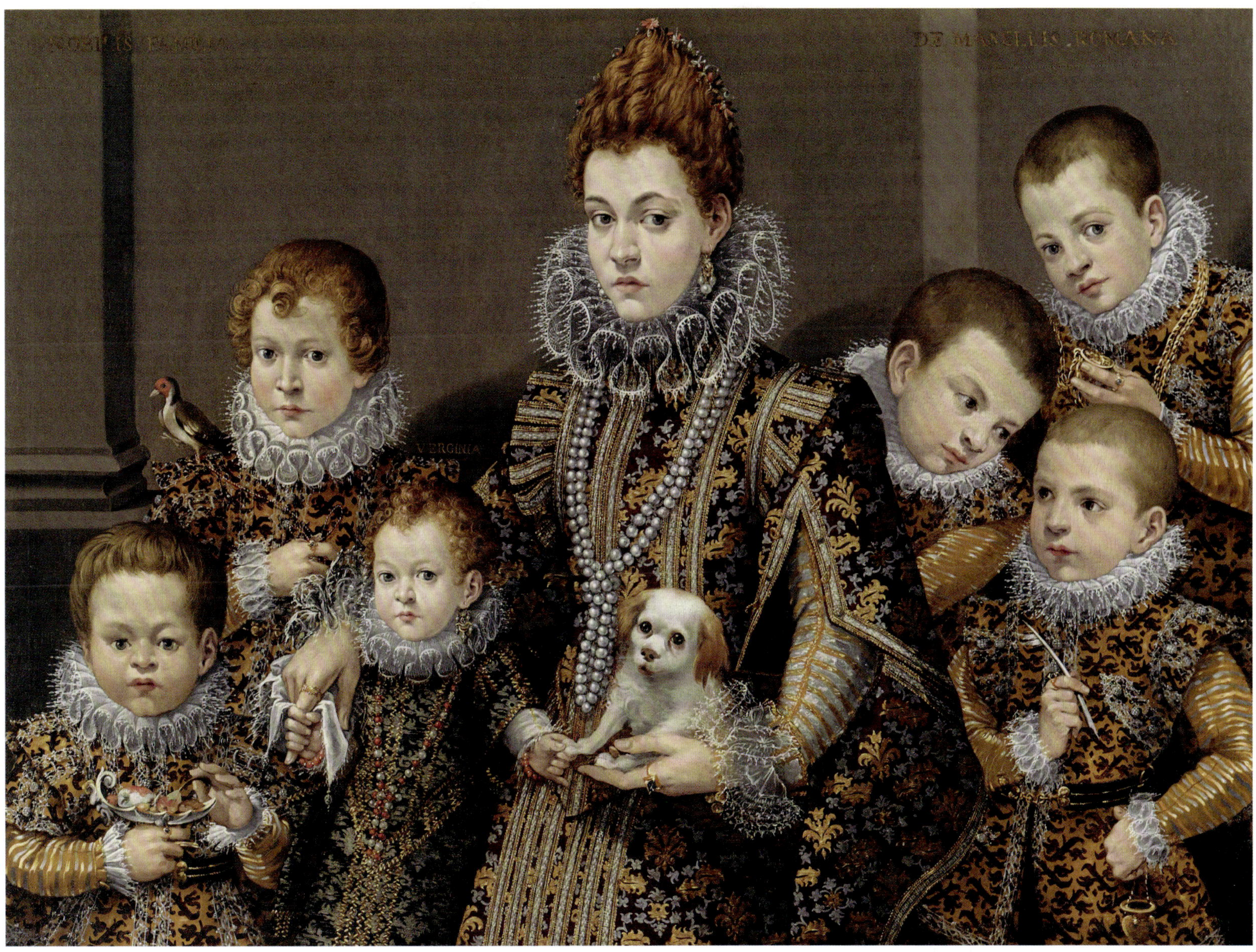

PORTRAIT OF BIANCA DEGLI UTILI MASELLI WITH SIX OF HER CHILDREN
1603–4, oil on canvas, 99 × 133.5 cm (39 × 52 ½ in)

Lavinia Fontana, born 1552, Bologna, Italy.
Died 1614, Rome, Italy.

Regarded as one of the first prominent woman artists in Europe, Fontana was a Mannerist painter, known for her portraiture of important figures in late Renaissance Italy, including the court of Pope Paul V. At the age of twenty-five, Fontana married another painter who soon became her assistant, both in her painting studio and within the domestic sphere – a gendered role reversal that was highly unusual in the sixteenth and seventeenth centuries. Fontana's father brought wealthy clients to his daughter, and she painted them in their finery, with symbolism woven into the fabric of her paintings as was then customary. This particular portrait presents us with a noblewoman surrounded by her six russet-haired children. The colour is echoed through their dress design, the contents of a silver bowl, and even in the pigment of the family's pet dog and perched bird-on-chain. Fontana displays the client's wealth explicitly through woven silk, fine jewellery and lace, all rendered with meticulous, exquisite detail. Each child holds something symbolic, perhaps a nod to each heir's future hopes and dreams.

HELEN FRANKENTHALER

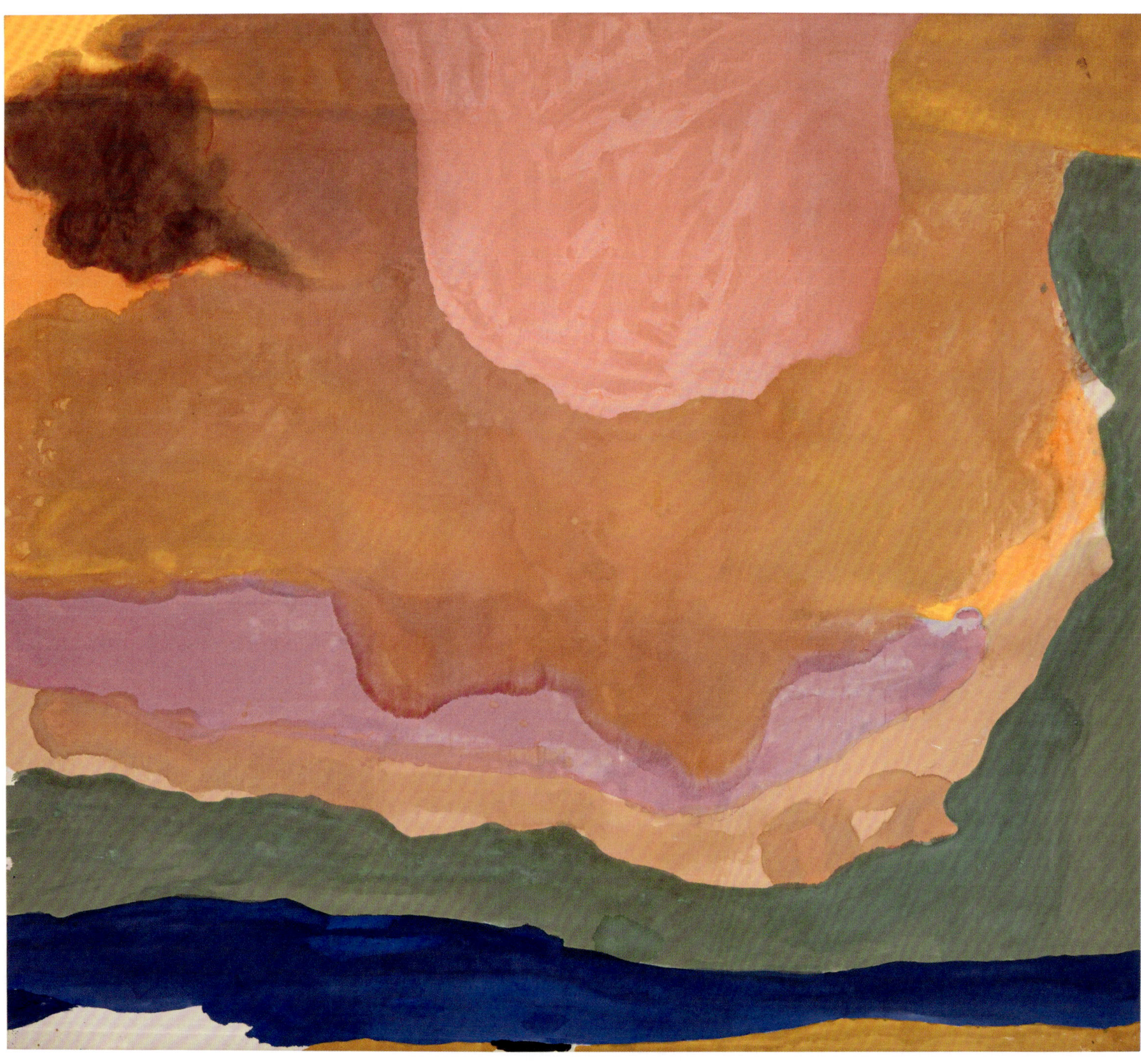

FLOOD
1967, acrylic on canvas, 315.6 × 356.9 cm (124¼ × 140½ in), Whitney Museum of American Art, New York; purchase, with funds from the Friends of the Whitney Museum of American Art

Helen Frankenthaler, born 1928, New York, USA. Died 2011, Darien, Connecticut, USA.

Widely seen as one of the most significant American artists of the twentieth century, Frankenthaler was a key figure in the evolution of Abstract Expressionism and Colour Field painting. Visiting Jackson Pollock's (1912–56) studio in 1951 inspired Frankenthaler to adopt a spontaneous approach to painting. *Mountains and Sea* (1952), her breakthrough work painted in a single day, signalled a new method called soak-stain. This technique involved affixing unprimed cotton canvas flat to the floor, and applying oil paint (thinned to the consistency of watercolour) with brushes and other tools to soak into the fabric. As Frankenthaler's practice developed, her colours, initially centred on the canvas in her early works, expanded outwards to cover the surface completely, recalling the 'all over' paintings of first-generation Abstract Expressionists such as Janet Sobel (p.283) and Clyfford Still (1904–80). Considered a second-generation Abstract Expressionist, along with Elaine de Kooning (p.89) and Grace Hartigan (p.131), Frankenthaler's work embraced references to the natural world. In addition to its title, *Flood*'s horizontal layers and earth tones evoke landscapes and organic matter, as well as inviting an emotional response from the viewer.

JANE FREILICHER

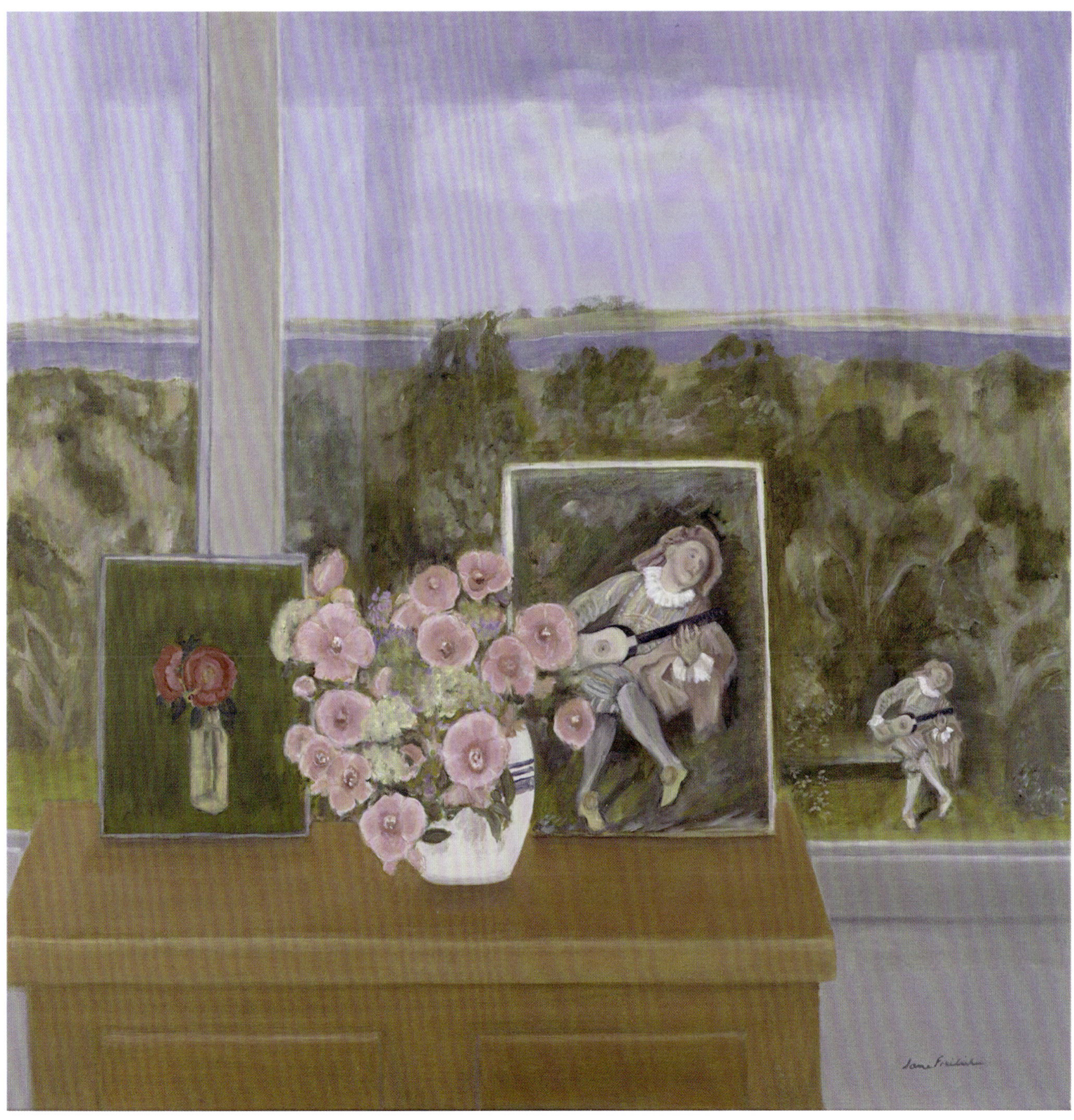

THE LUTE PLAYER
1993, oil on canvas, 91.4 × 91.4 cm (36 × 36 in), Metropolitan Museum of Art, New York, USA

Jane Freilicher, born 1924, Brooklyn, USA. Died 2014, New York, USA.

With a career that spanned more than sixty years, Freilicher was noted for her luminous views of Long Island and Manhattan landscapes, often juxtaposed with still lifes in the foreground. Freilicher was part of an avant-garde circle called the New York School, which included poets such as John Ashbery and Frank O'Hara and painters Grace Hartigan (p.131) and Joan Mitchell (p.203). Although she came to artistic maturity at the height of Abstract Expressionism, and had studied with German-born painter Hans Hofmann (1880–1966), renowned for his teachings on abstraction, Freilicher devoted her career to representational painting. In *The Lute Player*, a visual disjunction between truth and fiction occurs through the image of Jean-Antoine Watteau's painting *Mezzetin* (*c.*1718–20). Mezzetin, the stock comic character of Italian commedia dell'arte, appears in a reproduction of the eighteenth-century painting on the table, but also seems to be sitting outside the window in the exact same pose – exemplifying how Freilicher bestowed on her seemingly ordinary scenes an air of the surreal and the strangeness in the everyday. A long-time member of the American Academy of Arts and Letters, Freilicher was awarded its Gold Medal in Painting in 2005.

FEDE GALIZIA

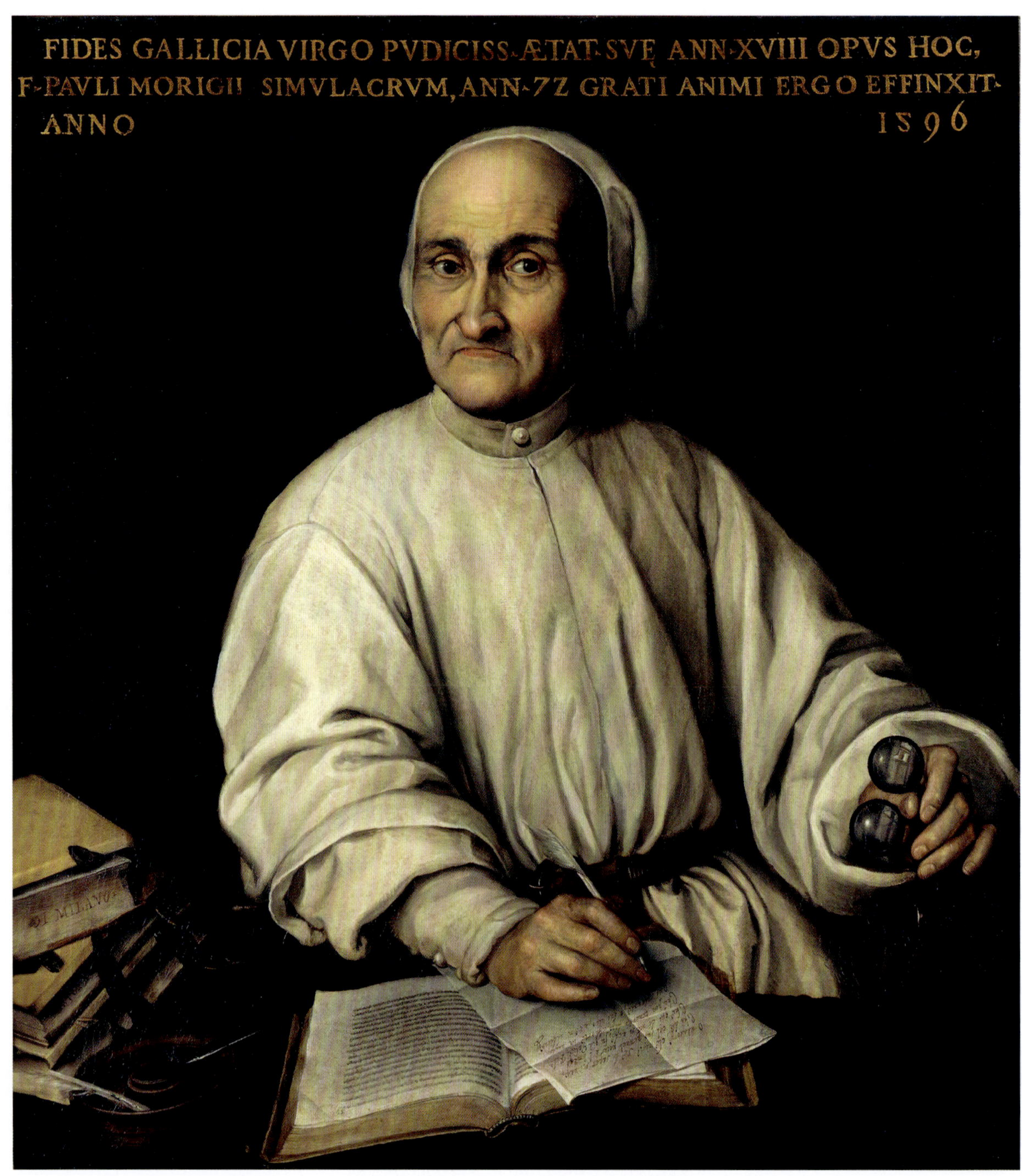

PORTRAIT OF PAOLO MORIGIA
*c.*1592–5, oil on canvas, 88 × 79 cm (34⅝ × 31⅛ in), Pinacoteca Ambrosiana, Veneranda Biblioteca Ambrosiana, Milan, Italy

Fede Galizia, born *c.*1578, Milan, Italy. Died *c.*1630, Milan.

Although she was trained by her father, the miniaturist and metalworker Nunzio Galizia (before 1550–1621), Fede Galizia did not remain in his shadow. Already at the age of twelve she was singled out for her excellence by the artistic biographer Giovanni Paolo Lomazzo. She worked in numerous genres: lifesize portraits; history paintings; religious altarpieces, including the high altarpiece for Milan's church of Santa Maria Maddalena; and, for the new breed of art collector, still-life compositions of fruit, which are counted among the very first still lifes by an Italian artist. In her early twenties, Galizia created this lively portrait of revered Jesuit scholar Paolo Morigia at work among his books. Morigia, who chronicled local Milanese society, appears to be interrupting his writing – a madrigal in praise of Galizia's painting skills – in order to acknowledge the artist, removing his glasses in order to see her better. Reflected on the lenses of his skilfully painted spectacles are a candle and a window with two faces peering through open shutters.

SANDRA GAMARRA

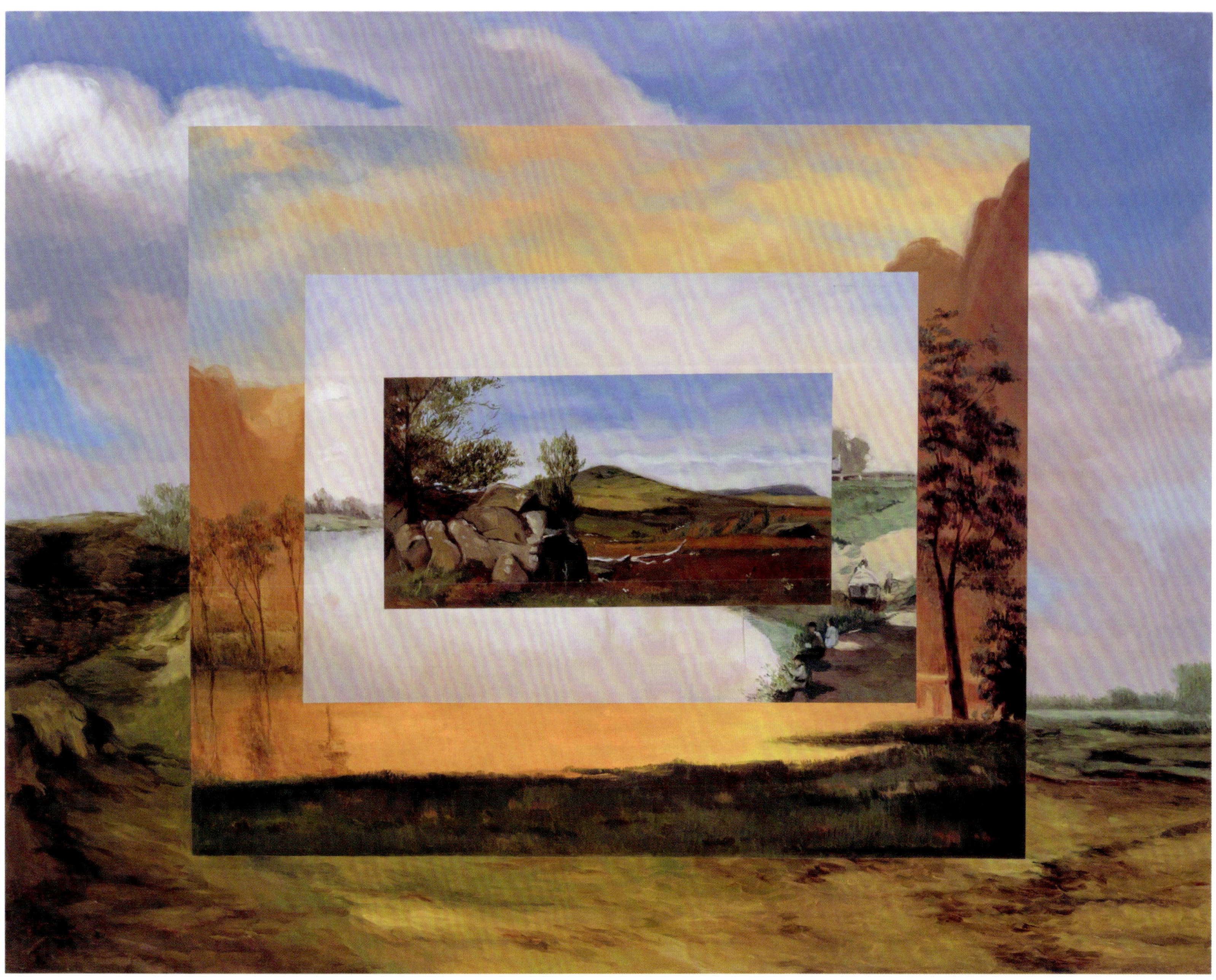

EL MARCO DEL PAISAJE III (THE LANDSCAPE FRAME III)
2017, oil on canvas, 100 × 130 cm (39.4 × 51.2 in), private collection

Sandra Gamarra, born 1972, Lima, Peru.

The visual representation of the environment, particularly in the European and North American traditions, has long been connected to the occupation and management of land – as territory, property, colony, tourist destination or extractive site. Gamarra brings a critical eye to these issues in works that both appropriate and subvert representations of the South American landscape. In Peru and Brazil – regions with which Gamarra has long engaged – the rolling hills of Machu Picchu or the verdant Amazon rainforest have been reproduced in souvenirs, postcards and travelogues, while simultaneously being destroyed through deforestation and industrial extraction. After completing a doctorate at the Universidad de Castilla–La Mancha in Cuenca, Spain, in 2003, Gamarra's work was brought to the attention of a wider audience through her inclusion in high-profile international exhibitions, including the Venice Biennale (2009), São Paulo Biennial (2010) and Berlin Biennale (2020). In works such as *The Landscape Frame III*, Gamarra activates the picture frame device, which has functioned throughout the history of painting to render the natural world 'picturesque' and thus commodifiable. Overlaying several landscapes into a single image, this attainability is provocatively obfuscated.

GIOVANNA GARZONI

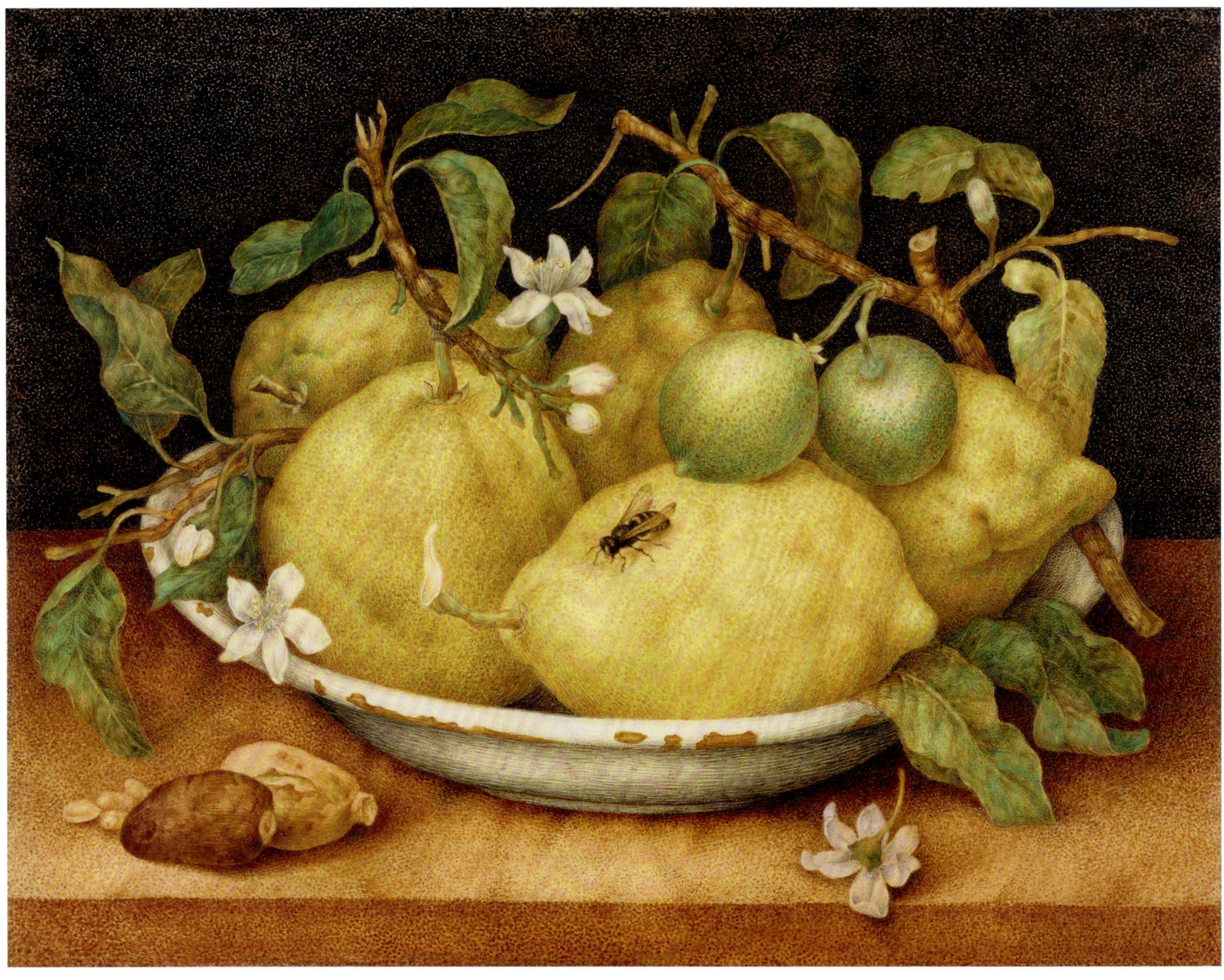

STILL LIFE WITH BOWL OF CITRONS
late 1640s, tempera on vellum, 27.6 × 35.6 cm (10 ⅞ × 14 in), J. Paul Getty Museum, Los Angeles, USA

Giovanna Garzoni, born 1600, probably Ascoli Piceno, Italy. Died 1670, Rome, Italy.

One of the first Italian women to practise the art of still life, Garzoni found great renown during her lifetime. After being taught oil painting by her uncle, Garzoni followed him to Venice. Aged seventeen, she collaborated with Palma il Giovane's (*c.*1548–1628) workshop, making a life-size painting of Saint Andrew for a Venetian church. By the age of twenty, she boasted additional talents in singing, instrumental music, calligraphy and miniature painting. The fame of her miniatures on vellum would take her to Rome, Naples, Turin, London, Paris and Florence. She lived out her final years in Rome, where she was buried with great honour in the church of the painters' guild. In this work, Garzoni applied a dense veil of tiny black dots to her vellum support, allowing its pearly glow to shine through. Filling the sheet are lifesize lemons and limes, exotic horticultural prizes grown with recently developed techniques. Painted in exquisite, delicate detail, the vivid greens and yellows capture the bright flavours of these luxurious fruits. By contrast, their surroundings are rustic: a chipped terracotta plate, ordinary pine nuts and an itinerant wasp, attracted by the flowers' neroli scent.

ARTEMISIA GENTILESCHI

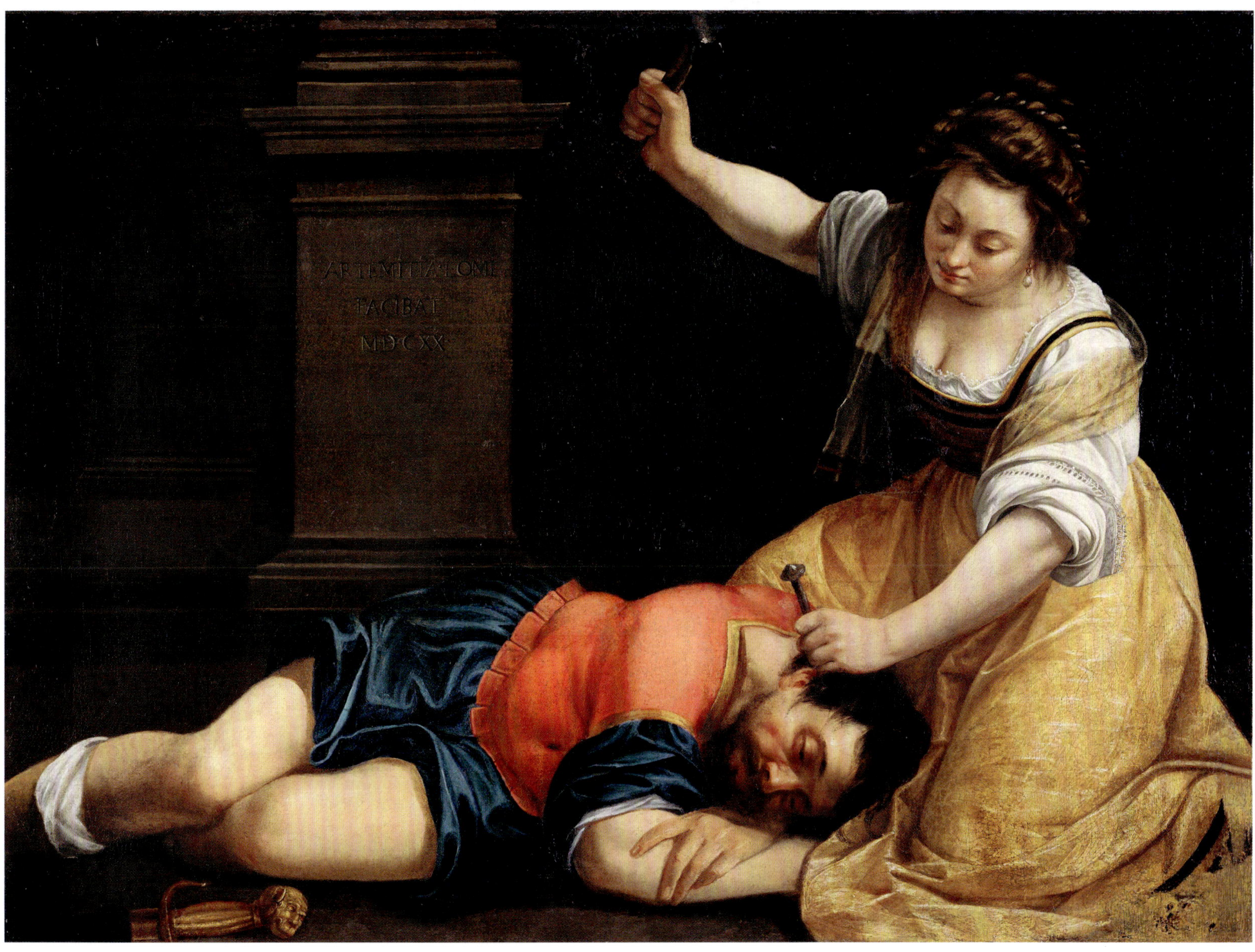

JAEL AND SISERA
1620, oil on canvas, 93 × 128 cm (36⅝ × 50⅜ in), Szépművészeti Múzeum, Budapest, Hungary

Artemisia Gentileschi, born 1593, Rome, Italy. Died *c.*1653, Naples, Italy.

Now widely considered among the most accomplished painters of the Baroque, Gentileschi's biography has often overshadowed her art. After being raped at the age of seventeen by the painter hired by her artist father to train her, she was subjected to a public trial in which she was tortured to ensure she was telling the truth. Her attacker was ultimately indicted, and Gentileschi went on to become one of the earliest women to forge a successful career as a painter and the first to become a member of the prestigious Accademia delle Arti del Disegno in Florence in 1616. In addition to portraits, she is celebrated for her monumental religious scenes presented from a distinctly female perspective. The Old Testament tale of Jael and Sisera was a popular story in the 'Power of Women' *topos*, a term defined in 1995 by art historian Susan Louise Smith to describe the medieval and Renaissance representations of men being dominated by women. Here Jael, defender of Israel, is about to drive a tent peg through the head of the sleeping Canaanite commander Sisera. Sleeves pushed up to the elbows reveal strong and active forearms – a detail that recurs across many of Gentileschi's paintings of women.

FRANÇOISE GILOT

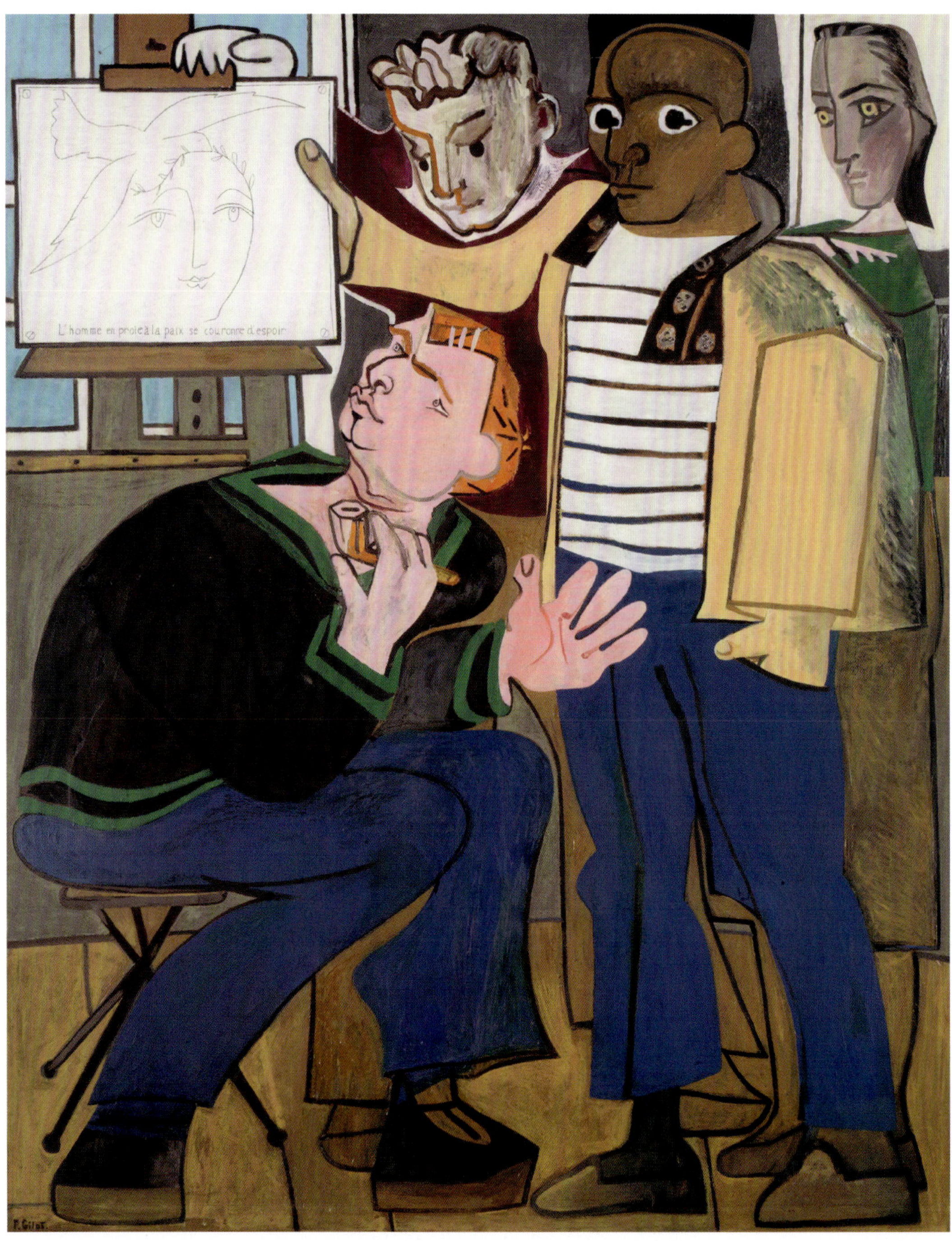

LES PEINTRES (THE PAINTERS)
1952, oil on board, 163.5 × 130.5 cm
(64 3/8 × 51 3/8 in)

Françoise Gilot, born 1921, Neuilly-sur-Seine, France.

Gilot knew from the age of five that she wanted to become an artist. The only child born to a wealthy family, in 1939 she enrolled at law school at her father's behest but after the Nazi Occupation of Paris, she abandoned her studies, resulting in temporary estrangement from her family. While working as a fashion designer in Paris, she began her artistic training under the painter Endre Rozsda (1913–99). Following her first exhibition in 1943 – also the year she met Pablo Picasso (1881–1973), with whom she had a decade-long relationship – Gilot became a key figure in the School of Paris. While influenced by movements such as Cubism and Fauvism, she continually sought new ways to communicate her original ideas. In the 1950s she briefly joined the Réalités Nouvelles (New Realities) movement of pure abstraction, but soon realized she preferred the figurative mode. Painted in homage to Picasso, who is depicted holding a drawing of his lover with a dove (one of her favourite symbols), *The Painters* exemplifies Gilot's use of figures to explore colour and composition, seen in the complementary yet contrasting shades and the complex interplay of vertical and horizontal lines.

LOUISE GIOVANELLI

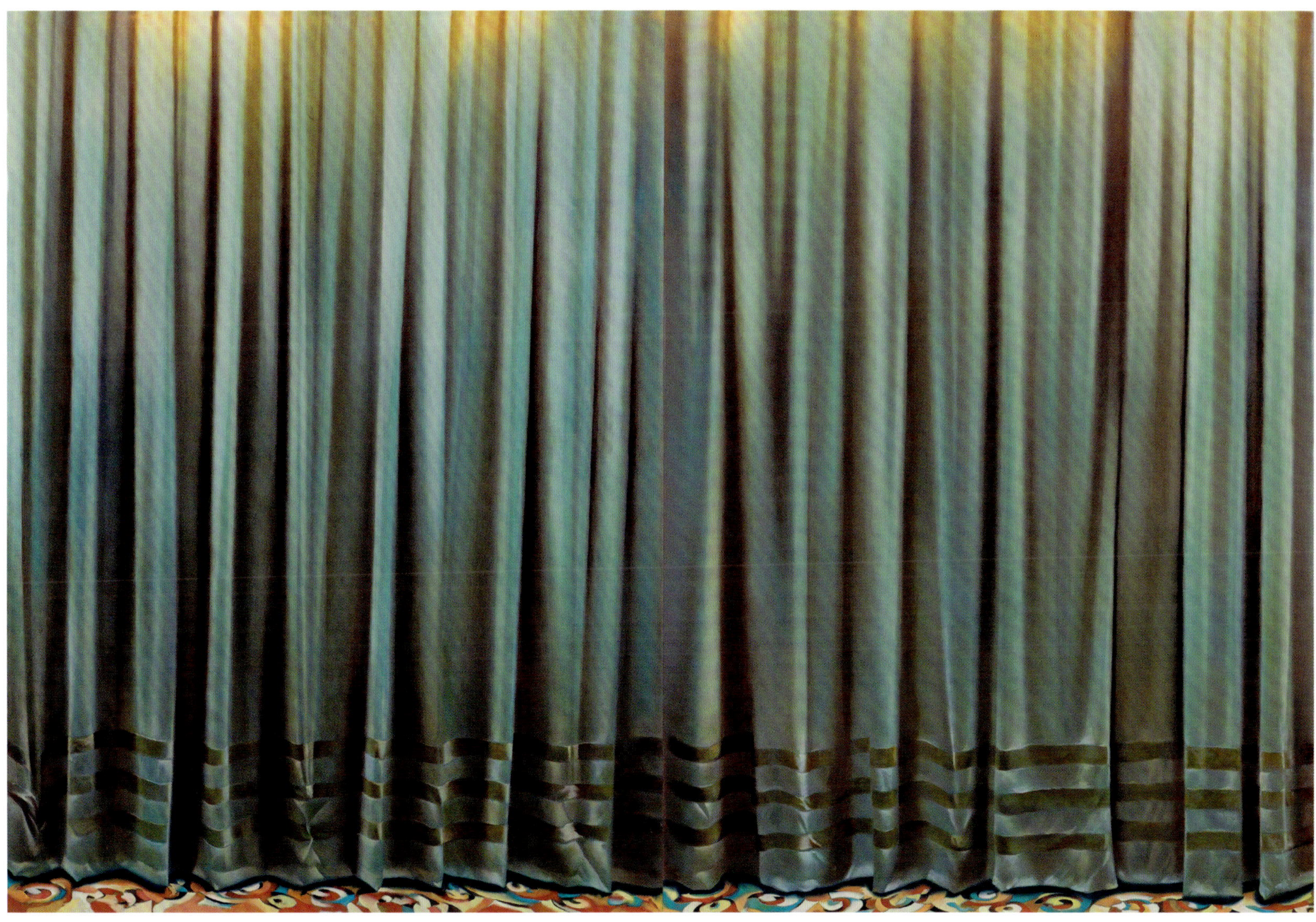

BE ALL, END ALL
2020, oil on canvas, diptych, 200 × 300 cm
(78 ¾ × 118 ⅛ in)

Louise Giovanelli, born 1993, London, UK.

Largely focusing on closely cropped images taken from film stills and historical works of art, Giovanelli's paintings are rooted in how we perceive texture, surface and atmosphere. After graduating from Manchester School of Art in 2015, Giovanelli studied with Amy Sillman (p.273) at Städelschule, Frankfurt, from 2018 to 2020. She often builds her compositions with washes of highly pigmented paint on bright white grounds (a technique central to the Renaissance and Flemish early modern paintings that Giovanelli admires). As each layer refracts the light, light itself becomes central to the painting, creating strikingly luminous surfaces that render the material qualities of her subject matter particularly intense. Focusing on materials and surfaces often associated with high cultural and monetary value – like shimmering silk, lustrous velvet and glimmering sequins – Giovanelli's paintings compel the viewer to consider how they relate to what they may often encounter but do not pause to reflect on. As with *Be all, end all*, a painting that forms part of a series of works on theatrical curtains, Giovanelli avoids presenting a clear narrative or message, creating an atmosphere of possibility, at once tense and sensuous.

GLUCK

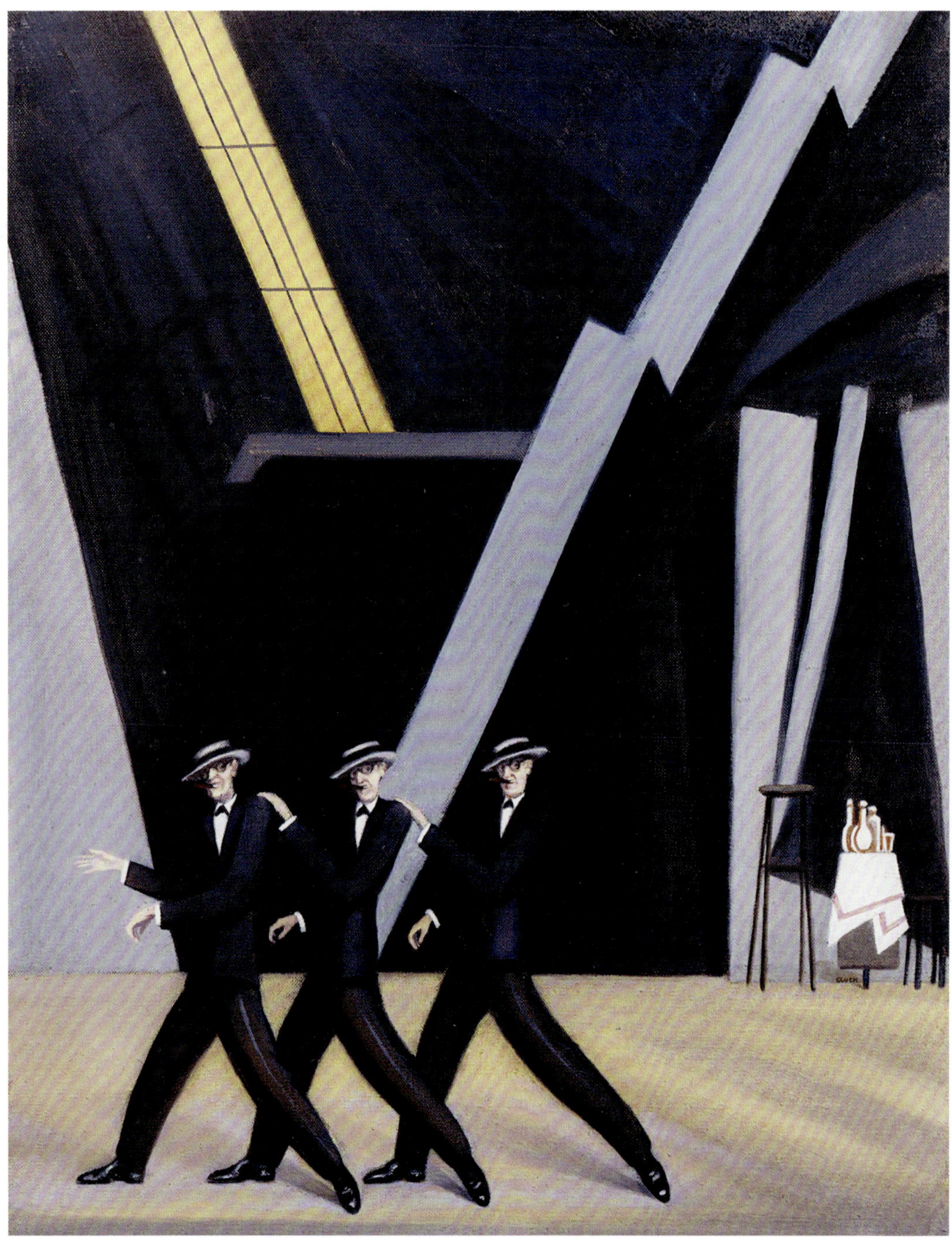

THE THREE NIFTY NATS
1926, oil on canvas, 49.5 × 39.5 cm (19 ½ × 15 ½ in)

Gluck, born 1895, London, UK. Died 1978, Steyning, West Sussex, UK.

Born Hannah Gluckstein, Gluck grew up in a wealthy Jewish family. A trailblazing gender nonconformist, Gluck rejected any forename or prefix – preferring the gender-neutral moniker by which she is now known – insisted on wearing men's clothes, smoked a pipe and cropped her hair short. She likewise rejected association with any named movement or style and only presented her work in solo exhibitions. After studying at St John's Wood School of Art in London, in 1916 Gluck moved to the Lamorna artist colony in Cornwall, where she would keep a studio throughout her life. Painted shortly after the 1925 'Art Deco' launch held in Paris, *The Three Nifty Nats* represents a stark contrast to the elaborate detail and curvaceous forms of the Art Nouveau works of the period. In this work, part of a series depicting C.B. Cochran's famous Trocadero cabaret *On with the Dance* (1925), Gluck presents a new mechanized vision in paint, embracing the energy and dynamism of modern technology with its machine-age streamlining and sleek geometrical composition. In line with the Art Deco aesthetic, Gluck was also streamlined in her approach to the sparing use of paint, the grain of canvas peeping through the minimal layers of pigment.

TANYA GOEL

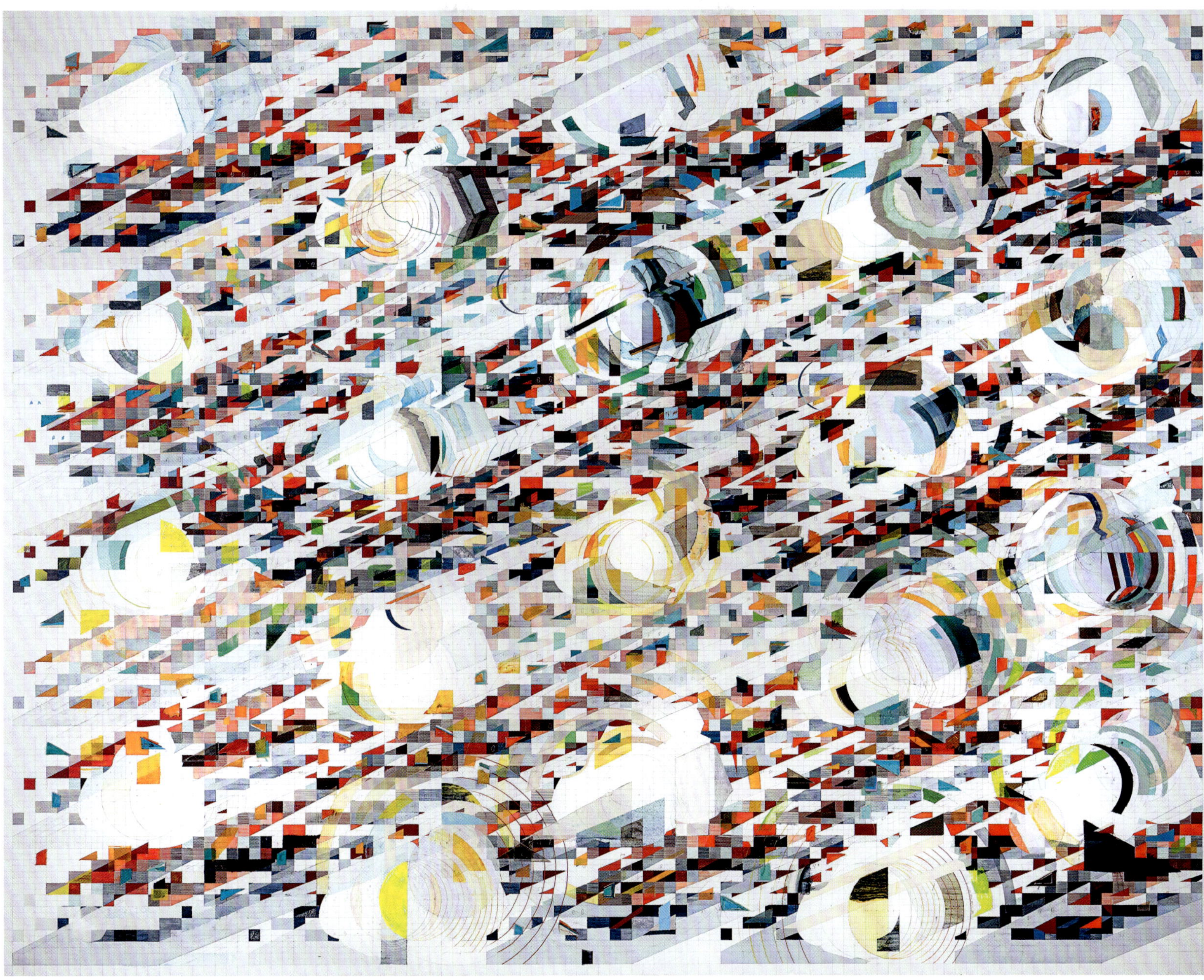

MECHANISMS 1
2019, mica, glass dust, acrylic and paper silk on canvas, 213 × 274 cm (84 × 108 in)

Tanya Goel, born 1985, New Delhi, India.

For Goel, painting is a way of visually recording the changes to the urban environment. Goel studied at the Faculty of Fine Arts at the Maharaja Sayajirao University of Baroda, India, and the School of the Art Institute of Chicago before receiving a master's degree from Yale School of Art in 2010. In 2012 the artist returned to her hometown of New Delhi after a decade living in different parts of the United States and was struck by the extent of architectural demolition occurring across the city. She began to visit construction sites, gathering samples of materials such as concrete, glass, soil and mica, which she ground up to use as pigment. The resulting paintings serve as a 'material archive' of the rapidly vanishing modernist structures built in Delhi in the mid-twentieth century – and a record of the failure of the utopian vision these buildings represented. Although abstract in composition, Goel's works, such as *Mechanisms 1*, have an underlying structure that references the well-ordered grids of modernist urban planning. Her canvases are planned in a similarly meticulous fashion, with the often brightly coloured pigments applied using a 'paint-by-letters' system; on close inspection, the artist's notes in pencil are visible on the surface of the painting.

NATALIA GONCHAROVA

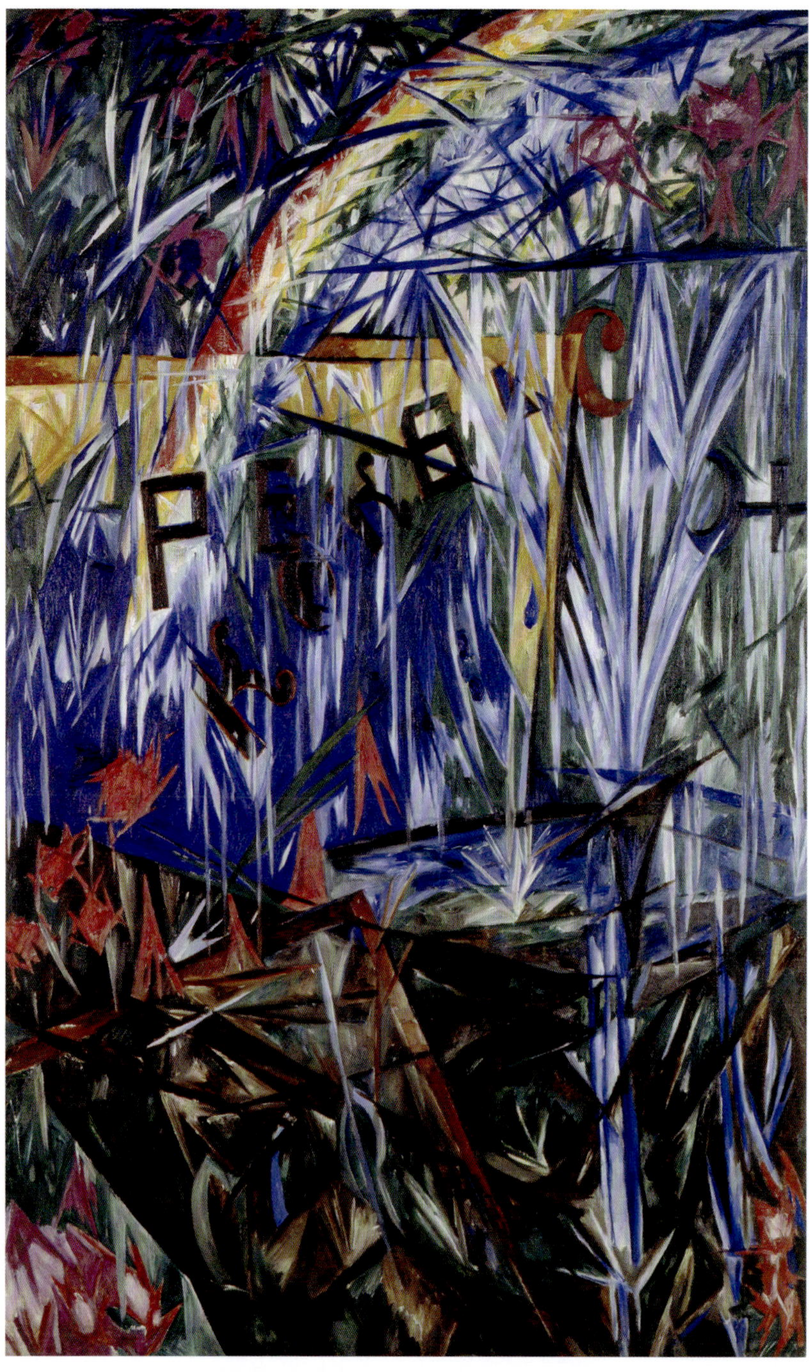

RAYONIST GARDEN: PARK
*c.*1912–13, oil on canvas, 140.6 × 87.3 cm (55 ⅜ × 34 ⅜ in), Israel Museum, Jerusalem

Natalia Goncharova, born 1881, Chernsky District, Tula Oblast, Russia. Died 1962, Paris, France.

Goncharova was a central figure in the development of Russian avant-garde art. Born in the Russian countryside, she moved to Moscow in 1892, and in 1901 began studies in sculpture at the Moscow School of Painting, Sculpture and Architecture, soon switching to painting. The following year, she withdrew from the school after a number of fellow students were expelled from the studio for emulating European modernist styles such as Impressionism and Fauvism. Goncharova was instrumental in the organization of several exhibitions that marked a departure from a European-influenced modernism, including 'Jack of Diamonds' (1910–11) and 'Donkey's Tail' (1912), which presented works embracing Russian folk art traditions. In 1913 she and her life partner, Mikhail Larionov (1881–1964), published the manifesto for Rayonism. One of Russia's first abstract art movements, it described itself as 'the true liberation of painting… a self-sufficient painting, with its own forms, colour and timbre'. *Rayonist Garden: Park* shows the typical shard-like rays of the style and represents a juxtaposition of life and death, with new green vegetation growing from old lifeless foliage.

BEATRIZ GONZÁLEZ

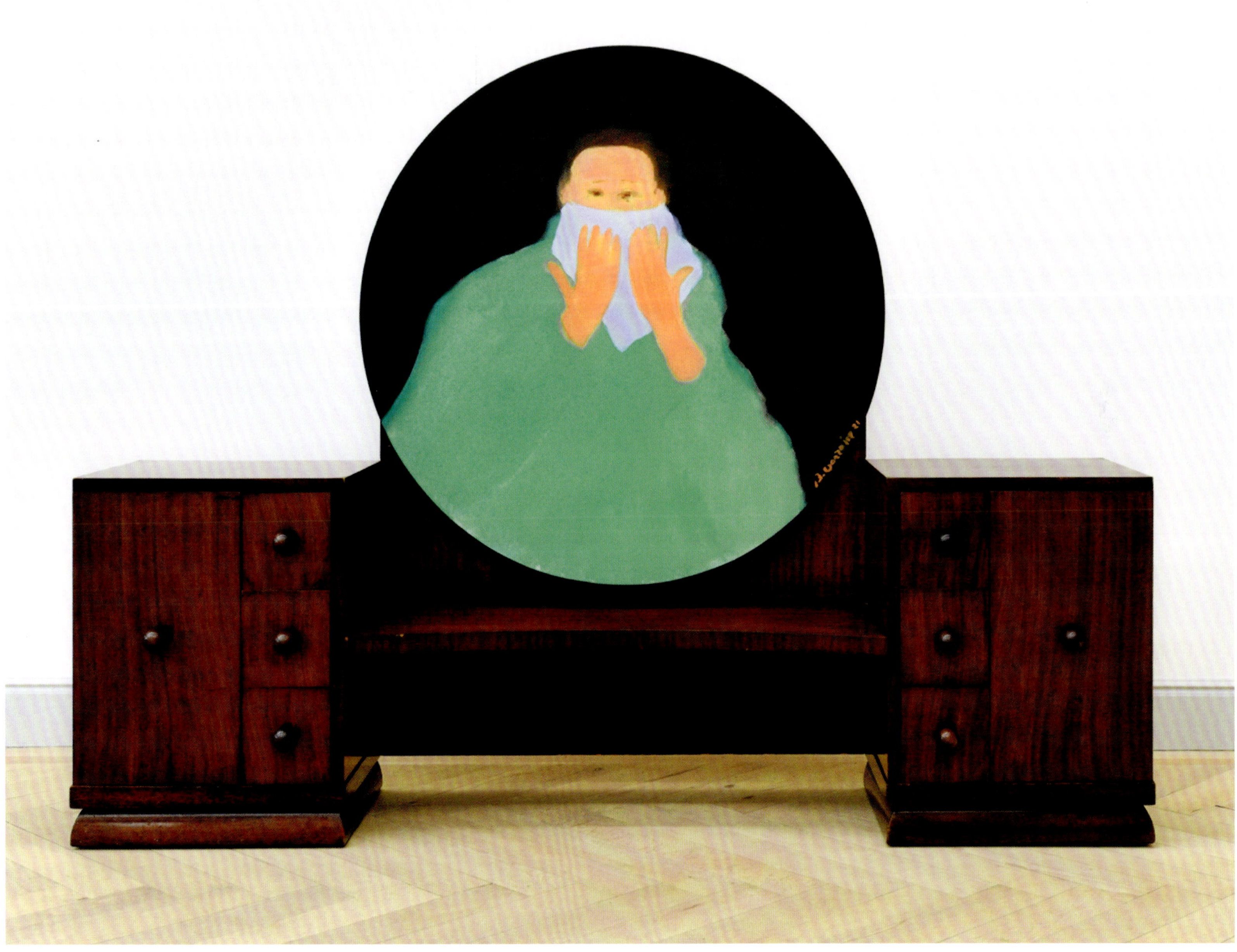

DUELO POR DESAPARECIDOS (MOURNING FOR THE MISSING)
2021, oil on canvas assembled in wooden furniture, painting: diam. 90 cm (35 ⅜ in), object: 126 × 169 × 38 cm (49 ⅝ × 66 ½ × 15 in)

Beatriz González, born 1932, Bucaramanga, Colombia.

One of Colombia's most celebrated artists, González emerged onto the country's art scene in the 1960s with a series inspired by Old Master paintings but soon began to make work appropriating imagery from magazines and newspapers, leading some to associate her with the Pop art movement. González grew up during La Violencia (The Violence), a ten-year period of intense political unrest in Colombian history from 1948 to 1958. These events, and the political unrest that followed, deeply influenced her practice, which consistently engages with pressing social issues in Colombian history. In the 1970s she began embedding her paintings into pieces of furniture – including beds, cribs and dressers culled from local markets. In this work, González replaces the mirror of an old-fashioned wooden bedroom dressing table with a tondo-shaped painting depicting a lone figure weeping into a handkerchief. The title refers to the enforced disappearances that have haunted Colombia over the past half-century; the work captures this tragic domestic reality, rendered in her characteristic informal style, full of empathy and humanity.

JENNA GRIBBON

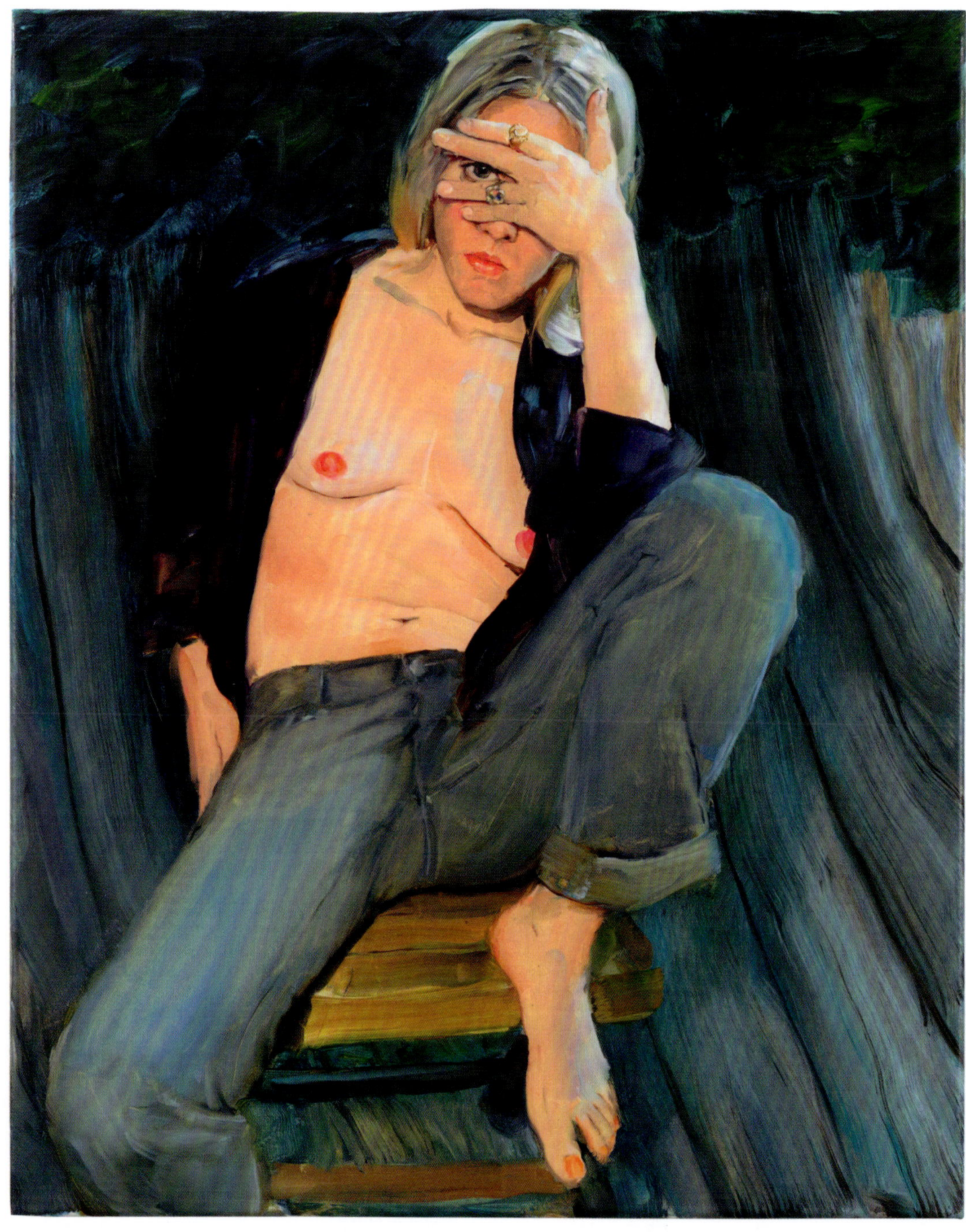

DECK PEEK
2021, oil on linen, 72 × 55.8 cm (28 × 22 in), private collection

Jenna Gribbon, born 1978, Knoxville, Tennessee, USA.

Gribbon's lush canvases offer intimate glimpses of a private world rendered in a fluid painterly style reminiscent at once of Alice Neel (p.219) and Jean-Honoré Fragonard (1732–1806). Raised in Tennessee, Gribbon attended college at the University of Georgia and then moved to New York, where she earned an MFA from Hunter College and, for a time, ran a salon-cum-studio space called the Oracle Club. Often Gribbon works from iPhone snapshots that allow her to capture fleeting moments and to emphasize her presence as a viewer and participant, her own limbs and hands sometimes straying into the frame. Gribbon often focuses her attention on her partner, Mackenzie Scott (a.k.a. Torres, a musician), seen in an infinite array of postures: in bed mid-coitus, clipping her toenails, flipping channels. The artist's friends and young son also make frequent appearances. In *Deck Peek* Gribbon depicts Scott covering her face with one hand, an eye peering through the gap between parted fingers. Though Scott is partly undressed, it is her face, not her body, that she obscures. Gribbon here makes visible both the discomfort and the eroticism of representation, an awareness shared by artist and sitter.

KATHARINA GROSSE

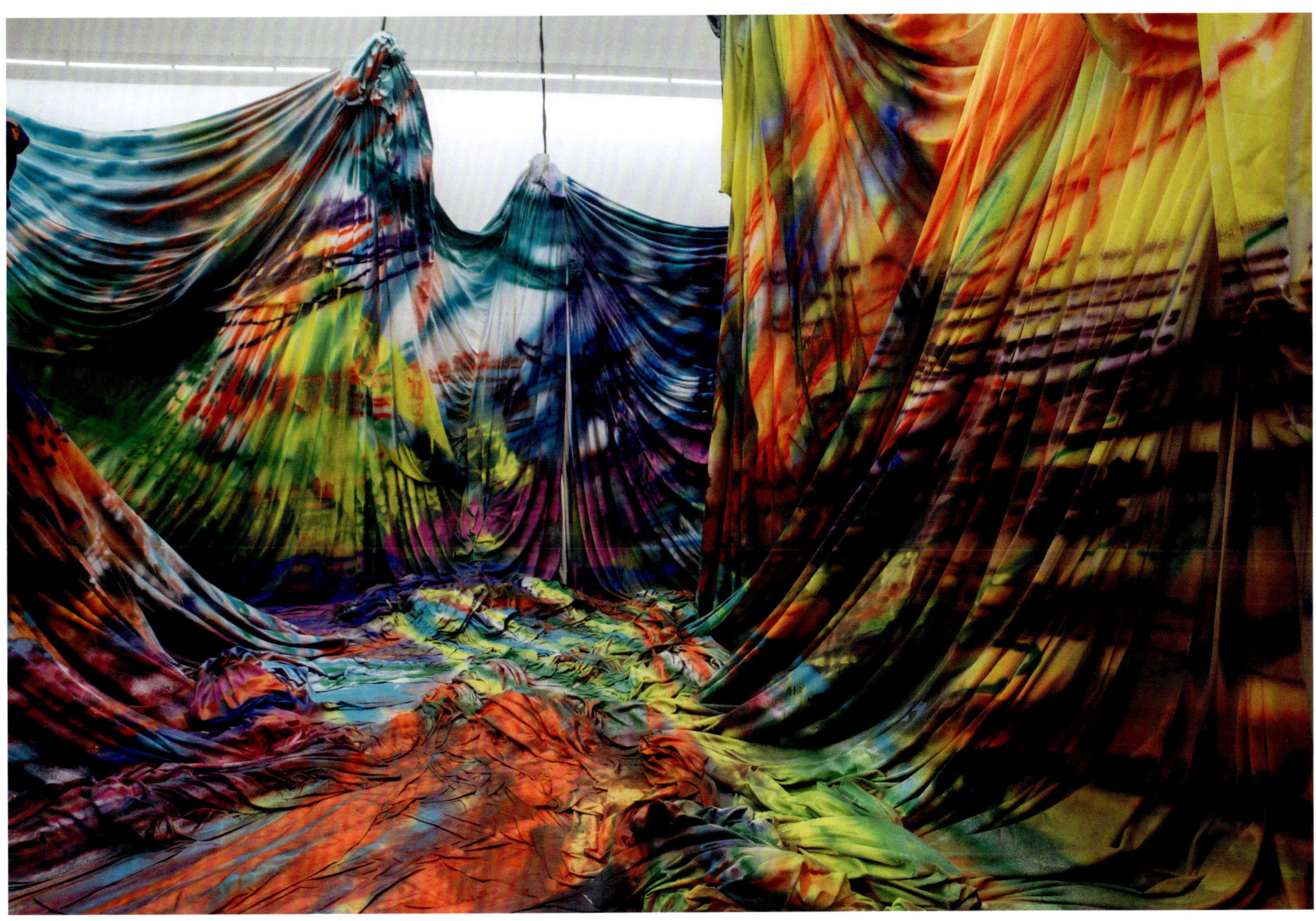

IS IT YOU?
2020, acrylic on fabric, 600 × 1,350 × 1,250 cm (236 ¼ × 531 ½ × 492 in), Baltimore Museum of Art, USA

Katharina Grosse, born 1961, Freiburg im Breisgau, Germany.

Grosse's paintings sweep across walls, floors, ceilings, objects and even entire buildings and landscapes. Falling within the field of expanded painting, her sprawling, site-specific works fill spaces both indoors and outdoors with swathes of vibrant abstract colour, creating immersive experiences into which the viewer can step. Growing up in rural south Germany, Grosse moved north to study at the Kunstakademie Münster and Kunstakademie Düsseldorf, where she was also a professor from 2010 to 2018. Her early abstract canvases featuring vertical transparent brushstrokes gave way in the late 1990s to works painted directly onto gallery architecture using an industrial spray gun, a method that distances the painting from the artist's hand and connects her work to street art and mural painting. Grosse sometimes uses large plastic and metal armatures as supports, or paints onto draped fabric. For the immersive painting *Is It You?*, installed at the Baltimore Museum of Art, Grosse hung enormous sheets of cloth from the gallery's ceiling, which she then spray-painted, enveloping viewers in a disorienting, undulating environment of flowing colour and form.

JENNIFER GUIDI

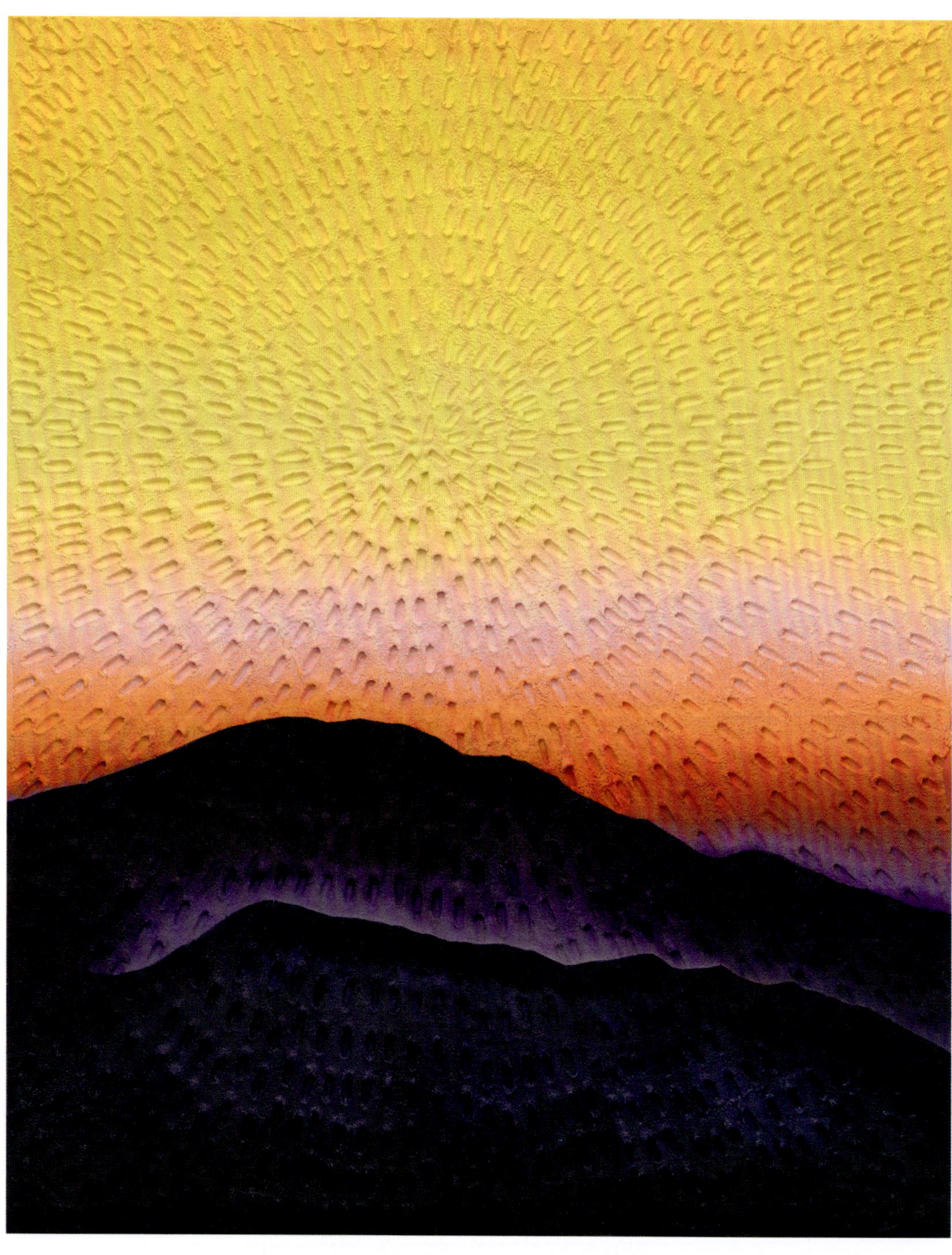

MAJESTIC MOUNTAINS (PAINTED YELLOW SAND SF #1H, YELLOW-PINK-LIGHT ORANGE-DARK ORANGE-PURPLE SKY, BLACK-PURPLE MOUNTAIN, NATURAL GROUND)
2021, sand, acrylic and oil on linen, 152.4 × 101.6 cm (60 × 48 in)

Jennifer Guidi, born 1972, Redondo Beach, California, USA.

The city of Los Angeles, where Guidi relocated to after receiving her MFA from the School of the Art Institute of Chicago in 1998, has profoundly influenced her radiant paintings, which are energized by the city's light, pulsating urbanity and striking natural features. While her early compositions were based on photographs of Los Angeles neighbourhoods, domestic interiors and portraits of friends and family, in the early 2010s Guidi began pursuing a more abstracted mode as she introduced layers of sand to her compositions, which she indents with uniform marks to form radial, mandala-like patterns. Light and colour are integral to these large-scale, painstakingly rendered paintings, which embrace the pared-down language of Minimalism while evoking the art and culture of ancient civilizations. Stemming from her interest in Eastern spirituality, Guidi considers each work an act of meditation, visually manifesting the sensory experience of being in nature. Some are purely abstract, employing elemental shapes such as circles and triangles, while others refer directly to natural forms, such as the moon, snakes or landscapes, as in this glowing mountain sunrise with its gradated hues and richly textured surface evoking a sunburst.

HULDA GUZMÁN

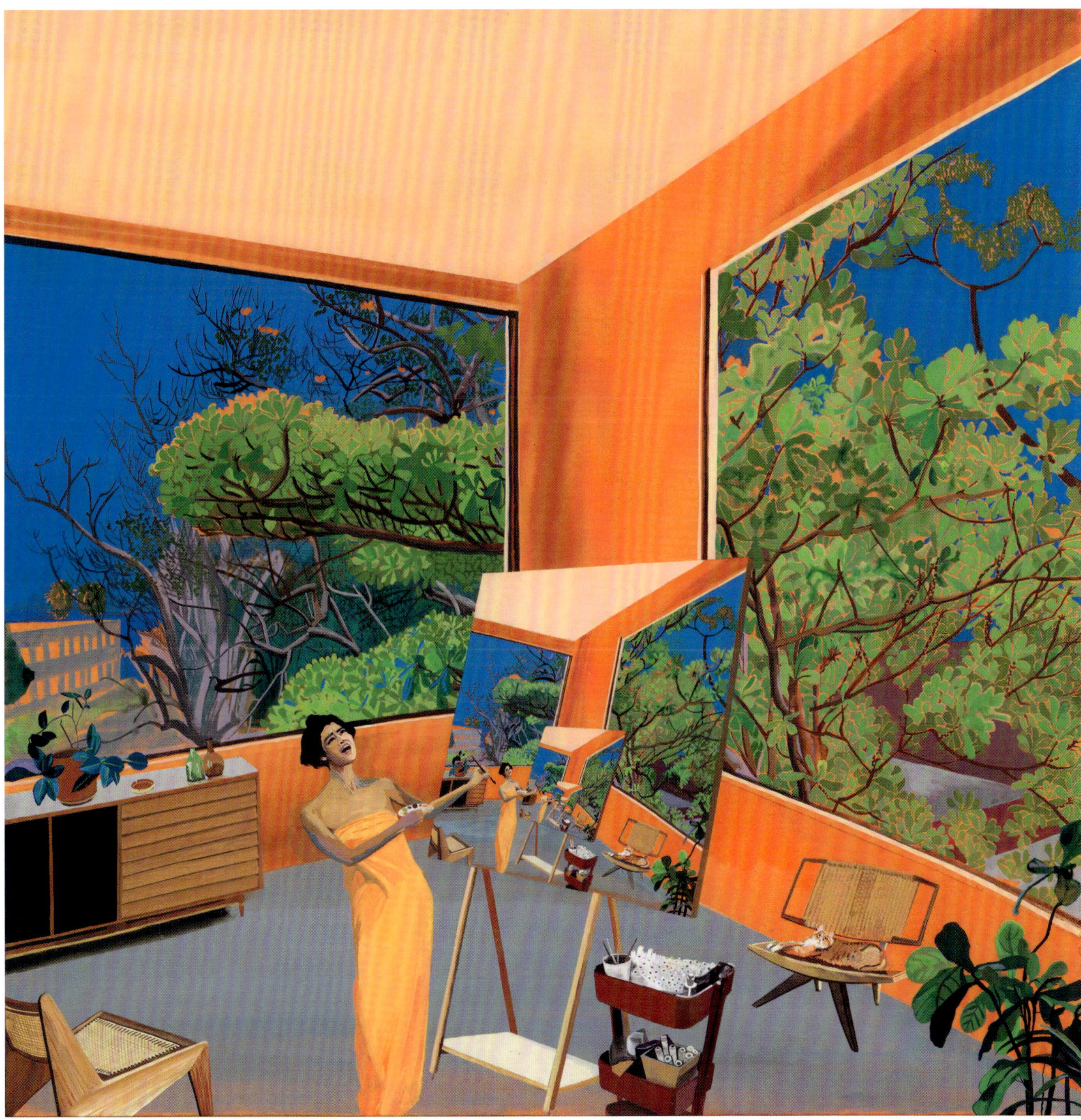

PINTANDO LA ALMENDRA (PAINTING THE TROPICAL ALMOND TREE)
2020, acrylic gouache on linen in artist's frame (not pictured), 114.3 × 114.3 cm (45 × 45 in), San Francisco Museum of Modern Art, USA

Hulda Guzmán, born 1984, Santo Domingo, Dominican Republic.

After attending Altos de Chavón School of Design in the Dominican Republic and Parsons School of Design in New York, Guzmán studied photography and mural painting in Mexico City before returning to the Dominican Republic, where she lives and works. With formal echoes of the work of Henri Rousseau (1844–1910) and Leonora Carrington (p.72), Guzmán's magical realist compositions explore Caribbean folk traditions and human relationships to physical and metaphysical environments. Biography and fantasy frequently commingle in her work: bright interiors, often the artist's home or studio accessorized with modernist furniture, become theatre sets engulfing small humans, cats, imaginary creatures and tropical flora, all spied in the middle of unknowable rituals. 'These paintings… question our own nature as creators of our "reality" and examine the manifested world in relation to and reflection of the inner world,' Guzmán informed *Garage Magazine* in 2020. This sentiment can be evidenced in this work, where the stability of perspective is questioned not just by the vertiginous walls of the artist's studio but also by her use of the 'looped' composition known as the Droste effect – a form of *mise en abyme* and a technique popular with the Surrealists.

IKE GYOKURAN

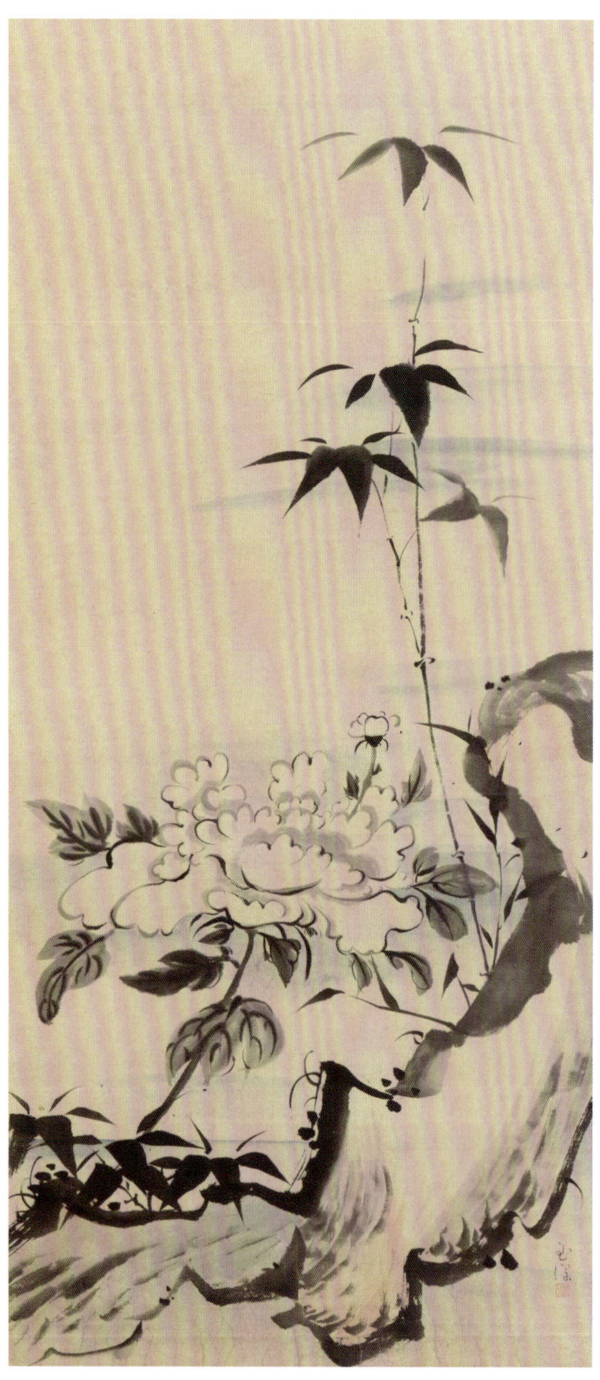

PEONY AND BAMBOO
*c.*1768, hanging scroll, ink and colour on paper, 93 × 41.7 cm (36 ⅝ × 16 ⅜ in), Metropolitan Museum of Art, New York, USA

Ike Gyokuran, born 1727, Kyoto, Japan. Died 1784, Kyoto.

Finding fame at a time when it was rare for Japanese women to become painters, Gyokuran became a revered figure in Japanese art history. She began painting at an early age, receiving tuition from the esteemed artist Yanagisawa Kien (1704–58), who was a regular at her mother's teahouse and likely introduced her to her husband, painter and calligrapher Ike Taiga (1723–76). Unusually for the time, the couple treated one another as equals, sharing a studio and mutually influencing each other. She introduced him to classical Japanese poetry, and he taught her *bunjinga*, a pen-and-ink painting style derived from Chinese art that sought to capture the essence of nature. Although many proponents of *bunjinga* shunned commercialism, Gyokuran painted folding screens, doors, scrolls and fans. She also painted small scenes, sometimes incorporating her own calligraphic poems. *Peony and Bamboo* shows her elegant and restrained graphic style: contrasting tonalities of ink delineate the natural forms with a combination of broad strokes and fine lines, while pale blue washes provide contrast and suggest depth.

MAGGI HAMBLING

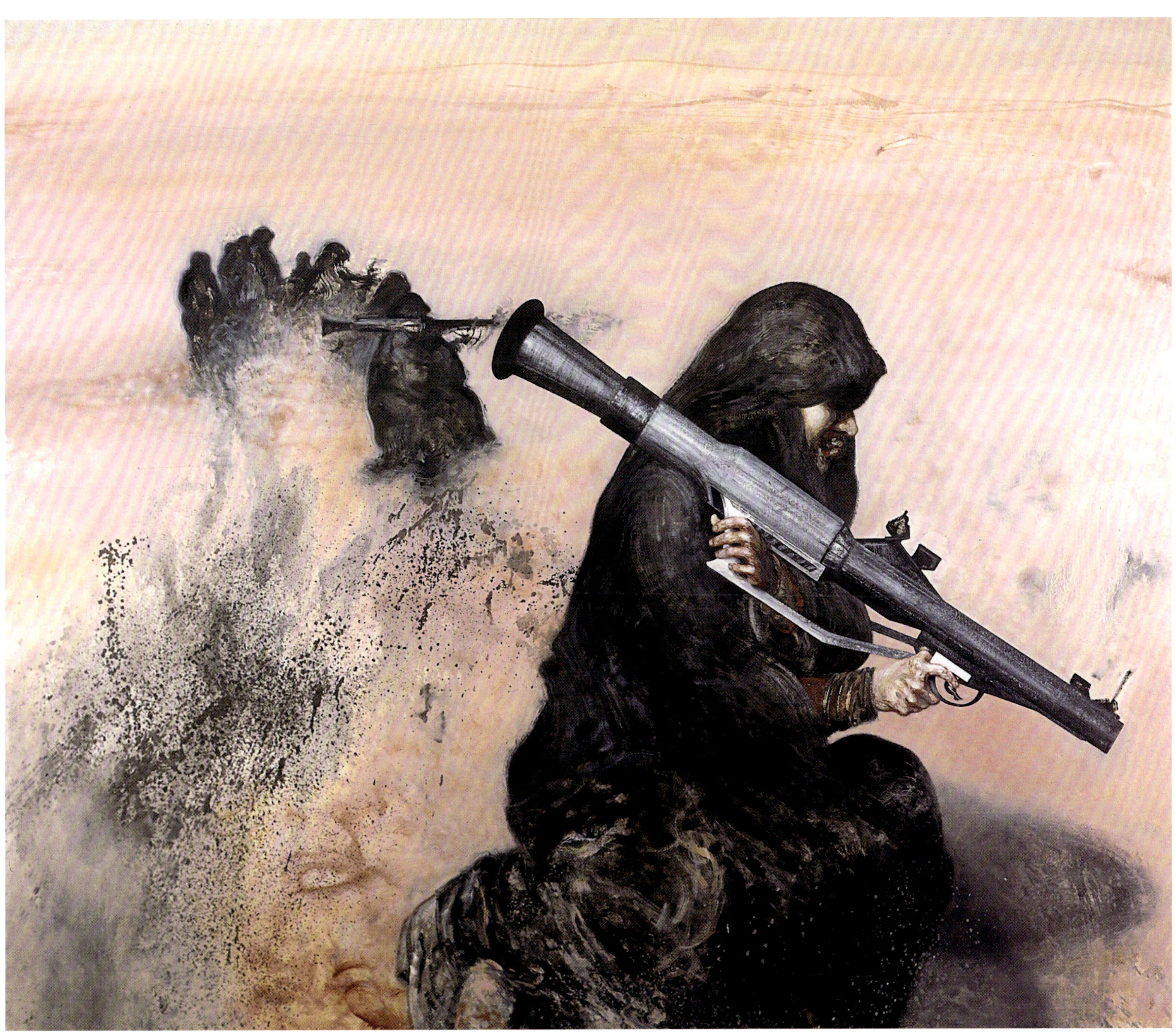

GULF WOMEN PREPARE FOR WAR
1986, oil on canvas, 122 × 145 cm (48 × 57 ⅛ in), New Hall Art Collection, Murray Edwards College, University of Cambridge, UK

Maggi Hambling, born 1945, Sudbury, Suffolk, UK.

Hambling is recognized for her piercing portraits – often of the dead and dying – as much as she is for her evocative landscapes, frothy seas and public sculptures. With gestural brushwork she creates intense images that bespeak her rebellious character. Outspoken and often goading controversy with her confrontational works, Hambling was honoured with a CBE in 2010 and was the first artist-in-residence at London's National Gallery in 1980. It was here, looking at Édouard Manet's *Execution of Emperor Maximilian of Mexico* (*c.* 1867–8), that she developed the central figure in this painting. Based on a newspaper photograph documenting preparations for the Iran–Iraq War (1980–8), Hambling modifies Manet's solider into an image of female strength enveloped in a rose-pink desert. In keeping with what critic John Berger described as her 'unflinching' approach, the image of a woman wearing a hijab and operating a rocket launcher is a striking depiction that subverts more common depictions of women – and Muslim women in particular – in art history and popular culture.

HARMONY HAMMOND

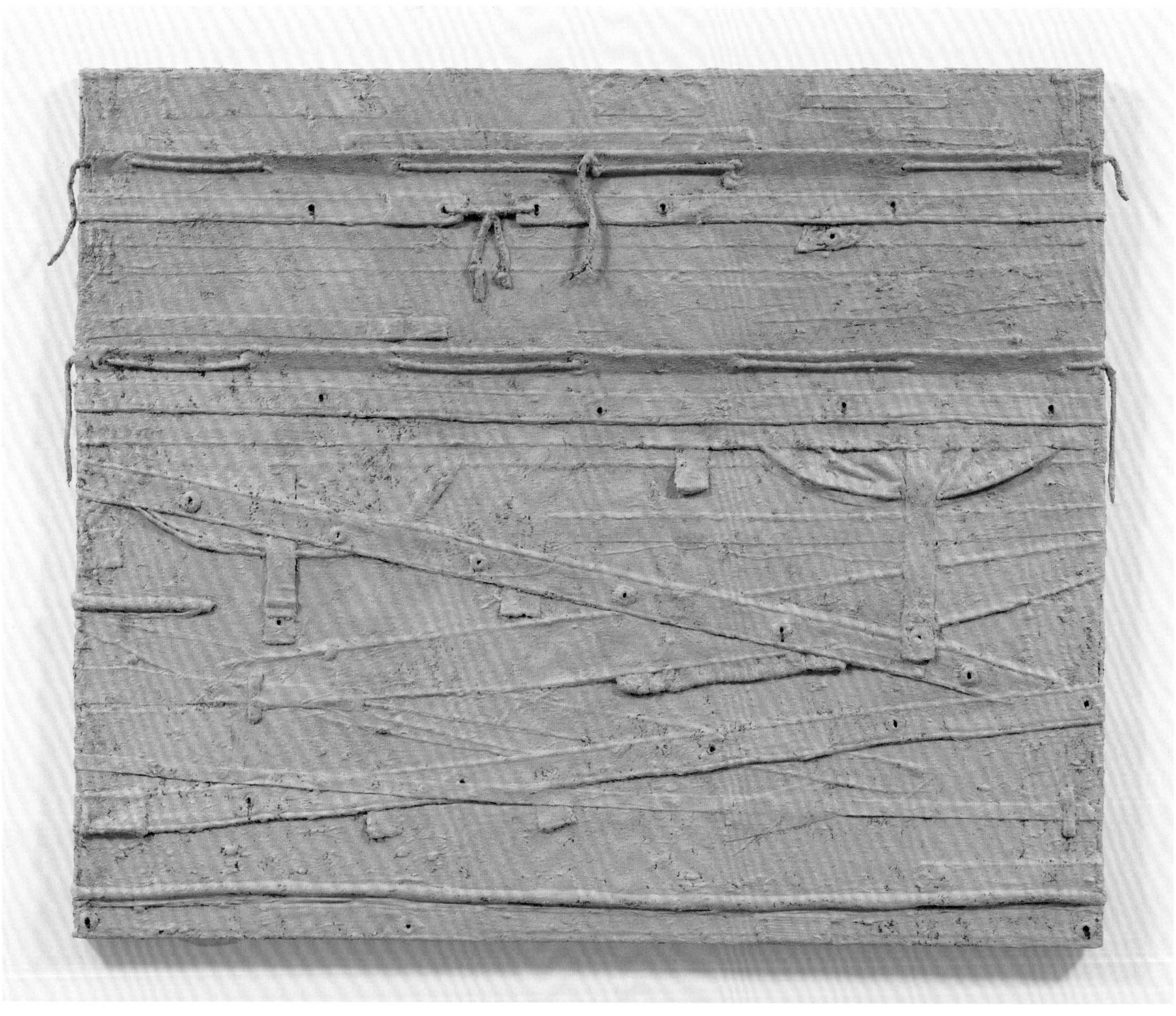

FRAGGLE
2014, oil and mixed media on canvas,
123.2 × 148.6 cm (48½ × 58½ in)

Harmony Hammond, born 1944, Chicago, USA.

A stalwart supporter of women's empowerment, Hammond is an activist, curator, writer and educator alongside her visual art practice. A co-founder of A.I.R. Gallery (see p.279), in 1976 she established the Heresies Collective with nineteen other women including Joyce Kozloff (p.164), Pat Steir (p.284) and critic Lucy Lippard. In 1978, she curated the ground-breaking 'A Lesbian Show' at the art space 112 Greene Street, the first exhibition to overtly showcase gay women artists, and in 2000, published the survey book *Lesbian Art in America: A Contemporary History*. Since 1984, Hammond has been based in New Mexico. Even without direct political messages, her Post-Minimalist abstract paintings reflect a feminist perspective through her incorporation of materials and processes that she described in a 2019 interview with *Elephant* magazine as being 'associated with women's traditional arts and the creative practices of non-Western cultures… thereby bringing women's textile arts into the modernist painting field'. *Fraggle* comprises scraps of clothing – laces, garters, bound strips of fabric – that Hammond monochromatically covers in paint. This material composite amassed on the surface expands the work beyond the conventional two-dimensional boundaries of painting.

GRACE HARTIGAN

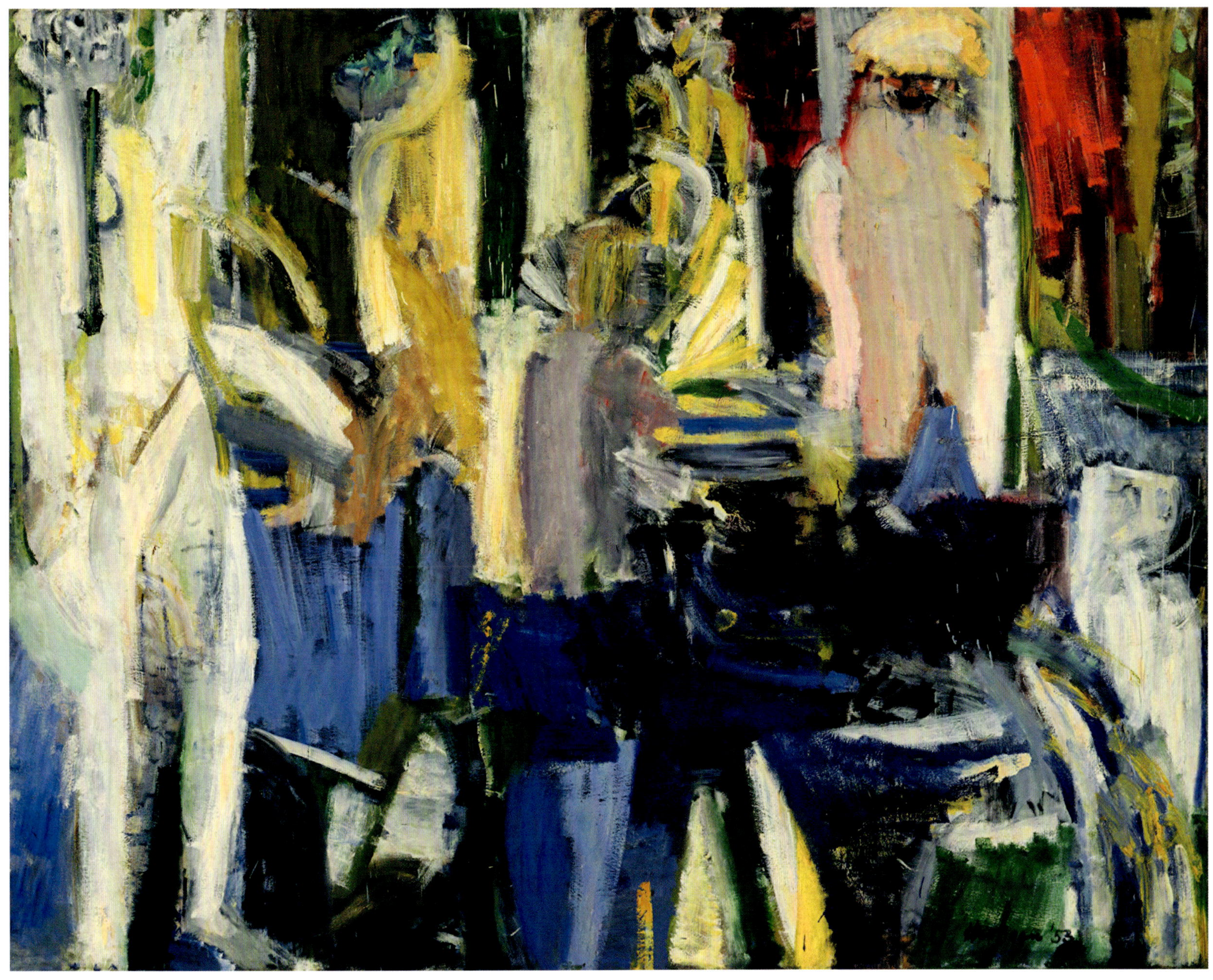

RIVER BATHERS
1953, oil on canvas, 176.2 × 225.5 cm (69 3/8 × 88 3/4 in), Museum of Modern Art, New York, USA

Grace Hartigan, born 1922, Newark, New Jersey, USA. Died 2008, Baltimore, USA.

A second-generation Abstract Expressionist, Hartigan combined gestural abstraction with art-historical and popular imagery. Hartigan's vast field of references included the compositions of Francisco Goya (1746–1828) and Diego Velázquez (1599–1660), Lower East Side bridal shops, colouring books and images of film stars, leading some to identify her work as anticipating the Pop art movement. In a 1956 artist statement, Hartigan distilled her artistic vision: 'I have found my "subject"… It concerns that which is vulgar and vital in American modern life.' Hartigan rose to swift prominence after moving to New York in 1945. There, she fell under the influence of painters like Jackson Pollock (1912–56) and Lee Krasner (p.165), and Willem (1904–97) and Elaine de Kooning (p.89). Exhibiting under the name George Hartigan until the mid-1950s, she eclipsed many of her female peers in the male-dominated Abstract Expressionist scene. *River Bathers*, an early large-scale slashing abstraction inspired by Henri Matisse's *Bathers by a River* (1916–17), was acquired by New York's Museum of Modern Art and shown in its twenty-fifth anniversary exhibition in 1954. In 1960 Hartigan moved to Baltimore, where she worked as an educator from 1965 until her death.

MARY HEILMANN

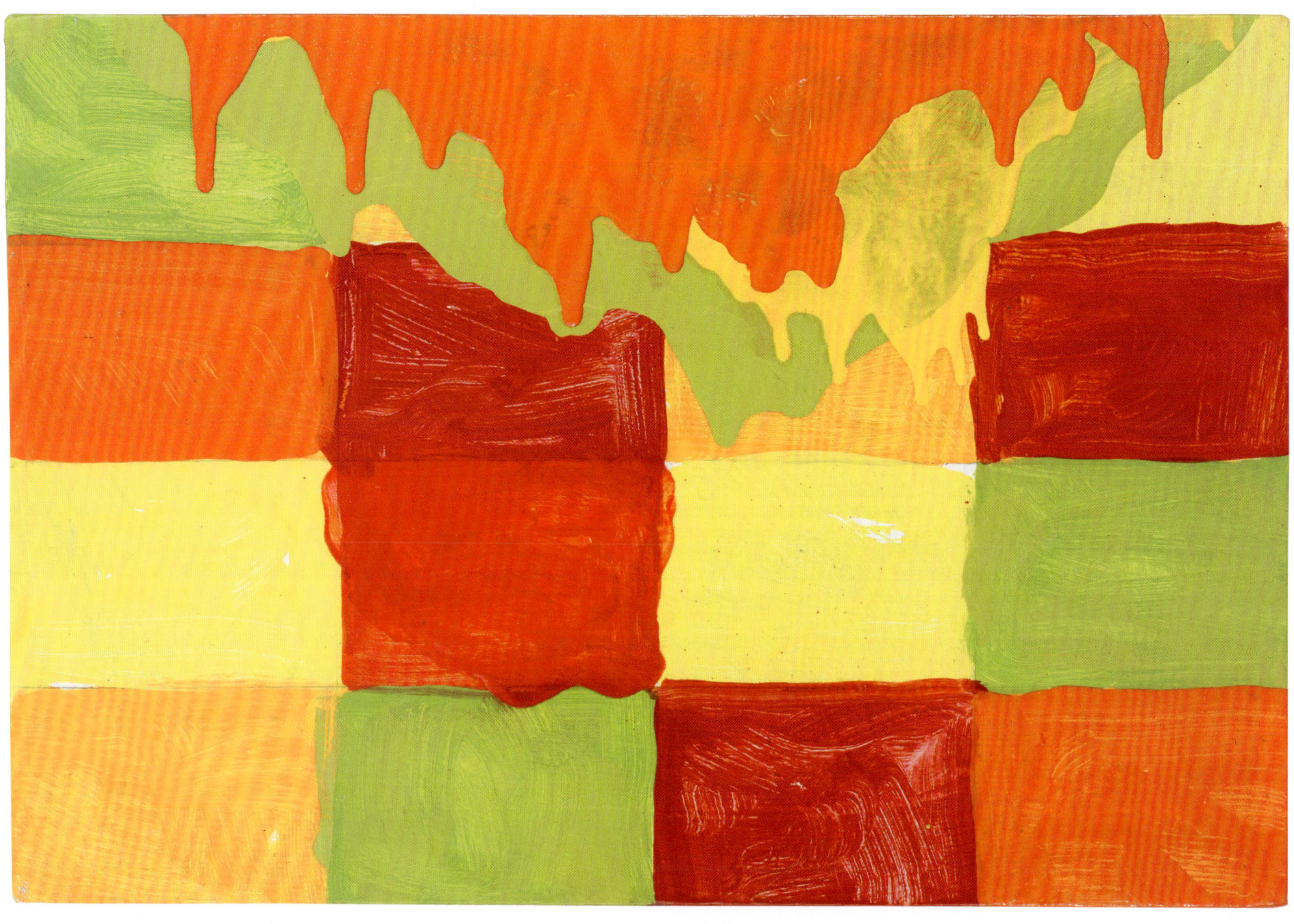

HAWAIIAN PLANET STUDY
2008, oil on canvas, 30.5 × 45.7 cm (12 × 18 in)

Mary Heilmann, born 1940, San Francisco, USA.

Heilmann's exuberant and tactile canvases, ceramics, works on paper and furniture incite sensorial responses from the viewer that are simultaneously meditative and immediate. Originally a student of literature and poetry, followed by training as a ceramicist and sculptor at the University of California at Berkeley, Heilmann began to identify strongly as a painter when she relocated to New York in 1968. Since the 1970s, she has been known for marrying taut geometric fields with vibrant gestural applications of paint, influenced by 1960s counterculture as well as the Minimalist art movement and the Beat Generation's celebration of nonconformity and spontaneous creativity. Heilmann's works are visual retellings of her life's ongoing journeys and poignant memories, evoking colourful vistas like the California coast, the eastern shores of Long Island, New York, and Hawaii's north shores. *Hawaiian Planet Study* is a jewel-toned chequerboard of red, green, orange and yellow rectangles; the top row of blocks has disintegrated into drips of paint that threaten to dissolve the boxes below. Unlike the grids seen in classic Minimalism, Heilmann's shapes are not straight and rigid, instead wavering into loose, playful and imperfect forms.

CATHARINA VAN HEMESSEN

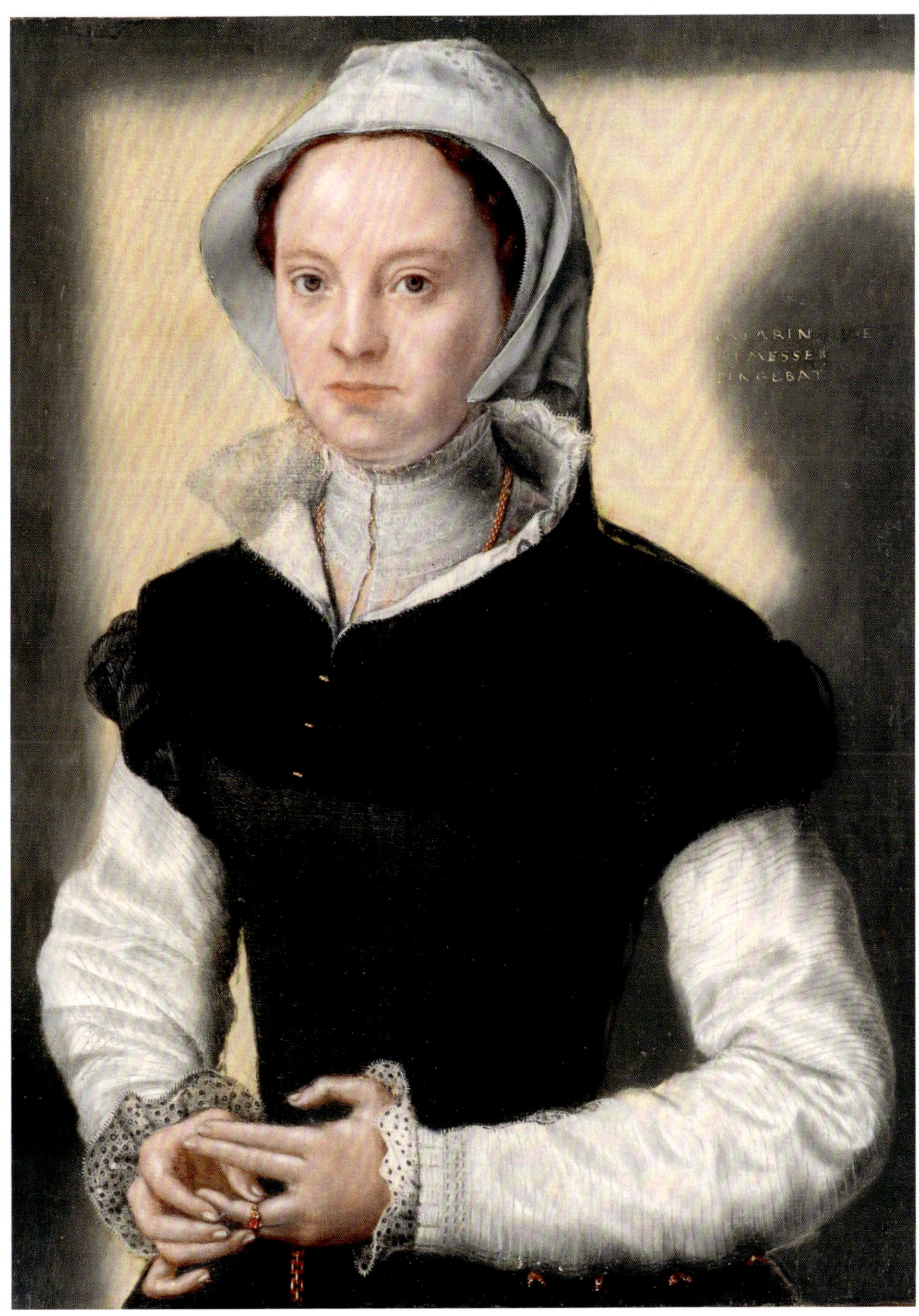

LADY IN 16TH CENTURY COSTUME
1548–9, oil on panel, 40.9 × 30.1 cm
(16 ⅛ × 11 ⅞ in), Bowes Museum, Barnard Castle, County Durham, UK

Catharina van Hemessen, born 1528, Antwerp, Belgium. Died *c.*1588, probably Antwerp.

A painter of the Flemish Renaissance, van Hemessen trained under her father, a successful genre painter, who encouraged his daughter to pursue a career as a portraitist. She became successful in her own right, mostly producing commissioned portraits of wealthy women; she was also supported by a female patron, Maria of Austria. Van Hemessen is best known for a remarkable 1548 self-portrait portraying herself seated at her easel, thought to be the first self-portrait of an artist at work in this way. *Lady in 16th Century Costume* was likely completed soon after: small in scale, and lush in details, the portrait is equally arresting in the unusually direct and exacting gaze of the female subject; it seems to capture an intimate moment of understanding and mutual recognition between artist and sitter, and is thus an early example of how women saw each other, beyond the male gaze. The subject plays with a ring on her wedding finger – a gesture that is both vulnerable and evocative. This portrait is thought to be one of the last works van Hemessen completed – conforming to the social expectations of the period, she seems to have ceased working after her marriage in 1554.

CARMEN HERRERA

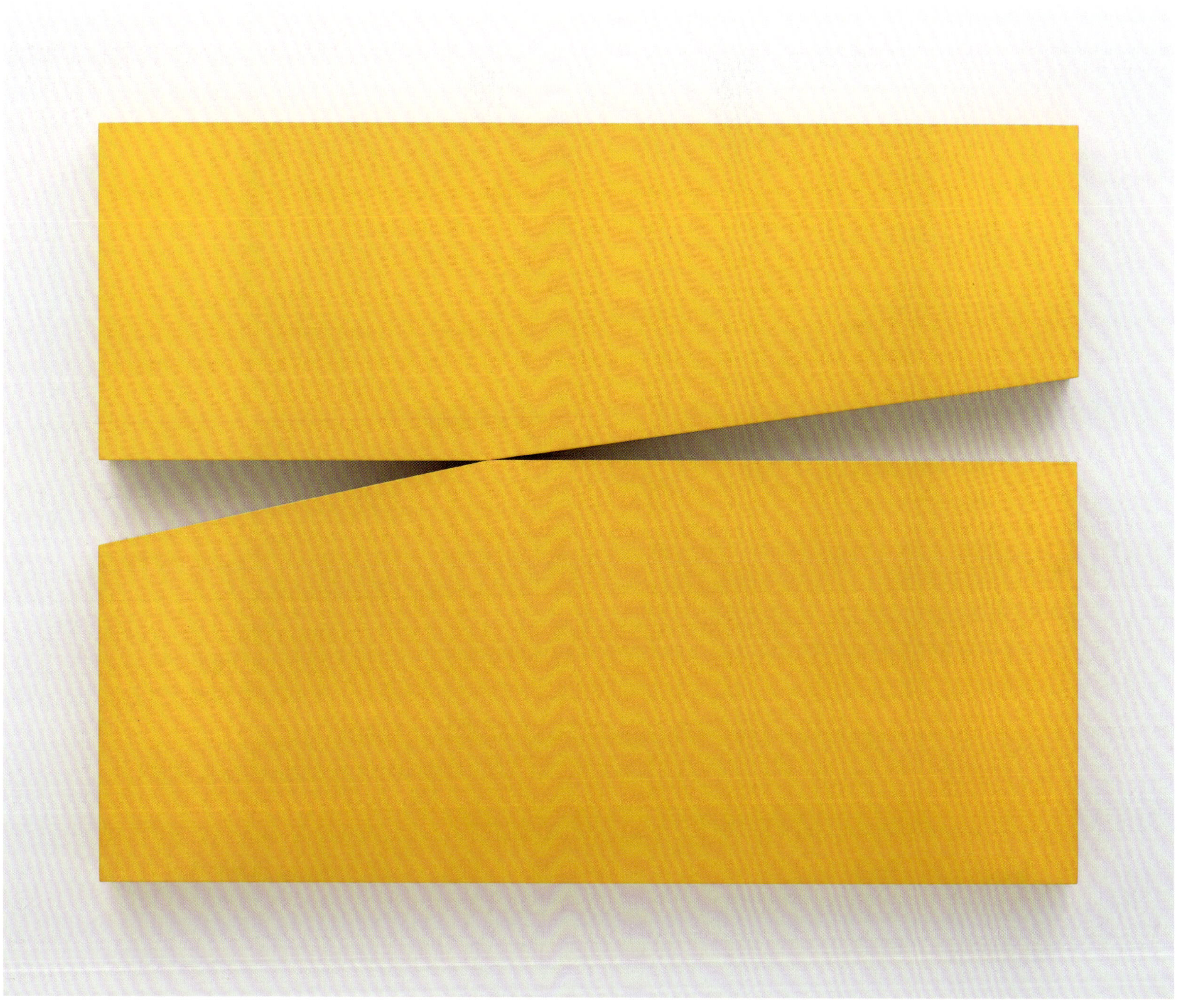

AMARILLO "UNO"
1971, acrylic on wood, 114.3 × 152.4 × 7.6 cm
(45 × 60 × 3 in)

Carmen Herrera, born 1915, Havana, Cuba.
Died 2022, New York, USA.

A student of architecture in her native Havana, Herrera's background informed her hard-edged, geometric abstract paintings, executed with exacting precision and seamless application of colour. Though she participated in salons in post-war Paris and was close friends with Abstract Expressionist painters in New York in the 1950s, it was not until 2004, at the age of eighty-nine, that she sold her first work at a commercial gallery. Herrera's 'Estructuras' ('Structures') series, begun in the early 1970s, marked a pivotal moment in her practice, when she extended her geometric drawings into wall-relief paintings. Herrera envisioned the wall surrounding her monochromatic paintings to be an integral component of the resulting work, the architectonic compositions interacting with the negative space of the white walls. Herrera's emphasis on line and pattern as a means to generate three-dimensional space anticipated the Op art movement, and prefigured works by Ellsworth Kelly (1923–2015) and Frank Stella (b. 1936). *Amarillo "Uno"* features two pieces of yellow-painted plywood that converge at a sharp angle and create a sense of tension. In 2016, a thirty-year retrospective at the Whitney Museum of American Art in New York helped to bring about an international reckoning with Herrera's overlooked oeuvre.

LUBAINA HIMID

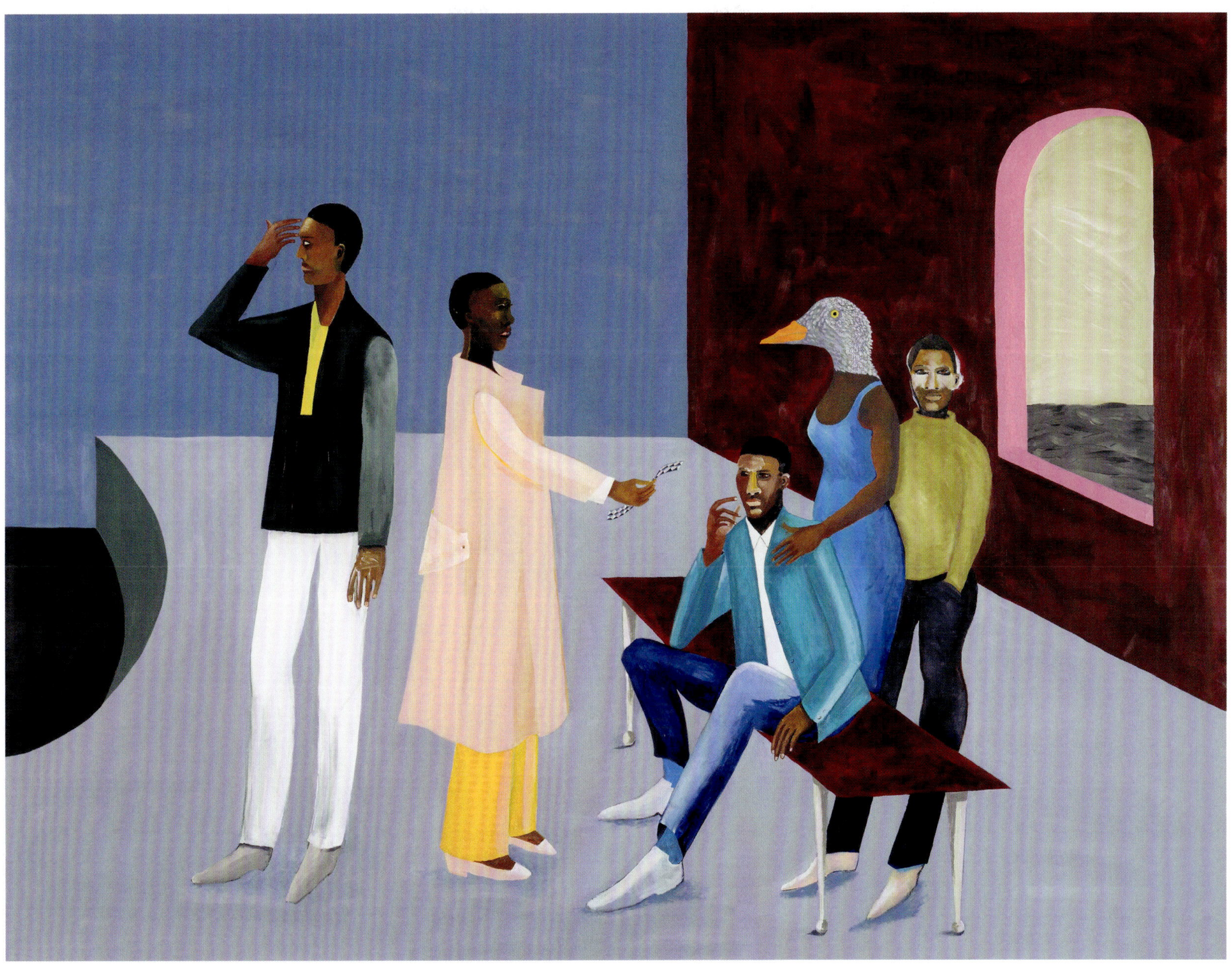

LE RODEUR: THE EXCHANGE
2016, acrylic on canvas, 183 × 244 cm (72 × 96 in)

Lubaina Himid, born 1954, Zanzibar, Tanzania.

Originally trained as a theatre designer, Himid's painting has a strong basis in scenography and narrative, with painted wooden cut-out figures a staple of her practice alongside scenes rendered in acrylic on canvas, as exemplified here. Having moved to the UK as a young child, Himid had a leading role in the British Black Arts Movement of the 1980s, both as artist and curator, which galvanized her interest in invisibility and loss within African diasporic history. Himid's 'Le Rodeur' series (2016–17) is titled after an illegal French slave ship, in which an outbreak of ophthalmia (an eye condition causing blindness) in 1819 spread among the 162 captured Africans aboard, with 36 eventually cast overboard. Speaking about this series in *History Today* in 2017, Himid said that she was 'struck by the horror of the incident but also by the dread of losing sight, especially as a visual artist'. She also explained that rather than represent the event overtly, she preferred to depict its themes of total horror and endless hauntings as narratives of their own.

LOIE HOLLOWELL

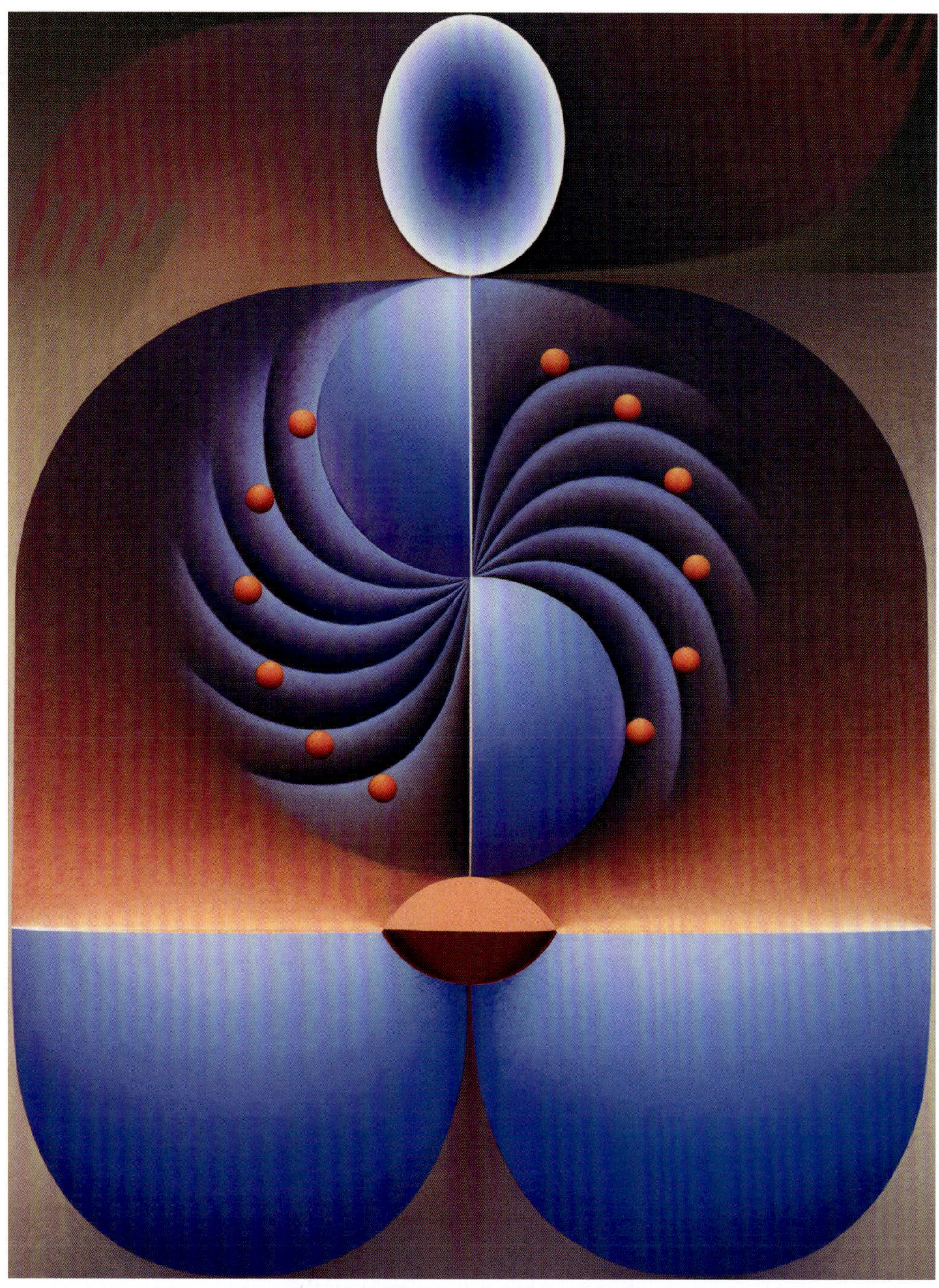

BOOB WHEEL
2019, oil paint, acrylic medium and high-density foam on linen mounted on panel, 183.5 × 137.5 × 8.9 cm (72 ¼ × 54 ⅛ × 3 ½ in)

Loie Hollowell, born 1983, Woodland, California, USA.

Hollowell's autobiographical paintings return to timeless themes of sexuality, the female body, pregnancy and birth. With their voluminous, sensual symmetry and flawless, illusory gradients, the artist's paintings recall the works of the Southern California Light and Space movement of the 1960s and 1970s, as well as feminist artists Judy Chicago (p.77) and Georgia O'Keeffe (p.227). Her works often incorporate timeless iconographic symbols such as mandorlas and lingams, curvilinear shapes that recall forms inherent both in female bodies and in nature. Hollowell's paintings are the result of an idiosyncratic process: taking a sculptural approach to reflect the corporeality of her subject matter, she adheres pieces of CNC-milled high-density foam onto panels, sealed with coats of gel medium before applying oil paint to the bas-relief surface. The resulting works play with the viewer's perception of dimensions and space. *Boob Wheel* was among a body of nine large-scale abstract works created in 2019, inspired by the physical changes the artist went through during pregnancy and early motherhood. The radiating, organic forms, along with the light that seems to emanate from the painting's surface, appear both rooted in the body and evocative of an ancient spirituality.

SHIRAZEH HOUSHIARY

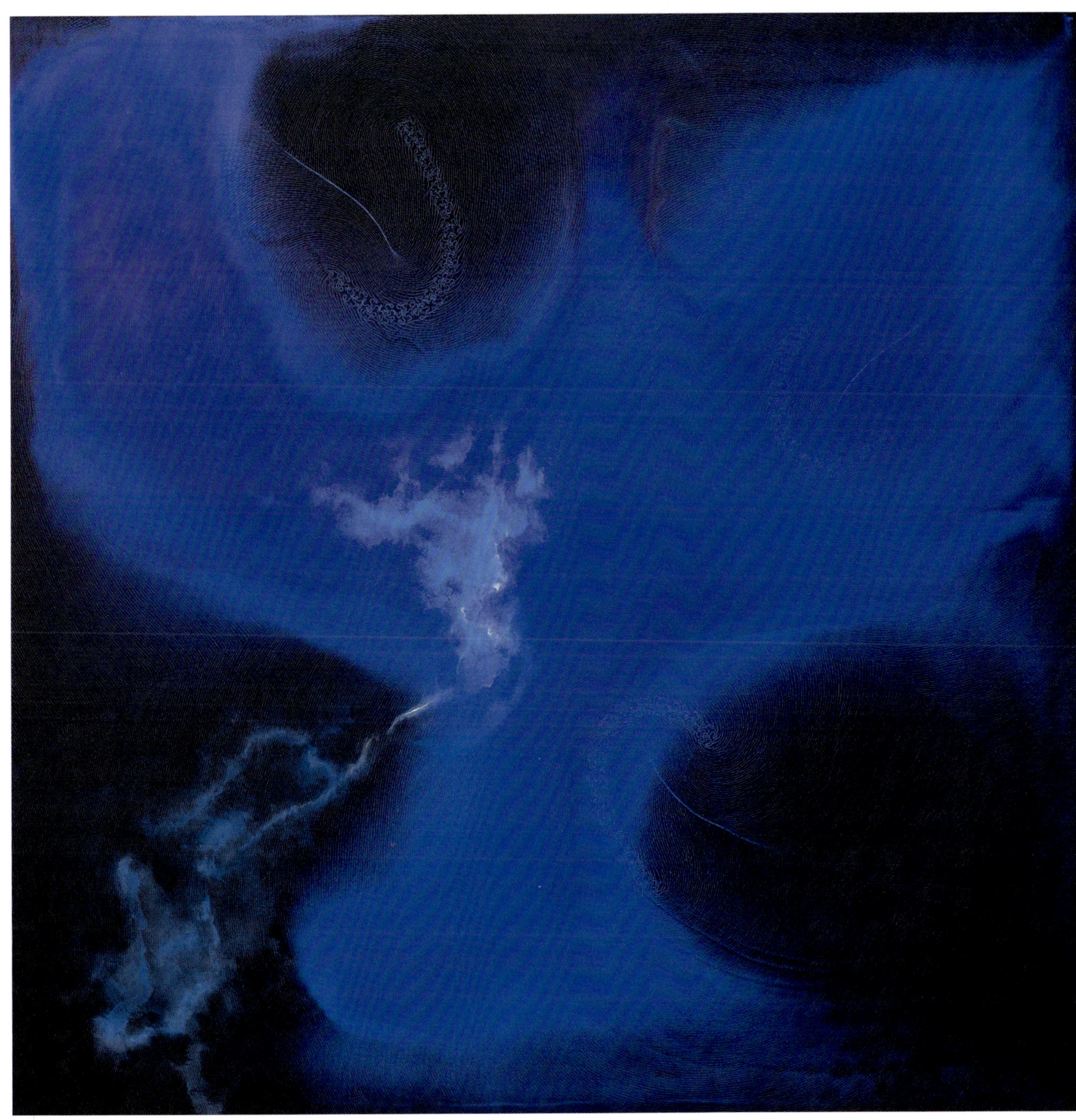

CHIMERA
2020, pigment and pencil on black Aquacryl on canvas and aluminium, 190 × 190 × 5.5 cm (74 ¾ × 74 ¾ × 2 ⅛ in)

Shirazeh Houshiary, born 1955, Shiraz, Iran.

Houshiary once considered becoming a mathematician, and she brings the laws of physics – of nature – into her work, which encompasses painting, sculpture, installation and film. Houshiary moved to London in 1974 to study at the Chelsea School of Art and, later, at the Cardiff School of Art and Design in Wales; in 1982 she exhibited at the Venice Biennale, and she was nominated for the Turner Prize in 1994. Her works address such abstract concepts as the ephemerality of existence and explore methods of perception, striving to make the incorporeal visible. Her works contain no narrative but nevertheless seem to move towards a meaning that can be sensed. *Chimera* was inspired by and created during the COVID-19 pandemic lockdown and the renewed appreciation of nature that those months engendered. The artist's painting technique mirrors this slow, still pace of life: each canvas is built from successive layers of pigment, pencil and Aquacryl, taking months to complete, with the finished work mirroring the movement of water and organic rhythms of nature.

SHARA HUGHES

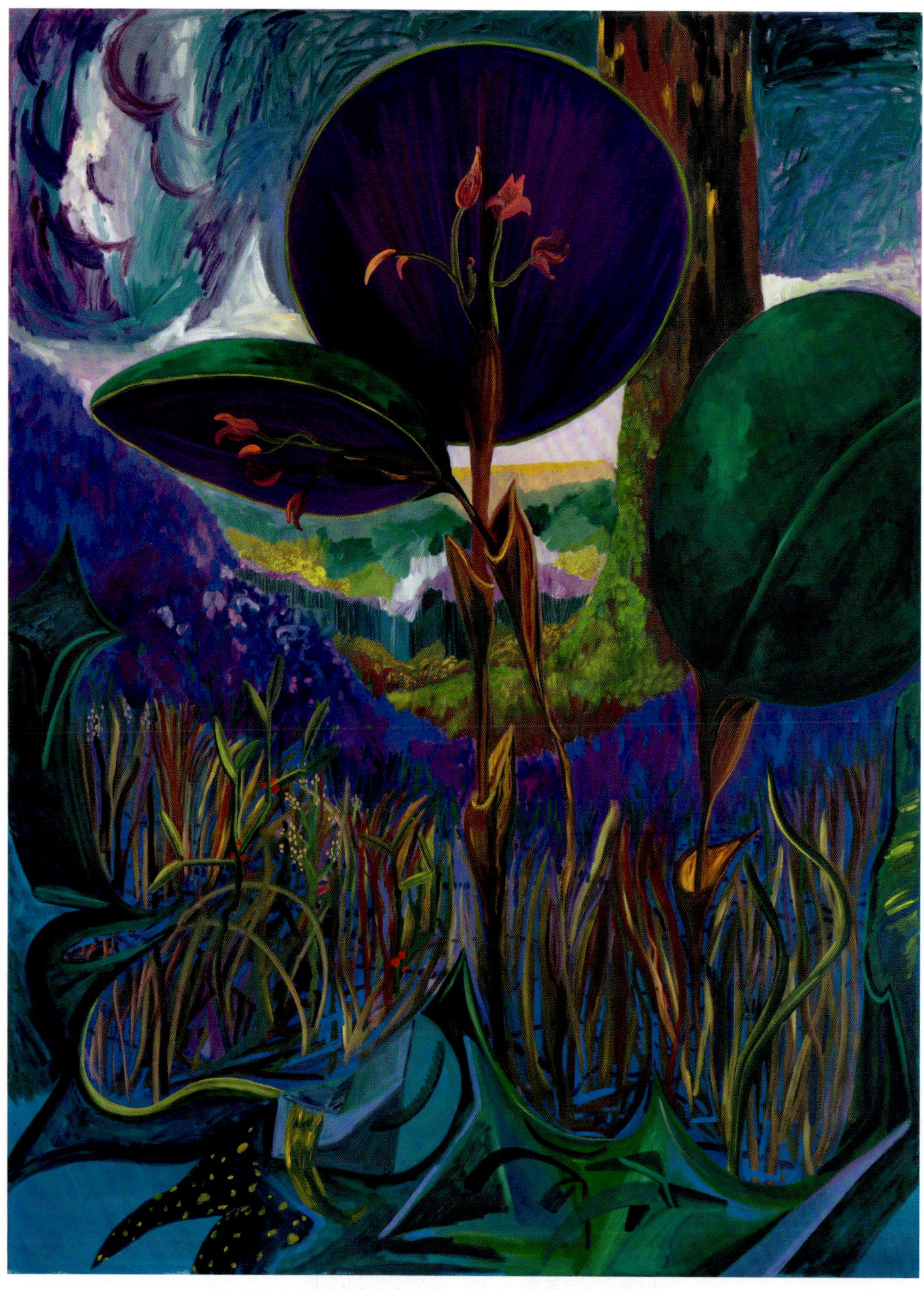

HARD HATS
2021, oil and dye on canvas, 243.8 × 182.9 cm (96 × 72 in)

Shara Hughes, born 1981, Atlanta, USA.

Rooted in an exploration of psychological states and the expressive possibilities of paint and colour, Hughes's paintings create dreamlike landscapes that she has described as forms of self-portraiture. A graduate of the Rhode Island School of Design and the Skowhegan School of Painting and Sculpture, Hughes initially began painting interiors based on narratives and art-historical references. More recently she has turned her attention to flowers, complicating their aesthetic and cultural associations by rendering them both powerful and vulnerable, frightening and sensual. Hughes usually begins with water-based paint to work quickly and abstractly, applying colour directly onto the canvas to create richly chromatic and fantastical images loaded with psychological undertones. She uses this painting process to find forms and explore her emotions, drawing out recognizable floral elements from intuitively conceived fields of abstract form and colour. As with *Hard Hats*, these vegetal and floral figures often appear as composite, monstrous beings whose scale suggests that the viewer is occupying an insect-like perspective.

LUCHITA HURTADO

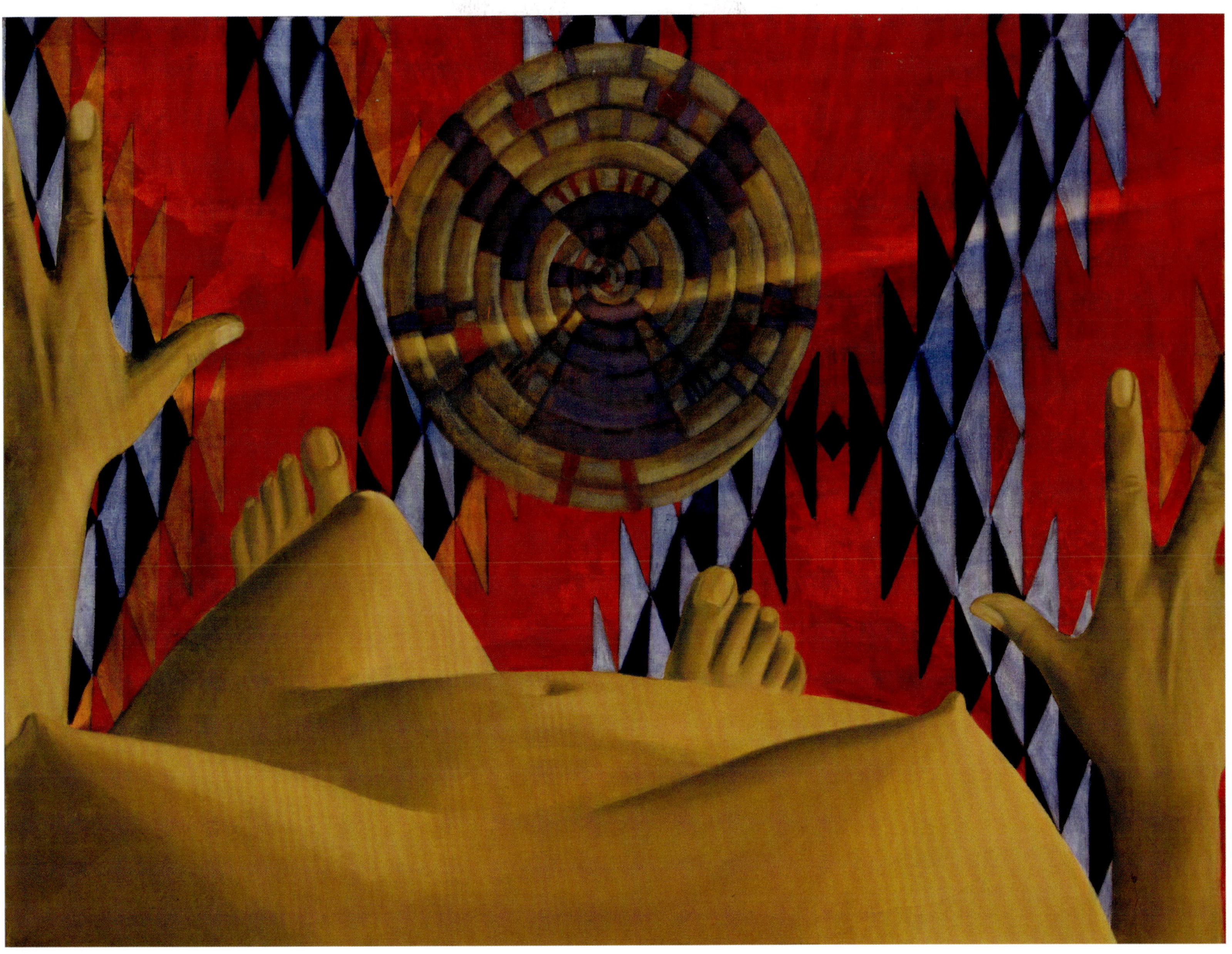

UNTITLED
1969, oil on canvas, 90.8 × 121.9 cm (35 ¾ × 48 in)

Luchita Hurtado, born 1920, Maiquetía, Venezuela. Died 2020, Santa Monica, California, USA.

Over more than eighty years of art-making, Hurtado continually adopted new strategies for exploring the relationship between humanity and nature. Her practice was informed by a spiritual understanding of the interconnectedness of life, which she described as 'planetarian'. Living in New York, Mexico City and Mill Valley, California, before settling in Santa Monica and Taos, New Mexico, Hurtado moved through artistic milieux – crossing paths with Diego Rivera (1886–1957) and Frida Kahlo (p.152), but also with Isamu Noguchi (1904–88) and Agnes Martin (p.191). The untitled canvas illustrated here is one of a number of self-portraits that Hurtado made exploring the subject of her own naked body from the neck down, as seen from the artist's own perspective looking down her torso towards her feet. This series, called 'I Am', plays with the artist's subjective, embodied experience of reality and subverts expectations of the nude genre. Hurtado's form is made strange – in some of these compositions, her skin might be mistaken for rolling sand dunes. Here, she sets herself against a background of geometric shapes, produced by the carpet and woven placemat at her feet.

KUDZANAI-VIOLET HWAMI

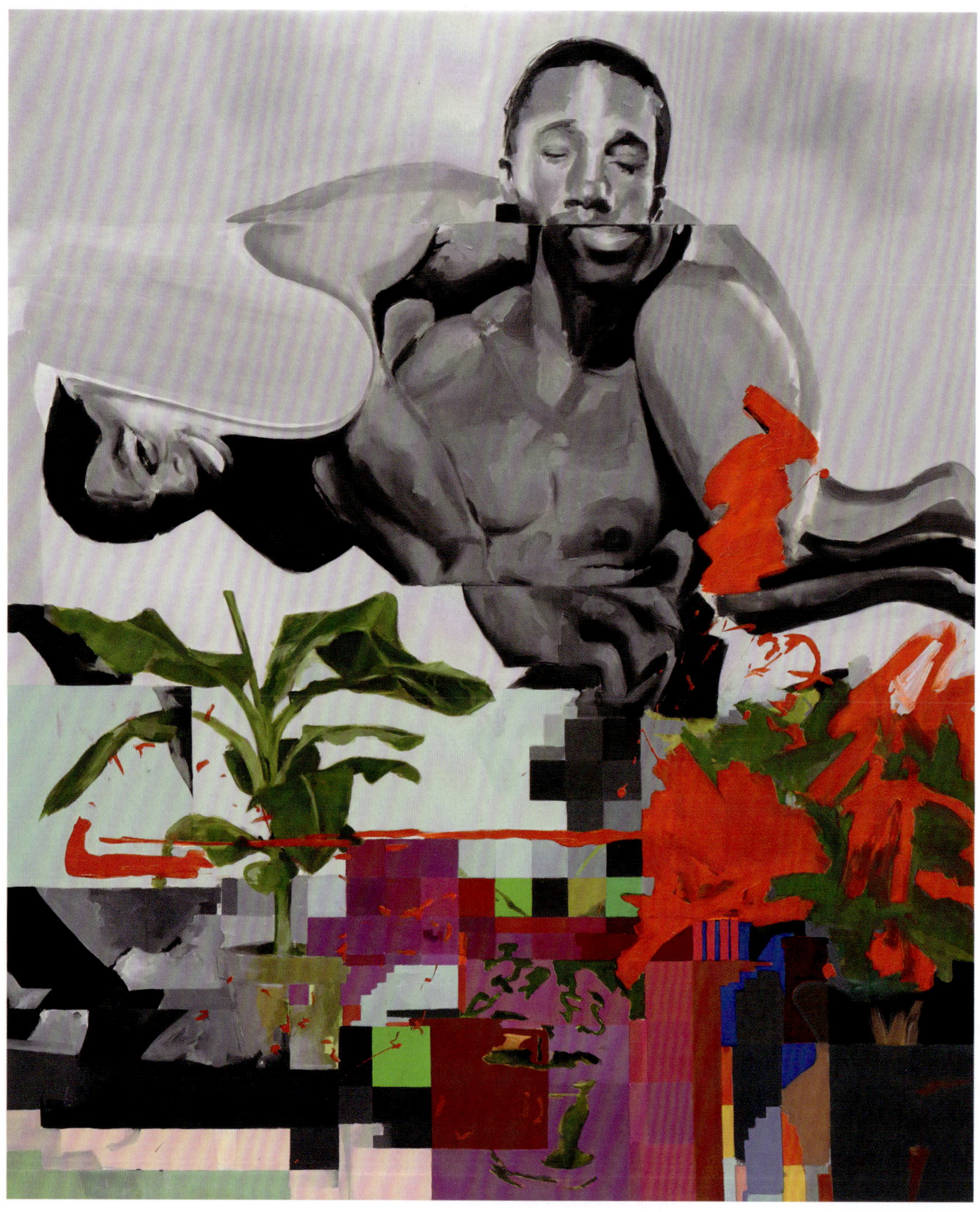

INNNSPIRIT-ED
2021, oil and acrylic on canvas, 143 × 119.5 cm (56 ¼ × 47 ⅛ in)

Kudzanai-Violet Hwami, born 1993, Gutu, Zimbabwe.

Embracing the freedom and playfulness afforded by collage, Hwami combines found images with gestural abstraction to create highly personal, narratively inflected works that subtly interrogate issues of spirituality, gender, race, sexuality and the body. After being raised in Zimbabwe and South Africa, Hwami moved to the United Kingdom in 2013, graduating from the Ruskin School of Art in Oxford in 2021. Inspired by the hybrid visual languages of artists such as Jean-Michel Basquiat (1960–88) and Robert Rauschenberg (1925–2008), Hwami mines a variety of visual sources, from family photographs and self-portraits to images of anonymous figures and vintage pornography discovered online. Each painting begins with a digital collage, which is then translated into paint. Figurative imagery is often disrupted by abstract passages, as in this large painting in which fragmented male bodies are juxtaposed with glitchy digital artefacts and thick red lines applied with oil sticks, which, despite appearing spontaneous, are all carefully plotted. By collapsing the past and present, Hwami's amalgamations reflect on her experiences of geographical displacement and the way that identities are increasingly constructed in digital spaces.

KAMALA IBRAHIM ISHAG

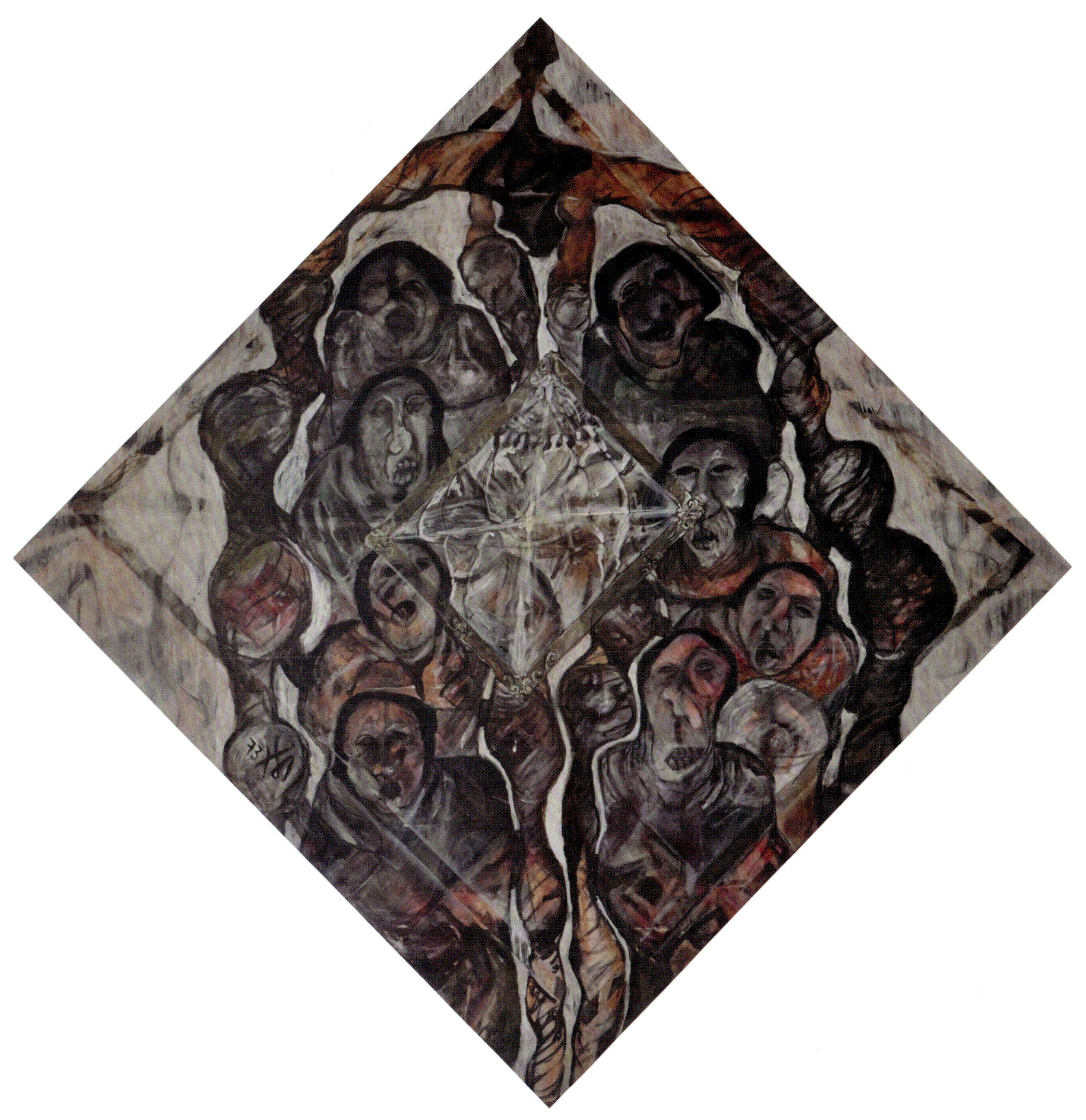

WOMEN AT A ZAAR CEREMONY
1973, oil on canvas (covered with board on backside), 134 × 134 cm (52 ¾ × 52 ¾ in), Barjeel Art Foundation, Sharjah, UAE

Kamala Ibrahim Ishag, born 1937, Omdurman, Sudan.

Described as Sudan's first female modernist painter, Ishag is known for figurative abstractions that often explore traditional spiritual practices. In the early 1960s, Ishag was a founding member, along with Ibrahim El-Salahi (b. 1930) and Ahmad Shibrain (1931–2017), of the Khartoum School, which espoused an aesthetic that distilled Arabic calligraphy into expressive, abstract forms, sometimes incorporating Sudanese folk art patterns. In the 1970s, she co-founded the Crystalist Group, whose interests in transparency, experimentation and interior knowledge challenged the male-dominated, rationalist modernism of the Khartoum School. 'The Crystalist Manifesto', published in *Al-Ayyam* on 21 January 1976, stated polemically: 'Man's essence is pleasure, and that should be the sole unit of measurement everywhere, including in the sciences, philosophy, and art.' Ishag's compositions include formal elements that nod to crystalline formations, such as rhombuses and glass. Her work sometimes focuses on the Zaar ceremony, an exorcism ritual performed by women to cure a person from demonic spirit possession. *Women at a Zaar Ceremony* depicts a cluster of healers with faces twisted in anguish, rendered in Ishag's distinctive palette of earthy hues. The figures appear to meld into one another, signifying otherworldly transformation.

YUKIE ISHIKAWA

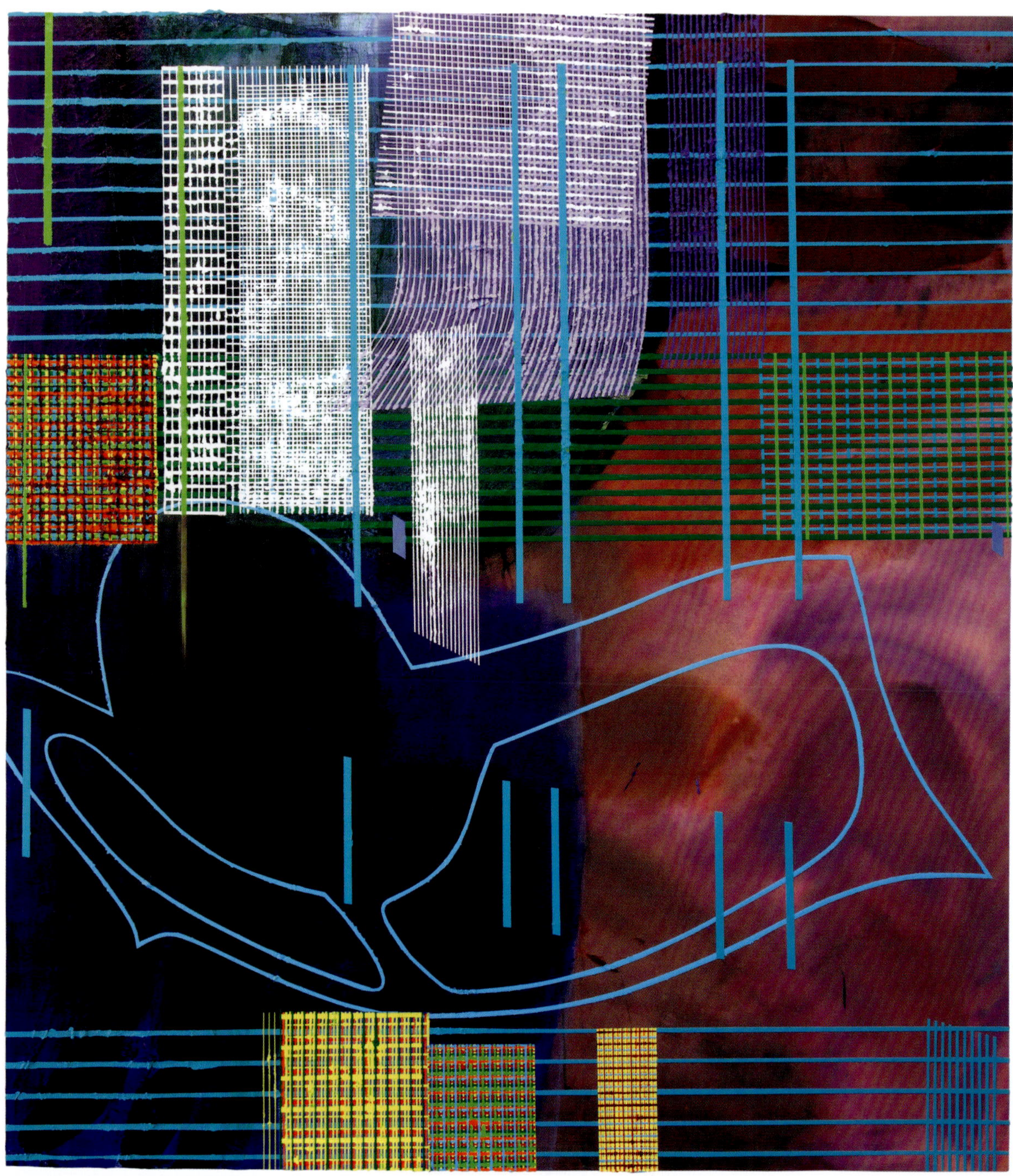

IMPERMANENCE – HYACINTH ORCHID
2018, acrylic and sand on canvas, 217 × 196.5 cm (85 ½ × 77 ⅜ in), private collection, Istanbul, Turkey

Yukie Ishikawa, born 1961, Tokyo, Japan.

Since the 1980s Ishikawa has cultivated a body of gestural paintings that reject histories of Euro-American modernism and Minimalism to create new possibilities of artistic expression. Ishikawa finds inspiration in the visual language of print culture (magazines, newspapers, books and corporate advertisements), though the artist renders these sources abstract by cropping, enlarging, layering and tracing them – harnessing material products of capitalism to create lyrical compositions where colour creates form. Since 2012 Ishikawa has developed her technique further with her 'Impermanence' series, reworking finished canvases from previous decades by adding layers of paint and sand. *Impermanence – Hyacinth Orchid* is emblematic of her ability to introduce new grids, lines and materials that do not destroy the previous image but generate new meaning through their interaction with the original painting's composition. Initially inspired by the ever-present construction in Tokyo and the constantly shifting views from her studio windows, this technique suggests the canvas, like the landscape, is a living and unfinished form.

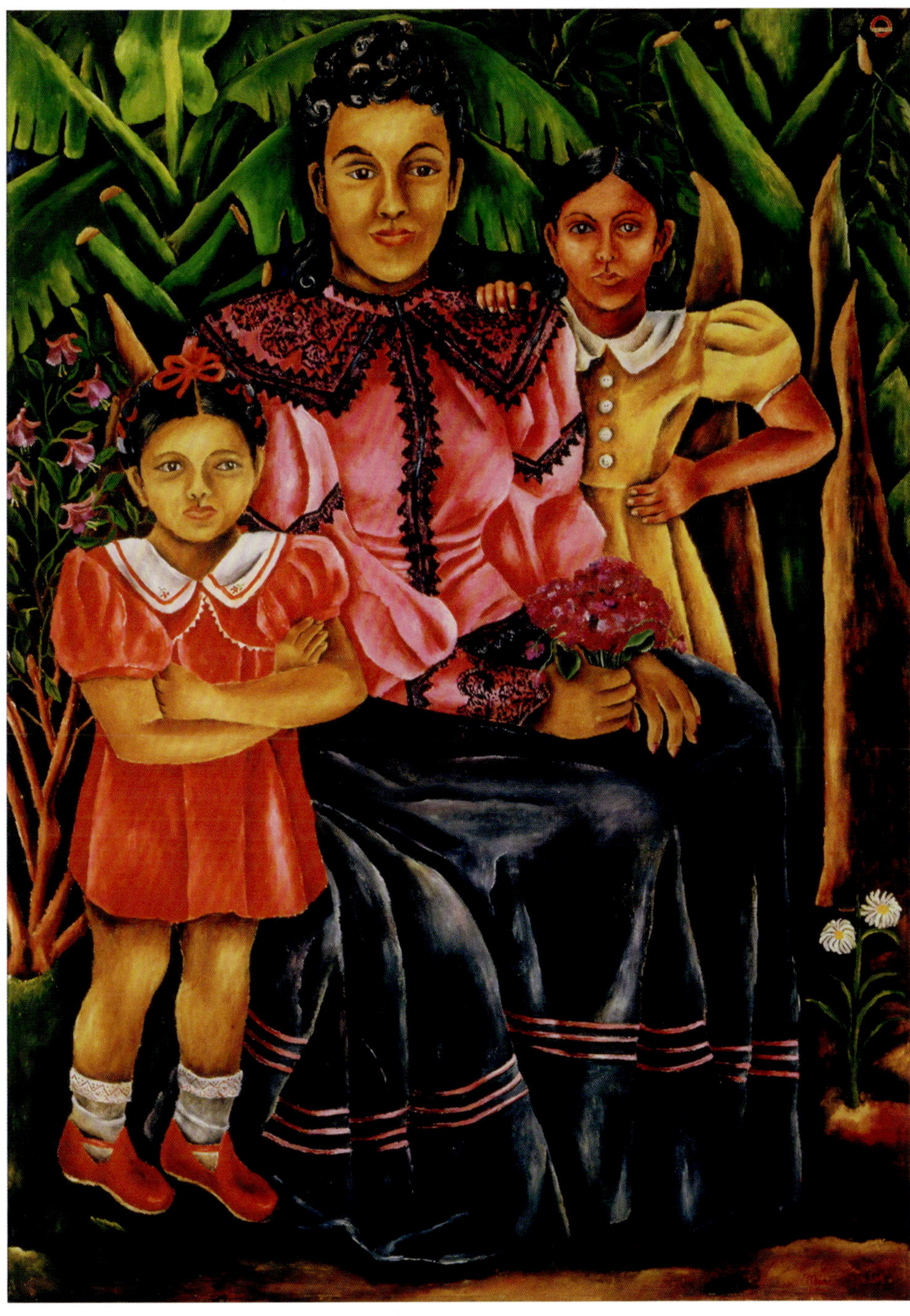

MIS SOBRINAS (MY NIECES)
1940, oil on plywood, 140.3 × 94.6 cm (55¼ × 37¼ in), Museo Nacional de Arte, Mexico City, Mexico

María Izquierdo, born 1902, San Juan de los Lagos, Mexico. Died 1955, Mexico City, Mexico.

Raised by a conservative family in a rural village in central Mexico, Izquierdo moved to Mexico City in 1926, enrolling at the San Carlos Academy of Fine Arts, where her career soon took off. This was thanks partly to the mentorship of celebrated artist Diego Rivera (1886–1957). He held her in such high favour that other students complained, causing her to leave the school. Izquierdo was also close to Rufino Tamayo (1889–1991); together, they developed an approach to painting that combined personal experiences with trends in European modern art, namely Surrealism. A conflict developed with Rivera and other promoters of Mexican muralism; although Izquierdo was interested in exploring her pre-Columbian heritage and contemporary Indigenous culture, they believed that art should be a purely political, nationalist tool. Some of Izquierdo's frequent subjects were local flora, horses and village circuses. Depicting the artist seated between her nieces, *My Nieces* is one of many self-portraits that emphasize Izquierdo's mestiza (mixed) heritage, reflecting her desire to place her own identity and experience at the centre of her work. The pinks, yellows and other bright colours invoke the palette of Mexican popular arts.

TESS JARAY

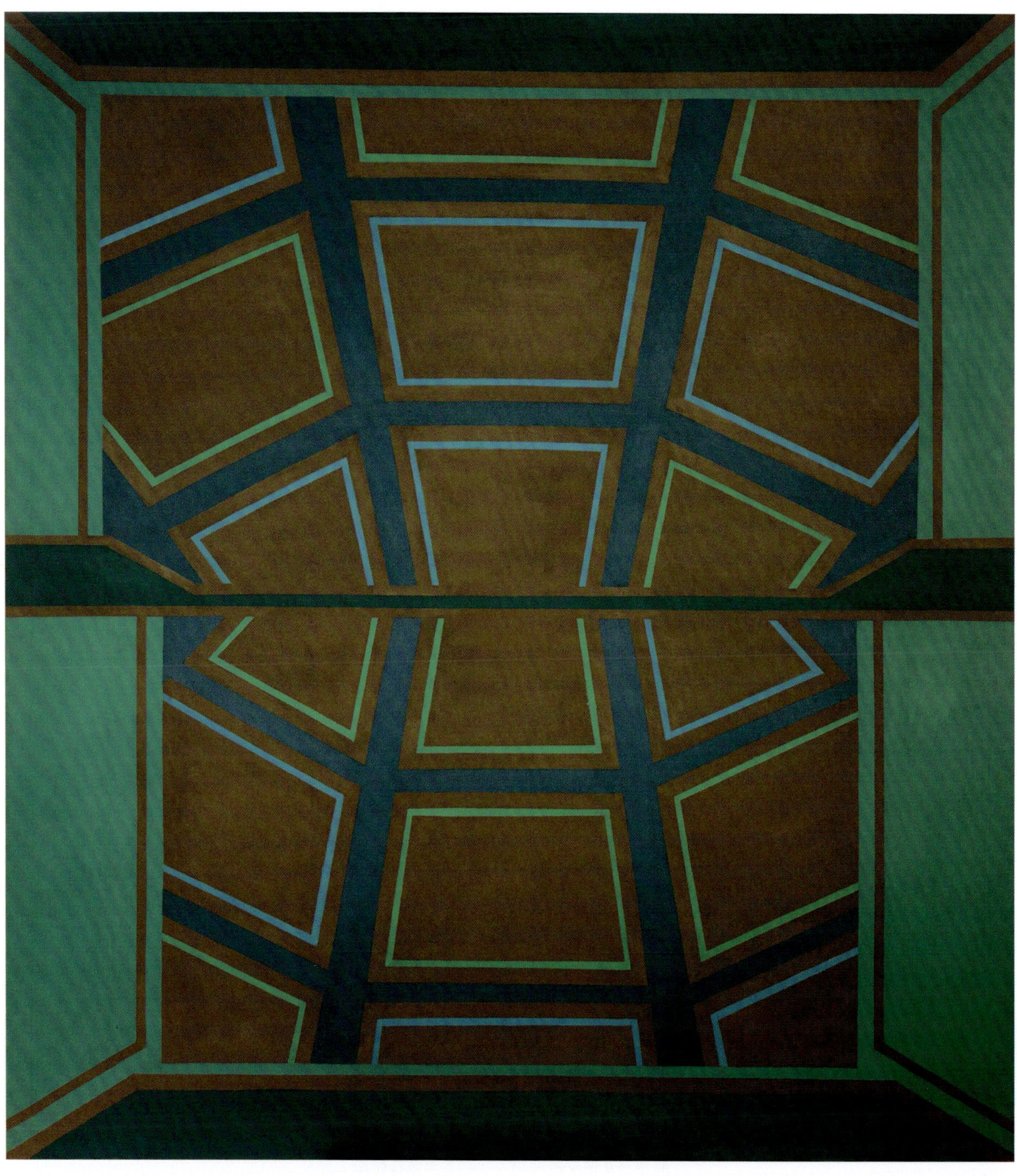

CUPOLA BLUE
1963, oil on canvas, 183 × 152 cm (72 ⅛ × 59 ⅞ in)

Tess Jaray, born 1937, Vienna, Austria.

Since the 1960s, Jaray's sumptuous explorations in paint have played with the stirring potential of scale, pattern and geometry. Growing up in the UK, Jaray was trained at Saint Martin's School of Art and the Slade School of Fine Art, where in 1968 she went on to become the school's first female art teacher. Jaray's works often take inspiration from architectural structures and details, transforming them into trompe l'oeil abstractions that have been associated with hard-edged painting, Op art and Minimalism. *Cupola Blue* is one such example, an oil painting from Jaray's early period, inspired by the Renaissance buildings the artist encountered on travels through Italian cities in the early 1960s. In this large-scale abstract work, Jaray concisely translates the formal grandeur of the domed construction into a condensed, flat space that is just as beguiling and emotive. Persistently fascinated with the possibilities of 'making space' – as she described in a 2021 *Art Newspaper* interview – Jaray's paintings oscillate between the need to contain the world and the desire to be overwhelmed by it, between restrained, precise lines and colours that overspill with emotion.

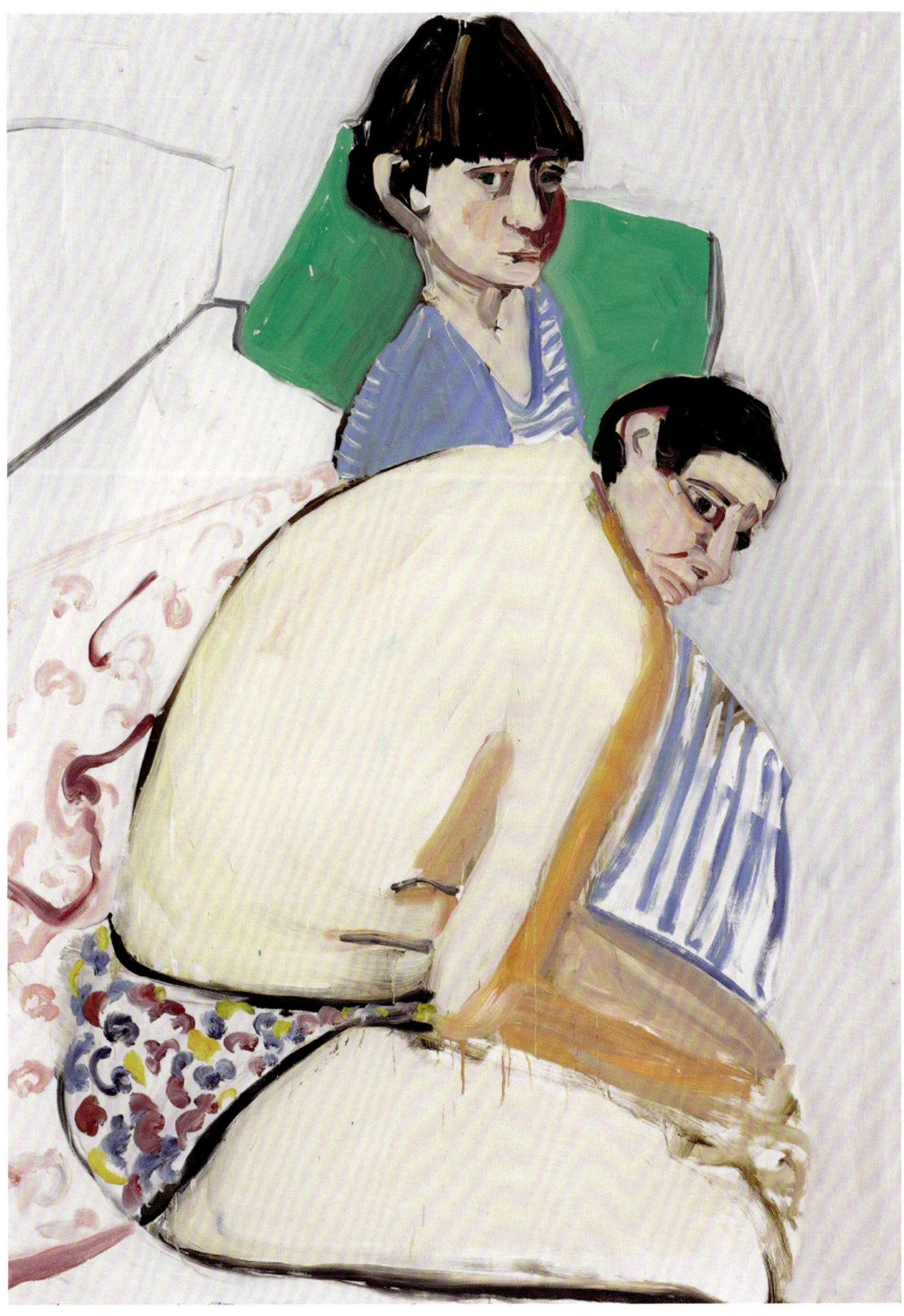

THE SQUID AND THE WHALE
2017, oil on board, 214 × 152 cm (84 ¼ × 59 ⅞ in)

Chantal Joffe, born 1969, St. Albans, Vermont, USA.

After graduating from London's Royal College of Art in 1994, Joffe has remained committed to figurative painting, which she imbues with an emotional intensity and psychological depth. In the 1990s, Joffe focused on the politics of pornography, provoking audiences with sexually explicit canvases. The female body has remained a central concern in her work, and her intimate compositions, both large-scale or small, are no less immediate or confrontational, touching on themes such as motherhood, the ageing process and the representation of women across culture. Working primarily from photographs and from life, Joffe paints her portraits of women and girls in an expressive, fluid style with large, casual brushstrokes. Distortions of scale and form are often introduced for expressive effect, as in *The Squid and the Whale*, one of many portraits of the artist and her daughter, Esme, born in 2004. Addressing the heartache caused by a child separating from its mother, the painting depicts the pair sitting on a bed; the mother's hunched back almost conceals the child, her downcast face expressing the emotional intensity of raising offspring from childhood to adolescence.

GWEN JOHN

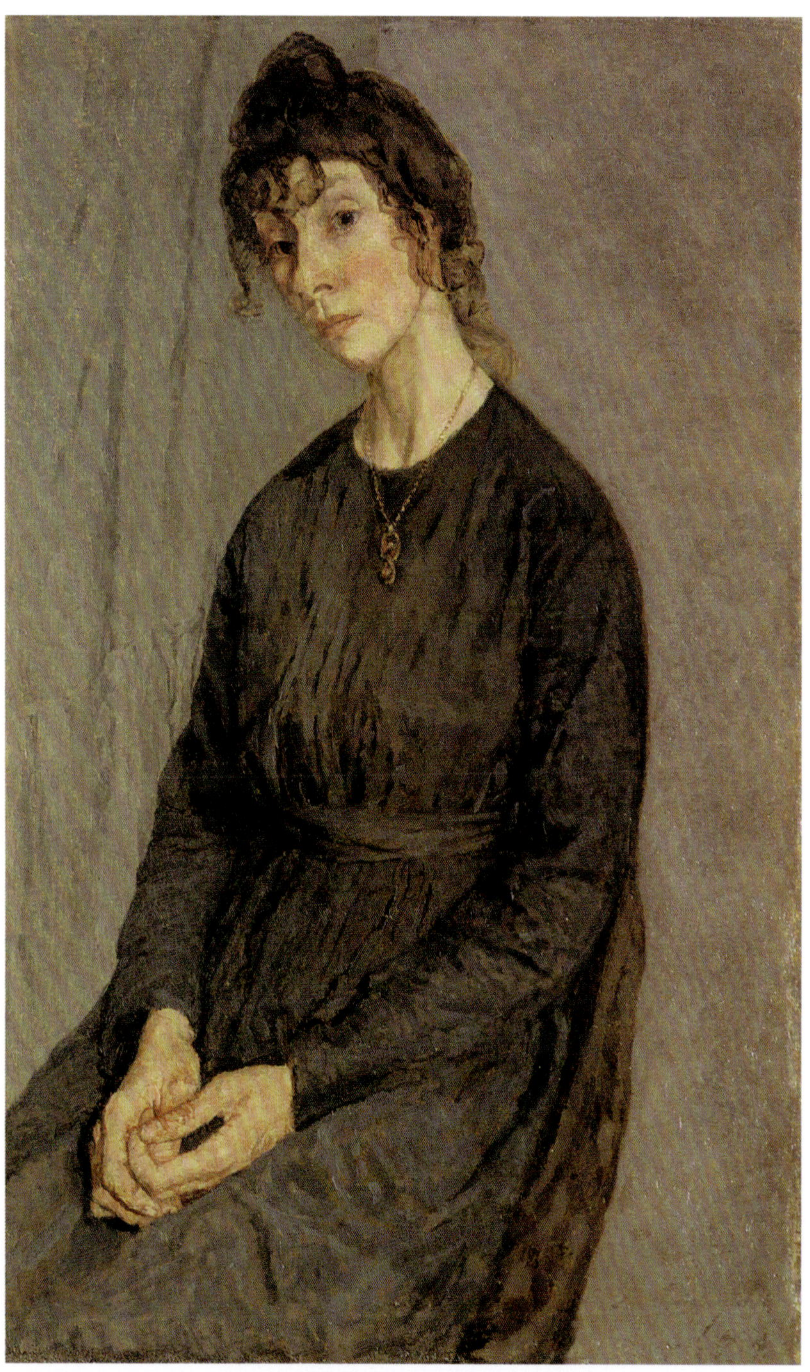

CHLOË BOUGHTON-LEIGH
1910–14, oil on canvas, 60.3 × 38.6 cm
(23 ¾ × 15 ¼ in), Leeds Art Gallery, UK

Gwen John, born 1876, Haverfordwest, Pembrokeshire, UK. Died 1939, Dieppe, France.

Although historically she has been perceived as a recluse, John frequently networked with her contemporaries and regularly exhibited and sold work during her lifetime. Often overshadowed by her brother Augustus John (1878–1961), a fellow student at the Slade School of Fine Art in London in the 1890s, John developed her own approach to modernism that focused on psychological studies of interiors and solitary figures. In 1904, she permanently settled in France, where she began a mutually impactful yet fraught relationship with sculptor Auguste Rodin (1840–1917) and became an integral member of bohemian circles. This painting depicts Chloë Boughton-Leigh, the daughter of poet Edward Ward-Boughton-Leigh and a close friend of John's. Chloë was the subject of a number of paintings in muted grey palettes in which she sits in quiet repose. Her clasped hands and distant gaze are suggestive of the artist's own propensity for self-reflection, indicated by John's increasing turn to Catholicism. In a letter from 1908, she wrote, 'I think that is a beautiful idea, that we dig out the precious things hidden in us when we paint – and quite true.'

CLAUDETTE JOHNSON

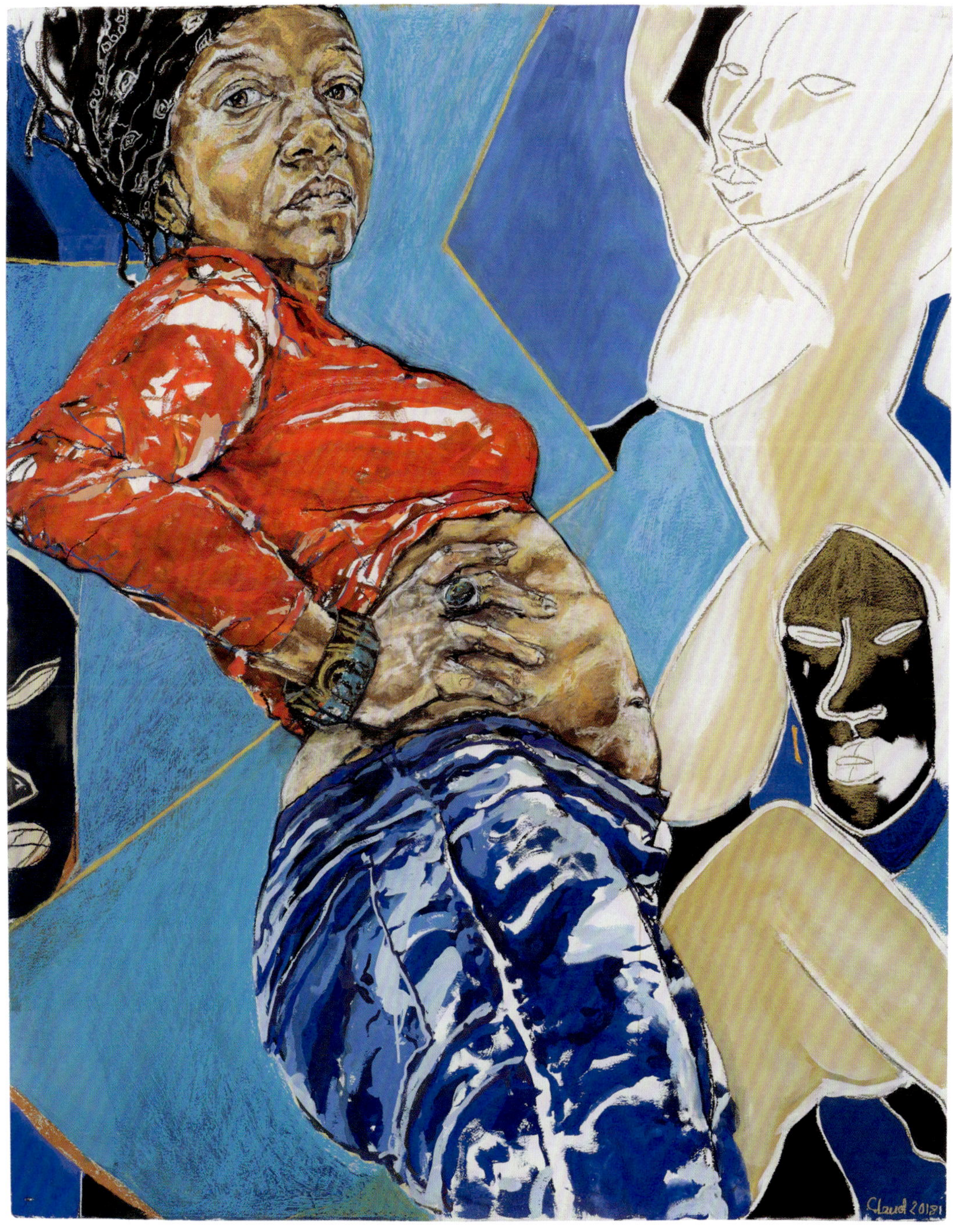

STANDING FIGURE WITH AFRICAN MASKS
2018, pastel and gouache on paper,
163 × 133 cm (64 × 52 in), Tate, London, UK

Claudette Johnson, born 1959, Manchester, UK.

With larger-than-life canvases that depict intimate encounters with her subjects, Johnson centres and reimagines the position of Black women in the history of art. As a student at Wolverhampton Polytechnic, UK, in the 1970s, Johnson was a founding member of the BLK Art Group, a collective of artists of Caribbean ancestry that programmed exhibitions critiquing institutional racism in the art world. Johnson continued to engage with these issues collectively in the 1980s, participating in group exhibitions with figures from the British Black Arts Movement. Johnson forms her figures through gestural lines, creating a complex formal relationship between vibrant pigment and blank, untouched areas of the painting surface. This work, rendered in layers of pastel and gouache, typifies Johnson's stylistic approach. The statuesque model looks down at her audience, relegating Cubist imagery from Pablo Picasso's iconic *Les Demoiselles d'Avignon* (1907) – which appropriated African masking traditions – to the margins of the frame, literally and figuratively repositioning historically marginalized Black women within mainstream visual culture.

LOÏS MAILOU JONES

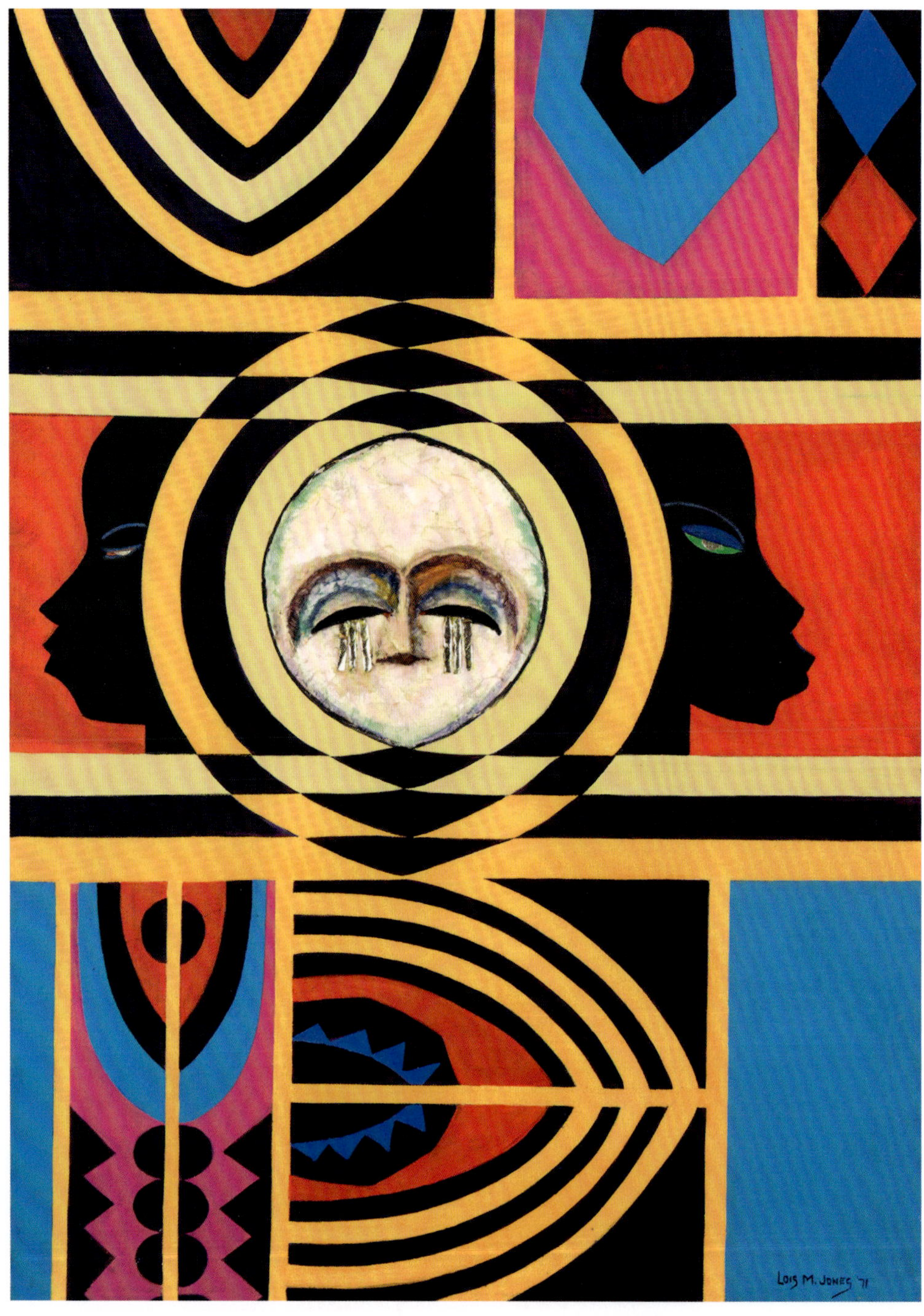

MOON MASQUE
1971, oil and collage on canvas, 104.1 × 76.4 cm (41 × 30 ⅛ in), Smithsonian American Art Museum, Washington DC, USA

Loïs Mailou Jones, born 1905, Boston, USA. Died 1998, Washington DC, USA.

A key figure of the Harlem Renaissance, Jones illustrated her deep-seated engagement with Africa and its diasporas through paintings, textiles and collages. A professor of art and design at Howard University in Washington DC for over forty years, Jones applied Black Studies and the struggle for civil rights to the visual arts. As quoted in a 1972 exhibition catalogue, she felt it was 'the duty of every Black artist to participate in the current movement which aims to establish recognition of the works by "Black Artists".' Jones's interest in stylized masks began early in her career, when she trained in Paris from 1937 to 1938, and grew during her travels to Africa throughout the 1970s. *Moon Masque* was exhibited at the Second World Festival of Black and African Arts and Culture (FESTAC) in Lagos, Nigeria, in 1977. The central heart-shaped Kwele mask from Zaire (now the Democratic Republic of the Congo) collaged with pieces of silver foil suggests the appearance of tears flowing from the eyes. It is flanked by two silhouetted profiles and surrounded by richly coloured textile patterns from Ethiopia. Jones deliberately combined motifs from various African cultures to resist one-dimensional conceptions of the region, and instead visualized a plurality of Black experiences and traditions.

JACQUELINE DE JONG

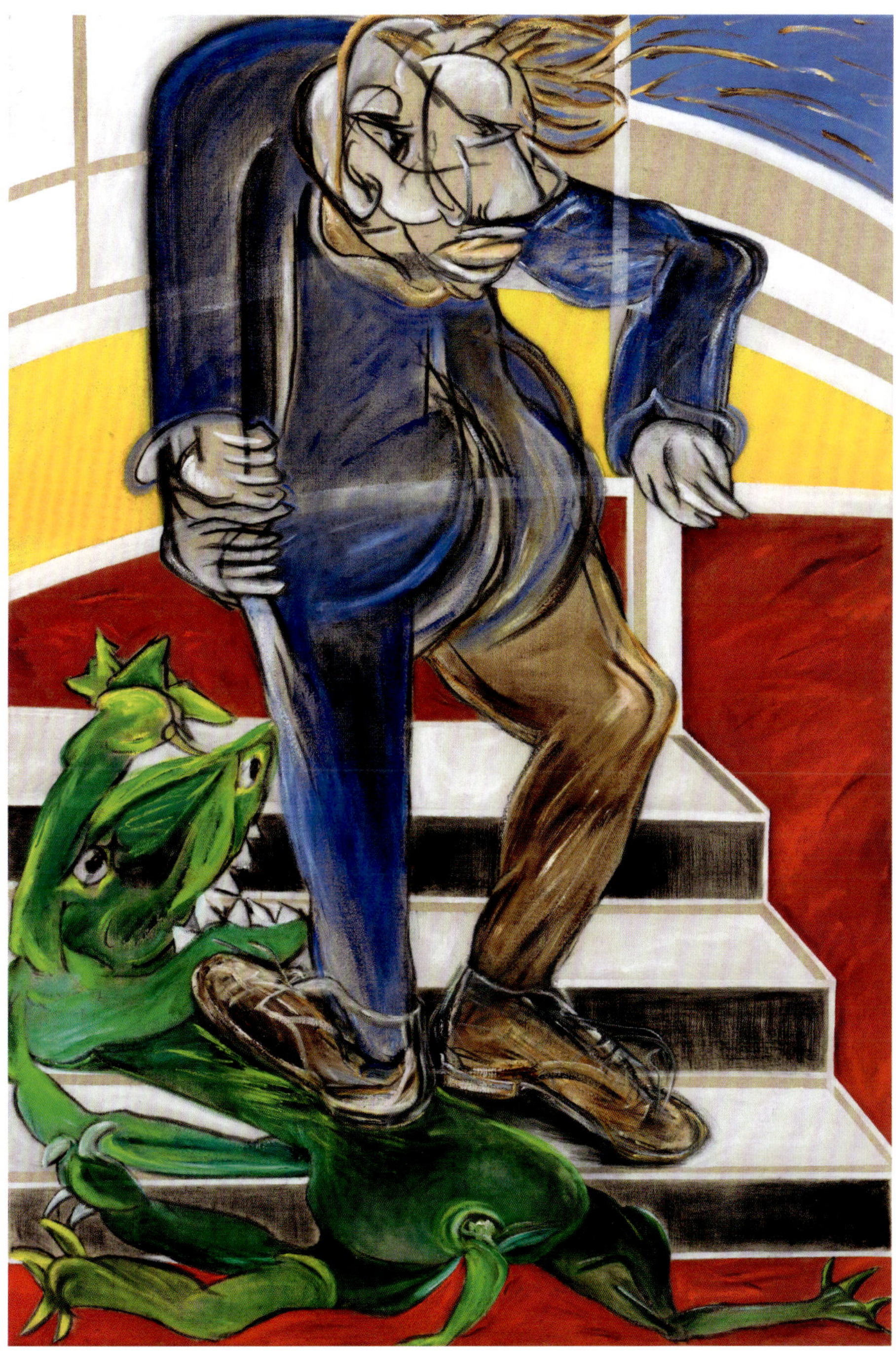

BIG FOOT SMALL HEAD (FOR THOMAS)
1985, oil on canvas, 200 × 160 cm
(78 ¾ × 63 in), collection of Rattan Chadha

Jacqueline de Jong, born 1939, Hengelo, Netherlands.

With works spanning painting, sculpture and graphic art, de Jong has experimented with diverse styles, from Art Brut to Pop to Expressionism. After escaping Nazi-occupied Amsterdam and being rescued at the Swiss border by the French Resistance, de Jong returned to the Netherlands after the war. In 1957 she moved to Paris, where she became involved with the avant-garde Situationist International movement. Like many female peers, de Jong's work was long overlooked but has seen a late flourishing of interest, resulting in significant exhibitions, including a 2019 retrospective at Amsterdam's Stedelijk Museum. Her hallucinatory canvases, executed in a vivid palette with bold brushstrokes, connect violence, humour and erotic desire and are often inhabited by monstrous hybrid creatures engaged in ambiguous encounters. This work, part of the 'Upstairs Downstairs' series originally commissioned for the stairwell of Amsterdam Town Hall, could be a contemporary take on the popular legend of Saint George and the Dragon. De Jong conveys the motion of struggle by depicting the protagonist's head and hand in multiple positions, yet far from being the dashing knight of lore, her dragon-slayer stands hunched, feet facing opposite directions as the splayed beast thrashes under his shoe.

JOSEPHINE JOY

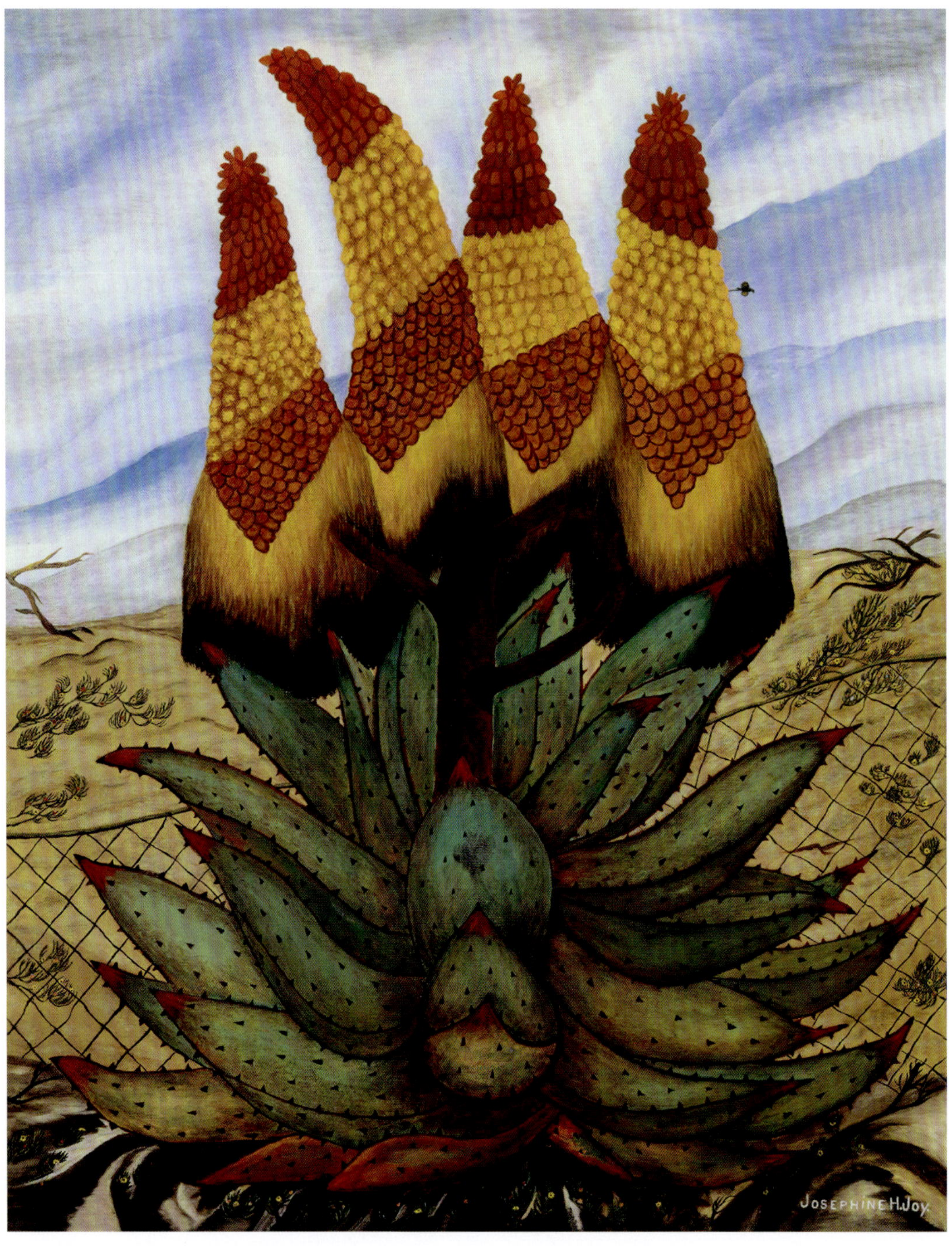

ALOES
c. 1935–8, oil on canvas, 76.2 × 61.3 cm (30 × 24 ⅛ in), Smithsonian American Art Museum, Washington DC, USA

Josephine Joy, born 1869, North River Mills, West Virginia, USA. Died 1948, Peoria, Illinois, USA.

Born Sally Hiett, Joy changed her first name to Josephine when she was sixteen and later took her second husband's surname. After growing up on a farm in rural Illinois, she lived in Chicago and Denver, Colorado, before settling in San Diego, where she developed her interest in painting and enjoyed sketching animals at the city's famed zoo. After her husband died in 1927 and the Great Depression struck in the 1930s, she earned her living as a Works Progress Administration (WPA) artist and gained national acclaim as part of a wave of interest in artists who had taken a non-academic route into art. In 1942 she was the first woman painter to have a solo exhibition at the Museum of Modern Art, followed by a critically acclaimed show at New York's Galerie St. Etienne in 1943. Joy painted plants and animals in a style combining naturalism with a playful twist of the imagination. Here, she gives glory to a sinuous aloe plant in full bloom, rendering it as though it were the eminent subject of a stately portrait.

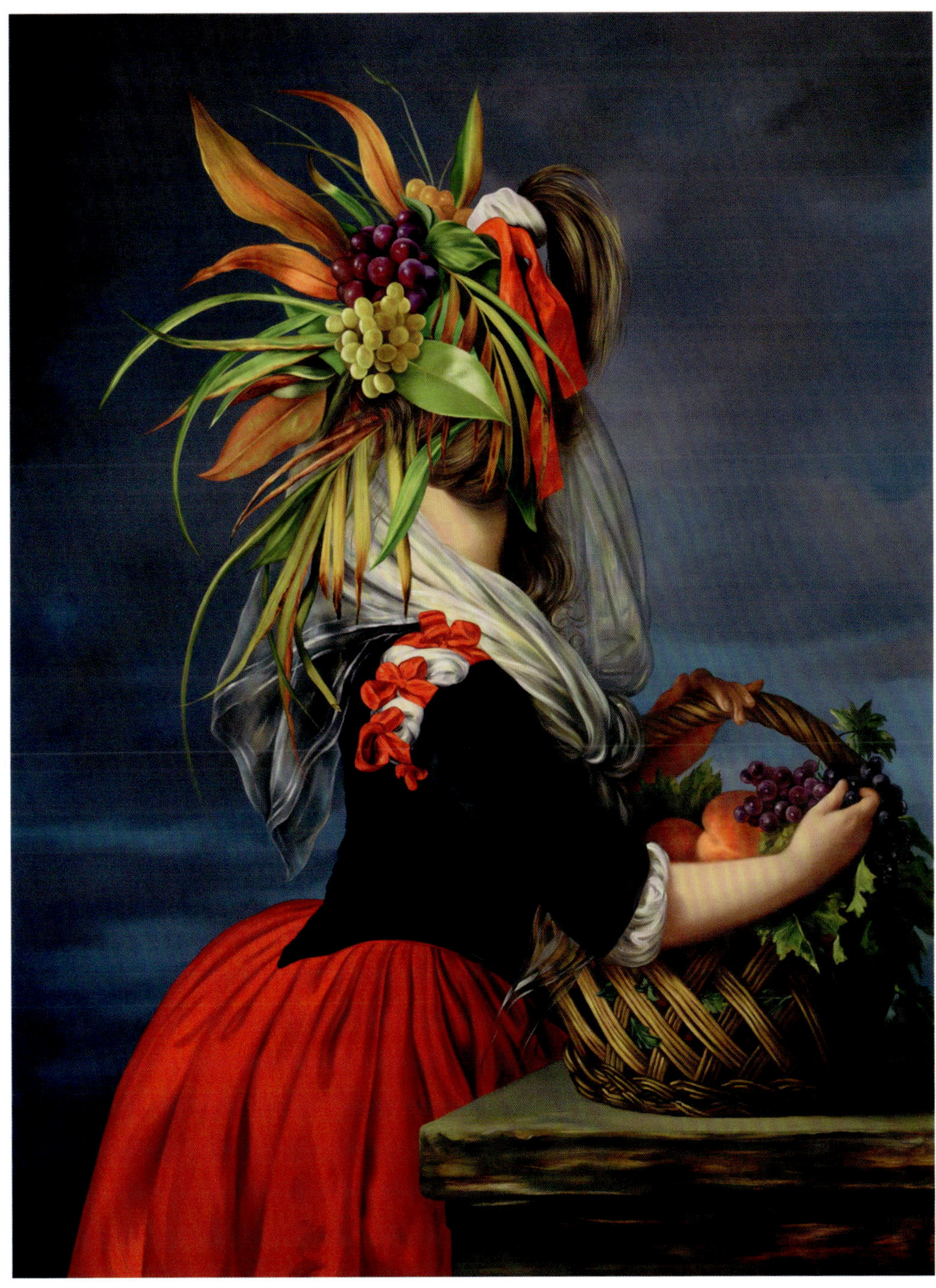

UNTITLED (AFTER ÉLISABETH VIGÉE LE BRUN)
2020, oil on canvas, 160 × 120 cm (63 × 47 ¼ in)

Ewa Juszkiewicz, born 1984, Gdańsk, Poland.

'Through the transformation and modification of historical portraits,' Juszkiewicz said in an interview for *Gagosian Quarterly* in 2020, 'I want to deprive them of their obviousness and disrupt the familiar order.' Although her references span the Renaissance to the twentieth century, the artist's primary focus is paintings of women from the eighteenth and nineteenth centuries, which for the past decade she has meticulously recreated in oil on canvas – but with a twist: the women's heads are obscured, swathed in folds of fabric, flora and fauna, or masses of hair. The surreal ornamentations are presented as a comment on the rigid conventions of female portraiture – particularly from the Rococo period – and on how women's individual identities are effaced by these idealized depictions. A regular source for Juszkiewicz is the oeuvre of Élisabeth Vigée-Lebrun (p.310). This painting reinterprets Vigée-Lebrun's 1784 portrait of the Comtesse de Caderousse, who is dressed as a peasant girl carrying a basket of fruit, reflecting the Marie Antoinette–inspired fashion for rustic simplicity at the time. Here, the countess's face is replaced by an explosion of hair, brightly coloured leaves and grapes, subverting a traditional image of female beauty and throwing into question social expectations of female appearance.

FRIDA KAHLO

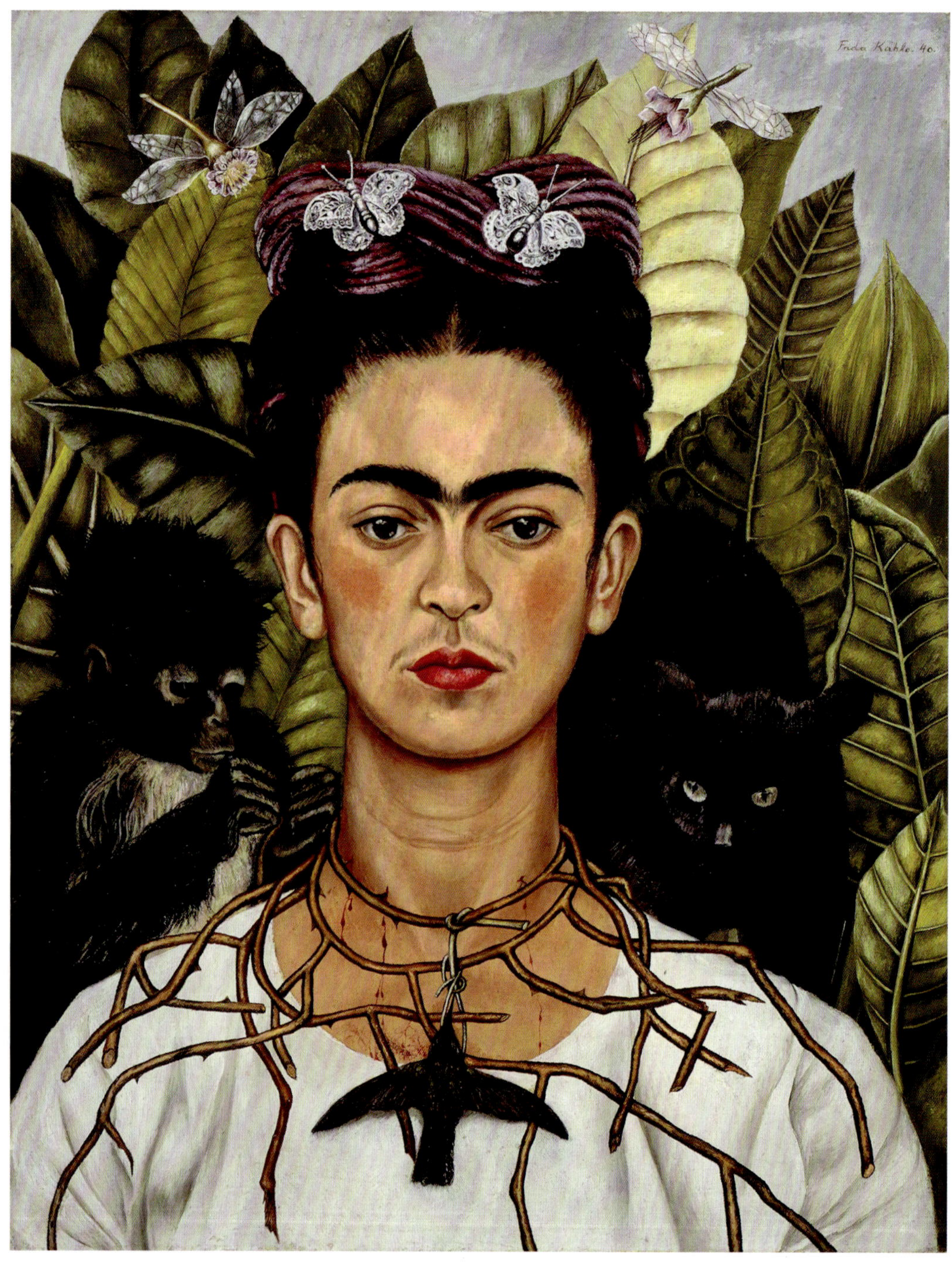

SELF-PORTRAIT WITH THORN NECKLACE AND HUMMINGBIRD
1940, oil on canvas mounted to board, *c.*62.6 × 47.9 cm (*c.*24 3/8 × 18 7/8 in), Nickolas Muray Collection of Mexican Art, Harry Ransom Center, University of Texas at Austin, USA

Frida Kahlo, born 1907, Coyoacán, Mexico City, Mexico. Died 1954, Coyoacán.

A global feminist icon and one of Mexico's most important modern artists, Kahlo produced about two hundred paintings over the course of her relatively short career. At the age of eighteen, Kahlo sustained multiple injuries, notably to her spine, following a horrific tram accident, after which she began painting to distract herself during her recovery. Kahlo's enigmatic figurative style draws on diverse Indigenous influences, notably Mexican votive paintings (*retablos*). Her merging of 'reverie, cruelty and sexuality', to quote Laura Mulvey and Peter Wollen from a 1982 essay, saw her feted by Surrealist commissar André Breton (1896–1966) in 1938. 'I detest Surrealism,' Kahlo countered in a 1952 letter. 'I wish to be worthy, with my paintings, of the people to whom I belong and to the ideas which strengthen me.' Her self-portraits, allegories of suffering and fortitude, exemplify this. Their power resides in Kahlo's blending of shared female experience with local symbols and personal anecdotes. In this painting, for example, the monkey may symbolize her husband, artist and fellow left-wing activist Diego Rivera (1886–1957), who had once gifted her a spider monkey. The thorns piercing her neck may testify to her lifelong endurance of physical pain – or to the emotional distress of her tempestuous marriage to Rivera, whom she had divorced a year earlier.

HAYV KAHRAMAN

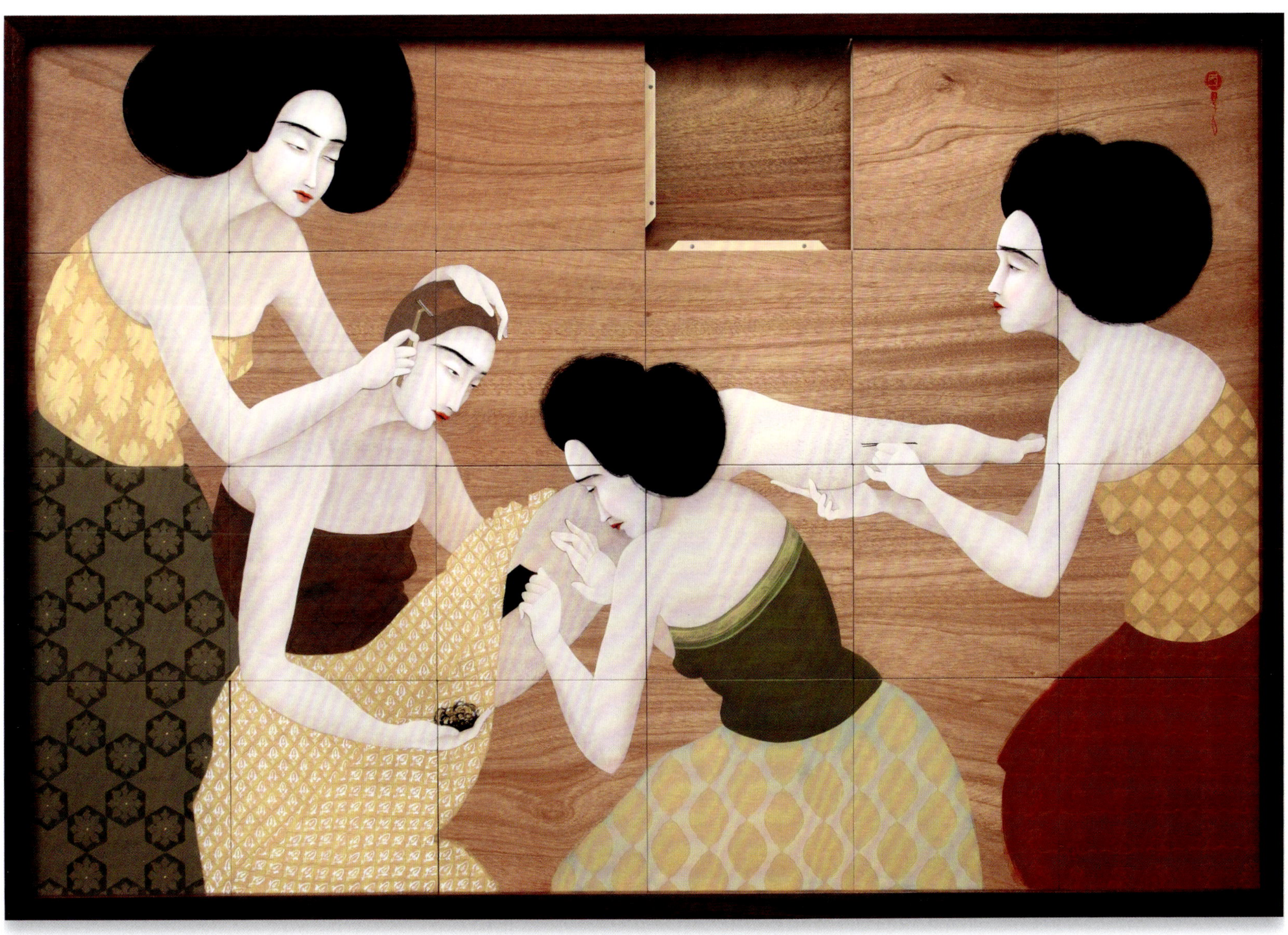

APPEARANCE OF CONTROL
2010, oil with gold paint on 23 wooden panels (sliding puzzle) in artist's frame, 167 × 246 cm (65 3/4 × 96 7/8 in)

Hayv Kahraman, born 1981, Baghdad, Iraq.

Kahraman describes her art as semi-autobiographical, combining activism and an archive of personal and collective female experience. A child during the Iran–Iraq War (1980–8) and the first Gulf War (1990–1), Kahraman fled Iraq with her family when she was eleven, becoming a refugee in Sweden before eventually settling in the United States, where she currently lives and works. A recurring motif throughout her work is the iconic figure identified by the artist simply as 'She', a cultural hybrid combining Kahraman's study of Italian Renaissance figuration with Persian miniatures, Japanese woodcuts and medieval Arabic illuminated manuscripts. The title *Appearance of Control* points directly to the work's ambiguity: does the scene depict acts of care or of bodily mutilation carried out to conform to imposed standards of beauty? Constructed as a sliding tile puzzle, the scene is left vulnerable to rearrangement and thus, further control of the women's bodies. Themes of control and violence are prevalent across Kahraman's oeuvre, though they are often subsumed by the aesthetic harmonies of her earth-tone colours, as well as the tessellated patterns, geometric compositions and delicate brushwork for which she has become known.

KATSUSHIKA ŌI

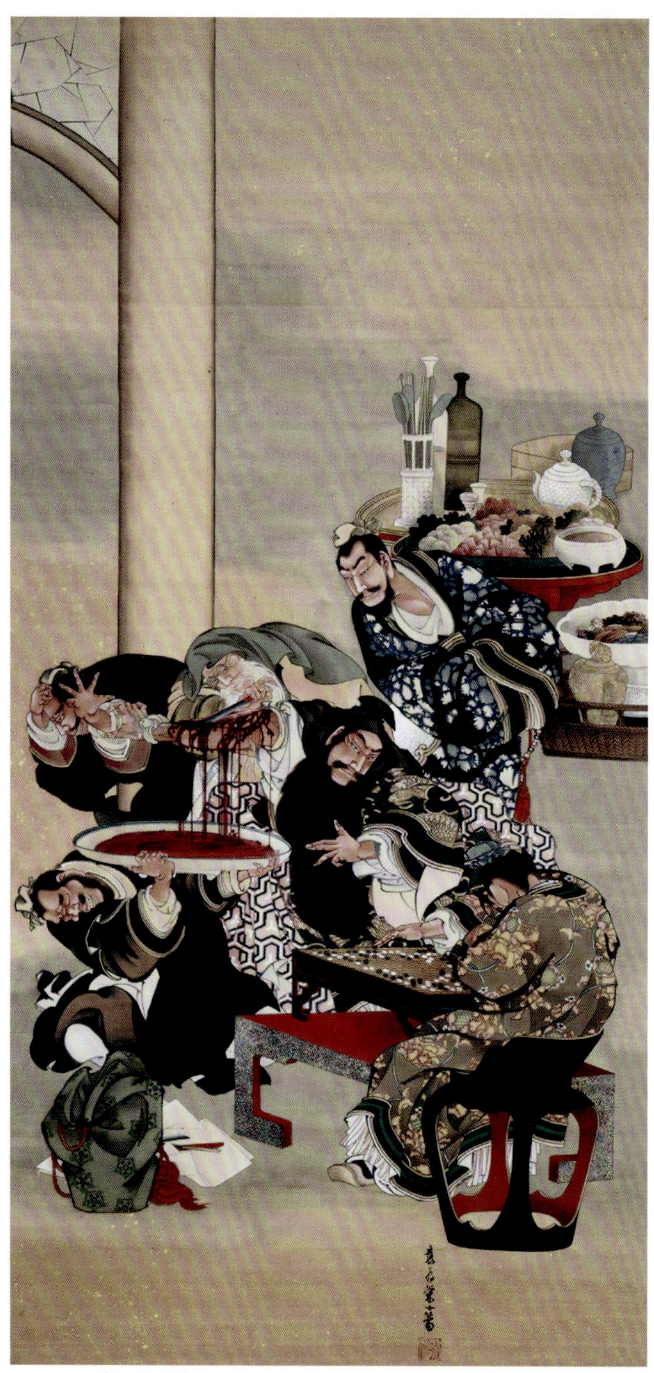

OPERATING ON GUANYU'S ARM
1840s, hanging scroll: ink, colour and gold leaf on silk, 140.2 × 68.3 cm (55 ¼ × 26 ⅞ in), Cleveland Museum of Art, Ohio, USA

Katsushika Ōi, born *c.* 1800, Tokyo, Japan. Died *c.* 1866, Tokyo.

The third daughter of the legendary painter and printmaker Katsushika Hokusai (1760–1849), Ōi was herself an acclaimed artist in the ukiyo-e style of painting. As children she and her siblings assisted their father in his workshop, from preparing paints to adding figures to his illustrations. She also produced her own paintings and drawings, garnering acclaim for her skilled portraits of the courtesans who inhabited the pleasure quarters of Edo Japan. Scenes from popular literature were another common subject for ukiyo-e artists: Ōi's largest-known painting, *Operating on Guanyu's Arm*, illustrates an episode from the fourteenth-century Chinese novel *The Romance of the Three Kingdoms*, in which a military leader undergoes a bloodletting after being poisoned. Painted on silk and richly pigmented, it would have been expensive to produce and commissioned by a wealthy patron, an indication of Ōi's professional reputation. Although only ten works have been attributed to her, it is believed that she collaborated closely with Hokusai on many of those signed with his name.

ANGELICA KAUFFMAN

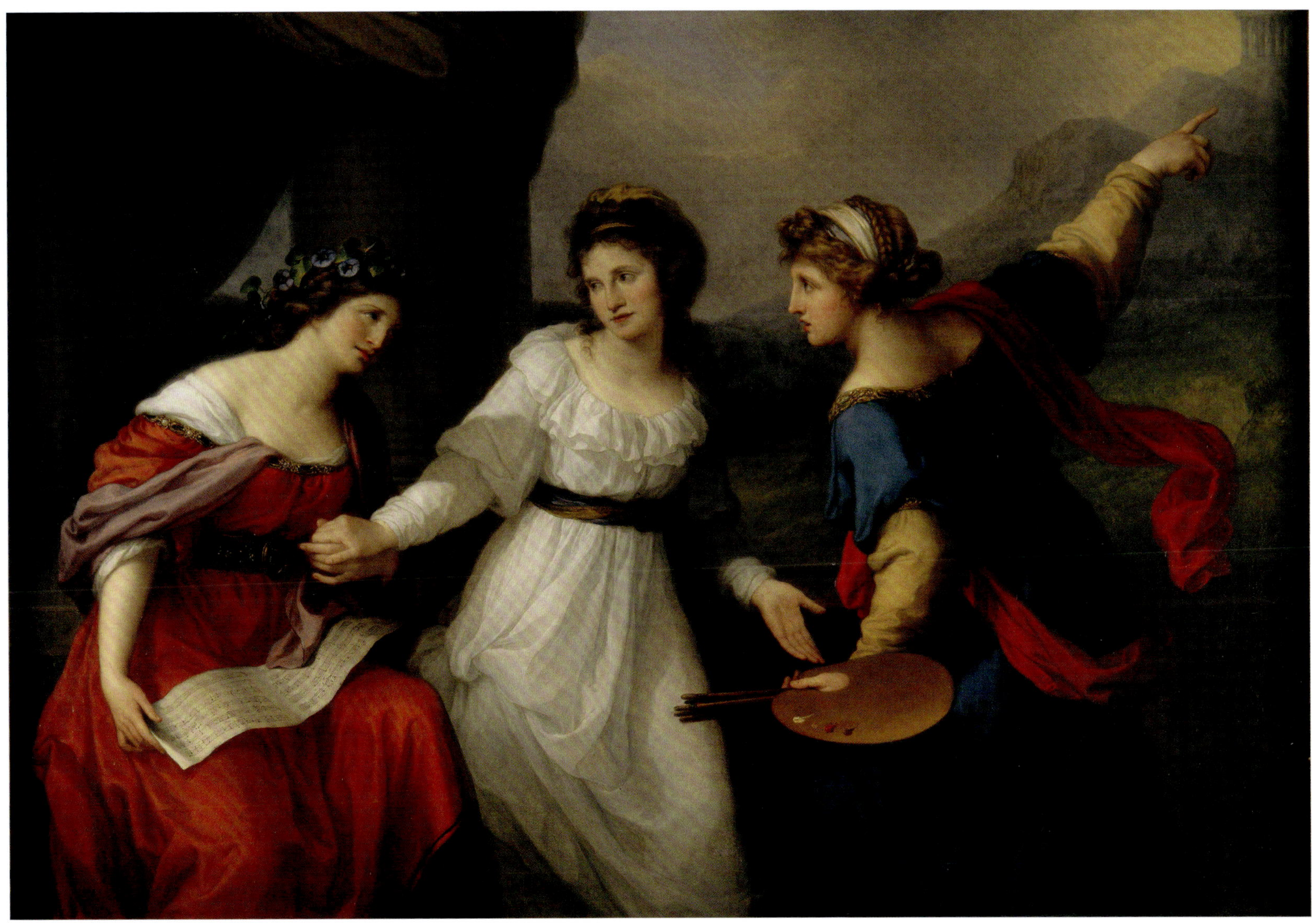

SELF-PORTRAIT OF THE ARTIST HESITATING BETWEEN THE ARTS OF MUSIC AND PAINTING
1794, oil on canvas, 147.3 × 215.9 cm (58 × 85 in), Nostell Priory, West Yorkshire, UK

Angelica Kauffman, born 1741, Chur, Switzerland. Died 1807, Rome, Italy.

One of two female founders of the Royal Academy of Arts in London, Kauffman rivalled her friend Joshua Reynolds (1723–92) as one of the most successful and celebrated artists in eighteenth-century Europe. Taught by her father, she was multilingual, highly cultured and well connected, so popular that her studio in Rome became a stop on the Grand Tour. She was famous for her portraits of European aristocracy – when she arrived in London in 1766, she was hailed as the successor to court painter Anthony van Dyck (1599–1641) – and for her history paintings, scenes of classical history and mythology that were considered the highest form of painting at the time. When she left London for Rome in 1782, she ensured the continuing visibility of her work in the form of prints. Kauffman had been a child prodigy in both music and painting, and she painted this allegorical self-portrait as a commission from Princess Holstein-Beck of Russia when she was fifty-three. A young woman in a virginal white dress stands between personifications of music and painting, undecided about which to pursue. The painting figure holds a palette and points towards a Greco-Roman temple, signifying Kauffman's Neo-Classical style.

IDA KERKOVIUS

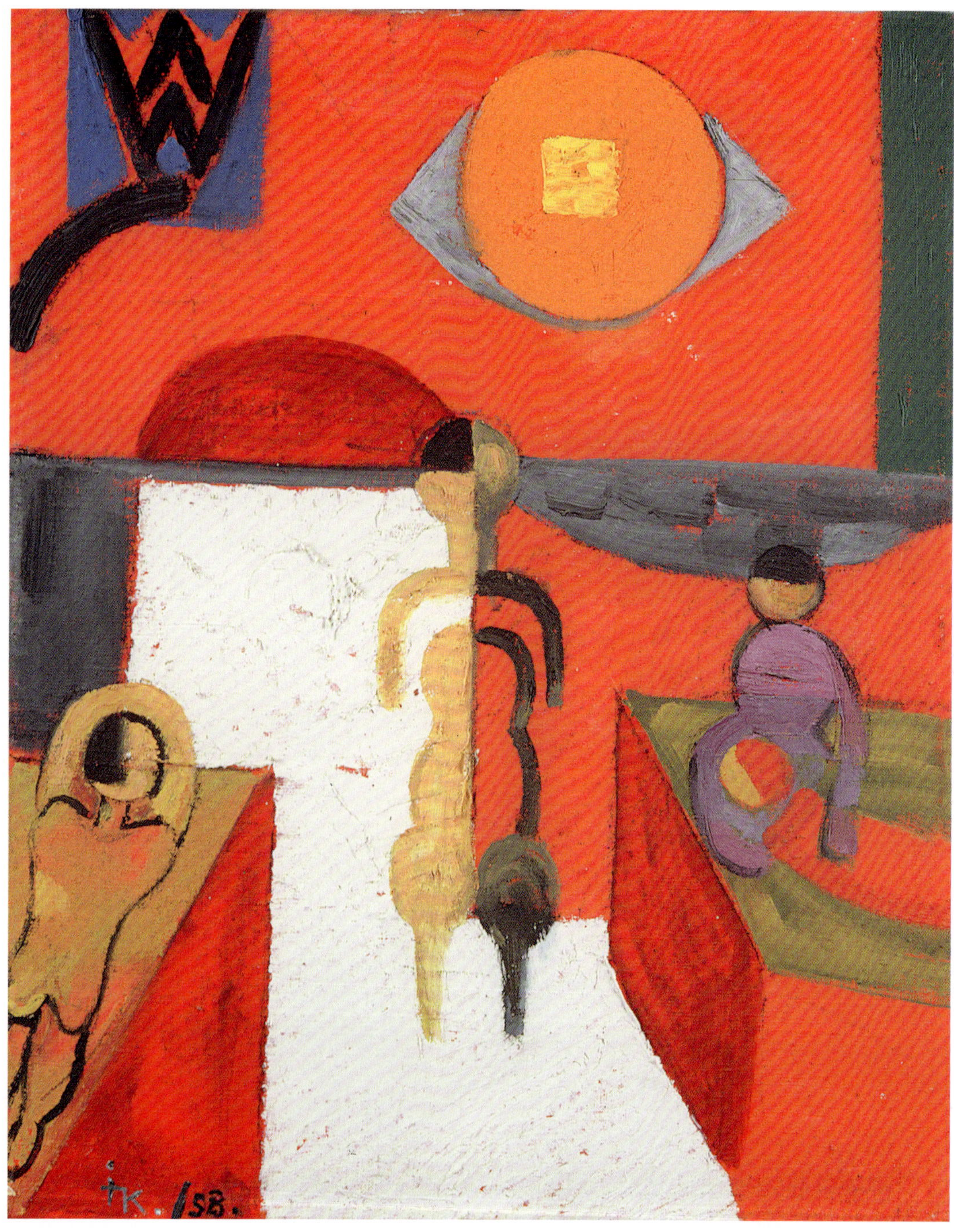

FIGÜRLICHE KOMPOSITION MIT SONNE (FIGURATIVE COMPOSITION WITH SUN)
1958, oil on canvas, 52 × 42 cm (20½ × 16½ in), Hamburger Kunsthalle, Hamburg, Germany

Ida Kerkovius, born 1879, Riga, Latvia. Died 1970, Stuttgart, Germany.

After a period of study in Dachau, Germany, with the painter Adolf Hölzel (1853–1934), Kerkovius joined the course at the Bauhaus in Weimar in 1920. There, she absorbed new theories of light and colour, and established a reputation in the school's industrial design programme, creating large-scale carpets from rectangular scraps of fabric or felt appliqué. Such commercial work would sustain her financially in the years that followed, but also suggested new possibilities for the compositional interplay of painting and textiles, evidenced in her vivid canvases some four decades later. Abstract yet suffused with symbolism, geometric yet tempered by subtle asymmetries, this 'composition' is a masterclass in European modernism. It also typifies a career jarred by two world wars – many of her pre–Second World War works were destroyed in a 1944 Stuttgart bombing – and subject to periods of obscurity and celebrity. Through it all, Kerkovius remained committed to the rigorous investigations of medium and human potential that animated the avant-garde movements of the early twentieth century.

RITA KERNN-LARSEN

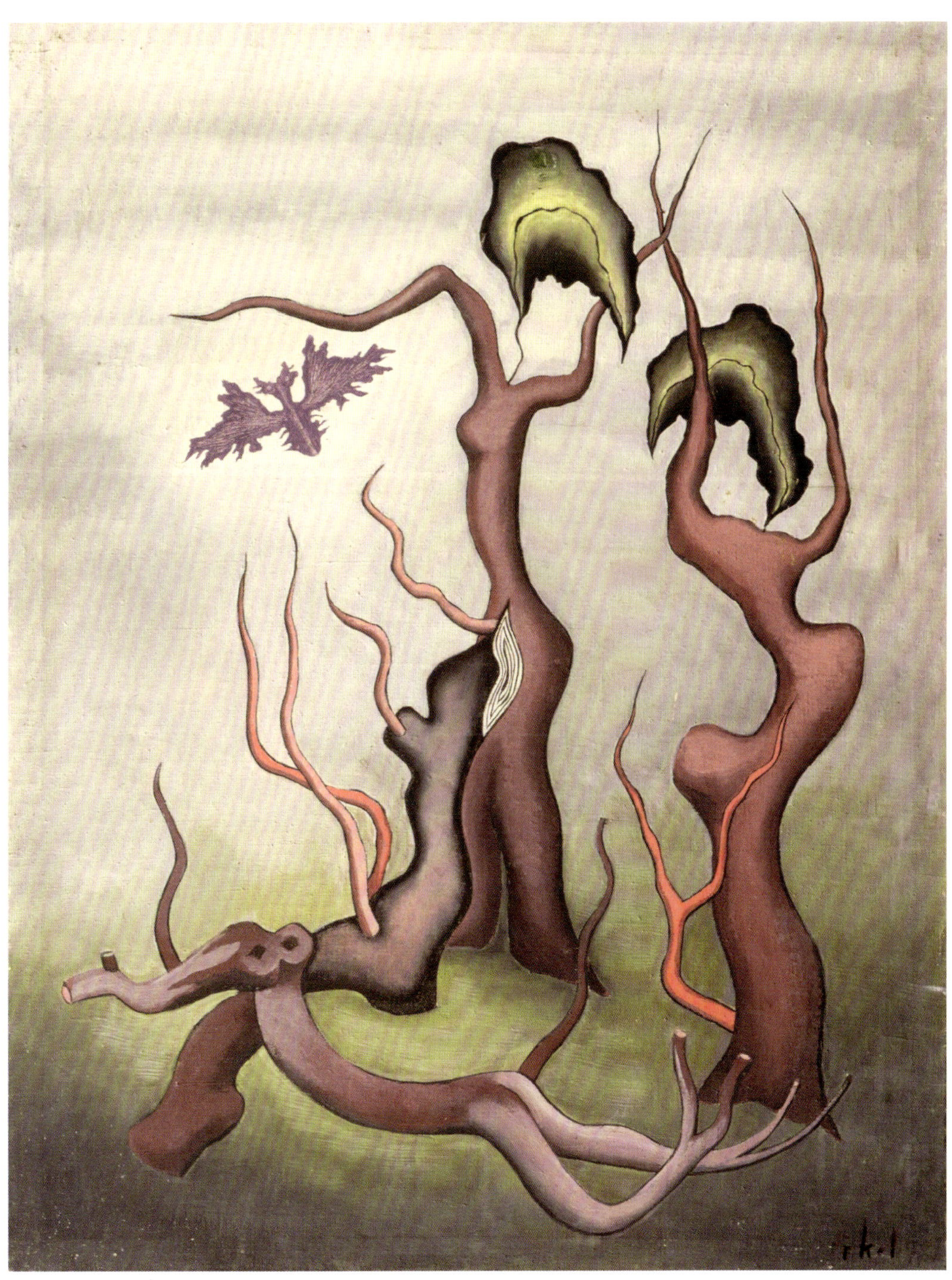

THE TWO YOUNG LADIES
1939, oil on panel, 65 × 60 cm (25 ⅝ × 23 ⅝ in), Israel Museum, Jerusalem

Rita Kernn-Larsen, born 1904, Hillerød, Denmark. Died 1998, Copenhagen, Denmark.

Kernn-Larsen took inspiration from dreams to paint images liberated from reality that transform the everyday into the unfamiliar. After studying at the Art Academy in Copenhagen, she moved to Paris in 1929 where she enrolled at the Académie Moderne and became a favourite pupil of Fernand Léger (1881–1955). She returned to Denmark in 1934 where she befriended members of the Danish Surrealist group and staged her first solo exhibition in Copenhagen. Her work appeared in landmark Surrealist exhibitions in London and Paris, including the International Surrealist Exhibition in 1938, the same year she became the first Surrealist to exhibit with Peggy Guggenheim at her fledgling London gallery, Guggenheim Jeune. *The Two Young Ladies* includes a pair of abstracted figures, women with branching arms, legs like tree limbs and verdant, crescent heads like leaves. The hybrid woman-tree, or *femme-arbre*, was a recurring theme in Kernn-Larsen's work and here is emblematic of her placement of abstracted, biomorphic figures in dreamlike landscapes.

SANAM KHATIBI

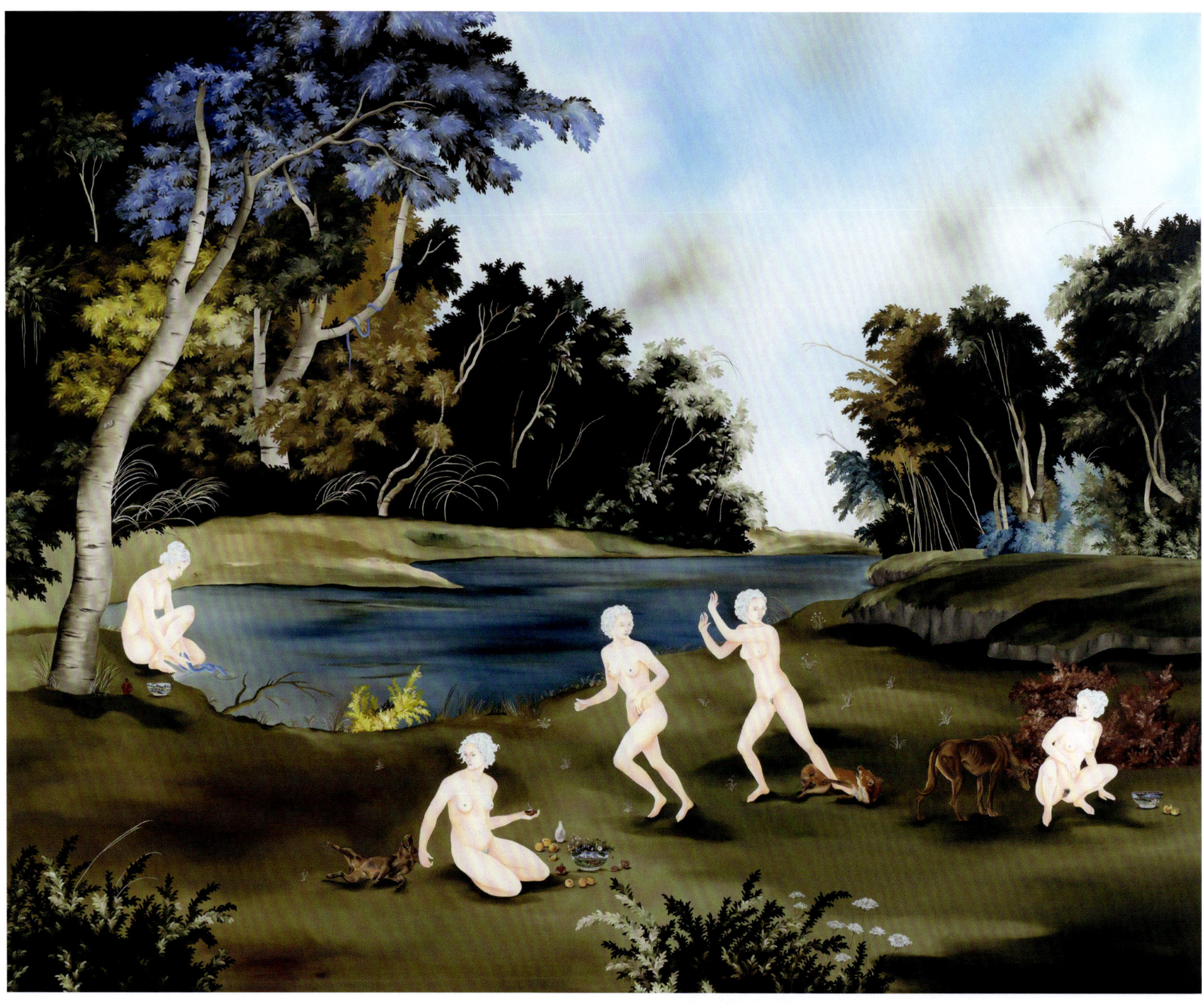

THIRTY DAYS OF HUNGER
2019, oil and pencil on canvas, 200 × 250 cm (78 ¾ × 98 ⅜ in)

Sanam Khatibi, born 1979, Tehran, Iran.

Born in Iran but raised in Copenhagen, London and Brussels, Belgian artist Khatibi's painting practice brings together her international upbringing with references ranging from the Bayeux Tapestry to the art of Hieronymus Bosch (*c.* 1450–1516). Exploring weighty themes such as power and human nature, her works frequently depict female protagonists in fantastical landscapes, blurring the lines of long-held dichotomies: dominance and submission, animal and human, past and future. In *Thirty days of hunger*, she depicts five porcelain nudes in a pastoral setting. Though most of the work is rendered in exquisite detail, Khatibi purposely leaves the hair of the women unpainted, outlining their features and limbs only with pencil. In doing so, she calls attention to the act of painting and the construction of women as fetishized objects of desire. Yet even as the work quotes art history – from arrangements evocative of Dutch still life to depictions of Adam and Eve reminiscent of Renaissance painting – its narrative remains unresolved. Without any explicit myth or allegory to tie it down, her work offers a vision of the future made up of components from the past, fashioning a matriarchal universe where laws of nature and expectations for being remain unfixed.

FIZA KHATRI

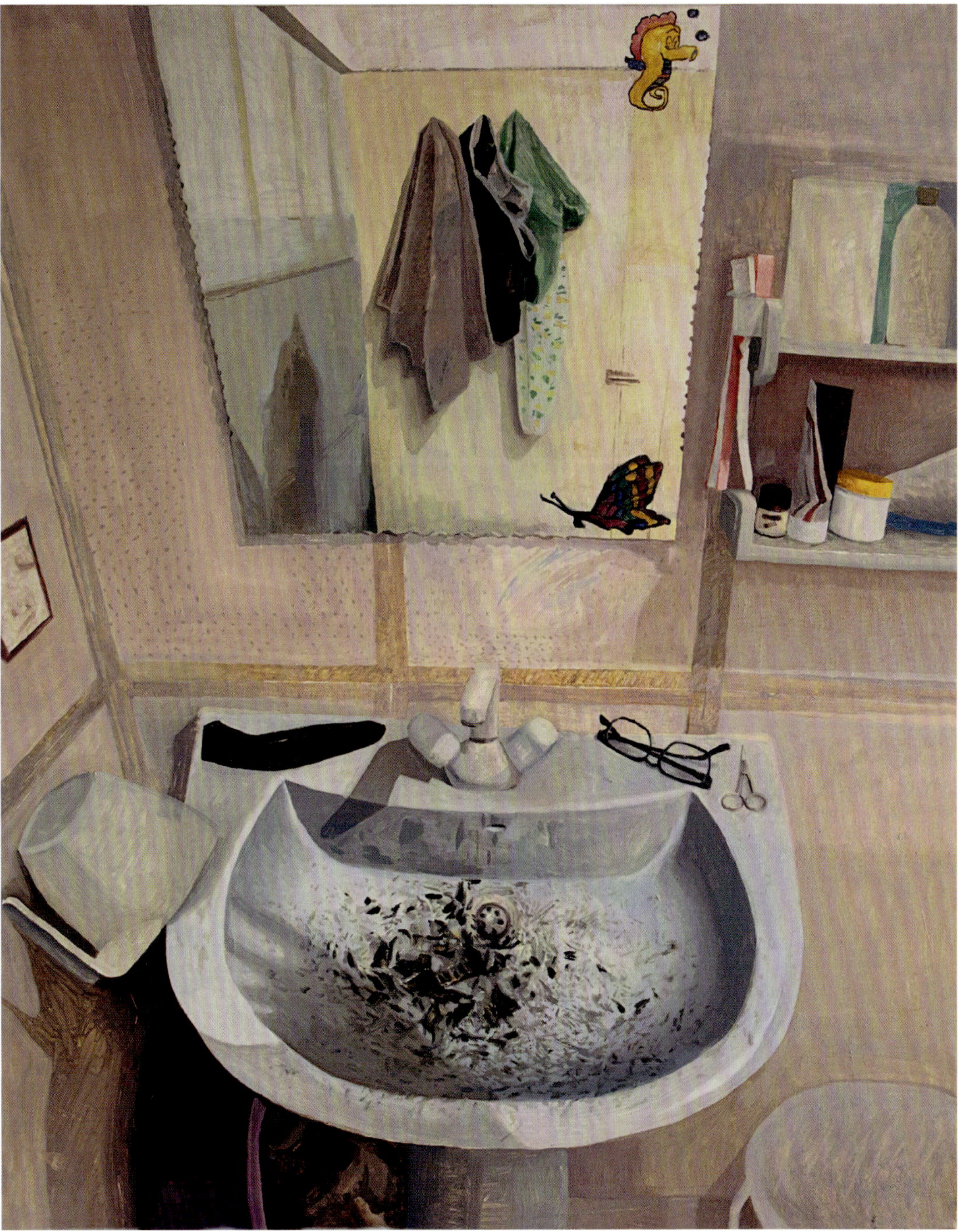

THE SINK
2020, oil on canvas, 76.2 × 61 cm (30 × 24 in)

Fiza Khatri, born 1992, Karachi, Pakistan.

Inspired by her immediate circle of friends, family and pets, Khatri's work explores themes of love, kinship and togetherness. Travelling from Pakistan to the United States in 2013, Khatri received a BA from Mount Holyoke College in Massachusetts and studied painting and printmaking at Yale School of Art. Her figurative paintings overflow with closely observed detail and lively brushwork, offering intimate glimpses into her everyday life and relationships: from meeting with friends over dinner or having her hair cut in a barber shop to posed portraits, domestic scenes and tender depictions of her beloved cats and dogs. Working from photographs, observation and her own memories of people and places, her open-ended images invite multiple interpretations. Many reflect her experiences of queerness. *The Sink*, which she considers a self-portrait, was painted following a relationship break-up. It depicts a bathroom basin filled with trimmings from the artist's own hair, which she cut off in a gesture to claim ownership over her own body.

KAREN KILIMNIK

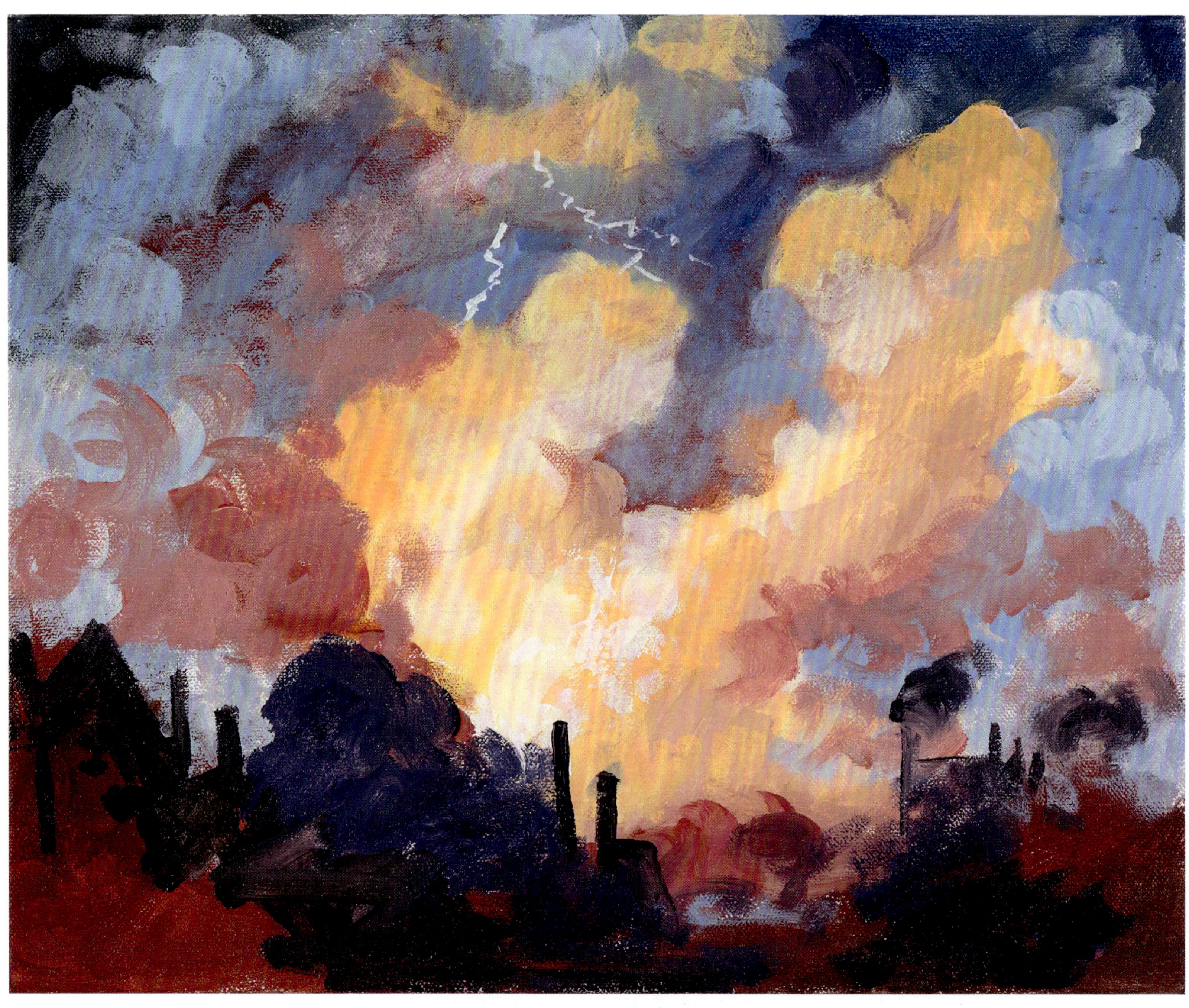

THE FACTORIES OF MARS AND MERCURY
2017, water soluble oil colour on canvas, 20.5 × 25.5 cm (8 × 10 in), Aïshti Foundation, Beirut, Lebanon

Karen Kilimnik, born 1955, Philadelphia, USA.

Influenced by traditions of Romantic painting, portraiture and landscape, Kilimnik gives equal weight to a range of disparate subjects in her work – from popular culture to Old Master paintings, via television shows, movies, books, magazines, animal portraits and fairy tales – such that distinctions between 'high' and 'low' culture dissolve. This creative levelling was apparent in her early works – following studies in art and architecture in Philadelphia, in the late 1980s and early 1990s she presented a series of exhibitions featuring paintings, photographs, drawings, installations, sculptures and films arranged around the exhibition space. Kilimnik's paintings include portraits, landscapes, houses and interiors, animals and scenes from the ballet, rendering mythology, femininity and historical and fictional themes through her confident, loose brushwork. Inspired by a Hubert Robert (1733–1808) painting, this work depicts a landscape that simultaneously rivets the viewer to the spot as it transports them up, up and away – from the factory of Mars (the god of war) to his planetary namesake.

KIYOHARA YUKINOBU

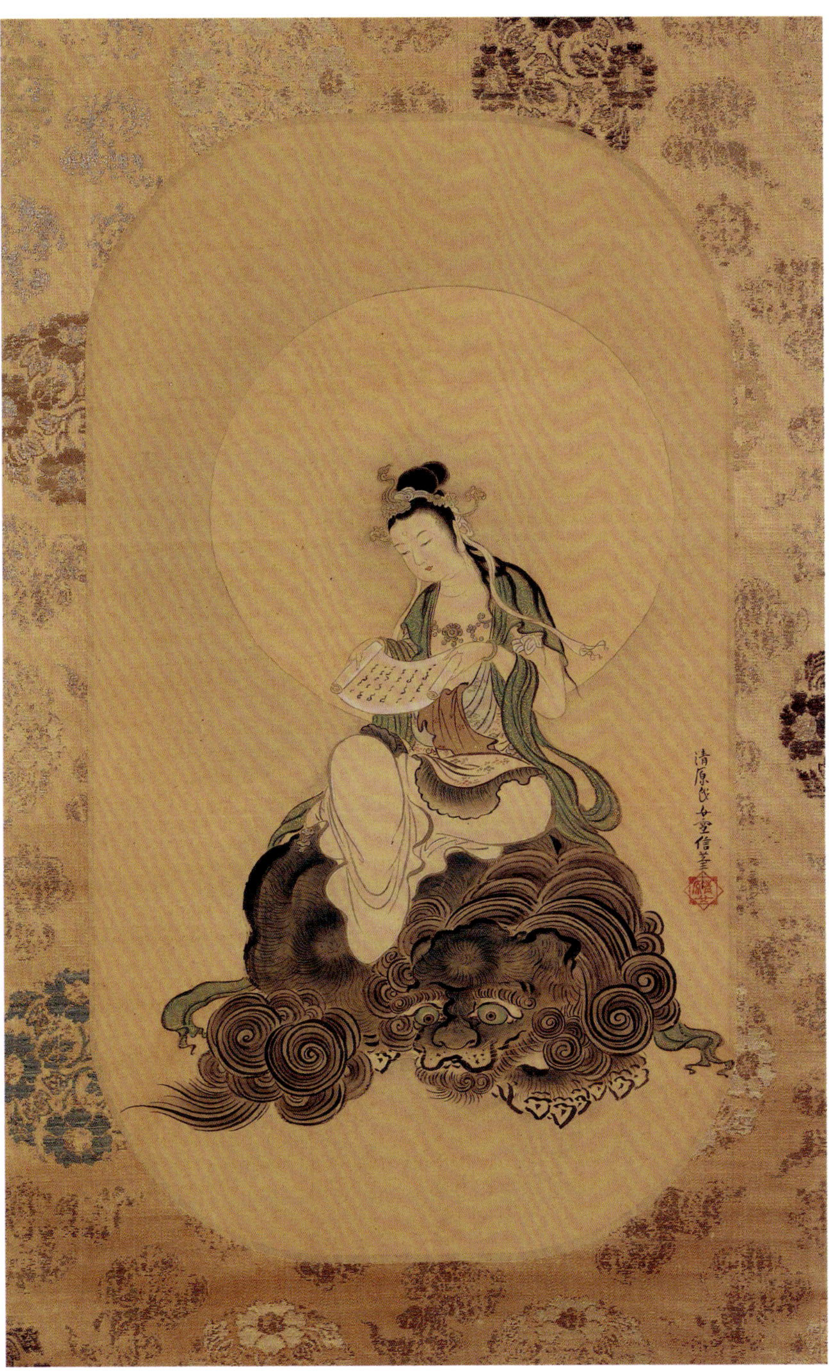

MONJU ON A LION
second half 17th century, ink and colour on silk, 60.9 × 36 cm (24 × 14 ⅛ in), Minneapolis Institute of Art, USA

Kiyohara Yukinobu, born 1643, Kyoto, Japan. Died 1682, Japan.

Recognized in her time as a 'woman highly accomplished in the arts' (*keishū*), Kiyohara was one of the first women painters in Japan to make a living from her work. She was affiliated with the Kanō school, a hereditary school of painters that was highly influential in Japan from the late fifteenth to the late nineteenth centuries. Kiyohara's father, Kusumi Morikage (*c.*1620–90), was a pupil of Kanō Tan'yū (1602–74), then head of the Kanō school; her mother, Kuniko, was Tan'yū's niece. Kiyohara probably trained under her father, learning the techniques of Kanō painting, which was influenced by Chinese brush and ink painting but incorporated Japanese colours and decorative elements. Her professional success is demonstrated by the fact that she signed and sealed many of her works, ranging from large folding screens to small silk scrolls such as *Monju on a Lion* (originally part of a triptych of scrolls depicting various deities). Religious scenes such as this were common in the Kanō school: Kiyohara distinguishes herself with the delicacy and detail of the brushstrokes rendering the finely clothed bodhisattva as he sits astride a blue lion.

EMILY KAME KNGWARREYE

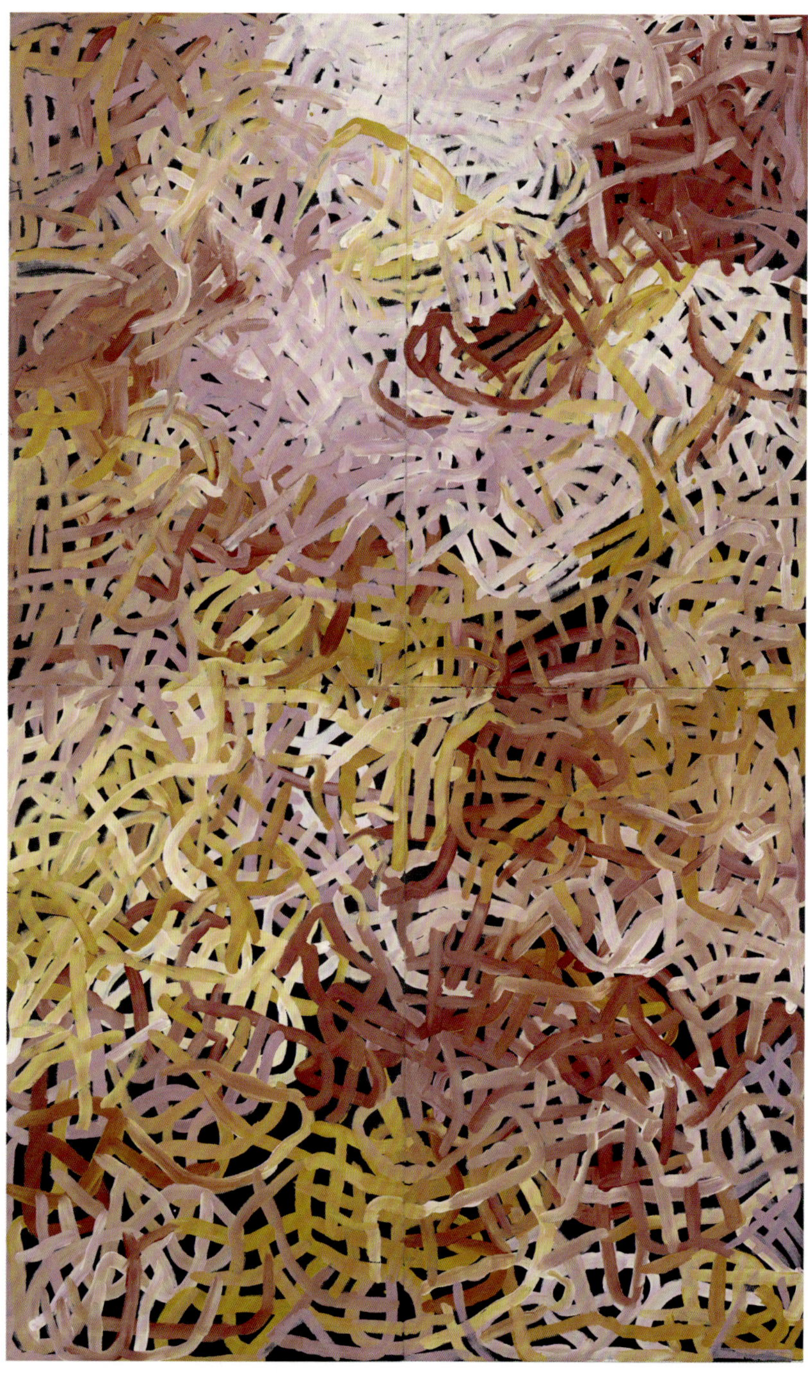

ANWERLARR ANGERR (BIG YAM)
1996, synthetic polymer paint on canvas, 401 × 245 cm (157 ⅞ × 96 ½ in), National Gallery of Victoria, Melbourne, Australia

Emily Kame Kngwarreye, born *c.*1910, Utopia, Northern Territory, Australia. Died 1996, Alice Springs, Northern Territory, Australia.

Raised in the Anmatyerre tradition of mark-making, Kngwarreye's works of the late 1970s and 1980s consisted of batik-based fabric designs, a technique developed through her activities with the communal Utopia Women's Batik Group in the Alhalkere clan country. It was not until her late seventies that she transitioned to painting, the medium in which she found she was able to express herself to her fullest potential. A prolific artist, she created thousands of paintings in the eight years she worked in the medium. As an Anmatyerre elder, Kngwarreye was a steward of women's Dreaming sites in Alhalkere, a role she expressed visually through painting. She explored relationships among spirits, people, plants, animals and the land, connecting with spirit ancestors through stories, art, ceremony and songs. *Anwerlarr angerr (Big yam)* is indicative of her use of layering, intertwining colours, the black background almost twinkly beneath. The seemingly endless interlocking lines illustrate Kngwarreye's instinctive and organic painting style and may represent the vines of the wild yam plant or the paths taken by ancestors on sacred Aboriginal land.

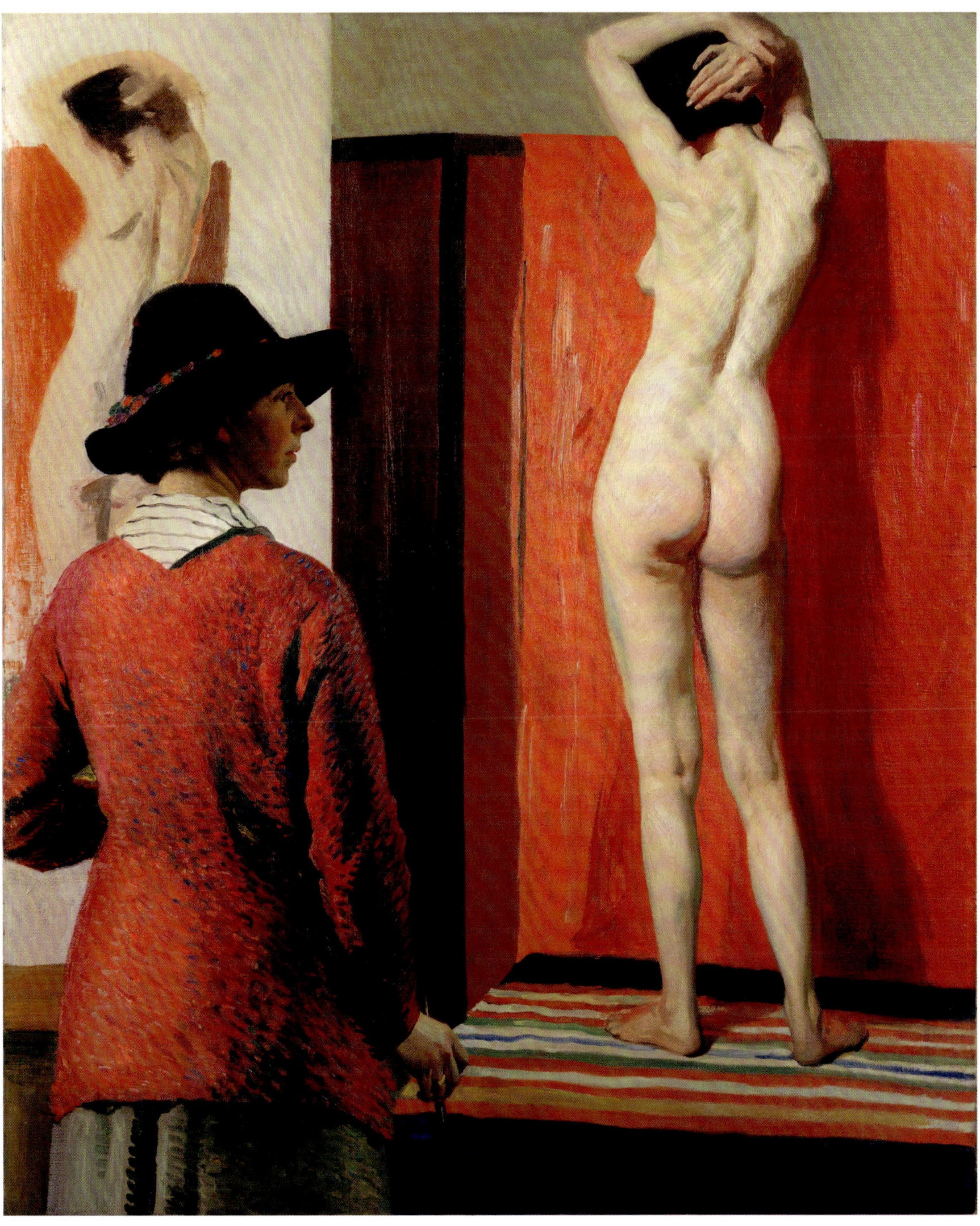

LAURA KNIGHT WITH MODEL, ELLA LOUISE NAPER ('SELF PORTRAIT')
1913, oil on canvas, 152.4 × 127.6 cm (60 × 50¼ in), National Portrait Gallery, London, UK

Laura Knight, born 1877, Long Eaton, Derbyshire, UK. Died 1970, London, UK.

An inventory of unprecedented achievements distinguished Knight's career: she was the first woman artist made a Dame of the British Empire, the first fully elected to the Royal Academy of Arts, London, and the first to hold a retrospective there. Trained in the academic tradition, she found in Impressionism's luminosity and movement a distinct pictorial style. For all the apparent miscellany of Knight's subjects – from ballet dancers to circus performers, travelling communities and the Auxiliary Air Force – in theme, they share a common interest in women's work. Her parallel commitment to representing poor and marginalized individuals lends her paintings the urgency of social documentary. Indeed, Knight was a prolific chronicler of state history, too – she completed several commissions for the War Artists Advisory Committee during the Second World War and was invited to depict the Nuremberg trials in 1946. Her career, however, was not without controversy. Reclaiming the female nude from the purview of men, this 'self-portrait' is as much a tender portrait of Knight and her friend as it was an affront to established taste. Then considered an improper subject for women artists, this figure study is renowned today for its formal elegance and conceptual complexity.

JOYCE KOZLOFF

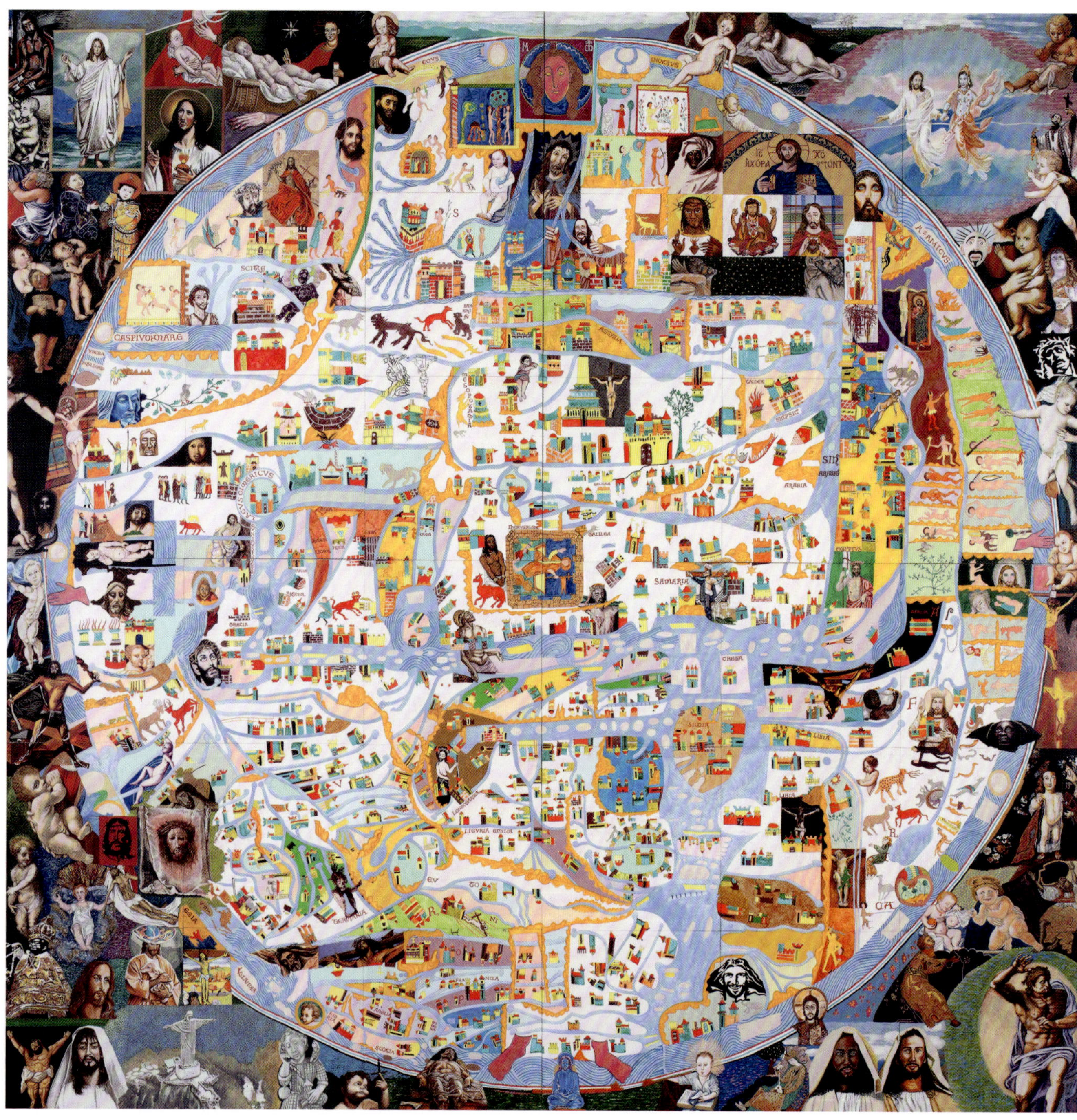

JEEZ
2012, acrylic on panel, 365.8 × 365.8 cm
(144 × 144 in)

Joyce Kozloff, born 1942, Somerville, New Jersey, USA.

One of the primary artists associated with the Pattern and Decoration movement of the 1970s, Kozloff's early paintings comprised kaleidoscopic fields of vibrant quilt and textile motifs – lending a serious modernist charge to artistic mediums that had long been dismissed as 'decorative arts' or 'women's work'. She was equally involved in the feminist art movement of the same decade, co-founding the influential collective and journal *Heresies* in 1976 along with artists including Harmony Hammond (p.130), Miriam Schapiro (p.259) and May Stevens (1924–2019). In more recent series, Kozloff has been inspired by cartography, a reference that enables her to critique and subvert Western visual paradigms related to colonization, religion and empire. Dense arrangements of fragmented images continue to fill the busy, flatbed surfaces of paintings such as *JEEZ*. Created in response to the ascendance of evangelical Christian doctrine in contemporary American politics, the work features a diverse array of artistic representations of the historical Jesus Christ, whose many visages – Byzantine and Baroque, painterly and kitsch, and racially coded as variously white, Black, Latino and other ethnicities – swirl around an abstracted medieval map.

LEE KRASNER

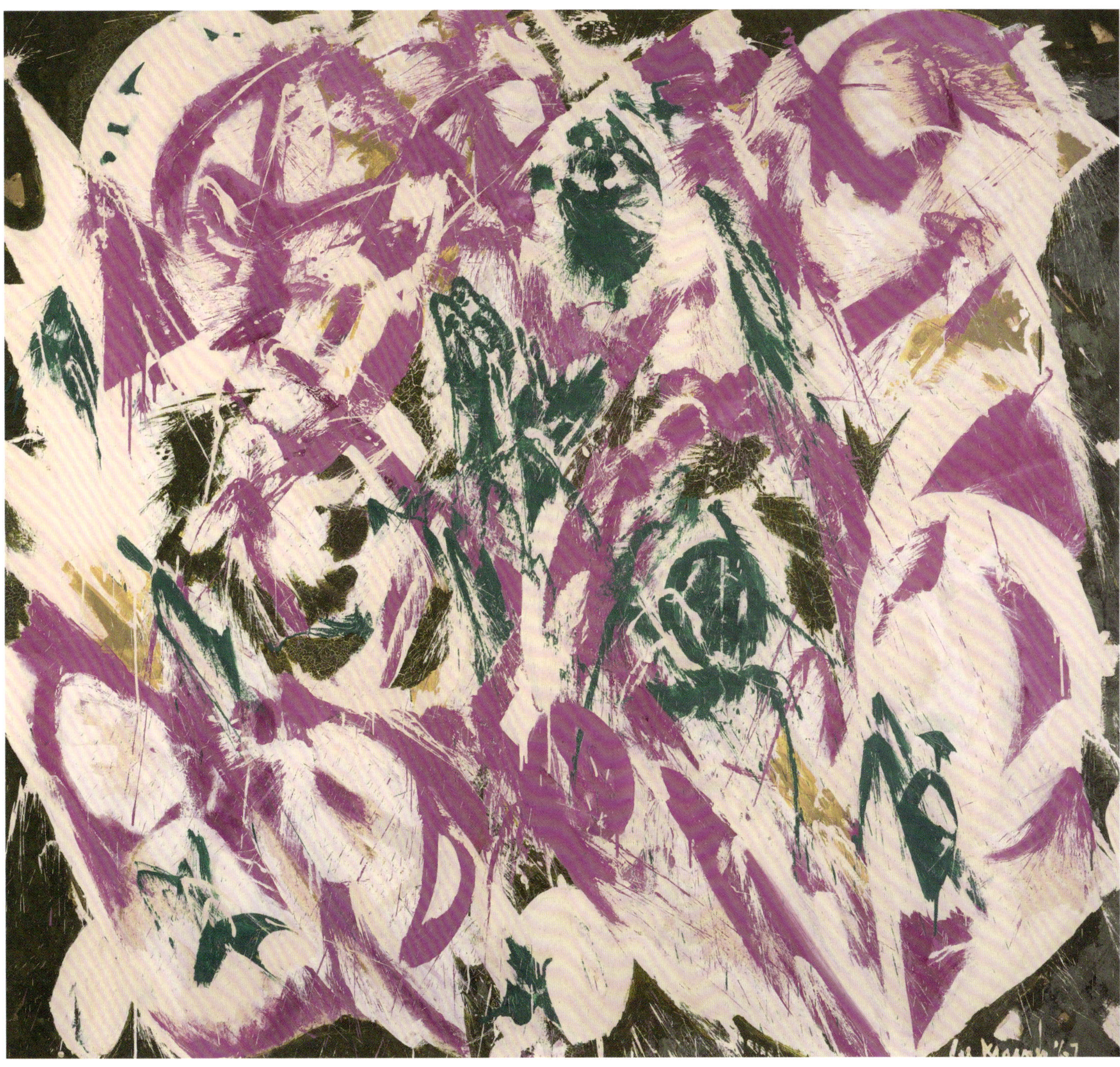

TOWARDS ONE
1967, oil on canvas, 174 × 190.5 cm (68 ½ × 75 in), Indianapolis Museum of Art, USA

Lee Krasner, born 1908, Brooklyn, USA. Died 1984, New York, USA.

Krasner was a member of the first generation of Abstract Expressionists and is one of the movement's best-known practitioners. She began producing abstract compositions after studying modernist artistic principles with Hans Hofmann (1880–1966), in whose classes she enrolled in 1937. Just a few years later, in 1941, she met Jackson Pollock (1912–56), and the two quickly became a couple. The pair influenced each other's work, with Krasner's paintings becoming more emotive and inwardly focused as she experimented with a variety of aesthetic approaches from the 1940s until the mid-1950s. By the latter part of that decade, following Pollock's death, the scale of Krasner's work expanded and her canvases became populated with large, curvilinear forms executed with loose, sweeping, gestural marks. By the 1960s, as seen in works such as *Towards One*, Krasner committed herself to a brilliant palette, often using bright pinks and greens, which gave her works an overall sense of ebullience, as if joy were triumphing over chaos.

ELLA KRUGLYANSKAYA

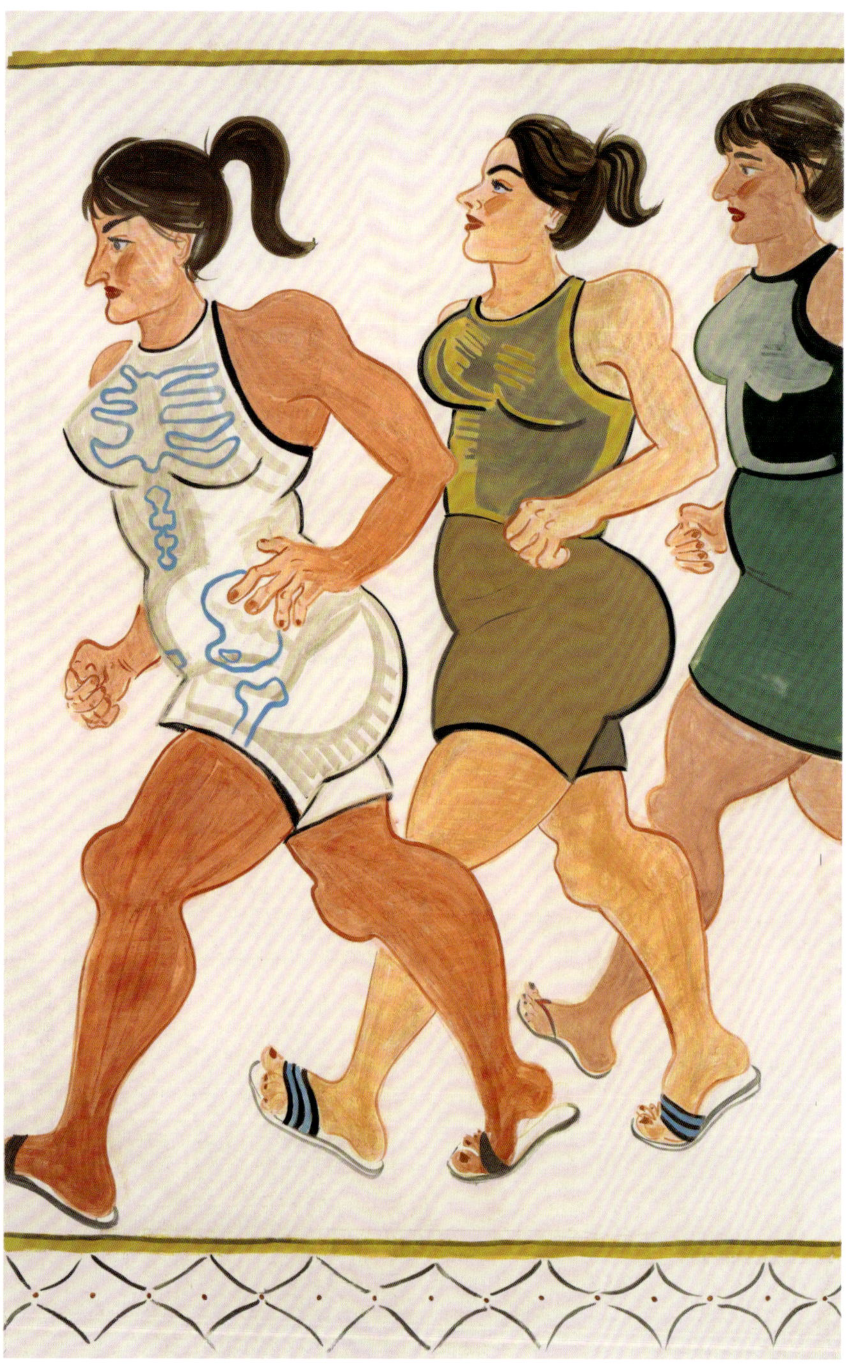

EXIT IN FLIP FLOPS
2016, fresco, 233 × 150 cm (91 ¾ × 59 in)

Ella Kruglyanskaya, born 1978, Riga, Latvia.

Kruglyanskaya's bold and bawdy paintings intervene in the traditional representations of women across visual history. Raised in Latvia, the artist moved to the United States in the mid-1990s, graduating with painting degrees from Cooper Union in 2001 and Yale School of Art in 2006 before eventually settling in New York, where she lives and works. Her playful images of strong, voluptuous women are born entirely from her imagination in a style that combines the painterly and the graphic. There is a robust physicality to Kruglyanskaya's protagonists; her women are strong, assertive and often humorous, sometimes engaged in banal, everyday tasks, at others participating in moments of undisclosed drama, as with the three running figures in this dynamic fresco. Though Kruglyanskaya describes her paintings as 'anti-style', a range of influences can be detected in her work, from ancient Etruscan wall painting to German Expressionism to 1950s film posters and cartoon strips – deliberately employing various aesthetics and the associations they conjure to communicate specific messages about women's experiences in the range of worlds they inhabit.

ELKE SILVIA KRYSTUFEK

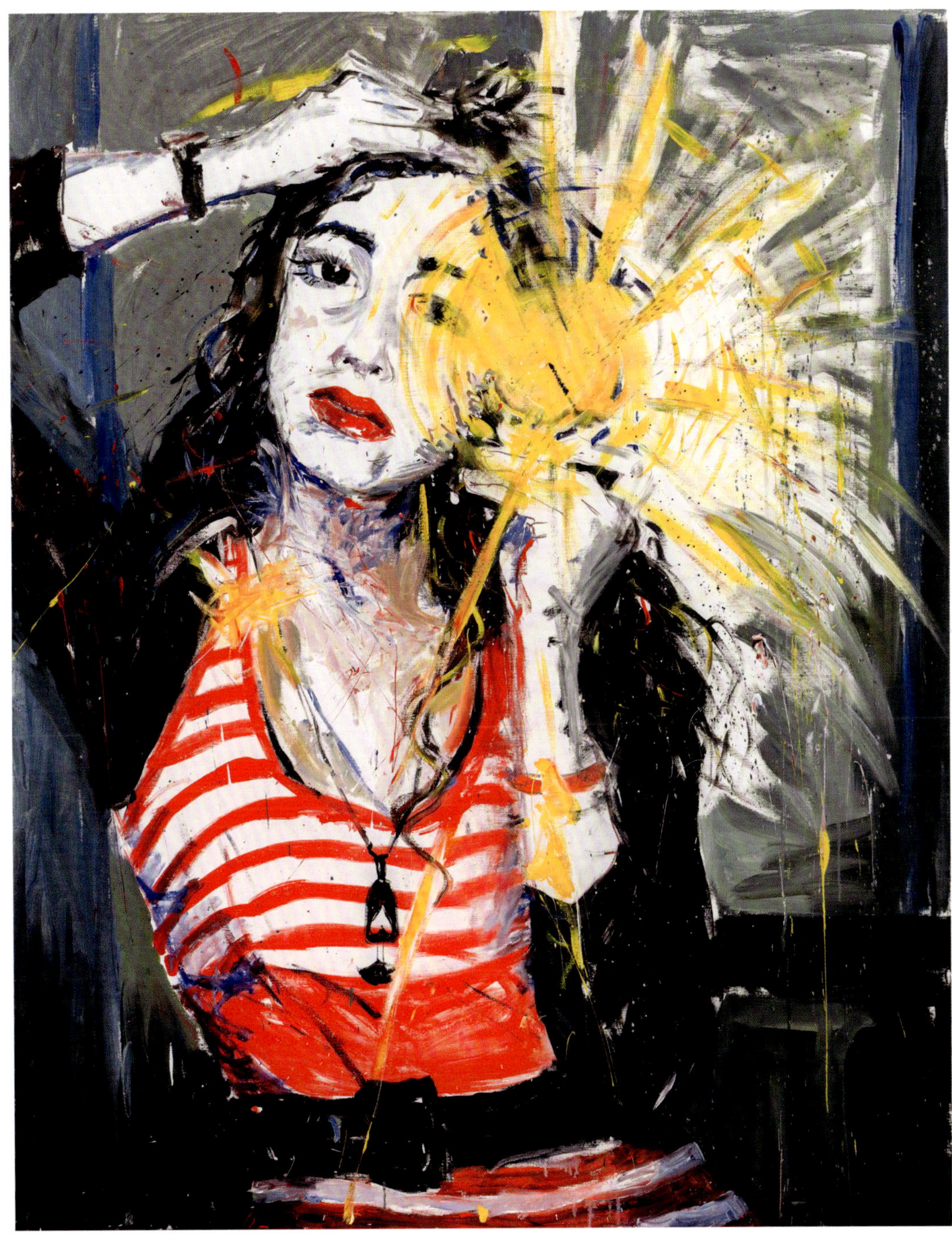

CHELSEA LIGHT
1998, acrylic and dispersion on canvas,
170 × 134.5 cm (66 7/8 × 53 in)

Elke Silvia Krystufek, born 1970, Vienna, Austria.

After studying with Art Informel pioneer Arnulf Rainer (b. 1929) at Vienna's Academy of Fine Arts from 1988 to 1992, Krystufek emerged on the art scene in the late 1990s with a multifaceted practice focused on issues such as personal struggles, social constructions and feminine identity. Despite also working across collage, video, drawing and installation, painting is the bedrock of her practice. Krystufek's paintings are predominantly self-portraits, made in front of a mirror, where the artist exhibits herself free from psychological or physical inhibitions, surrendering herself completely to the gaze of the viewer. This gesture, however, triggers a reverse phenomenon whereby the stereotyped vulnerability of the painted subject slowly evolves into a challenging, even openly confrontational statement about how the female body is perceived and represented in art. *Chelsea Light* exemplifies how Krystufek's multiple interpretations of herself reveal the complexities and contradictions that form a human being. Characterized by vigorous brushstrokes and powerful colours, it stages a battle where the artist's inner insecurities are counterbalanced by her trademark intense stare, successfully subverting the role of the observer and the observed.

YAYOI KUSAMA

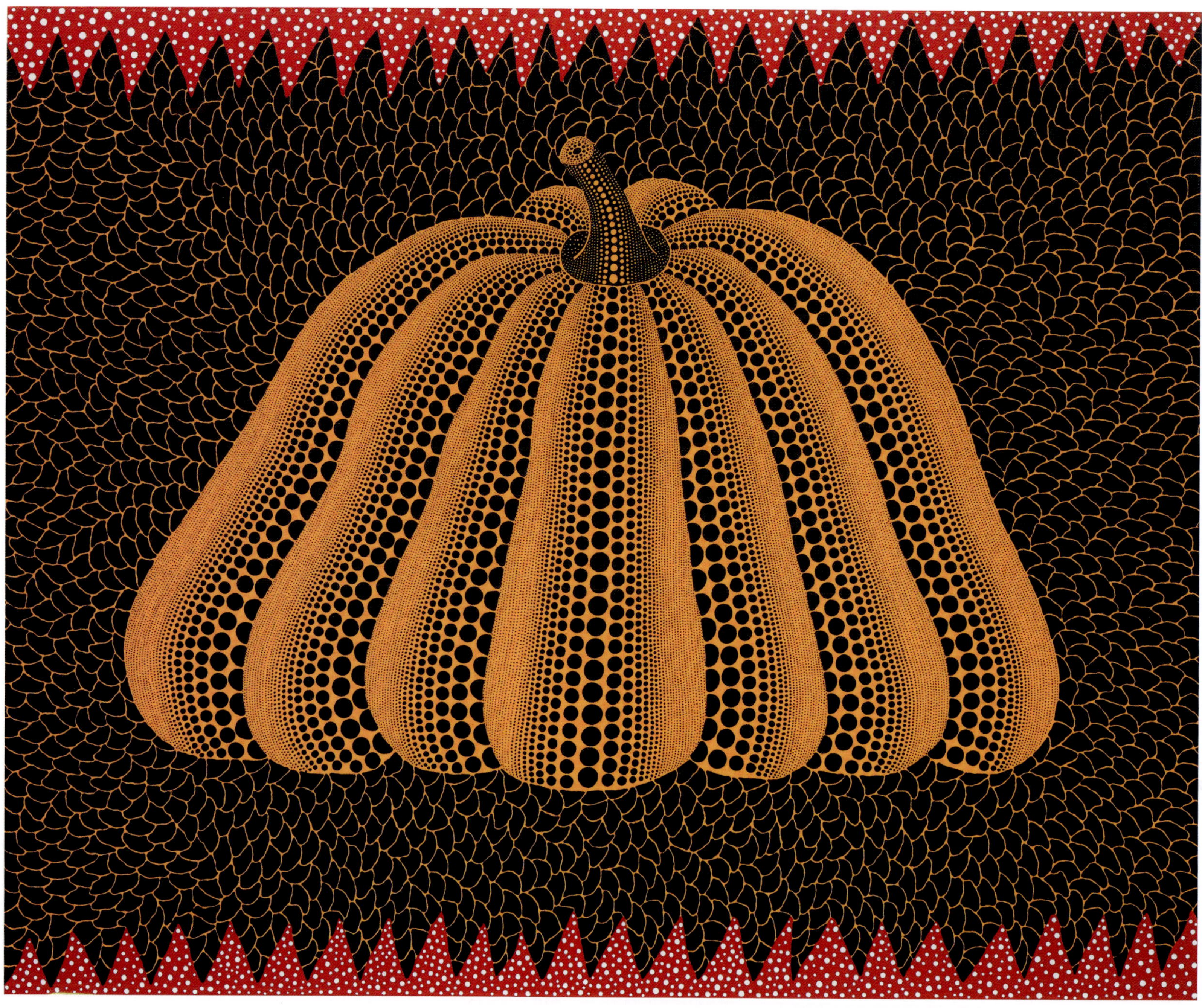

PUMPKIN [DRZRZ]
2018, acrylic on canvas, 130.3 × 162 cm
(51 ¼ × 63 ¾ in)

Yayoi Kusama, born 1929, Matsumoto, Nagano Prefecture, Japan.

Best known for her polka dot patterns, amoebic forms and immersive environments, Kusama has honed a recognizable style in works spanning painting, sculpture and installation. Many of her themes and motifs stem from the hallucinations that she has experienced since childhood – including proliferating fields of dots – finding that expressing them artistically helps to quell her fears and anxieties. As depicted in *PUMPKIN [DRZRZ]*, the pumpkin is one of Kusama's other key recurring subjects, one that has positive associations of comfort and stability for the artist. In 1948 she moved to Kyoto to attend art school, where she studied Japanese modernist Nihonga painting. She moved to New York in 1958 where she established herself at the heart of avant-garde artistic communities, staging happenings and performances and exhibiting alongside artists such as Donald Judd (1928–94) and Eva Hesse (1936–70). Although rooted in her idiosyncratic worldview, her bold and repetitive imagery played an important role in the development of art movements including Pop art and Minimalism. Kusama returned to Japan in 1973 due to health issues and continues to live and work in Tokyo.

ADÉLAÏDE LABILLE-GUIARD

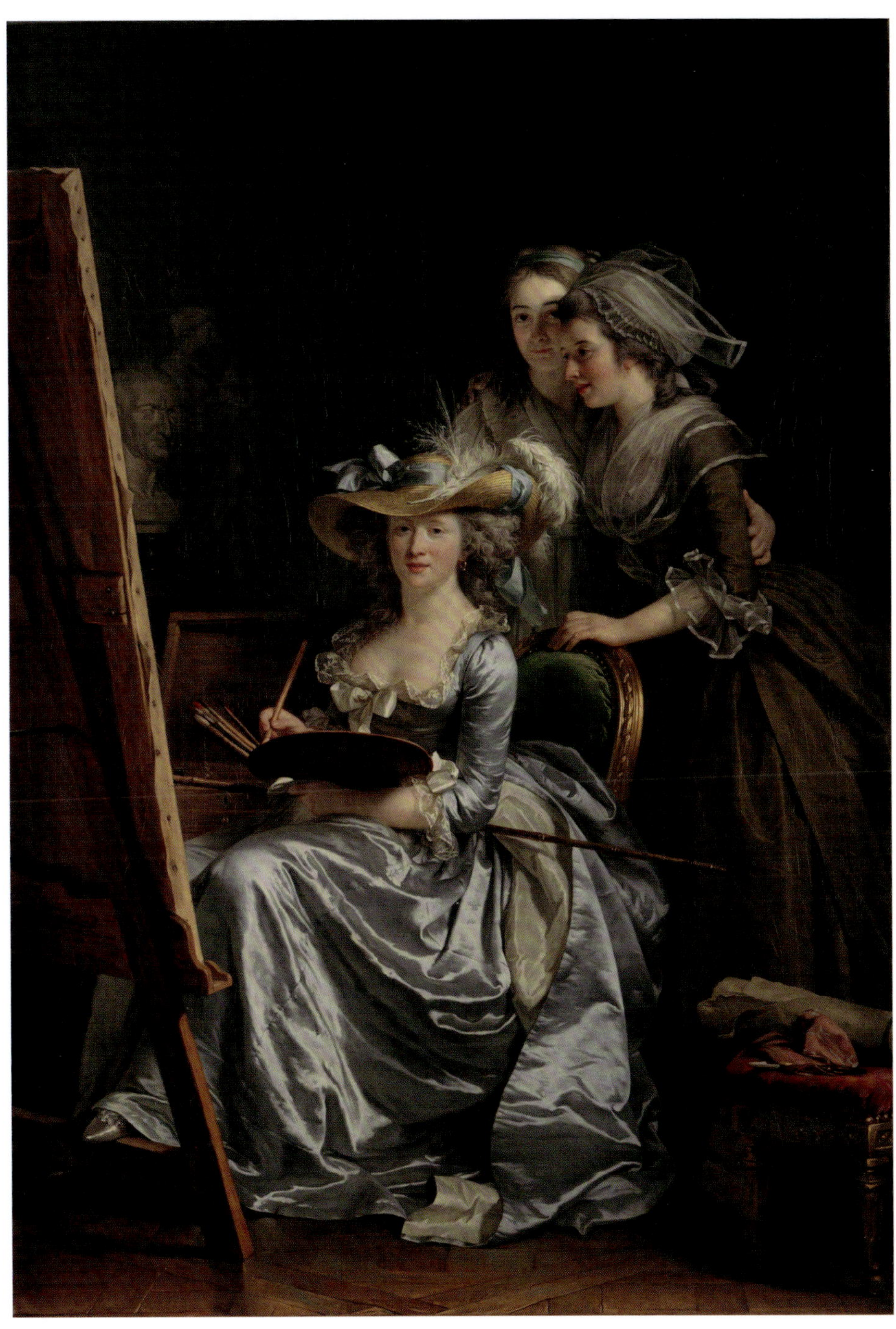

SELF-PORTRAIT WITH TWO PUPILS, MARIE GABRIELLE CAPET (1761–1818) AND MARIE MARGUERITE CARREAUX DE ROSEMOND (DIED 1788)
1785, oil on canvas, 210.8 × 151.1 cm (83 × 59½ in), Metropolitan Museum of Art, New York, USA

Adélaïde Labille-Guiard, born 1749, Paris, France. Died 1803, Paris.

The daughter of a shopkeeper, Labille-Guiard did not have a natural entrée to the art world. She began by painting in the tradition of miniatures and pastels, graduating to oil painting under the history painter and portraitist François-André Vincent (1746–1816). In 1783 she was admitted to the Académie Royale de Peinture et de Sculpture with her contemporary Élisabeth Vigée-Lebrun (p.310) at a time when King Louis XVI had restricted female membership to four. This monumental painting was exhibited at the 1785 Salon and established Labille-Guiard as a talent to rival her male counterparts. Though incongruously dressed for painting a self-portrait, in satin gown and feathered hat, the artist demonstrates her status as an academician and her prowess through an exquisite execution of textures. Moreover, in depicting herself teaching younger women (including Marie Gabrielle Capet, p.68) to paint, she announces her aim of promoting their advancement within the male-dominated Academy. The painting won her critical acclaim and the patronage of the king's aunts, but her timing was unfortunate: this momentum was dramatically derailed by the 1789 French Revolution.

JOY LABINJO

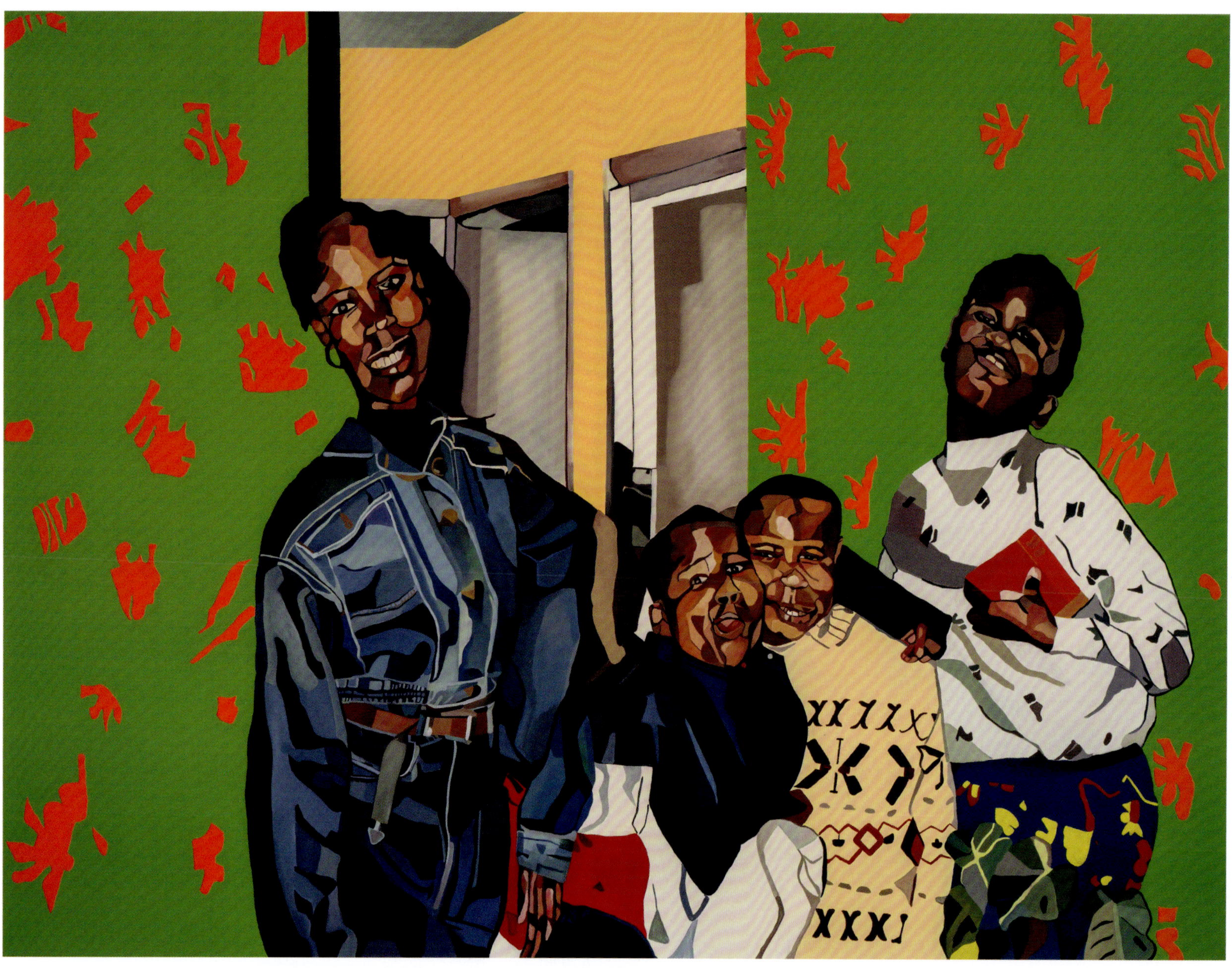

COME PLAY WITH US
2019, oil on canvas, 150 × 200 cm (59 × 78 ¾ in)

Joy Labinjo, born 1994, London, UK.

Labinjo's portraits explore community, intimacy and memory in her signature style of flattened perspective, vibrant colours and figures that appear almost sculptural in their geometric formations. In addition to her well-known snapshots of intimacy, Labinjo creates scenes that are politically charged, responding to experiences of abjection and destitution. Invested in her British Nigerian heritage, the artist looks to her own family albums, images circulated online and design, like Ankara prints, as sources of inspiration. Labinjo's practice is devoted to the vast range of the Black British experience, and she cites among her influences the pioneers Lubaina Himid (p.135), Claudette Johnson (p.147) and Sonia Boyce (b. 1962), who forged opportunities for Black feminist artistic life in the United Kingdom. Labinjo's early works, which include *Come play with us*, depict scenes of Black familial joy. Labinjo paints intuitively and allows her creative process to dictate the skin tone gradations for which she has become known. Bright colours, buzzing patterns and figural details communicate elation and comfort in these portraits.

LALAN

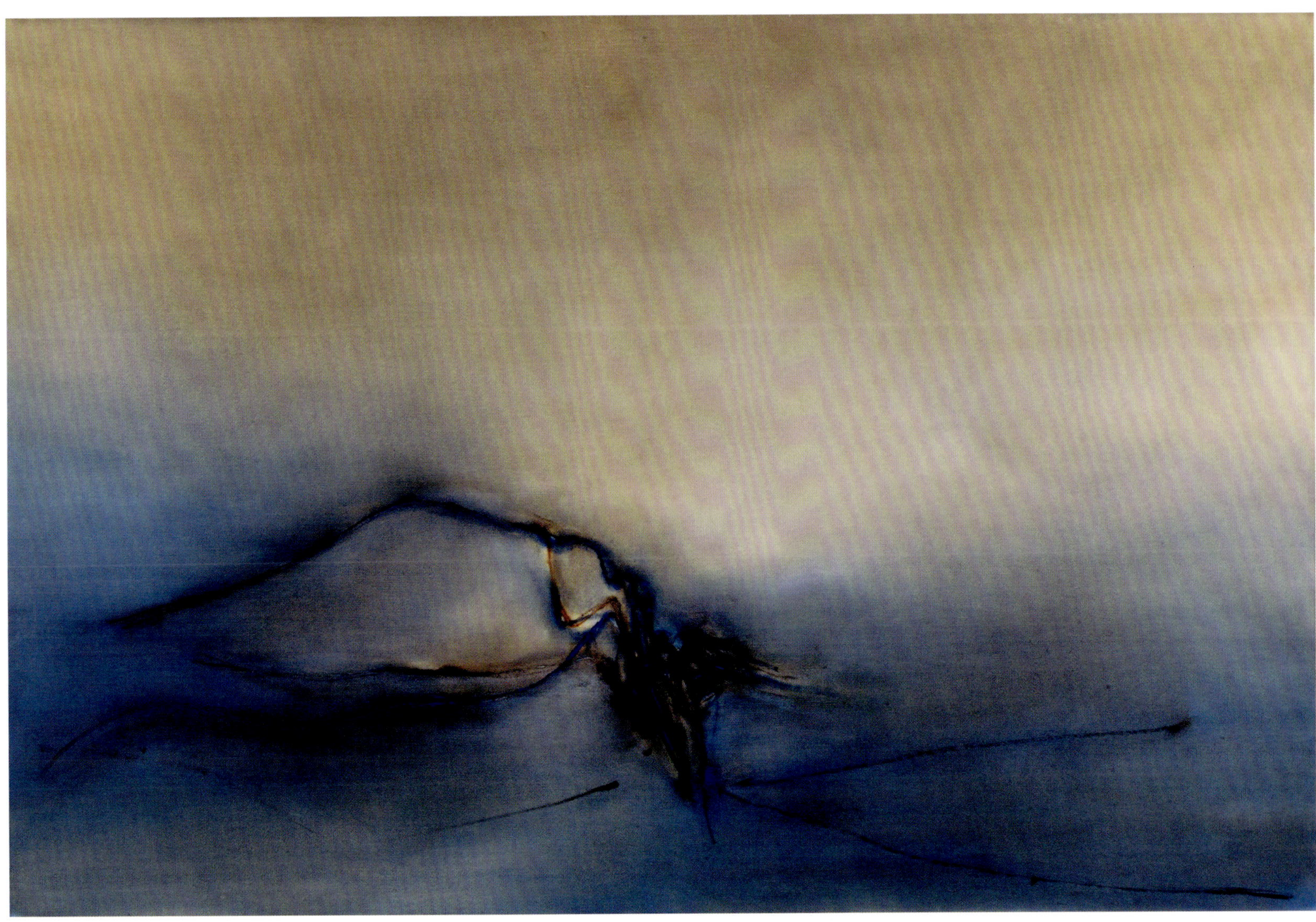

PHILTRE (POTION)
1969, oil on canvas, 130 × 195 cm (51 ⅛ × 76 ¾ in), Musée d'Art Moderne de Paris, France

Lalan, born 1921, Guiyang, Guizhou Province, China. Died 1995, Le Lavandou, Provence-Alpes-Côte d'Azur, France.

An artist whose integrated practice in music and dance mutually informed her paintings, Lalan (born Xie Jing-lan) tirelessly pursued a language combining figuration and abstraction. The artist studied classical European music in Hangzhou before relocating to Paris in 1948, where she continued her musical endeavours and learnt modern dance. She and her first husband, Zao Wou-Ki (1920–2013), became neighbours of Alberto Giacometti and joined the Paris avant-garde that included Henri Michaux, Sanyu and Pierre Soulages. She took up painting in 1957 and, seeking a new artistic identity, renamed herself Lalan after her childhood nickname, Lanlan. She channelled the sweeping gestures of modern dance, Chinese calligraphy and landscape painting in works like *Potion*, created when she started fusing lyrical abstraction with natural scenery. The dark outlines inherit their controlled movement from calligraphy – the beginning of each stroke is stressed before being let go, a technique that demands precision of execution from the shoulder to the wrist. Blue, grey and white meld together like mist over water, translating Chinese landscape painting techniques – ink wash and *cun* ('wrinkles', textured brushwork) – into oil, using the figurative to portray the abstract.

GIULIA LAMA

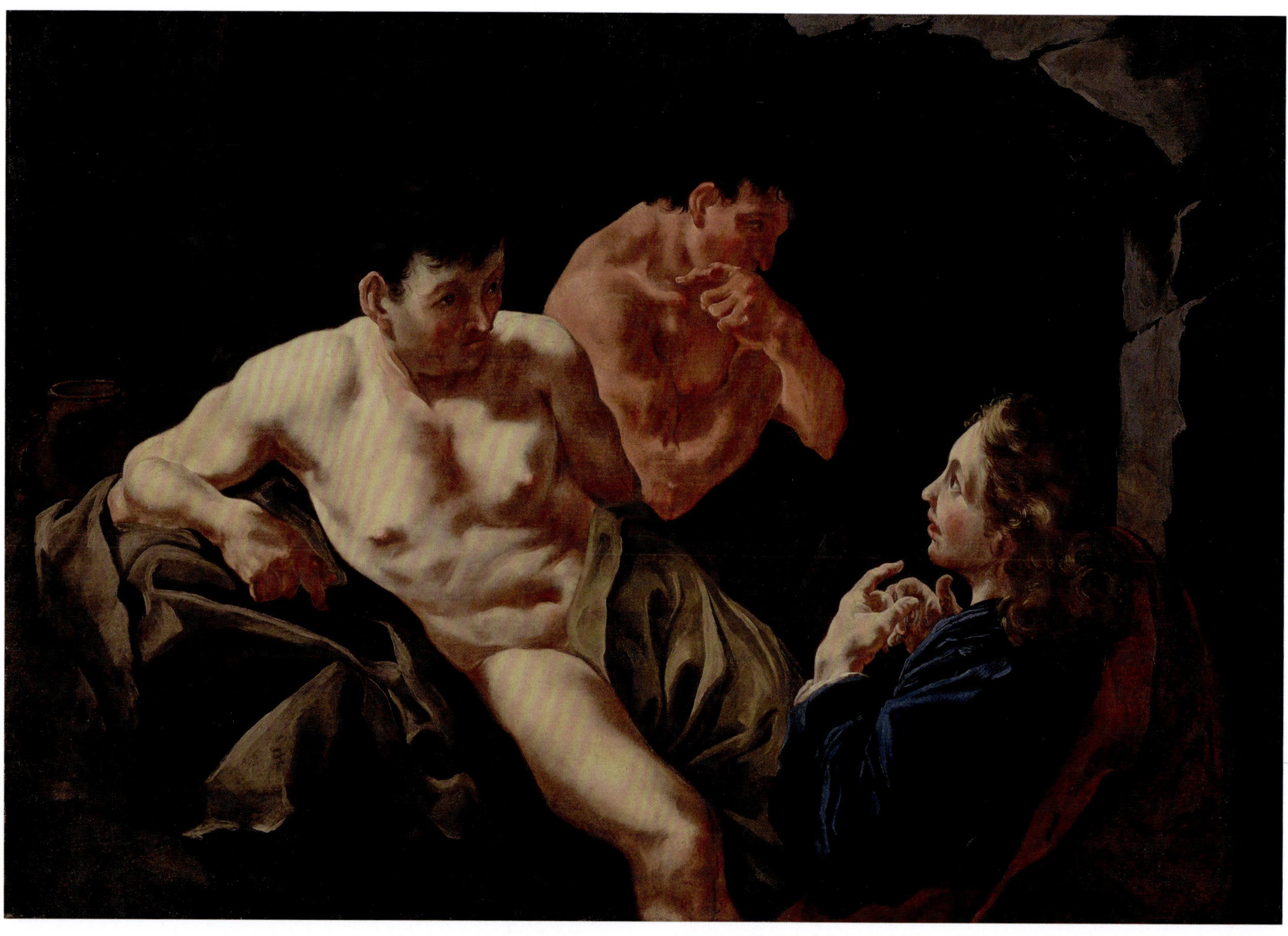

JOSEPH INTERPRETING THE EUNUCHS' DREAMS
*c.*1730, oil on canvas, 106.7 × 154.8 cm (42 × 60⅞ in)

Giulia Lama, born 1681, Venice, Italy. Died 1747, Venice.

Little is known about Lama's life and work, although the recent discovery of more than two hundred of her drawings proves that she was one of the first women artists to have studied nude models – an element of artistic training traditionally reserved for men. She was probably trained by her father, the painter Agostino Lama (1645–1714), and may have also studied alongside the important Venetian artist Giovanni Battista Piazzetta (1682–1754). Her visual style is similar to that of Piazzetta's early work in particular, characterized by dramatic compositions, a sombre palette, stark contrasts in lighting (tenebrism) and dark subject matter – a divergence from the then-popular Rococo style. Lama never married and seems to have led a reclusive life, although she forged a successful career as an artist – painting religious and mythological scenes and portraits – and as a poet, embroiderer and scholar. Only recently unearthed, her depiction of the biblical episode of *Joseph Interpreting the Eunuchs' Dreams* demonstrates her skill in rendering human physiognomy, evidenced in the naturalistic and dynamic pose of the seated eunuch at the centre of the canvas, probably based on a live model.

LOTTE LASERSTEIN

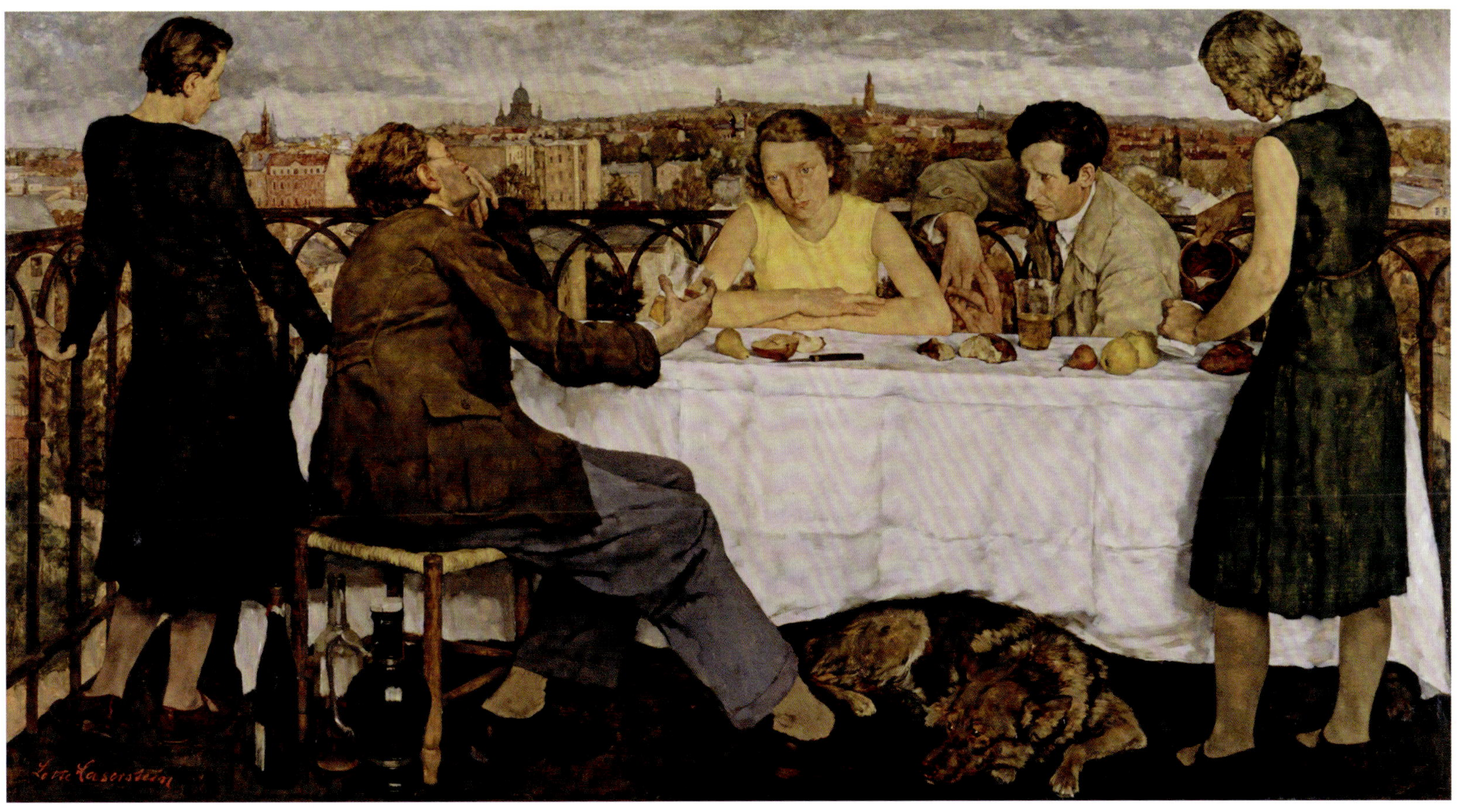

ABEND ÜBER POTSDAM
(EVENING OVER POTSDAM)
1930, oil on panel, 111 × 205.7 cm (43 ¾ × 80 ¾ in)

Lotte Laserstein, born 1898, Pasłęk, Poland.
Died 1993, Kalmar, Sweden.

As one of few women to graduate from the Berlin Academy of Fine Arts in 1925, Laserstein began to garner success in Germany, but by 1935 rising Nazism forced her to close her studio. In 1937 she fled to Sweden, where she would spend the rest of her life, becoming known for naturalistic, figurative works, including landscapes, female portraits and nudes that reinvented the image of woman and reimagined her as an independent agent, free of the male gaze, inhabiting an increasingly cosmopolitan society. *Evening over Potsdam* is among Laserstein's best-known paintings, completed in 1930 while she was still in Germany. It depicts a group of friends, including the artist's husband on the far left, and her long-time muse, athlete Traute Rose, who stands next to him in a sombre black dress. The ambience is ruminative: the figures languish on a rooftop, the German city bathed in the fading late afternoon sun in the background, the remnants of a long lunch scattered across the table. Reflecting a mood of uncertainty at the end of the Weimar Republic, the painting exemplifies Laserstein's frank, realist style and the enigmatic, psychologically charged atmosphere that distinguished her paintings.

MARIA LASSNIG

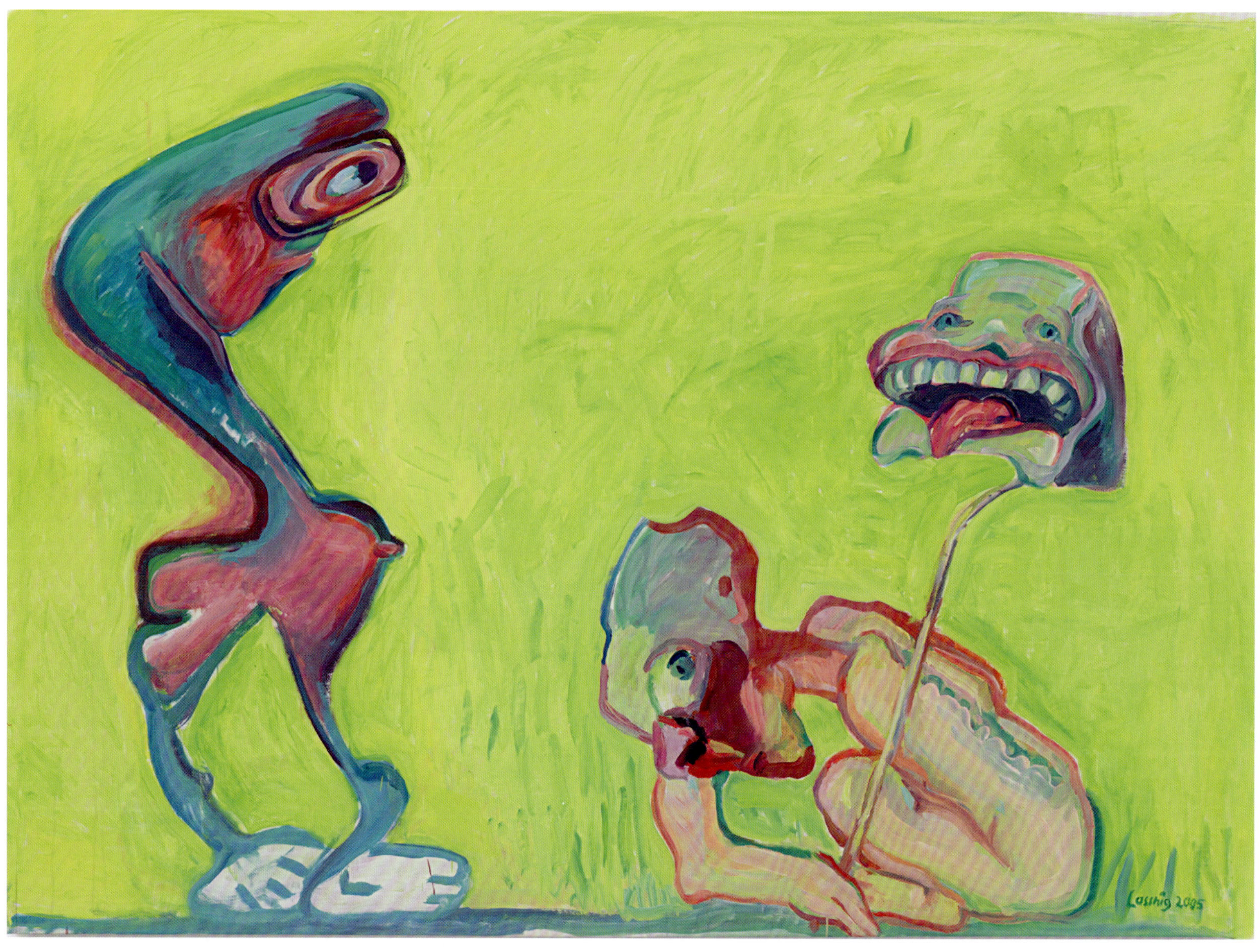

FOTOGRAFIE GEGEN MALERIE (PHOTOGRAPHY AGAINST PAINTING)
2005, oil on canvas, 150 × 200 cm (59 × 78 ¾ in), Ursula Hauser Collection, Switzerland

Maria Lassnig, born 1919, Kappel am Krappfeld, Austria. Died 2014, Vienna, Austria.

Lassnig was dedicated to painting throughout an artistic career that lasted over seventy years. Though she was little known outside the German-speaking world until she was in her eighties – despite representing Austria at the 39th Venice Biennale in 1980 – a flurry of solo exhibitions in Europe and the United States resulted in her being repositioned in the history of post-war figurative painting alongside contemporaries including Francis Bacon (1909–92) and Lucian Freud (1922–2011). Lassnig is best known for her self-portraits and *Körpergefühl* (body awareness) works, in which she sought to represent the lived experience of being within a physical body, but prolific later years saw her explore a range of additional subjects, including couples, footballers and country people. While the camera appeared in a number of her compositions, Lassnig was sceptical of photography's artistic merit, stating in her notebook in 2007 that 'Photography only sees the surface. The painter sees underneath.' Here the two are presented in direct opposition: a stooped figure of the painter holding a jeering, toothy mask that taunts photography's single eye.

MARIE LAURENCIN

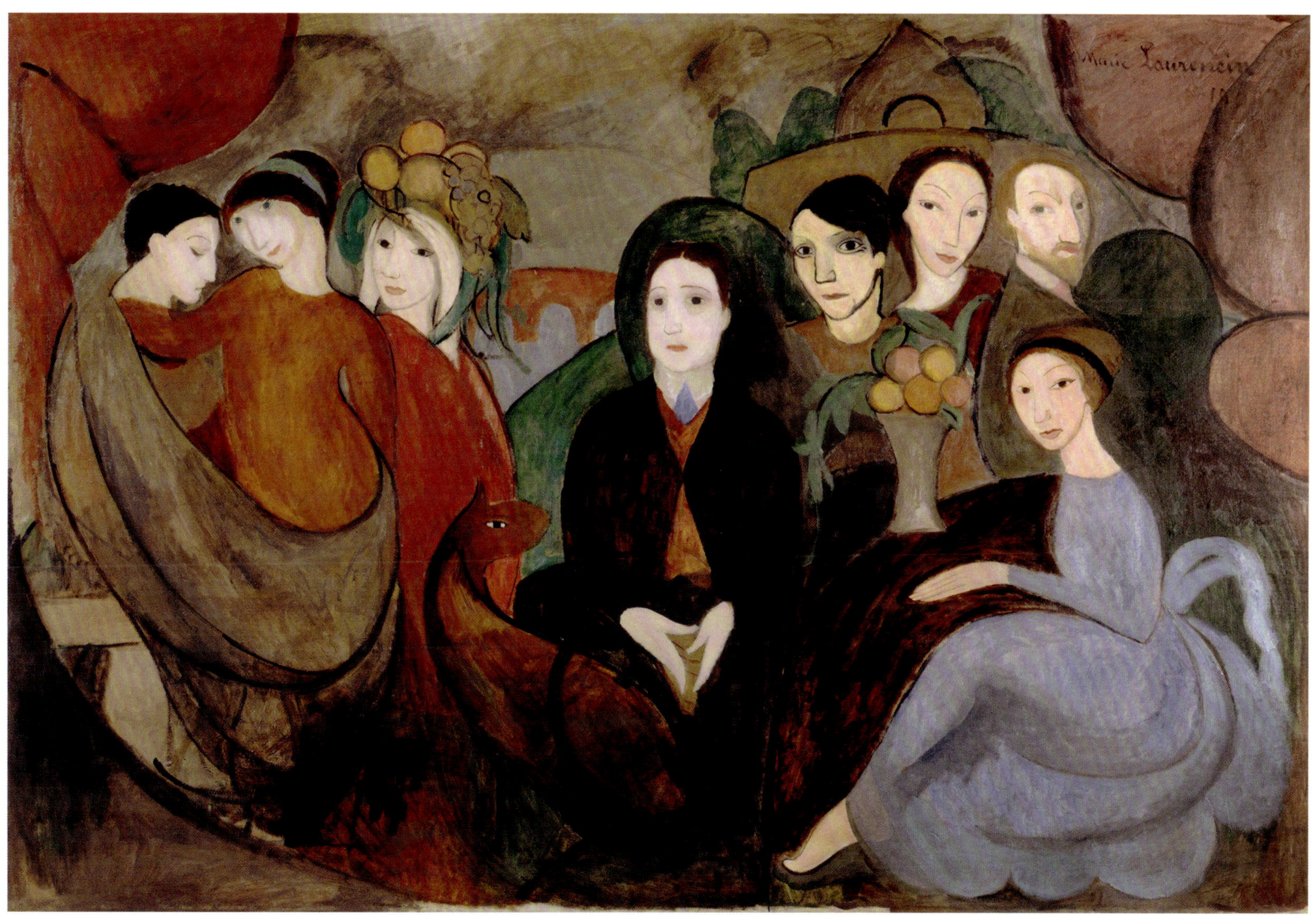

APOLLINAIRE ET SES AMIS (2ÈME VERSION) (APOLLINAIRE AND HIS FRIENDS [2ND VERSION])
1909, oil on canvas, 130 × 194 cm (51 ⅛ × 76 ⅜ in), Musée National d'Art Moderne, Centre Pompidou, Paris, France

Marie Laurencin, born 1883, Paris, France. Died 1956, Paris.

After training in porcelain painting at the École de Manufacture de Sèvres, Laurencin pursued oil painting, becoming a figure in the Parisian avant-garde. Having studied at the Académie Humbert in the early 1900s, Laurencin attended American expatriate Natalie Barney's neo-Sapphic gatherings of lesbian and bisexual women, discussing utopian ideas of female liberation and eroticism. An initial interest in Fauvism gave way to the spatial fragmentation of Cubism. Laurencin was acquainted with figures including Pablo Picasso (1881–1973), Gertrude Stein and Guillaume Apollinaire, Laurencin's lover and the central subject in this perspective-free painting, which also depicts Stein (who acquired the work) on the far left, Picasso centre right and a self-portrait of Laurencin on the bottom right. During the First World War, Laurencin and her husband were exiled in Spain, where she saw and admired Francisco Goya's (1746–1828) portraits of dark-eyed women. She returned to Paris in 1921, often painting portraits of doe-eyed, self-assured women in a style with sweeping lines and a soft colour palette. In the interwar period, Laurencin designed wallpaper and textiles, and also designed sets and costumes for Sergei Diaghilev's Ballets Russes.

DORIS LEE

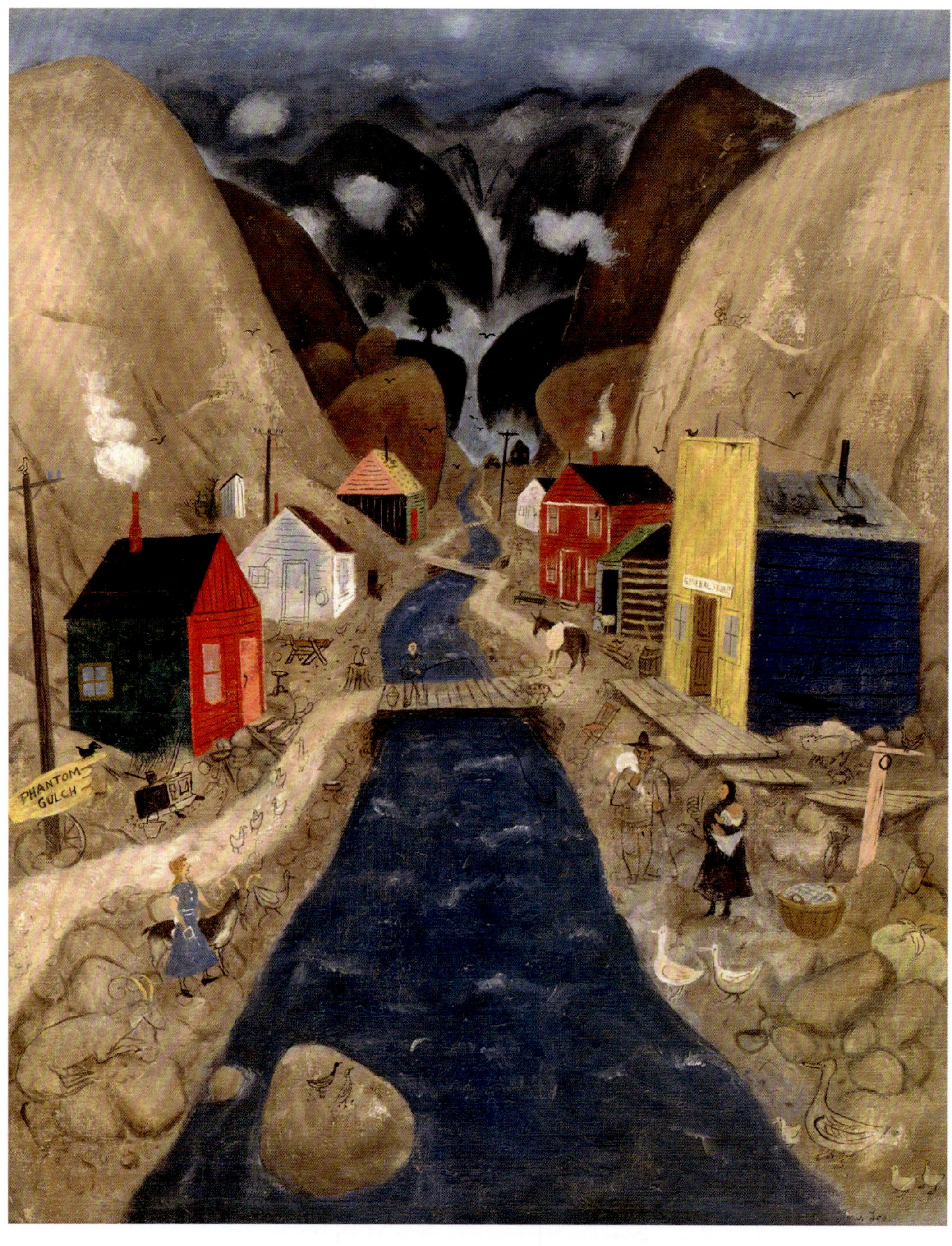

PROSPECTOR'S HOME
1945, oil on canvas, 68.6 × 55.9 cm (27 × 22 in),
Dallas Museum of Art, USA

Doris Lee, born 1905, Aledo, Illinois, USA.
Died 1983, Clearwater, Florida, USA.

Lee rose to fame in 1930s America with whimsical and wistful works that reimagined the grim reality of life during the Great Depression. One of the most revered artists of her era and a leading figure of Regionalist art, Lee's popularity could perhaps be attributed to the way she painted ordinary scenes with great optimism, projecting a nation Americans wanted to see: brightly coloured, exuberant and imbued with hope. Lee's flat, folk-style paintings were exhibited at the first-ever Whitney Biennial in New York in 1932, and her place in American art history was consolidated further when she was awarded the Art Institute of Chicago's Logan Purchase Prize in 1935; a prestigious prize at the Carnegie Institute show in Pittsburgh (now the Carnegie International) followed in 1944. Lee's works focus mainly on dreamlike depictions of bucolic scenes and American traditions, evoking a pastoral pace through paint in a playful and decorative manner, as seen in this 1945 work – most likely inspired by several summers between 1936 and 1939 when Lee was a visiting artist at Colorado Springs Art Center. Though her popularity waned with the rise of Abstract Expressionism in the 1950s, the appeal of her work endures, and she was the subject of a travelling retrospective in 2021.

MARIE-VICTOIRE LEMOINE

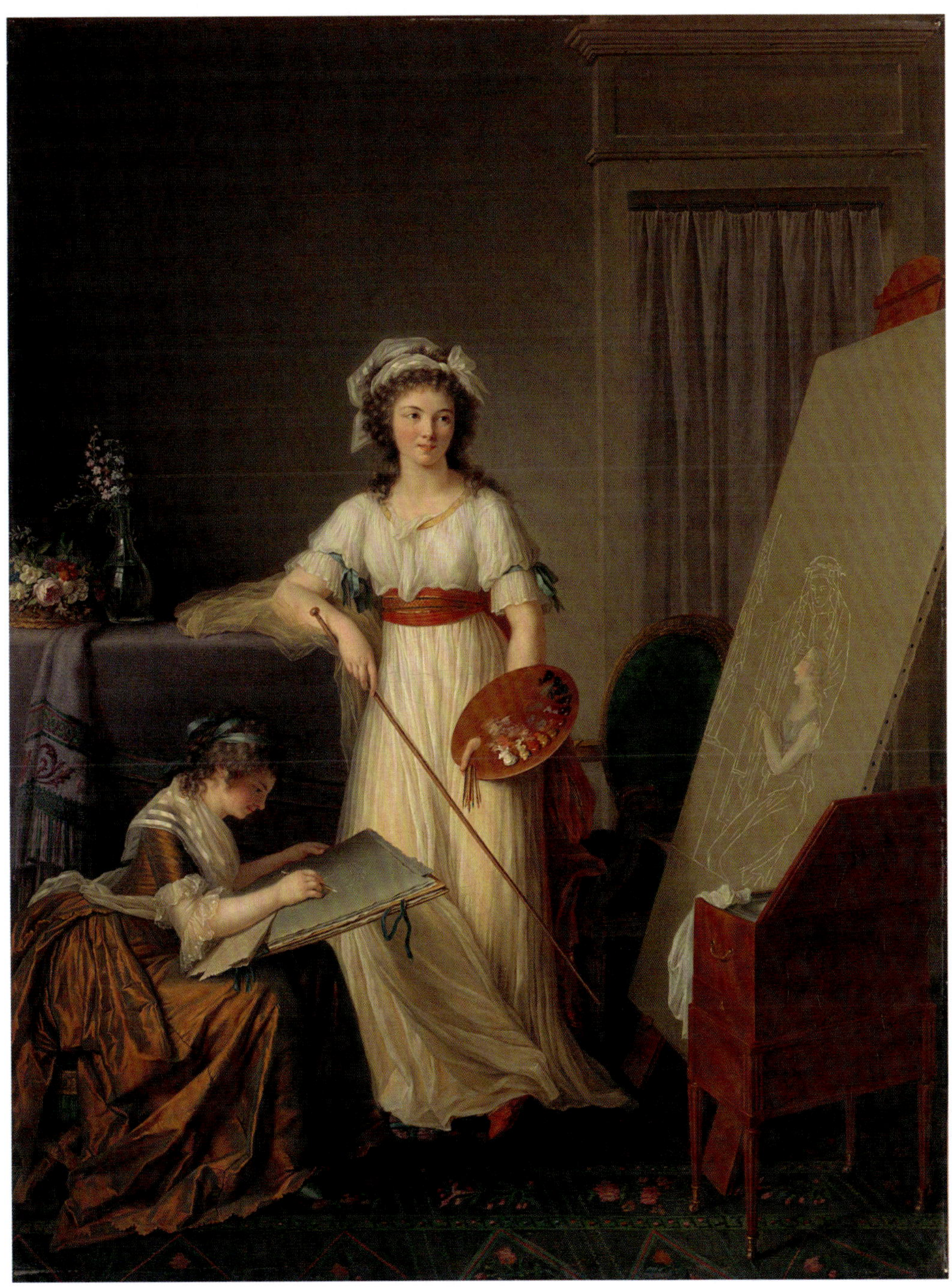

THE INTERIOR OF AN ATELIER OF A WOMAN PAINTER
1789, oil on canvas, 116.5 × 88.9 cm (45 ⅞ × 35 in), Metropolitan Museum of Art, New York, USA

Marie-Victoire Lemoine, born 1754, Paris, France. Died 1820, Paris.

Known for her portraits, miniatures and genre scenes, Lemoine studied under the French painter François-Guillaume Ménageot (1744–1816) in Paris. As her reputation grew, she received important portrait commissions from members of the French royal family and senior court figures. She first exhibited her paintings at the Salon de la Correspondance in 1779 with a portrait of Princesse de Lamballe, a confidante of Marie Antionette who was later killed in the September Massacres of 1792 during the French Revolution. Post-Revolutionary reforms at the Académie Royale de Peinture et de Sculpture led to Lemoine becoming one of the first women to exhibit at the Salon du Louvre, where in 1796 she showed this canvas depicting a woman painter and her pupil. Demonstrating her facility in portraiture and still life, it is thought to be a self-portrait with her sister, Marie-Élisabeth Gabiou (1761–*c.* 1811/14), who was also an artist. The unfinished history painting on the easel shows a devotee of the Greek goddess Athena and is included as a provocative gesture towards an establishment that deemed the genre unsuitable for women painters.

TAMARA DE LEMPICKA

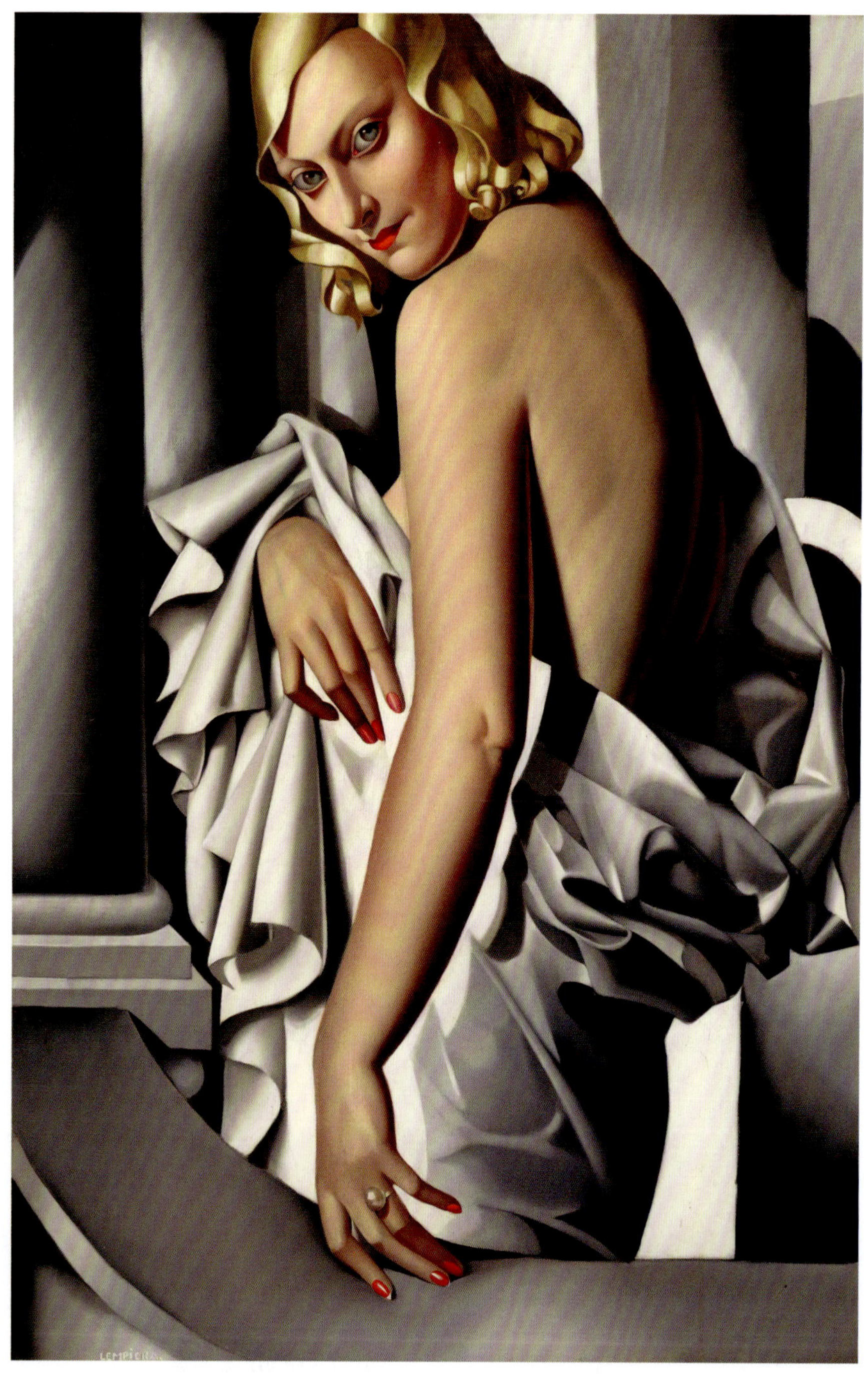

PORTRAIT DE MARJORIE FERRY
1932, oil on canvas, 100 × 65 cm (39 ⅜ × 25 ⅝ in)

Tamara de Lempicka, born 1898, Warsaw, Poland. Died 1980, Cuernavaca, Mexico.

By virtue of her stylized, glamorous portraits, Lempicka is remembered as the quintessential Parisian painter of the 1920s and 1930s. Born into a wealthy family in Poland, she lived in St Petersburg during the Bolshevik Revolution of 1917, following which she and her husband emigrated to Paris. There she became synonymous with the liberal spirit of the Jazz Age, embarking on a string of relationships with both other men and women, many of whom were her models and patrons. Successfully navigating a path through European and American high society, Lempicka developed an art practice at the forefront of modernism, fashioning a bold visual vocabulary that captured the Art Deco spirit. This painting of British-born Parisian cabaret singer Marjorie Ferry was commissioned by Ferry's fiancé, the engagement ring proudly on display. Wrapped seductively in a silky sheet, the subject's flawless skin chimes with the slick monochrome architecture, all encapsulating Lempicka's signature high classical style – a brand of modernism that has come to define the era.

SHANNON T. LEWIS

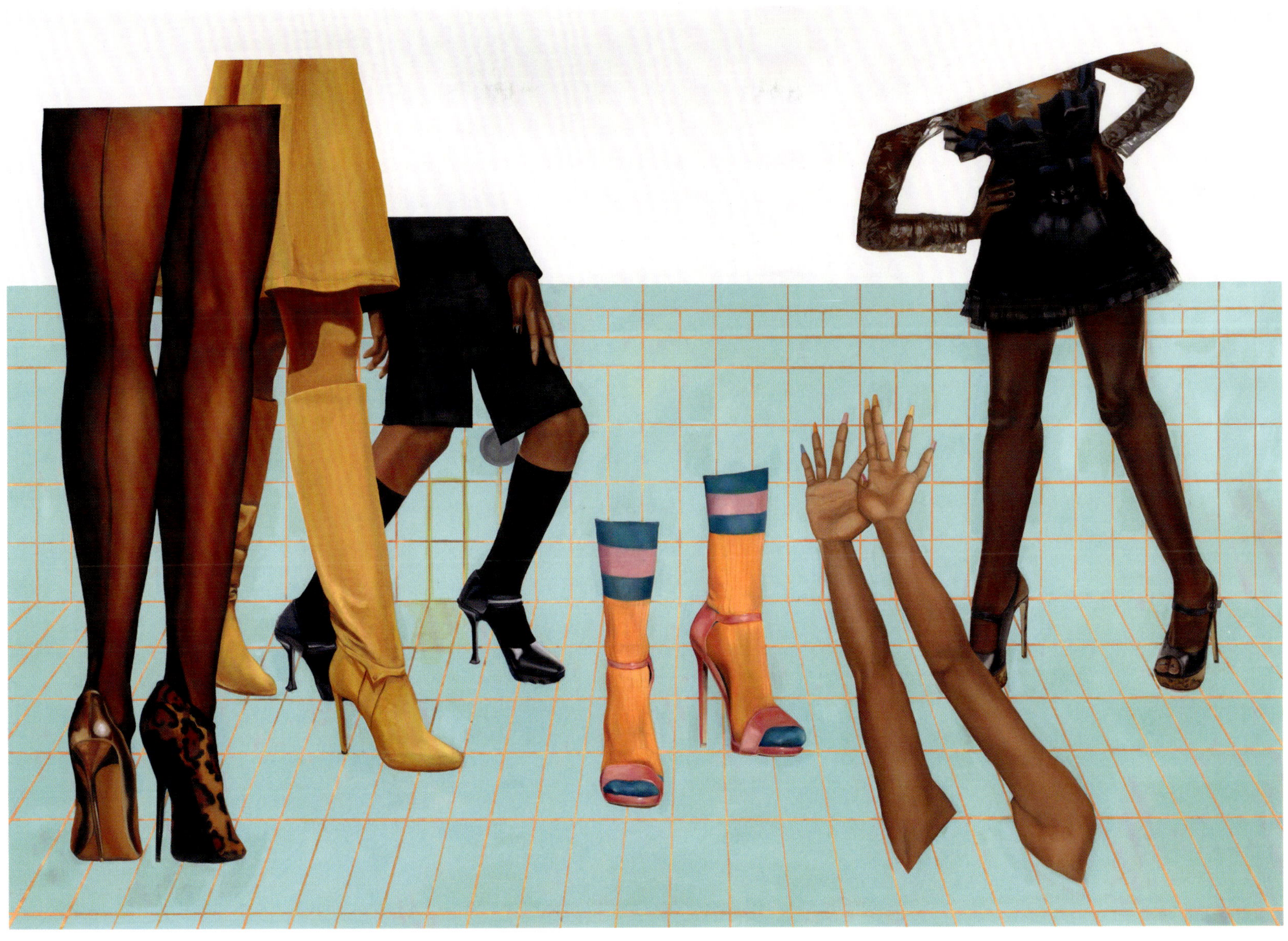

UP FROM THE ROOTS
2021, oil on linen, 140 × 200 cm (55 ⅛ × 78 ¾ in)

Shannon T. Lewis, born 1981, Toronto, Canada.

Inspired by photomontage techniques used by Dadaists and Surrealists, Lewis's artistic process begins with tearing out pages from fashion and architecture magazines, layering them with images culled from the internet and arranging them on disjointed backgrounds, which she then reproduces in paint. In a 2021 interview with *Juxtapoz* magazine about the intersection of gender and racial politics in her work, Lewis explained that her form of 'scrambling' allows viewers to 'deconstruct their own kind of conclusions'. The process of collage is also a metaphor for the artist's interest in multiplicity and migration and how identities are forced to perform and adapt. After completing a master's degree at Goldsmiths College, London, Lewis moved to Berlin. *Up From The Roots* presents a group of anonymous individuals in various stages of fragmentation, with some reduced only to their limbs. The vivid colours (orange socks, mustard boots) and the precise material details (a lace sleeve, ribbing on a sock, the seam on a pair of sheer tights) are juxtaposed with the intensity of the tiled turquoise background. The hyperrealist painting style that Lewis uses for these figures is intricate and exacting, enhanced by the eerie emptiness of the surrounding architecture.

JUDITH LEYSTER

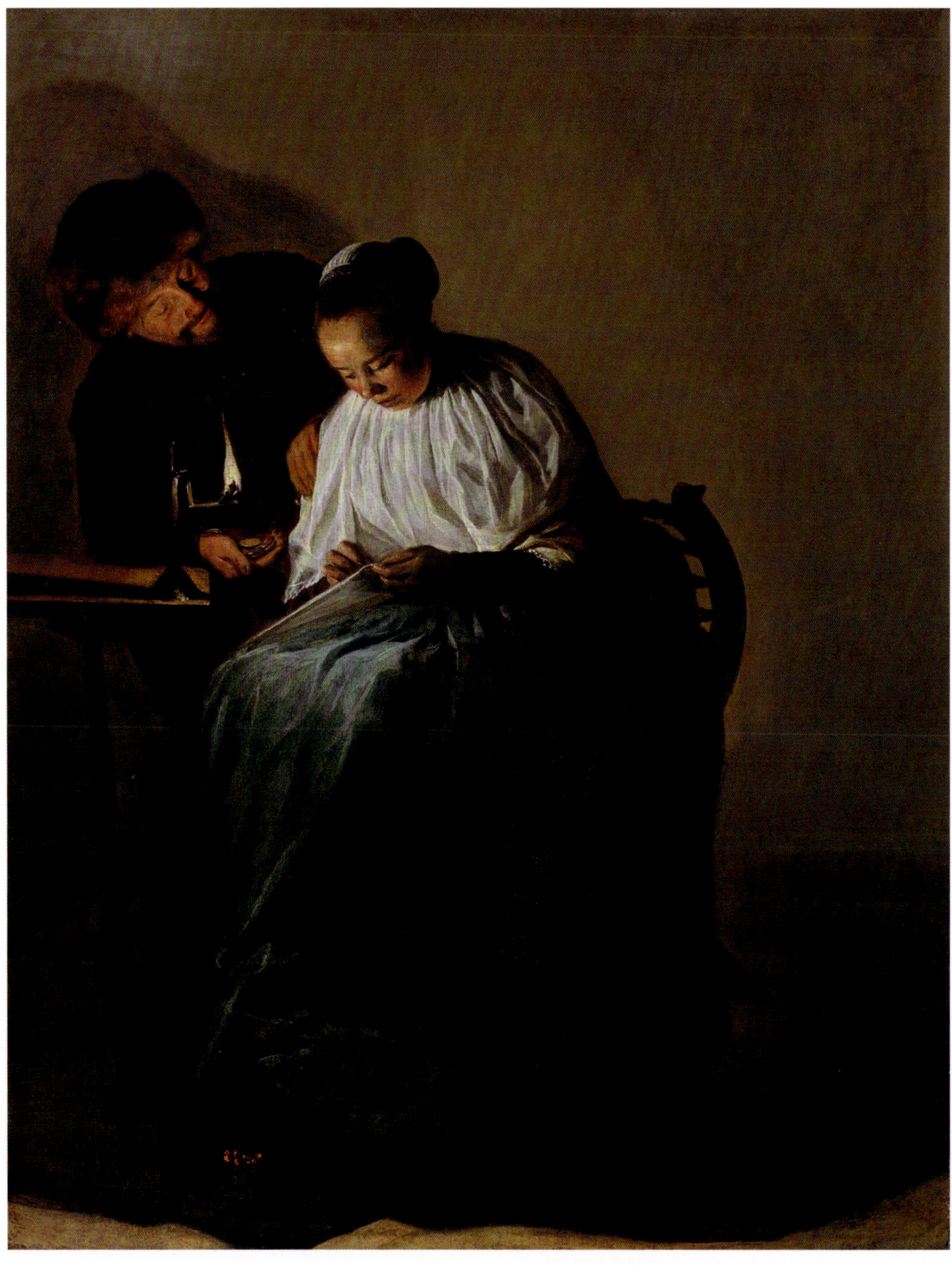

MAN OFFERING MONEY TO A YOUNG WOMAN
1631, oil on panel, 30.8 × 24.2 cm (12 ⅛ × 9 ½ in),
Mauritshuis, The Hague, Netherlands

Judith Leyster, born 1609, Haarlem, Netherlands.
Died 1660, Heemstede, Netherlands.

One of the few professional painters of the seventeenth century, Leyster was one of only two female painters accepted into Saint Luke's Guild of Haarlem during that century; that she subsequently had at least three students is an indication of her skill. Very little is known of her career or early training, though her paintings reveal the influence of the Utrecht School followers of Italian artist Caravaggio (1571–1610) in their flat backgrounds and sharp contrasts of light and dark. After her marriage to the painter Jan Miense Molenaer (*c.*1610–68) in 1636, Leyster painted very little and probably managed her husband's studio. Leyster was primarily a genre painter and, in a Calvinist country, secular genre scenes served to instil morality. This ambiguous painting has usually been interpreted as representing a virtuous woman who ignores the sexual propositions of an older man with money. She is dressed modestly and is engaged in domestic needlework; in the iconographic code of the time, the foot warmer visible beneath her feet indicates a married woman. Nevertheless, some scholars have seen moral decision in the work, painted when Leyster was twenty-two: a choice between virtue or vice.

LIANG YUANWEI

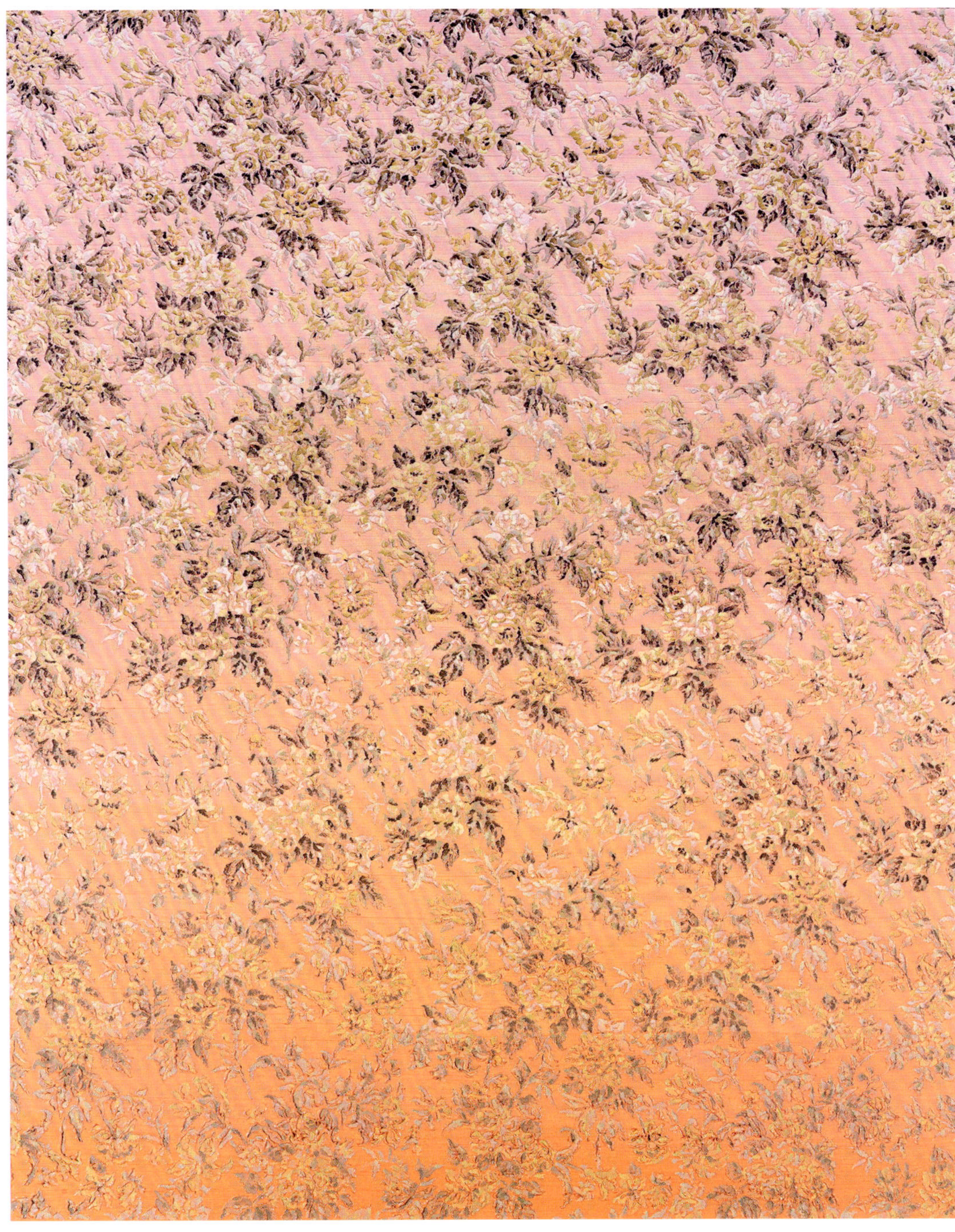

PIECE OF LIFE 13
2007, oil on linen, 162 × 130 cm (63 ¾ × 51 ⅛ in), White Rabbit Collection

Liang Yuanwei, born 1977, Xi'an, Shaanxi Province, China.

A graduate of Beijing's Central Academy of Fine Arts, Liang experimented with photography, installation and the dense, intricate paintings for which she has become known. The thick impasto canvases in Liang's 'Piece of Life' series reproduce ready-made textile designs modelled on fabric scraps, some taken from friends and family and others based on aprons and soft furnishings. Working intuitively across the canvas, she painstakingly builds up each image over long stretches of time, only deeming a composition complete when she feels she has successfully communicated her emotions. Nodding to the 'all over' paintings by American Abstract Expressionists, Liang ironically subverts their macho abstraction with domestic textile designs typically sewn and worn by women. In this example, delicate gold, white and brown flowers are set against a gradated ground that elegantly shifts from bubblegum pink to sunset orange. The balance and harmony that Liang strives for has drawn comparisons with historical Chinese art, including the flower paintings of the Song dynasty, while her subject matter pays homage to the unsung labour of Chinese women across time.

HUNG LIU

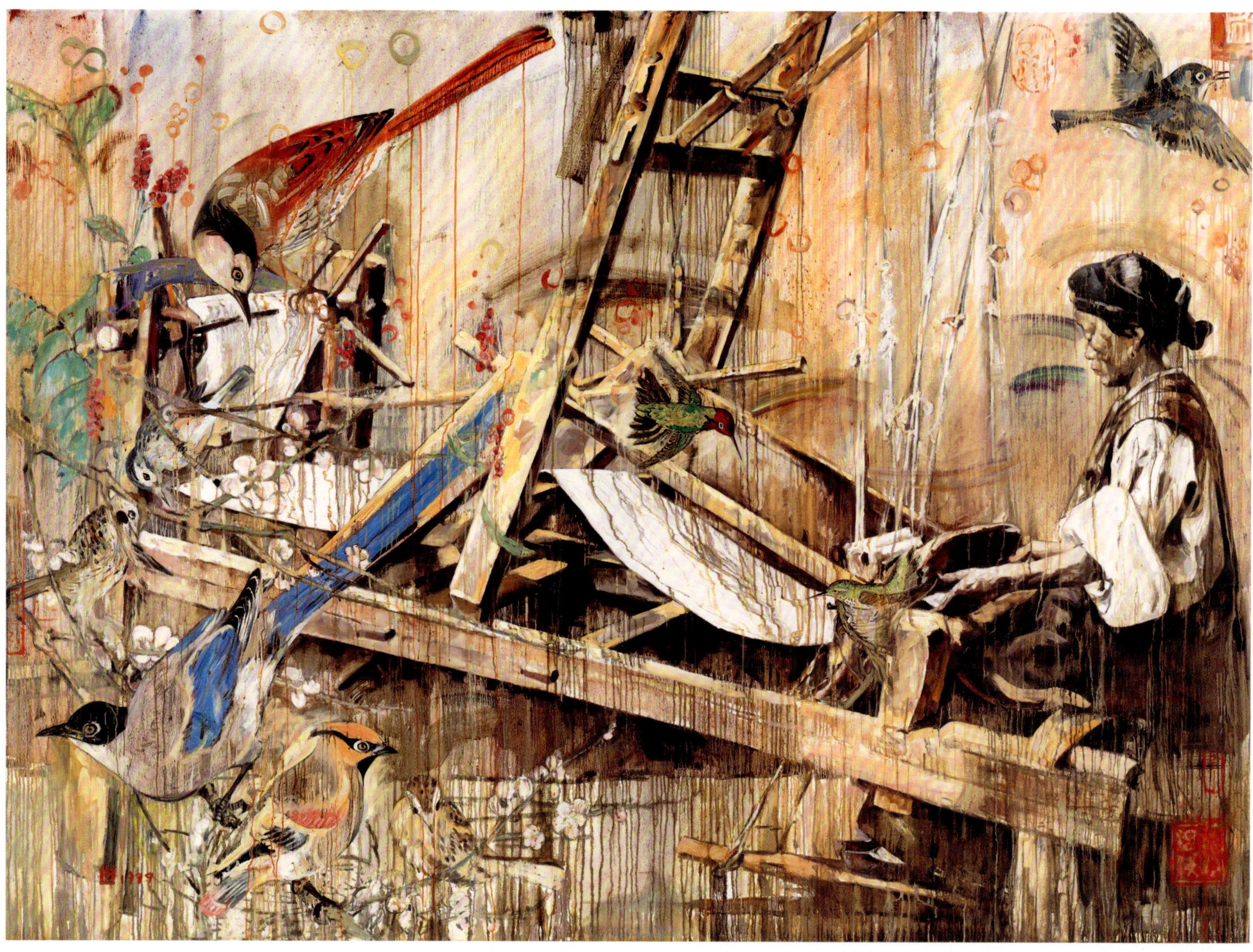

LOOM
1999, oil on canvas, 203.2 × 279.4 cm (80 × 110 in), San Francisco Museum of Modern Art, USA

Hung Liu, born 1948, Changchun, Jilin Province China. Died 2021, Oakland, California, USA.

Giving voice to characters marginalized by society and written out of history, including refugees, sex workers and street performers, Liu's sensitive paintings highlight their individuality through her empathetic approach. Liu practised in a Socialist Realist style and studied mural painting at the Central Academy of Fine Arts in Beijing, leaving China for the United States in 1984, where she studied with performance artist Allan Kaprow (1927–2006) at the University of California, San Diego. There she found a new artistic vocabulary by blending five thousand years of Chinese culture with her political reality as an immigrant. Long drips of thinned paint resembling tears cover her canvases, a style dubbed 'weeping realism'. *Loom* depicts a Chinese woman performing the daily work of creating fabric on a mechanical loom as some members of remote and minority communities in China still do. Liu emphasizes the woman skilfully operating the towering machinery to challenge Euro-American historical conventions of passive female models posing under the male gaze. The decorative surround of birds, inspired by Chinese flower and bird paintings and needlework – classical genres traditionally associated with femininity – provides a glimpse at images that may come to mind for the weaver as she works.

BERTINA LOPES

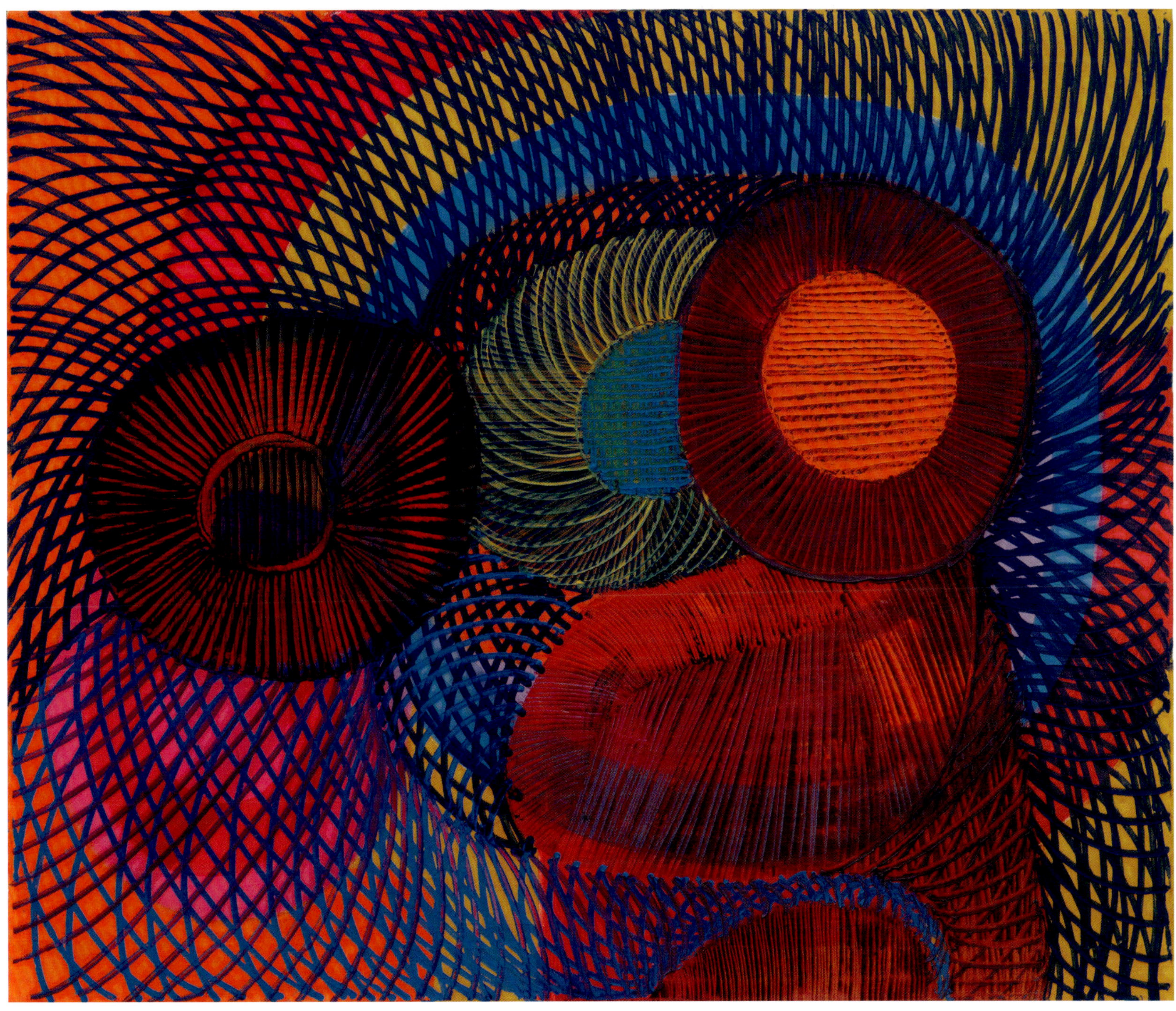

UNTITLED
1977, oil on canvas, 100 × 120 cm (39 ⅜ × 47 ¼ in)

Bertina Lopes, born 1924, Maputo, Mozambique. Died 2012, Rome, Italy.

Born in Maputo, educated in Lisbon and based in Rome, where she spent the majority of her professional life, Lopes is regarded as one of the artists who pioneered the concept of multiculturalism in the twentieth century. Classic elements of Mozambican art and European modernism merge in her work, establishing a critical relationship with the African-influenced Western art perpetuated by artists like Pablo Picasso (1881–1973) decades earlier, while activating a process of decolonization and reappropriation that would reach its apex in her paintings of the mid-1960s onwards. Although politically engaged, Lopes elected not to rely on openly aggressive strategies of representation, opting instead for the subtle power of metaphors. She often deployed traditional fairy tales and parables as a foundation for compositions conspicuous for their chromatic vivacity and elegant forms. In contrast with the gloomy mood and the menacing geometric structures that dominated the cycle of paintings that anticipated it, *Untitled* displays a renewed sense of serenity and hope, with kaleidoscopic grids and colours arranged in a circular way that reaffirms their rhythmical energy.

LEE LOZANO

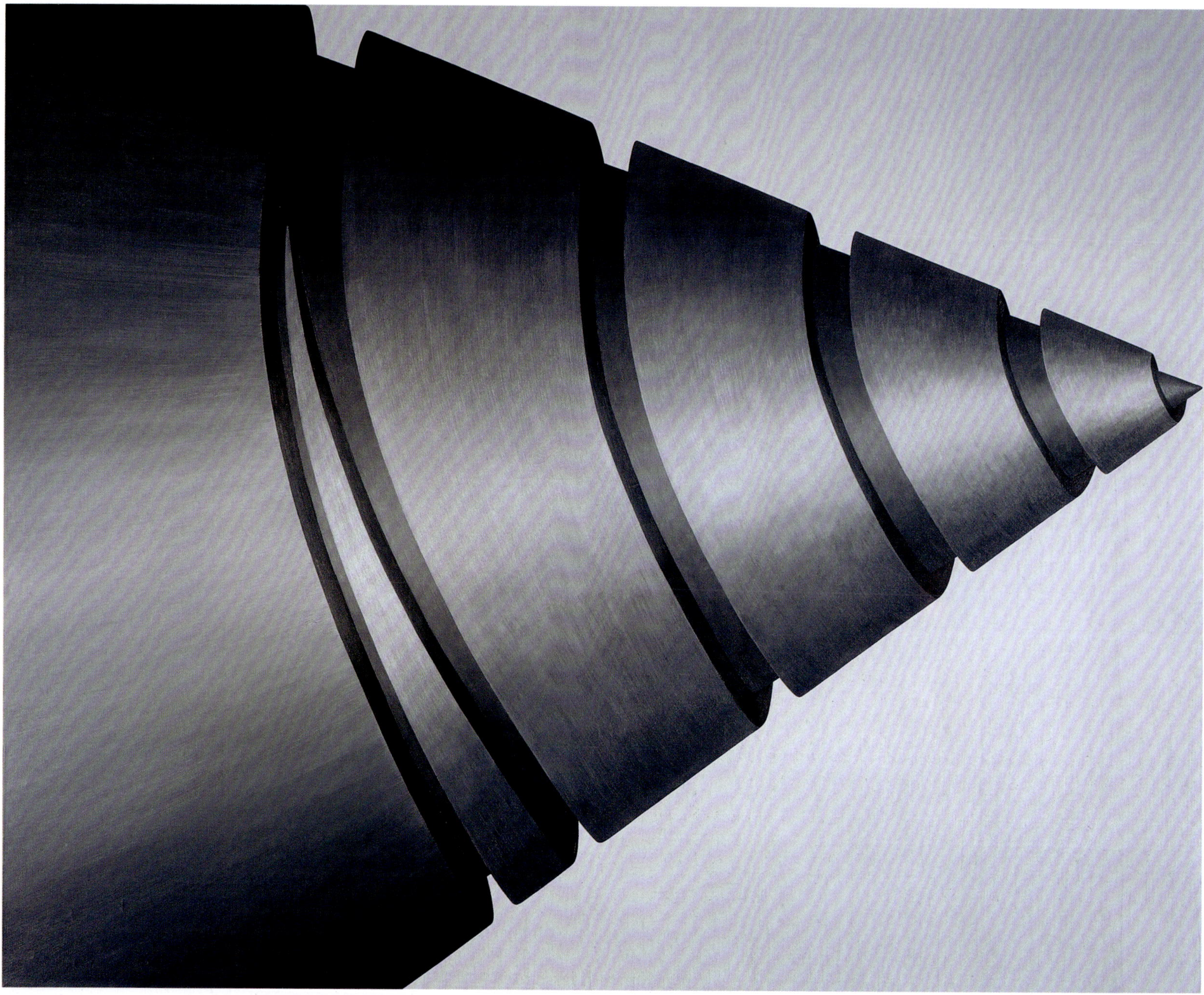

REAM
1964, oil on canvas, 198.1 × 243.8 cm (78 × 96 in), Blanton Museum of Art, University of Texas at Austin, USA

Lee Lozano, born 1930, Newark, New Jersey, USA. Died 1999, Dallas, USA.

Lozano is perhaps best known for her conceptual 'text' works, culminating in the early 1970s, when she cut ties with the art world and boycotted all women for the rest of her life, acts of disengagement that blur distinctions between artwork and life. During the mid-1960s, Lozano was working at the heart of new developments in Minimalism and hard-edged painting. Unlike many of her famed contemporaries, she insisted that her geometric works – often featuring arcs, inscribed circles and waveforms – were both inspired by scientific advances and transgressively suffused with beauty. Space, in particular, was an ongoing concern for Lozano, from developments in astrophysics to the weight and structure of the forms in her canvases. Ever averse to the cult of 'flatness' that so occupied American modernism, she later gouged holes into the surfaces of her austere, visually kinetic canvases. This large-scale painting comes from a series of works seemingly depicting hardware, such as screwdrivers and drill bits, in extreme close-up. Taken together, they are rife with sexual double-entendre and violate the time's reigning dictum against referencing forms from the real world. *Ream*'s repeated arcs and rigorous handling of volume augured Lozano's brief practice as one of her generation's leading talents – one who refused to play by the rules.

MA SHOUZHEN

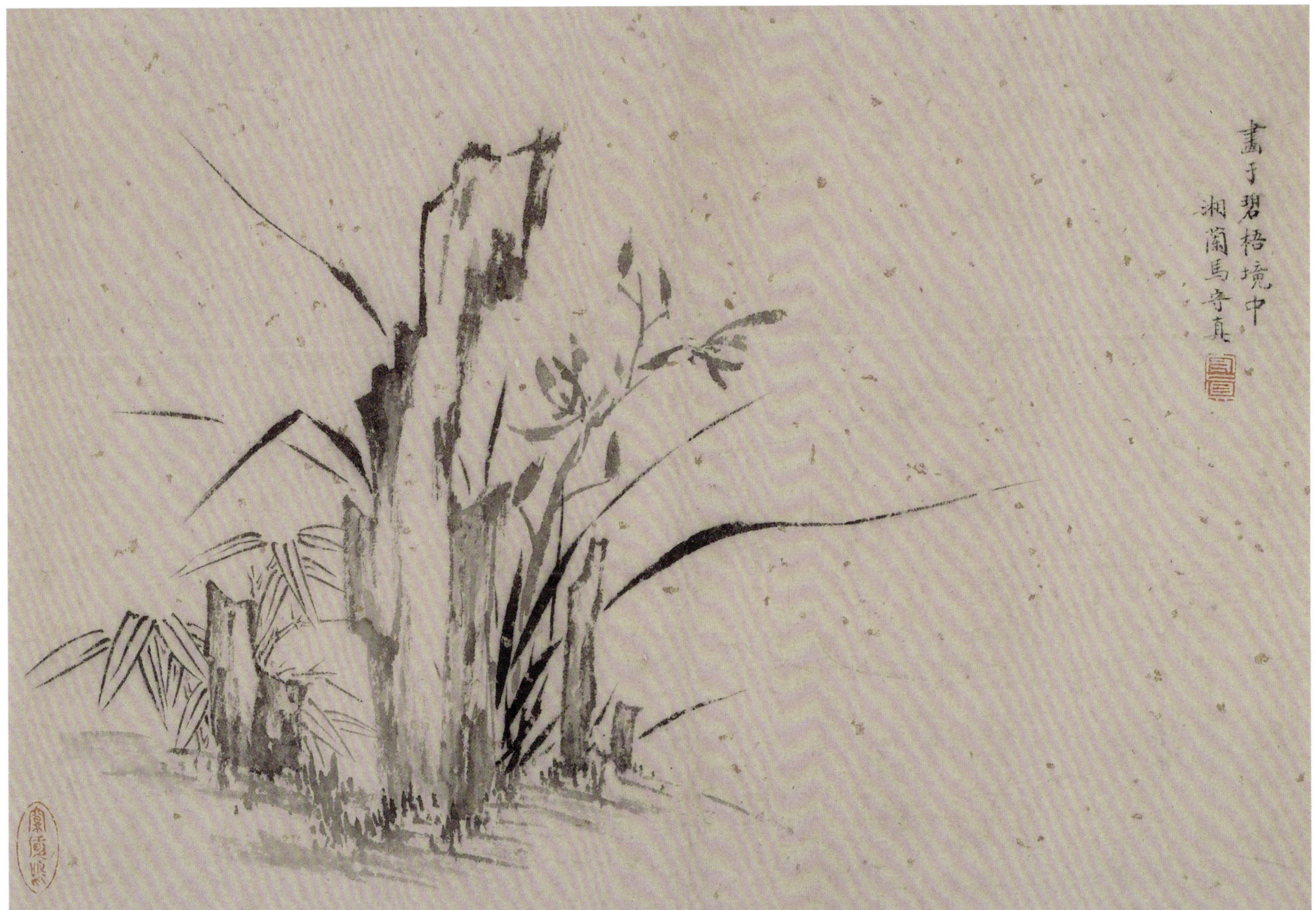

BAMBOO, ROCKS, AND ORCHIDS
late 16th century, ink on gold-flecked paper, 32.4 × 47.1 cm (12 ¾ × 18 ½ in), Freer Gallery of Art, National Museum of Asian Art, Smithsonian Institution, Washington DC, USA

Ma Shouzhen, born 1548, Nanjing, Jiangsu Province, China. Died 1604, Nanjing.

As an elite courtesan (*mingji*) in the late Ming dynasty, Ma was rigorously educated in the arts – poetry, dance, music and painting. Courtesans cultivated these talents in order to entertain the literati and would often produce works of art in collaboration with their clientele. Ma's main patron was the scholar and calligrapher Wang Zhideng (1535–1612), who wrote inscriptions on many of her paintings. Her visual art, which included fans, handscrolls and hanging scrolls, was widely admired; clients were known to travel from as far as Thailand to buy her works. This painting on gold-speckled paper is typical of her surviving oeuvre, which consists of landscapes featuring bamboo and orchids. The natural imagery is rendered in the *xieyi* (freehand) style popular among literati painters, characterized by sketchy brushstrokes in monochromatic ink. The resulting images are almost abstract yet highly expressive. Ma was particularly admired for her depictions of orchids, which led to her adopting the style name Ma Xianglan (Orchid Ma).

TALA MADANI

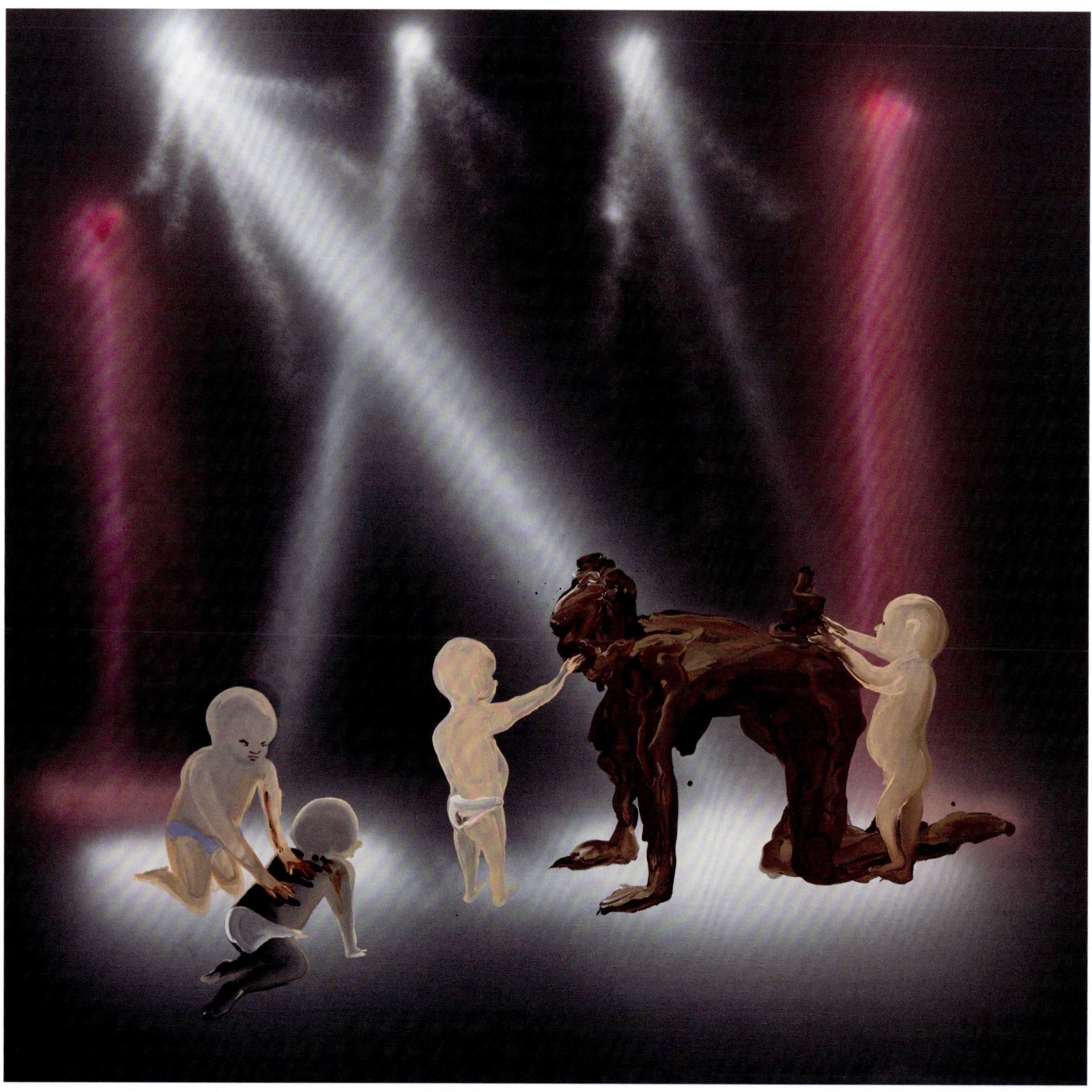

SHIT MOM (DISCO BABIES)
2019, oil on linen, 195.6 × 203.2 × 3.2 cm
(77 × 80 × 1 ¼ in)

Tala Madani, born 1981, Tehran, Iran.

Having moved to the United States aged thirteen, Madani studied political science before switching to visual arts at Oregon State University. She graduated from Yale School of Art with an MFA in painting in 2006 before relocating to Los Angeles, where she still lives and works. Her art, which encompasses painting, drawing and stop-motion animations, is often described as transgressive due to her representations of bodily functions, uninhibited desires and objectionable behaviours. Working without preparatory drawings, she paints directly onto the canvas to create loose compositions that retain spontaneity and informality. Gender stereotypes are a major theme, and she has frequently returned to masculinity and its preconceived roles as a subject ripe for satirical exploration, depicting interactions between (often bald) men that are at once comical and awkwardly pitiful. After several months away from painting following the birth of her second child, Madani created a body of work entitled 'Shit Moms'. In contrast with the archetypal and idealized representations of the mother figure in art history, here she is composed of faeces – leaving brown smeared trails in her wake – and shown distracted and wary, staged in scenarios with energetic infants whose antics humorously imply a failure to live up to societal expectations around motherhood.

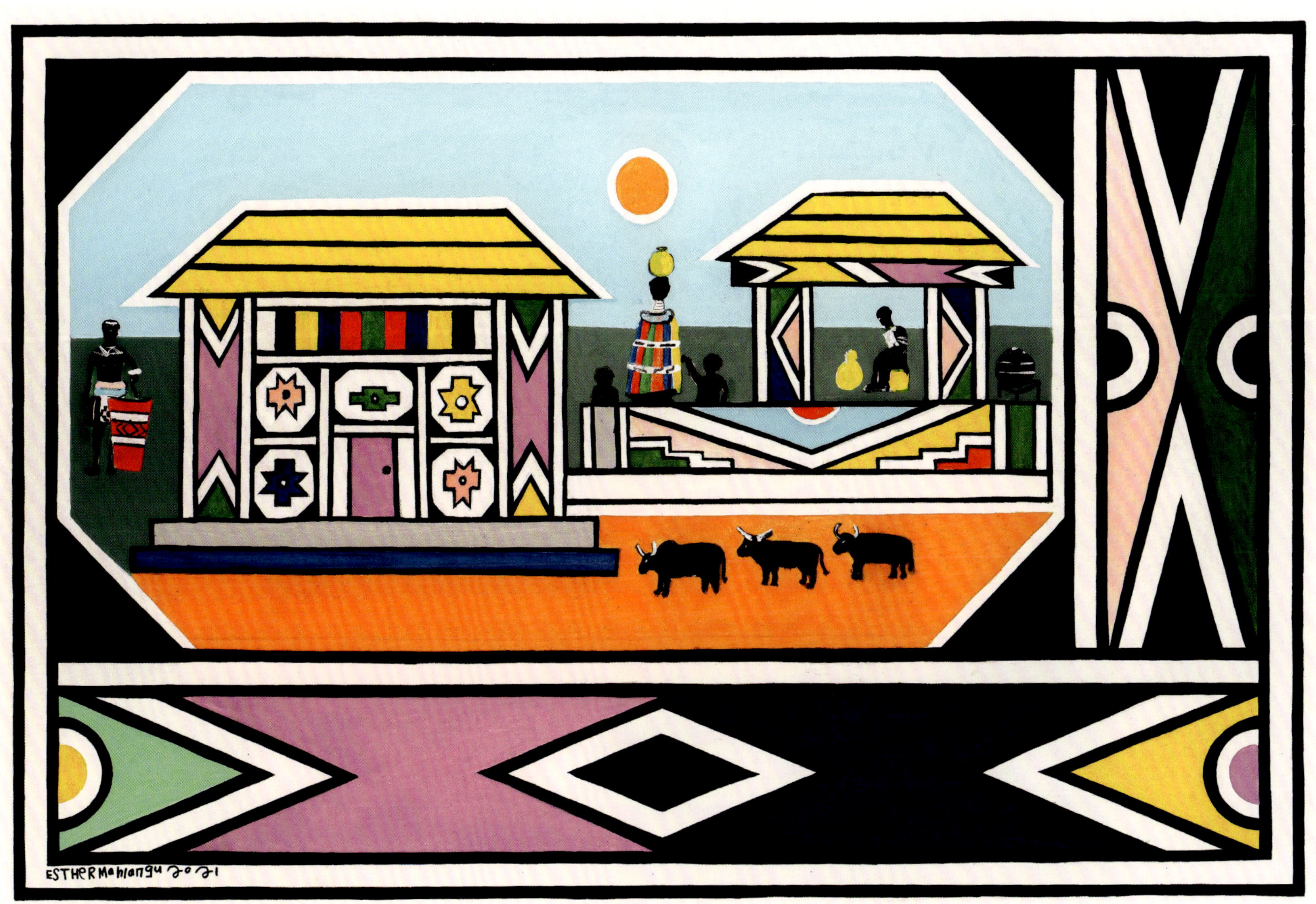

NDEBELE ABSTRACT
2021, acrylic on canvas, 120 × 180 cm
(47 ¼ × 70 ⅞ in)

Esther Mahlangu, born 1935, Middelburg, South Africa.

Following the centuries-old matrilineal custom of her Ndebele culture, Mahlangu was trained in traditional Ndebele arts by her grandmother and mother from a young age, first learning beadwork and then how to mix pigments from natural materials and to paint with chicken feathers. Ndebele painting is usually found on the exteriors of houses, and Mahlangu is known for being the first artist to transfer the designs from wall to canvas, and later a cornucopia of other objects, so that the tradition could be transported far beyond the community. In the 1980s, she began to exhibit her works internationally: a breakthrough came in 1989 after she painted murals on a house installed in the landmark 'Magiciens de la terre' ('Magicians of the Earth') exhibition at the Centre Pompidou in Paris, where her practice was exposed to new audiences. Mahlangu uses dazzling contrasts of colour and bold geometric compositions in her works – each shape, line and colour is also used symbolically to convey social, political and cultural meaning. Although best known for her abstract works, in this painting we encounter a figurative scene: a village with houses painted according to the traditional style, signalling the roots of the artist's practice.

JESSIE MAKINSON

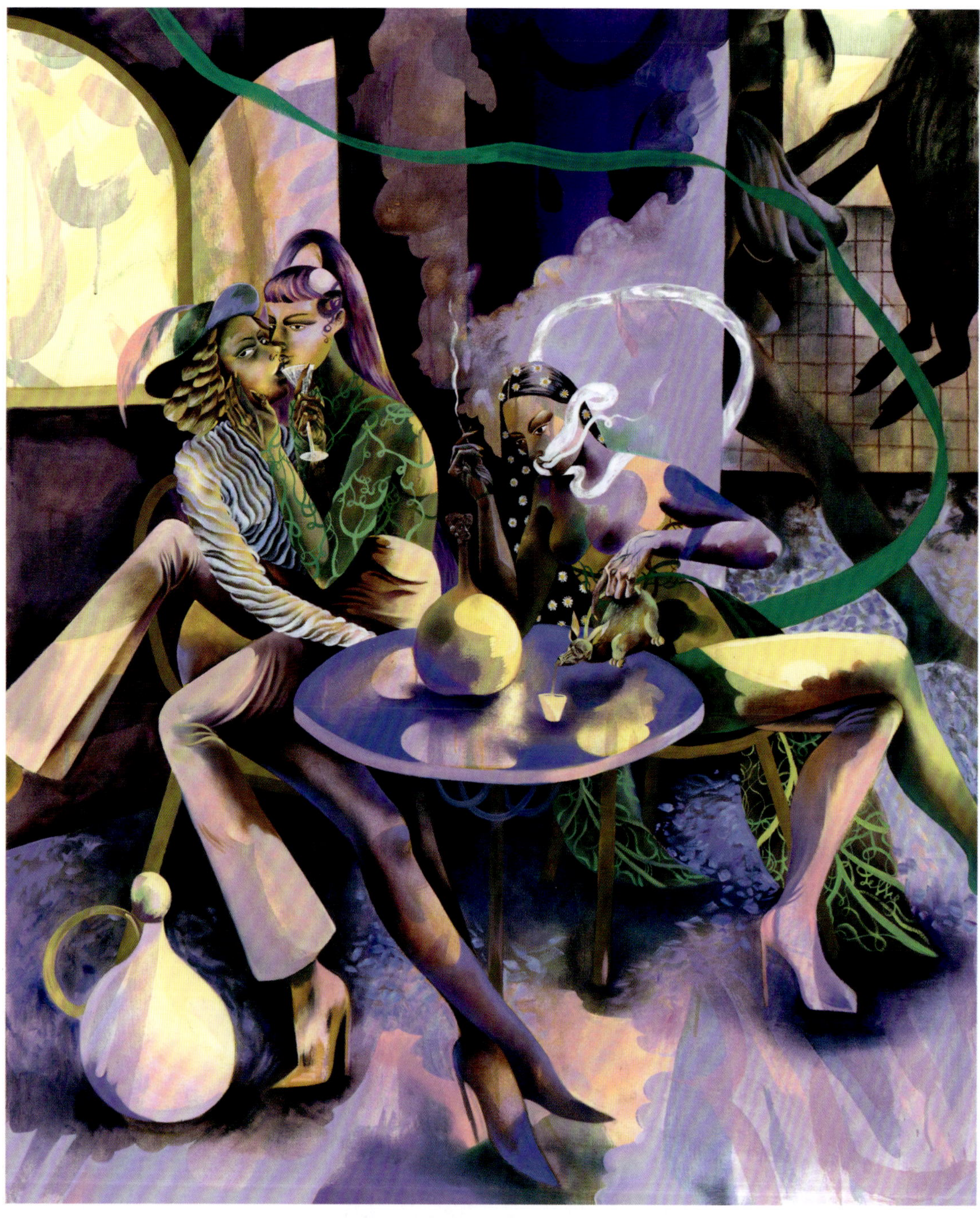

A POX ON THEM
2020, oil and pigment on canvas, 120 × 100 cm (41 ¼ × 39 ⅜ in), private collection

Jessie Makinson, born 1985, London, UK.

Influenced by art history, literature, ancient folklore and ecofeminism, Makinson's entrancing scenes feature groups of women in ambiguous setups, inhabiting spaces from fairy-tale landscapes to Renaissance-style architecture. Her confident, sensual protagonists often have their heads together as they revel, fight off unseen enemies and engage in mysterious rituals and transformations. A graduate of Edinburgh College of Art and the Royal Drawing School in London, Makinson begins each canvas by deciding on a colour palette and creating an underpainting. This process generates abstract shapes in which she discerns scenes, figures and spaces, transforming them intuitively into the characters, objects and settings that populate the finished canvas. Often the product of simple colour schemes rendered in a range of tones, the resulting images are fluent in supernatural allusions, projecting mystical and sexual energies. Makinson is fascinated by how post-humanism and science fiction imagine alternative ways of living that transcend individualism and patriarchal systems. Incarnating this subversive spirit, Makinson's women here find pleasure together as they level their gazes at each other, while animals in various guises hint at untamed desires and illicit rituals.

JEANNE MAMMEN

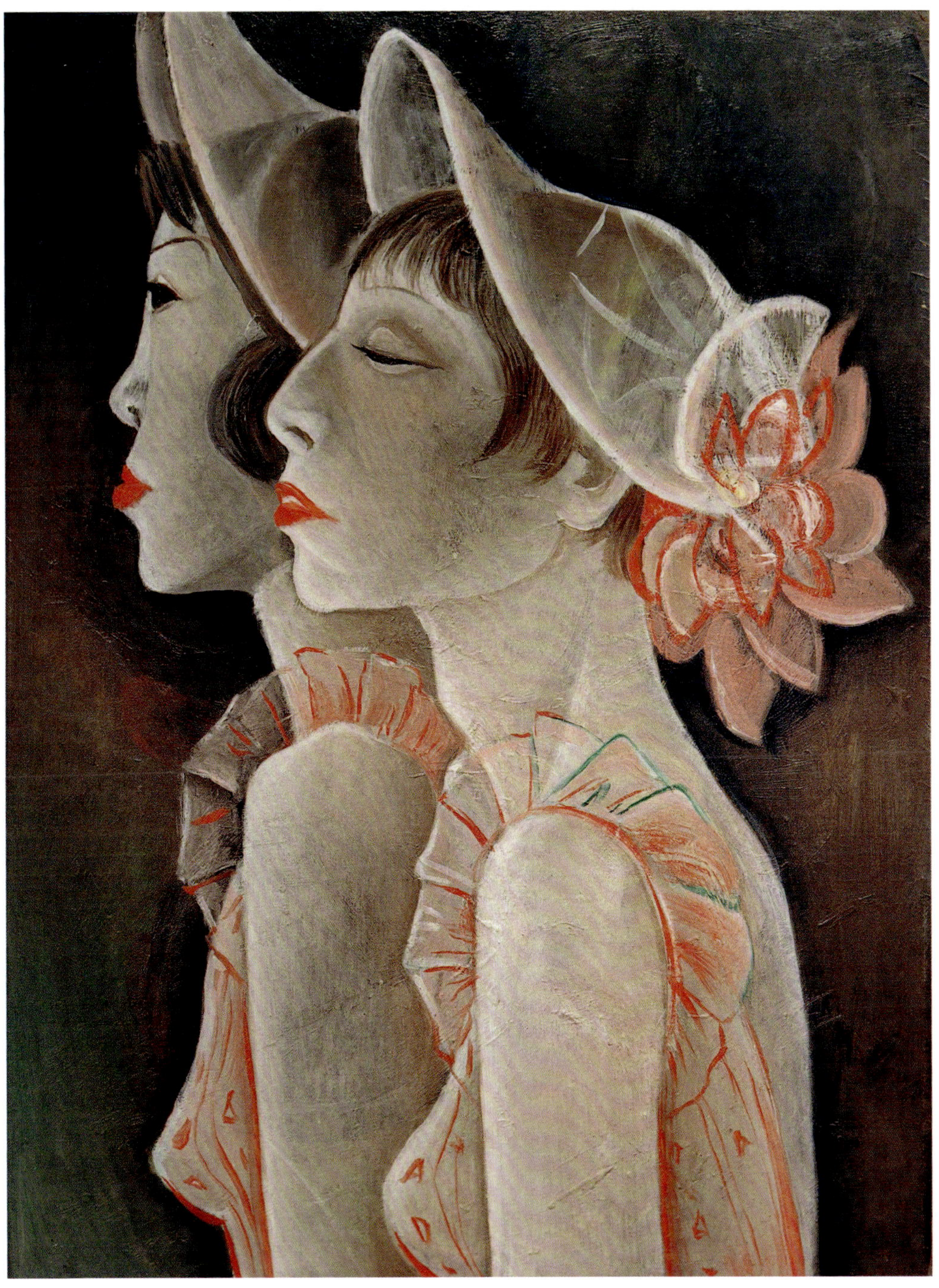

REVUEGIRLS (CHORUS GIRLS)
1928/9, oil on cardboard, 64 × 47 cm (25 ¼ × 18 ½ in), Berlinische Galerie, Berlin, Germany

Jeanne Mammen, born 1890, Berlin, Germany. Died 1976, Berlin.

Mammen is best remembered as a chronicler of the interwar years in Weimar Berlin. Having studied art in Paris and Brussels between 1906 and 1911, her work shows the influence of Henri de Toulouse-Lautrec (1864–1901) and shares features with her contemporaries associated with the Neue Sachlichkeit (New Objectivity) movement, including George Grosz (1893–1959) and Otto Dix (1891–1969). In her 1975 interview with art historian Hans Kinkel, Mammen professed a desire to be 'a pair of eyes, walking through the world unseen, only to be able to see others'. Mammen's observations focused on women, particularly the new woman of the Roaring Twenties: bobbed-haired flappers in Berlin's cabarets, theatres and jazz clubs; jaded sex workers in dark doorways; bourgeois ladies at pavement cafés. Chorus girls worked in the dance theatres, their long legs and diaphanous clothing an open invitation. Here Mammen depicts them in profile, their faces heavily made up, preparing to emerge on stage. When the Nazis assumed power in 1933, Mammen retreated to her studio and adopted abstraction, in solidarity with Cubist and Expressionist artists condemned as 'degenerate'.

MARGHERITA MANZELLI

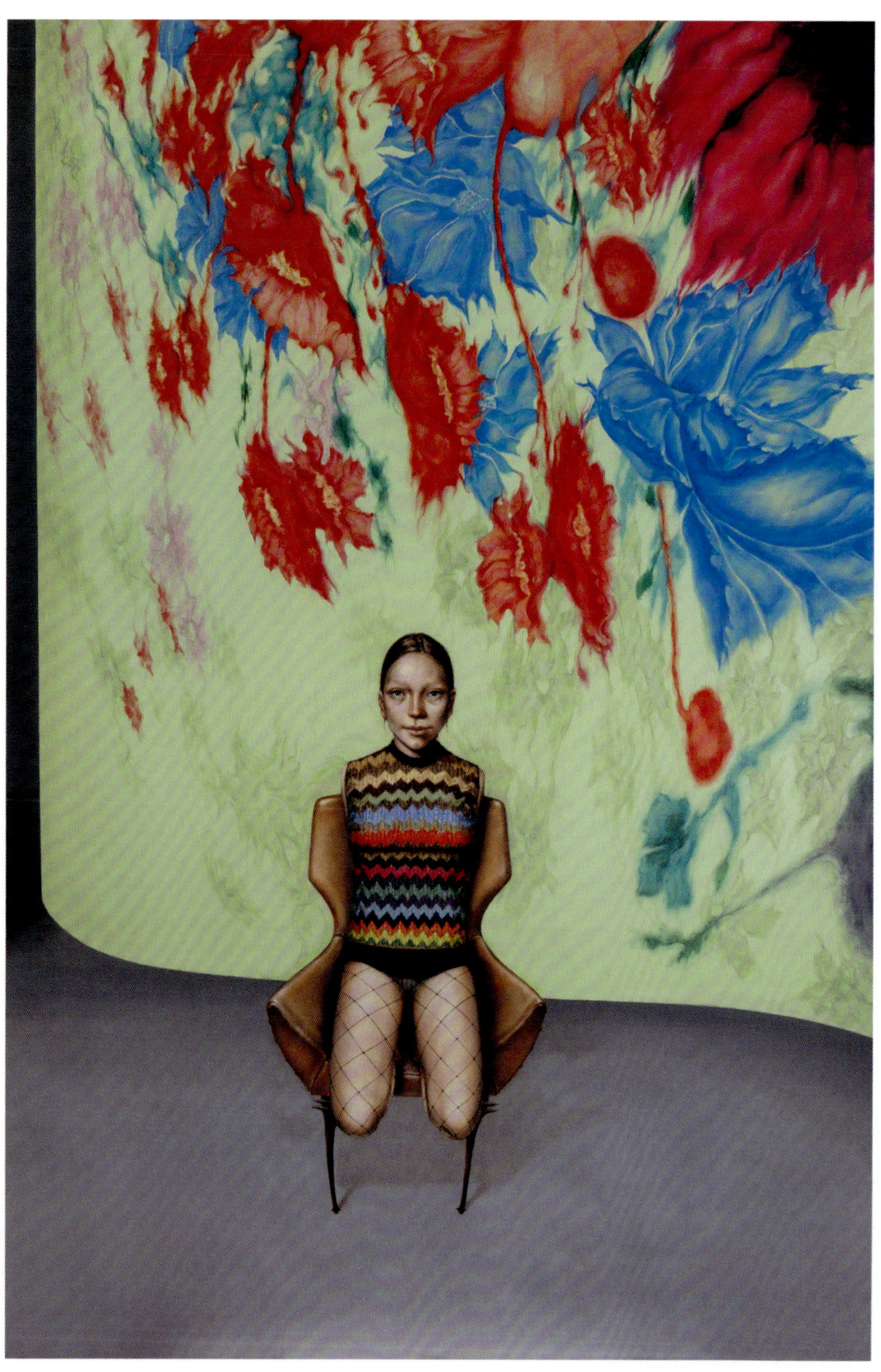

CHE OGNI GIORNO A MEZZOGIORNO MUORE (THAT DIES EVERY DAY AT MIDDAY)
2018, oil on linen, 299.7 × 200 × 5.1 cm
(118 × 78¾ × 2 in)

Margherita Manzelli, born 1968, Ravenna, Italy.

Manzelli's finely detailed portraits of female adolescents follow a painstaking and time-consuming process, and as a result, exhibitions of new works are infrequent. The artist has nevertheless gained international recognition and been featured in important group exhibitions including the 25th São Paulo Biennial (2002) and 'Pittura/Painting: From Rauschenberg to Murakami, 1964–2003' at the 50th Venice Biennale (2003). Although fictional, Manzelli's wide-eyed figures are distant self-portraits, each one reflective of the artist's interior world or memory. Many of her paintings evoke the sense of subjects who are knowingly performing for a viewer. As seen in this work, some are surreal scenes in which a solitary figure sits or reclines against a highly patterned background, with arms, hands or feet concealed as if tightly bound. Manzelli's works are often psychologically tense as she allows the gaze of the scantily dressed figure to confront that of the viewer – the act of looking becoming a subject in itself. Despite their fragility, the artist's emaciated, prepubertal figures appear self-possessed and perhaps even threatening, their enlarged, suggestive eyes conveying wisdom and innate power beyond their years.

AGNES MARTIN

WHITE FLOWER
1960, oil on canvas, 182.6 × 182.9 cm (71 7/8 × 72 in), Solomon R. Guggenheim Museum, New York, USA

Agnes Martin, born 1912, Macklin, Saskatchewan, Canada. Died 2004, Taos, New Mexico, USA.

Martin began pursuing her art career aged thirty, developing her style as she lived between New York and New Mexico. She emerged during the heyday of Minimalism in the 1960s and shares many formal qualities with her contemporaries associated with the movement. However, her art eschews the mechanical in favour of the individual mark and is conceptually centred around the spiritual and emotional rather than materiality and literalness. In paintings such as *White Flower* – the first work by Martin to enter a museum collection – she uses geometry as a vehicle to express and contemplate abstract, universal ideas of happiness and beauty, which she associated with perfection and transcendent reality. Her reductionist approach to creating harmonious compositions allowed her to remove ego from art-making, striving to communicate the immaterial absolute. Yet by not masking her hand entirely – as evidenced by the slightly wavering and humming hand-drawn lines that form her grids, and variations in her thin layers of translucent paint – Martin revelled in the paradox of creating physical objects to articulate metaphysical ideas, suggesting that sublime reality could be known or experienced but not obtained.

WANGARI MATHENGE

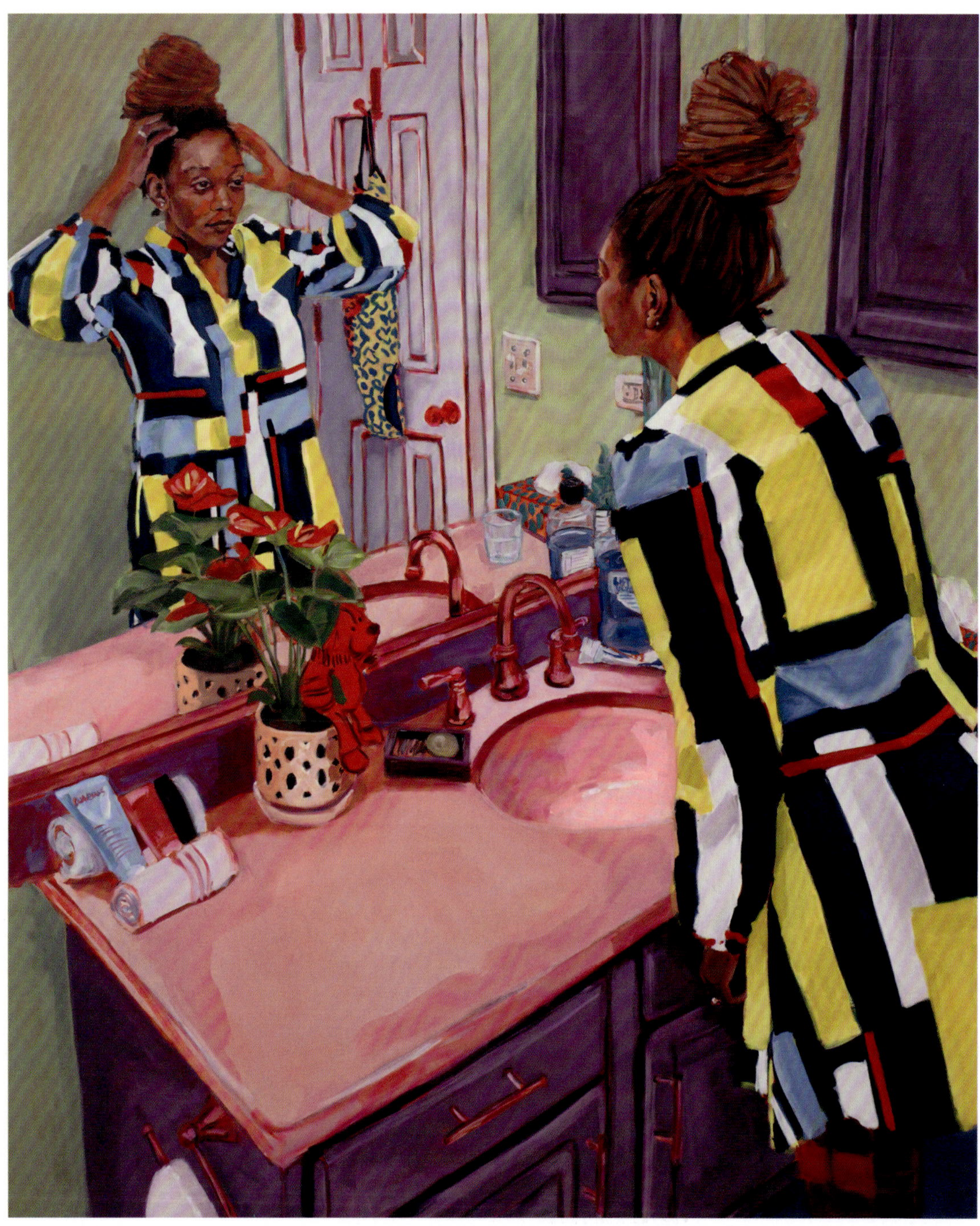

THE ASCENDANTS XVII (SHE IS HERE TOO BUT WHY ARE YOU?)
2021, oil on canvas, 193 × 160 cm (76 × 63 in), private collection

Wangari Mathenge, born 1973, Nairobi, Kenya.

Mathenge's works examine the diasporic experience through intimate figural compositions that draw from both personal memories and collective histories of immigration. Born in Kenya, the daughter of an intergovernmental agency employee who lived in the United Kingdom throughout the 1970s, Mathenge moved to the United States to study and currently lives and works in Chicago. Mining her and her family's experiences, the artist's series 'The Expats' and 'The Ascendants' explore the colonial legacies and racial hierarchies implied in the assumption of immigrant or expatriate social status, noting that the latter designation is often reserved for white people living abroad, but rarely for African emigrants in the West. In her dynamic compositions – which typically feature lusciously coloured domestic interiors and overlapping layers of textile patterns – women occupy positions of both introspection and power, refashioning spaces traditionally associated with women's labour into dignified sanctuaries of leisure. *The Ascendants XVII* features a female figure gazing into her own mirrored reflection, which appears different to her – an articulation of diasporic double consciousness and hybrid identity.

LOUISA MATTHÍASDÓTTIR

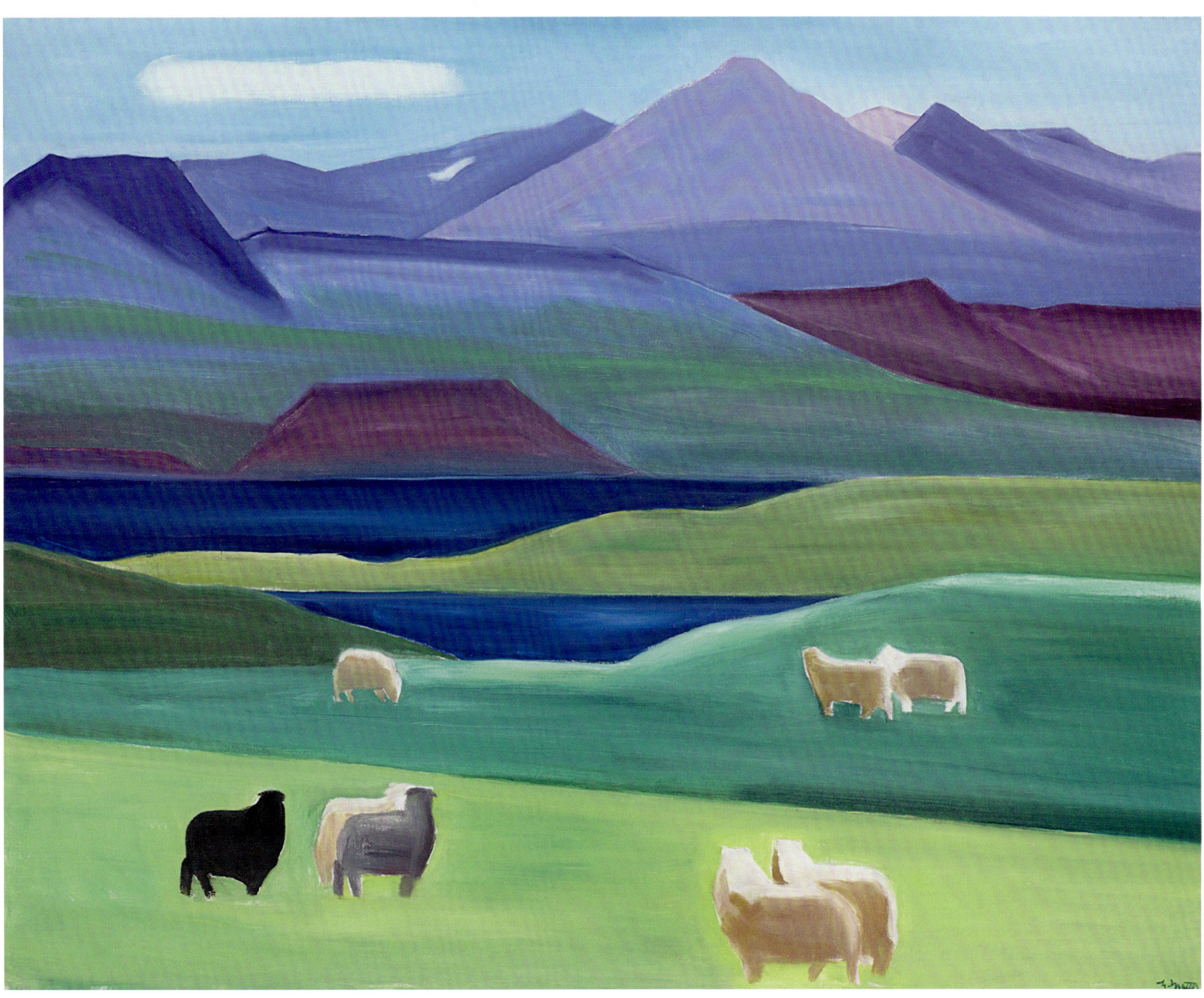

MOUNTAIN AND SHEEP
1989, oil on canvas, 132.1 × 167.6 cm (52 × 66 in)

Louisa Matthíasdóttir, born 1917, Reykjavík, Iceland. Died 2000, Delhi, New York, USA.

Working across genres including landscape, still life and portraiture, Matthíasdóttir cultivated a distinctive painting style defined by vibrant colour blocks that reduce scenes to their fundamental shapes and planes. Born in Reykjavík but educated in Copenhagen and Paris, the artist moved to New York in 1942, briefly enrolling at the Art Students League before transferring to Hans Hofmann's (1880–1966) fine arts school where she studied alongside artists including Larry Rivers (1923–2002) and Jane Freilicher (p.113). While her earlier works were informed by Expressionist painting, by the 1960s she had developed the signature style for which she has become best known, emphasizing geometric forms and smooth, broad brushstrokes in her idyllic landscapes of the Icelandic countryside. *Mountain and Sheep* depicts a scenic vista, with the topography rendered in shades ranging from green to mauve. As in most of her works, the painting's quiet simplicity gives way to an enigmatic quality, described by the poet John Ashbery in a 2000 exhibition catalogue as having a 'strange flavour, both mellow and astringent, which no other painter gives us'.

DÓRA MAURER

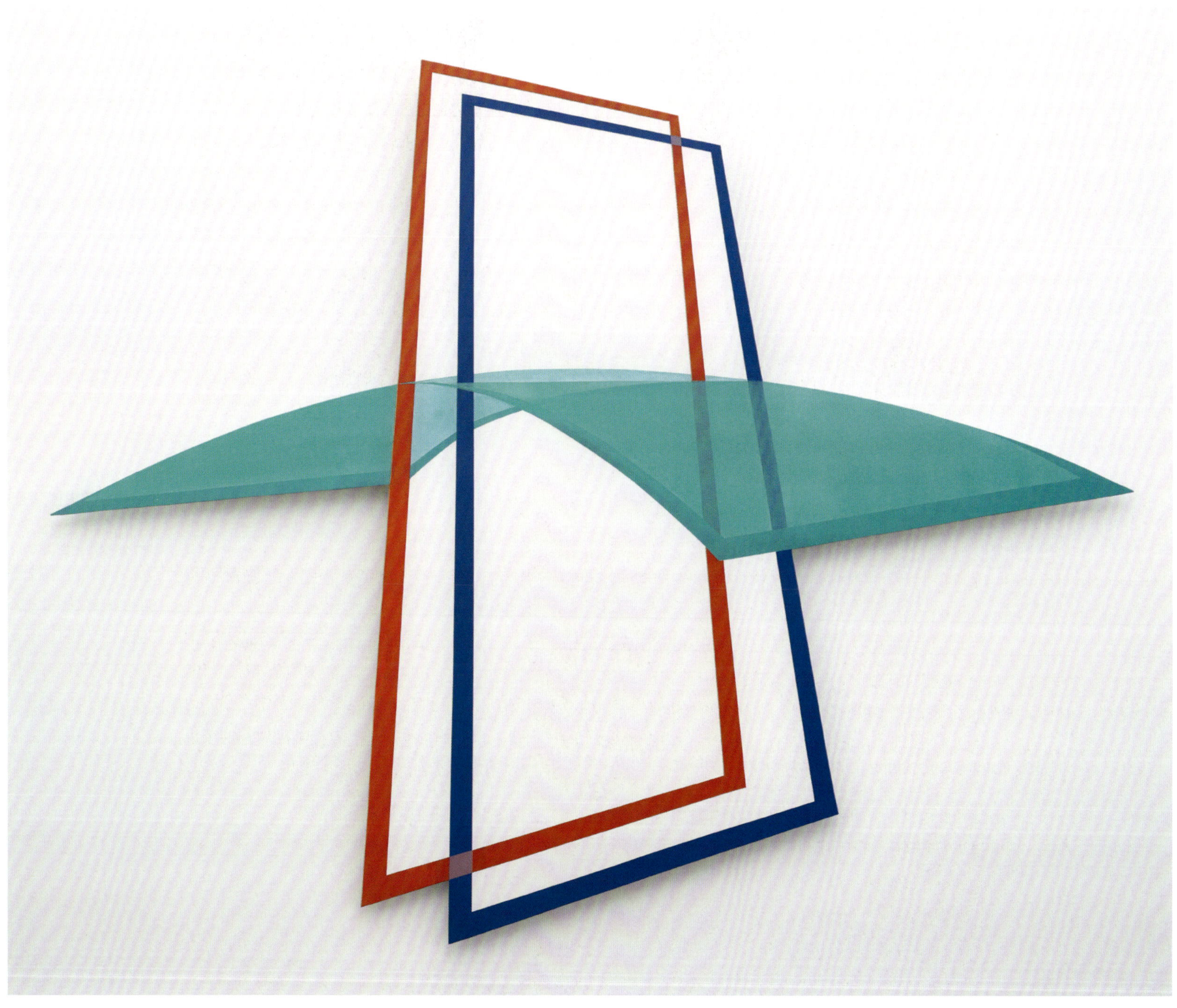

IXEK 11
2014, acrylic on canvas and wood, 160 × 200 cm
(63 × 78 ¾ in)

Dóra Maurer, born 1937, Budapest, Hungary.

Maurer is widely regarded as a foundational figure in the Hungarian avant-garde. Born on the eve of the Second World War, Maurer grew up in communist Hungary, and her early artistic practice was thus mediated by a backdrop of political suppression and creative limitation. These terms, perhaps, set the stage for her embrace of a stark conceptual style in place of narrative, symbolism or subjective expression. In her early photographs and short films of the 1960s and 1970s, Maurer explored the formal and kinetic possibilities of basic objects and shapes, creating sequential series that documented subtle shifts in motion, perspective or action. The artist's practice in abstract painting both distils and extends this interest in motion study. Her irregularly shaped canvases, such as *IXEK 11*, were inspired by the colour studies of Josef Albers (1888–1976). In these works, Maurer renders overlapping or intersecting geometric planes, enacting a careful study of perspective, form and two- and three-dimensionality, while subversively breaking through the medium's traditional mandate of representing an illusory 'window' to another world.

DINDGA McCANNON

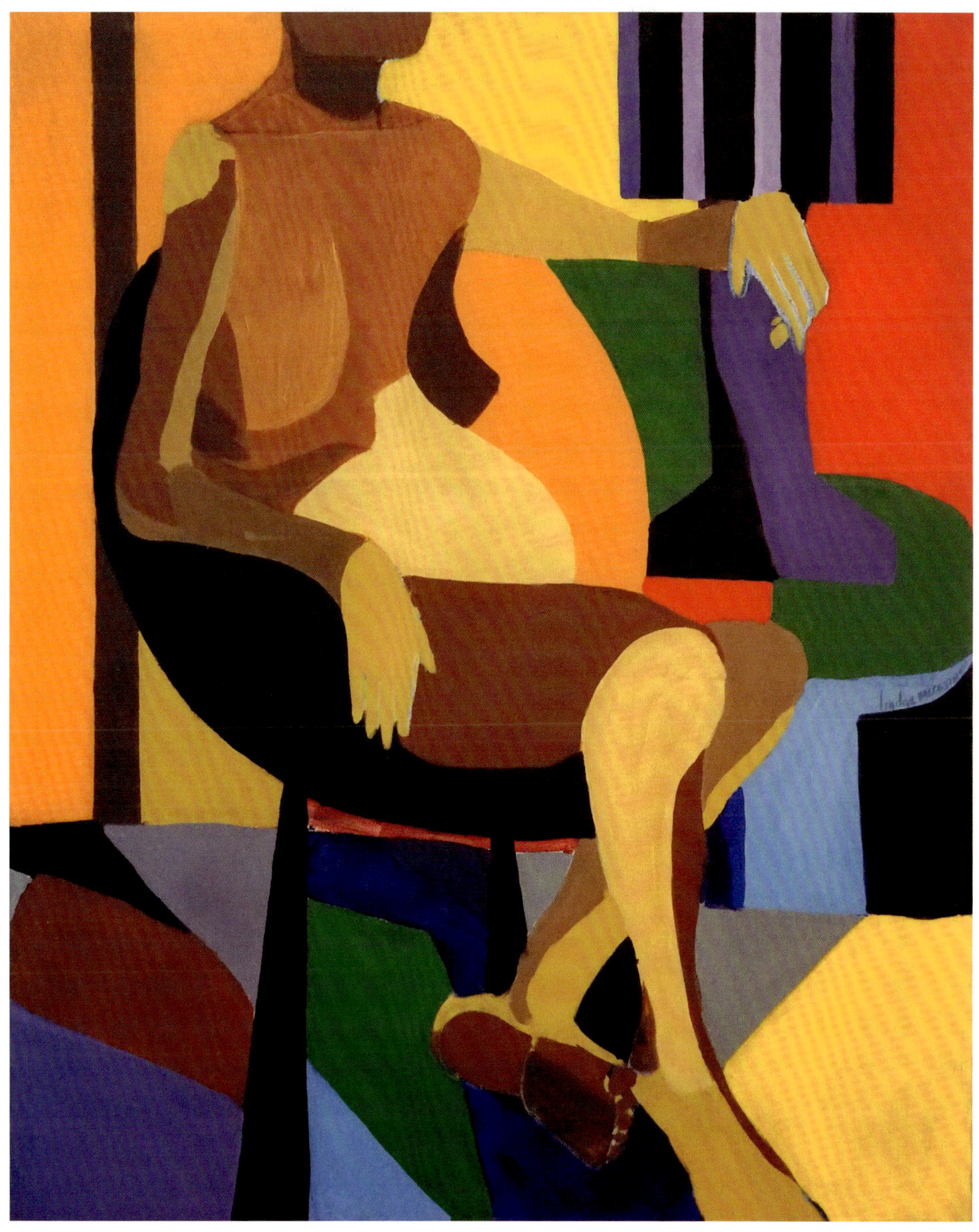

WOMAN #1
1975–7, acrylic on canvas, 106.7 × 83.8 cm (42 × 33 in)

Dindga McCannon, born 1947, New York, USA.

Working across mediums including painting, printmaking, textile assemblage and found-object quilting, McCannon was drawn to art from an early age, learning to sew from her mother and grandmother. A key figure in the American Black Arts Movement, McCannon found artistic community with the Harlem-based Weusi Artist Collective in the late 1960s, which helped her mount her first show at seventeen. In 1971, she co-founded, with Faith Ringgold (p.249) and Kay Brown (1932–2012), 'Where We At' Black Women Artists, a feminist collective that promoted Black women in the arts. Early in her artistic career, McCannon had left the art programme at New York's City College, frustrated with the white-centric approach to art-making that left no space for her Afrocentric vision. She turned instead to the Art Students League of New York, where she was able to learn from prominent Black artists including Richard Mayhew (b. 1924), Jacob Lawrence (1917–2000) and Harlem Renaissance painter Charles Alston (1907–77). One of many works focusing on the history and stories of women, *Woman #1* shows a seated female nude comprised of blocks of solid colour, exploring the interplay between depth and flatness and evoking the vibrancy of McCannon's own community.

JULIE MEHRETU

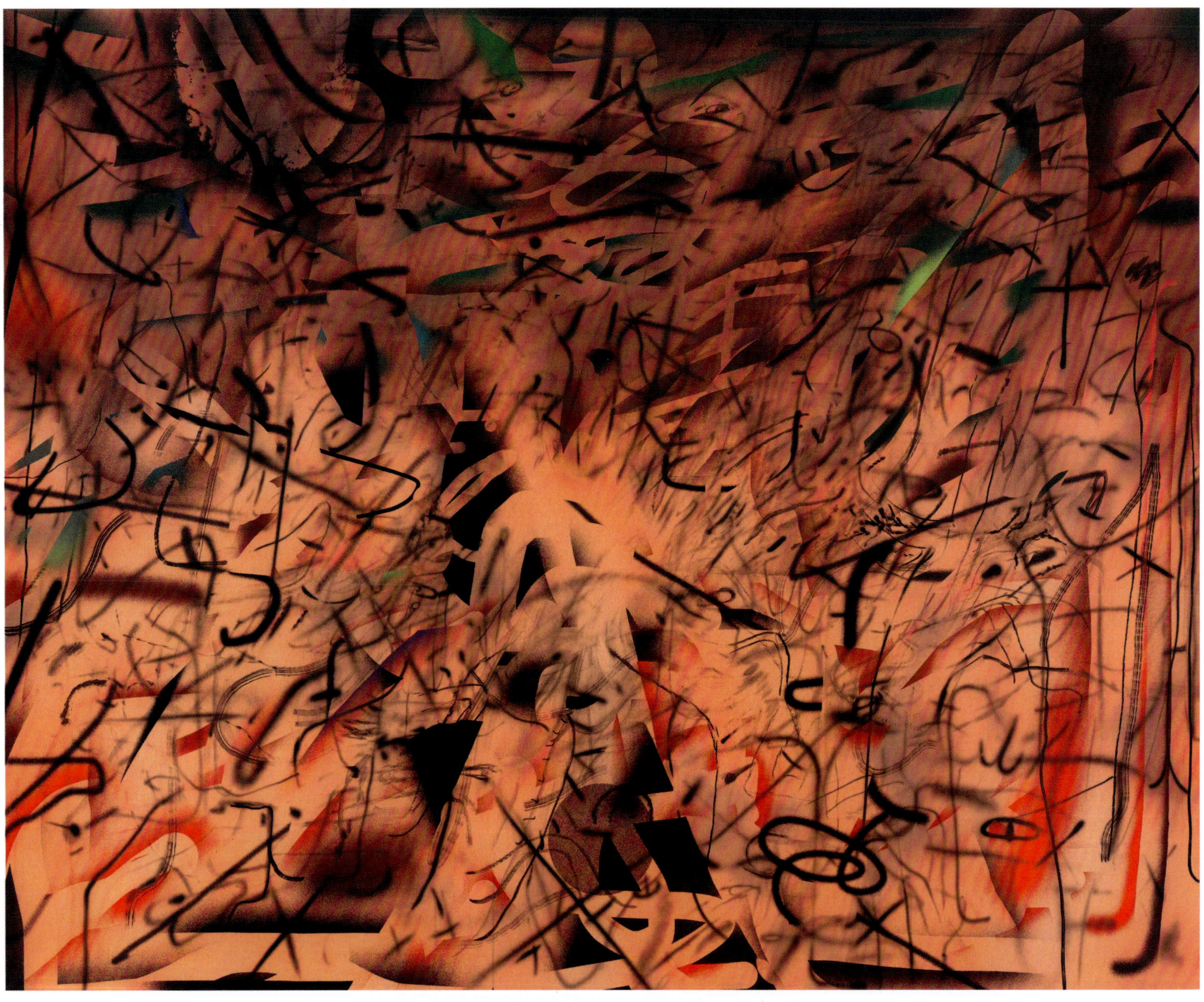

HINENI (E. 3:4)
2018, ink and acrylic on canvas, 243.8 × 304.8 cm, (96 × 120 in), Musée National d'Art Moderne, Centre Pompidou, Paris, France

Julie Mehretu, born 1970, Addis Ababa, Ethiopia.

Building on a global history of abstraction, Mehretu's paintings telescope between the intimate and the immense. Early works emphasized the power of small marks, as they accumulated into squalls that many have compared to maps or topographies. Sometimes, her work is literally architectural, adumbrating plazas in Berlin or realized in the skyscrapers and sanctuaries of Manhattan, where the artist lives and works. Elsewhere, such scale is less spatial than conceptual, with Mehretu visualizing the social and meteorological systems that affect us all. In the late 2010s Mehretu began translating media photographs into fields of colour, generating substrates to be layered with the gesture of the calligrapher or graffiti artist. *Hineni (E. 3:4)* is a vision of wildfires sweeping through California – a symptom of an accelerating climate crisis – and a response to the burning of Rohingya houses in Myanmar. Its title, Hebrew for 'Here I am', evokes Moses's assent to the divine burning bush. In so recomposing a tumultuous world, Mehretu further elaborates a practice that bridges temporalities and terrains, the discrete and the sublime, into a unified pictorial language.

PRABHAVATHI MEPPAYIL

I/hundred thirty one
2018, copper wire embedded in gesso panel, 121.9 × 121.9 × 5 cm (48 × 48 × 2 in)

Prabhavathi Meppayil, born 1965, Bangalore, India.

Meppayil's paintings and installations unite Minimalist aesthetics with the tools of artisanal craft. Born to a family of goldsmiths, the Indian artist often utilizes the instruments of the trade to create her subtle, nearly monochromatic works. She regularly employs the *thinnam* – a small tool used to create impressions in metal jewellery – to 'draw' repetitive marks in gesso. Meppayil's influences include Indian process-based modernists like Sheela Gowda (b. 1957) and Nasreen Mohamedi (1937–90), as well as American Minimalists; in particular, her work has frequently been compared to that of Agnes Martin (p. 191), who incorporated the geometric grid into her pale paintings exploring light and atmospheric conditions. Meppayil, whose painstaking process also includes the use of precious metals, achieved wider recognition after she was included in the 2013 Venice Biennale exhibition 'The Encyclopedic Palace'. In *l/hundred thirty one*, the artist embedded tiny copper wires into a panel that she covered with layers of gesso. She then sanded some of the layers away, revealing glimpses of oxidized metal of different shades that appear when viewed at various angles. This work calls attention to labour and temporality, and requests the viewer's attention in return.

GLADYS MGUDLANDLU

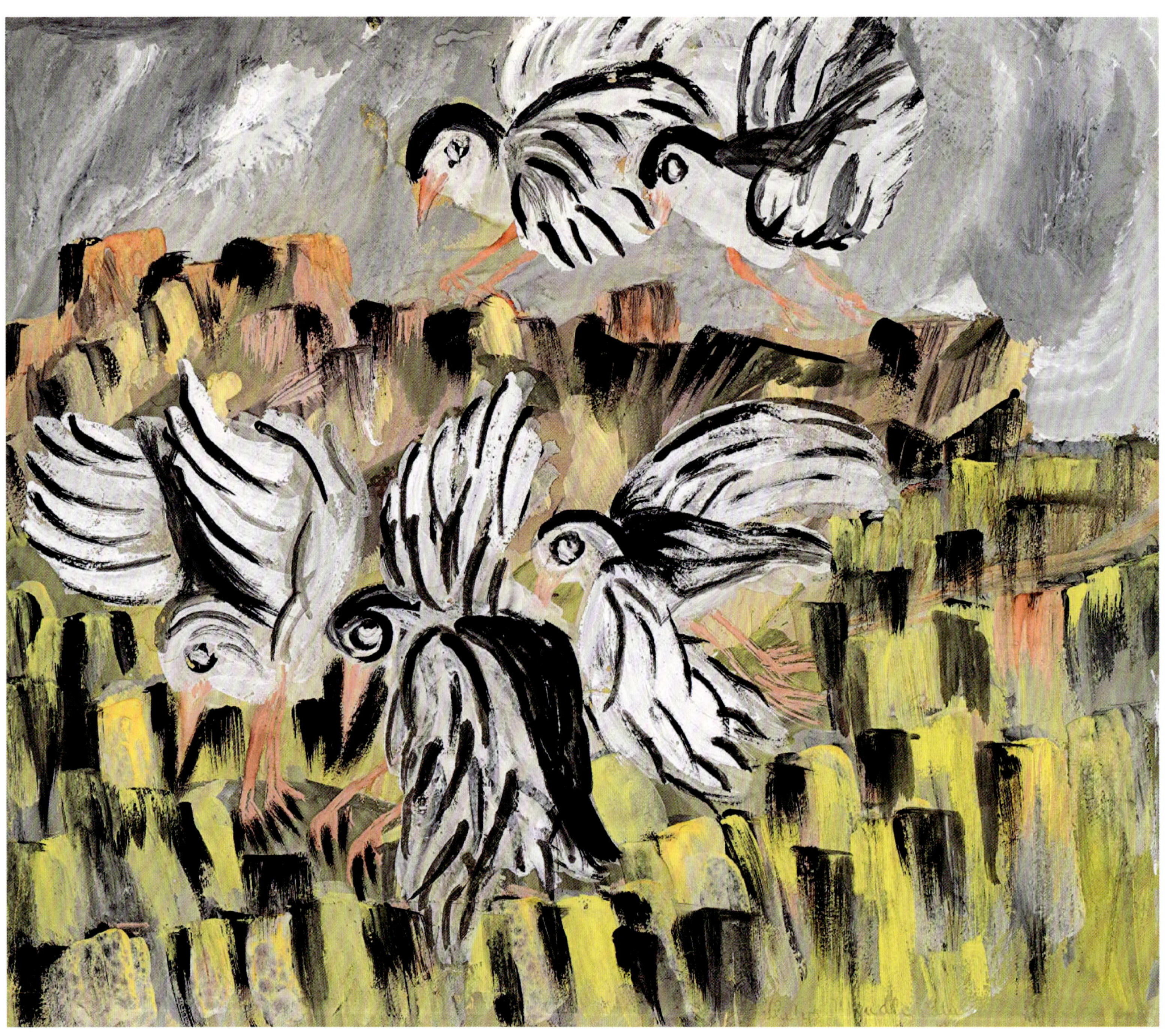

BIRDS OVER A FIELD
1962, gouache on paper, 49.5 × 58 cm
(19 ½ × 22 ⅞ in)

Gladys Mgudlandlu, born 1917, Peddie, South Africa. Died 1979, Gugulethu, Cape Town, South Africa.

Born and raised in rural South Africa, Mgudlandlu started to paint professionally in 1957 after the death of her grandmother, who had trained her from a young age in the tradition of Mfengu and Xhosa mural painting. Mgudlandlu found great fame during her lifetime, and in 1962 she was one of the first Black South African women to have a solo gallery exhibition. Though her work was considered to be 'naive' folk art by her mostly white patrons, Mgudlandlu's formally complex compositions reveal her understanding of Western art-historical traditions such as Impressionism and Expressionism. Sometimes referred to as the 'Bird Lady' (or *uNontaka* in her native Xhosa), Mgudlandlu often turned her focus on the animals in her work – or adopted a bird's-eye view in her depictions of landscape. In this work, a group of birds moves gracefully across a field in what may at first appear to be an ordinary rural scene. A more sustained look reveals a frenetic strangeness – the birds' wide-open eyes and vegetation that ranges from peach to hazmat yellow – leading some writers to interpret her works as commentaries on the forcible removal of Black South Africans from their land during apartheid.

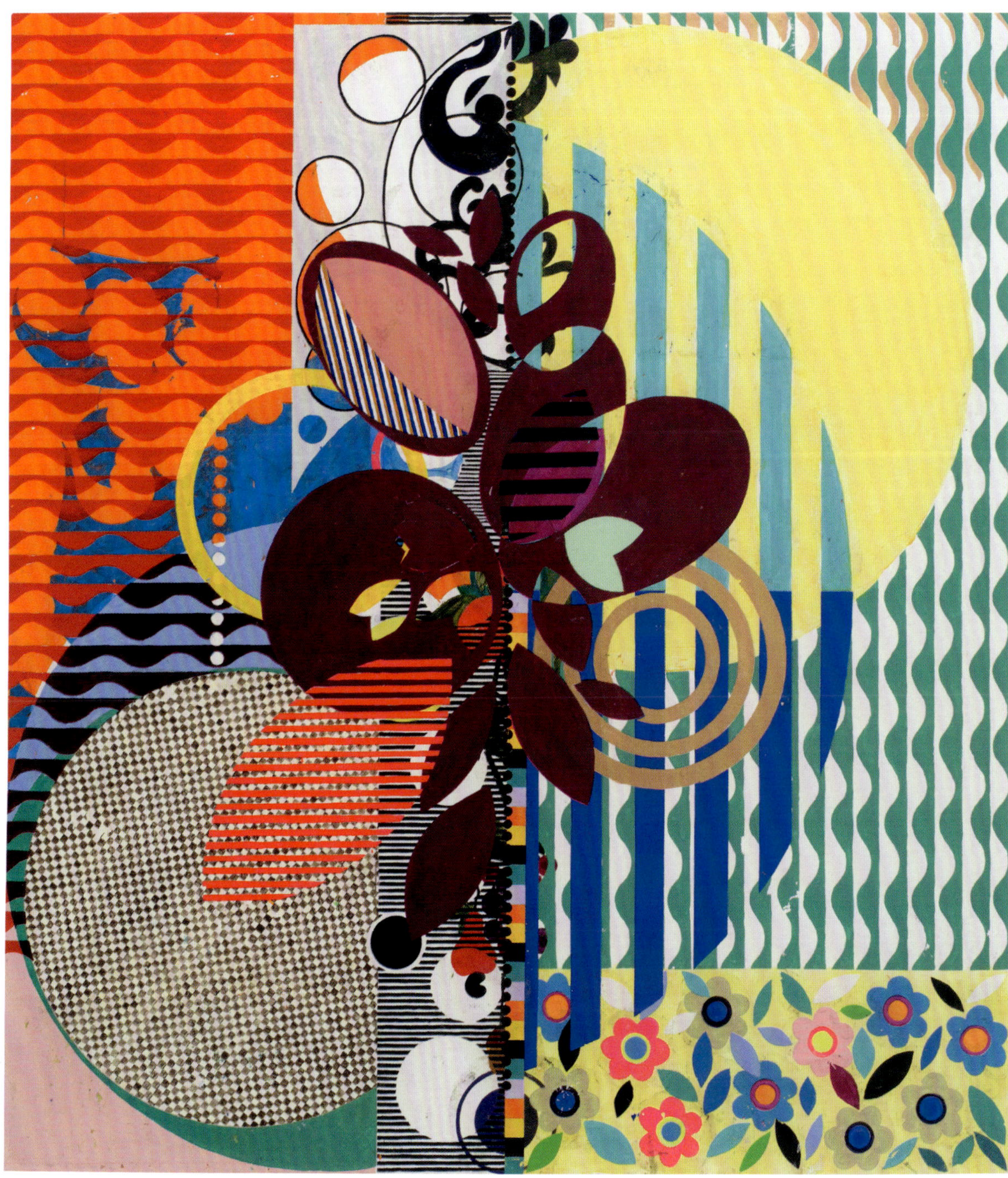

QUEIMADINHO
2014/15, acrylic on linen, 180 × 160 cm
(70 ⅞ × 63 in)

Beatriz Milhazes, born 1960, Rio de Janeiro, Brazil.

Celebrated for her distinctive formal language, Milhazes creates vibrant, energetic paintings and collages that fuse imagery of tropical vegetation, modernist abstraction and the decorative arts of her native Brazil. Part of the Geração 80 (80s Generation) – a group of Brazilian artists who found new vitality in the medium of painting – Milhazes is known for her signature use of stencil-like transfers, in which she layers acrylic paint on plastic decals, which are then applied to her canvases and peeled off. Making visible the physical layers of paint and the imperfections of the transfers, this technique takes influence from the process of natural erosion. Milhazes's influences include Brazilian modernists Tarsila (p.297) and Hélio Oiticica (1937–80), the abstractions of Piet Mondrian (1872–1944) and Henri Matisse's (1869–1954) late cut-outs. She also draws inspiration from craft, fashion and the traditions of Carnival. The interplay between Brazilian themes and international modernist idioms is evident in *Queimadinho*. Here, Milhazes has layered a central geometric leafy pattern over optical patterns of wavy lines and, in the lower right, a cluster of flowers inspired by vintage decor.

LISA MILROY

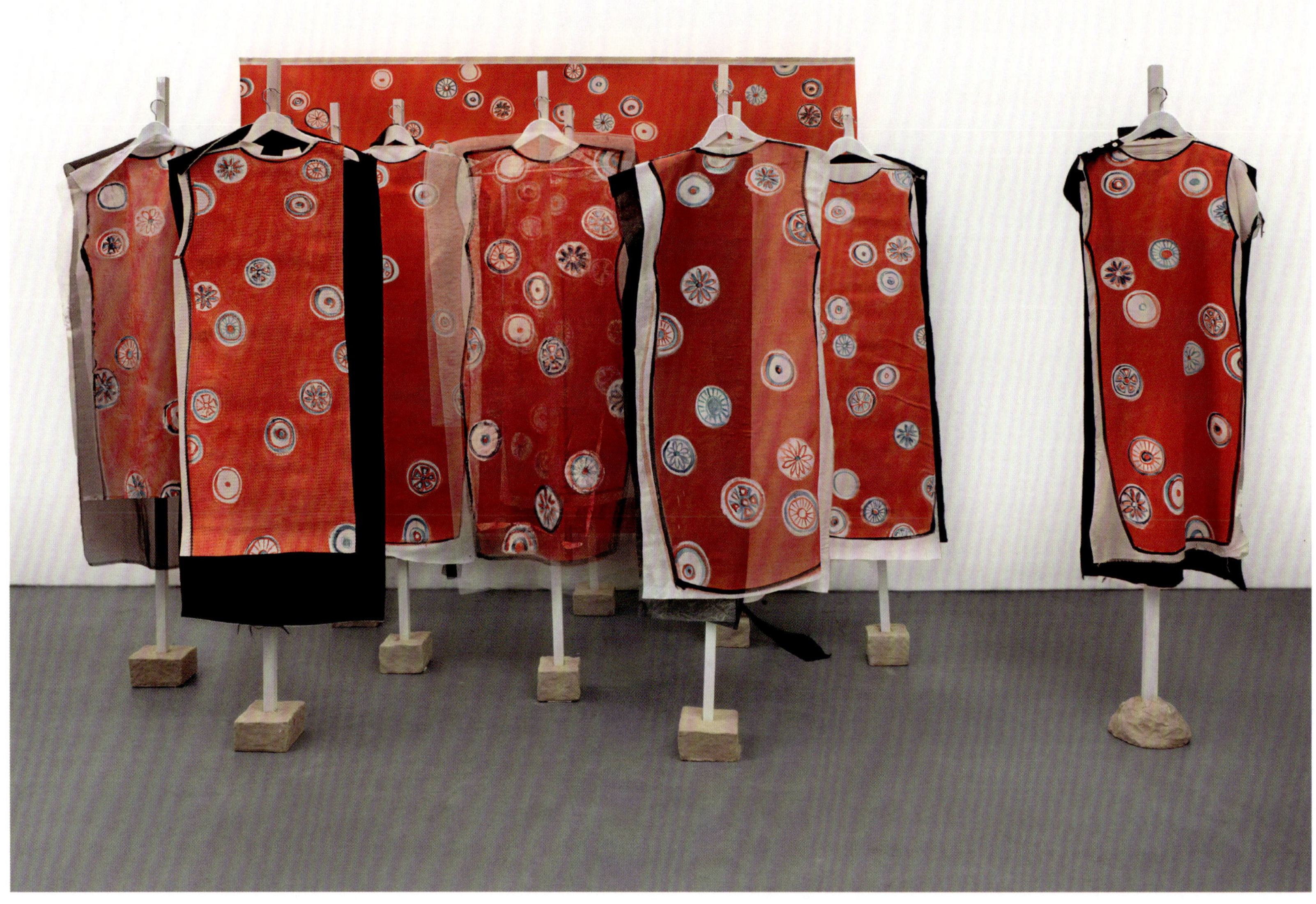

PARTY OF ONE
2013, installation painting and painting performed: 9 dress 'object-paintings', 1 wearable dress painting, 10 wooden stands, clay bases and oil on unstretched canvas, 182 × 234 × 200 cm (71 5/8 × 92 1/8 × 78 3/4 in), Tate, UK

Lisa Milroy, born 1959, Vancouver, Canada.

After studying at Saint Martin's School of Art and Goldsmiths College in London, Milroy achieved recognition in the mid-1980s for her oil paintings of shoes, clothes, plates, hardware, postage stamps and other everyday objects variously arranged on an off-white ground and painted with quick, gestural brushstrokes. Having situated the still-life genre at the heart of her practice, she experimented with fast and slow applications of paint to evoke a range of moods and atmospheres, expanding her imagery in the 1990s to include landscape, architecture and figures. Her interest in the relationships between stillness and movement, thought and action, and presence and absence as they pertain to the experience of making and looking at paintings, led to the development of large-scale installation and performance-based works. Probing the nature of painting, *Party of One* (2013) comprises nine 'object-paintings' in the form of red, patterned dresses, which hang installed in front of a painted backdrop. A tenth, wearable dress is donned by a performer, who steps within the installation to assume various positions among the 'object-paintings' and then exits the installation to travel around the gallery, animating and extending Milroy's painting in both time and space.

AD MINOLITI

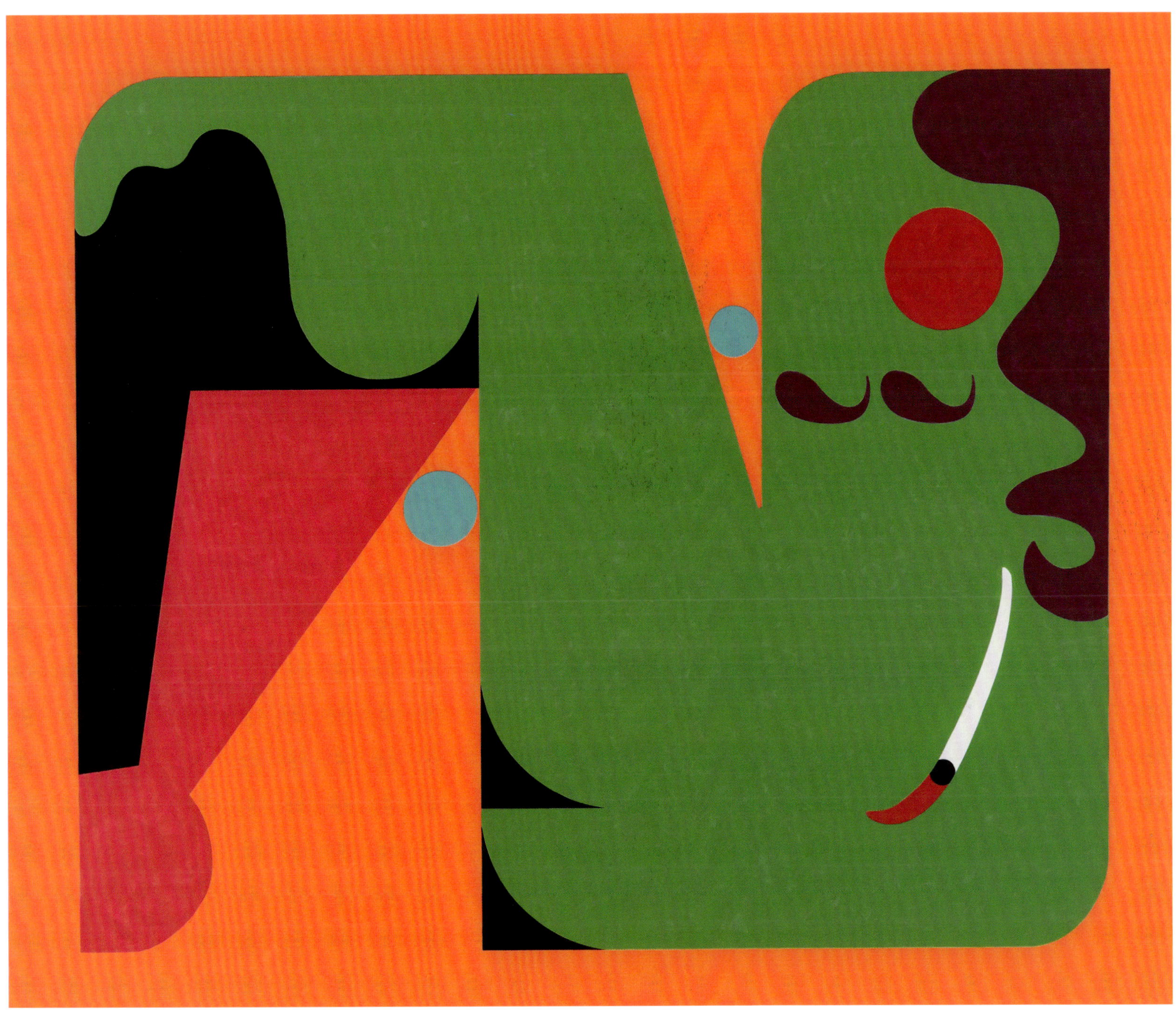

KING 1
2019, acrylic on canvas, 150 × 180 cm (59 × 71 in)

Ad Minoliti, born 1980, Buenos Aires, Argentina.

Minoliti's paintings employ a vivid visual language grounded in the legacy of Latin American geometric abstraction, which are often displayed within total environments alongside sculptures and murals. For their ongoing participatory project 'The Feminist School of Painting' (begun in 2018), Minoliti accessorizes these displays with chairs and rugs to create spaces for learning and play in workshops that Minoliti facilitates in collaboration with other artists, thinkers and activists. Minoliti, who trained in painting at the National School of Fine Arts Prilidiano Pueyrredón and the Artistic Research Center of Buenos Aires, brings the history of painting into dialogue with important texts of queer and feminist theory, including Donna Haraway's 'A Cyborg Manifesto' – a 1985 essay proposing a dismantlement of the categories of male and female, human and animal, animal and machine. Complicating such binaries is central to Minoliti's artistic project. In *King 1*, Minoliti references 1970s graphic design with areas of flat, vibrant colour and a tangle of geometric shapes that hint at body parts without fully subsuming the figure into a traditional representational aesthetic.

MARILYN MINTER

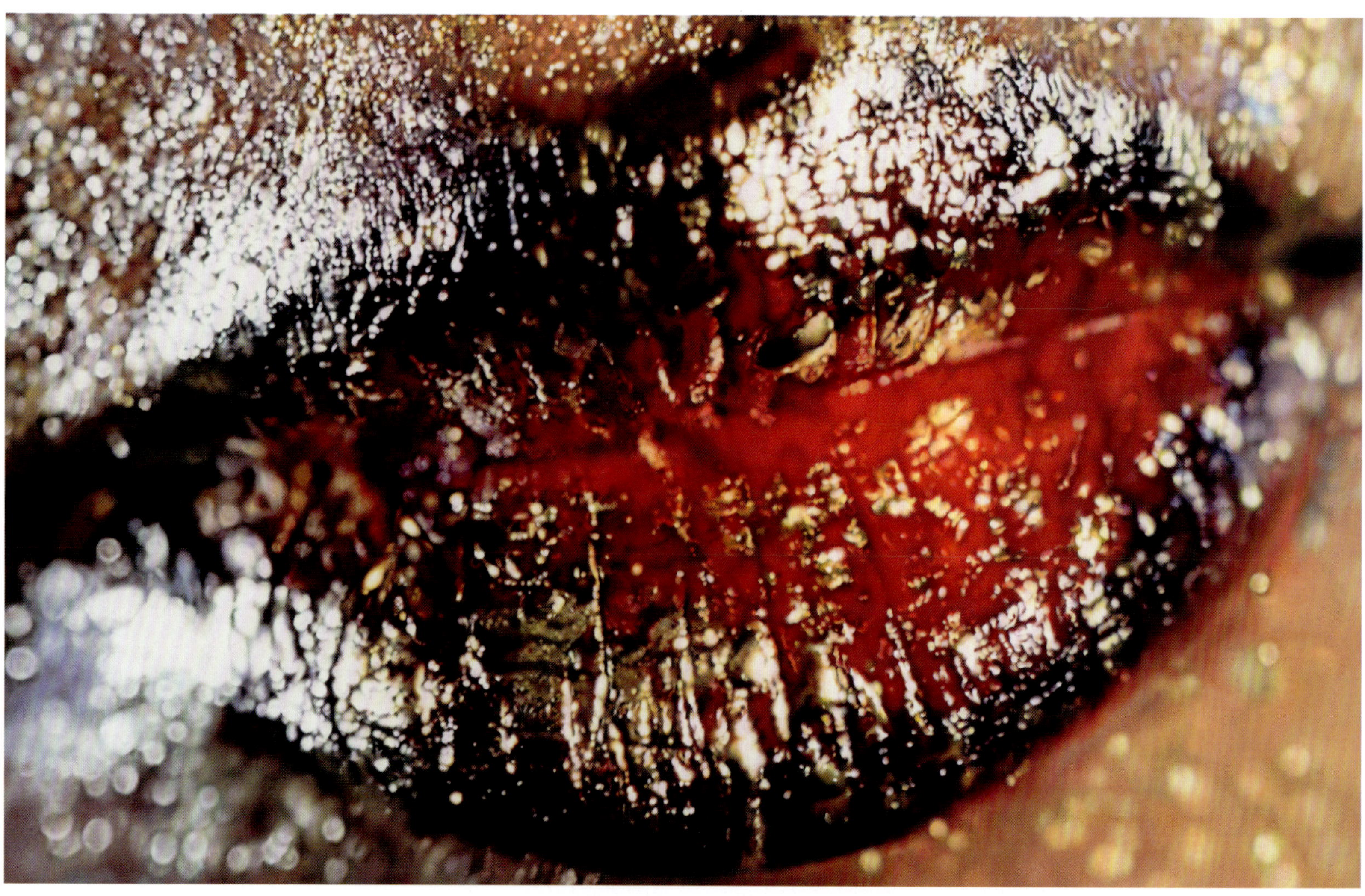

BIG RED
2010, enamel on metal, 152.4 × 243.8 cm
(60 × 96 in)

Marilyn Minter, born 1948, Shreveport, Louisiana, USA.

Through erotically charged imagery, often in extreme close-up, Minter addresses the commodification of women's bodies, particularly in the worlds of fashion, beauty and pornography. Her hyper-realism mimics the aesthetics of these industries, yet her compositions also feature dirt, stray hairs, visible pores, bodily fluids or other 'imperfections' usually airbrushed away in commercial imagery. *Big Red*, for example, initially appears like a perfect beauty shot of a heavily made-up mouth. Yet closer inspection reveals sweat beading on the upper lip and the lipstick bleeding. Having initially depicted the banalities of feminine daily life in her work of the 1970s, when Minter moved on to more lascivious subjects in the 1980s, she sparked a critical and ideological backlash, being seen by some as antifeminist. This response prompted her deeper interest in exploring societal mores. Since the mid-1990s, her process has begun with elaborate photoshoots, often featuring Minter herself, to create the source material for her paintings, which are mostly rendered in enamel on metal to further reinforce a high-gloss finish. Her inclusion in the 2006 Whitney Biennial in New York was the catalyst for a re-evaluation of her work, and in 2015 she had a major retrospective that toured to four US cities.

JOAN MITCHELL

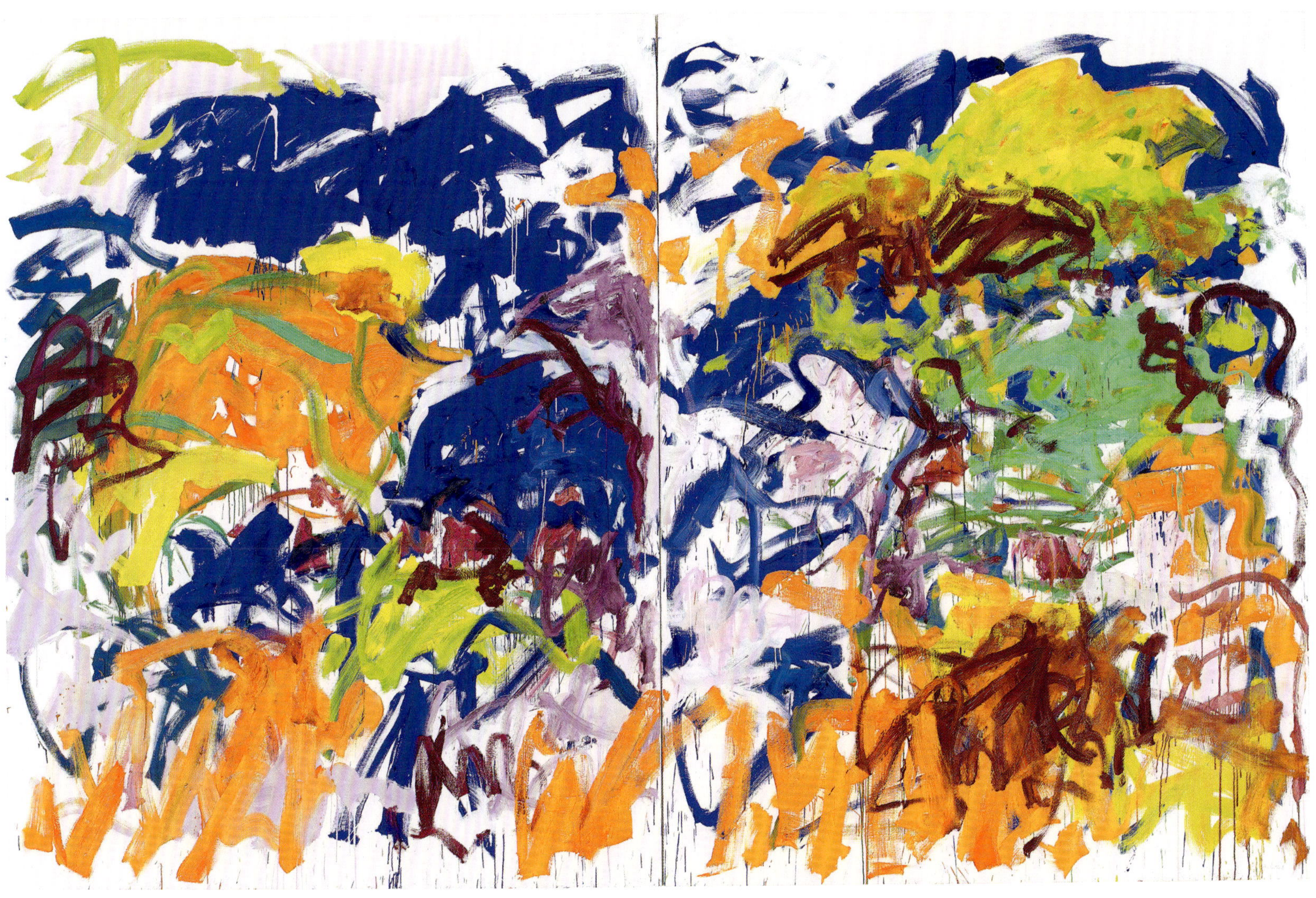

ICI
1992, oil on canvas, 260 × 400.1 cm
(102 ⅜ × 157 ½ in), Saint Louis Art Museum, USA

Joan Mitchell, born 1925, Chicago, USA.
Died 1992, Paris, France.

In her youth, Mitchell competed as a figure skater, diver and horse rider, early evidence of a drive that would later translate to her painting. As one of the few women in the Abstract Expressionist movement and the New York School, Mitchell used large canvases and vivid colour to express feeling through abstraction, with many of her works influenced by landscapes and nature. Mitchell moved to New York in 1949 and became established within the avant-garde, befriending writers Frank O'Hara and John Ashbery and spending time at the Cedar Tavern, a hang-out of artists and critics including Clement Greenberg and Willem de Kooning (1904–97). In 1959, she left New York for France, moving first to Paris and then, in 1968, to Vétheuil, where she would remain for the rest of her life. It was there that Mitchell painted the abstract landscape titled *Ici* (French for 'here'). Created the year of her death, *Ici* combines Mitchell's bold, swift brushstrokes with bursts of bright colours drawn from nature. The painting is a culmination of Mitchell's practice, its ambiguous title perhaps a declaration of the artist's own presence in the landscape of the canvas.

JESSE MOCKRIN

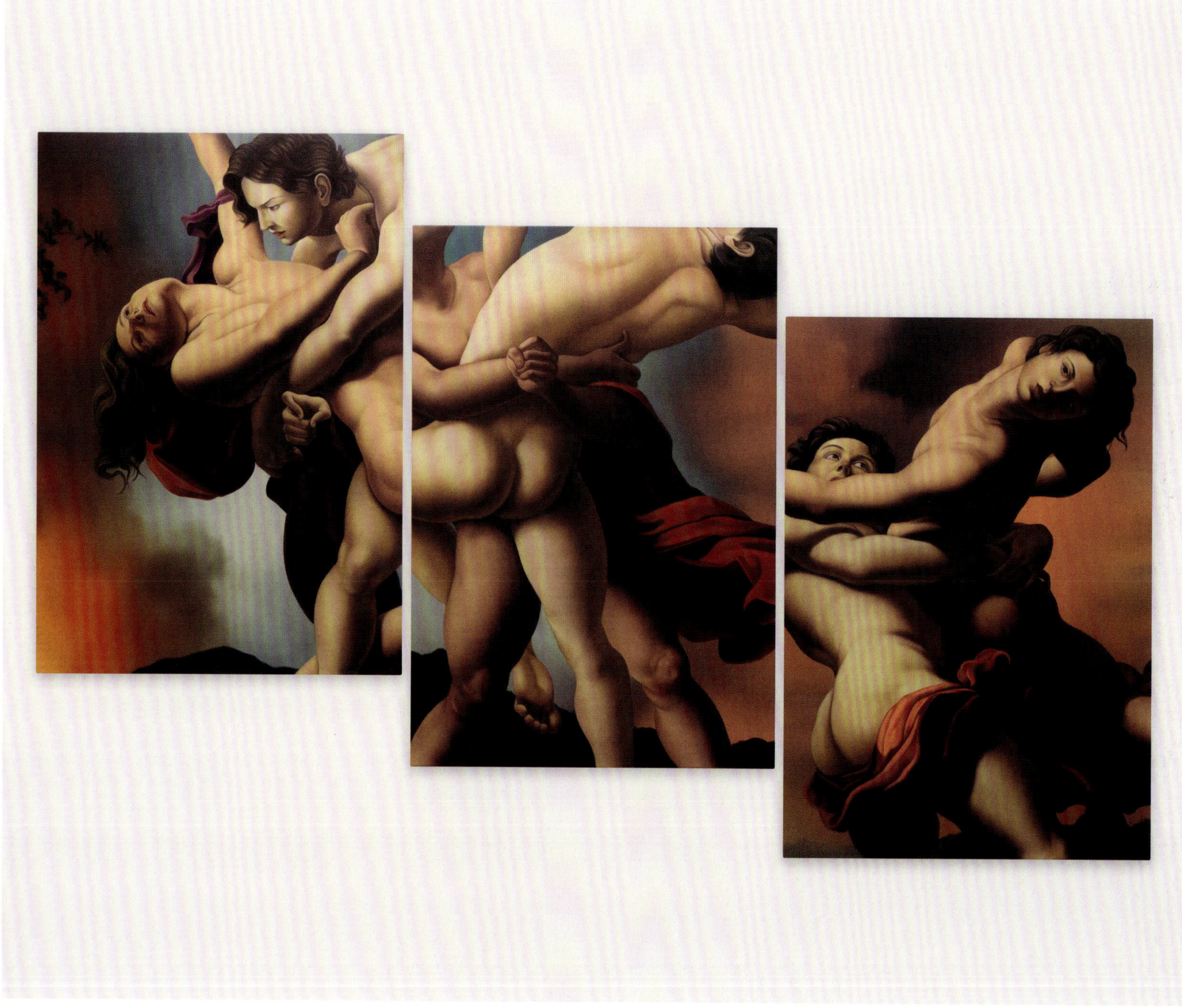

OVERMASTERED
2020, oil on cotton, each: 124.5 × 86.4 cm (49 × 34 in); overall: 165.1 × 259.1 cm (65 × 102 in)

Jesse Mockrin, born 1981, Silver Spring, Maryland, USA.

The human body is central to Mockrin's highly polished paintings, which plunder and reinterpret canonical works by artists including Peter Paul Rubens (1577–1640), Nicolas Poussin (1594–1665) and Titian (*c.* 1488–1576). Often depicting classically posed figures against pitch-black backgrounds, Mockrin's frequently eroticized scenes echo their sources but bring to them a contemporary twist, fragmenting their bodies and sometimes positioning their faces outside of the frame. Mythological themes of rape and abduction have inspired several works, including *Overmastered*, in which entangled figures wrestle and writhe across three canvases. The triptych alludes to the Rape of the Sabine Women, an episode from Roman mythology represented repeatedly in Western art history. However, knowing the origin of Mockrin's sources is less important than the issue of why such representations of violence against women have endured for so long without question. As with many of her paintings, Mockrin leaves the gender of her figures ambiguous. She stated in a 2021 interview with Art of Choice, 'I am so heavily invested in the depiction of the human figure, and in how the construction of gender codes change over time, that I end up looking to art history as the place to see human history made visible.'

PAULA MODERSOHN-BECKER

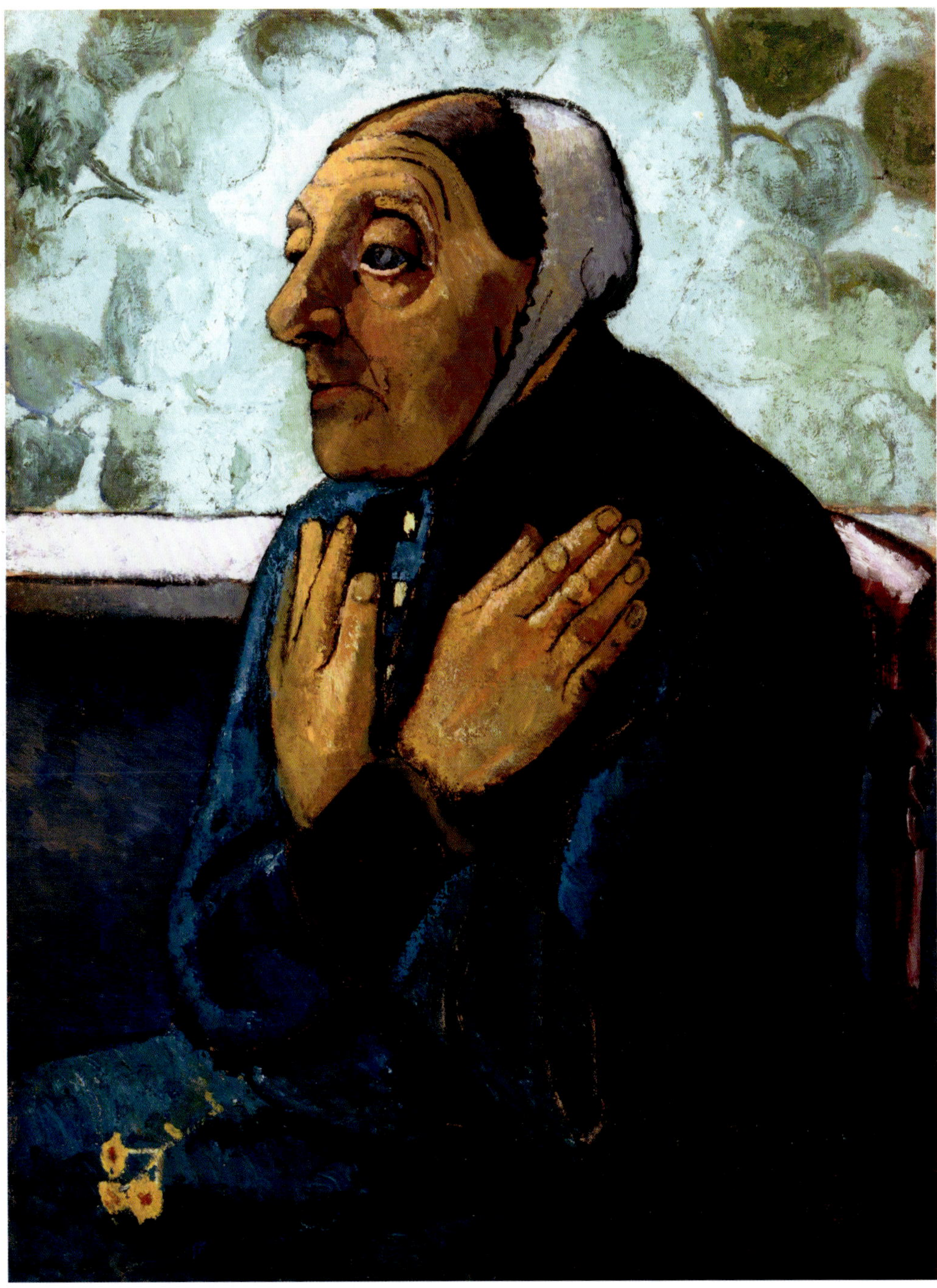

OLD PEASANT WOMAN
*c.*1905, oil on canvas, 75.6 × 57.8 cm (29 ¾ × 22 ¾ in), Detroit Institute of Arts, Michigan, USA

Paula Modersohn-Becker, born 1876, Dresden, Germany. Died 1907, Worpswede, Germany.

At the turn of the twentieth century, Modersohn-Becker retaliated against German society's gendered expectations not only by pursuing a career as a painter, but more critically through her fearless and approachable portraiture of women, from young girls to farmers' wives. One of the first women artists to embrace Expressionism, Modersohn-Becker's unidealized portraits focus on colour and form, prizing these characteristics over sentimentality, and call attention to marginalized communities. *Old Peasant Woman*, made on Modersohn-Becker's return to the Worpswede artist colony after a year in Paris and one of her last paintings before her premature death, signals the social virtues and material experimentations most important to the artist. Modersohn-Becker often altered the viscosity of her paints to manipulate their effects and saturations, and would drag the end of her brush through wet paint to produce highly tactile and layered impasto surfaces. Though the artist experienced little recognition during her lifetime, she is considered among the first modern women artists to paint herself and other women unclothed, subverting the academic trope of the female nude as the exclusive domain of the male artist.

LOUISE MOILLON

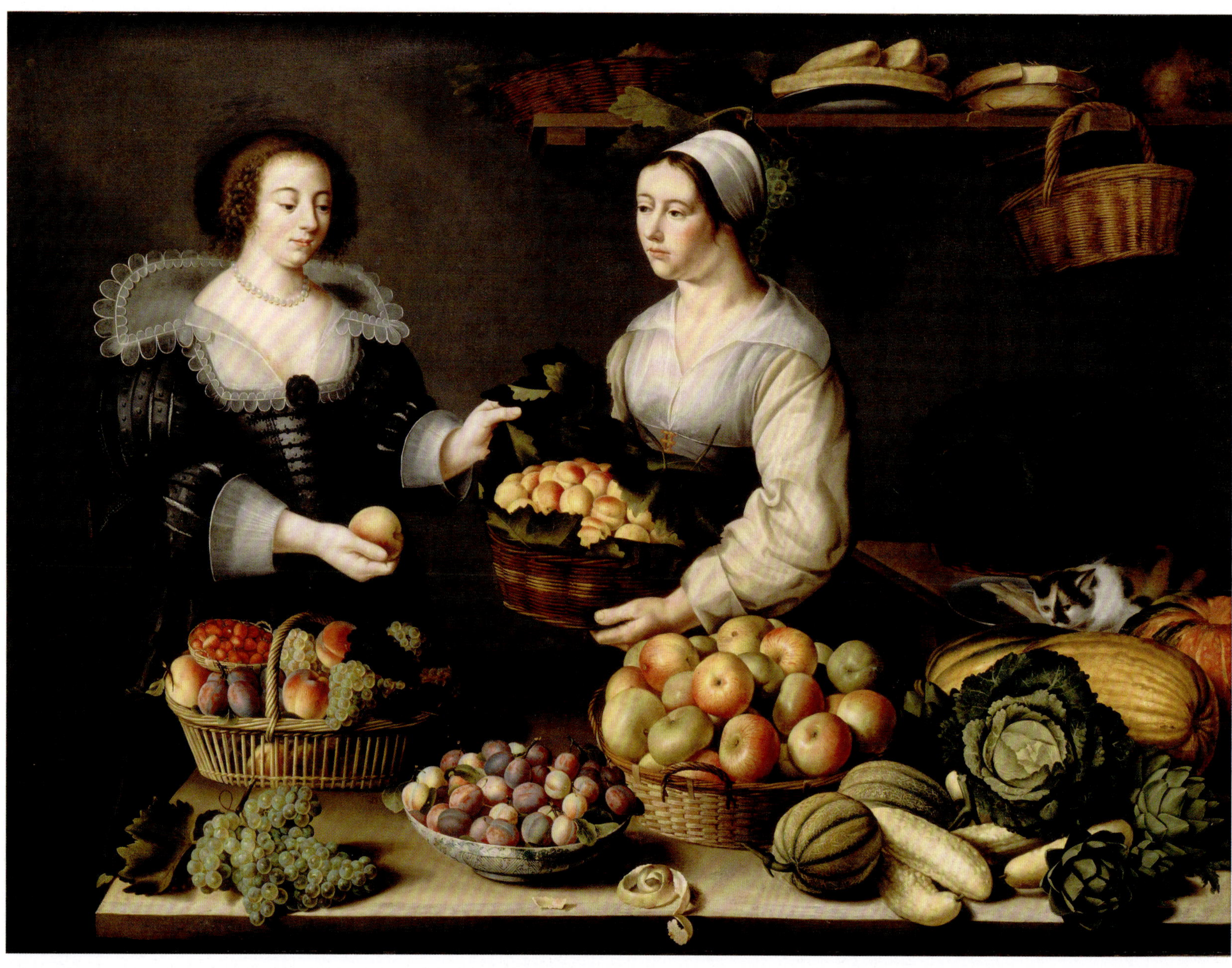

LA MARCHANDE DE FRUITS ET LÉGUMES (THE FRUIT AND VEGETABLE SELLER)
1630, oil on canvas, 120 × 163 cm (47¼ × 64⅛ in), Musée du Louvre, Paris, France

Louise Moillon, born 1610, Paris, France. Died 1696, Paris.

A highly successful painter of still lifes, Moillon is credited with helping to popularize the Dutch genre in her native France. Her initial exposure to still life was through Dutch Protestant refugee artists who had settled in her family's neighbourhood of Saint-Germain-des-Prés in Paris. She studied under her father, the Protestant artist and gallerist Nicolas Moillon (1555–1619), and her stepfather, the artist François Garnier (*c.*1600–72), alongside whom she exhibited her first painting in an exhibition in Grenoble in 1629. Moillon's painting sold immediately, catapulting her to celebrity; her many clients included Louis XIII and Charles I of England. This large canvas demonstrates Moillon's ambitious vision, with an array of fruits and vegetables of different shapes and textures, rendered with the artist's intricate attention to detail and characteristic chiaroscuro. Signature elements include the item (here, a fruit rind) toppling off the table in the foreground and the figures positioned behind the table – the latter an unusual addition to still-life painting of the period.

BERTHE MORISOT

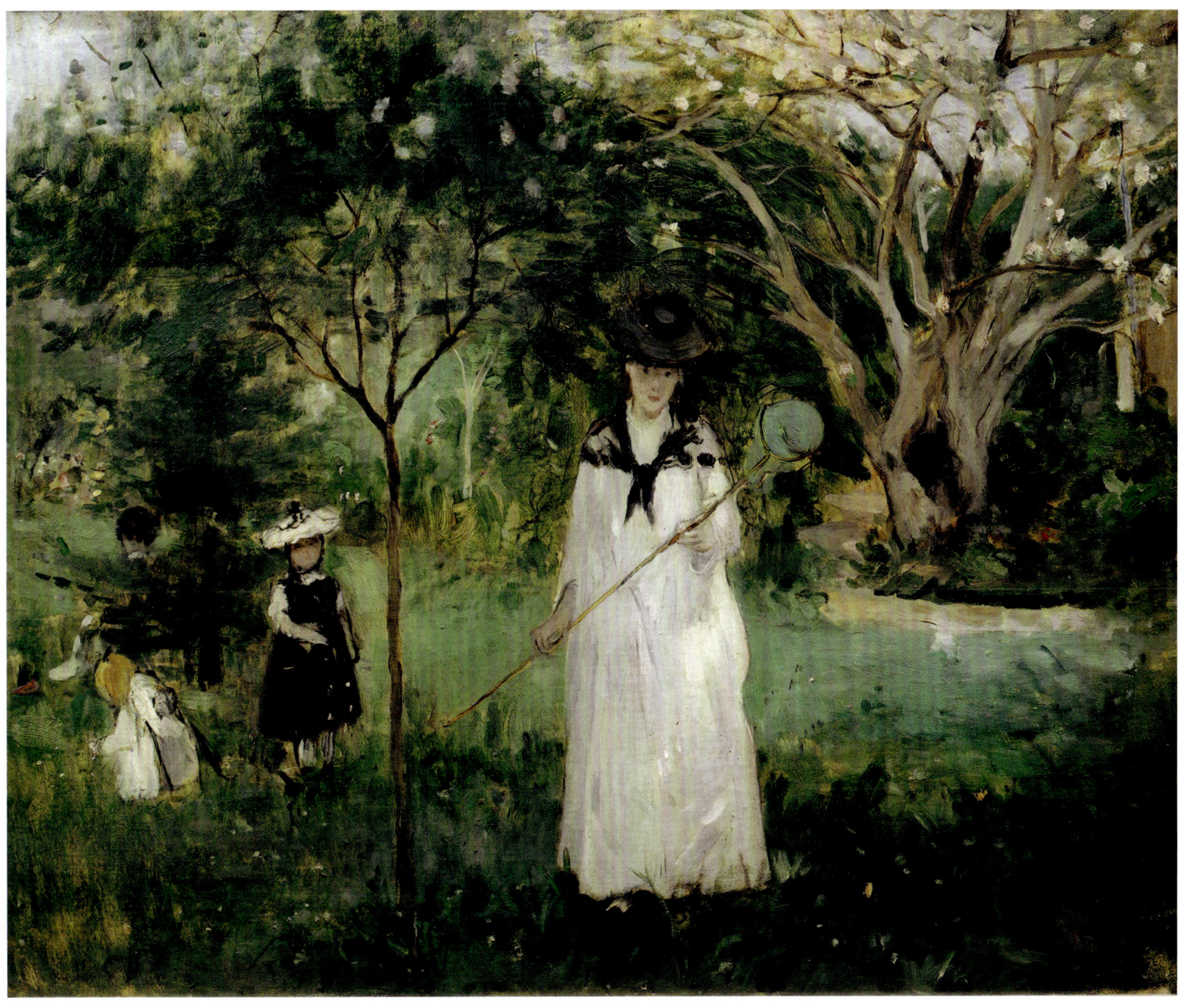

CHASSE AUX PAPILLONS (CHASING BUTTERFLIES)
1874, oil on canvas, 46 × 56 cm (18 ⅛ × 22 in), Musée d'Orsay, Paris, France

Berthe Morisot, born 1841, Bourges, France. Died 1895, Paris, France.

The only woman in the inaugural group of Impressionist painters and its longest-lasting member, Morisot manifested in her work the struggle between a woman's independence and marriage and motherhood in modern bourgeois society, choosing the female experience as her main subject. She studied painting with tutors, including landscapist Jean-Baptiste-Camille Corot (1796–1875), and started showing at the Paris Salon in 1864. The profession of an artist was seen as improper for upper-middle-class women, yet her family championed her career. Édouard Manet (1832–83) became Morisot's closest comrade and she modelled for him as part of their artistic dialogue. She married his brother Eugène (1833–92), who sacrificed his own painting career to support hers. In this garden scene, Morisot places her sister Edma as the focal point, hiding the horizon behind a carpet of green and allowing just a hint of clear sky for perspective. The sway in her skirt, the embroidery on her scarf and the transparency of the net are conveyed through spare, loose brushstrokes. This unfinished quality is a signature of Morisot's style and associated with the brisk execution of Impressionist paintings.

SABINE MORITZ

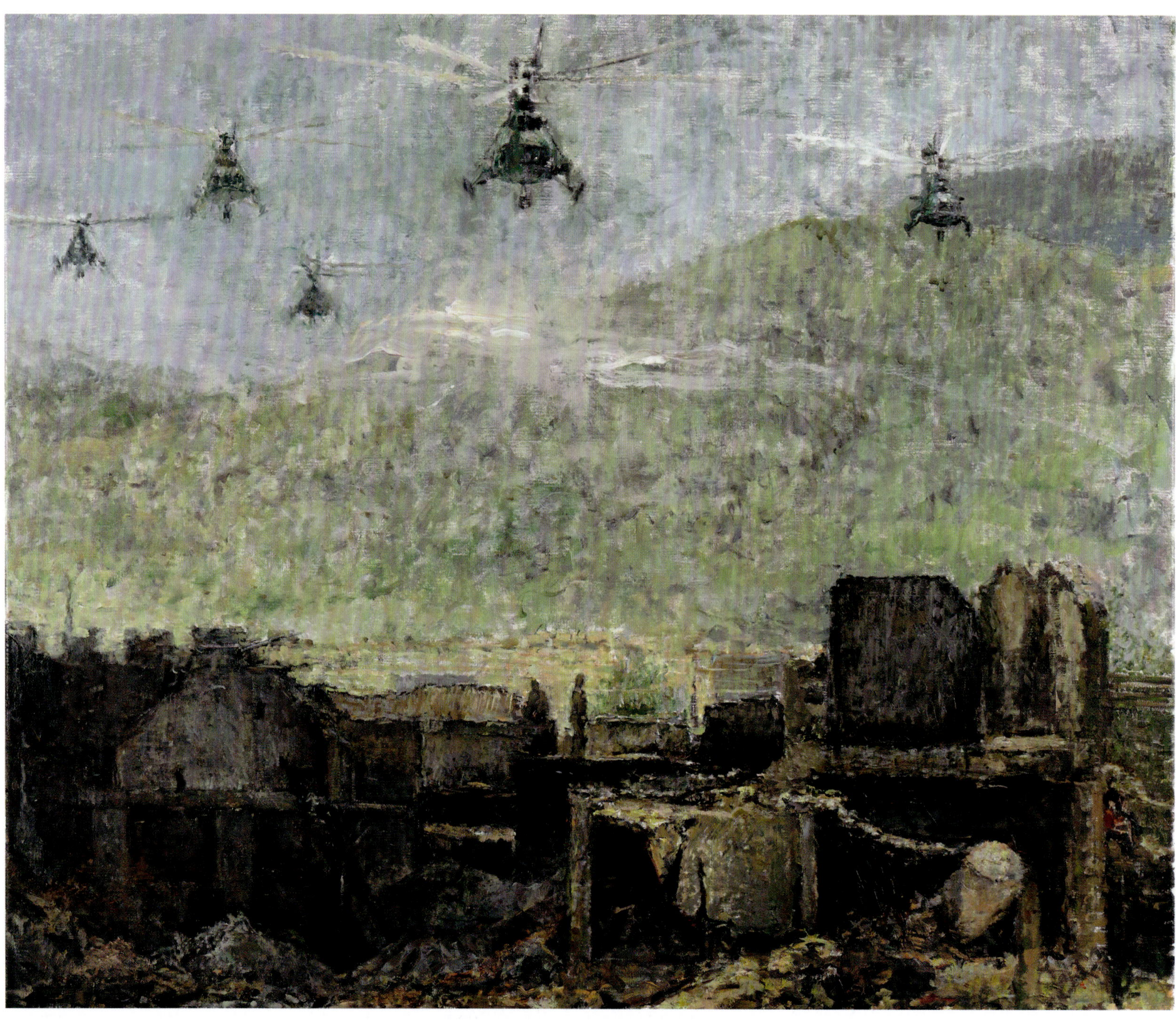

PARADE I
2007, oil on canvas, 100 × 120 cm (39 ⅜ × 47 ¼ in)

Sabine Moritz, born 1969, Quedlinburg, Germany.

Moritz's work is concerned with memory, repeating themes and images among her paintings and drawings to represent how they fade, shift and evolve over time. Growing up in East Germany, Moritz experienced the hardships associated with the Cold War regime. After immigrating to West Germany in 1985, she enrolled at the Hochschule für Gestaltung Offenbach in 1988 and continued her studies at the Kunstakademie Düsseldorf in 1991, taking classes with Markus Lüpertz (b. 1941) and Gerhard Richter (b. 1932). *Parade I* belongs to a larger body of work based on press clippings from a variety of publications following the terror attacks of September 11, 2001. While the paintings make clear reference to war, they abstract the original photographs, withholding their specifics with thick brushstrokes that render the scene almost as a distant memory. Rejecting graphic images of war, Moritz evokes what is to come, the state of being in limbo before or after the violence, evoking a paradoxical sense of calm. In 2015, Moritz began painting abstractions, creating images that summon emotions without real-life referent.

SARAH MORRIS

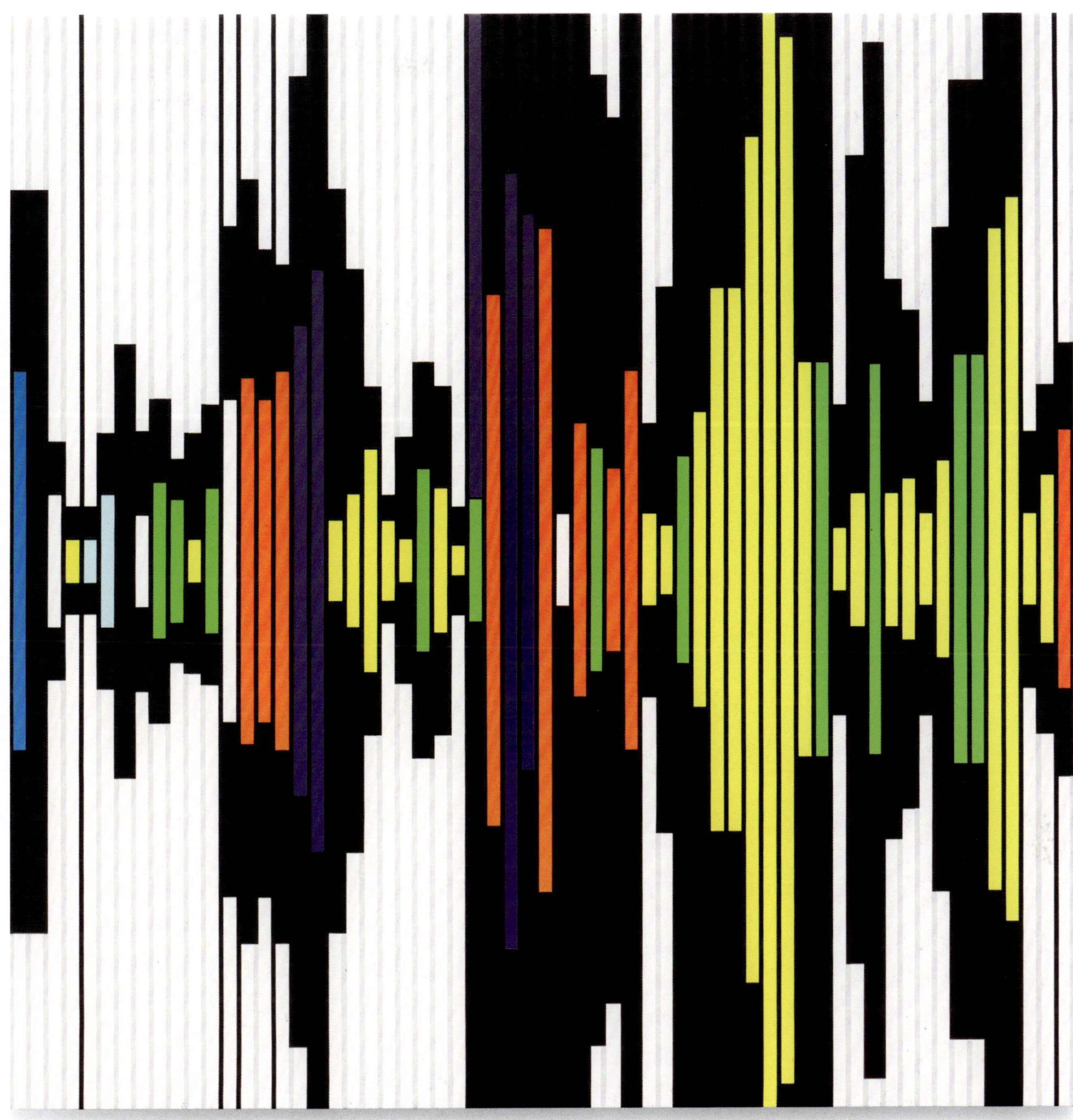

BAD SCHOOL [SOUND GRAPH]
2018, household gloss paint on canvas, 214 × 214 cm
(84 ¼ × 84 ¼ in)

Sarah Morris, born 1967, Sevenoaks, Kent, UK.

An American national born in the United Kingdom, Morris began her career with a series of text paintings, but in the mid-1990s pivoted to making abstract canvases and films. For her series 'Midtown' (1998–2001), for example, Morris made a cinéma vérité documentary of the streets of Midtown Manhattan alongside a suite of grid-like paintings abstractly portraying its soaring corporate towers. This bifurcated way of working remains the basis of her polished, analytical practice, in which she often isolates a city, architectural site or cultural protagonist and subjects it to close scrutiny and aesthetic defamiliarization. Morris slowly and deliberately gestates her paintings, each one rendered on a square canvas using household gloss paint, a serial method that repudiates preciousness and painterly expressionism. The origin of the work illustrated here is a digital sound file from a 2017 interview she gave with German author and film director Alexander Kluge, which formed part of the series' companion film, *Finite and Infinite Games* (2017). To create the graphic, Morris fed the file through a synthesizer and various computer programs to generate a visual representation of the frequencies, which she then transposed to canvas.

MARY MOSER

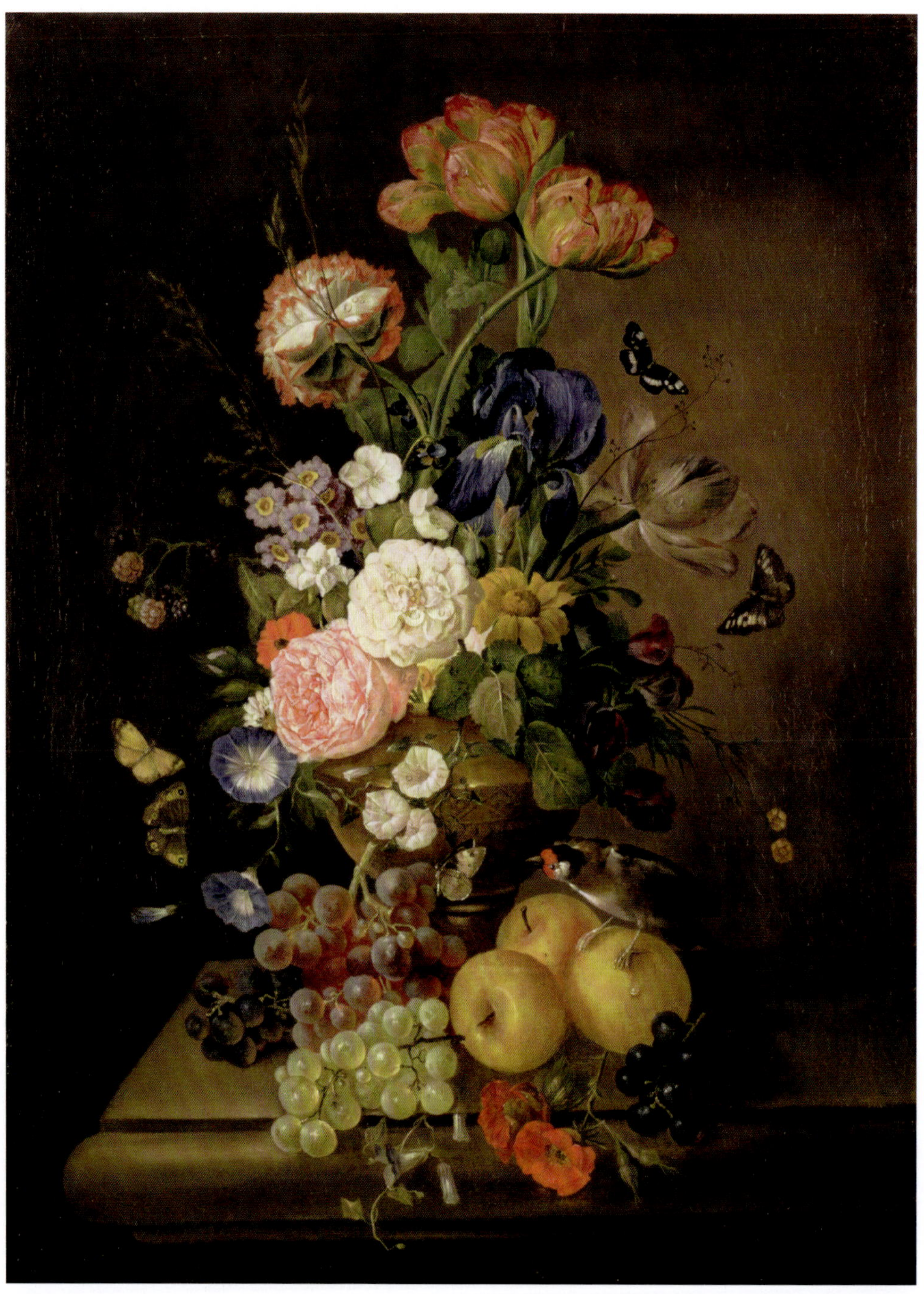

VASE OF FLOWERS
date unknown, oil on canvas, 72.1 × 53.6 cm (28⅜ × 21⅛ in), Fitzwilliam Museum, University of Cambridge, UK

Mary Moser, born 1744, London, UK.
Died 1819, London.

Moser was widely celebrated for floral paintings in the classical Dutch style. Aged just fourteen, her talent was recognized by London's Society of Arts, whose members awarded her a medal for her drawings. Well connected and well educated, thanks to her father – an enamellist and engraver – in 1768 Moser was one of only two women (alongside Angelica Kauffman, p.155) invited to become a founding member of the Royal Academy of Arts in London. Flora remained the recurrent theme of Moser's best-known works, notably her ambitious installation at Frogmore House, Windsor, commissioned by Queen Charlotte in the 1790s and comprising epic murals and canvases faithful to typically English arrangements – an ode to the elaborate and timeless yet transient beauty of flowers. This work, simply titled *Vase of Flowers*, exemplifies her mastery of the still-life genre. The scene bursts with life: a finch, often associated with joy, is poised on a pile of yellow apples, while butterflies flutter around the vibrant blooms, giving an animated and lively feel to the painting.

ANNA MARY ROBERTSON ('GRANDMA') MOSES

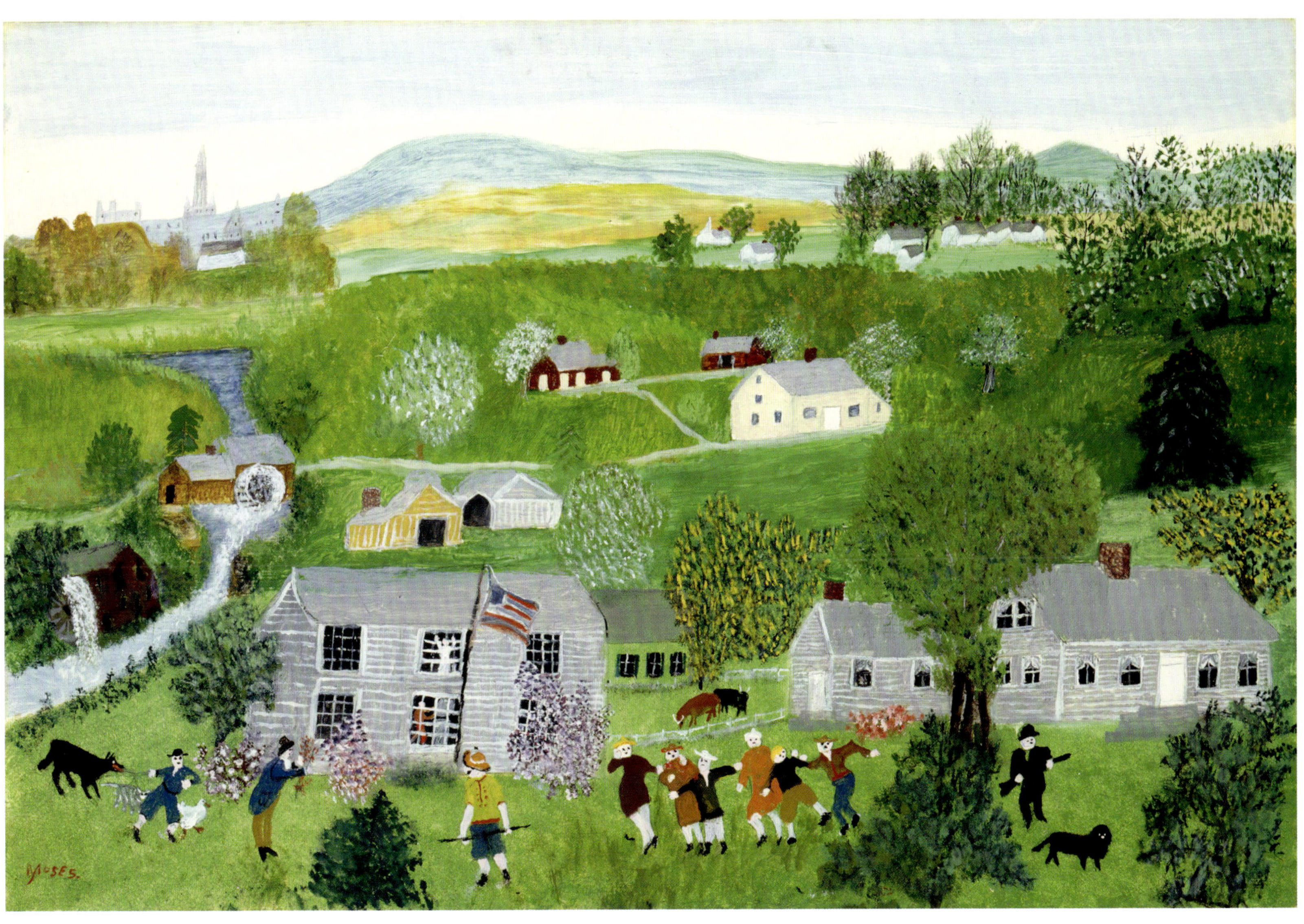

SUMMER PARTY
1959, oil on Masonite, 40 × 59.9 cm (15 ¾ × 23 ⅝ in), Museum of Fine Arts, Houston, USA

Anna Mary Robertson ('Grandma') Moses, born 1860, Greenwich, New York, USA. Died 1961, Hoosick Falls, New York, USA.

Grandma Moses (so dubbed by a reviewer of her first solo show in 1940) began painting in her late seventies, after arthritis meant that she could no longer hold a needle to do embroidery. Her professional career was launched in 1938, at the age of seventy-eight, after Louis Caldor, a New York art collector, discovered her work in a drugstore in Hoosick Falls, New York. The following year, Caldor helped secure the artist's inclusion in the exhibition 'Contemporary Unknown Painters' at the Museum of Modern Art, New York. Her first solo show was held at the Galerie St. Etienne in New York the next autumn. Her folk art has been compared to the work of Pieter Bruegel the Elder (*c.* 1525–69) in its glowing colours and nostalgic scenes of farm life, and she claimed that she painted to remind people of how life once was, deliberately omitting images of modern technology such as tractors and telephone poles. Moses's subject matter focused on childhood memories from her life in rural New York and Virginia – of summer holidays (such as this outdoor party scene), barn dances and views of farms and weather.

MARLOW MOSS

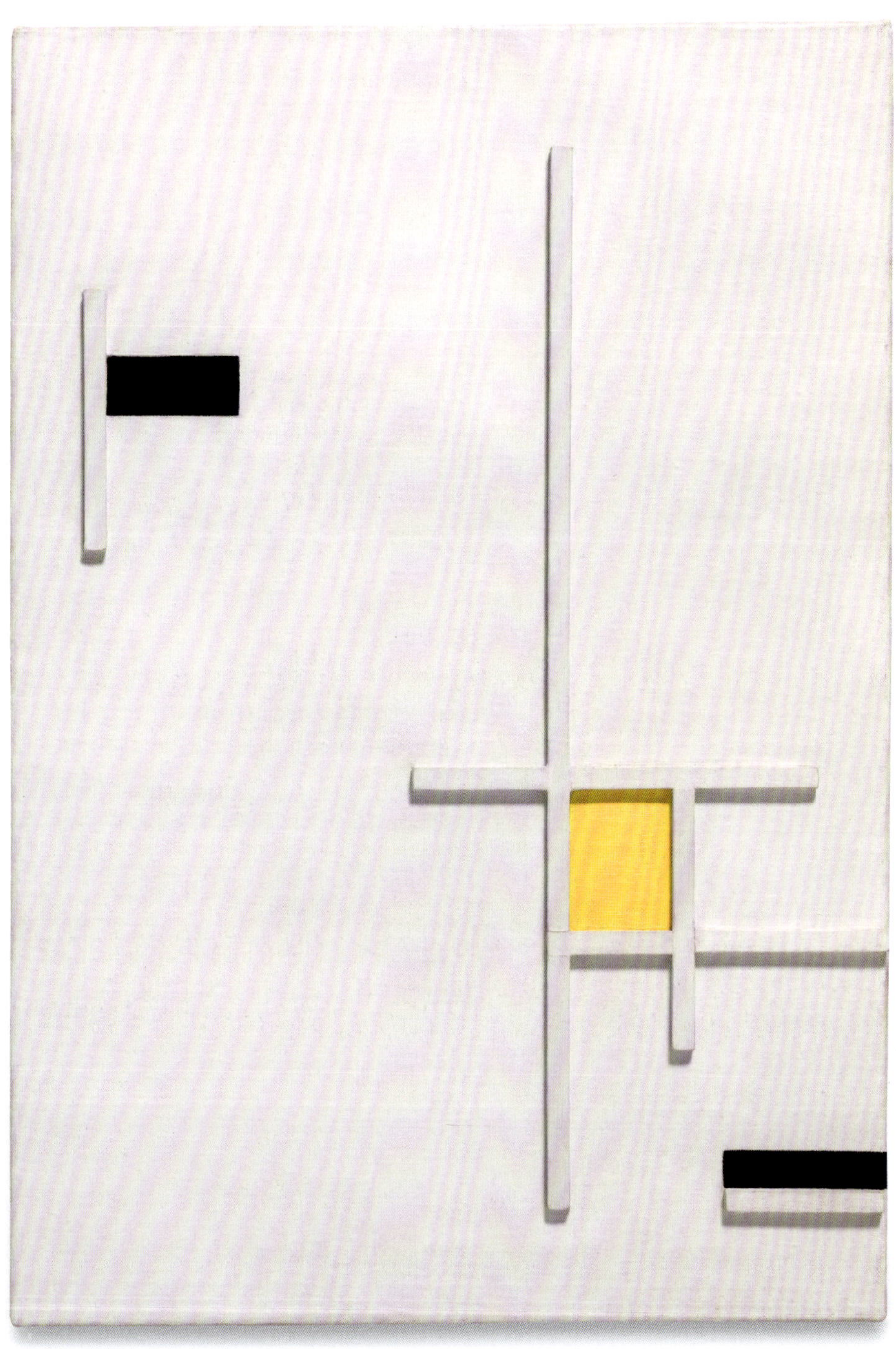

COMPOSITION IN YELLOW, BLACK AND WHITE
1949, oil and wood on canvas, 50.8 × 35.6 × .6 cm (20 × 14 × ¼ in), Tate, London, UK

Marlow Moss, born 1889, London, UK. Died 1958, Penzance, Cornwall, UK.

An avant-garde British Constructivist artist, Moss's radical legacy has been long overlooked. Called a 'maverick' and a 'radical modernist', Moss embarked on studies at the Slade School of Fine Art in London but abandoned them and, in 1927, moved to Paris. There, she developed a distinct sartorial style, wearing cravats and riding breeches, smoking cigars and donning a short haircut – refusing to conform to the conventions of her assigned gender. It was in Paris that she encountered the work of Piet Mondrian (1872–1944) and began a long-standing exchange with the Dutch artist; the influence was mutual, and Moss's artistic breakthrough of the introduction of double lines, arranged in parallel in her schematic paintings, was later adopted by Mondrian. Moss was fascinated by ideas of universality, of subsuming the self in the search of truth, seeking beauty of form. This sense of distilling the intrinsic qualities of line, colour and space is inherent in *Composition in Yellow, Black and White*, a painted relief from the later period of Moss's work – an example of her restraint and precision, and her desire to understand beauty, beyond the subjective experience.

JILL MULLEADY

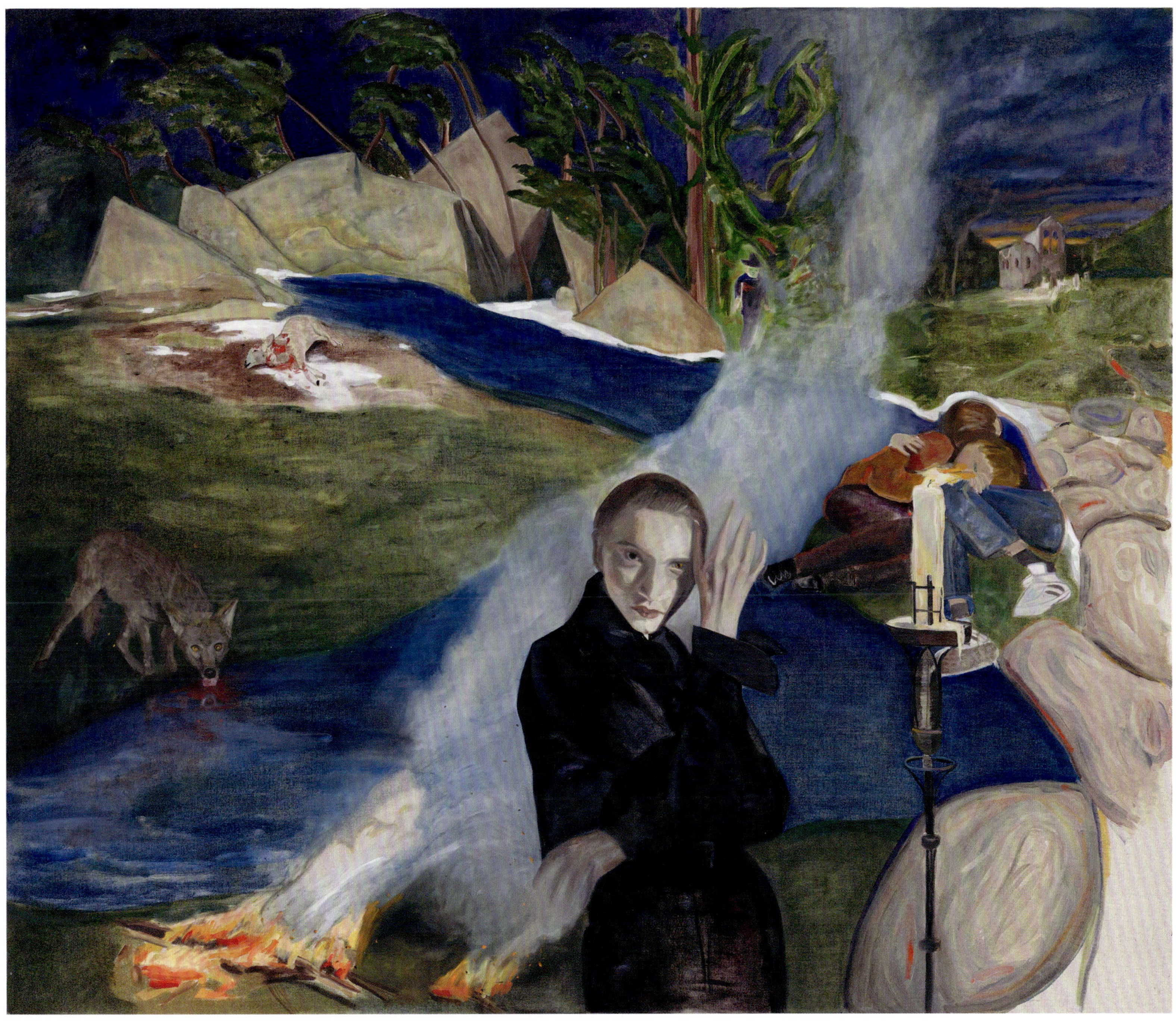

GARDENS OF THE BLIND
2020, oil on linen, 168 × 200 cm (66 ⅛ × 78 ¾ in)

Jill Mulleady, born 1980, Montevideo, Uruguay.

Born in Uruguay, Mulleady grew up in Buenos Aires and studied at the Chelsea College of Art in London before moving to Los Angeles in 2013, where she lives and works. Mulleady has cited the experimental theatre director Antonin Artaud and the erotic artist and writer Pierre Klossowski (1905–2001) as key inspirations for her practice. This interest in dramaturgy, and the influence of avant-garde art history, cinema and theatre, is evidenced by her expansive, cinematic compositions and framing, in addition to the unsettling and violent scenes that she conjures. Mulleady's canvases are often populated by ghostly or otherworldly characters as well as real-life historical figures such as the sexual libertine, the Marquis de Sade. The sadistic relationship between pleasure and pain associated with de Sade can be seen in *Gardens of the Blind*, where references to both sex and violence are inferred by the embracing couple and the bleeding lamb, arranged on either side of the murky river that slices through the picture plane. Mulleady's imposition of the pale androgynous character and the candle stand in the foreground rejects traditional artistic conventions regarding pictorial perspective, with the composite image manifesting as a strange dream or memory, amplifying the sense of apprehension and unease.

GABRIELE MÜNTER

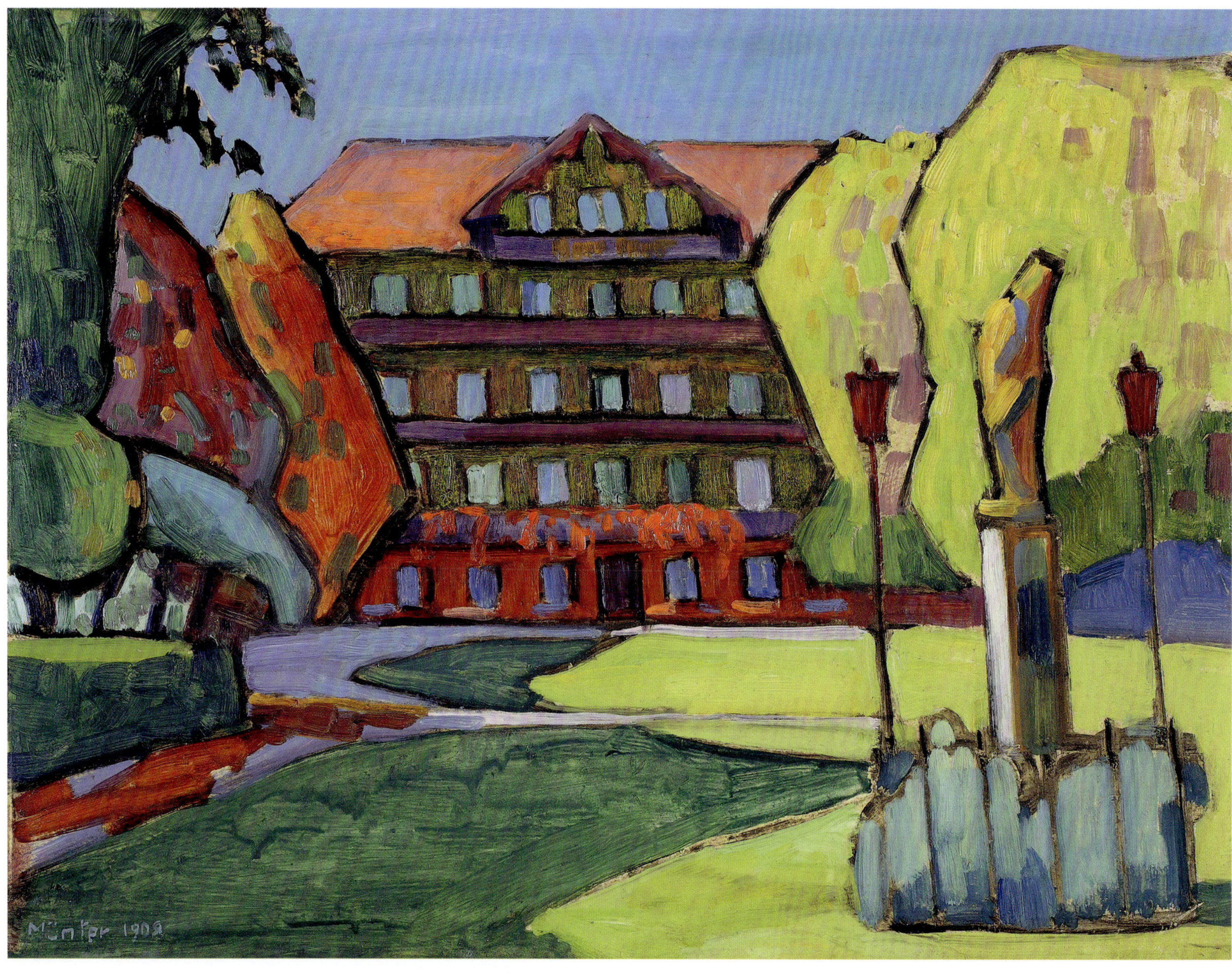

TUTZING
1908, oil on artist's board, 37.5 × 49.5 cm (14 ¾ × 19 ½ in), San Diego Museum of Art, USA

Gabriele Münter, born 1877, Berlin, Germany. Died 1962, Murnau, Germany.

A founding member of the German Expressionist group Der Blaue Reiter (The Blue Rider), along with her lover and early teacher Wassily Kandinsky (1866–1944), Münter studied art in Dusseldorf before moving to Munich and ending up at the Phalanx School, an avant-garde institute founded by Kandinsky. She spent the summer of 1908 with him and others at Murnau, in the foothills of the Bavarian Alps, where she developed a style based on luminous blocks of colour and traditional Bavarian folk art, influenced by the work of Vincent van Gogh (1853–90) and Henri Matisse (1869–1954). In the 1930s she hid paintings of Der Blaue Reiter artists in her house in Murnau to avoid their confiscation by the Nazis. Painted that first summer at Murnau, this scene of a Benedictine monastery in Tutzing, a small town between Murnau am Staffelsee and Munich, is characterized by Münter's opulent colours outlined with thick black lines, using a compressed perspective that appears flat to the viewer. In its simplified forms, bold lines and rich colours, it typifies Münter's distinctive absorption of van Gogh and Paul Gauguin (1848–1903), as well as medieval reverse-glass painting.

ELIZABETH MURRAY

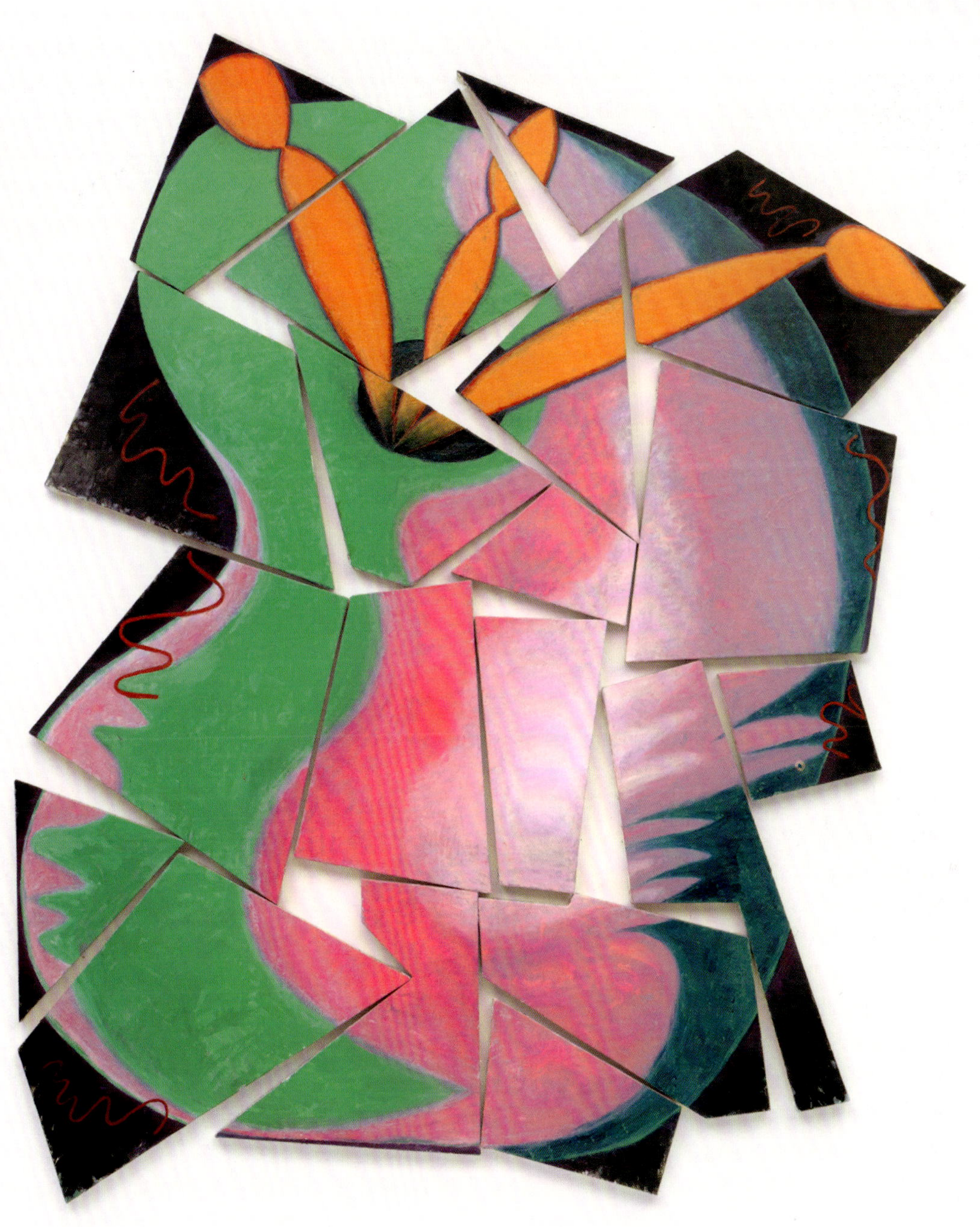

PAINTERS PROGRESS
1981, oil on canvas, 19 panels, 294.5 × 236.2 cm (116 × 93 in), Museum of Modern Art, New York, USA

Elizabeth Murray, born 1940, Chicago, USA. Died 2007, New York, USA.

Having initially planned to become a commercial artist due to a childhood interest in cartoon-making, Murray decided to become a painter after encountering a still life by Paul Cézanne (1839–1906) while studying at the School of the Art Institute of Chicago. Murray graduated in 1962, coinciding with the height of the Chicago Imagists (see Gladys Nilsson, p.222, and Christina Ramberg, p.243), and their irreverent approach to image-making, influenced by cartoons, is also seen as an influence on Murray's work. The artist remained dedicated to painting throughout her career and demonstrated that, despite the medium's long history, it was still possible to create something entirely new. In 1978, she began to develop her signature style of irregular-shaped paintings in bright hues that revealed, as art critic Roberta Smith stated in her *New York Times* obituary, 'her blithe indifference to the distinctions between abstraction and representation or high and low'. This colourful, fractured rendering of an artist's palette with brushes entered the collection of New York's Museum of Modern Art soon after completion and was featured in Murray's comprehensive retrospective at the museum in 2006.

ISHBEL MYERSCOUGH

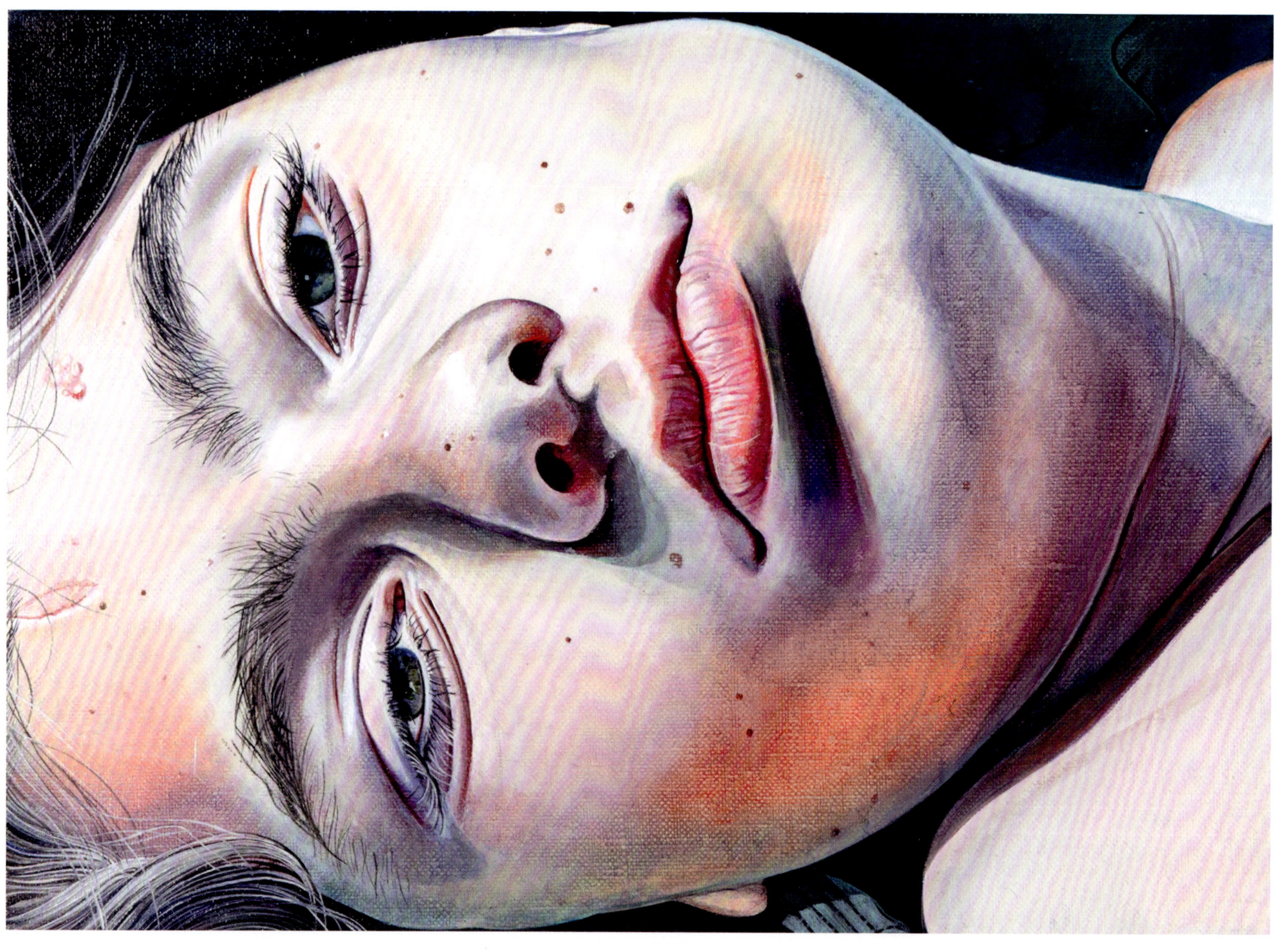

YOUTH I
2019, oil on canvas, 21 × 30 cm (8 ¼ × 11 ¾ in)

Ishbel Myerscough, born 1968, London, UK.

A graduate of the Glasgow School of Art (1991) and Slade School of Fine Art (1995), Myerscough has spent her career producing highly detailed, intimate portraits of friends and family. Individually and cumulatively, the bodies and faces of her subjects reveal the artist's exploration of the pillars of the human experience: love, longing, grief and the passing of time, focusing particularly on how signs of ageing are marked on the body. Myerscough often depicts her subjects resting and reclining on beds and sofas, sometimes with their eyes closed, capturing them in tender, vulnerable moments of repose. *Youth I* features an intimate view of an adolescent woman's face, her freckles, scars and strands of hair meticulously observed, while light reflects otherworldly colours onto her skin. Myerscough's work has been in constant dialogue with that of British painter Chantal Joffe (p.145), a long-time friend who is frequently depicted in her canvases and with whom she shared a joint exhibition at the National Portrait Gallery in London in 2015.

CASSI NAMODA

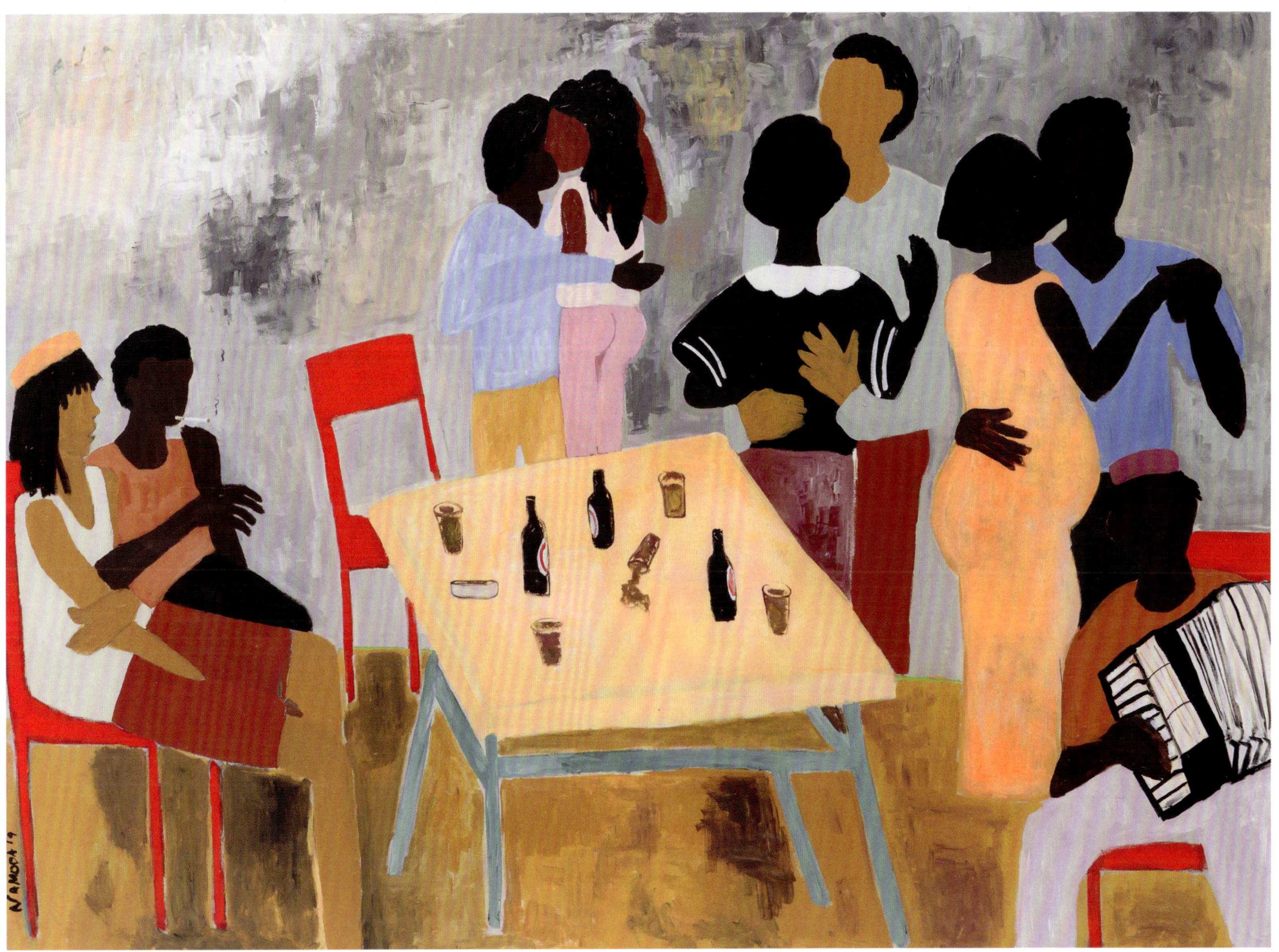

LITTLE IS ENOUGH FOR THOSE WITH LOVE / MIMI NAKUPENDA
2019, acrylic on canvas, 167 × 233 cm (66 × 92 in), private collection

Cassi Namoda, born 1988, Maputo, Mozambique.

Drawing from Luso-African literature and cinema, found and archival photographs, as well as dreams and personal memories, Namoda produces vividly coloured tableaux that represent both daily life and the mystical traditions of the African diaspora. Born in Mozambique, Namoda was raised internationally, travelling and living between Indonesia, Kenya, Haiti, Benin, Uganda and the United States. These experiences have imbued her with a deep and intuitive knowledge of mythologies and cultures from around the world, which inform her approach to visual narrative. At times, her work makes direct reference to the gods and goddesses of ancient Greece or Afro-diasporic syncretic spiritual systems, while elsewhere she renders vignettes of daily life in Lusophone Africa in complex narrative canvases. Titled in English and Swahili from an East African proverb, *Little is Enough for Those with Love / Mimi Nakupenda* pictures a group of figures dancing and socializing at an informal gathering. Each body, form and gesture is concisely rendered in loose passages of flatly applied acrylic, with an earthen and jewel-toned palette, conveying an almost ethereal ambience of warmth and intimacy.

YUKULTJI NAPANGATI

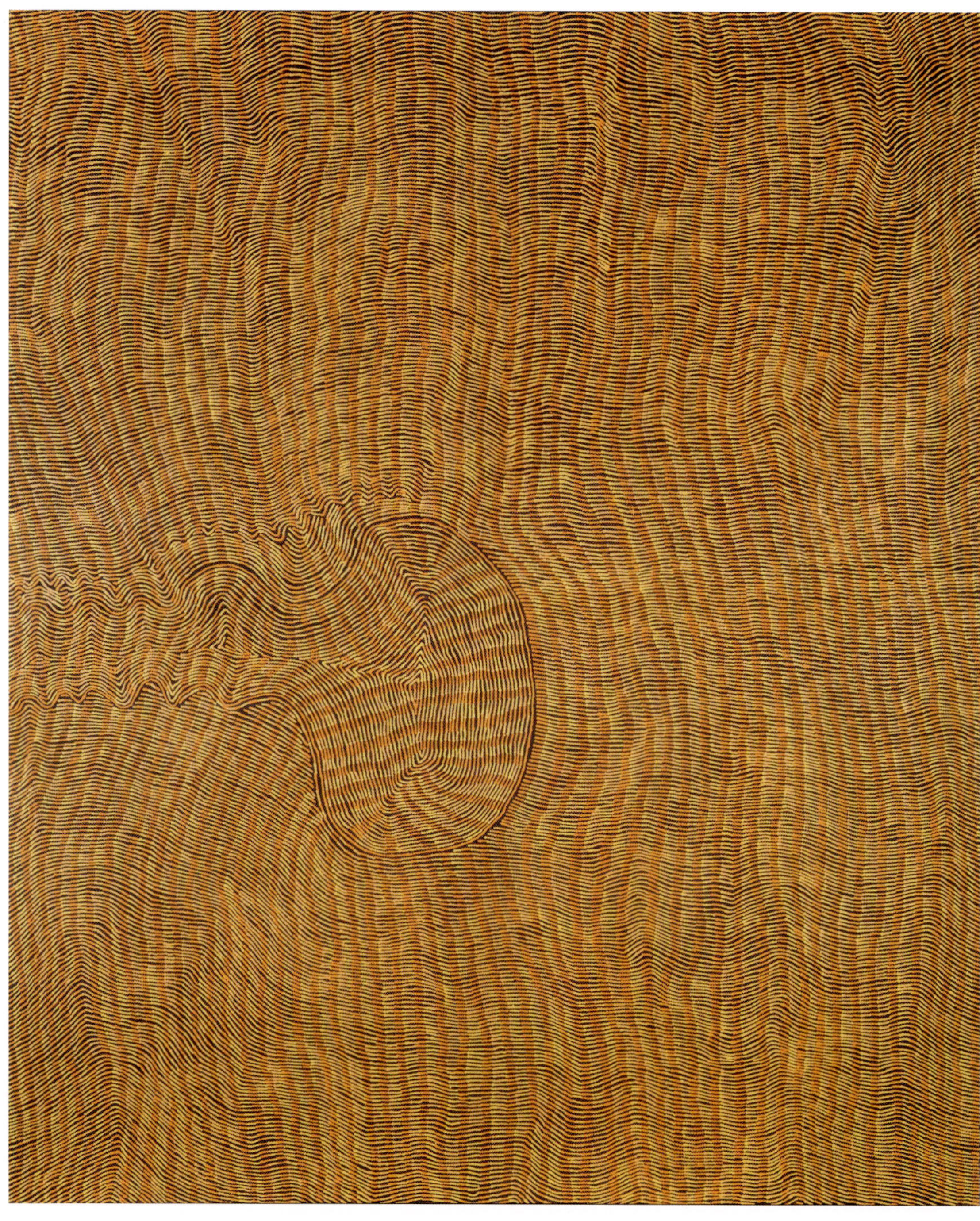

UNTITLED
2016, acrylic on linen, 189.4 × 159.4 cm
(74 ⅝ × 62 ¾ in)

Yukultji Napangati, born *c.* 1971, Wilkinkarra (Lake Mackay), Australia.

From the micro (grains of sand or a fingerprint's curving lines) to the macro (aerial views of a vast arid landscape), Napangati's abstract paintings reflect her intimate connection to the land. Napangati is a member of the Pintupi peoples, an Aboriginal group of Western Australia, where she grew up living and playing on desert land. Napangati left the traditional hunting-and-gathering life in 1984 with eight other members of the group who were dubbed the 'Pintupi Nine' by the media, becoming one of the last Indigenous groups to make first contact with modern Australia. Napangati began painting in 1996 as part of an initiative with other Pintupi women to create work independently of the men in the group. A key figure in the Papunya Tula Aboriginal painting group, Napangati paints with the canvas laid horizontally, applying dots in close succession – often in golden hues of yellow, orange or red, as evident in this work – which together become undulating lines and spirals, appearing almost shimmering, mirage-like. Visualizing ancestral time, Napangati depicts the lands associated with her Dreamings – cultural values, traditions and knowledge passed down through generations.

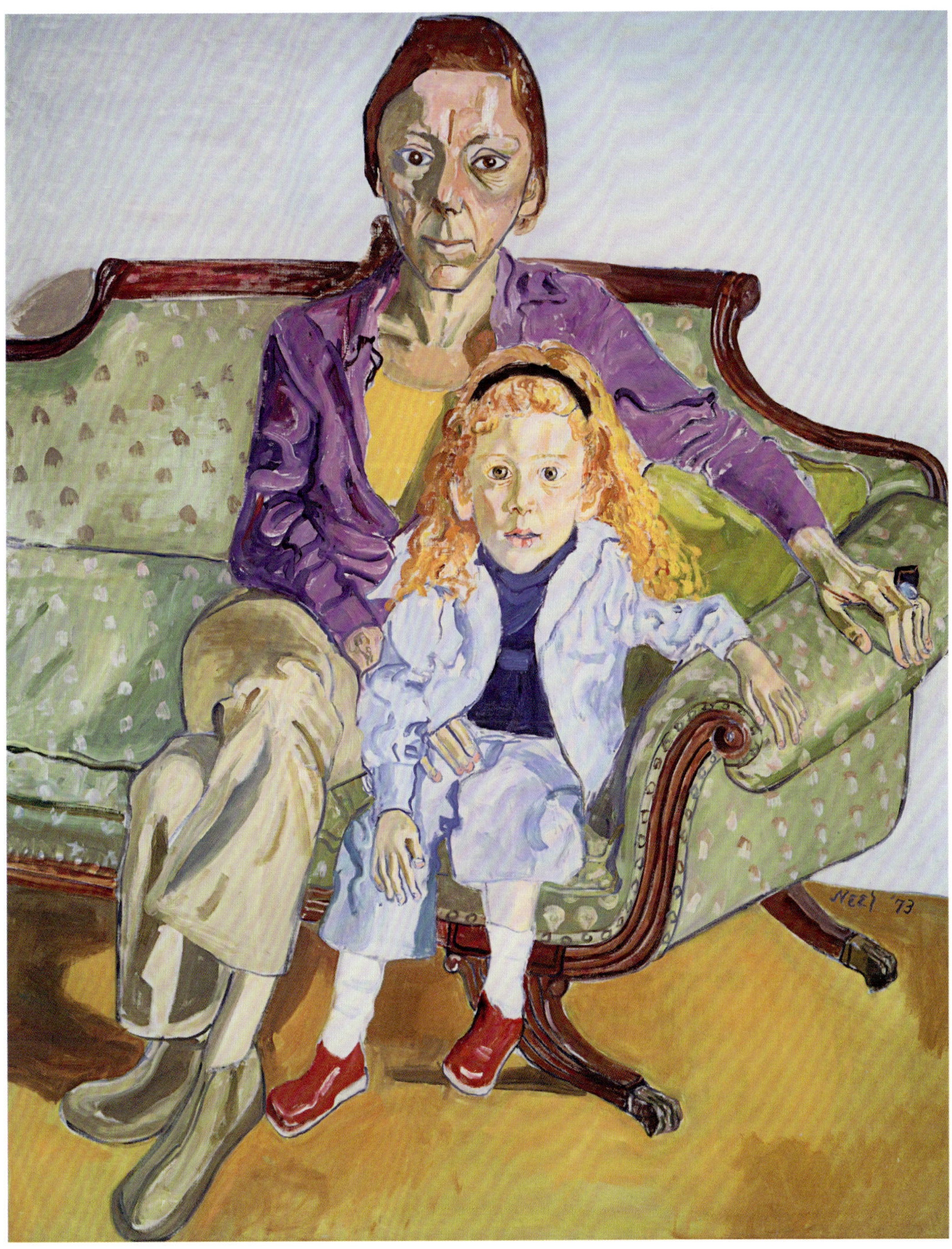

LINDA NOCHLIN AND DAISY
1973, oil on canvas, 141.9 × 111.8 cm (55 ⅞ × 44 in), Museum of Fine Arts, Boston, USA

Alice Neel, born 1900, Gladwyne, Pennsylvania, USA. Died 1984, New York, USA.

Neel is counted among the most important American painters of the twentieth century. A 1925 graduate of the Philadelphia School of Design for Women, Neel moved to New York in 1927, the city she would call home for the rest of her life. During a time when Abstract Expressionism and Pop art dominated the art market in New York, Neel remained committed to figurative painting. She created a new Social Realist style, defined by distorted proportions, flat compositions and thick, expressive brushstrokes. Neel gained widespread acclaim for her ability to capture enigmatic subjects and their inner lives with honesty and vulnerability. At the heart of her practice was the desire to make visible women of all ages whom she admired, as well as artists, activists, civil rights leaders and countercultural figures. This oil painting depicts pioneering art historian Linda Nochlin and her four-year-old daughter Daisy; their intense gazes, deliberately disproportionate heads and bright-blue outlines are emblematic of Neel's singular style. Two years before this painting was complete, Nochlin's seminal 1971 essay, 'Why Have There Been No Great Women Artists?', created a paradigm shift in the feminist art movement.

PLAUTILLA NELLI

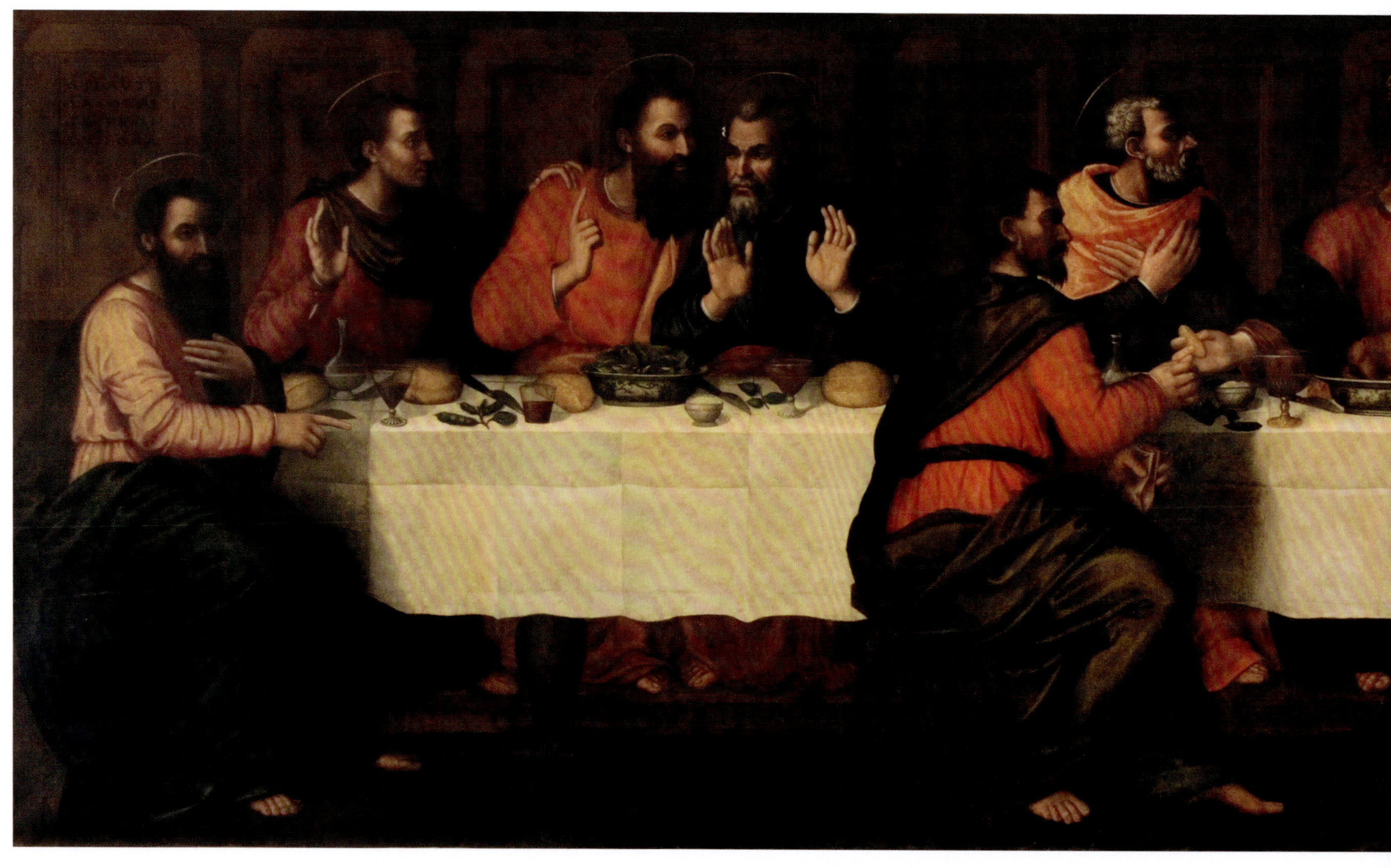

LAST SUPPER
*c.*1568, oil on canvas, 192 × 671 cm
(75 ⅝ × 264 ⅛ in), Santa Maria Novella Museum,
Florence, Italy

Plautilla Nelli, born 1524, Florence, Italy. Died 1588, Florence.

Nelli's training and activity took place within the Dominican convent of Santa Caterina da Siena, Florence, where she was a nun and later a prioress. Her paintings brought income to her community – many were sold to churches and secular collectors – and Nelli received great renown during her lifetime, being one of only four women included in Giorgio Vasari's second edition of *The Lives of the Most Excellent Painters, Sculptors and Architects* (1568). This ambitious *Last Supper*, created for the convent's refectory, is the first-known representation of this classic Christian scene by a female artist. Scholars believe that Nelli provided the drawings for all the figures and painted the heads shown in three-quarter view, while those in profile were executed by less experienced hands, whose painting she oversaw in the workshop. After the convent was dissolved in the early nineteenth century, the work was sold to a monastery and was reported to have been rolled up and placed in storage for three decades before being hung in a private room in the Santa Maria Novella monastery in Florence. Following substantial restoration funded by the non-profit Advancing Women Artists organization, it went on public view to great acclaim in October 2019.

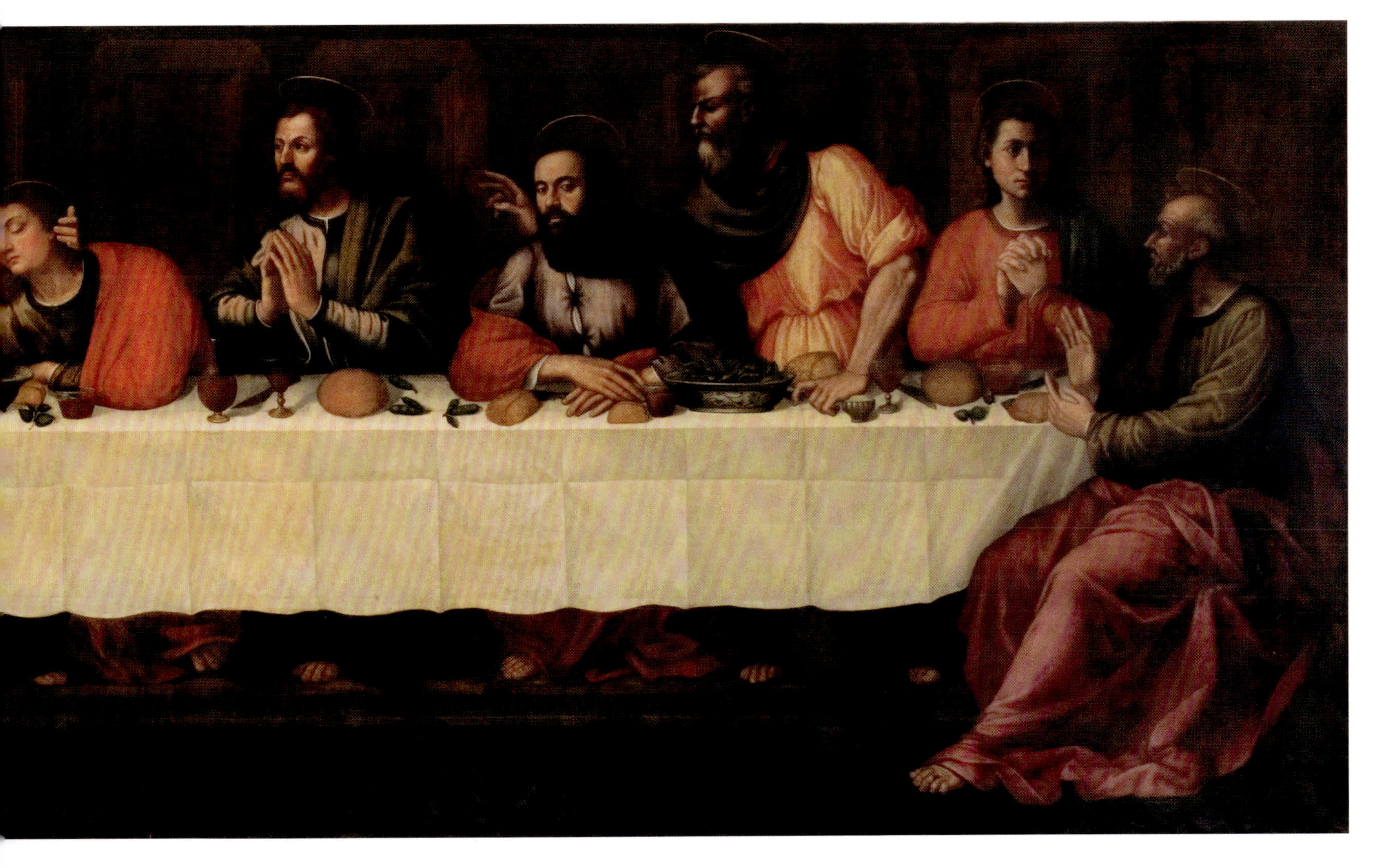

GLADYS NILSSON

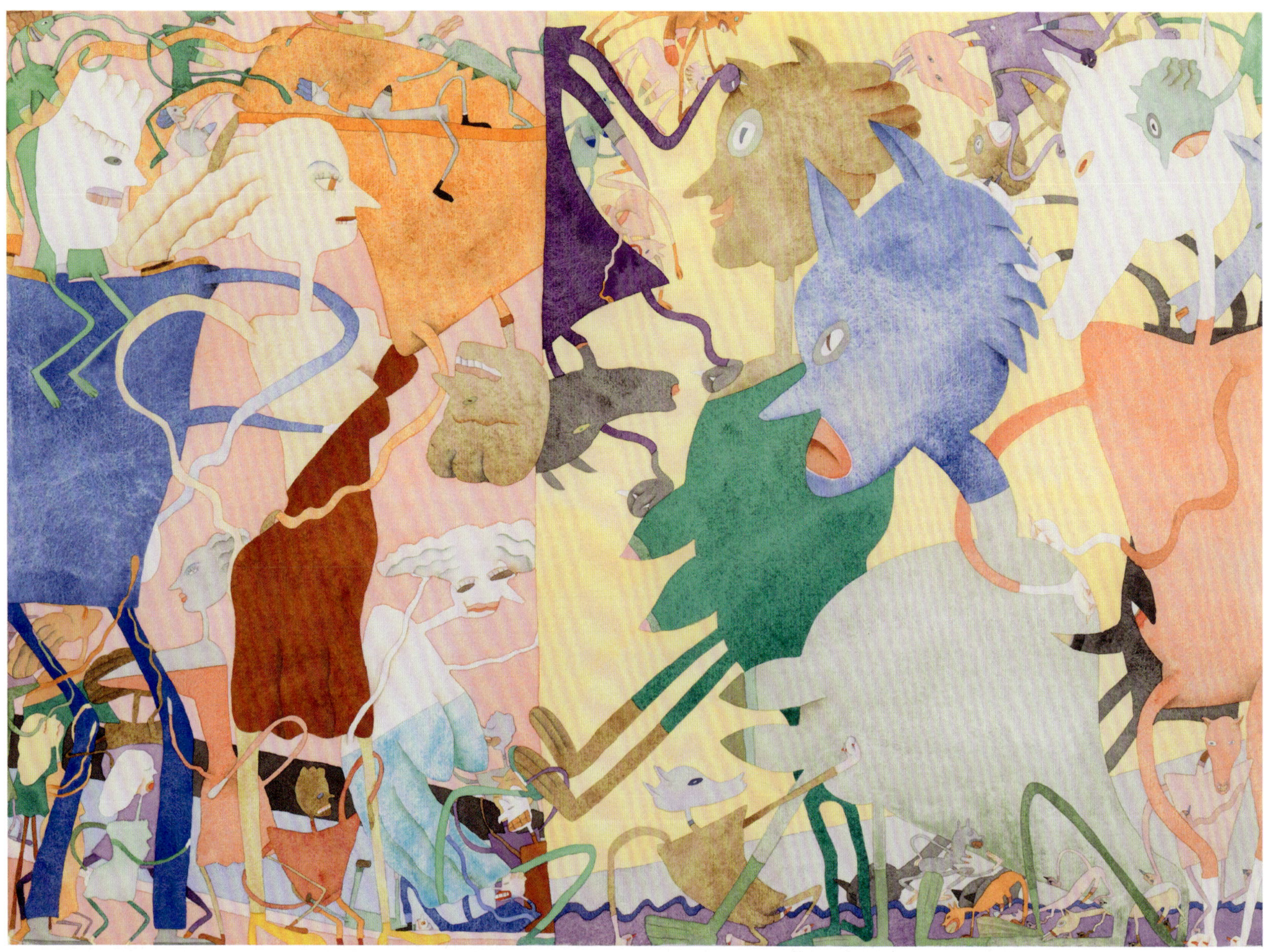

HALF EN HALFE
1970, watercolour on paper, 55.9 × 77.5 cm (22 ⅛ × 30 ½ in), collection of Garth Greenan, New York, USA

Gladys Nilsson, born 1940, Chicago, USA.

After completing studies in painting at the School of the Art Institute of Chicago, Nilsson received early critical recognition in the mid-1960s as a pivotal member of the provocative Hairy Who collective. Later known as the Chicago Imagists, the group challenged prevailing Pop art and Minimalist tendencies with their unconventional and often humorous works featuring fantastical imagery, vernacular references and bright, graphic forms. Primarily working in watercolour, which she adopted as a safer alternative to oil paint during pregnancy, Nilsson is known for her densely layered figurative tableaux populated by casts of bizarre figures. Her colourful compositions are rooted in closely observed human interactions, which she transforms with a surreal, cartoonish style that draws from German Expressionism, Ancient Egyptian art, fifteenth-century Italian painting and Cubism, among other sources. In *Half en Halfe* a mob of outlandish, animalistic creatures confront a human couple surrounded by other strange characters. Exaggerated features, entangled limbs and shifts in scale add further ambiguity to the strange scene.

ALIZA NISENBAUM

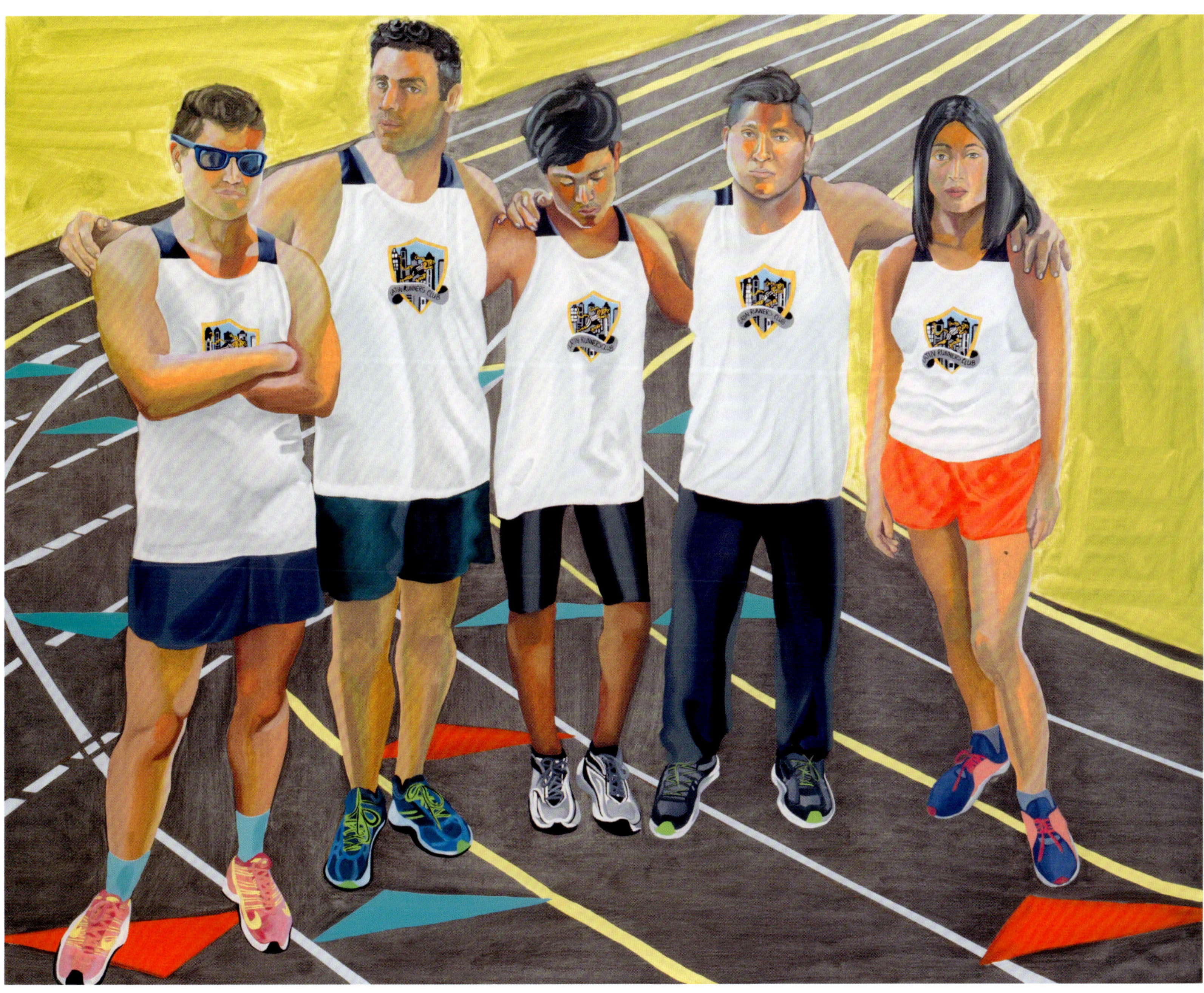

LATIN RUNNERS CLUB
2016, oil on linen, 190.5 × 241.3 cm (75 × 95 in)

Aliza Nisenbaum, born 1977, Mexico City, Mexico.

After volunteering for artist-activist Tania Bruguera's (b. 1968) Immigrant Movement International in Queens, New York in 2012, where she taught English to Mexican and Central American immigrants, Nisenbaum abandoned abstraction in favour of portraiture, painting her students as a way of getting to know them better. Nisenbaum often concentrates on subjects from transcultural backgrounds, from public service workers to undocumented immigrants to personal friends. She has gained a reputation internationally for vibrant, large-scale group portraits that echo the colourful, stylized mural paintings of her native Mexico. Such works empower those who are not usually commemorated in painted portraits, in this case a running club decked out in their logoed shirts. Human connection and community engagement lie at the heart of Nisenbaum's practice, which considers how to merge art production with an ethically driven politics of care. Regarding making art as a form of collaboration, she proposes a new kind of artist-model relationship – one that invites dialogue with individual sitters, allowing them to be the first witnesses of the finished product and even request changes if desired.

ELIZABETH NOURSE

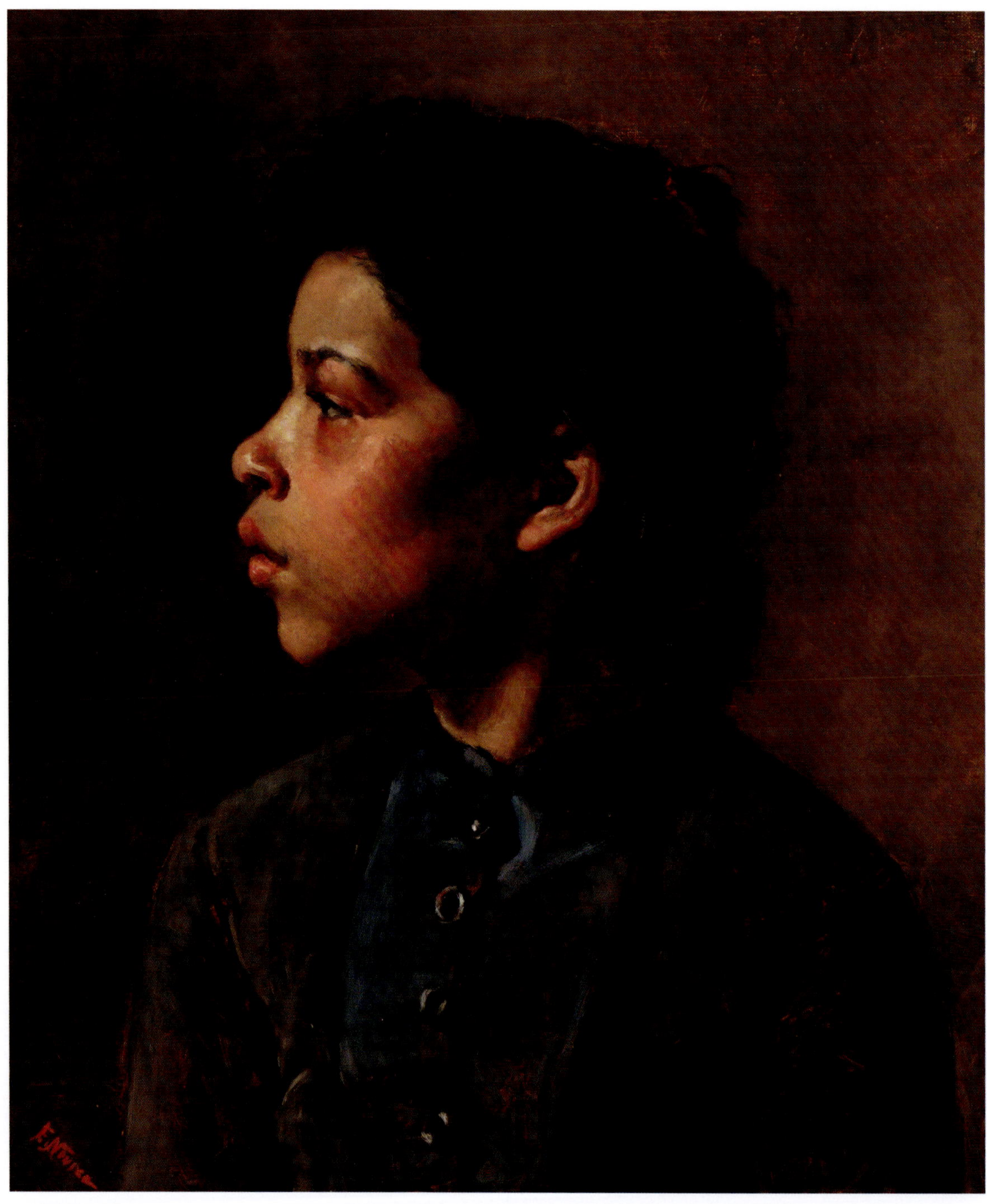

HEAD OF A GIRL
*c.*1882, oil on canvas mounted on academy board, 47.5 × 41 cm (18 ⅞ × 16 ⅛ in), Cincinnati Art Museum, Ohio, USA

Elizabeth Nourse, born 1859, Mount Healthy, Ohio, USA. Died 1938, Paris, France.

Following an artistic education in her native Ohio, Nourse moved to Paris in 1887 with her twin sister in order to pursue her career in what was at the time the global epicentre of painting. In Paris, Nourse became an acclaimed Salon painter and was one of the first American women to be elected a member of the Société Nationale des Beaux-Arts. Nourse's interest in peasant themes aligned with the Salon painters of her day, including those of her friend and fellow artist Mary Cassatt (p.73). Both artists focused on painting women – wives, mothers, female workers and children – but Nourse also addressed contemporaneous social issues and race, often painting portraits of Black subjects. Here, we can see the artist's mastery of depicting delicate details through paint. Nourse's rendering of her sitter's skin in particular demonstrates her technical skills, as she portrays tiny hairs, pores and the complex play of light on the girl's face. Nourse's acclaim lasted throughout her life; in 1921 she was described by the *Chicago Times* as the 'first woman painter of America', after receiving the prestigious Laetare Medal for enriching the heritage of humanity in the arts and sciences.

LEILA NSEIR

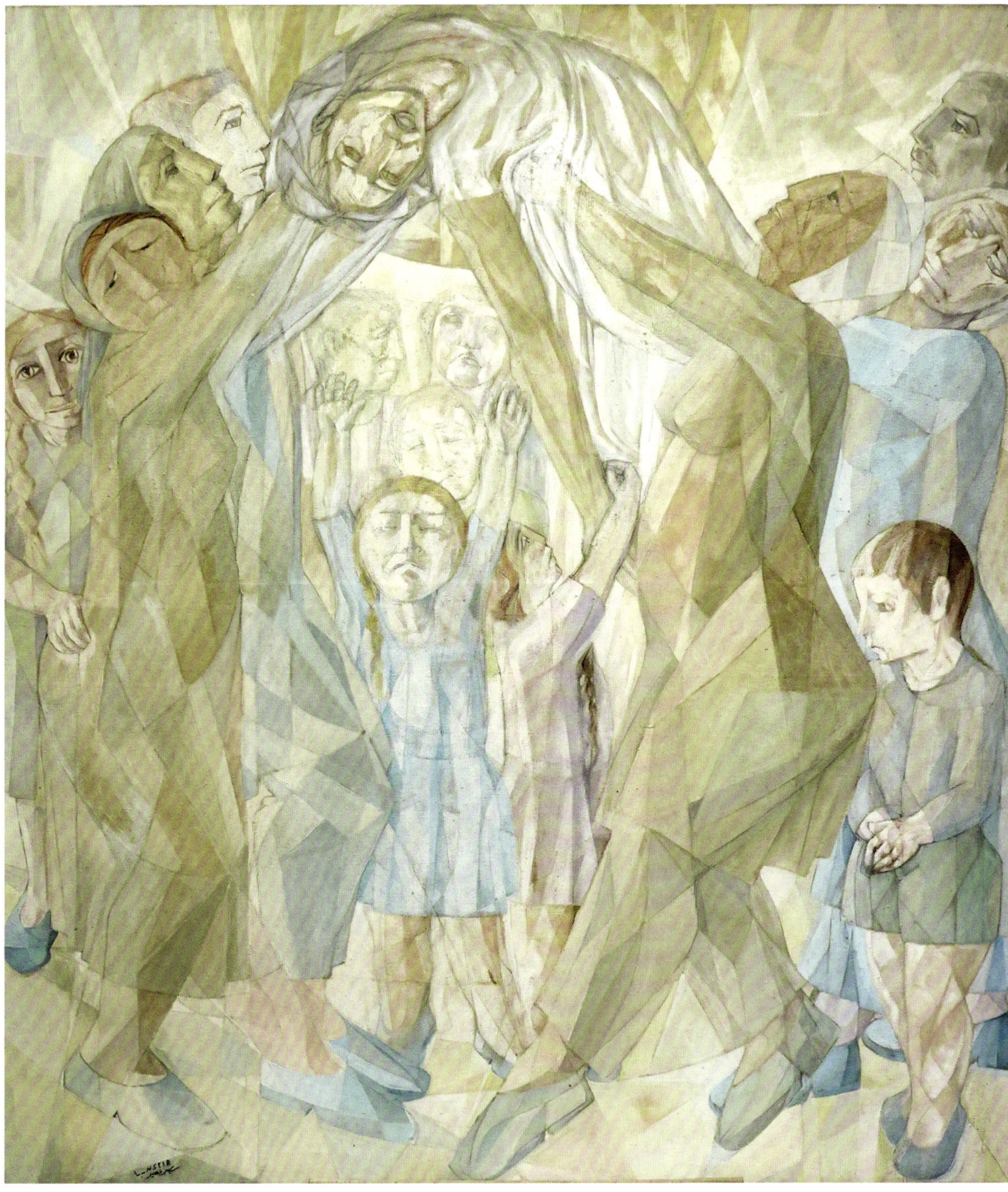

THE MARTYR (THE NATION)
1978, oil on canvas, 160 × 140 cm (63 × 55 ⅛ in), Barjeel Art Foundation, Sharjah, UAE

Leila Nseir, born 1941, Al-Haffah, Syria.

The struggles of the working class that Nseir witnessed while growing up in rural Syria inspired in her a concern for marginalized people and a desire to challenge prejudices. Nseir graduated from the Faculty of Fine Arts in Cairo in 1963, where she studied with a government scholarship as part of a generation of politically and socially engaged artists. Emerging at the height of Syrian modernism, she initially painted in a realist style and later experimented with Expressionism and Surrealism before developing a distinctive post-Cubist language of vibrant interlocking forms. While many of her paintings draw on Egyptian mythology to address contemporary issues, in the 1970s she represented contemporary images of oppression and imperialist aggression, foregrounding women in varying states of struggle and distress. This painting subverts the stereotype of the male freedom fighter by depicting a female martyr being carried by women through a crowd of mourners as children reach up to touch her. Nseir was one of the first women artists in Syria to achieve institutional recognition, and in 1968 and 1999 was honoured by the Ministry of Culture for her contributions to Syrian art.

JOSEFA DE ÓBIDOS

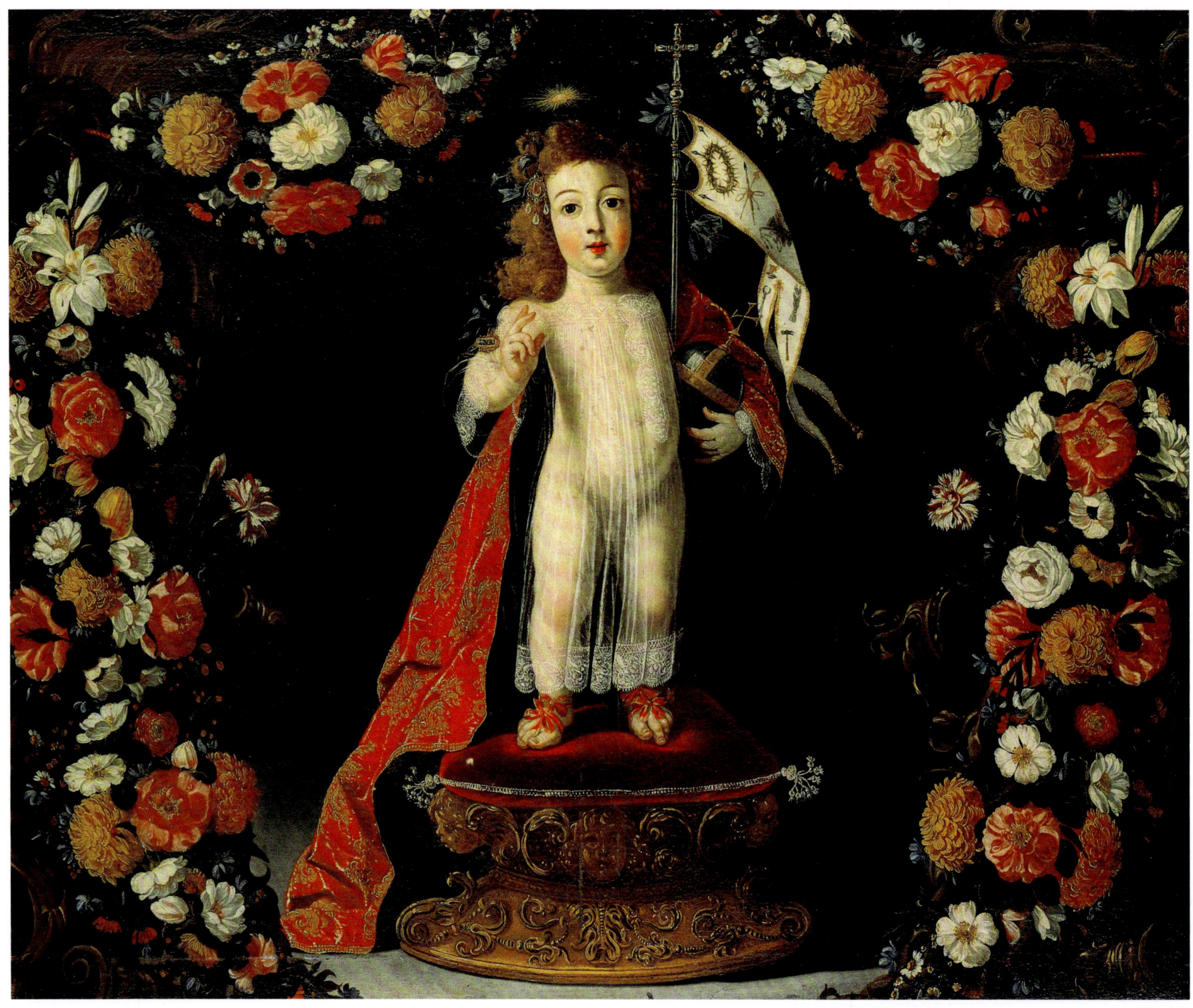

MENINO JESUS SALVADOR
(CHILD JESUS SAVIOUR)
1673, oil on canvas, 95 × 116.5 cm (37 ⅜ × 45 ⅞ in), Igreja de Nossa Senhora da Assunção (Cascais), Lisbon, Portugal

Josefa de Óbidos, born *c.*1630, Seville, Spain. Died 1684, Óbidos, Portugal.

A key figure in Portuguese Baroque painting, Óbidos was renowned during her lifetime despite working in a provincial town and in a male-dominated field. Born Josefa de Ayala, she signed her works with her first name and where she worked – 'Josefa em Óbidos' – a mark of both pride and professional shrewdness. Like many women artists of her time, she trained under and worked in the studio of her father, Baltazar Gomes Figueira (1604–74), who was known for his still-life painting. She showed skill and inventiveness from an early age, drawing on a range of visual materials, in particular her father's considerable collection of prints. As appreciation for her talents grew, she was commissioned to create large-scale public works, prompting her to emancipate herself from both her father and the possibility of marriage. 'Emancipation' was a legal status of the time that allowed women to sign contracts and sell directly without male surveillance, an independence that led to several commissions as well as opportunities to speculate financially, from which Óbidos amassed sizeable wealth. From the mid-1670s she focused on images of the Christ Child, as seen here, a favourite motif of hers from the Catholic sacred repertoire.

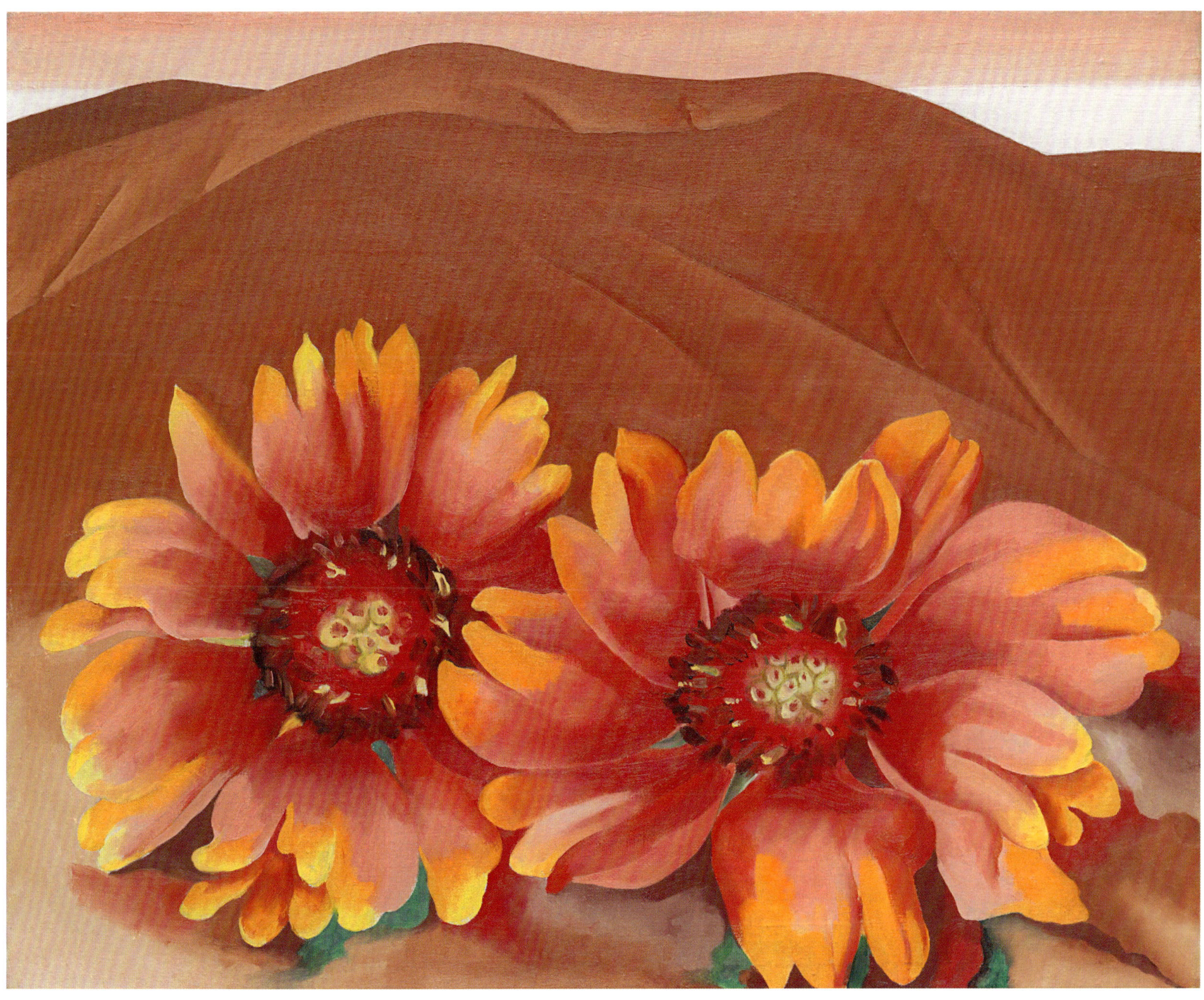

RED HILLS WITH FLOWERS
1937, oil on canvas, 50.8 × 63.5 cm (20 × 25 in),
Art Institute of Chicago, USA

Georgia O'Keeffe, born 1887, Sun Prairie, Wisconsin, USA. Died 1986, Santa Fe, New Mexico, USA.

A central figure in the development of American modernism, O'Keeffe first gained renown in 1916, when she exhibited a radical series of abstract charcoal drawings that expressed her inner, intangible emotions. Within two years, oil paint became her primary medium, allowing her to use colour alongside form to translate her feelings and sensory experiences in paintings characterized by their undulating rhythms, feathered brushwork and vibrant palette. O'Keeffe would continue to produce abstract work throughout her career, but by the mid-1920s she was executing representational canvases, gaining particular notice for her paintings of flowers. Many of these paintings were closely cropped and enlarged, reflecting the influence of modernist photography and her interest in calling attention to the details of the natural world. In 1929, the artist began to work at least part of the year in New Mexico. Inspired by the stark desert environment, landscape became increasingly prominent in her work. *Red Hills with Flowers* combines two of her recurring motifs – mountains and wildflowers – in a painting that simultaneously conveys the vastness of place and emotional intimacy through an extreme contrast in scale and an array of warm tones.

LAURA OWENS

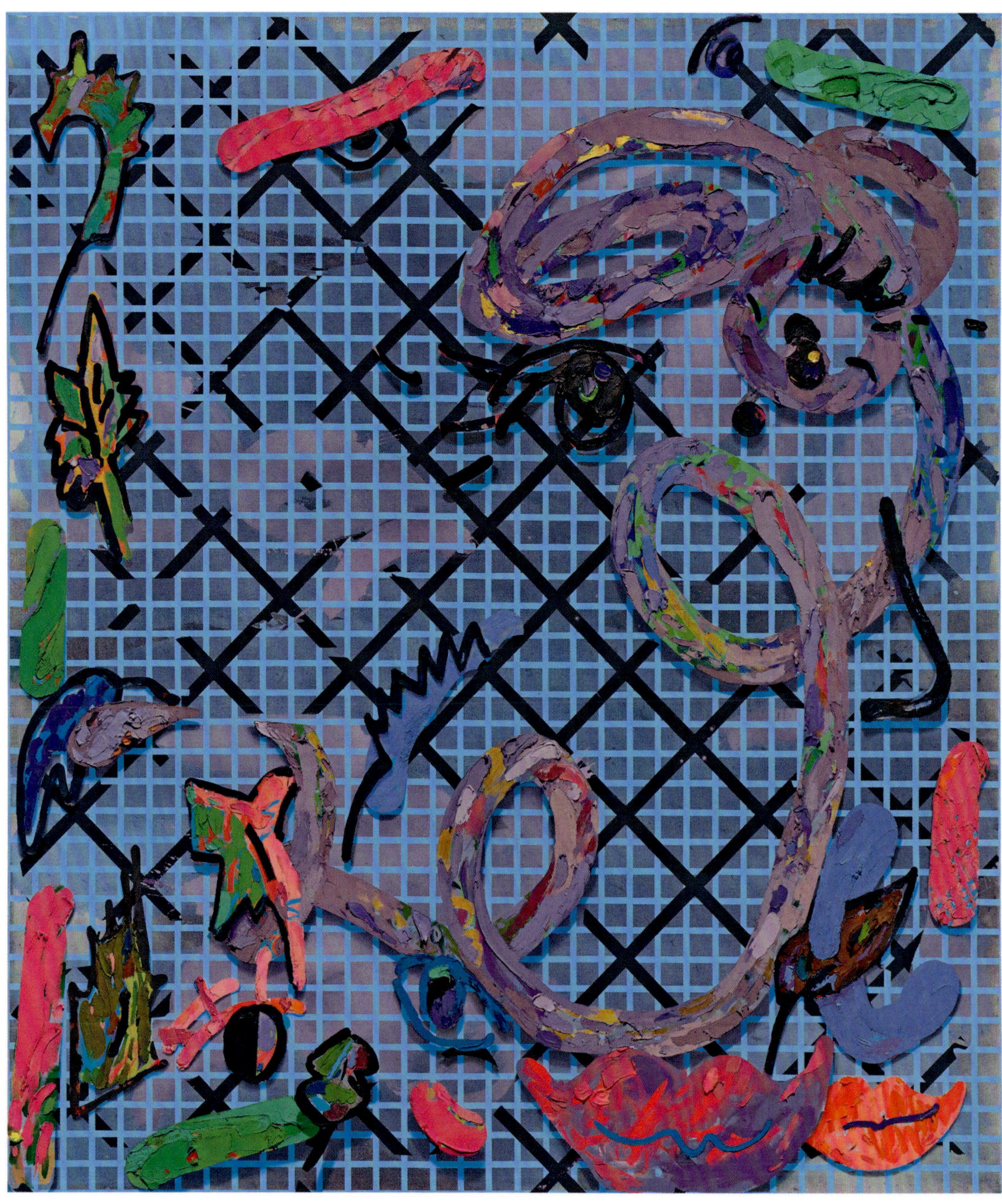

UNTITLED
2013, acrylic, oil and Flashe on canvas,
349.3 × 304.8 cm (137 ½ × 120 in)

Laura Owens, born 1970, Euclid, Ohio, USA.

Since she entered the Los Angeles art scene in the mid-1990s, Owens has experimented with the academic language of abstract painting through investigations into mark-making, illusionistic depth and materiality. The artist engages formal tools like the grid and the gestural brushstroke in her idiosyncratic style that combines devices from painting, technology, popular culture and craft. Owens's works constitute a self-referential network of symbols and formal manoeuvres: for example, marks that are a background textile pattern in one painting become the central subject of another. Well versed in the history of art, she queries and upends centuries-old tenets of academic painting, all the while remaining devoted to the medium and its possibilities. Owens's early works explore how a painting exists *in situ*: illusionistic shadows and grids sometimes literally break from the frame to intrude on the real space of the gallery. Beginning in the early 2010s, the artist merged her previous examinations of painterly techniques with digital technologies, importing source material onto a computer and generating stencils that are then transferred onto her canvases. These marks are subsequently painted or otherwise manipulated by the artist as she creates superficial shadows and cartoon-like doodles, as seen in this work.

JENNIFER PACKER

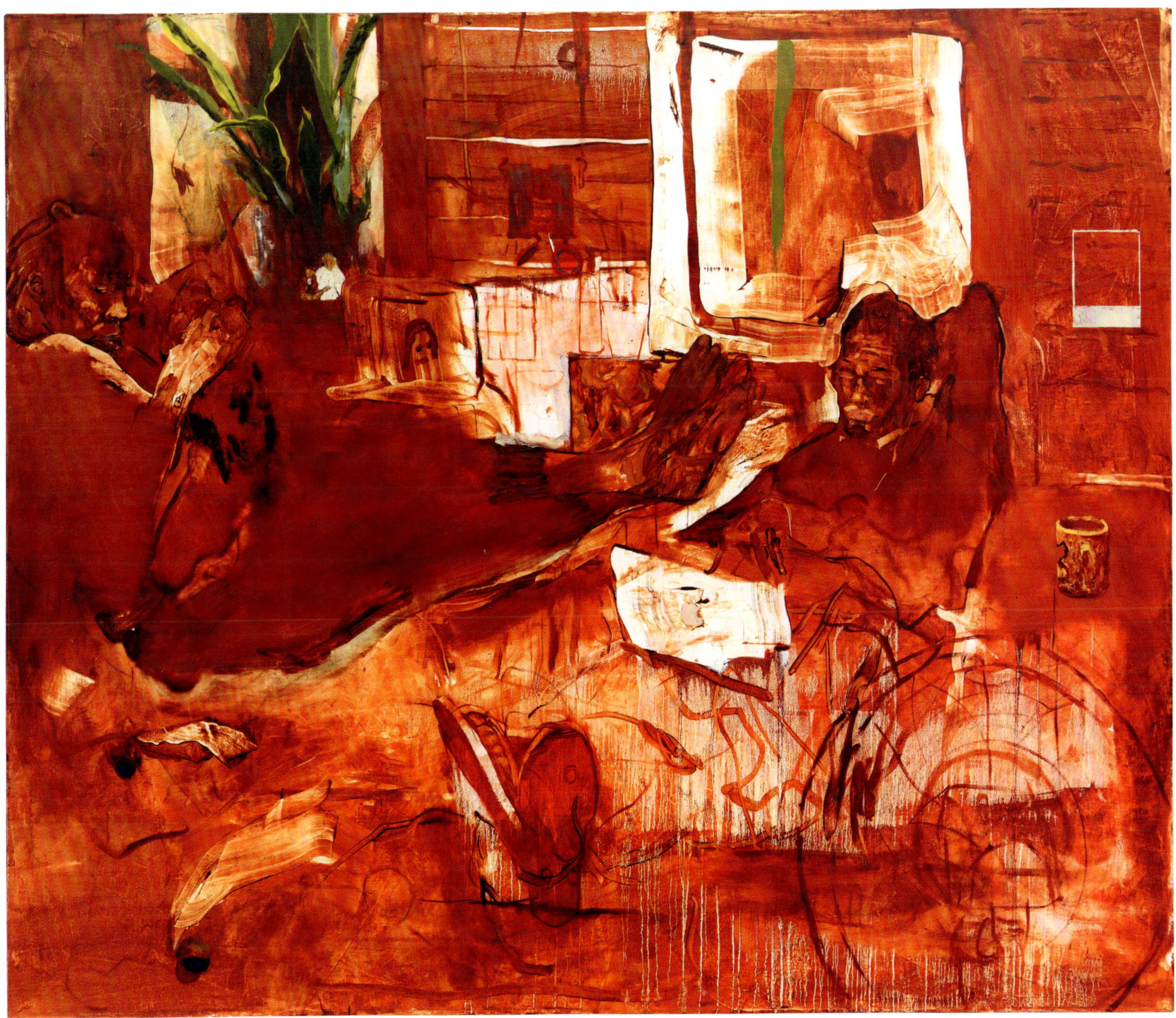

GRACES
2017, oil on canvas, 152.4 × 182.9 cm (60 × 72 in), Art Institute of Chicago, USA

Jennifer Packer, born 1984, Philadelphia, USA.

Packer's sensitively rendered paintings interrogate the ethics and politics of representation in contemporary painting. Bearing witness to Black people in everyday existence, the intimacy of her works counter dominant art-historical precedents of portraying Black sitters, while probing the possibilities – and limits – of portraiture. In a 2020 interview for the Serpentine Gallery, London, Packer stated, 'My inclination to paint… is a completely political one. We belong here. We deserve to be seen and acknowledged in real time.' Packer graduated from the Yale School of Art MFA programme in 2012, and her first solo institutional exhibition, 'Tenderheaded', took place at the Renaissance Society at the University of Chicago in 2017, where this painting was on display. In it, a figure lounges on a bed, while other details slowly materialize through a mirage of colour and haze: an Apple laptop is visible alongside a mug and, in the background, a plant. A second figure in what could be the interior of a university dormitory room emerges. Depicted with layered, gestural brushstrokes and washes of dripping paint, her subjects are simultaneously visible and hard to decipher, reflecting the representational limitations of painting itself.

PAN YULIANG

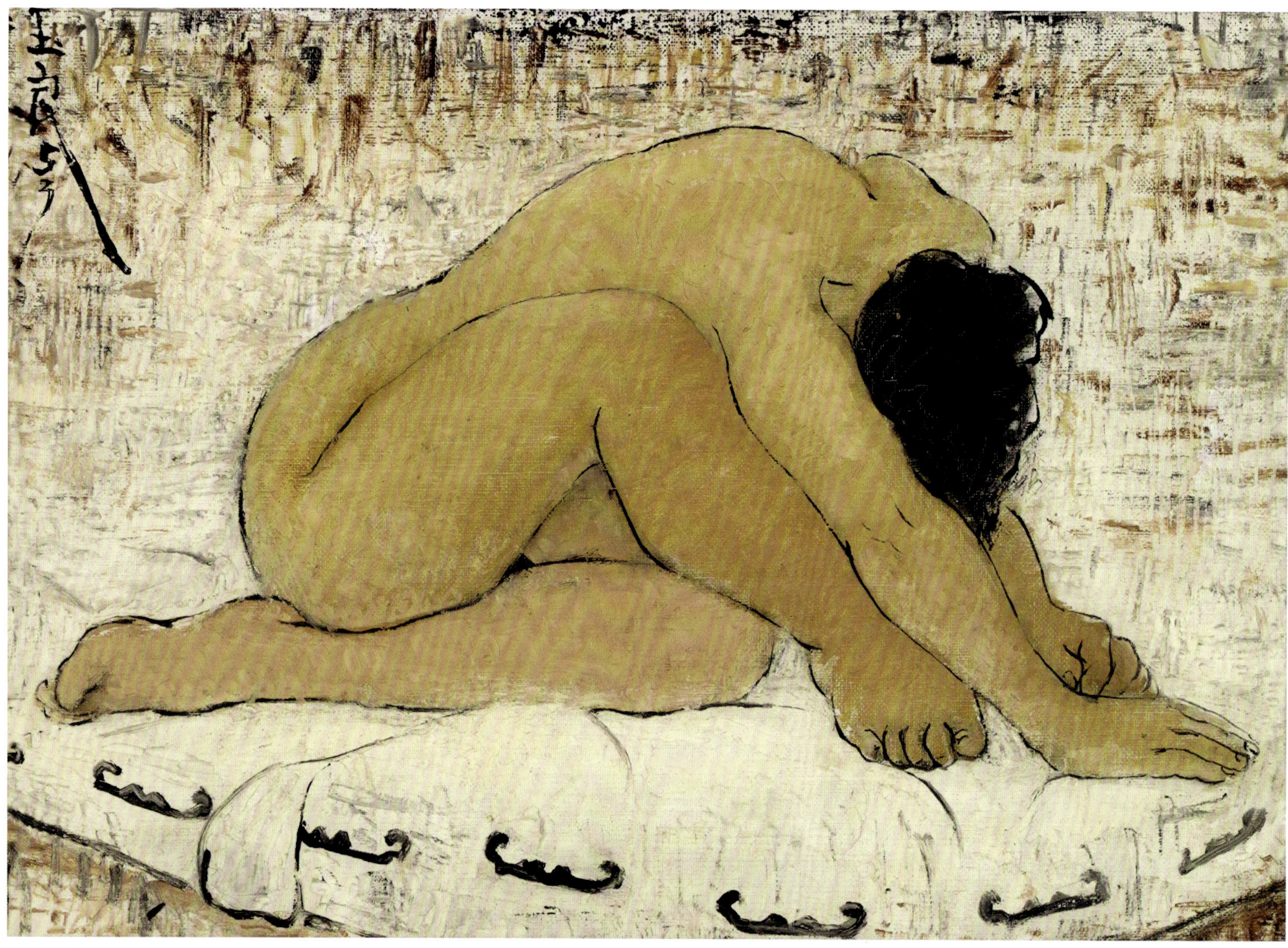

NU ASSIS (SEATED NUDE)
1953, oil on canvas, 33 × 46.4 cm (13 × 18¼ in), Musée Cernuschi, Paris, France

Pan Yuliang, born 1895, Yangzhou, Jiangsu Province, China. Died 1977, Paris, France.

Born as Chen Xiuqing, after her parents' death Pan was renamed Zhang Yuliang by her uncle, who had forced her to work in a brothel at the age of fourteen. In 1913 a wealthy civil servant bought her freedom and they relocated to Shanghai, where in 1920 she became an early female student at Shanghai Art Academy. Here, she was introduced to *xiyanghua* (Western-style painting), as practised by the modernist art circles of the time, and was later invited to study at the École Nationale Supérieure des Beaux-Arts, Paris. A prolific artist who left behind more than four thousand works, Pan's paintings combine the graphic style of Chinese brush and ink painting with the loose brushstrokes and variegated palettes of French Impressionism. The subjects of her portraits – for which she often used herself as a model – are circumspect in what they reveal to the viewer, expressing agency over their own bodies. In this example, a cloud of hatched marks frames a woman who conceals her face by hunching forward with her head bowed. It is one of the many works Pan produced in Paris, where she had settled in 1937. Though desolate with homesickness, she never returned to China.

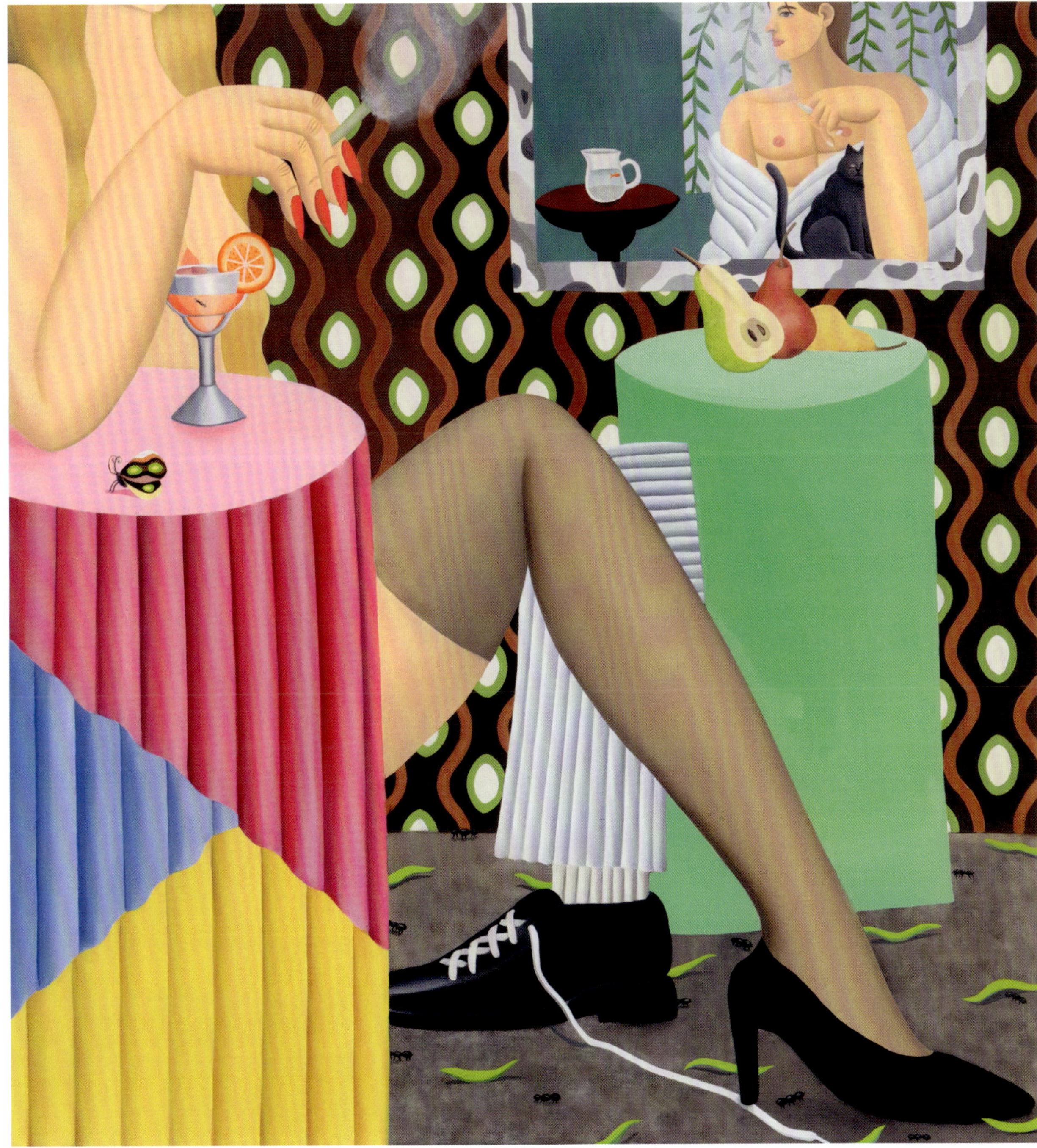

ANGEL NEXT DOOR
2020, oil on canvas, 132.1 × 121.9 cm (52 × 48 in)

GaHee Park, born 1985, Seoul, South Korea.

Moving to the United States to specialize in painting, Park graduated from the Tyler School of Art and Architecture in Philadelphia in 2012, followed by an MFA at Hunter College in New York in 2015, before moving to Montreal, Canada. After growing up in a conservative environment in Seoul and being religiously educated, Park was drawn to art as a means of expressing taboo subjects, including sexuality, nudity and the grotesque, which feature thematically in her work, intertwined with seemingly traditional still-life compositions. Naked bodies often interlock in her paintings, fostering a sense of intimacy and close communion, while portions of fruit are cut open to reveal their flesh and seeds. With psychological undercurrents, her works suggest hidden desire, secret affairs and spaces of fantasy removed from propriety. Painted in bright hues with bold shapes, Park's style is defined by a flatness that favours the surface plane and distorts perspective. The title *Angel Next Door* creates narrative overtones, suggesting the erotic imaginings of a near neighbour. The viewer is only permitted to see fragments of an interior space that includes a seemingly disembodied lower leg and floor crawling with ants – the insect a recurring motif in her art.

CELIA PAUL

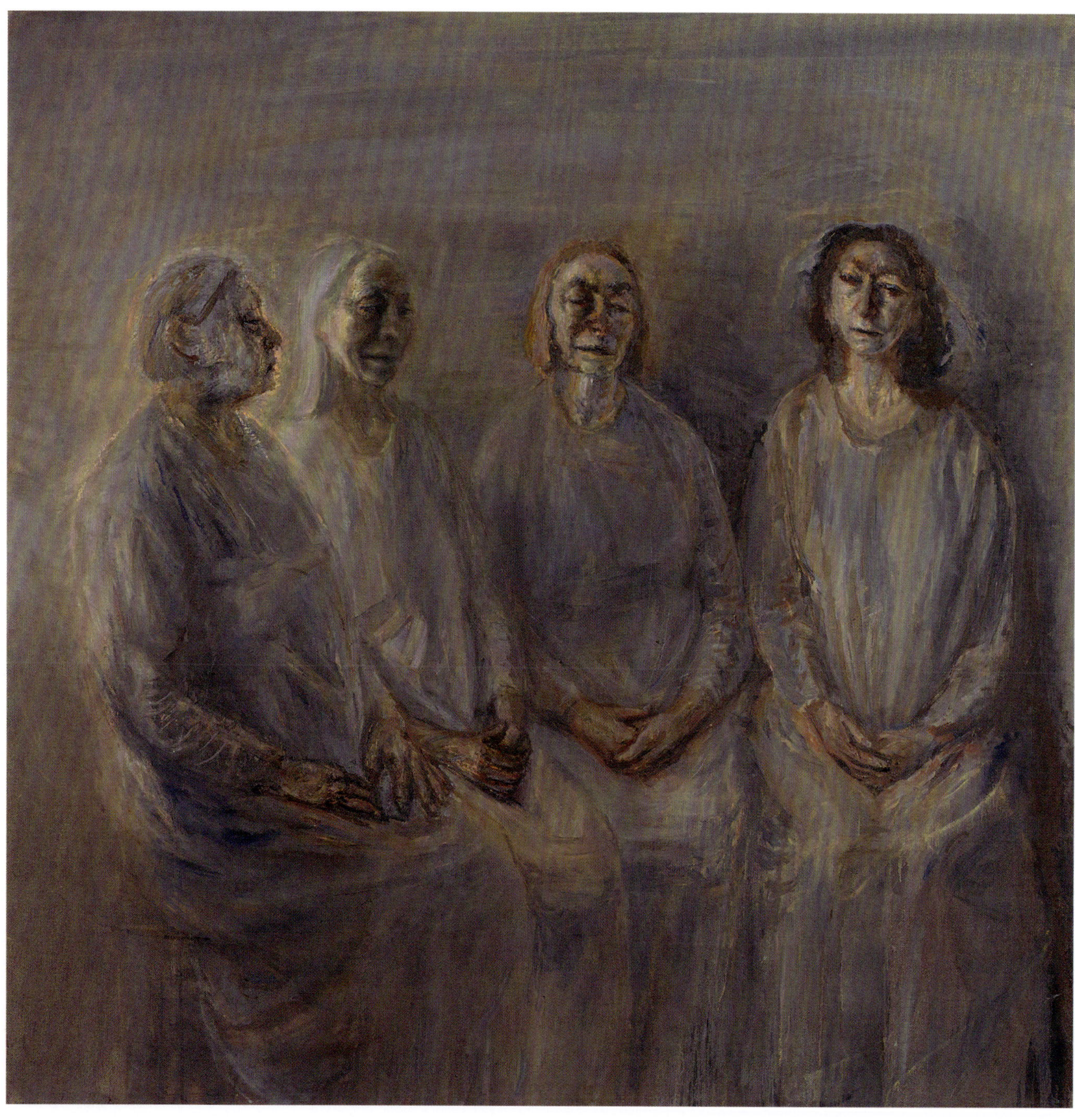

MY SISTERS IN MOURNING
2015–16, oil on canvas, 147.4 × 148 × 3.5 cm
(58 ⅛ × 58 ¼ × 1 ⅜ in)

Celia Paul, born 1959, Thiruvananthapuram, India.

The fourth of five daughters born to Christian missionaries in South India, Paul is a chronicler of her life and family, composing portraits and landscapes of exquisite emotional depth. In 1976 she began studies at the Slade School of Fine Art in London, where she worked with famed British painter Lucian Freud (1922–2011). A deep-rooted spirituality pervades her evocative, quasi-abstract landscapes and her quiet and contemplative portraits, which are characterized by muted, earthy colours. Solitary figures or groups sit or stand with distant, sometimes melancholy expressions in modest, undecorated rooms. Paul only ever paints people and places that she shares an intimate connection with – including herself – her most frequent subjects being her sisters and her mother, whom she painted regularly from 1977 until her death in 2015. This intimate portrait of her siblings depicts them grieving after the loss of their mother. Clothed in identical smocks, the mourning women are painted with a reduced palette of ash-grey and chalky blue, emanating ethereal glows as they each express subtly different emotional states, from acceptance to intense sorrow.

HILARY PECIS

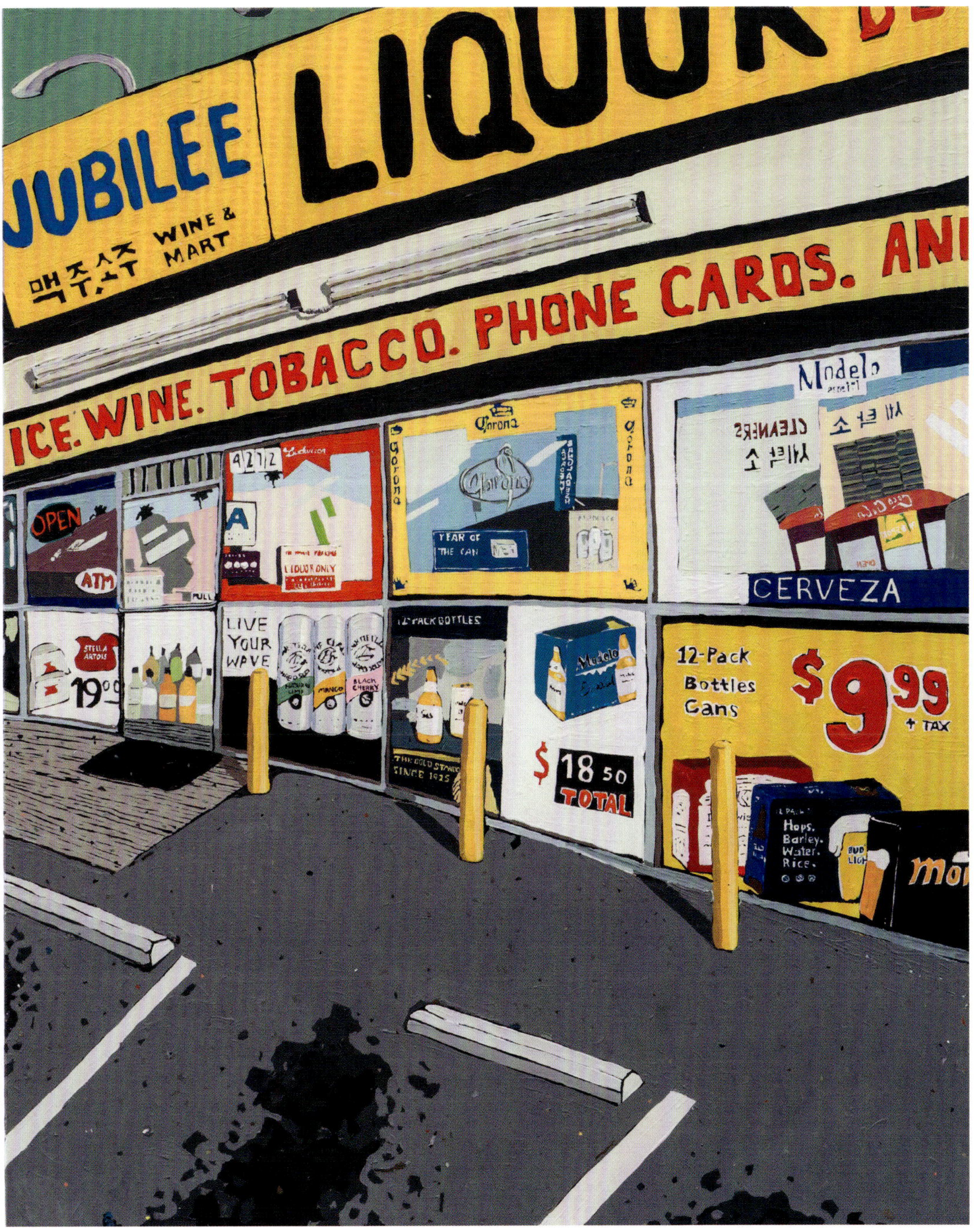

JUBILEE
2021, acrylic on linen, 81.3 × 66 cm (32 × 26 in)

Hilary Pecis, born 1979, Fullerton, California, USA.

California is a constant source of inspiration for Pecis, who knew from the age of six that she was an artist. After working as a registrar at a commercial gallery for many years, in 2019 Pecis devoted herself full-time to her studio practice. Pecis graduated with a BA and MFA from the California College of Art, and her early works primarily consisted of elaborate digital collages. She is now known for her signature style of representational paintings that update the historical genres of domestic interior, landscape and still life. The human figure is generally absent from Pecis's scenes, which none the less exude humanity and personality, displaying the lovingly curated minutiae of life. A series of paintings of her friends' bookshelves are akin to portraits, their thoughtful arrangements of books, artworks and objects defining 'who they are or who they aspire to be', as she told *Cultured* magazine in 2021. Pecis is a runner who renders landscapes and street-scenes as she sees them during her runs, rather than as they might appear in photographs. In *Jubilee* Los Angeles's dazzling light shines on a liquor store car park and its array of advertisements.

CLARA PEETERS

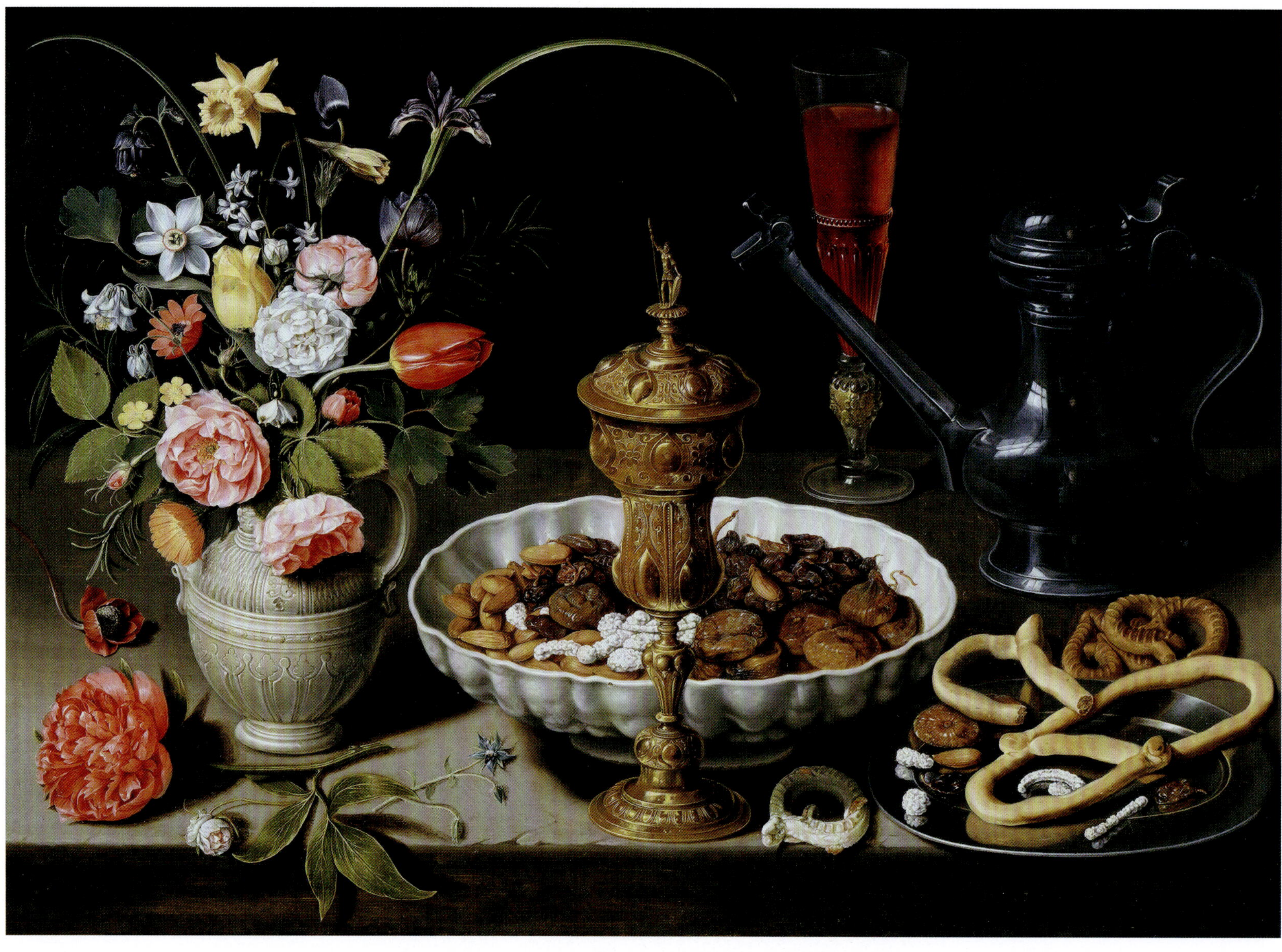

STILL LIFE WITH FLOWERS, A SILVER-GILT GOBLET, DRIED FRUIT, SWEETMEATS, BREAD STICKS, WINE AND A PEWTER PITCHER
1611, oil on panel, 52 × 73 cm (20½ × 28¾ in), Museo del Prado, Madrid, Spain

Clara Peeters, born *c.*1594, Antwerp, Belgium. Died *c.*1659, probably Antwerp.

A pioneer in the genre of still life, Peeters started working in the first decade of the seventeenth century when the taste for such works was beginning to grow in popularity. She was one of the few women active as a professional painter in early modern Europe and one of the only known Flemish women known to have painted still lifes. Peeters's work was widely distributed both during and after her lifetime, suggesting that she achieved an international reputation. Her limited biography has been pieced together from her paintings, which used panel and copper supports from Antwerp, leading scholars to believe that she worked in the city. In this work Peeters depicts both precious and common objects arranged in a seemingly random fashion on a table, including an intricate gilt goblet and pewter jug on which the artist has painted her self-portrait (four times on the goblet and three times on the jug). Such attention to visual detail – seen also in the shine of sticky dried fruit and the refractions and reflections on glass and metal – are testaments to Peeters's supreme artistic skill.

AGNES PELTON

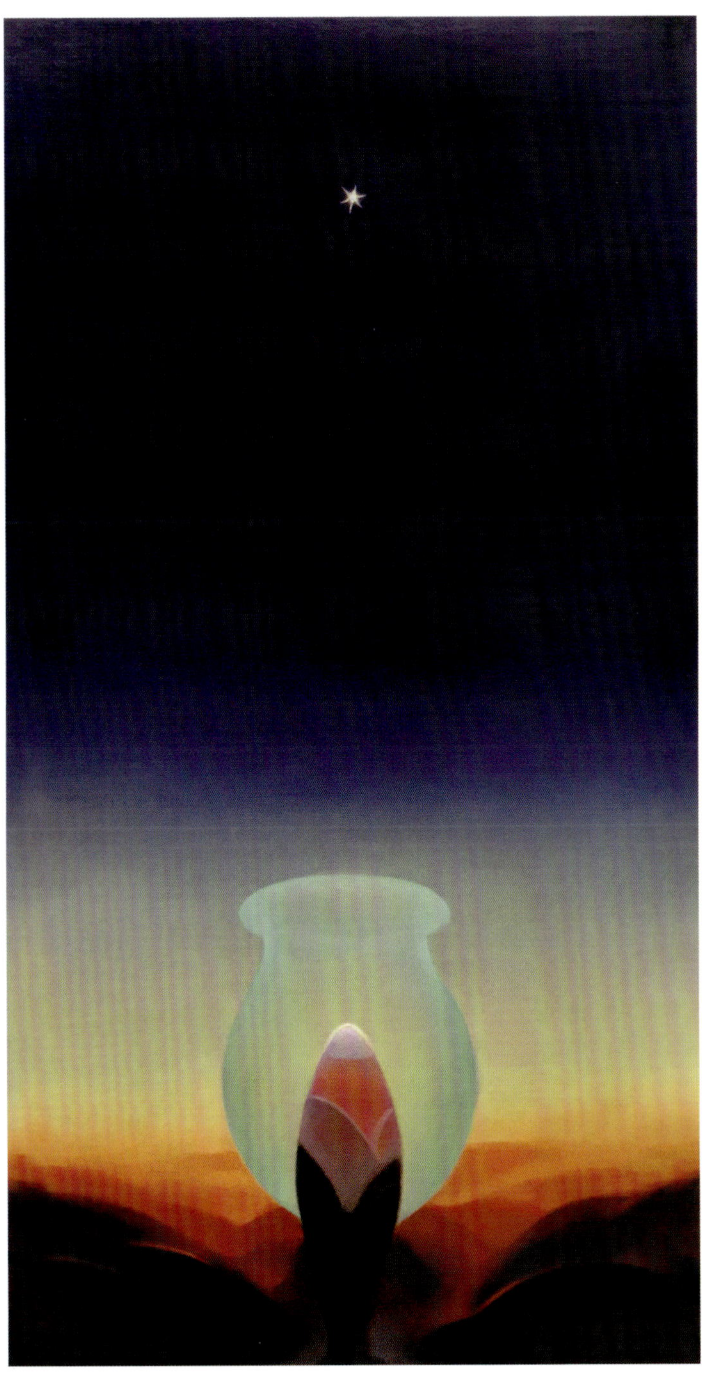

STAR GAZER
1929, oil on canvas, 76.2 × 40.6 cm (30 × 16 in), private collection

Agnes Pelton, born 1881, Stuttgart, Germany. Died 1961, Cathedral City, California, USA.

Replete with abstract, biomorphic and levitating motifs, Pelton's paintings capture a spiritual reality experienced by the artist in moments of contemplative stasis. Having moved to the United States as a child, Pelton graduated from Pratt Institute, New York, in 1900 before studying drawing at the British Academy of Arts in Rome in 1910. After a visit to New Mexico in 1919, Pelton began representing the American Southwest, which would remain a focus of her work throughout her life (she later relocated to the California desert). Her best-known works are the metaphysical and abstract paintings that she began in the mid-1920s, exemplified here. Achieved through a laborious process of layering thin glazes that took weeks or even months to complete, the illuminated lotus orb in *Star Gazer* is situated in a hazy, symmetrical landscape beneath a single, bright star that serves as a metaphor for individual passion and possibility. Pelton believed in the ability of art and poetry to transcend physical limits and was a member of the Transcendental Painting Group (1938–42), which was formed in New Mexico to promote non-objective abstraction.

ELIZABETH PEYTON

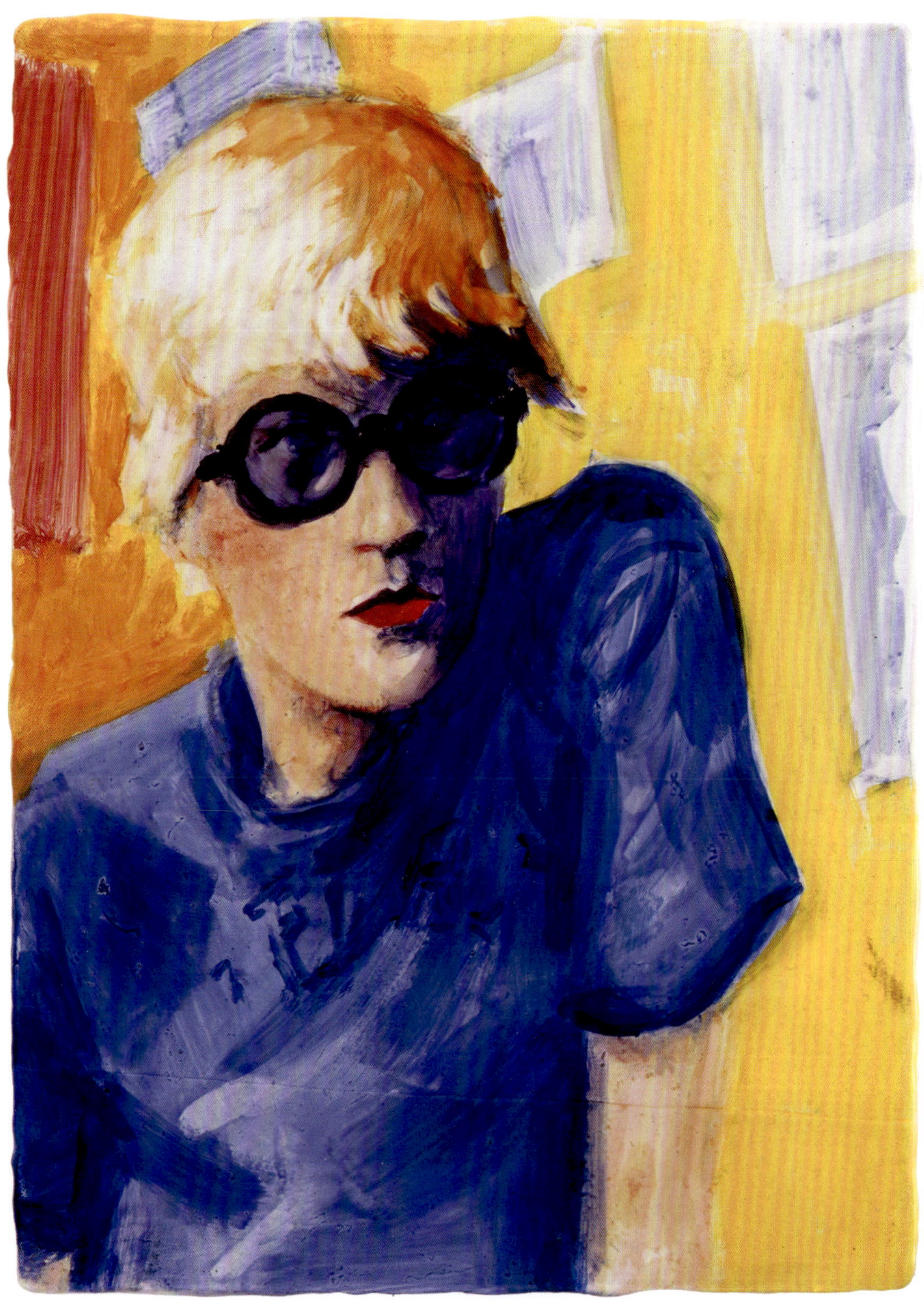

DAVID HOCKNEY, POWIS TERRACE BEDROOM
1998, oil on board, 25 × 18 cm (9 ¾ × 7 in)

Elizabeth Peyton, born 1965, Danbury, Connecticut, USA.

Since the mid-1990s, Peyton has been known for small-scale portraits of people from her own life and beyond it, ranging from fellow artists to historical personae. In oil paintings, as well as pencil drawings, monotypes and various forms of printmaking, Peyton alternates between precise and expressive registers. She simultaneously achieves a vitality of touch that eclipses questions of genre. Deriving from both photographic sources and from life her portraits have featured subjects as diverse as Kurt Cobain, Angela Merkel, David Hockney (b. 1937, as seen in this work) and the tenor Jonas Kaufmann. Throughout her career, she has returned to ideas of subjectivity and emotion, probing the boundary between interior self and outward persona. Still life has formed a prominent strand of her practice, with books and flowers articulating themes of time and memory. Since the 2010s, Peyton has made numerous paintings and works on paper inspired by opera, including scenes from Richard Wagner's *Tristan and Isolde*. As she explained in a 2013 interview with writer Dodie Kazanjian, 'I was looking for a way to make figurative work in a non-literal way and Wagner opened a door for me in how to be expressive about human feeling without being literal.'

HOWARDENA PINDELL

UNTITLED
1970, acrylic on canvas, 175.3 × 201 cm (69 × 79 ⅛ in), Whitney Museum of American Art, New York, USA

Howardena Pindell, born 1943, Philadelphia, USA.

Over the course of her long career, Pindell has moved between abstraction and figuration in her paintings, videos and sculptures, while also pursuing activities as a curator, educator, activist and writer. After completing her MFA at Yale School of Art in 1967, Pindell began drawing and painting her signature layered circular forms – first by hand and then with spray paint over stencils made using a hole punch, as in the exquisitely detailed *Untitled*. These labour-intensive, quasi-pointillist paintings, sometimes adorned with the left-over punched card discs or other materials such as glitter and talcum powder, were a response to the prevailing trend of Minimalism at the time, while also referencing the mugs stamped with red circles that African Americans were forced to drink from during segregation. Outside the studio, Pindell was involved in Black and women's activism, co-founding the women artists' cooperative A.I.R. Gallery (see p.279) in 1972. But it was after a near-fatal car crash in 1979 that she decided to communicate her personal experiences and political beliefs directly in her work, both on canvas and video.

LIUBOV POPOVA

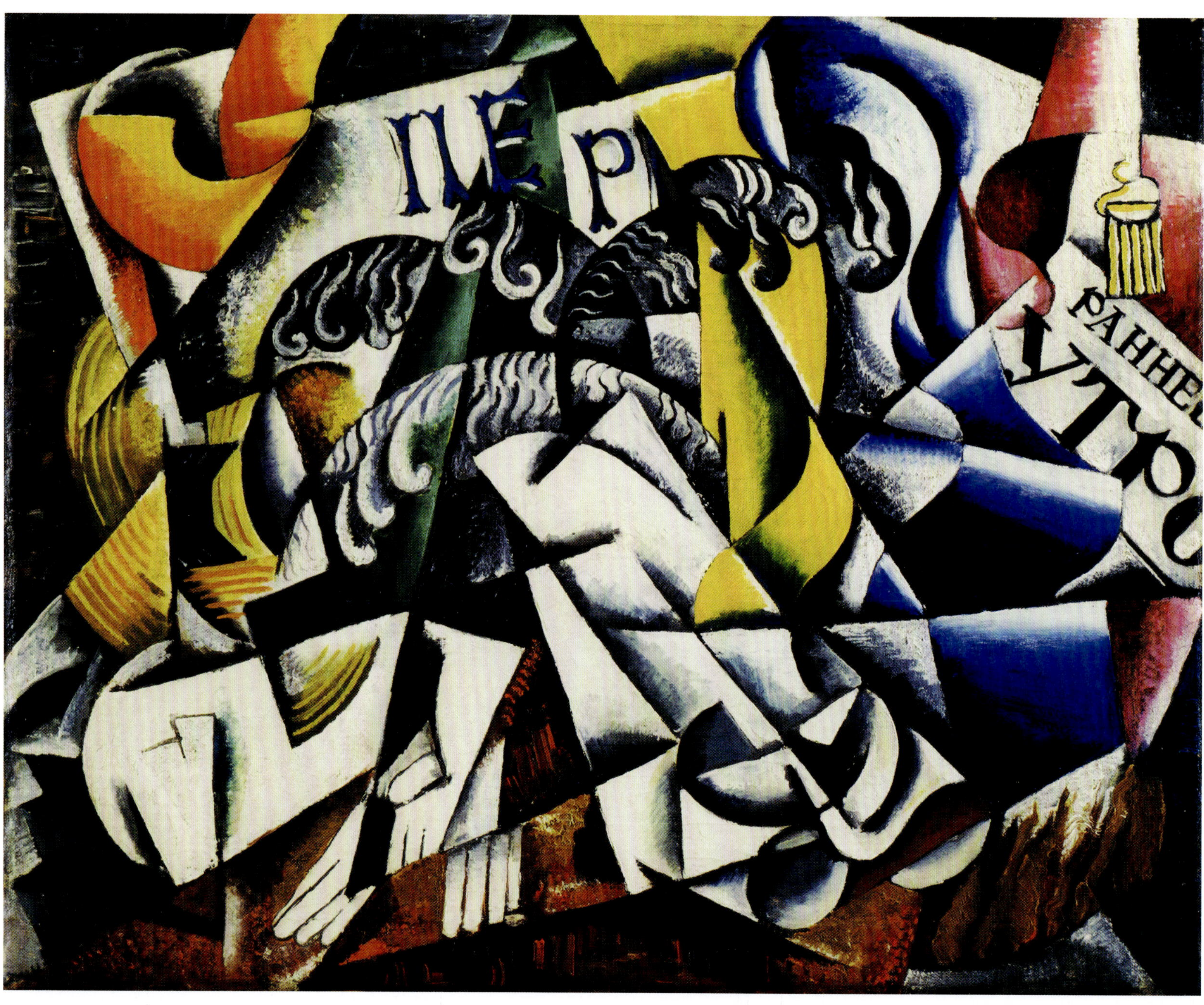

OBJECTS FROM A DYER'S SHOP
1914, oil on canvas, 71 × 89 cm (27 ¾ × 35 in), Museum of Modern Art, New York, USA

Liubov Popova, born 1889, Moscow, Russia. Died 1924, Moscow.

Popova was an instrumental figure in the development of Russia's twentieth-century avant-garde. Born to a wealthy family, she studied painting through private lessons and travelled extensively across Russia, Italy and France, where she was exposed to traditions ranging from Russian icons and Italian Old Master paintings to French Cubism and Italian Futurism – eventually creating a unique hybrid style called Cubo-Futurism. Referred to by her contemporaries as the 'artist-constructor' in an exhibition catalogue published shortly after her death, Popova built a network around herself, including artists Vladimir Tatlin (1885–1953) and Nadezhda Udal'tsova (1886–1961), and stirred up conversations among those who attended her home salons. In this work, Popova fragments and reassembles a still life into an energetic cluster of shape and colour, with free-floating letters alluding to the name of a Russian newspaper and glimpses of objects seen in a dyer's shop. Popova would embrace pure abstraction in the later part of the 1910s and ultimately renounced painting in favour of applied arts, including textiles and theatre and book design.

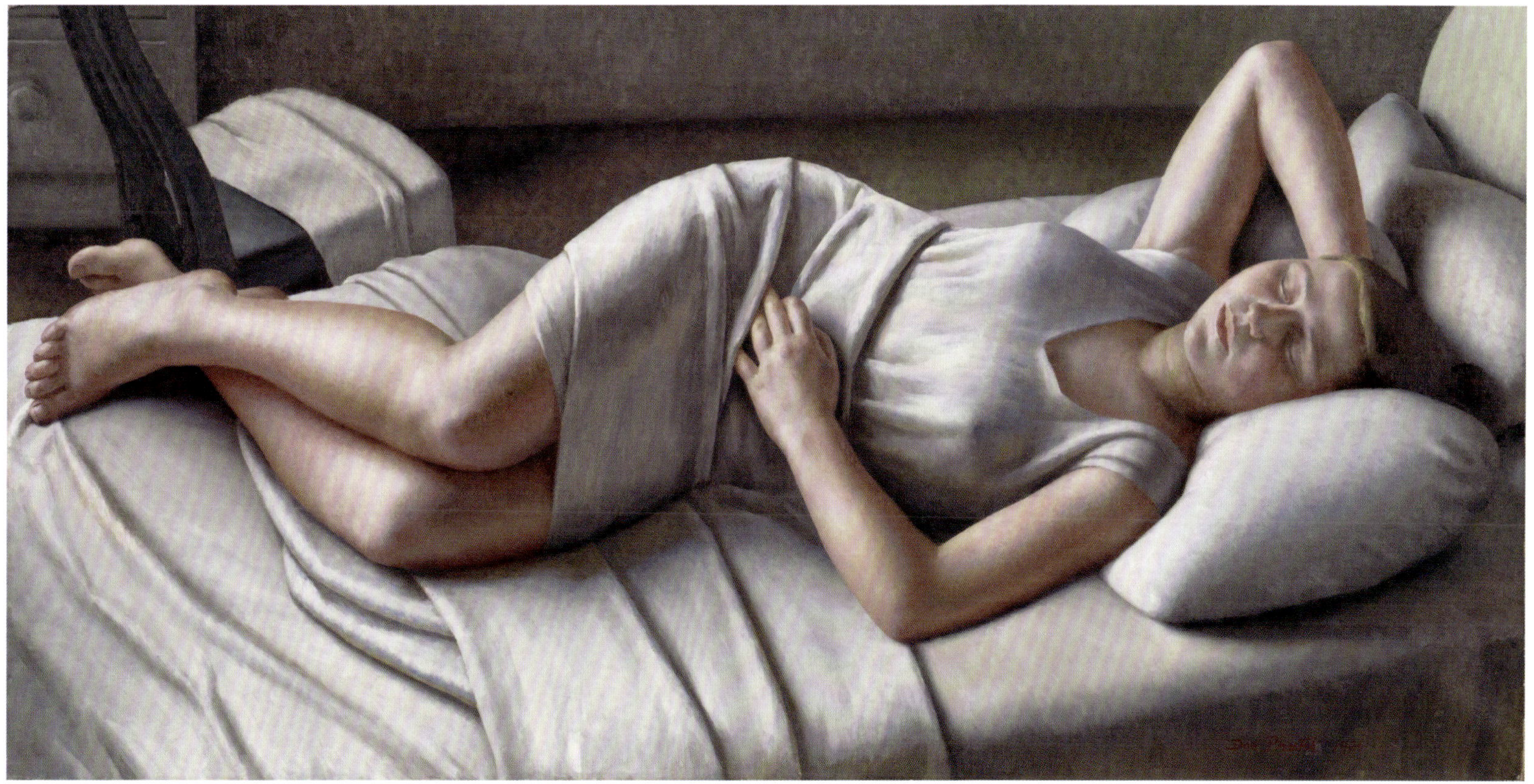

MORNING
1926, oil on canvas, support: 76.2 × 152.4 cm (20 × 60 in), Tate, London, UK

Dod Procter, born 1890, London, UK. Died 1972, Redruth, Cornwall, UK.

Based in Cornwall for most of her career, Procter is known for her figurative depictions of young women painted in a direct, realist style. Arriving in Newlyn in 1907, she studied at the Forbes School of Painting and then at the Slade School of Fine Art in London before travelling to Paris to study at the Académie Colarossi, one of the few art schools that allowed female students to attend life drawing classes. Though her real name was Doris, in 1923 she started exhibiting under the gender-neutral name of Dod as her work increasingly became focused on female identity and sexuality. Her breakthrough painting, *Morning* – exhibited at the 1927 Royal Academy Summer Exhibition – depicts Cissie Barnes, the teenage daughter of a local Cornish fisherman. Procter emphasizes the morning sunlight falling on the girl's solid, curvaceous body, which is painted with sculptural simplicity. This and similar works represented a retort to the long tradition of reclining females in academic painting. Its bold approach to depicting a working-class woman proposed a new role for women in British art.

CHRISTINA QUARLES

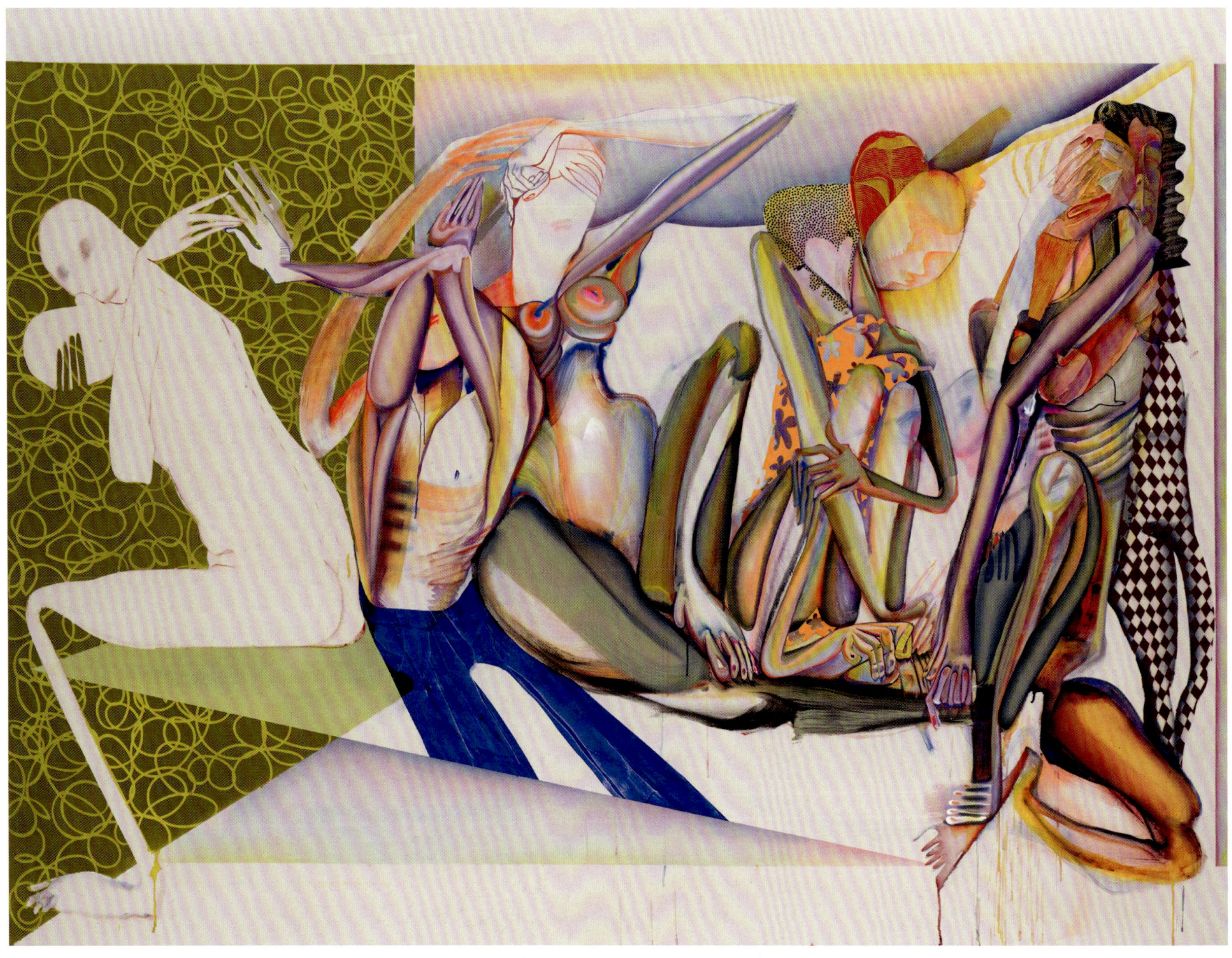

SWEET CHARIOT
2020, acrylic on canvas, 182.9 × 243.8 × 5.1 cm (72 × 96 × 2 in)

Christina Quarles, born 1985, Chicago, USA.

The fleshy, not-quite-human figures that populate Quarles's canvases are stretched, tangled and distorted to impossible lengths. The physical distress their bodies endure is a manifestation of feelings of ambiguity and displacement – a sense of being constricted in a body that is defined by others – which Quarles herself has often experienced as a mixed-race woman who is frequently misidentified as white. Raised in Los Angeles, where she still lives and works, Quarles developed her distinctive style at Yale School of Art, where she graduated with an MFA in painting in 2016, and the Skowhegan School of Painting and Sculpture, where she completed a residency the same year. Her process begins with gestural drawing, which she then manipulates with a computer program to create the extreme, angular forms seen in her finished canvases. Such contorted forms are present in this work, in which overlapping, alien-like figures are rendered in swathes of psychedelic colours and wrapped in clashing patterns. This explosion of visual information stands in contrast to the hunched figure on the left – existing only in outline, they embody the feeling of alienation experienced when one is told they do not belong.

FIONA RAE

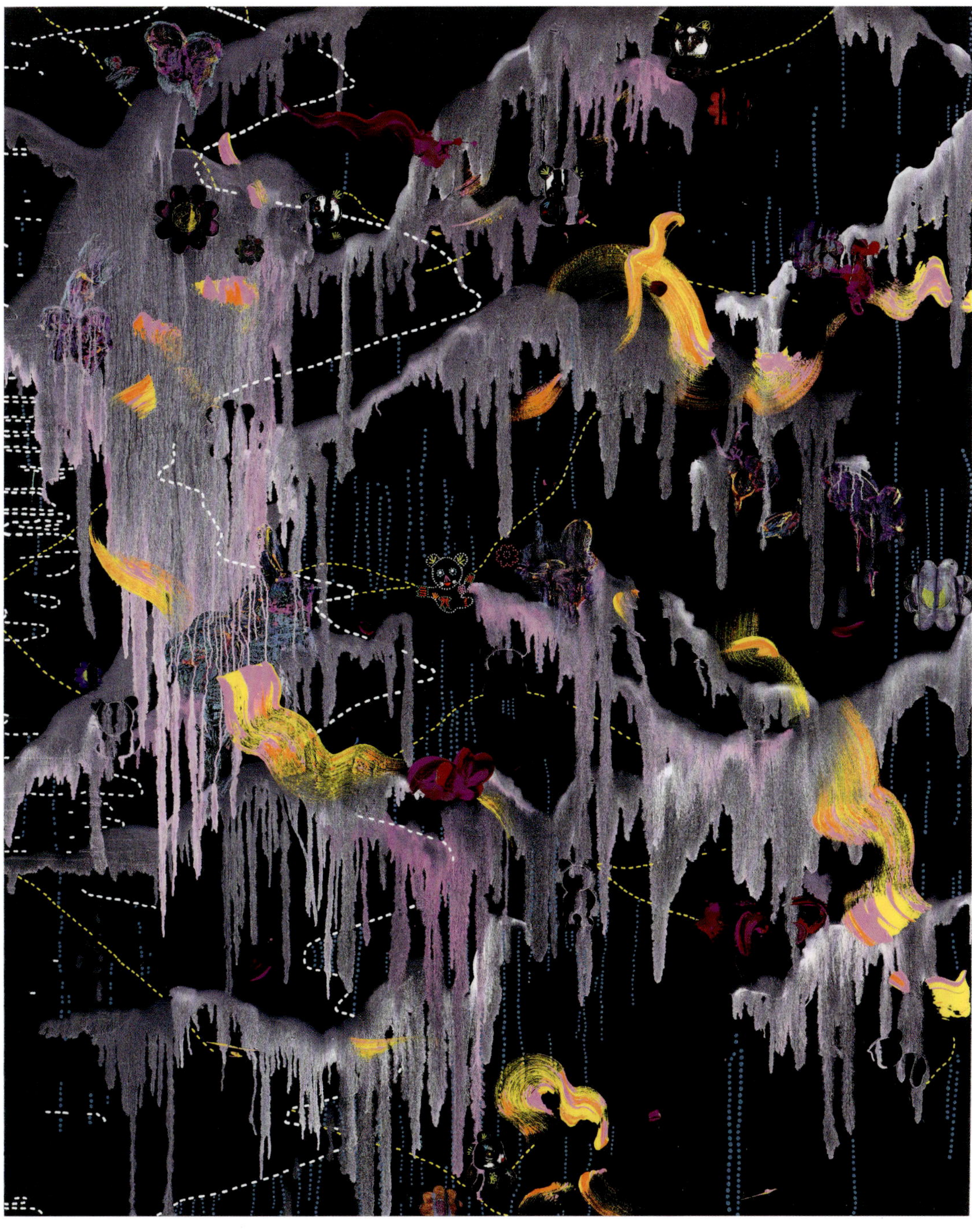

I ALWAYS WISH YOU EVERY HAPPINESS WITH MY WHOLE HEART IN THE DISTANCE
2012, oil and acrylic on canvas, 213.4 × 175.3 cm (84 × 69 in)

Fiona Rae, born 1963, Hong Kong, China.

Rae studied at London's Goldsmiths College, completing a BA in Fine Art in 1987 along with many artists who would later be associated with the Young British Artists (YBAs) movement. In 1988 she took part in the infamous 'Freeze' exhibition, organized by Damien Hirst (b. 1965), and was shortlisted for the Turner Prize in 1991. Rae's abstract paintings play with the notion of kitsch, combining bright colours with complex patterns, distinct black lines and, sometimes, cartoonish characters. Engaging with the history of abstraction, Rae references the flatness of modernism, the fragmented planes of Cubism and the energetic hues of Expressionism, all viewed through the lens of contemporary popular culture. Since the early 2000s, Rae has made paintings that relate to the computer screen, the digital space translating into a graphic flatness comprised of signs, symbols and fonts. An artificial dimension is suggested in this work, which recalls a pixelated landscape that simultaneously merges snowcapped mountains, rivers and the branches of a weeping willow upon the surface plane. Appointed as the first female Professor of Painting at London's Royal Academy Schools in 2011, Rae was part of a watershed moment that ended the institution's historical marginalization of women artists.

CAROL RAMA

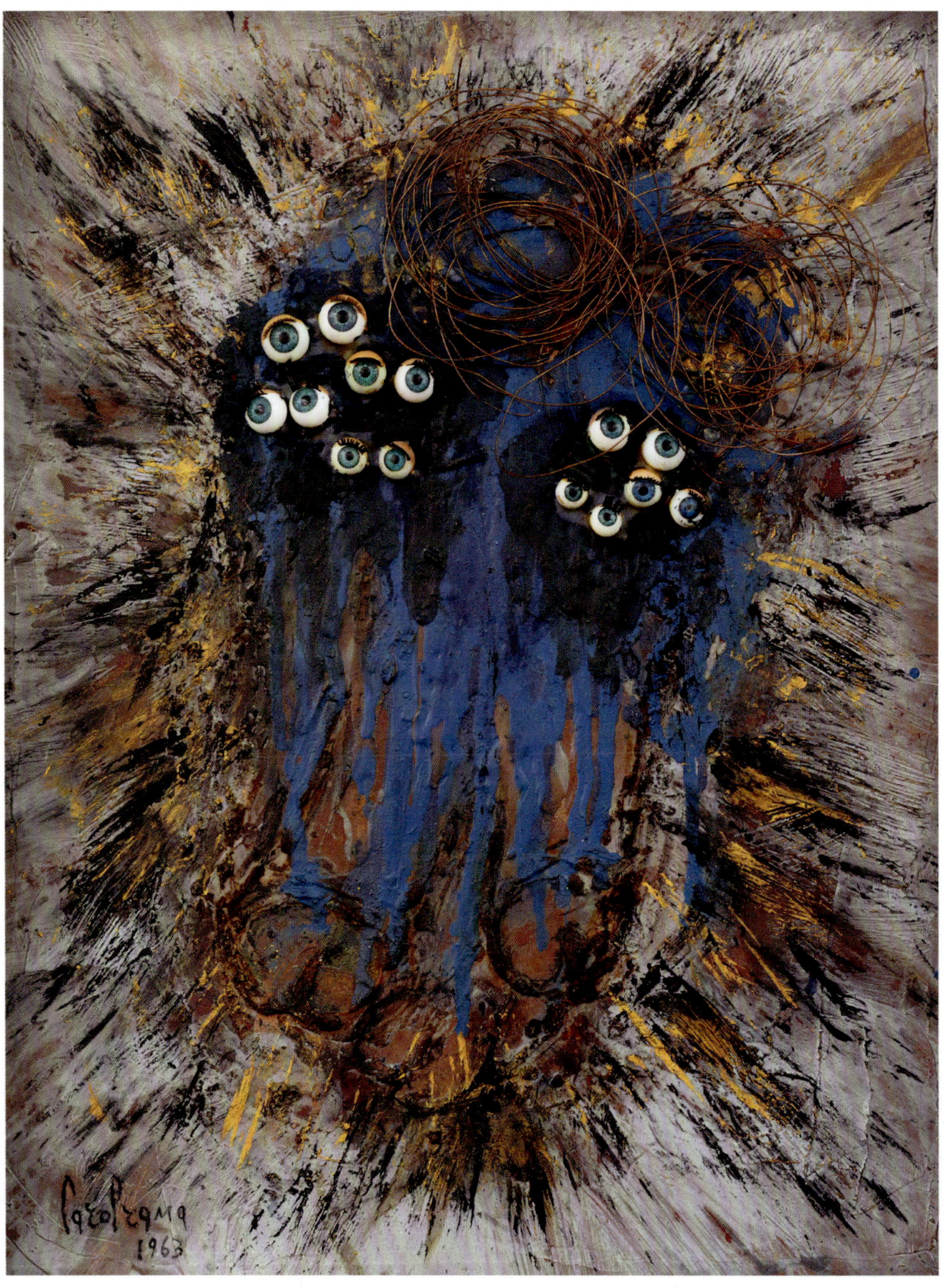

BRICOLAGE
1963, oil, glass dolls' eyes, gilded paint, copper wire and glue on Masonite with artist's frame (not pictured), 47.5 × 36.5 cm (18 ¾ × 14 ⅜ in), Nuyten Dime Collection

Carol Rama, born 1918, Turin, Italy. Died 2015, Turin.

A lifelong resident of Turin who occupied the same apartment and studio for more than seventy years, Rama started making art in the mid-1930s with no formal art training. Her early watercolours conveyed her fascination for the fluidity and disobedience of the body and her first exhibition, at Turin's Galleria Faber in 1945, included explicit images of bodies in sexual ecstasy. The show was deemed obscene and shut down by the government before it opened its doors, but the unruly human body – whole or in parts, expressing pleasure or pain – remained a constant in her work, staunchly resisting normality and freely expressing needs, desires and traumas. In the 1960s, Rama began incorporating a variety of organic and inorganic materials into her paintings – teeth, animal claws, syringes and rubber tyres – in works Rama's close friend and poet Edoardo Sanguineti called 'bricolages' for the way, like his poems, they assembled disparate elements to create an uncanny impression. Here, industrially produced dolls' eyes stare back at the viewer from dark blue pools that sit atop what appear to be painted penises, suggesting voyeurism and explosive sexuality, while an aura of black and gold rays of paint and copper wire halos lend the work a transcendent quality.

CHRISTINA RAMBERG

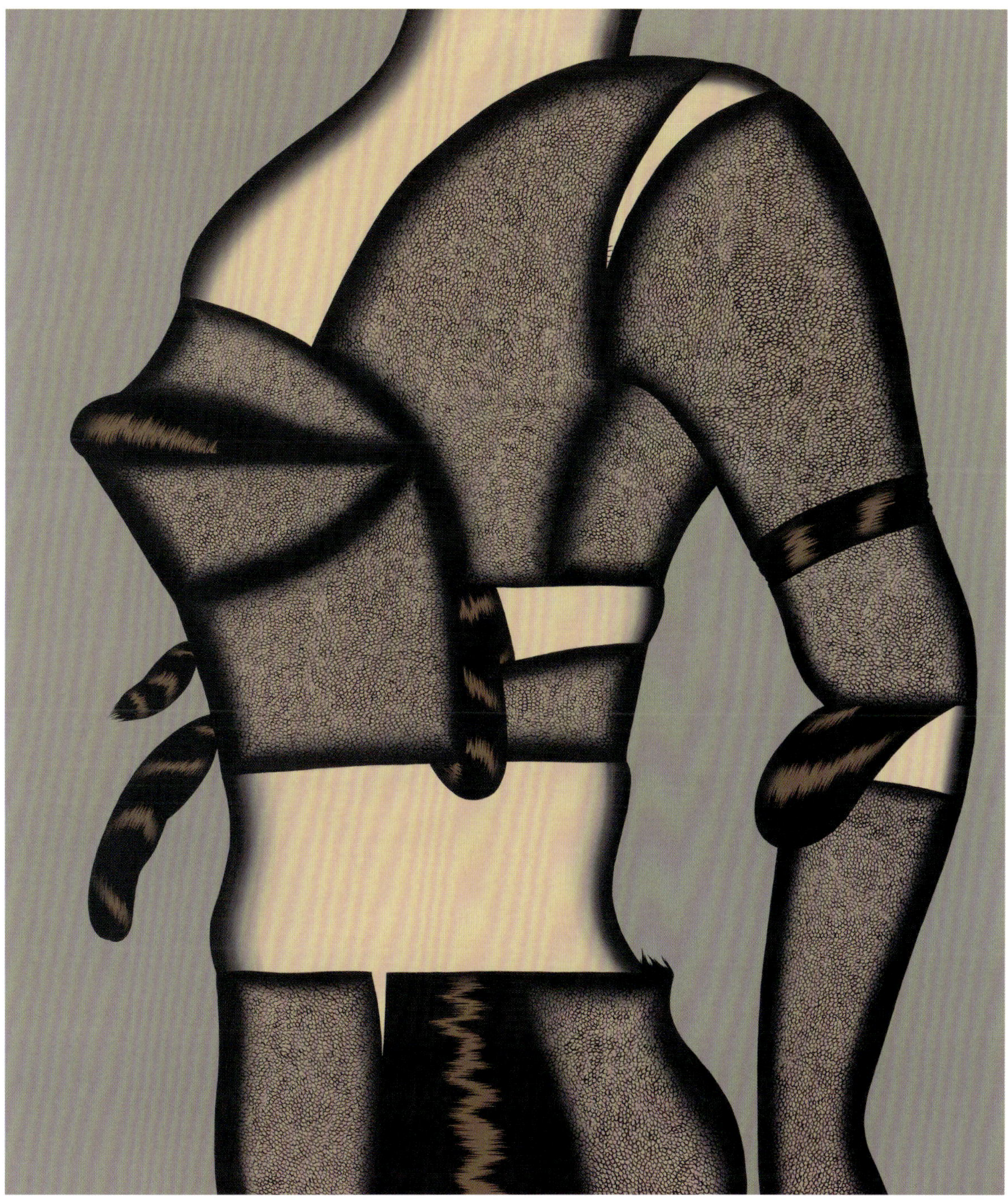

ISTRIAN RIVER LADY
1974, acrylic on composition board, 89.9 × 79.4 × 4.1 cm (35 ⅜ × 31 ¼ × 1 ⅝ in), Whitney Museum of American Art, New York, USA

Christina Ramberg, born 1946, Fort Campbell, Kentucky, USA. Died 1995, Chicago, USA.

A student at the School of the Art Institute of Chicago in the late 1960s, Ramberg was a key figure in the thriving art scene that emerged in the city in those years. She is associated with the Chicago Imagists, a group of artists with differing styles but a shared interest in figurative painting (as opposed to the Minimalism and Conceptualism that predominated on the East Coast of the United States at the time). Ramberg had her first solo show at Phyllis Kind Gallery in Chicago in 1974; by this stage, she had already developed her distinctive visual language, as typified by *Istrian River Lady*. In her paintings, female body parts – torsos, feet, heads – are bound and fragmented, shown from behind or from the neck down to render them anonymous. Here, the figure of a woman is cropped so that only her torso is visible, tightly encased in an armour-like corset and stylized braids of hair. The bold lines, flat planes and restricted colour palette, influenced by comic strips, emphasize the geometry of the composition – and indeed, in the 1980s, before a degenerative illness forced her to stop working, Ramberg began to experiment more directly with geometric abstraction, both through painting and quilt-making.

HILLA REBAY

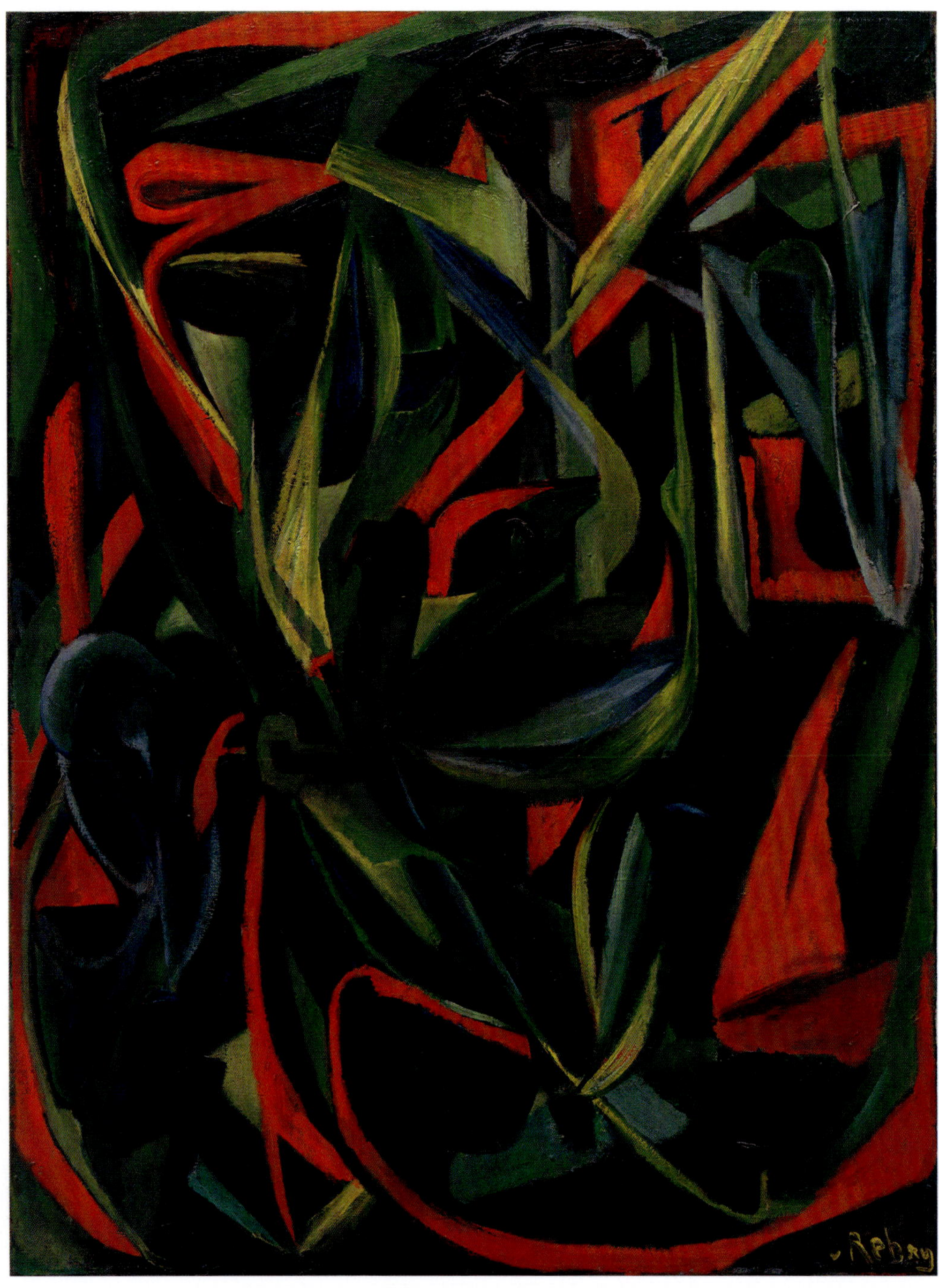

COMPOSITION I
1915, oil on canvas, 132.4 × 99.4 cm (52 ⅛ × 39 ⅛ in), Solomon R. Guggenheim Museum, New York, USA

Hilla Rebay, born 1890, Strasbourg, France. Died 1967, Westport, Connecticut, USA.

Born into an aristocratic family, Rebay displayed an early aptitude for art, combined with an interest in spirituality. Studies in Cologne and Paris were followed by a period at the Debschitz School in Munich, an experimental art school also attended by Sophie Taeuber-Arp (p.294), who would become a close friend and introduce her to the work of the artist group Der Blaue Reiter (The Blue Rider) and Russian abstractionism. Influenced by these rising avant-garde artistic innovations, Rebay entered a European arts scene inhabited by progressive artists and theorists. As the First World War erupted, an introduction to artworks freed from material representations, combined with new philosophies on spiritual abstraction, would further inform her artistic direction, as seen in this work of bold colour and dynamic composition. Rebay was particularly influenced by the work of Wassily Kandinsky (1866–1944), whose 1911 text *On the Spiritual in Art* she would later publish for the first time in English. A fascination with creating, collecting and championing abstract art would continue after immigrating to the United States in 1927. Rebay was instrumental in the establishment of the Museum of Non-Objective Painting in New York (later renamed the Solomon R. Guggenheim Museum), where she served as founding director.

ANITA RÉE

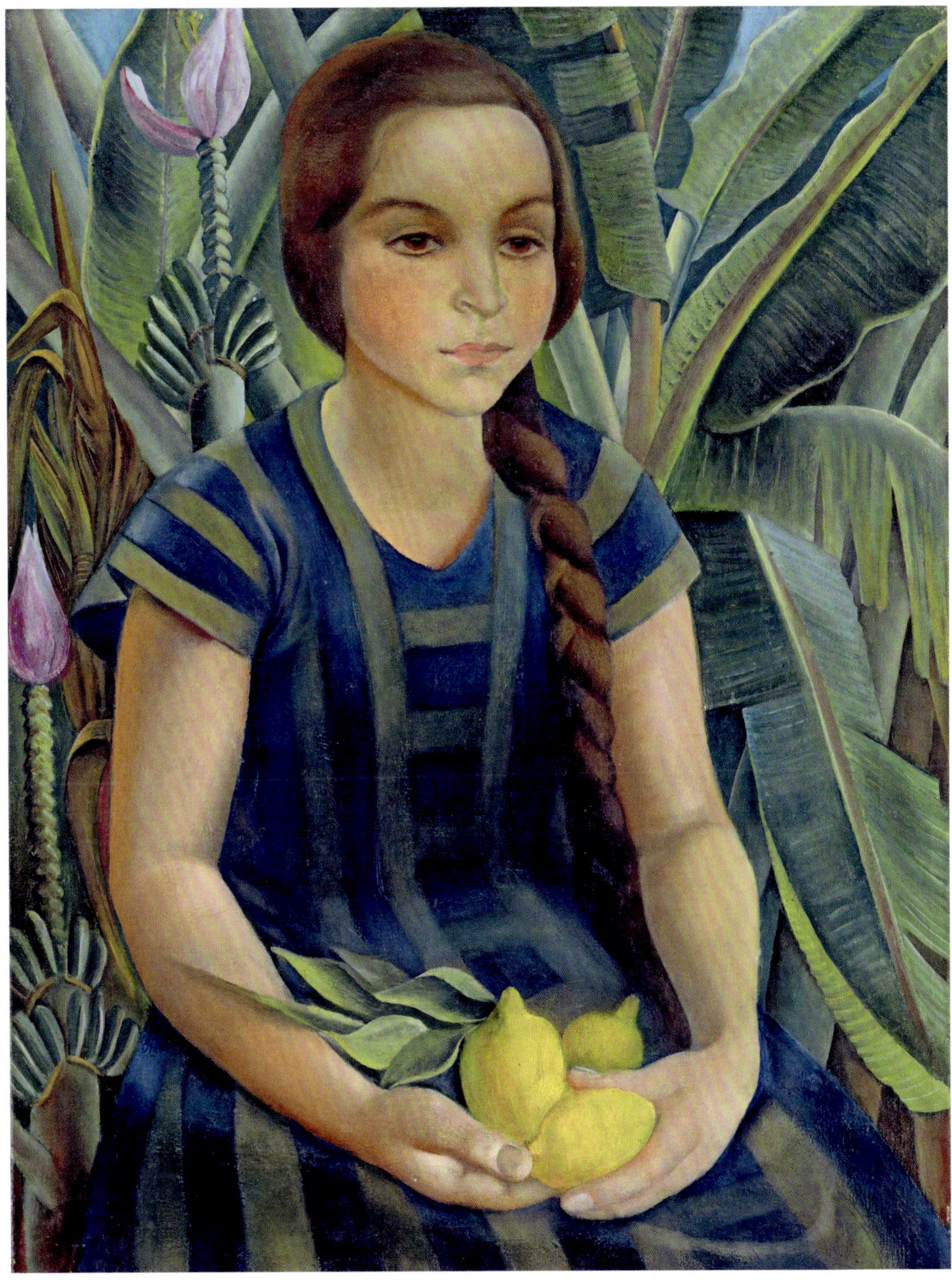

TERESINA
1922–5, oil on canvas, 80.5 × 60 cm (31 ¾ × 23 ⅝ in), Hamburger Kunsthalle, Hamburg, Germany

Anita Rée, born 1885, Hamburg, Germany. Died 1933, Kampen, Sylt, Germany.

A leading figurative painter in Weimar-era Hamburg, Rée was born to a wealthy Jewish family. The exclusion of women from art academies led her to study privately under Impressionist painter Arthur Siebelist (1870–1945) from 1905, and though she did not commit to a single style, her landscapes and portraits show the influence of Impressionism, as well as Cubism and Italian Renaissance painting. Rée's German and Venezuelan heritage fuelled a preoccupation with identity, and many of her portraits reflect an interest in people of foreign origins – or of the self as a foreign being in itself. In 1922, after visiting Paris, Tyrol and the Amalfi Coast, she settled in Positano, Italy, where she painted landscapes and portraits emphasizing her sitters' individuality in the Neue Sachlichkeit (New Objectivity) style – as seen in this portrait of a wistful peasant girl clutching fresh lemons, the major local crop. Her acclaimed Italian paintings led to numerous portrait commissions on her return to Hamburg. However, with the rise of Nazism and increasing antisemitism, she exiled herself to the island of Sylt, eventually taking her own life. The Nazis designated her paintings 'degenerate', though many were saved by a caretaker at the Hamburger Kunsthalle.

PAULA REGO

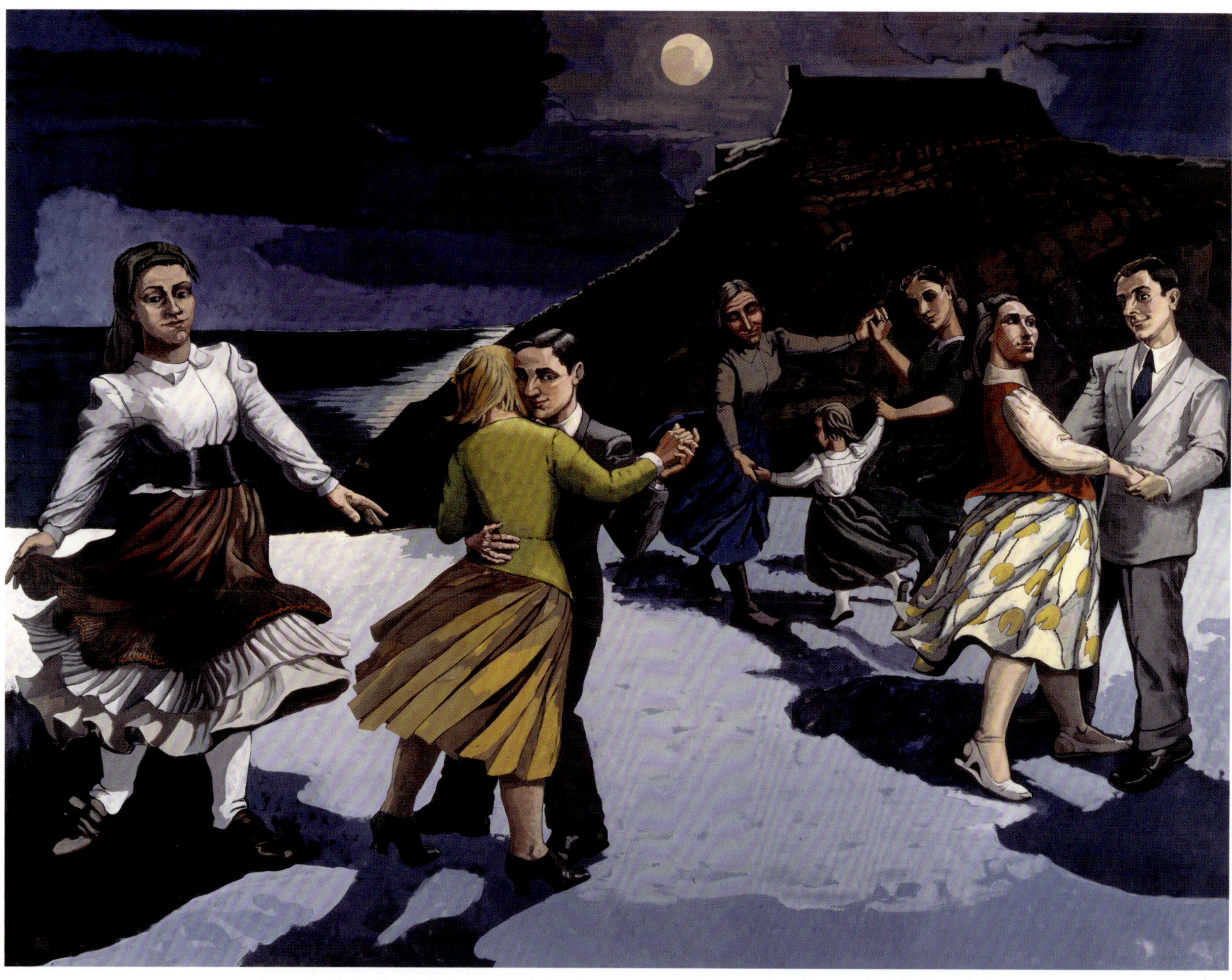

THE DANCE
1988, acrylic on paper on canvas, 213.3 × 274.3 cm (84 × 108 in), Tate, London, UK

Paula Rego, born 1935, Lisbon, Portugal.

Childhood memories, Portuguese folk tales and issues relating to women's rights are among the many reference points in Rego's enchanting yet disquieting narrative paintings. Growing up under Portugal's repressive Estado Novo (New State) regime, she was sent to finishing school in England, after which she attended the Slade School of Fine Art from 1952 to 1956, where she met her future husband, the painter Victor Willing (1928–88). Themes of fear, innocence and the dynamics of power pulse through her intense, psychologically charged compositions, many of which spark with erotic undercurrents. Strongly influenced by Surrealism, Rego's dreamlike paintings express an inner world where fiercely independent women and girls frequently appear as protagonists. This monumental moonlit scene features eight dancing figures on a beach. Two women and a girl twirl in a circle behind Rego's husband, who appears twice with different partners, while a much larger woman in traditional Portuguese costume dances alone. Representing the stages of a woman's life, from childhood to old age, the painting is also a memorial to Willing, who died before its completion.

SEUNDJA RHEE

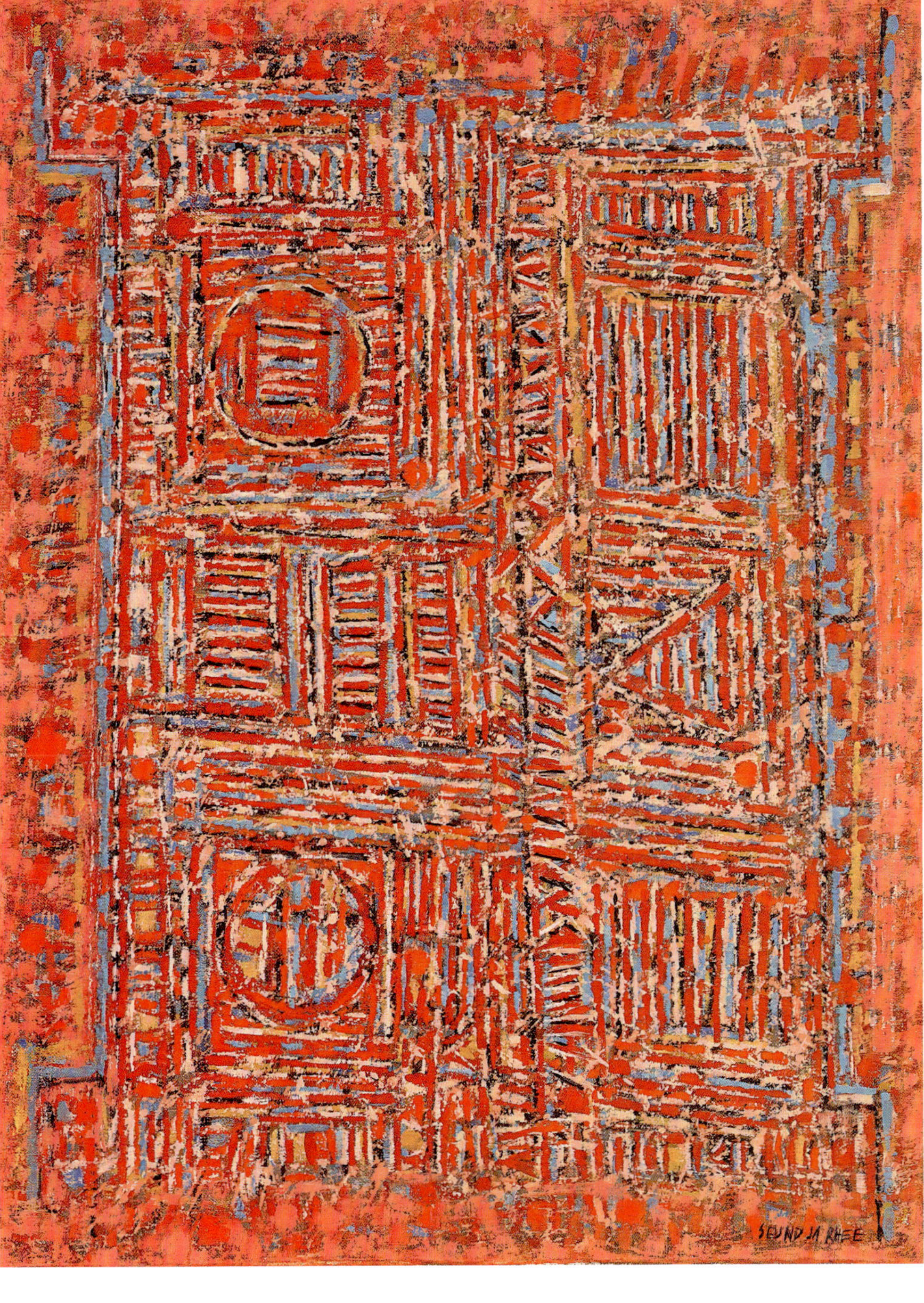

RED EARTH
1961, oil on canvas, 60.6 × 45.7 cm (23 ⅞ × 18 in)

Seundja Rhee, born 1918, Jinju, South Gyeongsang Province, South Korea. Died 2009, Paris, France.

A year after the start of the Korean War (1950–3), Rhee left South Korea for France, intent on pursuing her ambitions as an artist abroad. Arriving in Paris in 1951, aged thirty-three, she later enrolled at the Académie de la Grande Chaumière, where she studied painting with modernist artist Henri Goetz (1909–89) and began to adopt a language of abstraction in her work. Although she spent her formative artistic years in France, Rhee's work remained rooted in Korean sensibilities and images. The dazzling, mosaic-like compositions she began to make in the 1960s, for which she would become known, were grounded in the Eastern philosophical concepts of yin and yang, whereby apparently opposing elements are in fact shown to be complementary and interconnected. In her paintings, Rhee often took the Earth and mountains as points of departure in a palette of reds and blues – the colours of the Korean flag. *Red Earth* is an early painting from her 'Woman and Earth' series and represents a period in which Rhee began to employ repetition and geometric forms in her work, applied in a dense web of thick, expressive layers of paint.

BRIDGET RILEY

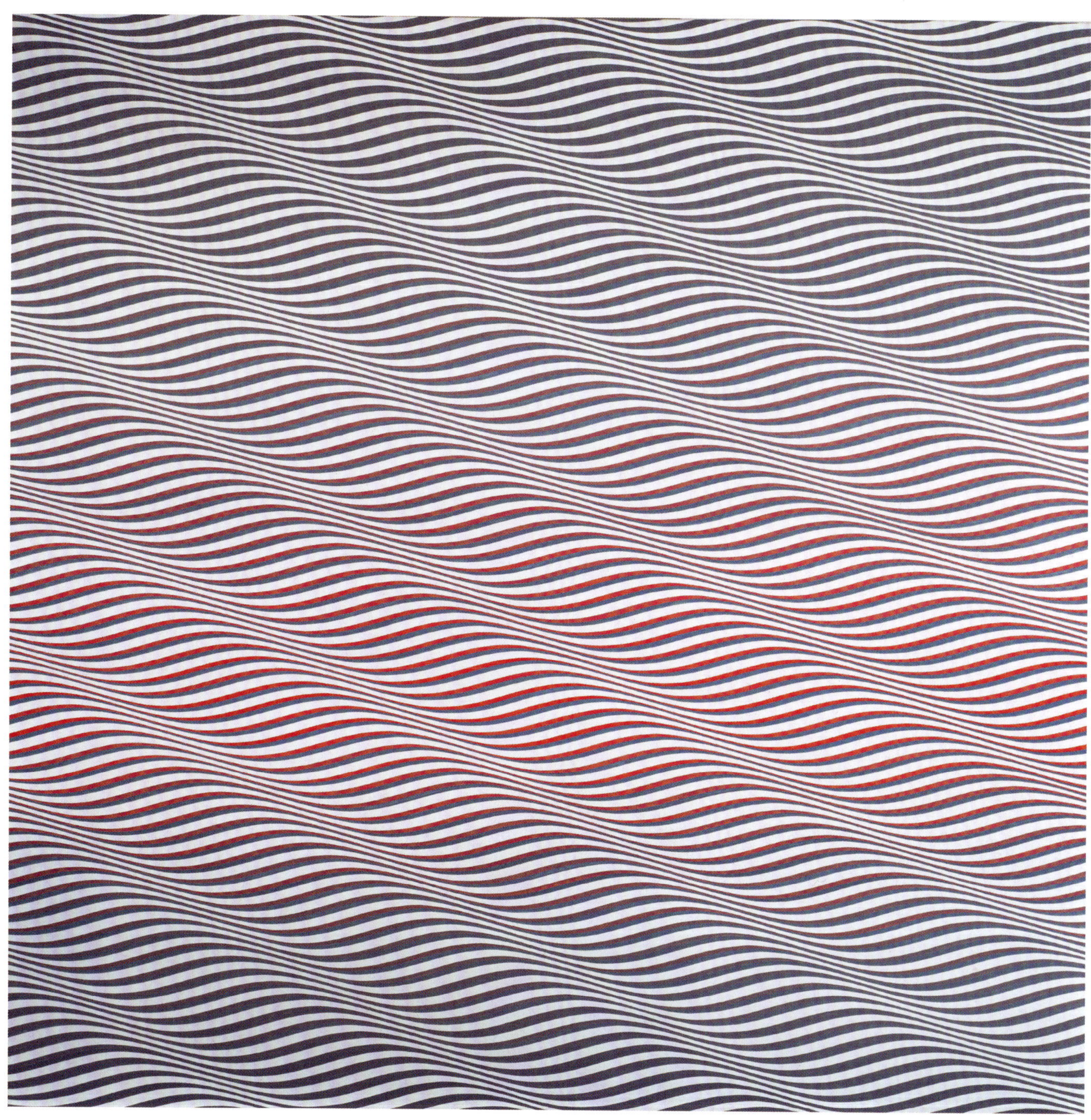

CATARACT 3
1967, emulsion and PVA on linen, 221.9 × 222.9 cm (87 ⅜ × 87 ¾ in), British Council Collection, UK

Bridget Riley, born 1931, London, UK.

Coming to prominence in the 1960s, Riley was a leading figure in the international Op art movement, using the interplay of line, shape and pattern to create the illusion of movement. Her striking geometric compositions featuring squares, circles, ovals and stripes draw inspiration from diverse sources, in particular the pointillist paintings of Georges Seurat (1859–91) and the Cornish coast, which she explored as a child after being evacuated from London during the Second World War. As with Seurat, nothing in Riley's paintings is left to chance, and each composition is painstakingly planned out on paper before being committed to canvas. Having initially worked in black and white, she introduced colour to her practice in 1967. This iconic work from her 'Cataract' series (1967) is painted with mathematical precision; its undulating red and turquoise bands appear to vibrate, creating a shimmering effect that evokes the waves of the sea. Soon after completing the series, Riley represented Great Britain at the 1968 Venice Biennale, where she became the first woman to win the prestigious International Prize for Painting.

FAITH RINGGOLD

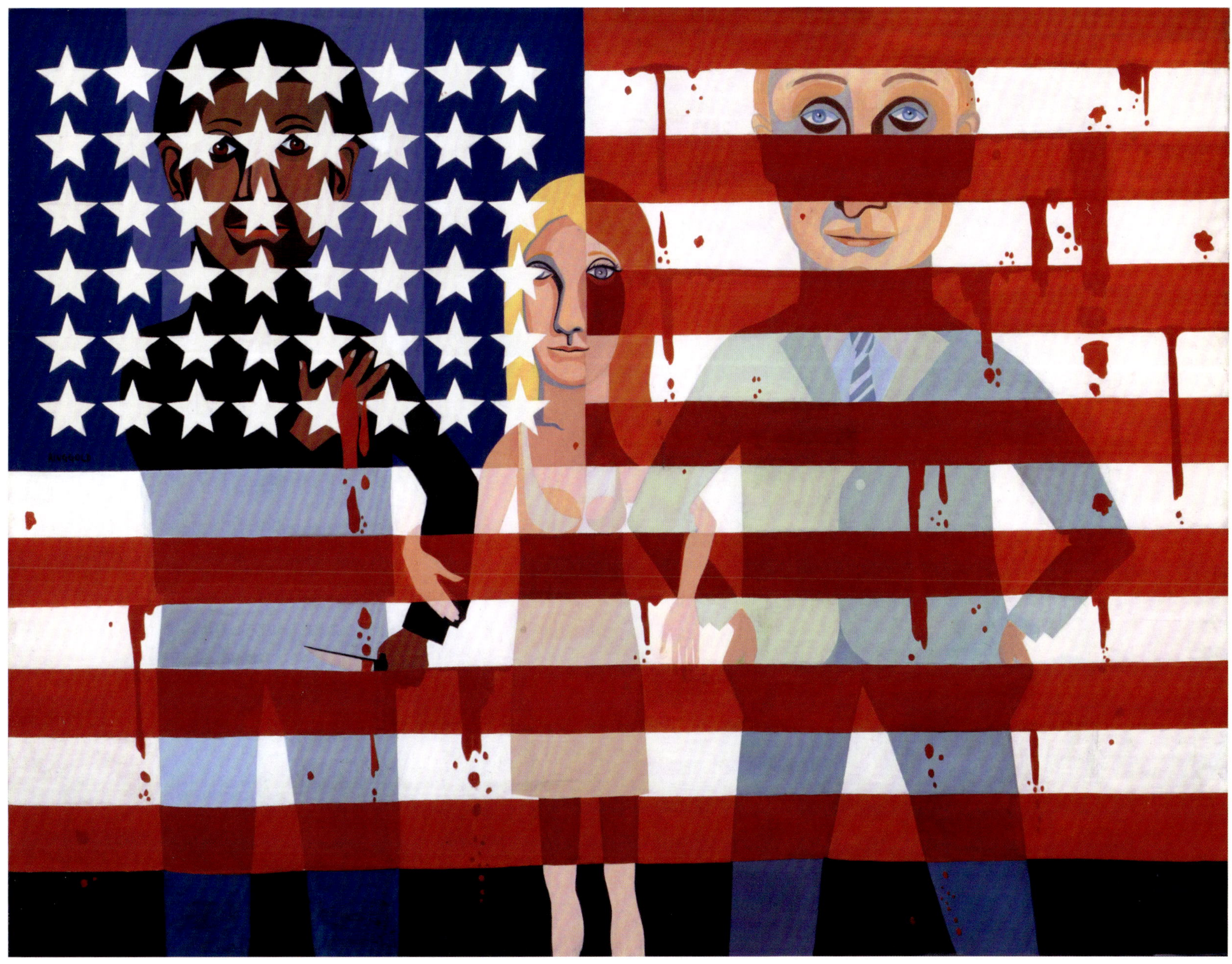

AMERICAN PEOPLE SERIES #18: THE FLAG IS BLEEDING
1967, oil on canvas, 182.9 × 243.8 cm (72 × 96 in), National Gallery of Art, Washington DC, USA

Faith Ringgold, born 1930, New York, USA.

Ringgold's varied creative practice encompasses painting, sculpture, performance, textiles, works on paper and children's books. Executed over the course of her extensive career, her self-consciously Black and feminist works are social, political and personal statements that celebrate and record the Black experience while denouncing the harsh actualities of race in the United States. Against the backdrop of the civil rights movement, Ringgold developed her mature, 'Super Realist' style – characterized by flat passages of high key colour – and committed herself to subject matter that interlaced her politics with her artistic practice. This union premiered in her 'American People Series' (1963–7), a group of paintings that unflinchingly depict racial strife between white and Black Americans. The series culminated with three mural-sized paintings, including *American People Series #18: The Flag Is Bleeding*, which portrays an American flag dripping with blood superimposed over a white couple linking arms with a Black man who holds a knife and places his hand over his heart. The monumental canvas embodies the contradiction between American ideals of equality and the country's realities of racism and racial hierarchies.

MARY ROBERTS

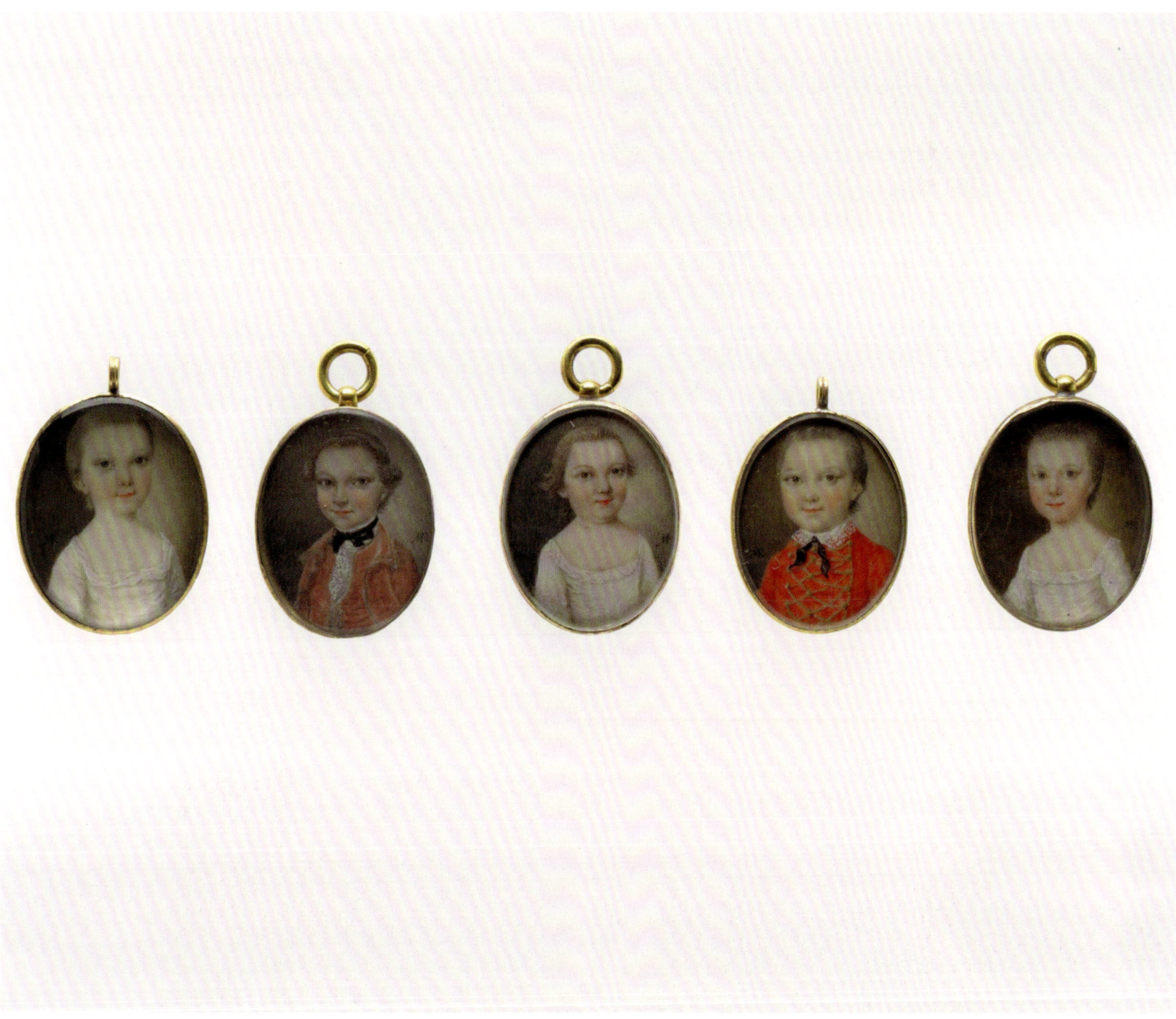

HESTER, WILLIAM, THOMAS, WILLIAMS AND HENRIETTA MIDDLETON
*c.*1752–8, watercolour on ivory, each: 3.8 × 2.5 cm (1 ½ × 1 in), Metropolitan Museum of Art, New York, USA

Mary Roberts, died 1761, Charleston, South Carolina, USA.

Little is known today about Roberts's biography, but she has the distinction of being North America's first woman miniaturist as well as the first-known American miniaturist to paint on ivory. She seems to have gone into business as an artist following the death of her husband, Bishop Roberts, himself an artist, in 1740. Roberts's use of watercolour on ivory was a technical feat, requiring immaculate precision and skill, the smooth surface of ivory being resistant to paint. In the eighteenth century, ivory became the fashionable material for miniature painting in England, and it is possible that Roberts developed her own technique by mimicking imported examples. Miniatures like these were often given as gifts to mark births, marriages or deaths, sometimes accompanied by a lock of the subject's hair or an inscription set into the frame. The small size of these portraits enabled them to be cradled in the hands, tucked in pockets or worn on the body as intimate mementoes. The group of miniatures seen here depicts children who, though cousins, were separated by the vast expanse of the Atlantic, united in painted form by Roberts's consistent style and composition.

MARIETTA ROBUSTI

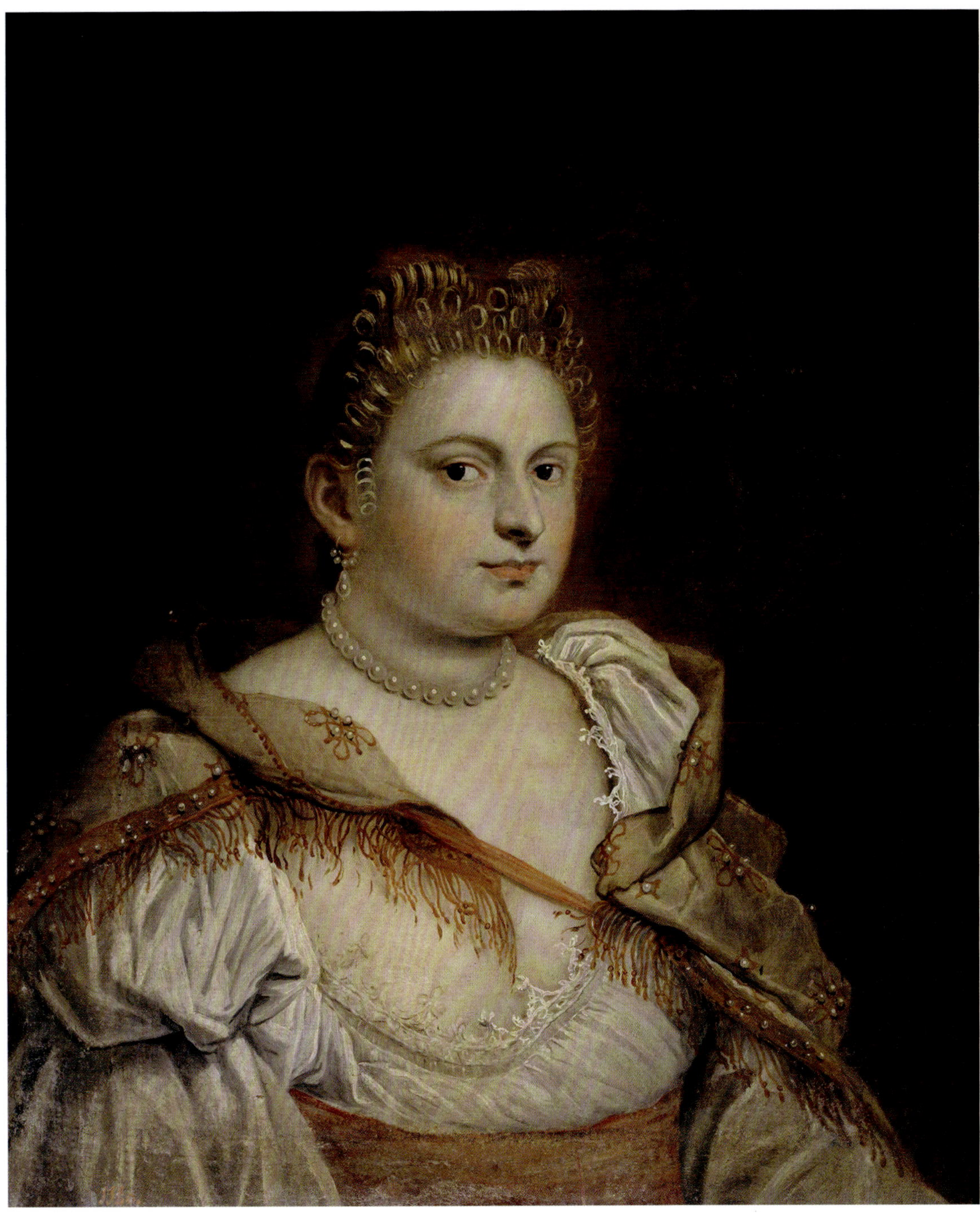

DAMA VENECIANA (VENETIAN LADY)
16th century, oil on canvas, 77 × 65 cm
(30¼ × 25⅝ in), Museo del Prado, Madrid, Spain

Marietta Robusti, born *c.*1550–60, Venice, Italy.
Died 1590, Venice.

The daughter of one of Renaissance Venice's premier painters, Tintoretto (Jacopo Robusti, *c.*1518–94), Robusti wanted so dearly to follow in her father's footsteps that he dressed her as a boy in order to fit in with her brothers and the apprentices in his bustling workshop. One of her surviving drawings from her apprenticeship shows two studies of male heads based on ancient sculptures in her father's workshop, testifying to her ability to quickly capture an accurate likeness and illustrating how early women artists often learnt to draw the male body through recourse to sculpture. After marrying, Robusti continued to answer the demand for her stylized portraits, gaining such renown that she received her own nickname, 'La Tintoretta'. This painting, rendered in a warm, golden palette suited to night-time viewing by candlelight, shows a fashionable Venetian woman who is likely a courtesan in light of her exposed (and overpainted) breast and direct gaze. The details suggest how women envisioned the ideal of female beauty: an elaborate hairstyle modelled after those seen on ancient Roman portrait busts; a glowing, porcelain complexion; a choker of large, perfect pearls; and luxurious clothing such as this satin shawl embroidered with pearls.

ERNA ROSENSTEIN

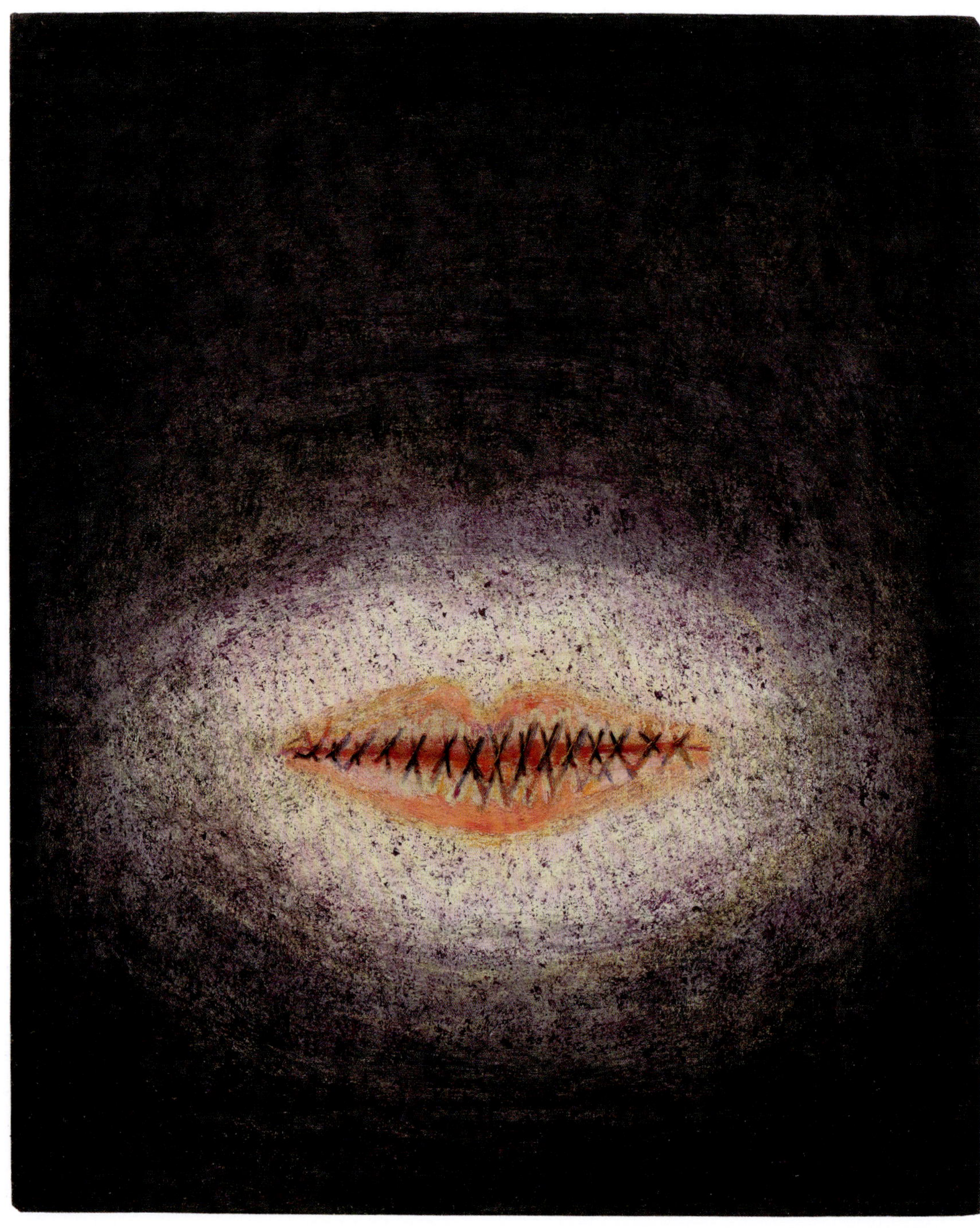

USTA (LIPS)
1989, oil and string on canvas, 46.4 × 38.7 × 1.9 cm
(18 ¼ × 15 ¼ × ¾ in)

Erna Rosenstein, born 1913, Lviv, Ukraine.
Died 2004, Warsaw, Poland.

Born to an upper-middle-class Jewish family, Rosenstein grew up in Kraków, where she studied at the Academy of Fine Arts between 1934 and 1937. It was there that she became associated with the avant-garde Grupa Krakowska, headed up by revolutionary artist and theatre director Tadeusz Kantor (1915–90). In 1938 Rosenstein visited the International Surrealist Exhibition in Paris and the 'Degenerate Art' exhibition in Berlin; these shows had a profound influence on her work, which would come to incorporate Surrealist, Expressionist and abstract elements. None of Rosenstein's pre-war work survives: after the Nazi occupation, her family was sent to the Lwów ghetto where, while attempting to escape, her parents were murdered. The memory of witnessing this traumatic event haunts many of Rosenstein's paintings and assemblages, including *Usta* (*Lips*), in which the literally sewn-together and disembodied lips demonstrate her use of symbolic imagery to explore a painful past. After the war Rosenstein stayed in Poland but refused to work in the Socialist Realist style mandated under Stalinism, committing instead to her experimental fusion of avant-garde styles.

SUSAN ROTHENBERG

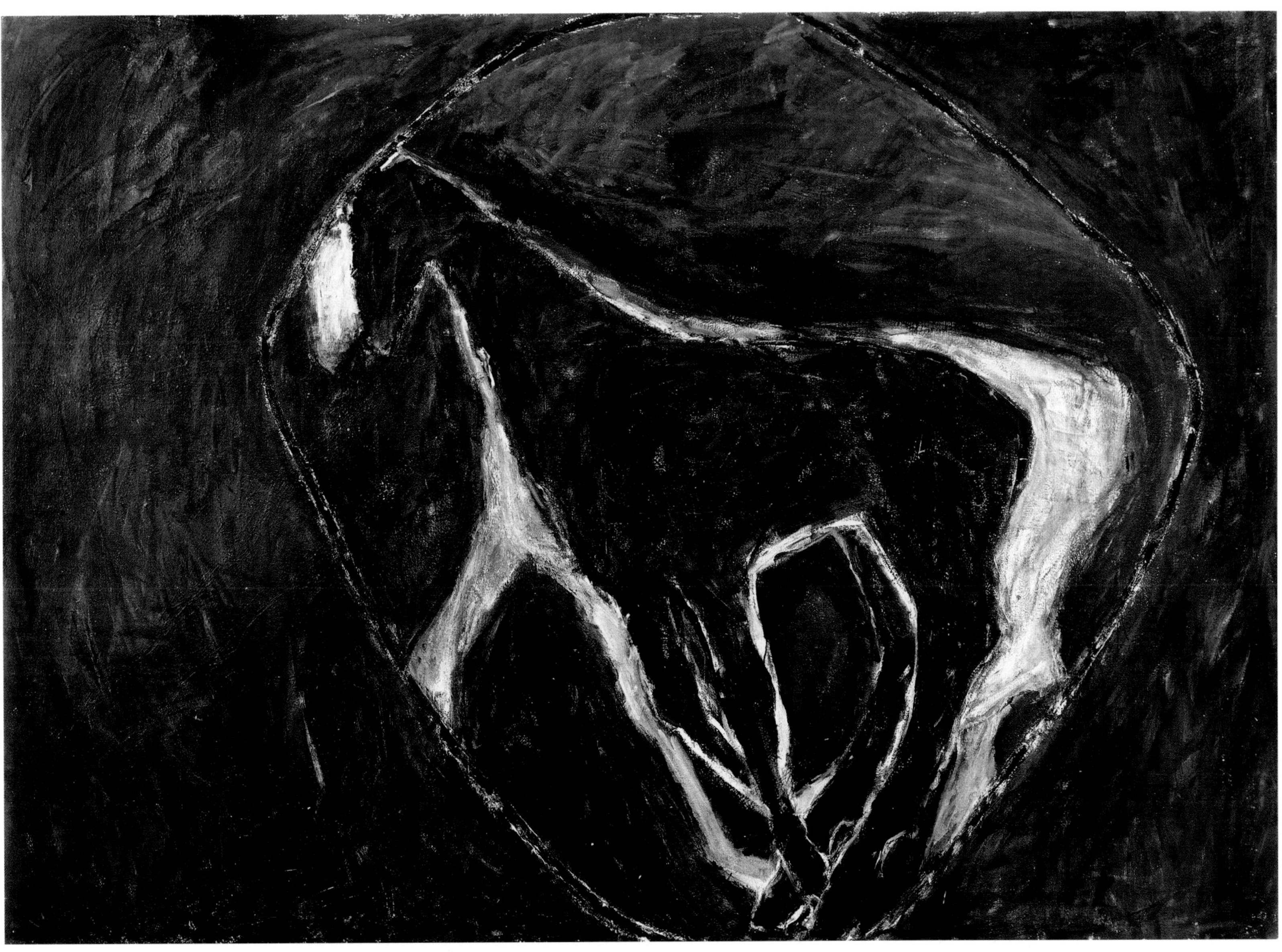

KELPIE
1978, acrylic and Flashe on canvas, 196.8 × 280 cm (77½ × 109 in)

Susan Rothenberg, born 1945, Buffalo, New York, USA. Died 2020, Galisteo, New Mexico, USA.

Although she dreamed of becoming a sculptor, Rothenberg switched to painting while still a student at Cornell University in the late 1960s, a time when the medium was waning in popularity thanks to the dominant movements of Minimalism and Conceptualism. Rothenberg's breakthrough moment came in 1975 at the 112 Greene Street art space in New York, when she exhibited three large canvases depicting the pared-down, quasi-abstract form of a horse, the subject for which she would become best known. She had chosen the horse as a replacement for the human figure, explaining in a 1992 interview with *The Buffalo News*, 'People look at the image of a horse and they have associations – of power, movement, heaviness. It's a living thing.' As seen in *Kelpie*, Rothenberg typically placed the horse's schematic silhouette in a flat, abstract ground, restricting herself to a simple colour palette. After moving to New Mexico in the 1990s, Rothenberg's subject matter shifted, ranging from birds to fragmented human body parts and scenes from everyday life, often rendered in short strokes of thickly layered paint.

RACHEL RUYSCH

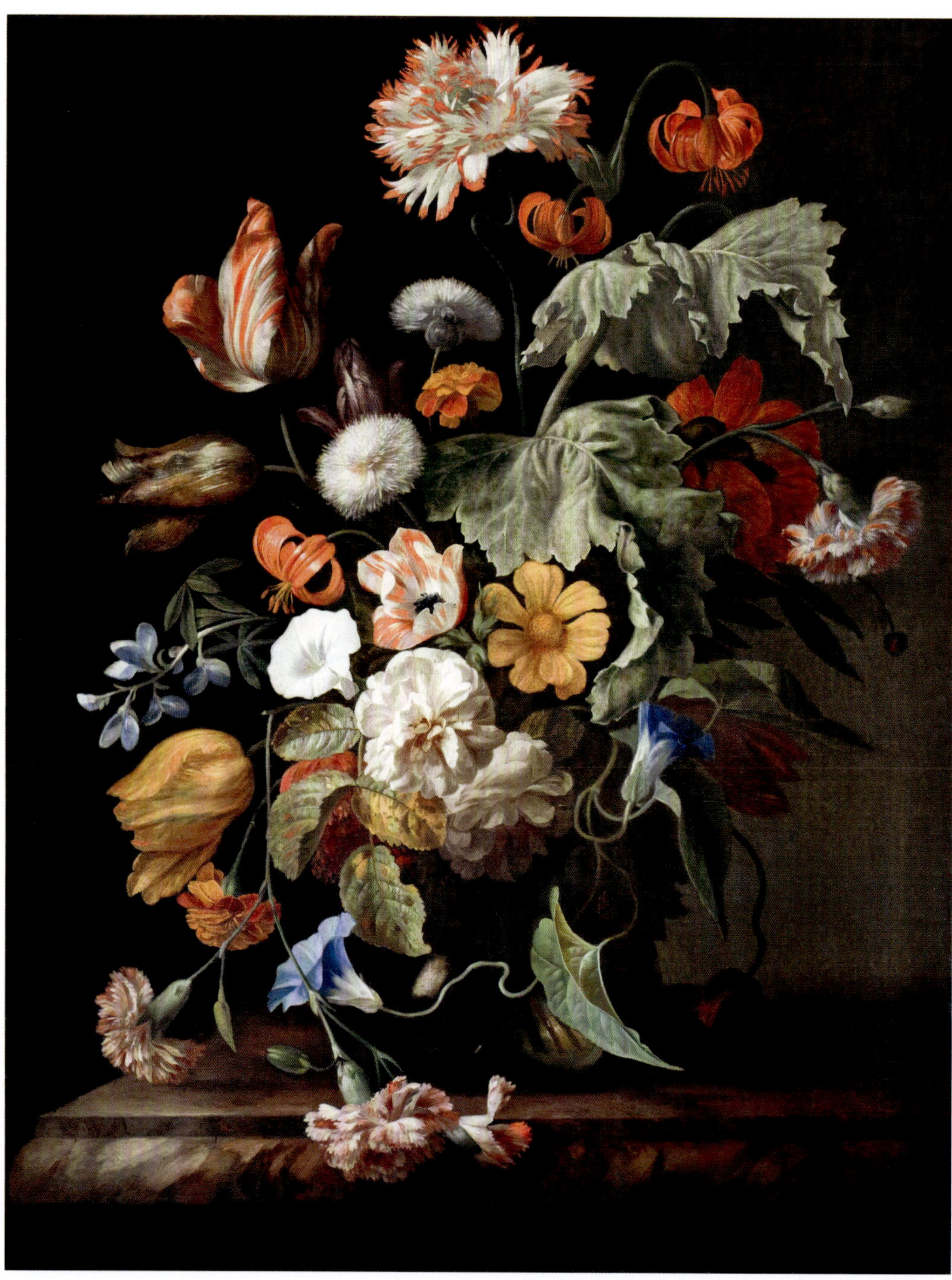

BLOMSTERSTYCKE (STILL-LIFE WITH FLOWERS)
date unknown, oil on canvas, 75 × 58.5 cm
(29½ × 23 in), Hallwylska Museet, Stockholm,
Sweden

Rachel Ruysch, born 1664, The Hague, Netherlands.
Died 1750, Amsterdam, Netherlands.

One of the most admired still-life painters of her time, Ruysch was encouraged to develop her artistic skills by her father, a professor of anatomy and botany. Her carefully observed studies of his botanic samples equipped Ruysch with an advantageous knowledge of her future subject matter. By the age of fifteen the artist gained an apprenticeship to flower painter Willem van Aelst (1627–83), and she soon began selling her own artworks. Ruysch produced still-life compositions focused on native and imported flora, including the newly arrived and mania-inducing tulip, with meticulous detail and a distinct colour palette. Her marriage to fellow painter Juriaen Pool (1666–1745) and the birth of her ten children did not end an unusually successful career for a woman of the age. Around the turn of the century, Ruysch and her family moved to The Hague, where she became the first female member of the city's artists' society, Confrerie Pictura. In 1708 she was named court painter to the Elector Palatine of Bavaria, Johann Wilhelm. Ruysch continued to receive commissions from prominent international clients into her early eighties, a testament to her reputation as one of the foremost flower painters of the Dutch Golden Age.

KAY SAGE

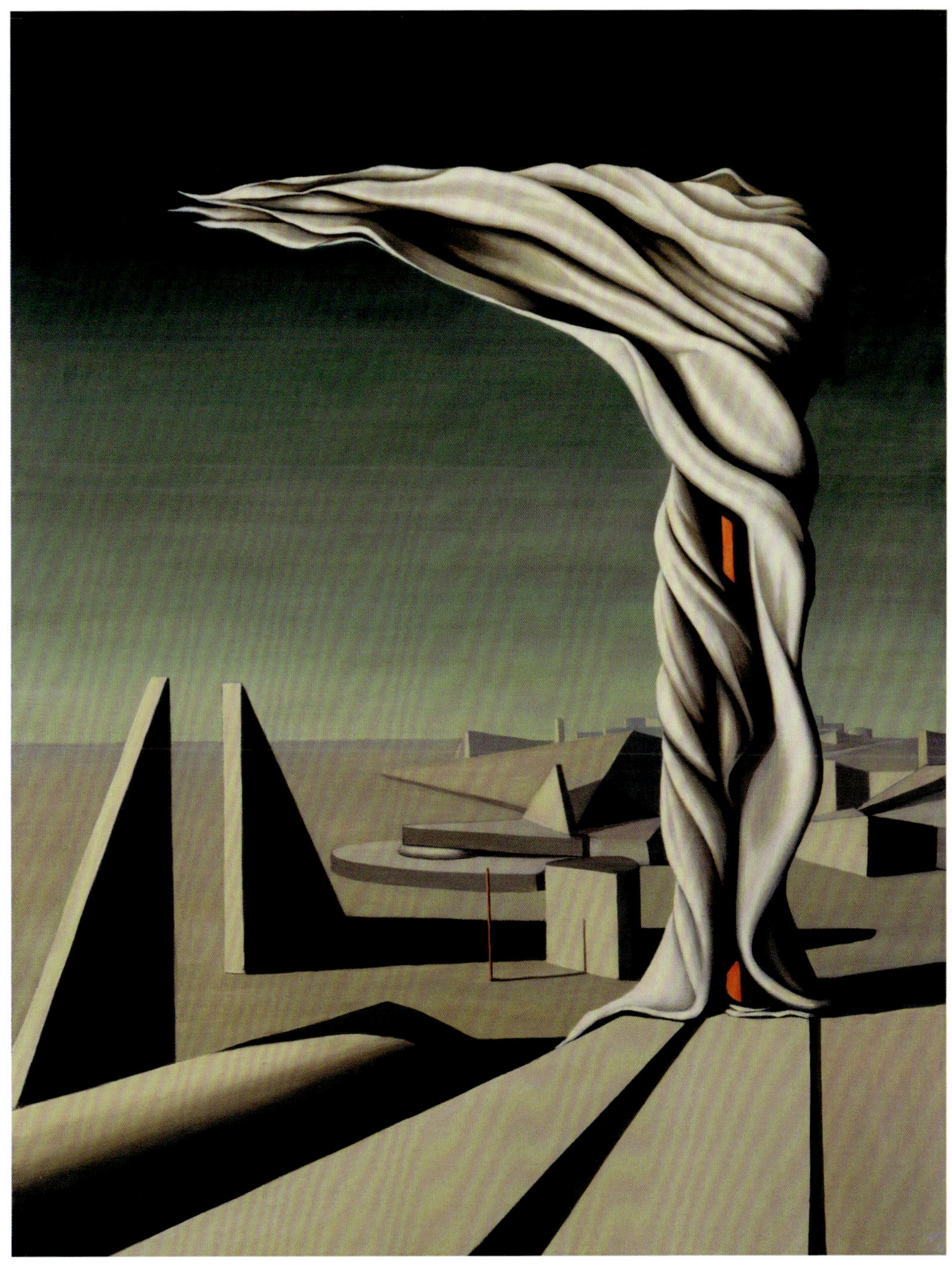

I SAW THREE CITIES
1944, oil on canvas, 92 × 71 cm (36 ¼ × 28 in), Princeton University Art Museum, New Jersey, USA

Kay Sage, born 1898, Albany, New York, USA. Died 1963, Woodbury, Connecticut, USA.

Sage's brooding metaphysical landscapes stage uncanny juxtapositions of movement and stasis against logically perspectival grounds. One of the few North American artists associated with Surrealism, Sage exhibited six Surrealist oil paintings in the 1938 Salon des Surindépendants in Paris, where her work caught the attention of André Breton (1896–1966) and her eventual husband, Yves Tanguy (1900–55). Sage's still, ominous scenes are haunted with psychological intensity and often boast a muted, restrained palette. Characteristic of her most important works made between 1940 and 1955 – when she returned to the United States from Europe ahead of the Second World War (staying until her husband's death in 1955) – *I Saw Three Cities* is tense and precarious, devoid of human life, toggling between the fantastical and the logical. The cold stasis of the landscape is punctured by flowing fabric surrounding a red rod, a humanoid reference to the ancient Greek statue *Nike of Samothrace* (*c.* 190 BCE, in the Louvre). Sage harnessed the visual vocabulary of Surrealism to create otherworldly landscapes, inhabited only by shadows and dreamlike entities, that nod towards the possibility of human life beyond their frames.

CHARLOTTE SALOMON

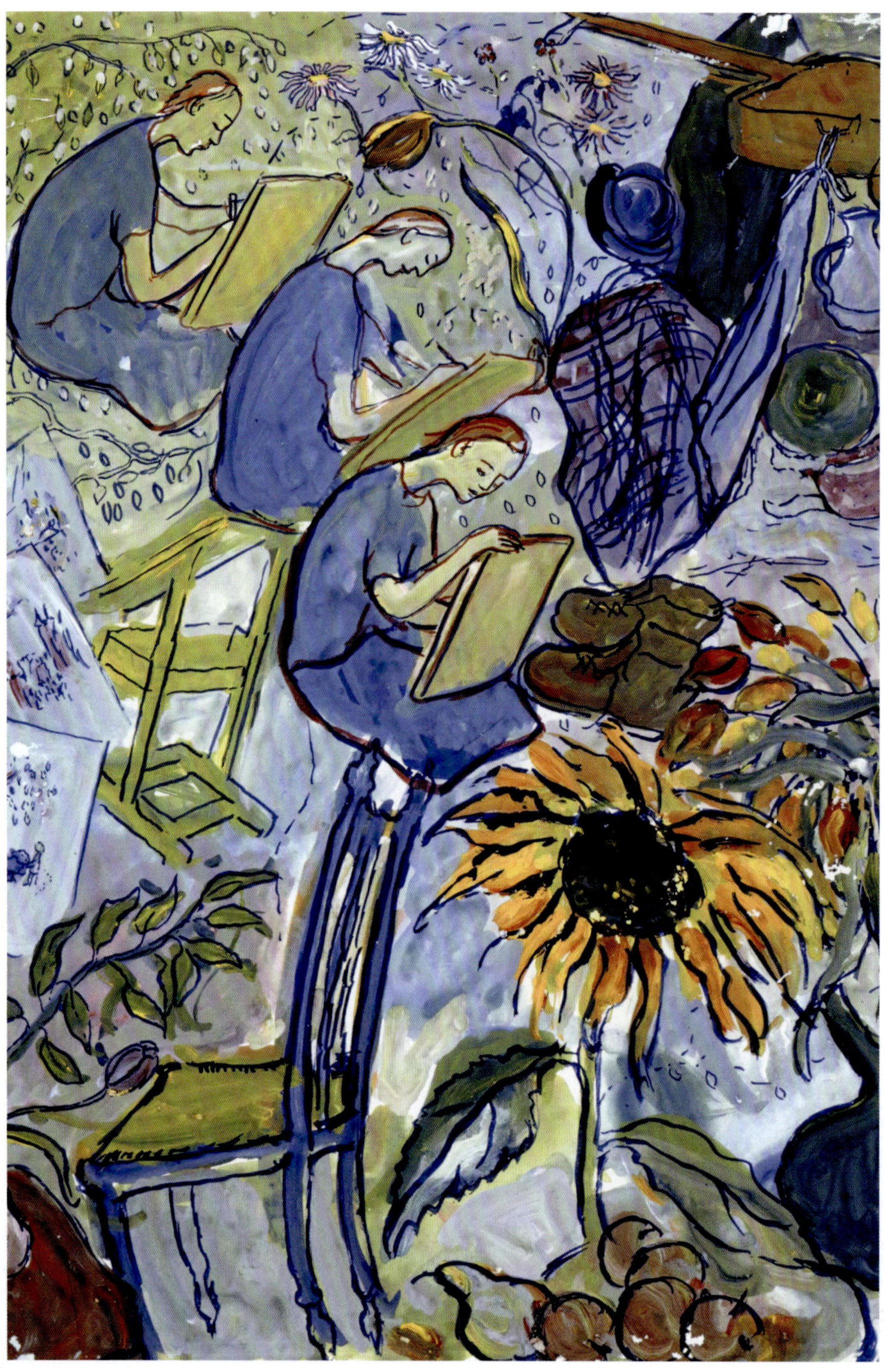

FROM LEBEN? ODER THEATER? EIN SINGSPIEL (LIFE? OR THEATRE? A SONG-CYCLE)
*c.*1940–2, gouache on paper, 32.5 × 25 cm (12 ¾ × 9 ⅞ in), Joods Historisch Museum, Amsterdam, Netherlands

Charlotte Salomon, born 1917, Berlin, Germany. Died 1943, Auschwitz, Poland.

While hiding from the Nazis in the South of France, German-Jewish artist Salomon completed a series of around eight hundred gouache paintings enigmatically titled 'Leben? oder Theater? Ein singspiel' ('Life? Or Theatre? A Song-Cycle'). Salomon had studied painting in Berlin before the policies of Hitler's Third Reich forbade her from attending class. Begun as a way to ward off mental disintegration, Salomon's series re-created the moments of her own life in a continuous narrative made up of both images and text, preserving events of historical import and adding in elements of fantasy. The work illustrated here conveys the escape and solace that Salomon found in art-making. She depicts the protagonist – a semi-fictional version of herself – through three unfolding figures lost in concentration as they work, while Van Gogh–like imagery swirls against a soft colour field. This style of presenting successive views on a single page evokes the aesthetic of storyboards, suggesting cinema as a source of inspiration for the artist. Salomon was captured by Nazis in October 1943 and killed in the gas chambers at Auschwitz. After the end of the war, her father and stepmother – who had survived, hiding in the Netherlands – found her paintings and donated them to Amsterdam's Jewish Historical Museum in 1971.

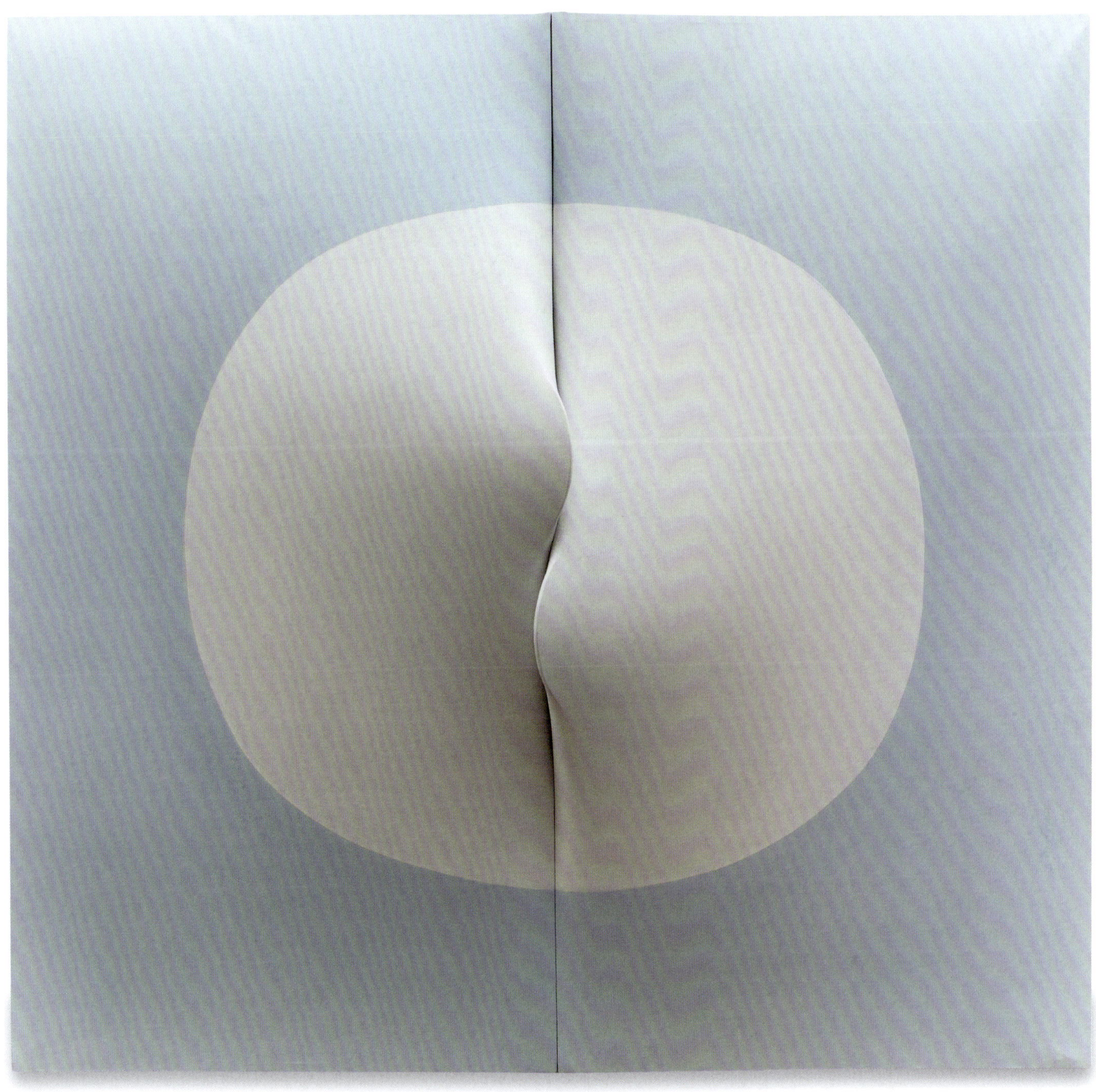

LUNAR V [MOON V]
c.1973, acrylic on stretched canvas, 189.9 × 201.9 × 25.4 cm (74 ¾ × 79 ½ × 10 in), private collection

Zilia Sánchez, born 1926, Havana, Cuba.

An early proponent of non-figurative art in Cuba in the 1950s, Sánchez developed her signature technique of stretching canvas over handmade wooden armatures after noticing the laundered sheet from her father's deathbed being blown against a pipe. She studied painting at the Escuela Nacional de Bellas Artes de San Alejandro in Havana, where she also designed theatre sets and furniture. During the Cuban Revolution, she represented Cuba at the 1958 Mexico Biennial and the 1959 São Paulo Biennial, after which she moved to New York in 1963 before settling permanently in Puerto Rico in the early 1970s. The undulating curves, folds and contours of her relief paintings bring a sensuality to the cool objectivity of Minimalism. Their protruding shapes are evocative of breasts and other female body parts, and though the two interlocking forms in this blue and white example are more ambiguous, they are no less evocative; with characteristic balance and symmetry, they emerge from a vertical crease, suggesting an intimate embrace. Identifying as a queer artist, Sánchez described her paintings in a 2016 *Ocula Magazine* interview as interior self-portraits that 'show what I am hiding'.

JENNY SAVILLE

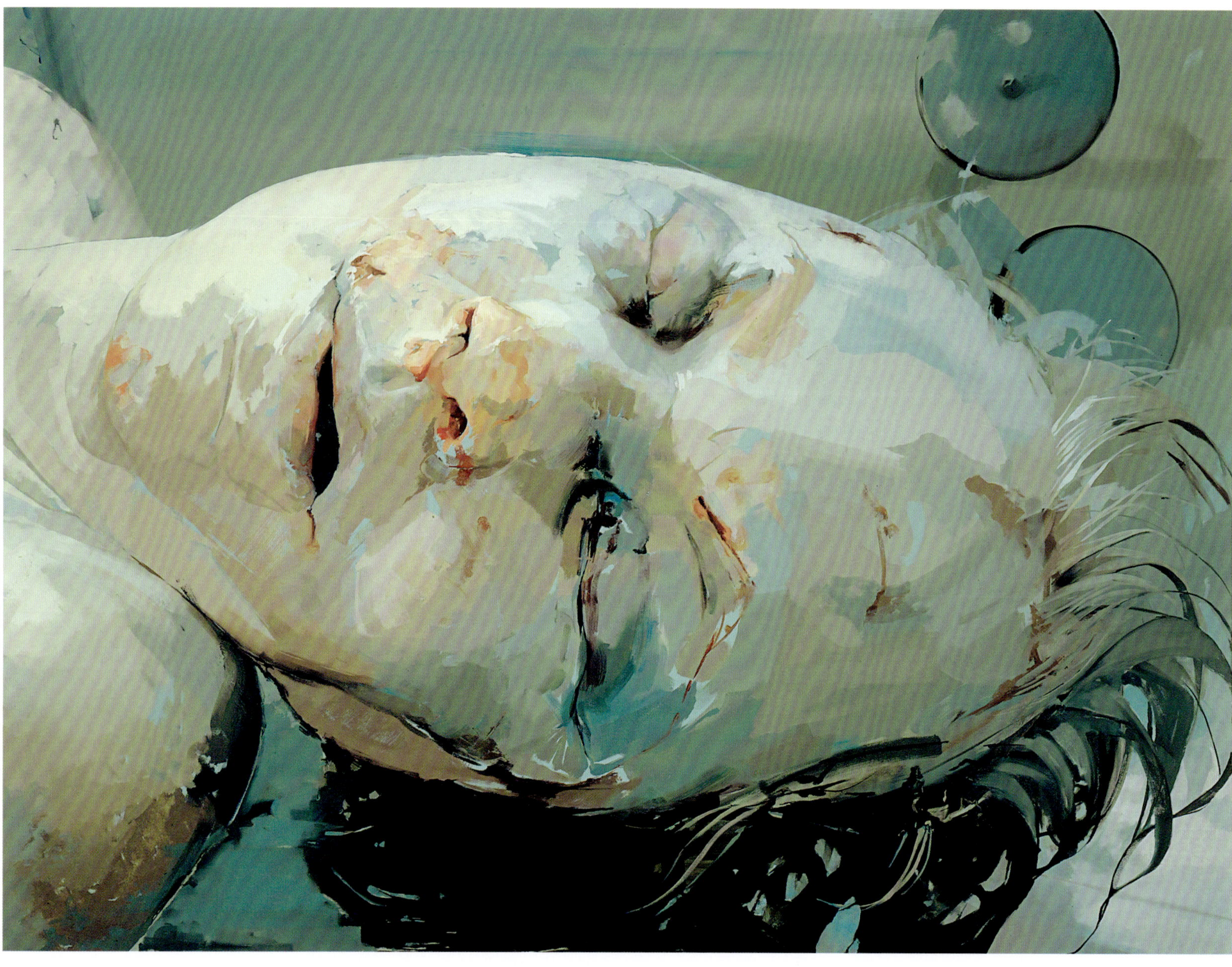

STILL
2003, oil on canvas, 274.3 × 366.1 cm
(108 × 144 ⅛ in), Metropolitan Museum of Art,
New York, USA

Jenny Saville, born 1970, Cambridge, UK.

Through the large-scale, visceral figurative paintings for which she is known, Saville investigates the complexities of the body with lavish attention paid to the materiality of human flesh. After graduating from Glasgow School of Art in 1992, Saville rose to prominence through her inclusion in the 'Young British Artists III' exhibition at London's Saatchi Gallery in 1994 and 'Sensation: Young British Artists from the Saatchi Collection' at the Royal Academy of Arts, London, in 1997. In 1994, while on a fellowship in Connecticut, Saville observed a New York plastic surgeon at work, a formative experience that deepened her fascination with flesh and how bodies are resilient yet vulnerable. These influences can be seen in *Still*, in which a woman's wounded face and shoulders are rendered in muted grey, green and blue hues. Based on a photograph of a woman in a morgue, the work is emblematic of Saville's heavy layers of brushwork that draw a connection between the materiality of flesh and oil paint itself, while challenging traditions of the perception of bodies and their representation in the history of figurative painting.

MIRIAM SCHAPIRO

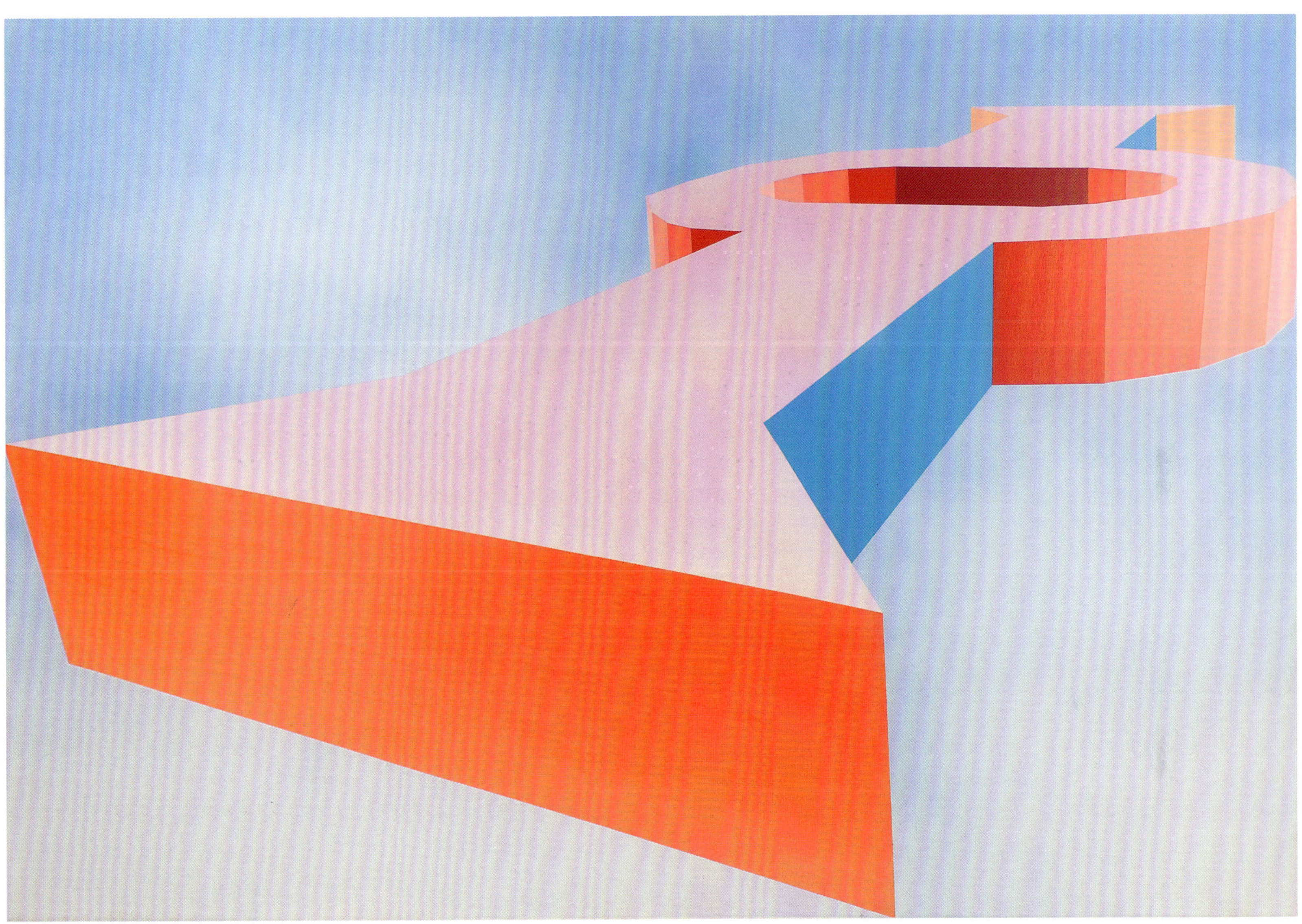

KEYHOLE
1971, acrylic and spray paint on canvas,
28.2 × 41.7 cm (71 ½ × 106 in)

Miriam Schapiro, born 1923, Toronto, Canada.
Died 2015, Hampton Bays, New York, USA.

A leading and foundational figure of American feminist art and of the Pattern and Decoration movement, Schapiro is best known for her 'femmages', a term she coined with painter Melissa Meyer (b. 1946), joining the words 'female' and 'collages'. Begun in the early 1970s, these works combine painting with modes of making historically associated with women and the domestic sphere, including craft and decorative arts practices such as quilting and lacemaking. By incorporating objects and approaches identified with women, Schapiro pointed out and challenged the hierarchies, values and norms of the art world, stretching the boundaries of the modern paradigm with which her early work engaged. Schapiro began her career as an Abstract Expressionist in the 1950s before pivoting to a hard-edged minimal vocabulary the following decade. By 1970, she was producing brilliantly coloured large-scale abstractions, like *Keyhole*, with the assistance of a computer, making her one of the first painters to embrace this technology in the service of art-making. Working with physicist David Nalibof, who commissioned a bespoke program to digitally transform her drawings, these paintings are Schapiro's first works created through collaboration, something that would become a central feature of her later feminist practice.

HÉLÈNE SCHJERFBECK

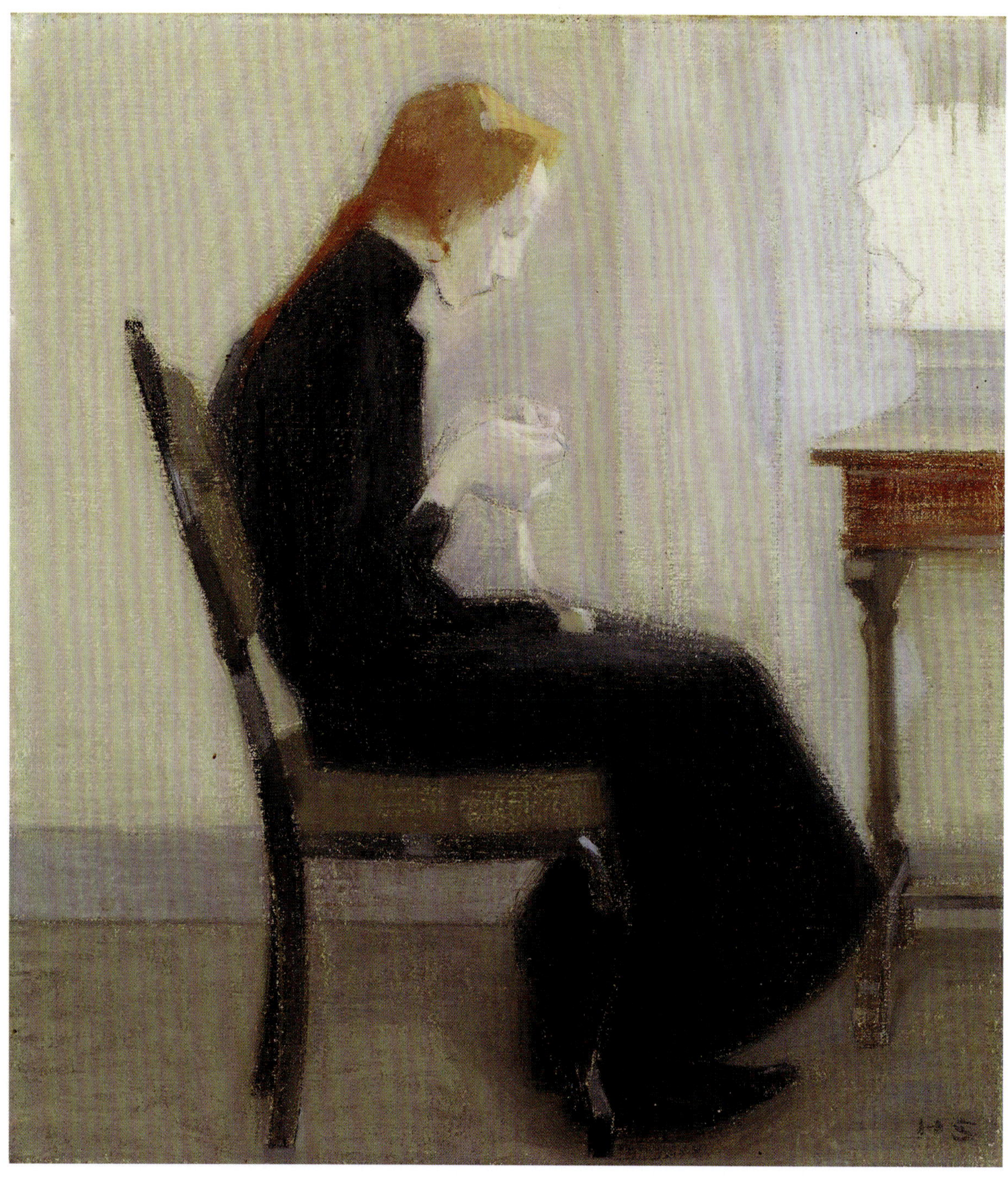

VIRKKAAVA TYTTÖ (GIRL CROCHETING)
1904, oil on canvas, 37 × 33 cm (14½ × 13 in), Sampo Group collection, Helsinki

Hélène Schjerfbeck, born 1862, Helsinki, Finland. Died 1946, Saltsjöbaden, Sweden.

Across her lifetime, Schjerfbeck's style evolved from realist landscapes and everyday scenes to melancholic, quasi-abstract portraits and still lifes. Growing up in Finland, Schjerfbeck was from a poor family and suffered from a lifelong limp that prevented her from attending school. Enabled by a government grant, she moved to Paris in 1880, studying French Realism and *en plein air* painting and in 1881 enrolled at the Académie Colarossi, where she studied until 1884. Returning to Finland, Schjerfbeck's work became increasingly Expressionist and experimental, employing techniques like scraping back paint to leave uneven surfaces, purposefully omitting details to evoke a certain mood and using blocks of colour to make faces appear mask-like. This can be seen in *Girl Crocheting*, in which a woman's red hair contrasts with the bold shapes of her pale face and black dress against an equally angular grey background. Schjerfbeck painted self-portraits from her early twenties into her eighties and, towards the end of her life as her health deteriorated, these began to depict her inner world as well, showing skeletal features rendered with the darkness of death.

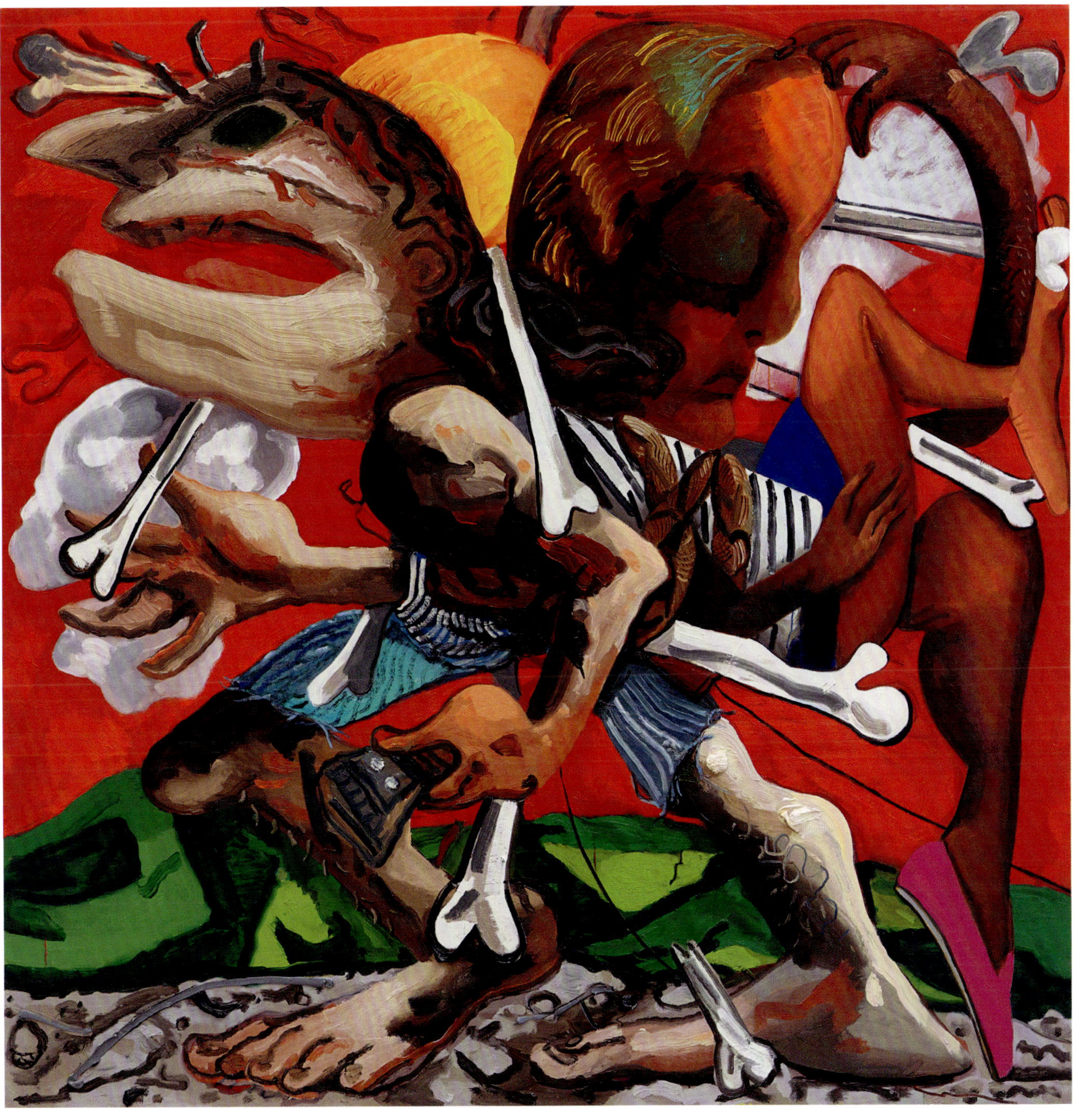

BOUND
2019, oil on canvas, 223.5 × 223.5 cm (88 × 88 in)

Dana Schutz, born 1976, Livonia, Michigan, USA.

Known for her humorous, unsettling and psychologically penetrating scenes, Schutz paints vivid figurative compositions that are left open to interpretation. Her career launched in the early 2000s with series that included the 'Sneeze' paintings (2001), which challenged the conventions of portraiture in their depiction of a physical event; and the 'Self Eaters' (2004), which depict unlikely scenarios of figures devouring themselves. Painting with a vibrant palette and energetic brushwork, the surfaces of her canvases are actively built up, sometimes with a thick impasto, displaying a fluency in the material possibilities of paint. Though her narratives are largely imaginary, they often resonate with the anxieties of modern life. In this large-scale painting, Schutz imagines an introvert tied to the back of an extrovert, surrounded by bones and a lurid red sky. Here, a young woman is being carried away by a hulking female figure, and the abductee scratches her head as if pondering or accepting her fate. The painting's combination of the grotesque and the fantastic typifies Schutz's approach, inviting viewers to decode the image's idiosyncratic iconography.

TSCHABALALA SELF

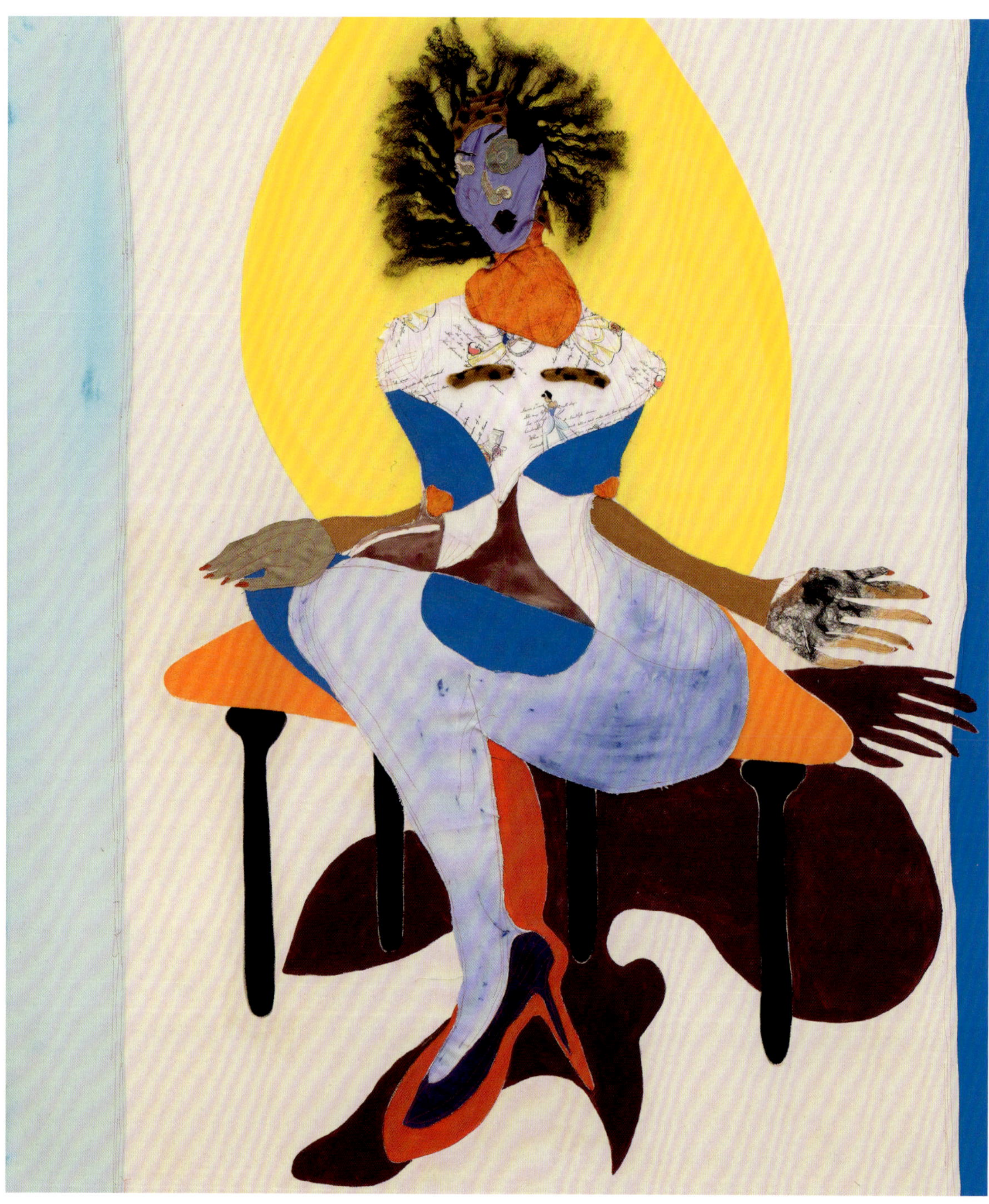

PRINCESS
2017, fabric, acrylic, Flashe, oil and human hair on canvas, 213.4 × 182.9 cm (84 × 72 in)

Tschabalala Self, born 1990, New York, USA.

Self graduated from Yale School of Art's MFA programme in 2015 and was soon recognized on an institutional level for her stylistic flair and innovative approach to painting. Drawing inspiration from artists such as Romare Bearden (1911–88) and Faith Ringgold (p.249), Self collages a variety of mediums and techniques – including painting and printmaking, as well as weaving and quilting – into large-scale canvases that dovetail abstraction, figuration and self-portraiture. The tapestry-like effect of this method alludes to the composite nature of identity – constructed by a complex process of self-fashioning that entails piecing together ideals, images and ideas formed both within oneself and by the outside world. Self is particularly concerned with the position of Black women in contemporary visual culture and often bases her figures on her own experiences and those of women she knows. This work takes on the feminine ideal of the 'princess', reinterpreting the trope as a surreal seated figure in bright colours with exaggerated lines and human hair, imposing and arresting. The figure remains enigmatic and ambivalent; as Self explains in an artist's statement: 'My subjects are fully aware of their conspicuousness and are unmoved by the viewer. Their role is not to show, explain, or perform but rather "to be."'

JOAN SEMMEL

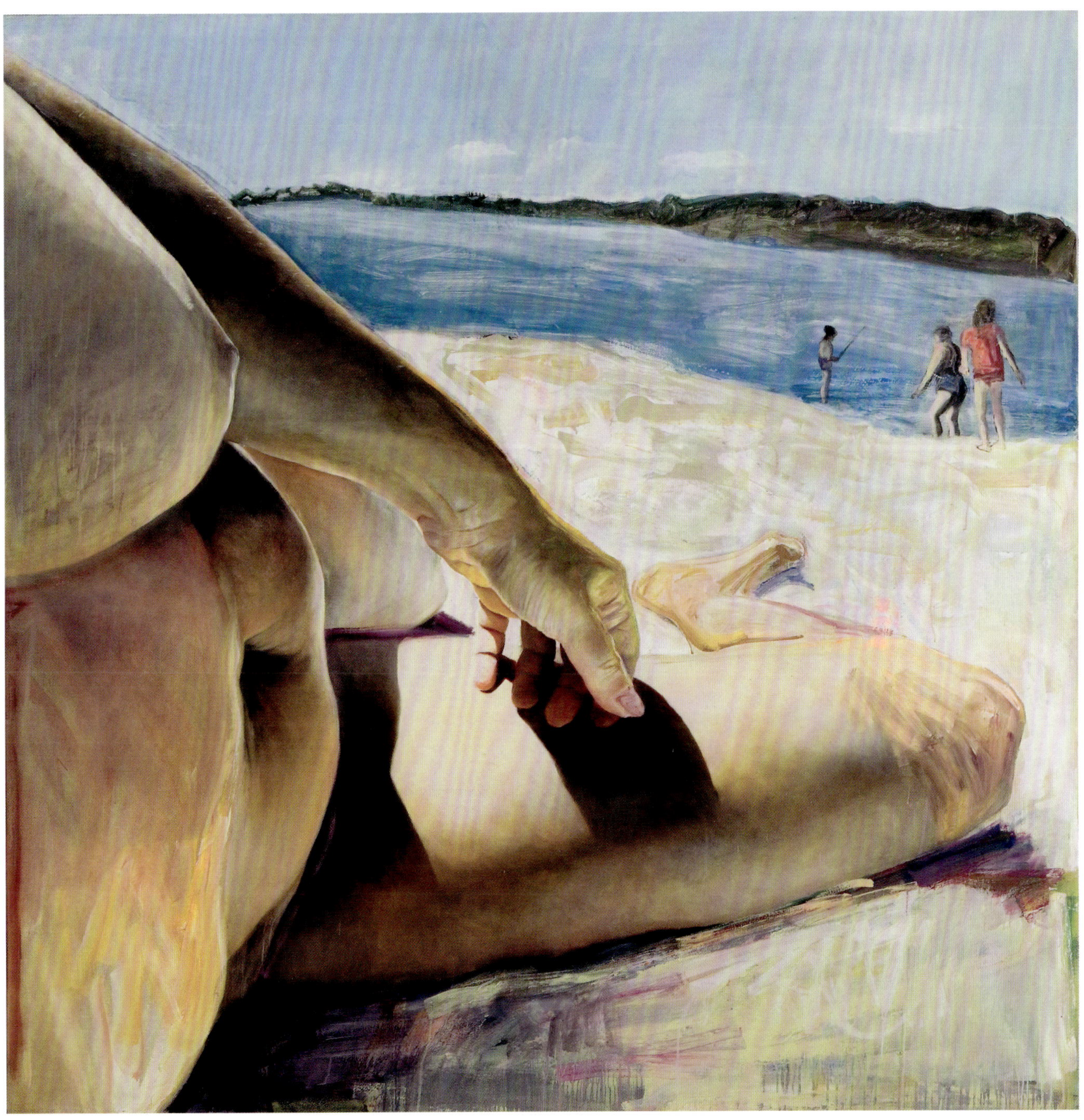

BEACHBODY
1985, oil on canvas, 172.7 × 172.7 cm (68 × 68 in)

Joan Semmel, born 1932, New York, USA.

A self-proclaimed feminist artist, Semmel is known for her paintings of nude women, often including herself, that subvert the male gaze and revolutionize how the female body is perceived. Semmel began investigating this theme in the early 1970s upon her return to New York after a seven-year period in Spain. Until then she had been making and exhibiting Abstract Expressionist paintings, but in the United States she felt suffocated by objectifying images of women – in pornography, popular culture and paintings in museums. She joined activist groups including the Art Workers' Coalition and the Guerrilla Girls, and developed her signature technique of using photography to capture images that she then translates into bold, gestural and often brightly coloured paintings. Semmel works in series, creating a sequence of paintings on a particular subject, from heterosexual couples having sex to plastic mannequins. *Beachbody* is from Semmel's 'Beach' series, made at her studio in East Hampton. It is a typically frank depiction of the artist's body, as seen from the perspective of a camera positioned below her head – a way of emphasizing her agency in the construction of her own image.

SÉRAPHINE DE SENLIS

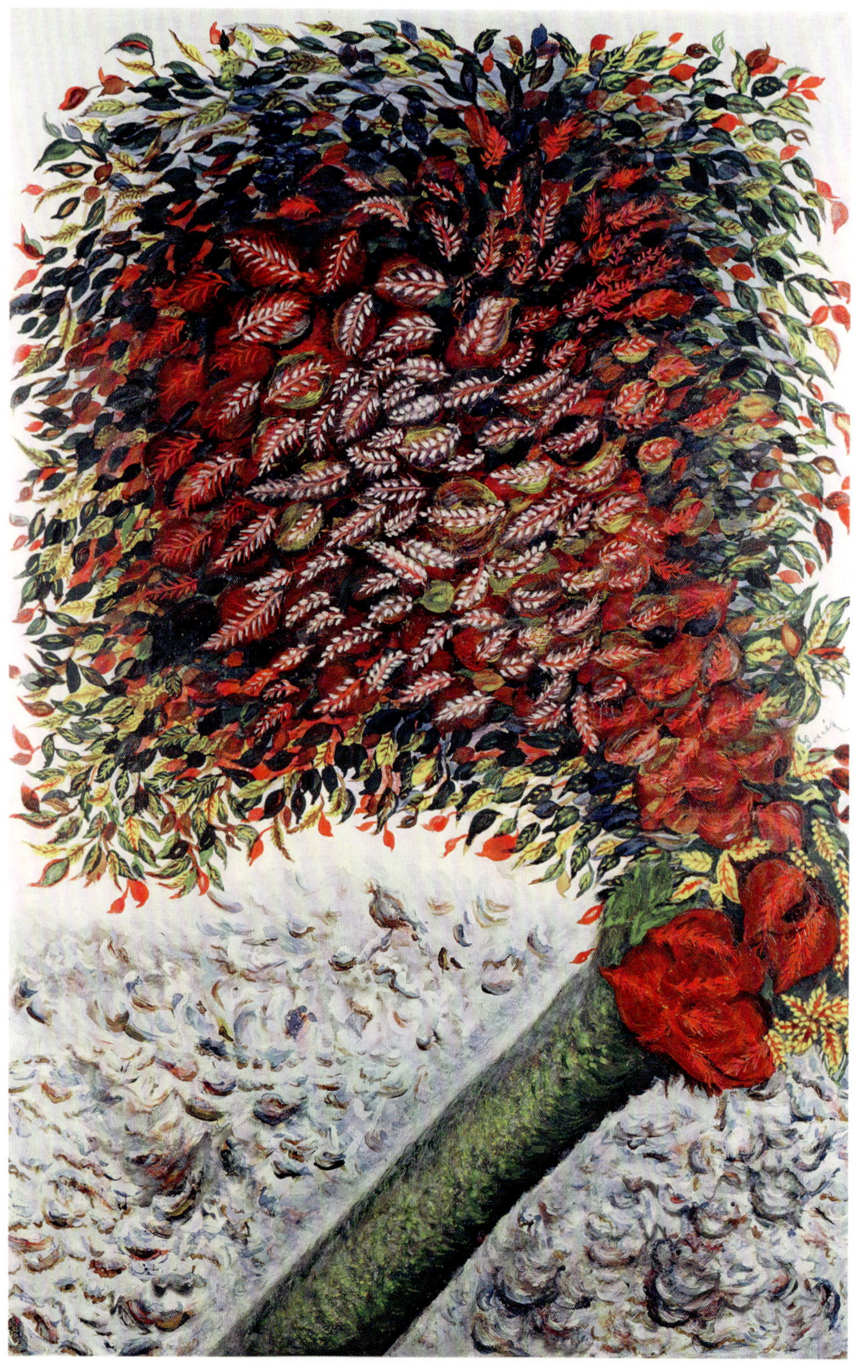

ARBRE ROUGE (THE RED TREE)
1928–30, oil on canvas, 193 × 130 cm (76 × 51 ⅛ in), Musée National d'Art Moderne, Centre Pompidou, Paris, France

Séraphine de Senlis, born 1864, Arsy, France. Died 1942, Clermont, France.

Before she began to paint, Senlis (born Séraphine Louis) spent twenty years as a lay sister at a convent in northern France. In 1901 she moved to the town of Senlis, France – which she eventually adopted as her artist's name – to work as a housekeeper for middle-class families, painting small canvases by candlelight, largely in secret. Senlis often made her own colours using Ripolin, the first commercially available enamel paint, as a base. Her body of work was discovered in 1912 by her employer, Wilhelm Uhde, a German art dealer and collector. Although they were separated by the First World War, Uhde and Senlis re-established contact in 1927 and, under his patronage, she began to paint on a large scale and achieved prominence as an artist. *The Red Tree*, which dates from this time, is typical of Senlis's work in its fantastical botanical arrangements depicted in saturated colours. Light seems to filter through the leaves, evocative of stained-glass windows in the local cathedral. In 1932 Senlis was committed to a psychiatric hospital and subsequently died in relative obscurity; however, several post-war exhibitions have brought her posthumous fame, as well as the 2008 biopic *Séraphine*, directed by Martin Provost.

MARIA SEREBRIAKOVA

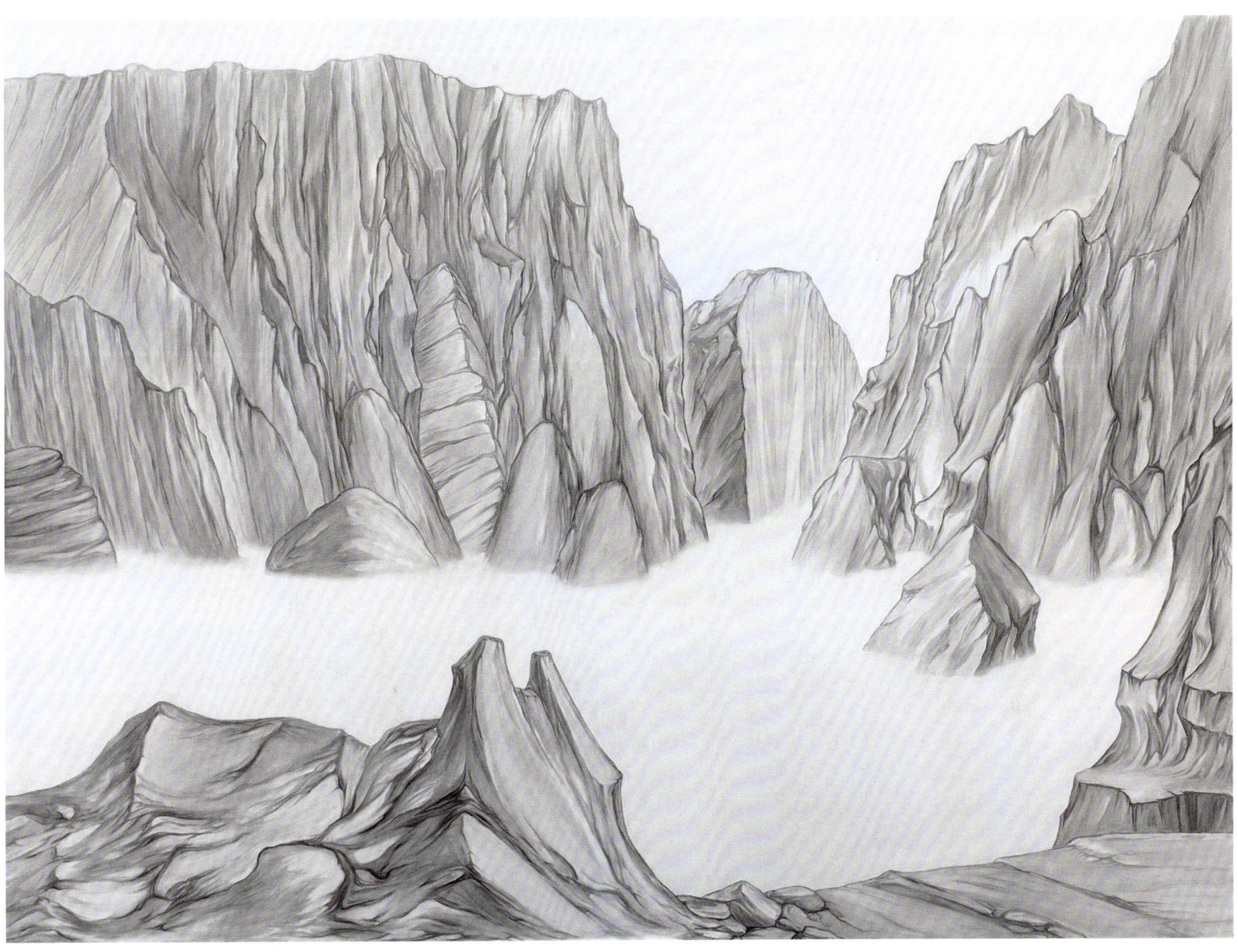

MEMORY TRACES
2014, oil on canvas, 205 × 280 cm
(80¾ × 110¼ in)

Maria Serebriakova, born 1965, Moscow, Russia.

For Serebriakova, art provides a way of communicating ideas that cannot readily be expressed by words. Although working across several different art forms, painting has remained central to her practice since she came to prominence in Moscow in the late 1980s, as the Soviet Union was beginning to disintegrate. Relocating to Germany in 1998, she has continued to work with restraint, painting dreamlike scenes with a subdued palette dominated by grey and washed-out tones. Her compositions, which include deserted landscapes, isolated dwellings and nebulous figures in ambiguous settings, suggest moments from half-remembered dreams or hazy recollections, images conjured from the subconscious mind. The carefully rendered rock formations in the large-scale painting *Memory Traces* could depict any number of mountainous landscapes but describe a hinterland that exists only in Serebriakova's imagination. For her, such spaces represent different mental states pertaining to experiences of isolation, loneliness and introspection. Yet, while her bleak borderlands propose sites of psychological withdrawal and disaffection, they also represent places of opportunity, where problems might also find resolution.

ZINAIDA SEREBRIAKOVA

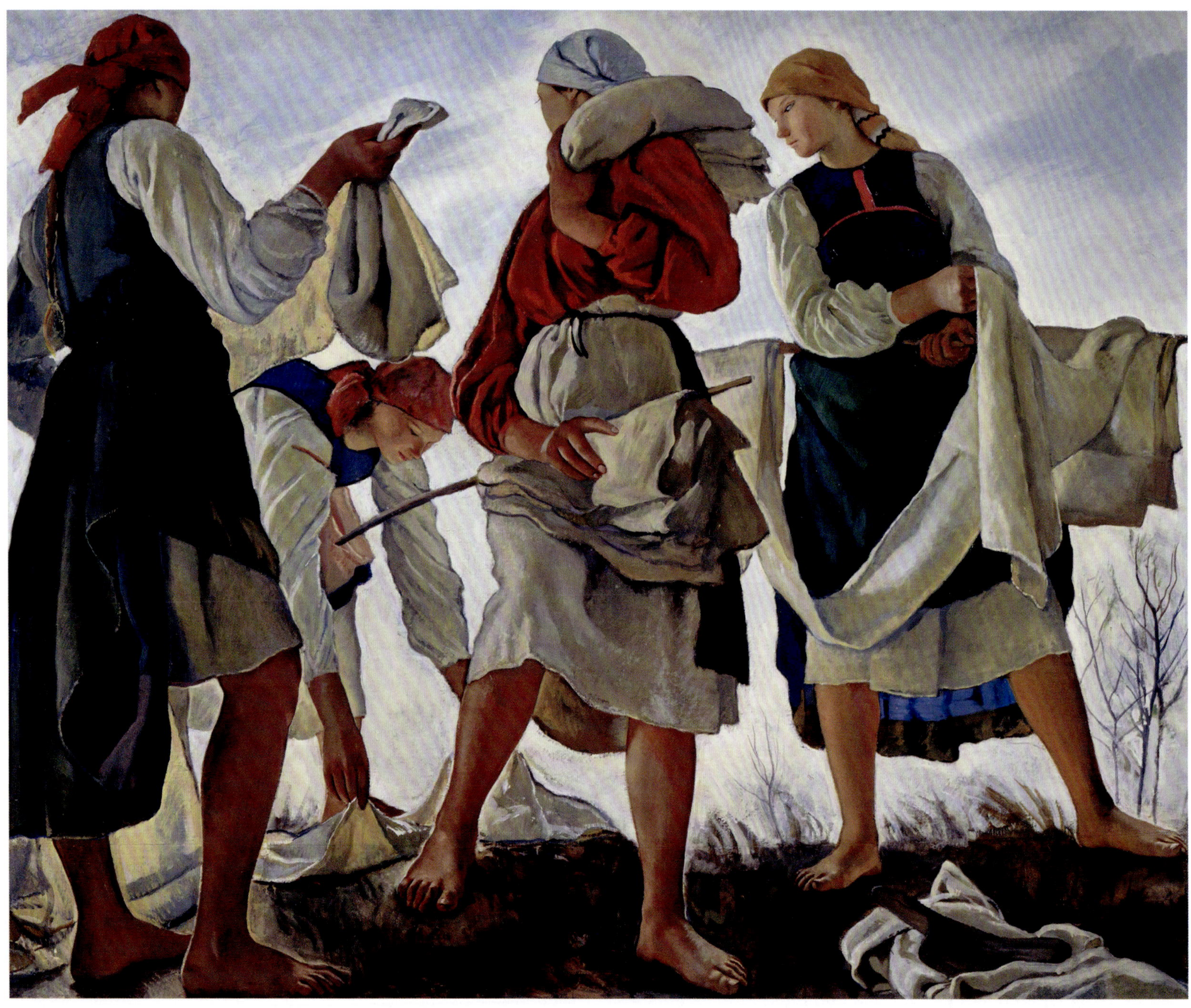

BLEACHING THE LINEN
1917, oil on canvas, 142 × 175.5 cm (55 ⅞ × 69 ⅛ in), State Tretyakov Gallery, Moscow, Russia

Zinaida Serebriakova, born 1884, Neskuchnoye, Kharkiv, Ukraine. Died 1967, Paris, France.

Born to a family of gifted artists, Serebriakova's burgeoning creativity was encouraged from an early age. After studying at the Académie de la Grande Chaumière in Paris, Serebriakova lived on the family estate in the rural retreat of Neskuchnoye. There, she developed the thematic content of her artworks by exploring family portraiture and nudes, in addition to the seasonal rituals of the local peasant community. The rise of the Bolsheviks in 1917 significantly affected the artist's lifestyle: the confiscation of assets, along with her husband's unexpected death from typhus and the destruction of her home by fire, left Serebriakova destitute. While continuing to paint, the artist was forced to abandon her children and relocate to France, where she remained for the rest of her life. Her classical painting style, simultaneously Impressionist and Socialist Realist, remained constant, in contrast to the avant-garde experimentation of the time. Created when she lived in the Ukrainian countryside, this painting depicting peasant women's labour employs a low horizon, allowing her subjects statuesque-like status.

NILIMA SHEIKH

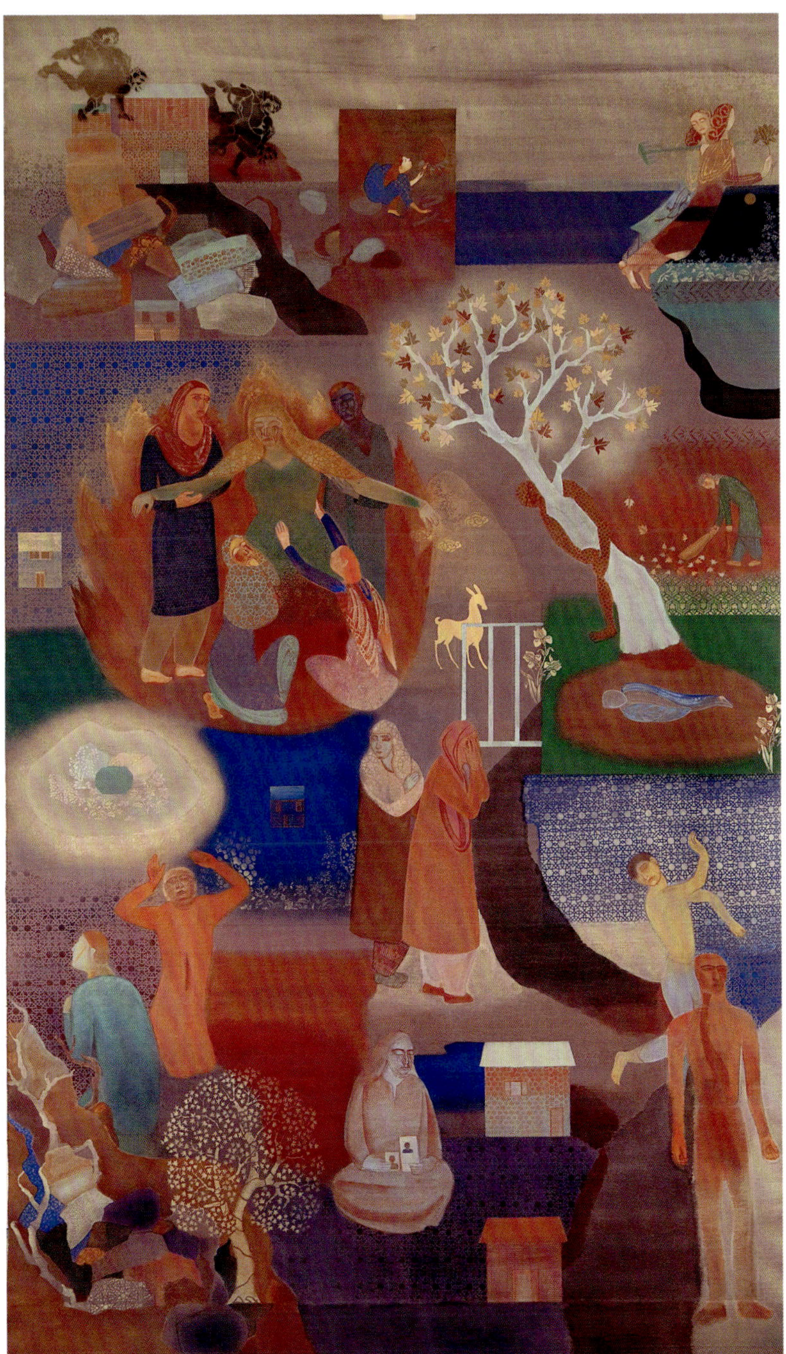

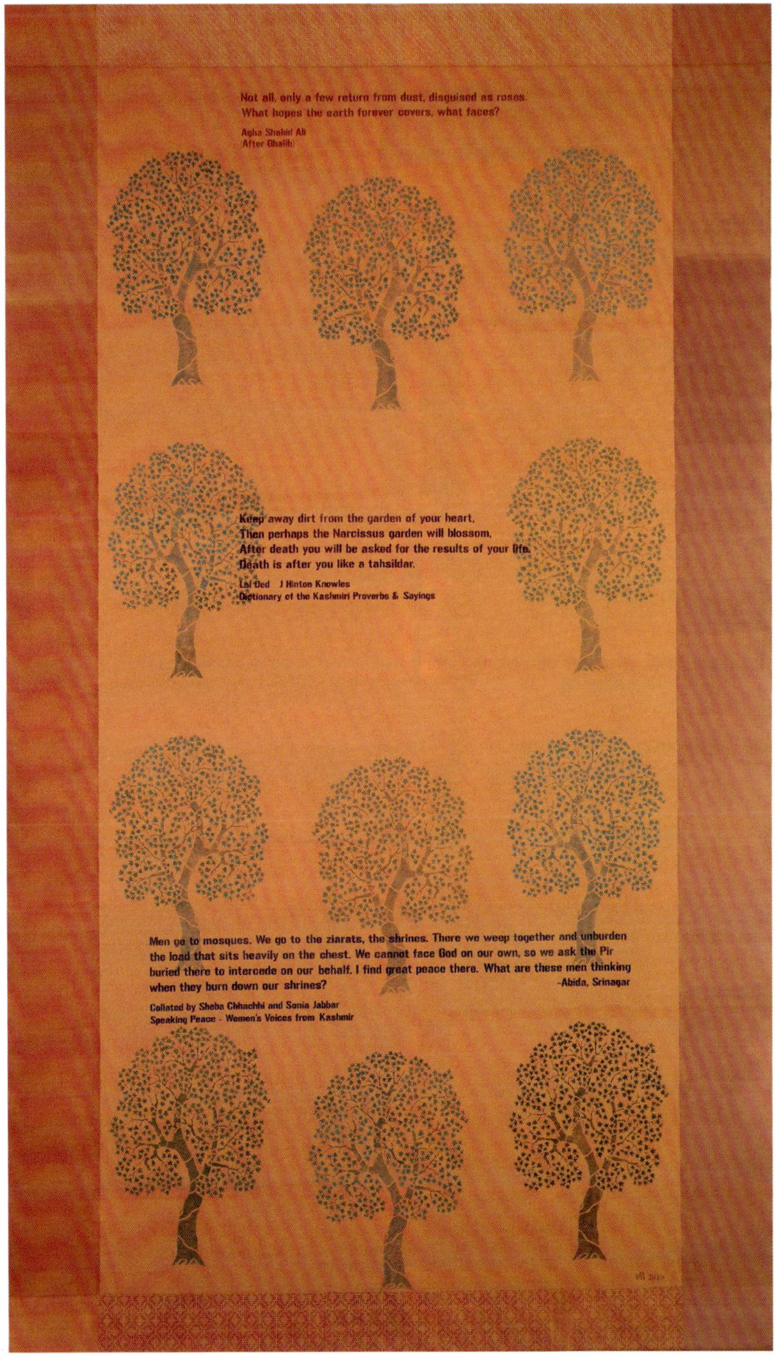

GOING AWAY
2010, casein tempera on canvas, 305 × 183 cm (120 × 72 in)

Nilima Sheikh, born 1945, New Delhi, India.

Over the course of her career, Sheikh has used painting to explore her concerns around India's national politics, femininity and incidences of violence. Having first studied history, she trained in painting at Maharaja Sayajirao University of Baroda in northwest India, graduating in 1971. It was here that she interacted with a group of artists who were experimenting with the narrative and figurative potential of painting, often drawing on the writings of Rabindranath Tagore along with Rajput and Mughal court styles. Sheikh's painting is known for synthesizing many of India's artistic traditions to create images that traverse different settings and universes. In this double-sided scroll painting she deploys the light, floral folk motifs of Pichwai textile design, stencilling aspects of the vegetation. Executed in delicate tempera paint, the work balances arresting figurative scenes with written extracts from Kashmiri poets and historians. Sheikh has described the process as additive; here it is used to visualize the contrasting beauty of Kashmir and the trauma that courses through the region as it struggles to be recognized as an independent state.

AMY SHERALD

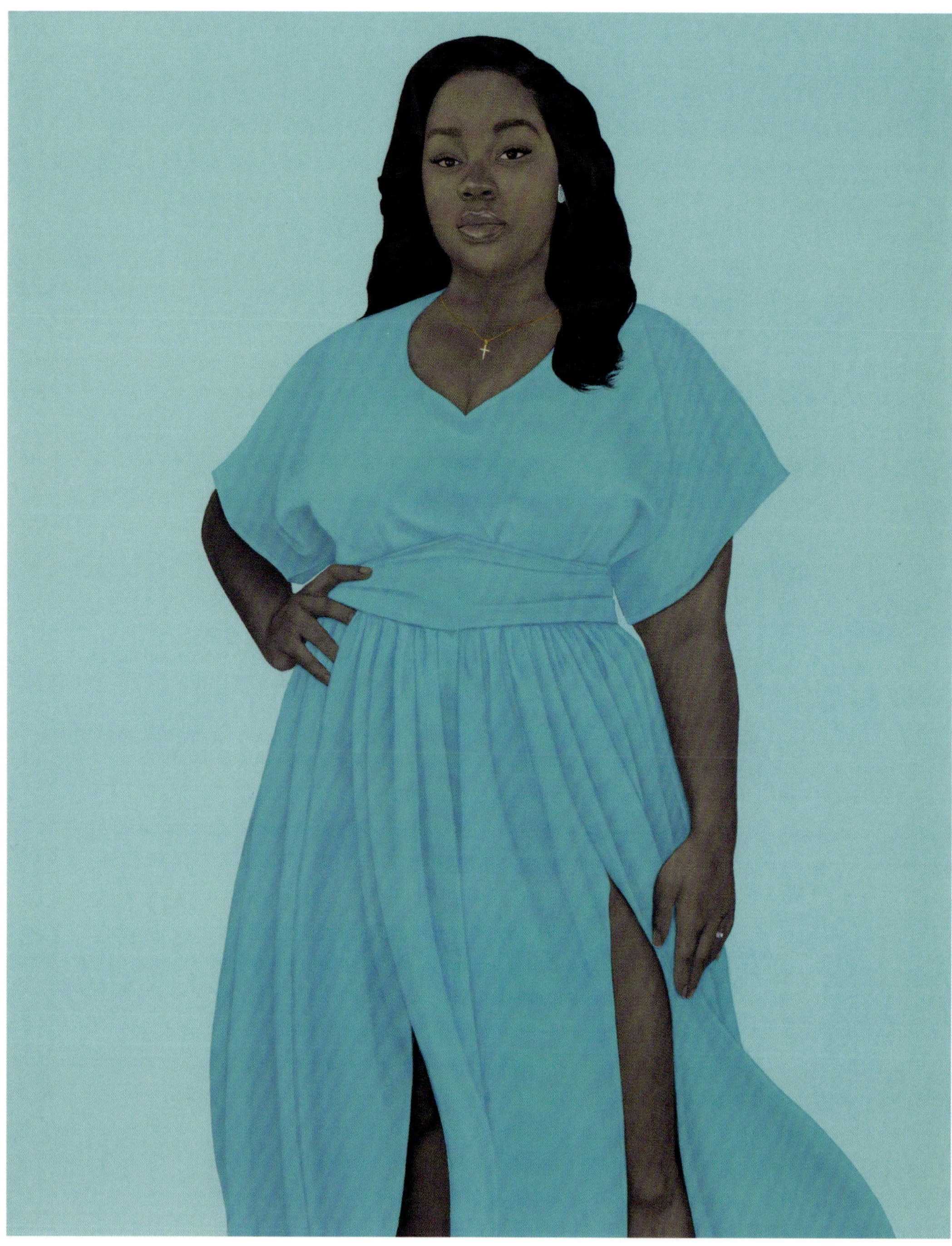

BREONNA TAYLOR
2020, oil on linen, 137.2 × 109.2 cm (54 × 43 in), Smithsonian National Museum of African American History and Culture, Washington DC, USA, and Speed Art Museum, Louisville, Kentucky, USA

Amy Sherald, born 1973, Columbus, Georgia, USA.

Sherald's arresting portraits of Black subjects are powerful anchors in the lineage of portraiture and art history, arenas that have often excluded Black life. A graduate of the Maryland Institute College of Art – where she studied with Abstract Expressionist painter Grace Hartigan (p.131) – Sherald rose to fame in 2017 when she was selected by then First Lady Michelle Obama to paint her official portrait. Following this, she received her second commission: the cover of the September 2020 issue of *Vanity Fair*, which focused on activism. Sherald created this portrait of Breonna Taylor, a twenty-six-year-old healthcare worker who was killed by police in her home in Louisville, Kentucky, in March 2020, galvanizing Black Lives Matter protests around the world. Rendered in the artist's signature use of greyish tint to represent skin tones, Taylor's piercing gaze unflinchingly meets the viewer's. Sherald took great care in her representation, working closely with Taylor's family to develop an intimate sense of who she was. The artist also incorporated details from photographs of Taylor, such as the engagement ring her boyfriend was planning to propose with, which had been photographed by artist LaToya Ruby Frazier (b.1982).

AMRITA SHER-GIL

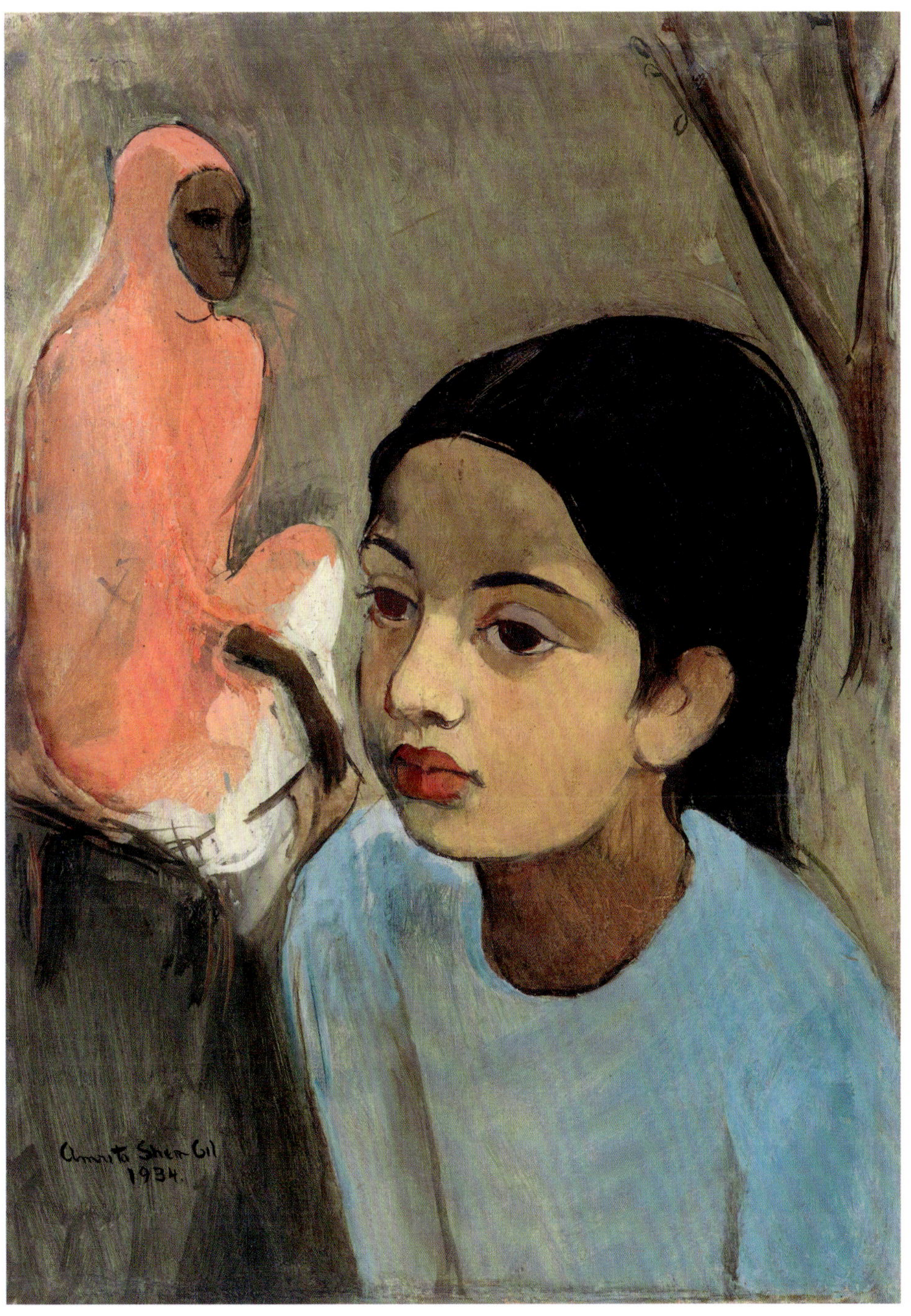

THE LITTLE GIRL IN BLUE
1934, oil on canvas, 48 × 40.6 cm (18.9 × 16 in)

Amrita Sher-Gil, born 1913, Budapest, Hungary. Died 1941, Lahore, Pakistan.

Sher-Gil, who was born to a Punjabi-Sikh father and Hungarian mother, is known for her figurative paintings of anonymous women and girls that focus on their internal contemplations. After moving with her family to Shimla, India, in 1921, Sher-Gil returned to Europe at the age of sixteen to study in Paris at the Académie de la Grande Chaumière followed by the École Nationale Supérieure des Beaux-Arts. In France, she encountered the work of Post-Impressionist painters, including Suzanne Valadon (p.306) and Paul Gauguin (1848–1903), and by 1933 had been elected an Associate of the Grand Salon, making her the youngest and only Asian artist to have received this recognition. Returning to India in 1934, she realized a new artistic mission: 'to interpret the life of Indians, and particularly poor Indians, pictorially'. These years mark her most important artistic output, as she travelled across the region, seeking influences and subject matter. As exemplified in *The Little Girl in Blue*, Sher-Gil posited a diasporic modernism torn between places and routed through her solemn portraits. Despite her short life, Sher-Gil has become one of India's most celebrated modern artists, with the Government of India declaring her a National Treasure in 1976.

UEMURA SHŌEN

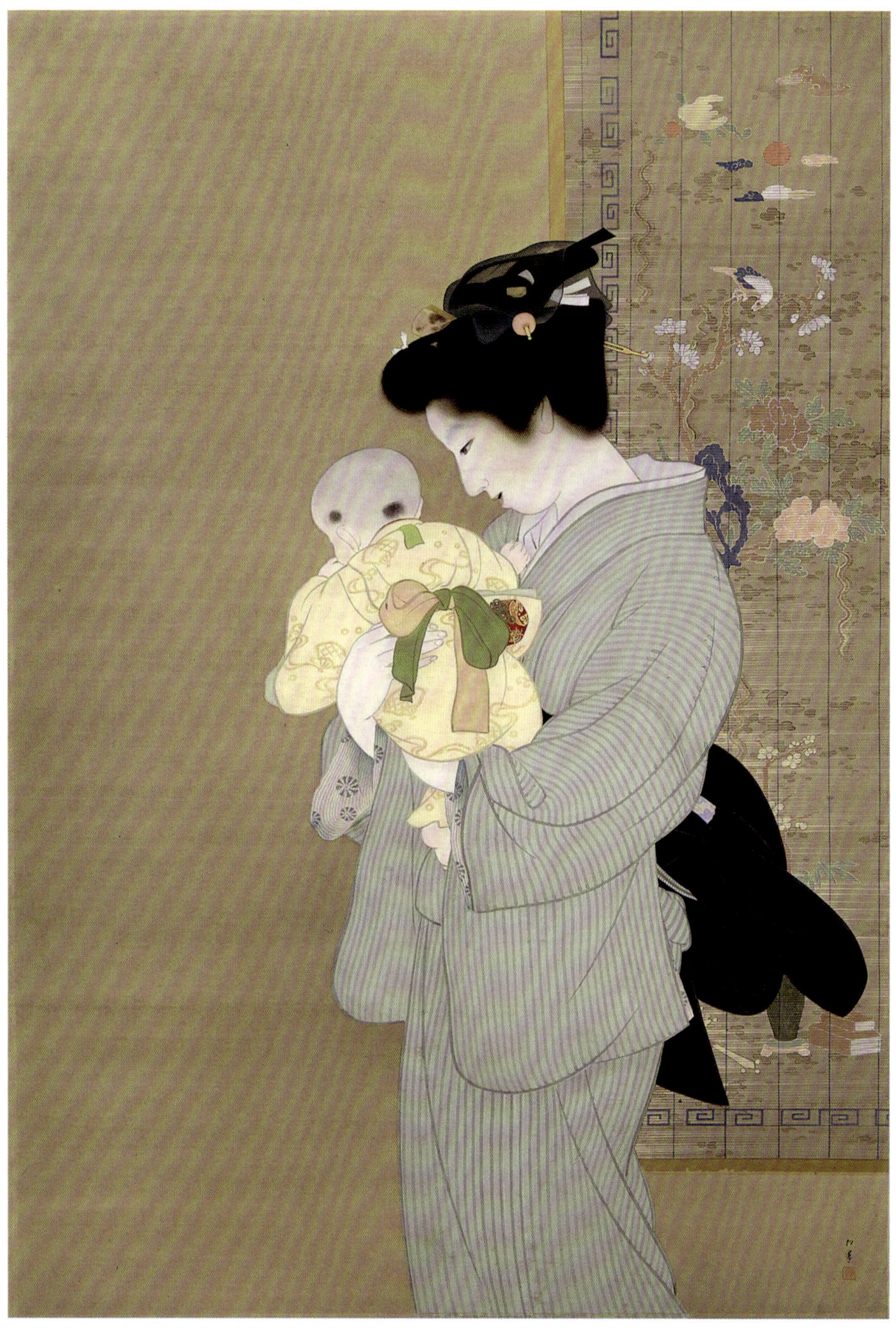

MOTHER AND CHILD
1934, watercolour on silk, 168 × 115.5 cm (66 1/8 × 45 1/2 in), National Museum of Modern Art, Tokyo, Japan

Uemura Shōen, born 1875, Kyoto, Japan. Died 1949, Nara Prefecture, Japan.

One of the first women to train as an artist in the art schools of the Meiji era (1868–1912), Shōen was acclaimed for her paintings in the *bijin-ga* genre (beautiful female figures). Rather than portraying courtesans as was the tradition, Shōen reinterpreted the genre by painting women engaged in everyday tasks, emphasizing qualities she regarded as female virtues of grace and inner strength. Shōen studied with Chinese-style landscape painter Suzuki Shōnen (1848–1918) – her artist's name was derived from his as a mark of distinction – earning accolades for her talent and skill as well as commissions from the imperial household. Shōen exhibited *Mother and Child* following the death of her own mother, who had been the artist's staunchest supporter and confidante. The painting depicts an elegantly dressed upper-class merchant woman from Kyoto holding her baby in front of a decorative bamboo shade. The subject's shaved bluish eyebrows, a feature that the artist fondly associated with her mother, indicate that she was a married woman who had borne a child. A true trailblazer, in 1948 Shōen became the first woman to receive the Order of Culture, the most esteemed award for a living artist in Japan.

PAULA SIEBRA

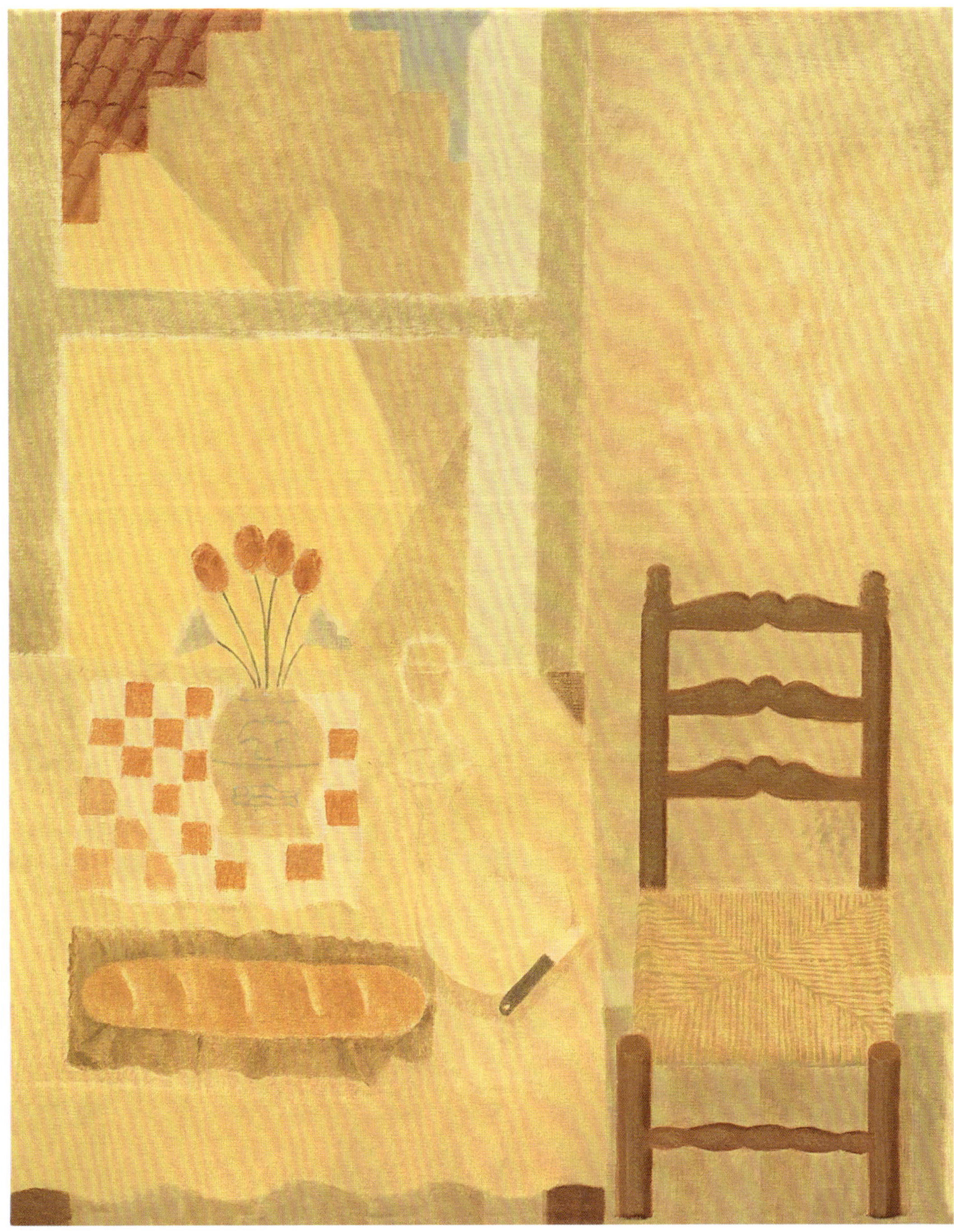

INTERIOR COM CADEIRA, FLORES E JANELA (INTERIOR WITH CHAIR, FLOWERS AND WINDOW)
2021, oil on canvas, 50 × 40 cm (19 ¾ × 15 ¾ in), private collection

Paula Siebra, born 1998, Fortaleza, Ceará, Brazil.

Imbued with a connection to Brazilian life and culture, Siebra's quiet, intimate paintings depict scenes from everyday life. Siebra's palette is comprised of earth colours to evoke moods of remembrance or daydreaming. Whether depicting a still life, domestic interior or landscape – all three of which are combined in this view of a chair sitting, anthropomorphically, next to the breakfast table – the artist often simplifies forms into distinct shapes, painting with soft, delicate brushstrokes to flatten perspective. Gaining recognition with a 2020 solo exhibition, 'Arrebalde', at Mendes Wood DM in São Paulo, Siebra conjured remnants of a mercantile realm on her canvases with ceramic jugs, bowls and glass bottles of sand, as well as vases filled with blooming flowers sitting on fabrics of lace. Her practice recalls the work of Latin American painters of the twentieth century, from Amadeo Luciano Lorenzato's (1900–95) rich landscapes to Alfredo Zalce Torres's (1908–2003) scenes of social and cultural activities. While suggesting the quotidian with an atmosphere of calm, Siebra creates a sense of long-lasting time, archived within the depths of memory, waiting to be rediscovered.

SHAHZIA SIKANDER

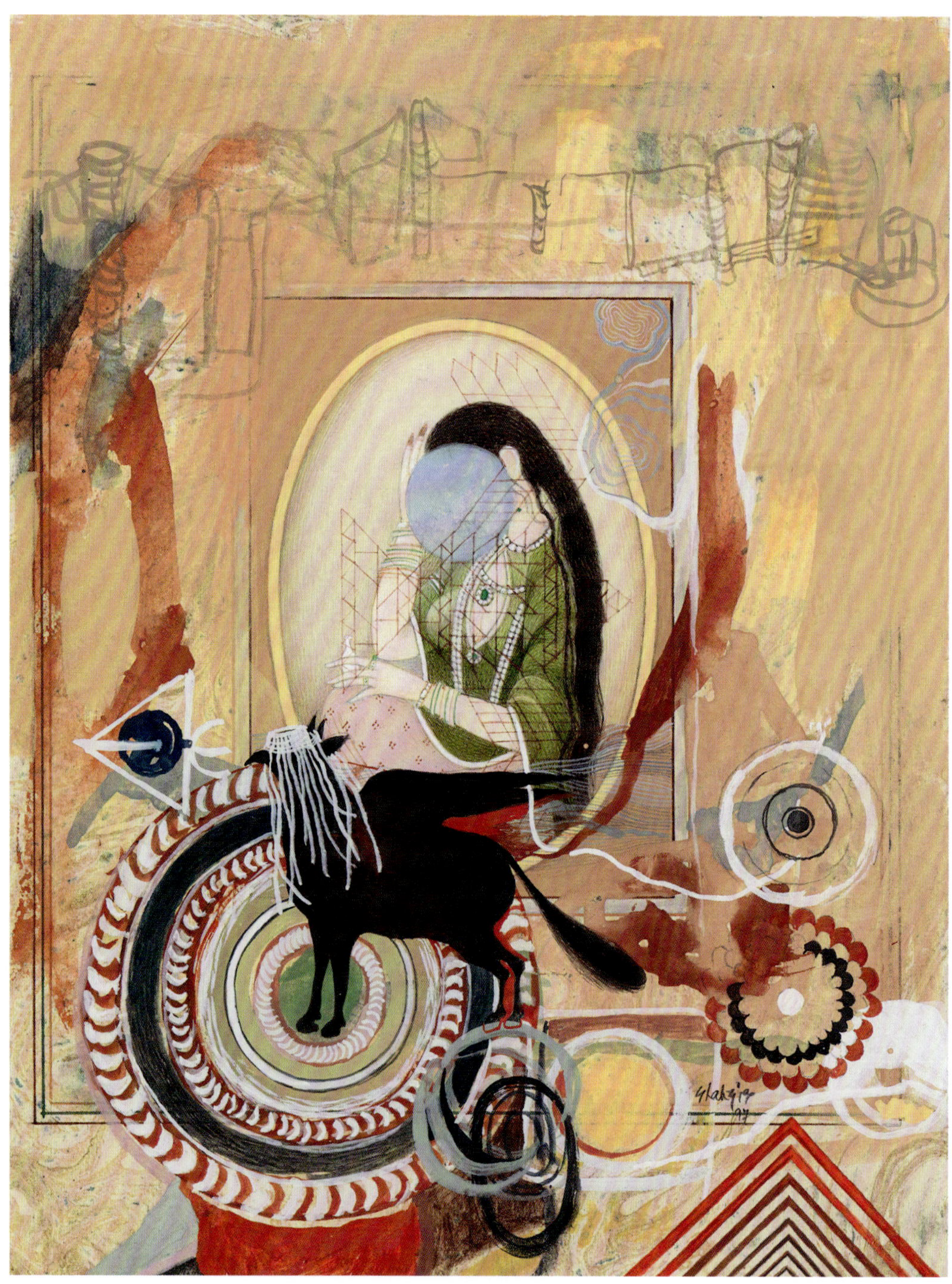

READY TO LEAVE
1997, vegetable colour, dry pigment, watercolour, ink and tea on wasli paper, 25.1 × 19.2 cm (9 ⅞ × 7 ½ in), Whitney Museum of American Art, New York, USA

Shahzia Sikander, born 1969, Lahore, Pakistan.

As a student at the National College of Arts in Lahore, Sikander learnt Indo-Persian miniature painting, a traditional Mughal-era genre. Thanks to her bold experiments deconstructing and reimagining its conventions she is now considered a pioneer of neo-miniaturism. Hindu mythology provides a rich source of imagery for Sikander's paintings, which she connects to contemporary concerns, opening up new avenues for interpretation. A move to the United States in 1993 to study at the Rhode Island School of Design prompted Sikander to develop her interests in themes of feminism, the immigrant experience and globalization. Following the terror attacks of September 11, 2001, rising Islamophobia led Sikander to explore her identity as a Muslim woman in the US and began to include symbols of nationalism and resistance in her paintings. As she explained in a 1997 statement published in the journal *Signs*, this work features both a *chalawa*, the Punjabi word for an animal poltergeist, and a griffin, the eagle-lion chimera from Greek mythology. Together they help express the feeling of 'becoming the other, the outsider, through the polarizing paradigm of East/West'.

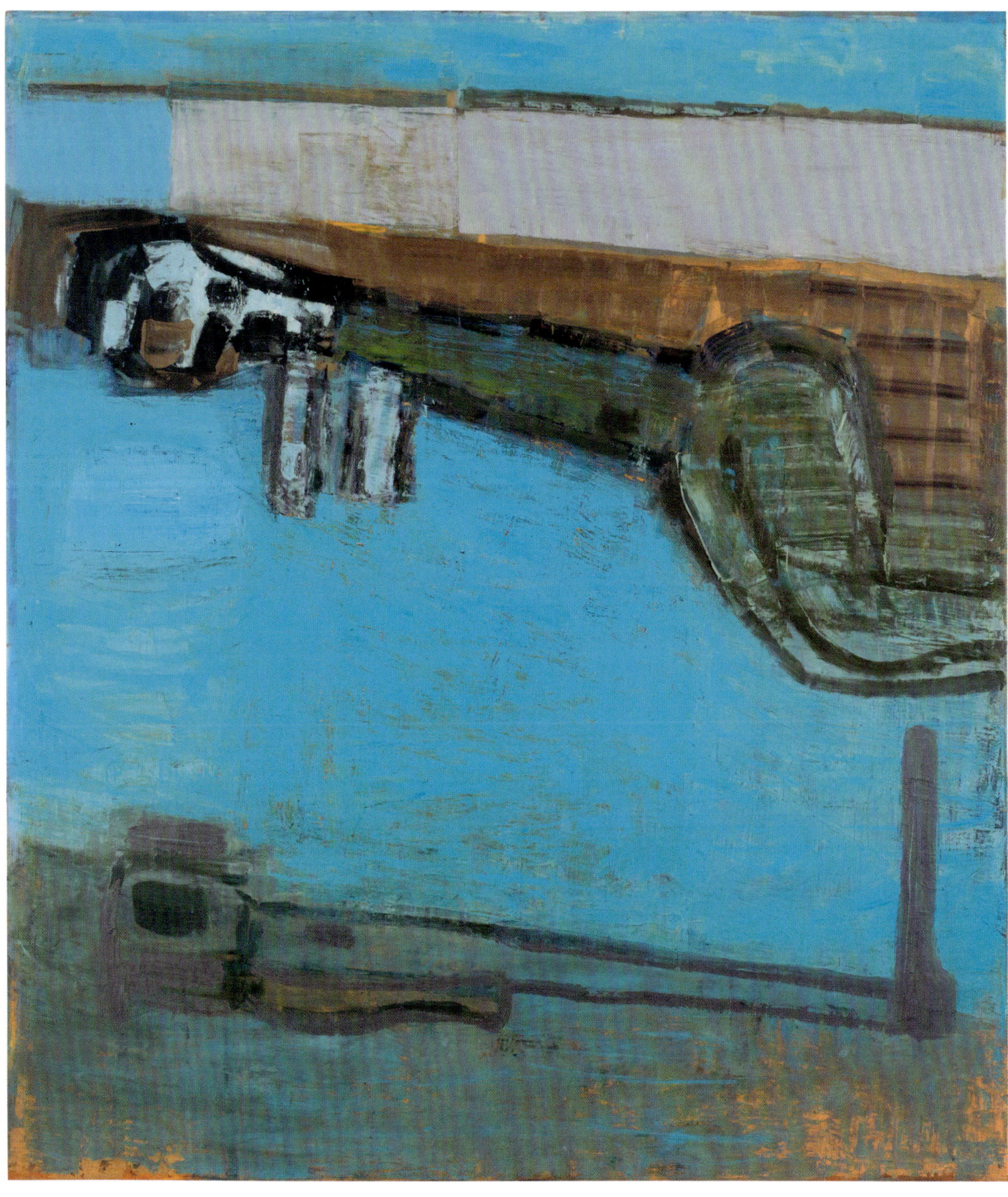

TV IN BED
2017–18, oil on canvas, 190.5 × 167.6 cm
(75 × 66 in)

Amy Sillman, born 1955, Detroit, Michigan, USA.

At once influenced by and critical of Abstract Expressionism, Sillman's ambiguous compositions pursue gestural abstraction with a queer, feminist bent. Precarity and discomfort are central to her pictorial preoccupations, which champion an 'aesthetics of awkwardness, struggle, nonsense, contingency', as she wrote in her 2011 essay 'Ab Ex and Disco Balls'. Sillman's is a process of accretion and – in her words – *ruination*, the artist building layers of paint on canvas only to scrape them back, efface them, working with and against her medium. It is, too, a process in collapsing difference: in her paintings, foreground and background threaten to merge, 'abstract' and 'figurative' prove imperfect adjectives, and even the brightest colours find an unsettling undertow. To Sillman, writing in her serial zine *The OG* in 2017, 'art offers *change above all*: insistent, unremitting change that won't resolve into finality or finesse'. Rendered with crude swathes of colour – and the artist's idiosyncratic humour – *TV in Bed* describes a close, almost claustrophobic scene. With the television's blue-screen glare occupying the majority of the canvas, the scene's disorienting perspective recalls the sensation of the eponymous activity: mindless, lethargic and, perhaps, a bit surreal.

LORNA SIMPSON

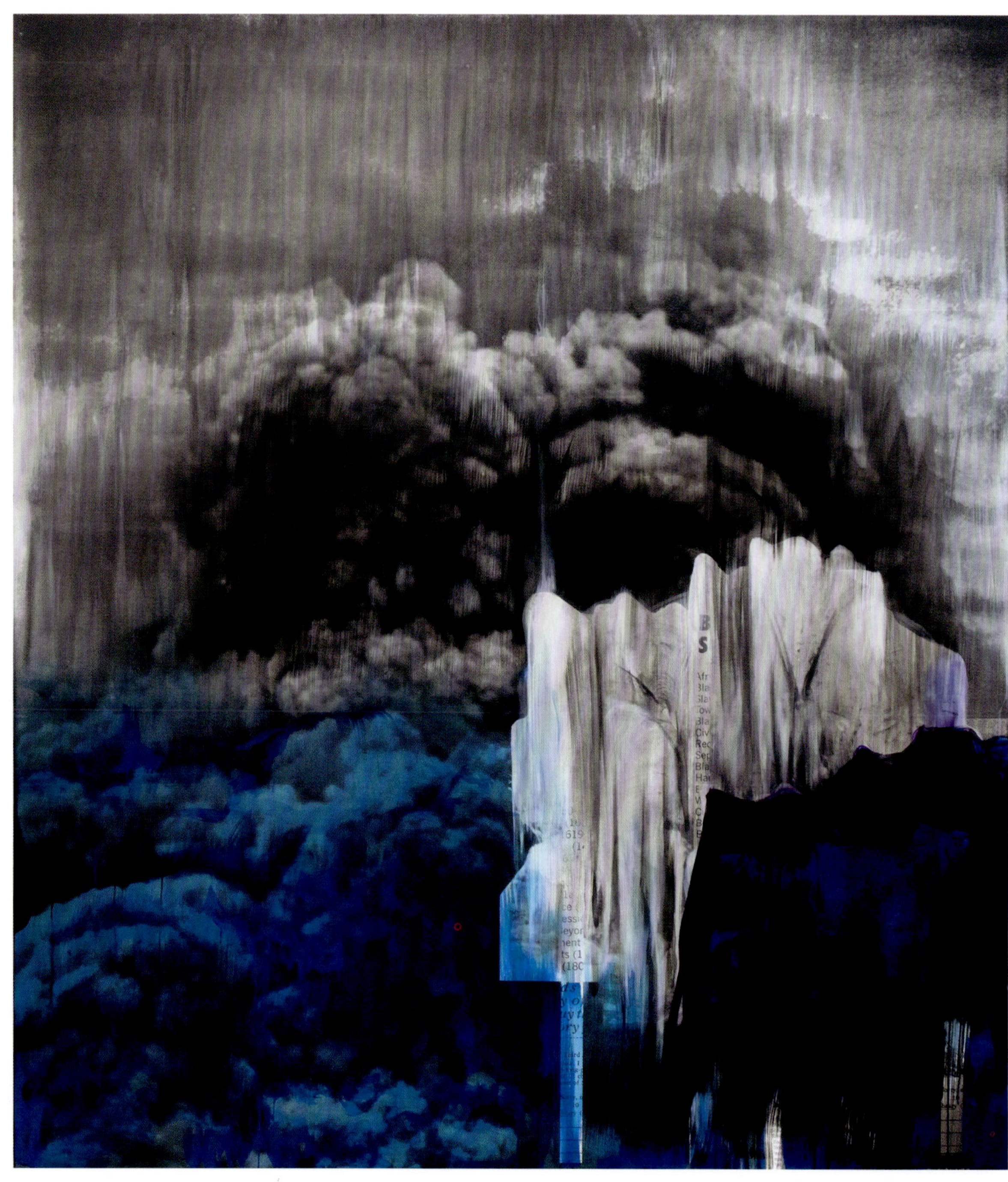

ICE 5
2018, ink and acrylic on gessoed fibreglass, 274.3 × 243.8 × 3.2 cm (108 × 96 × 1¼ in)

Lorna Simpson, born 1960, Brooklyn, USA.

Simpson first garnered acclaim in the 1980s for her conceptual photography practice. These works function in theoretical and formal capacities, combining images and language in an ambiguous manner to question the objectivity of both. Drawing on her own identity and experience as a Black American woman, and frequently employing Black women as her subject, Simpson's art challenges traditional ideas and assumptions around race, gender, representation and history. The artist has continued to engage with these themes throughout her career and across a wide range of media including painting, which she first began to exhibit in 2015. The paintings in Simpson's 'Ice' series, including *Ice 5*, are based on Associated Press photographs of ice, glaciers and smoke that have been transformed by washes of blue, grey and black ink and acrylic, while fragments of articles from vintage issues of *Ebony* and *Jet* peer through, rendered barely legible. While playing with the boundaries between representation and abstraction, the dark tones and dramatic brushwork in these works evoke environmental catastrophe, linking deep geological time with human history.

AVERY SINGER

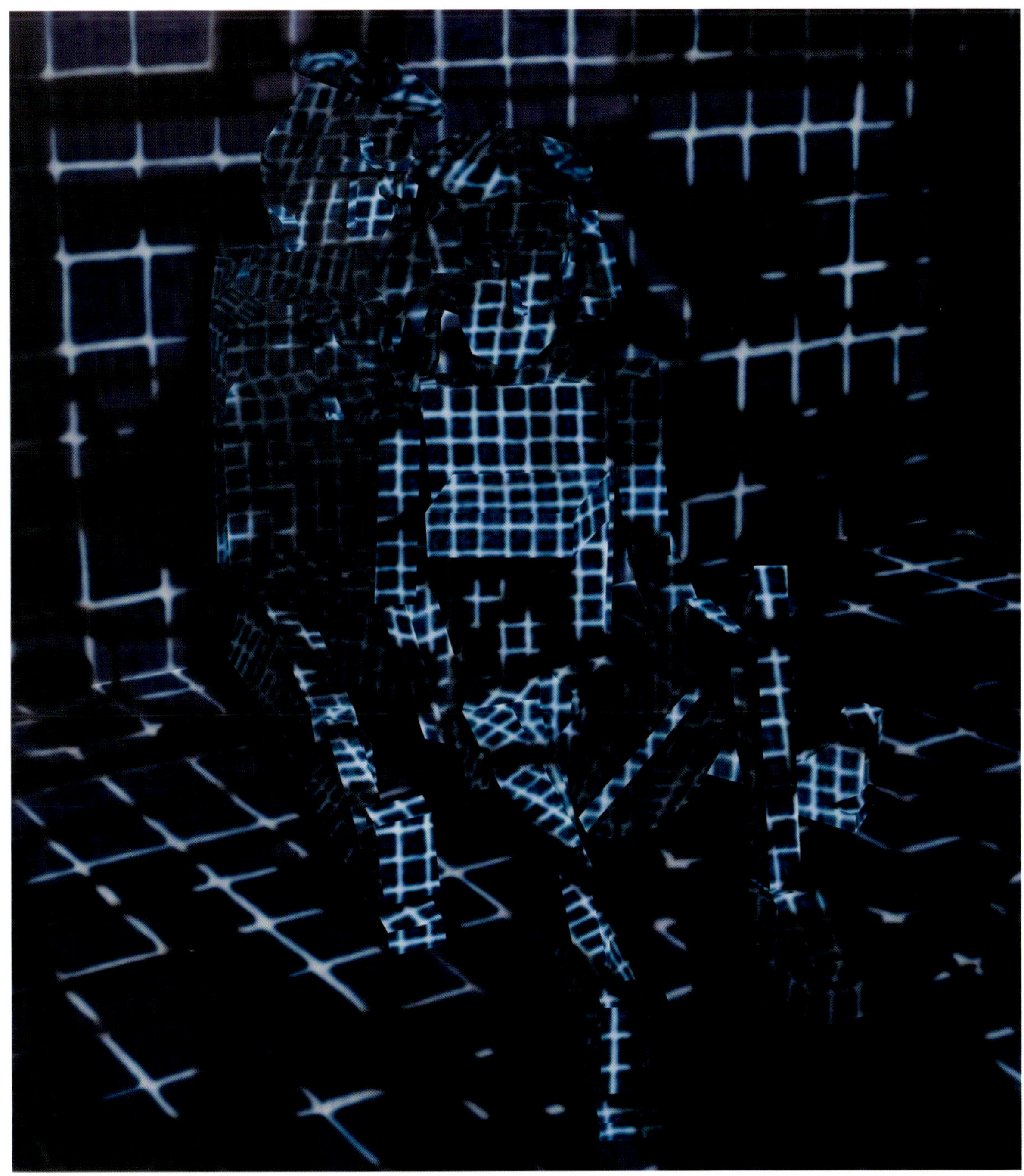

UNTITLED
2019, acrylic on canvas stretched over wood panel, 241.9 × 216.5 × 5.7 cm (95 ¼ × 85 ¼ × 2 ¼ in)

Avery Singer, born 1987, New York, USA.

The daughter of two artists, Singer graduated from Städelschule, Frankfurt, in 2008 and Cooper Union, New York, in 2010, where she experimented with photography, film, performance art and sculpture before discovering her chosen medium through an experiment with SketchUp, a 3D modelling software traditionally used to simulate architectural spaces. Singer employs this software to create an under-drawing over which she meticulously applies layers of paint via computer-controlled airbrush, masking the surface with tape and sometimes liquid rubber to create canvases that appear simultaneously digital and analogue. As seen in *Untitled*, Singer's translation of computer-generated visuals to a material surface results in large-scale trompe l'oeil paintings whose dramatic perspectival depth – accentuated with carefully modelled shadows and gridded patterns that fall like projections on her figures – mimic the illusionism of historical painting traditions. Like windows into an alternate reality, her works simultaneously eschew those modes of representation, removing traces of the artist's hand and exploring painting's place in a hyper-digital age.

ARPITA SINGH

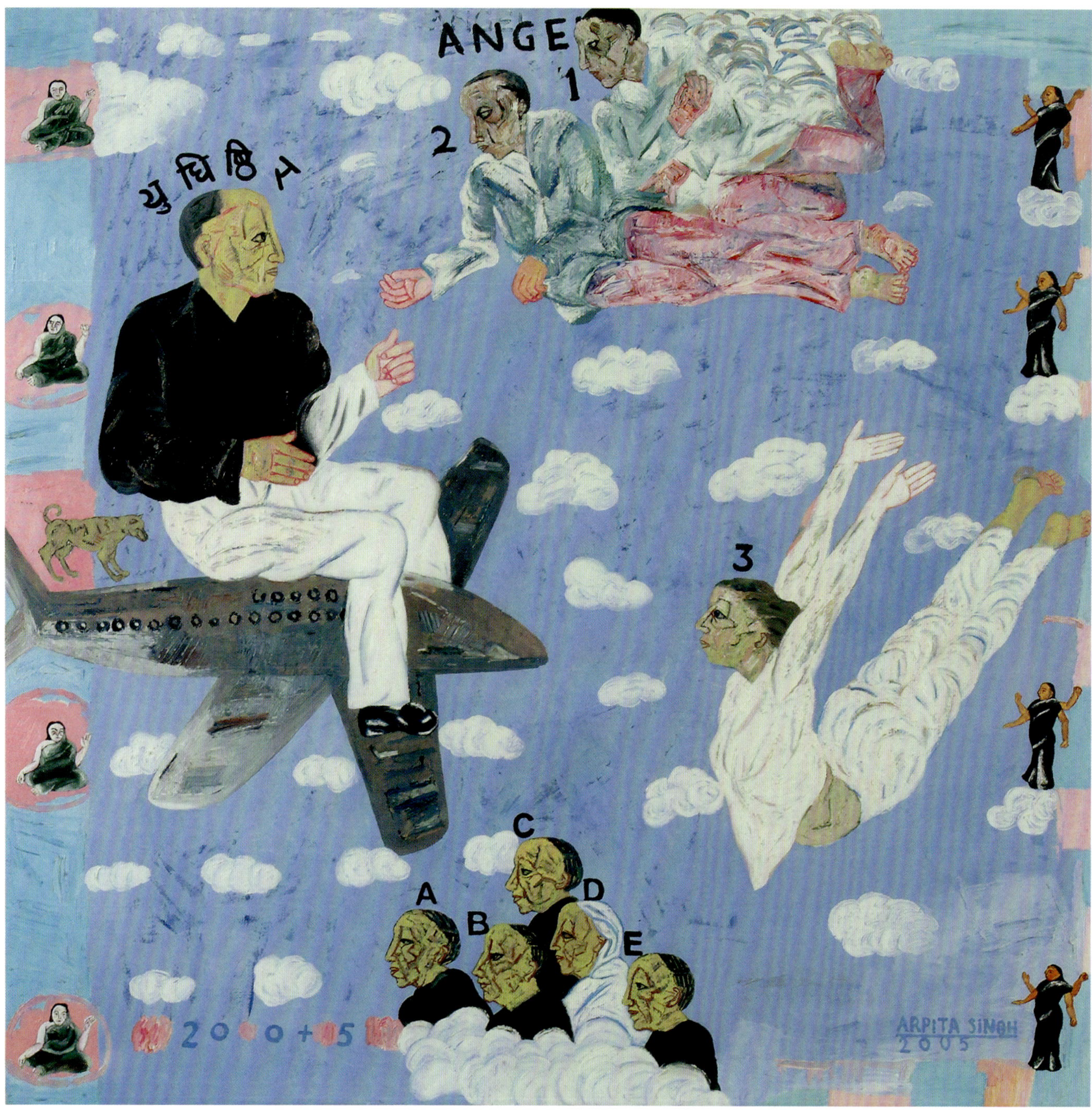

THIRTY SIX CLOUDS: YUDHISHTHIRA APPROACHING HEAVEN
2005, oil on canvas, 121.9 × 121.9 cm (48 × 48 in)

Arpita Singh, born 1937, Baranagar, India.

A leading member of the second generation of modernists that emerged in India in the 1960s, Singh remains one of the country's most acclaimed modern artists. After graduating from art school in Delhi in 1959, she worked for four years as a designer at the Weavers' Service Centre, part of the Ministry of Textiles, where she learnt the techniques of Kantha embroidery. This experience had a strong impact on her canvases, which emphasize colour and pattern over traditional linear perspective. Her earliest works are figurative but for a period following her first solo exhibition, which took place in 1972, she experimented with monochromatic abstraction – creating works using only lines and dots. In the 1980s she returned to figuration, creating enigmatic narrative scenes that draw both on the dreamlike paintings of Marc Chagall (1887–1985) and on South Asian mythology and visual culture. *Thirty Six Clouds: Yudhishthira Approaching Heaven*, rendered in Singh's signature thickly impastoed pinks and blues, refers to the Sanskrit epic *Mahabharata*. The figures float freely on the canvas, alongside numbers and words in different scripts – there is also a large airplane, on which Yudhishthira rides, adding a humorously contemporary twist to this ancient story.

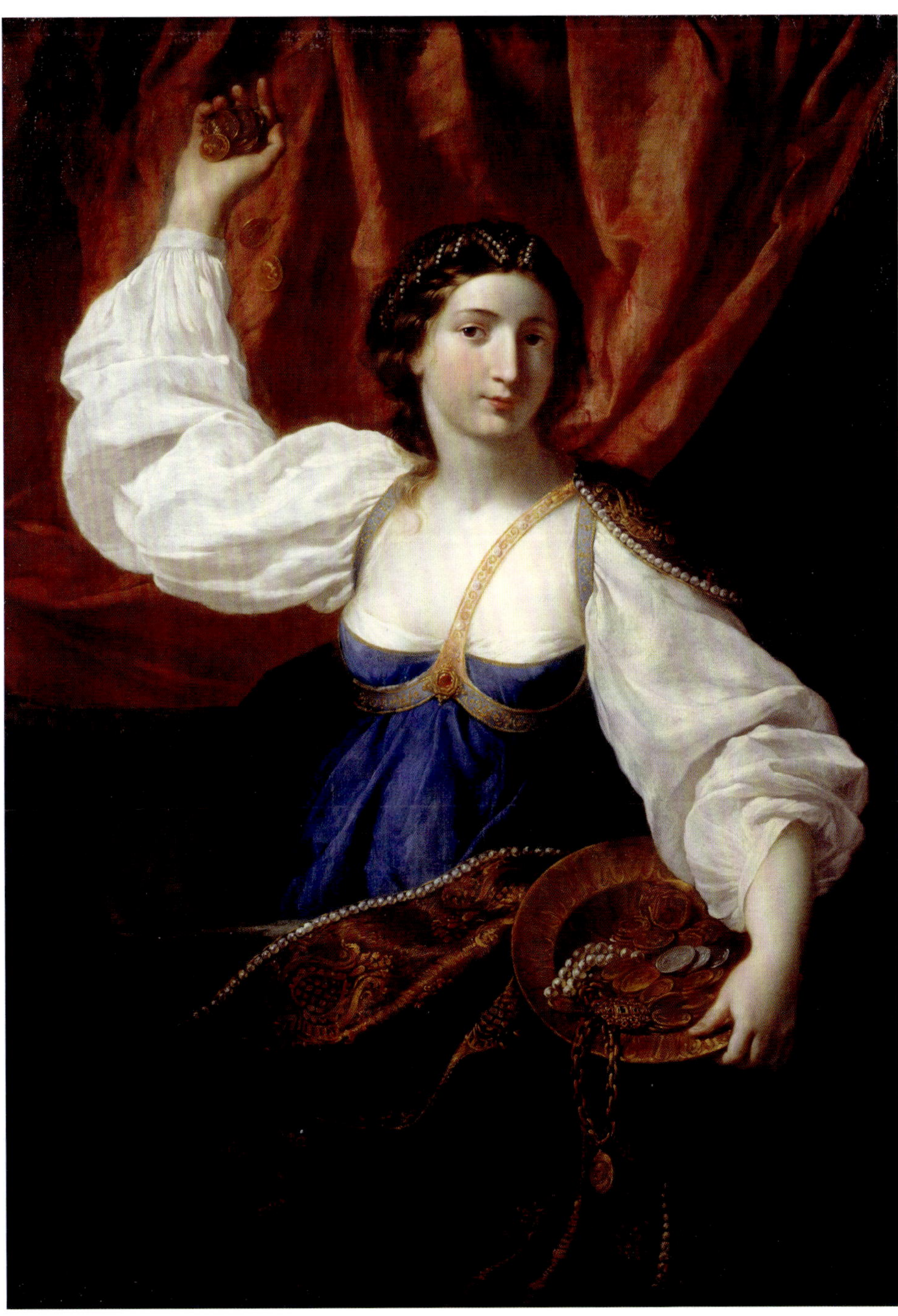

LA LIBERALITÀ (LIBERALITY)
*c.*1657, oil on canvas, 134 × 96 cm (52 ¾ × 37 ¾ in), Musée des Beaux-Arts de Nîmes, France

Elisabetta Sirani, born 1638, Bologna, Italy. Died 1665, Bologna.

Refining her elegant Baroque painting style in the progressive city of Bologna, Sirani was a revered and prolific talent championed by her artist father, Giovanni Andrea Sirani (1610–70). A *maestra* of her time, Sirani was known for her swift execution of finely rendered portraits, religious scenes and history paintings. After her father was left unable to paint, Sirani became the main source of income for the family, taking over his studio and establishing a school of art for young women. Across secular, religious and allegorical scenes, Sirani's favoured subjects were *femmes fortes* ('heroic women') from mythology and ancient history, whom she depicted in scenes that highlighted their virtue and courage. With this self-portrait, Sirani claimed her autonomy as an artist, creating a vision of abundance and generosity in which jewels and gold drip from a tray, and coins tumble down from her hands. Although she died suddenly at the age of twenty-seven, Sirani created close to two hundred works over the course of her ten-year career and, with patronage from high-profile collectors including the Medici family, she was wealthy and able to provide for her large family.

GAZBIA SIRRY

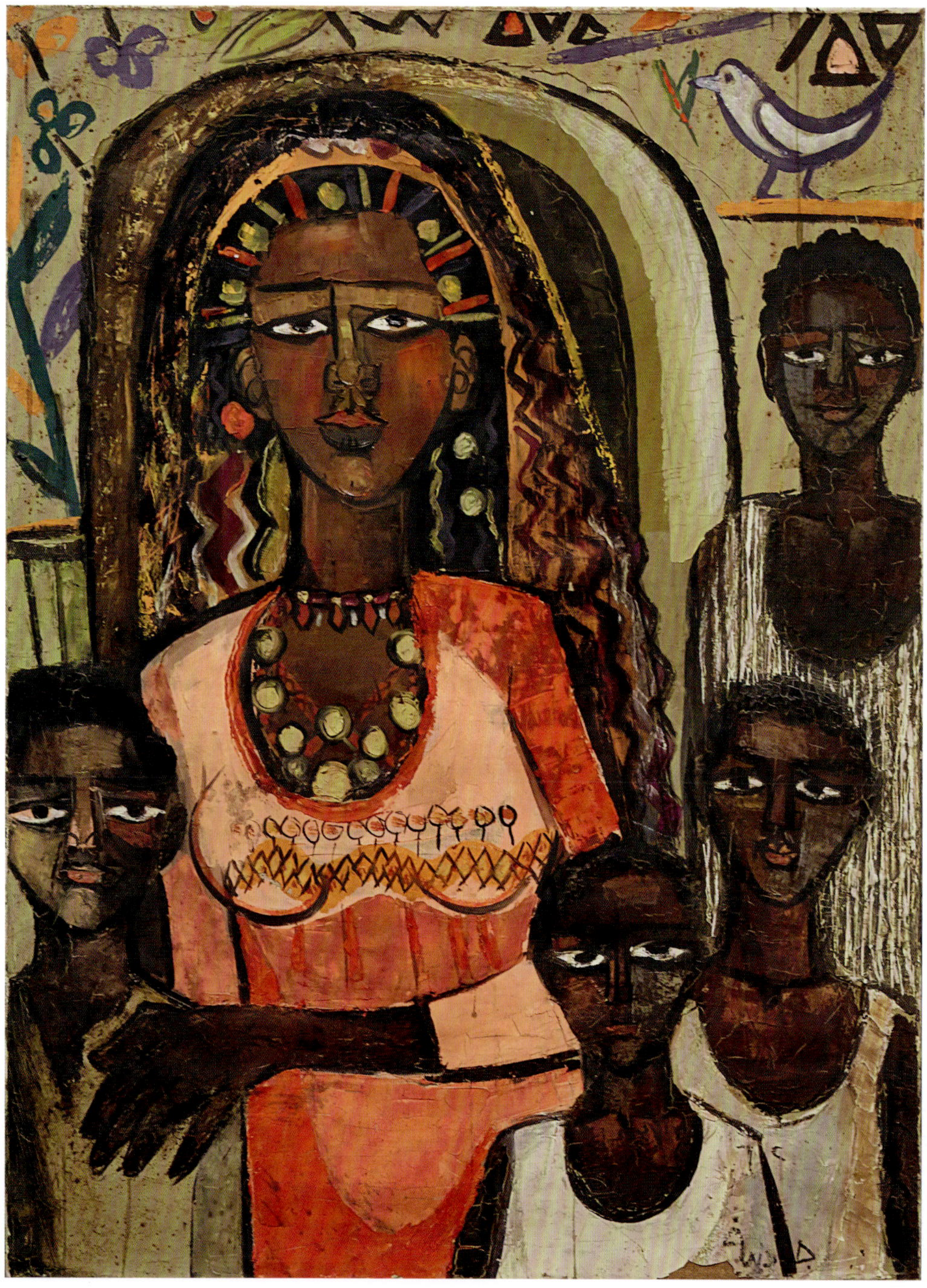

PORTRAIT OF A NUBIAN FAMILY
1962, oil on canvas, 72 × 53 cm (28 ⅜ × 20 ⅞ in), Barjeel Art Foundation, Sharjah, UAE

Gazbia Sirry, born 1925, Cairo, Egypt. Died 2021, Cairo.

Known for blending incisive political commentary with Arabic ornamentation, modernist abstraction and figurative styles borrowed from ancient pharaonic imagery, Sirry was one of the pioneering modern artists in North Africa and the Arab world. Having trained in Cairo, Rome and London, Sirry came to prominence after the Egyptian Revolution of 1952 and sought to express nationalist political sentiment in her work. Despite facing institutional barriers as a female artist, Sirry contributed to the complex discourses of nation, culture and identity during an era defined by the social reforms of President Gamal Abdel Nasser and enduring British colonial interference. *Portrait of a Nubian Family* is indicative of her best-known figurative style. Using dark outlines and an earthen colour palette, the painting recalls the flat and geometric compositions of ancient Coptic art. Centring on a mother, who wears an eye-catching pink garment and gold jewellery, the painting is a homage to those villagers who were displaced by the construction of the Aswan Dam in the early 1960s. Sirry's work shifted to abstraction towards the end of the 1960s as she became disillusioned with the Egyptian government's silencing of dissidents.

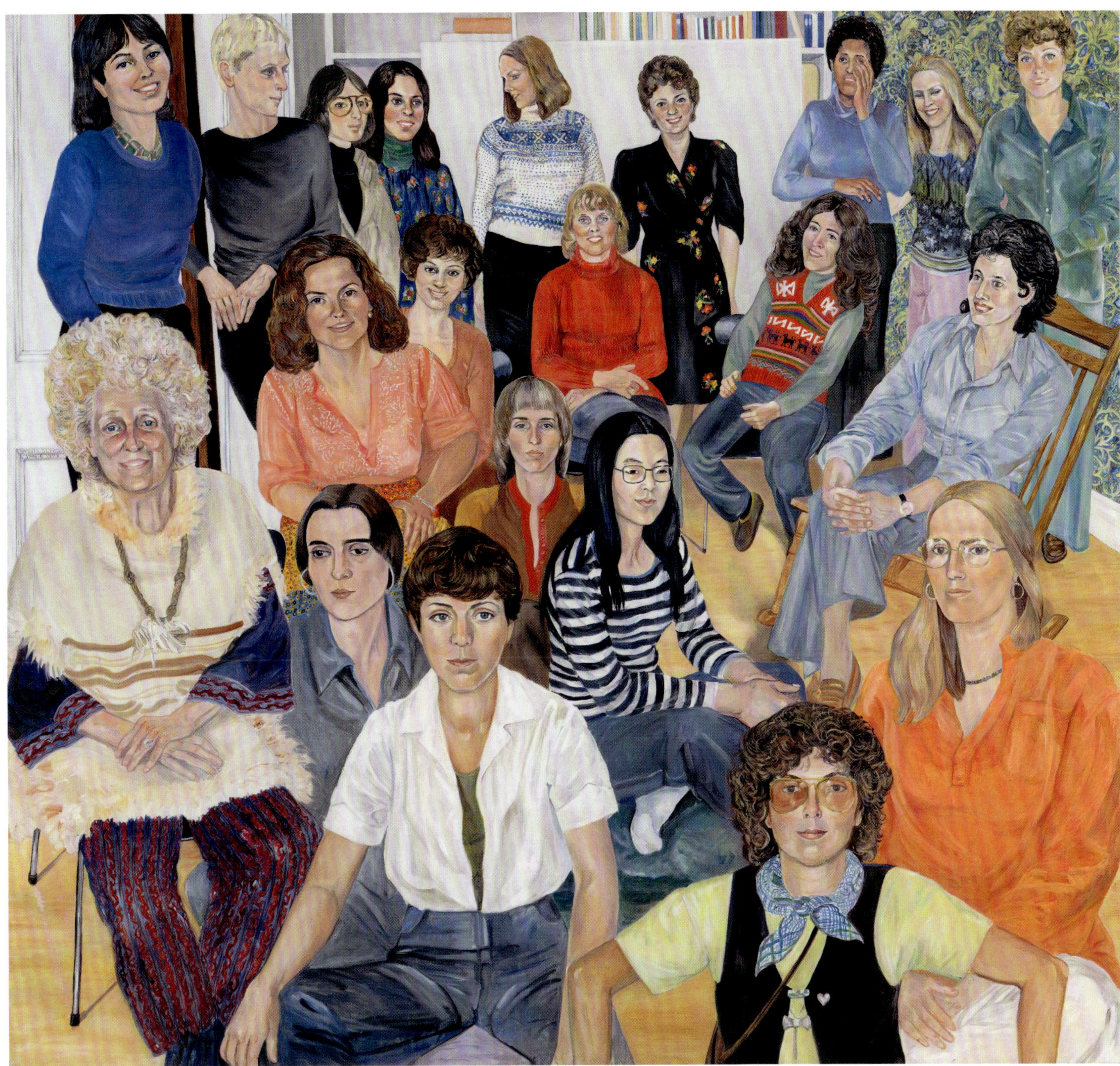

A.I.R. GROUP PORTRAIT
1977–8, oil on canvas, 190.5 × 208.3 cm (75 × 82 in), Whitney Museum of American Art, New York, USA

Sylvia Sleigh, born 1916, Llandudno, Wales, UK. Died 2010, New York, USA.

Welsh-born painter Sleigh rose to prominence during the women's liberation and feminist art movement in 1970s New York, where she had moved in 1961. She was a founding member of SOHO20 and later joined the alternative all-women and artist-directed cooperative gallery spaces Artists in Residence (A.I.R.) Gallery, which was founded in 1972 by artists including Judith Bernstein (p.54) and Harmony Hammond (p.130). While Sleigh is best known for her paintings of naked men, whom she depicted in postures typically associated with the female nude – a gesture that aimed to reverse stereotypes in art history – she also painted large group portraits and affectionate portraits of fellow women artists and writers. In the colourful *A.I.R. Group Portrait* she captures many of the numerous women associated with the gallery, including Dotty Attie (p.36) and Howardena Pindell (p.237). Sleigh's realist approach captured the individual style and appearance of her sitters, each made unique by their physiognomy and pose, and their choice in garments, hairstyles and glasses. Akin to a history painting, the canvas reads as a snapshot of a particular era as well as a document of a vital feminist art movement.

EMILY MAE SMITH

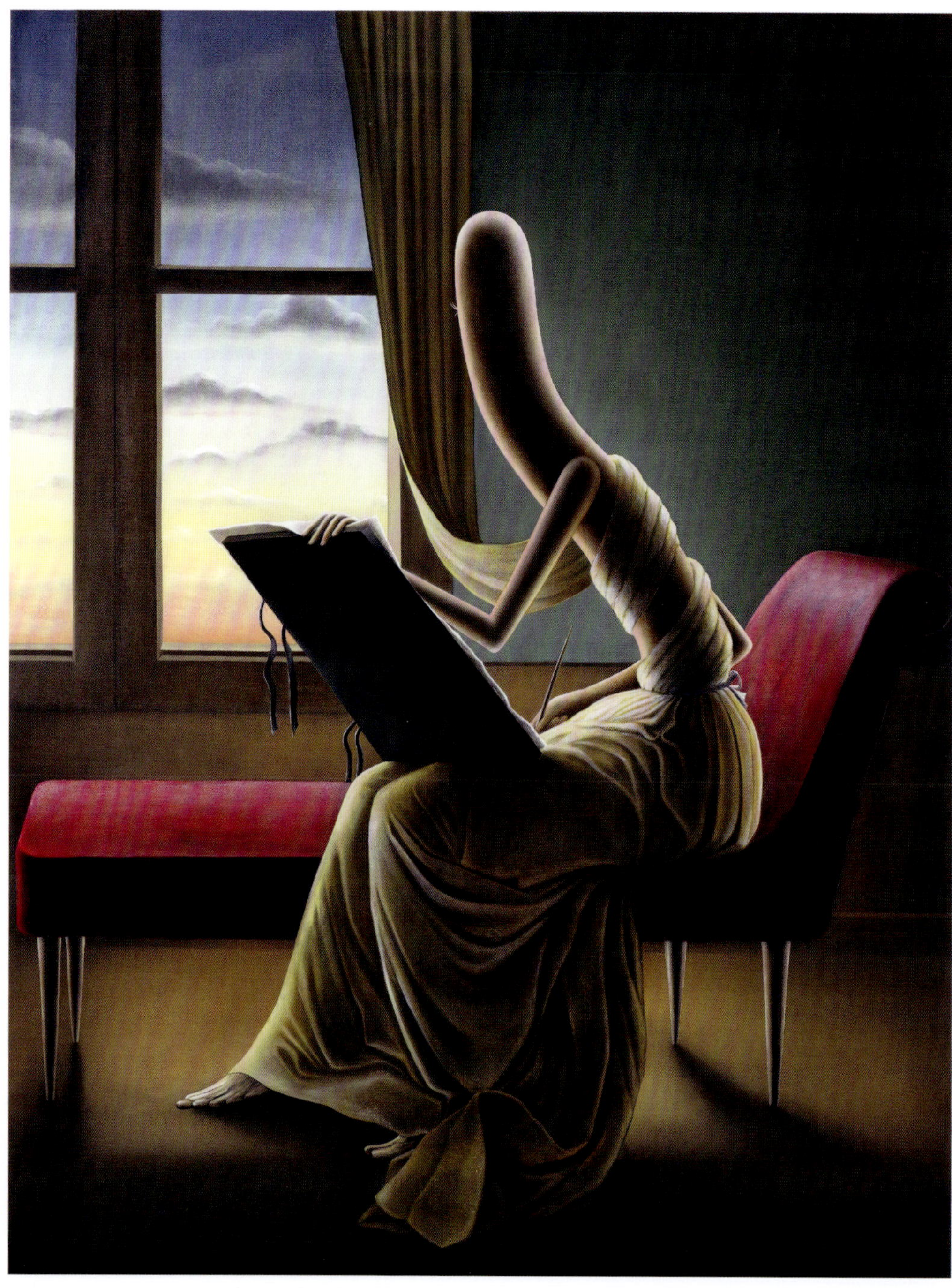

THE DRAWING ROOM
2018, oil on linen, 121.9 × 94 cm (48 × 37 in)

Emily Mae Smith, born 1979, Austin, Texas, USA.

Smith's surreal style of figuration plays with visual elements derived from Western painting, notably riffing on the movements of Symbolism, Surrealism and Pop art. In lieu of the female nude, her wry works have consistently featured an anthropomorphic broom character, influenced by the animated dancing brooms in the Disney film *Fantasia* (1940). 'The broom has become this really handy tool for me to work around the gendered connotations that you might get from painting the naked female figure,' Smith told *Elephant* in 2018. A multifaceted symbol of female labour and the domestic realm, while also suggestive of the artist's paintbrush or the phallus, Smith's broom has been shown in various scenarios. In *The Drawing Room* it is configured as a female artist rendering the sunset – a reference to the famous 1801 painting *Young Woman Drawing* by the French portrait artist Marie-Denise Villers (p.311), which until the 1960s had been incorrectly attributed to Jacques-Louis David (1748–1825). Smith's nod to the original work, along with her replacement of its central figure with her singular protagonist, embodies the story of this moment in feminist art history.

JAUNE QUICK-TO-SEE SMITH

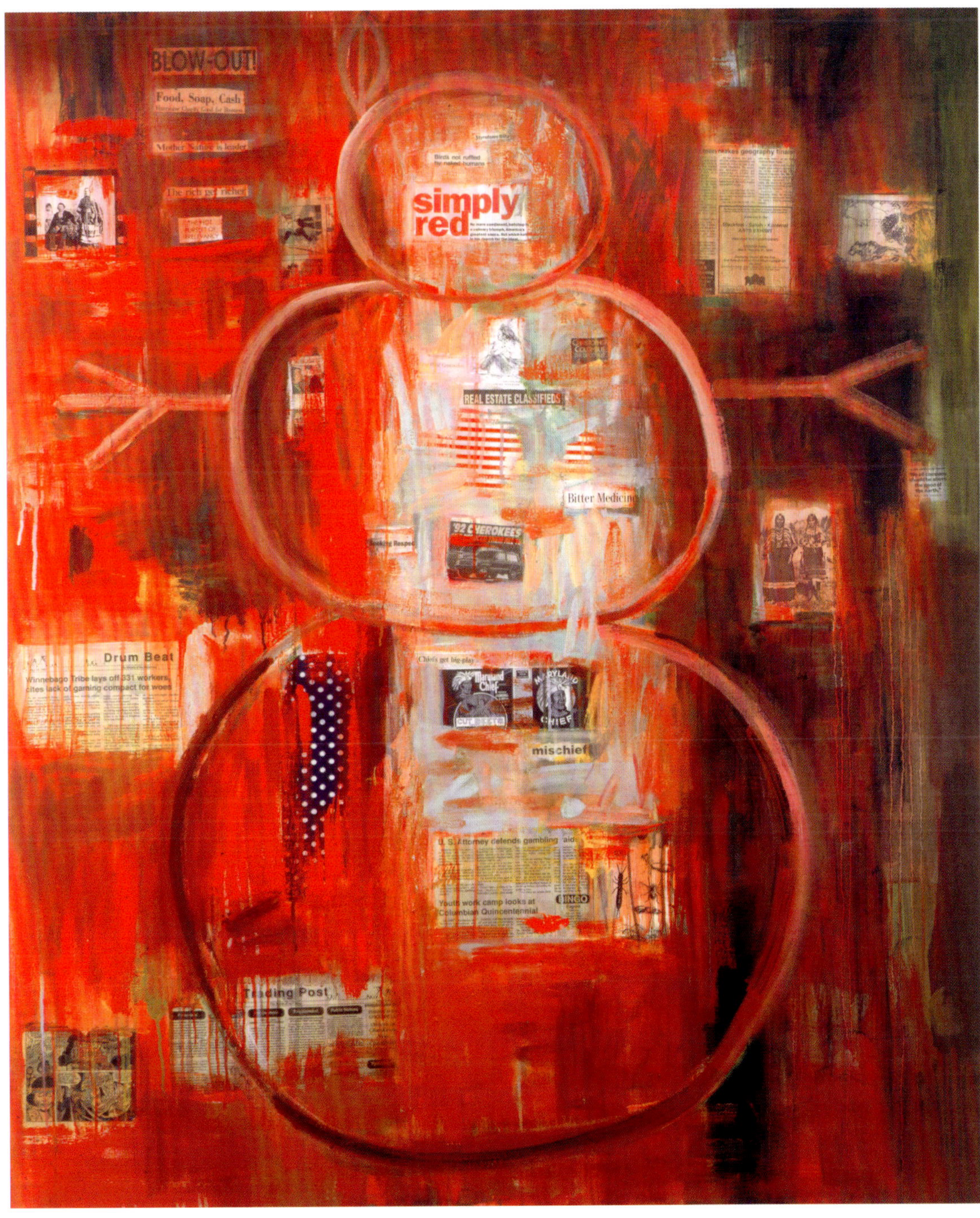

I SEE RED: SNOWMAN
1992, mixed media on canvas, 167.6 × 127 cm (66 × 50 in), collection of Beth Rudin DeWoody

Jaune Quick-to-See Smith, born 1940, St. Ignatius Indian Mission, Confederated Salish and Kootenai Nation, Montana, USA.

Across the flatbed surfaces of her mixed-media paintings, Smith merges scrawling, painterly designs with found images and newspaper clippings bearing reference to her personal history and to the colonial and First Nations histories of North America. An enrolled Salish member of the Confederated Salish and Kootenai Nation of Montana, Smith aims to challenge the pernicious stereotypes and historical erasures that have impacted Indigenous communities. Her 'I See Red' series of the early 1990s takes as a starting point the titular hue's use as a racial slur, evoking the violence of colonial dispossession and its ongoing effects today. In *I See Red: Snowman*, cut-out slogans making coy reference to the colour are placed in dynamic juxtaposition with advertisements, ethnographic photographs and sports logos that convey derivative, generalizing tropes of Native Americans. At the same time, the artist's painterly style – marked by gestural brushstrokes, drips and splatters – seems to recall Abstract Expressionism, a movement credited with the ascension of American painting to a world stage, but whose leading artists often appropriated Indigenous visual and spiritual practices.

MARY T. SMITH

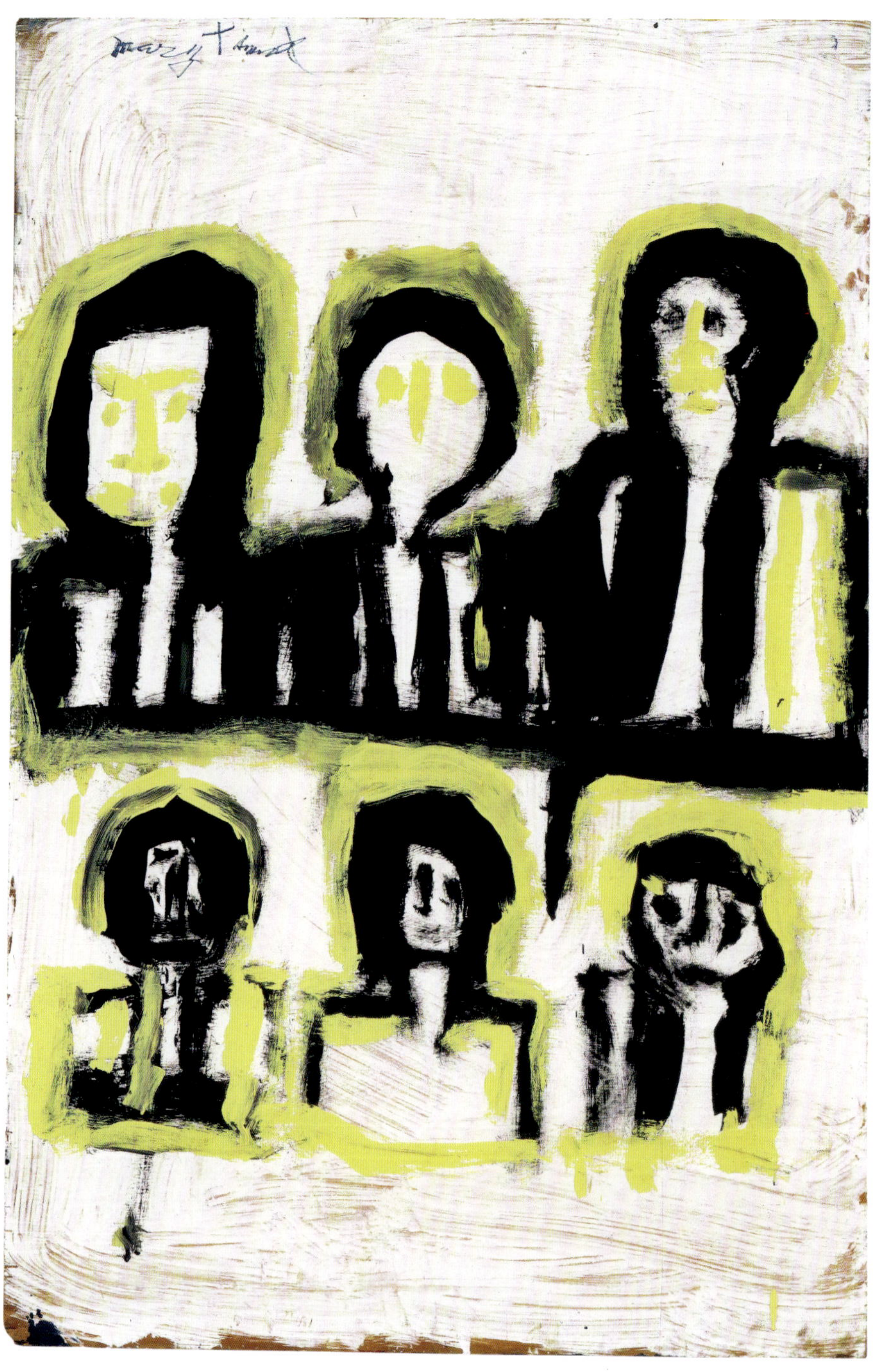

UNTITLED
1987, commercial paint on plywood, 121.9 × 81.3 cm (48 × 32 in), Metropolitan Museum of Art, New York, USA

Mary T. Smith, born 1905, Copiah County, Mississippi, USA. Died 1995, Hazlehurst, Mississippi.

Born to a sharecropping family in the American South, Smith and her twelve siblings grew up performing farm labour. A hearing impairment dogged her from childhood, leading to many hours spent alone, drawing. In the late 1970s, after retiring from a life spent working as a domestic servant, she turned to art, expressing the ideas that had developed during her childhood art-making. Taking corrugated tin from a nearby garbage dump, she constructed several structures in her yard, including a makeshift studio where she painted onto scraps of wood and iron sheets, displaying them in an outdoor gallery filled with portraits of friends and neighbours, as well as religious subjects reflecting her deeply held Christian faith. Smith's highly stylized figures, created with household paint in a pared back colour palette, are rendered with broad, brushy strokes, often accompanied by short, pithy texts – some in her own personal improvised writing system that was unintelligible to others. Her simple and direct style is exemplified by this image of six anonymous figures painted with thick black and yellow outlines on a monochrome background.

JANET SOBEL

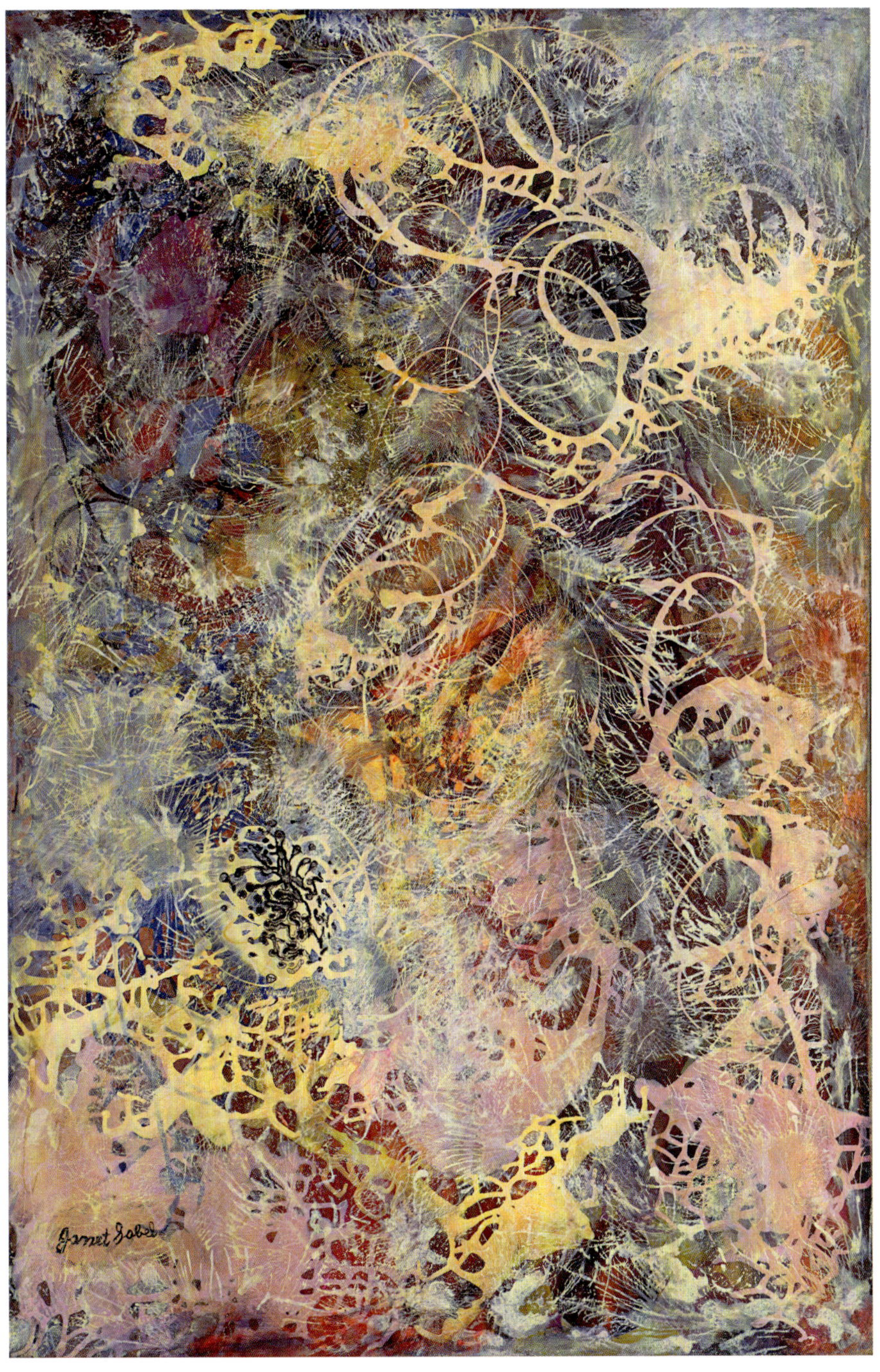

MILKY WAY
1945, enamel on canvas, 114 × 75.9 cm (44 7/8 × 29 7/8 in), Museum of Modern Art, New York, USA

Janet Sobel, born 1893, Dnipro, Ukraine. Died 1968, Plainfield, New Jersey, USA.

Sobel is known as the originator of the revolutionary 'drip' style, one of the most important developments in twentieth-century painting, exemplified in one of her best-known works, *Milky Way*, completed two years before Jackson Pollock (1912–56) would create his first drip painting. Sobel immigrated to the United States from Ukraine in 1908. She had never taken an art class when, at the age of forty-five, she began experimenting with enamel paint at home, splattering it and letting it drip onto scraps of paper with glass pipettes. Her expressive vigour and the physicality of her painting – she often worked lying on her stomach – aligns with the methods later favoured by the Abstract Expressionists. Sobel's work caught the attention of Peggy Guggenheim, who included Sobel in the landmark exhibition 'The Women' at The Art of This Century gallery in New York in 1945 and subsequently presented a solo exhibition in 1946. It was at these exhibitions, as art critic Clement Greenberg recorded, that Pollock encountered and took inspiration from Sobel's work. He went on to become one of the world's most widely acclaimed artists, while Sobel faded into obscurity despite a rich repository of more than one thousand works.

PAT STEIR

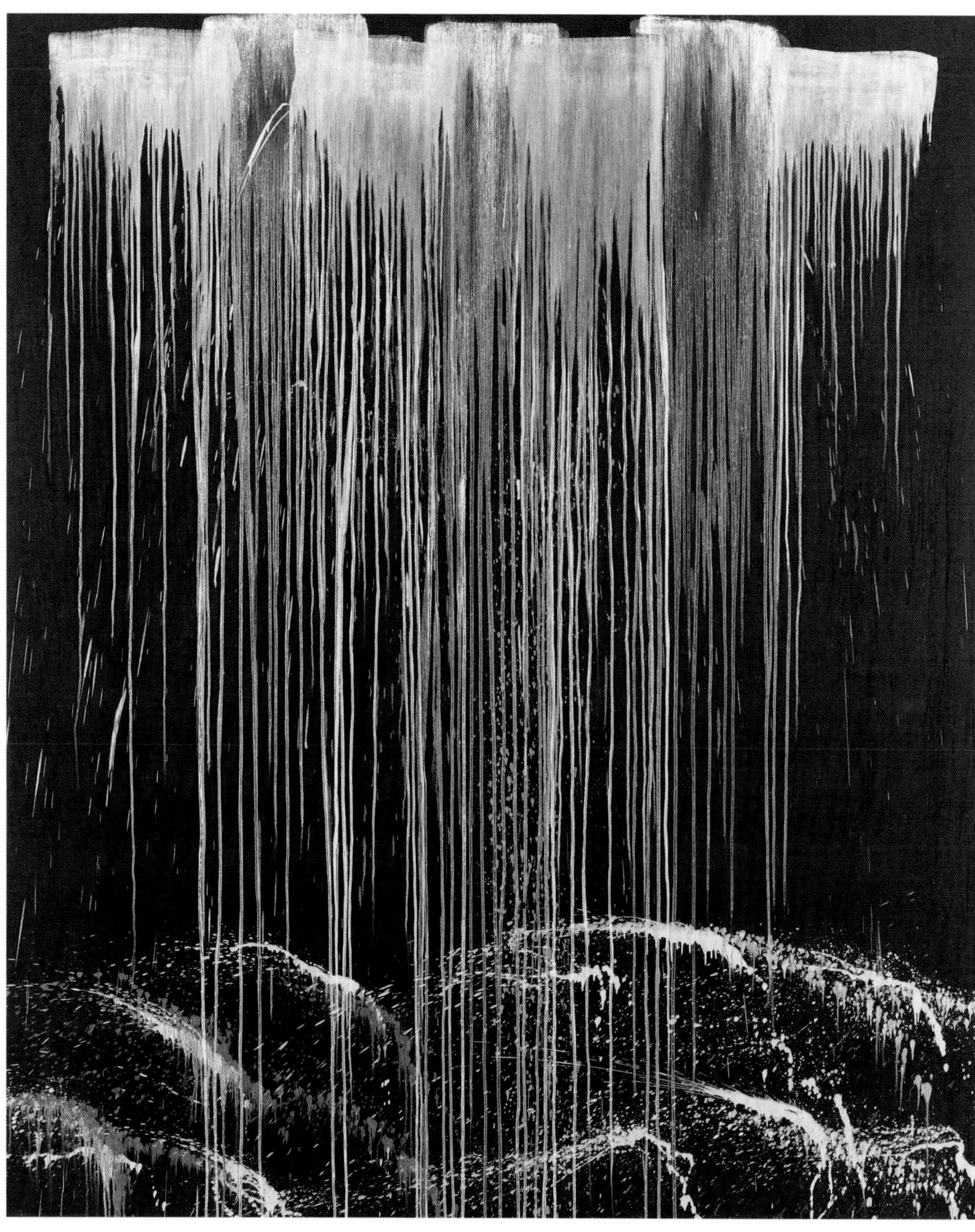

ELEPHANT WATERFALL
1990, oil on canvas, 346.7 × 288.3 cm
(136½ × 113½ in)

Pat Steir, born 1940, Newark, New Jersey, USA.

At once gestural and reserved, Steir's large-scale paintings are composed of chance and a quiet spiritual enquiry. Associated with Minimalism and the Conceptual art movement in the 1960s and 1970s, the collected canvases of her mid and late style reveal the influence of Japanese *hatsuboku* and Chinese *shuimo* paintings, in which scenes are evoked with washes of ink and few loose, intuitive brushstrokes. Pursuing a similar fluidity and restraint in her work, Steir applies oil to dark ground with oversoaked brushes, the excess pigment running in turpentine rivulets down the picture plane. 'The paint itself makes the picture,' the artist said in a 1995 monograph. 'Gravity makes the image.' While Steir is often referred to as a conceptual abstract artist, she prefers the term 'non-objective' to describe her work – it is not, she suggests, an abstraction of anything, but rather a notation of movement and time. In her 'Waterfall' series, begun in 1988, however, Steir traverses the pictorial and performative, the literal and metaphoric – each painting at once a waterfall and its invocation. Where earlier works in the series, such as *Elephant Waterfall*, are largely monochromatic, later iterations shift towards saturated colour.

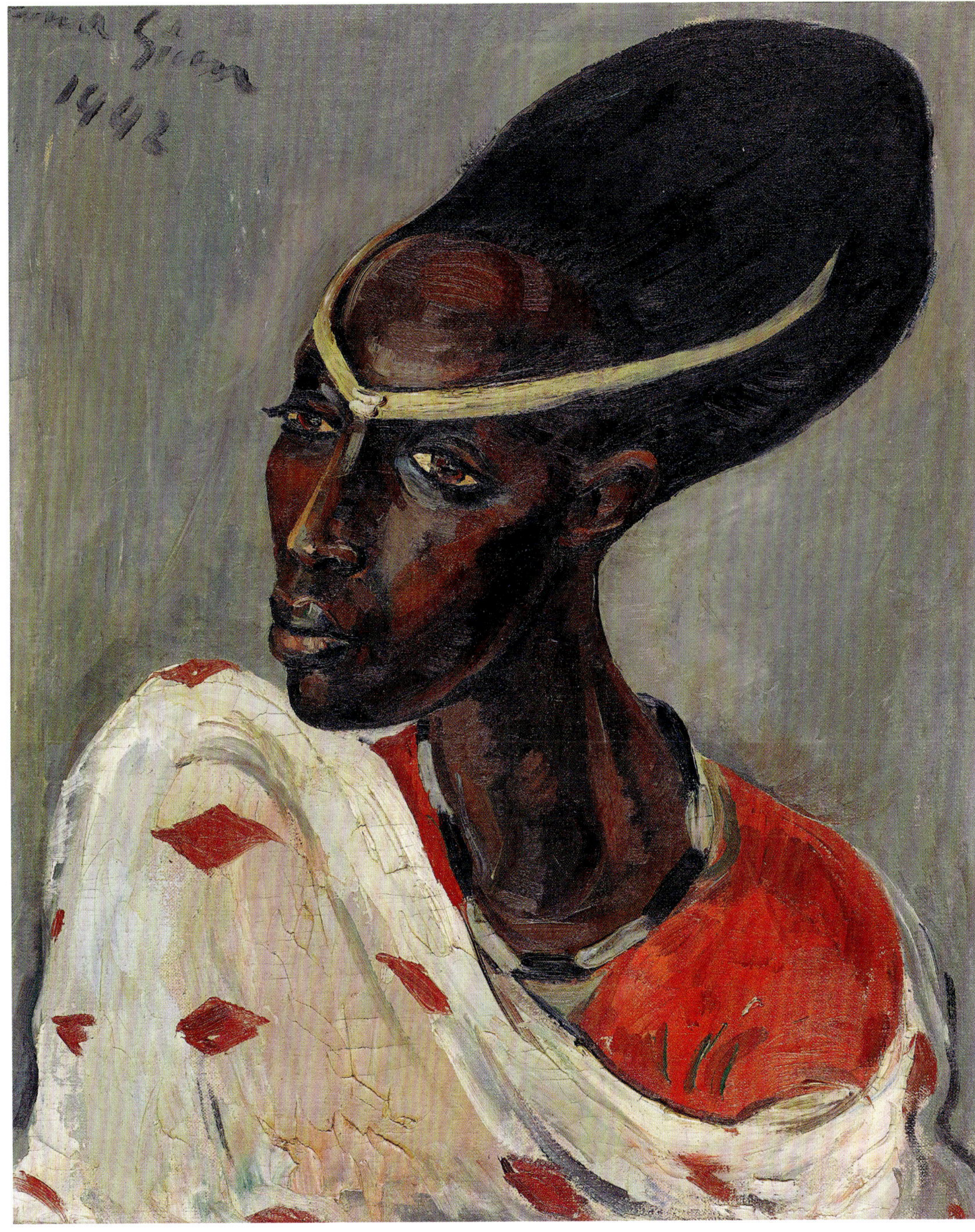

WATUSSI PRINCESS (EMMA BAKAYISHONGA)
1942, oil on canvas, 69 × 55 cm (27 × 21 ½ in)

Irma Stern, born 1894, Schweizer-Reneke, South Africa. Died 1966, Cape Town, South Africa.

An early South African modernist, Stern holds a prodigious position in the country's art history. Born to German parents in rural South Africa, Stern spent her formative years in Berlin, where she studied under German Expressionist Max Pechstein (1881–1955), whose primitivist style inspired her own. Returning to Cape Town in 1920, Stern paired modernism's formal enquiries with so-called 'native studies', an art movement aligned with ethnographic scholarship. Stern's work has been criticized for the artist's colonial sentiments, expressed in her works' romantic and simplistic imaginings of the 'dark continent'. As such, few of her Black subjects are named, thus reduced from individuals to ethnic emblems, but Stern nevertheless transcribes their visages with sensitivity and care, lending emotional depth in her impasto renderings. Stern's approach was one of form and feeling, her canvases rich in tone and expression, as seen in *Watussi Princess*, made during the artist's first trip to the Belgian Congo (now Democratic Republic of the Congo). 'Here I had found the quintessence of beauty,' Stern wrote of the Watussi nobility in her journal in 1942. The retrospective retitling of the work to include the sitter's name has since endowed this portrait with the weight of historical record.

HEDDA STERNE

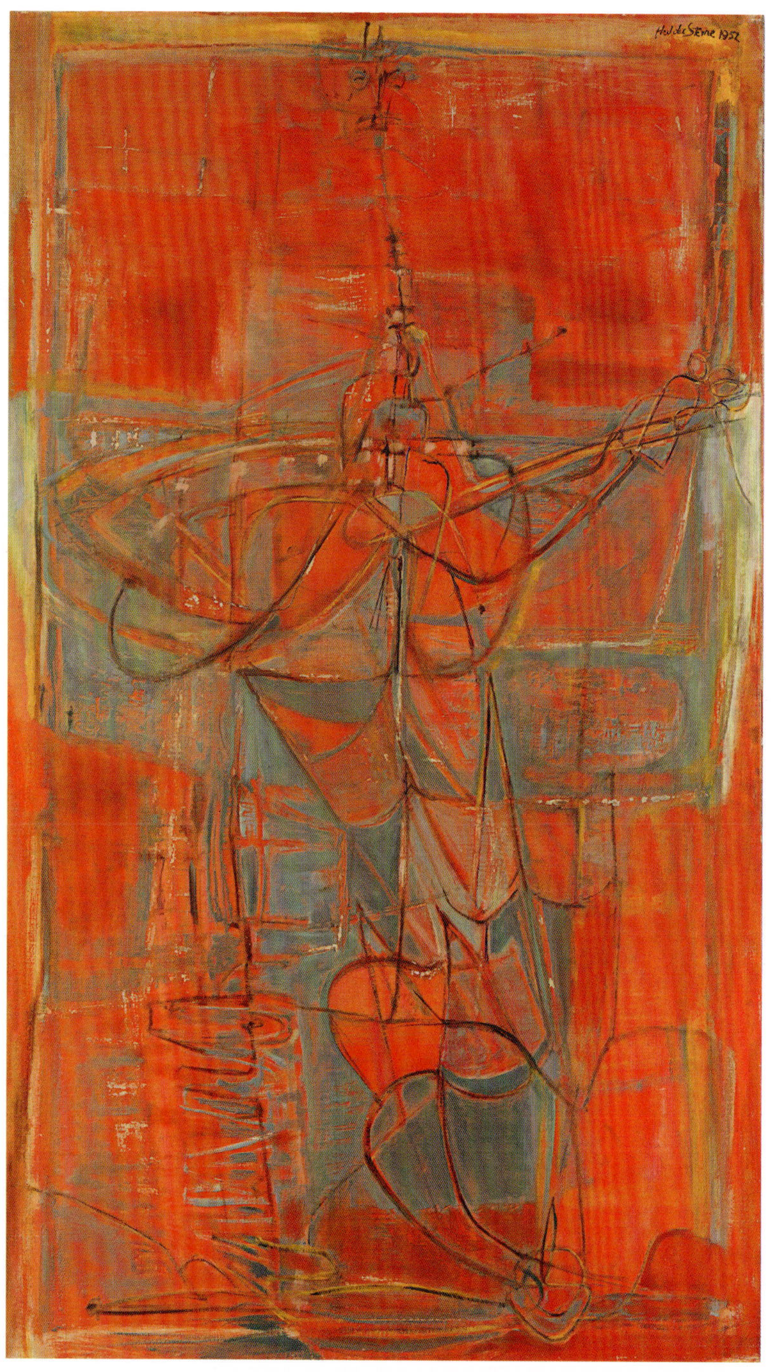

NUMBER 31, VERMILLION MACHINE
1952, oil on canvas, 132.4 × 76.8 cm (52 ⅛ × 30 ¼ in), Metropolitan Museum of Art, New York, USA

Hedda Sterne, born 1910, Bucharest, Romania. Died 2011, New York, USA.

A reluctance to align with one style may have contributed to Sterne's exclusion from the art-historical canon, although she considered being the only woman in the 1951 *Life* magazine photograph of New York School painters was what distracted attention away from her art; as she stated in a 2010 *New York Review of Books* article, 'I am known more for that darn photo than for eighty years of work.' During her long career – she was still drawing aged one hundred despite almost total loss of eyesight – she made both figurative and abstract compositions, and though she was associated with both Abstract Expressionism and Surrealism, she remained largely independent. As a teenager, Sterne took art classes in Vienna and Paris, then studied art history and philosophy at the University of Bucharest. After narrowly escaping the Bucharest pogrom, in 1941 she fled Europe for New York, where her paintings were soon exhibited regularly by Peggy Guggenheim, including in the influential '31 Women' (1943). *Number 31, Vermillion Machine* is informed by Sterne's fascination with mechanized power in her adopted country, which prompted an interest in capturing the visual qualities of machines in motion.

FLORINE STETTHEIMER

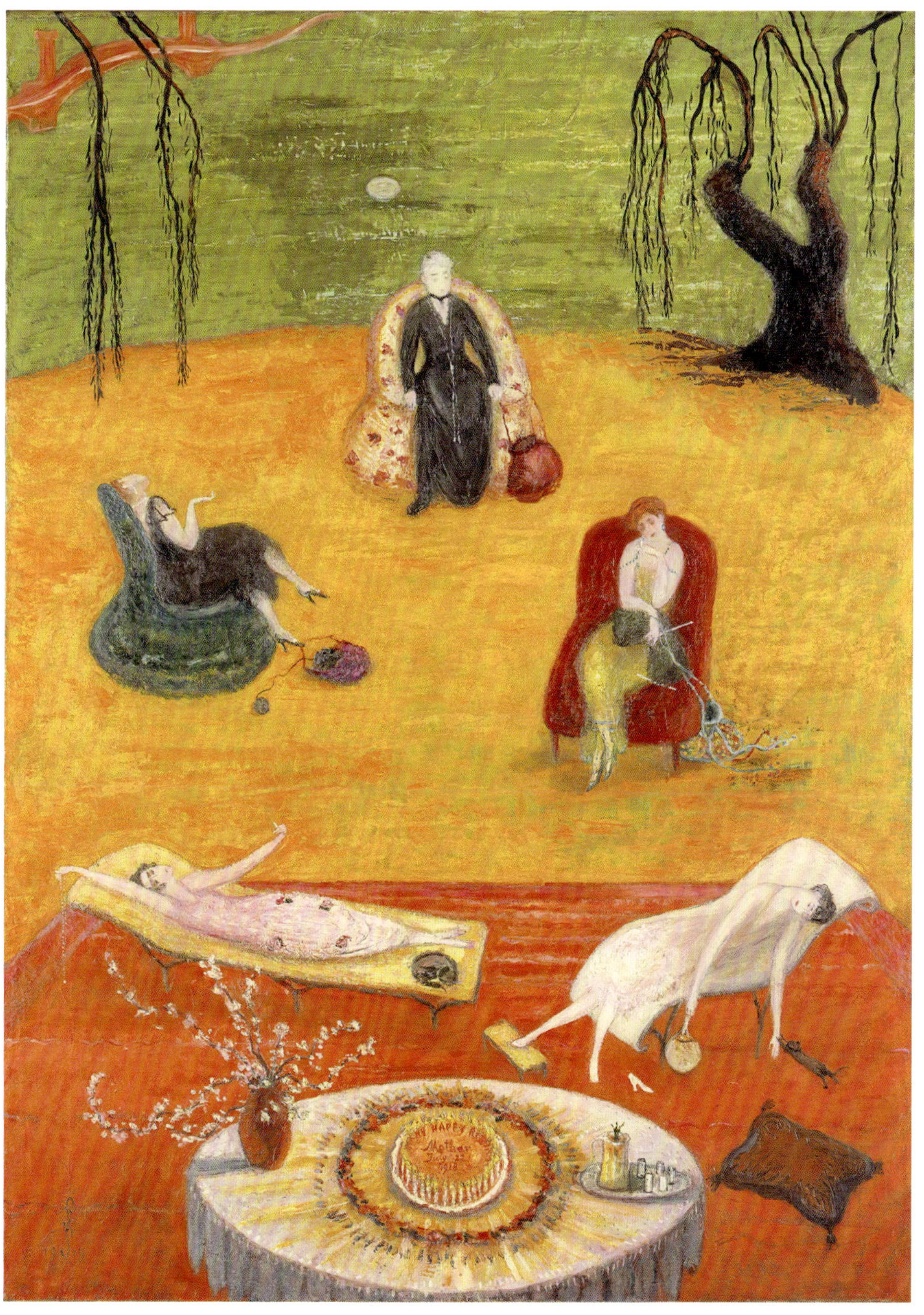

HEAT
1919, oil on canvas, 127 × 92.7 cm (50 × 36½ in), Brooklyn Museum, USA

Florine Stettheimer, born 1871, Rochester, New York, USA. Died 1944, New York, USA.

Painter, poet and salon doyenne of Jazz Age New York, Stettheimer was trained privately and at the Art Students League in New York. After living in Europe for almost twenty years, Stettheimer returned to New York at the outbreak of the First World War. In 1916 she held her only solo exhibition at the Knoedler Gallery; due to its poor reception, she decided against a public career, and as a result her work was little known during her lifetime. Along with her mother and sisters, Stettheimer held salons for the New York's avant-garde from their uptown apartment, hosting figures such as Hilla Rebay (p.244), Marcel Duchamp (1887–1968) – who would later help organize her first posthumous retrospective at the Museum of Modern Art – and Gertrude Stein, for whose experimental opera *Four Saints in Three Acts* (1934) Stettheimer designed the costumes and sets. Stettheimer's mature style was theatrical and richly coloured, the canvas structured like a stage occupied by friends and family members. In the earlier work *Heat*, Stettheimer presents a portrait of her mother, her sisters and herself arranged in a wide circle and lazing about in a dreamlike landscape, its otherworldly yellow ground evoking the mood of a sweltering summer day.

BECKY SUSS

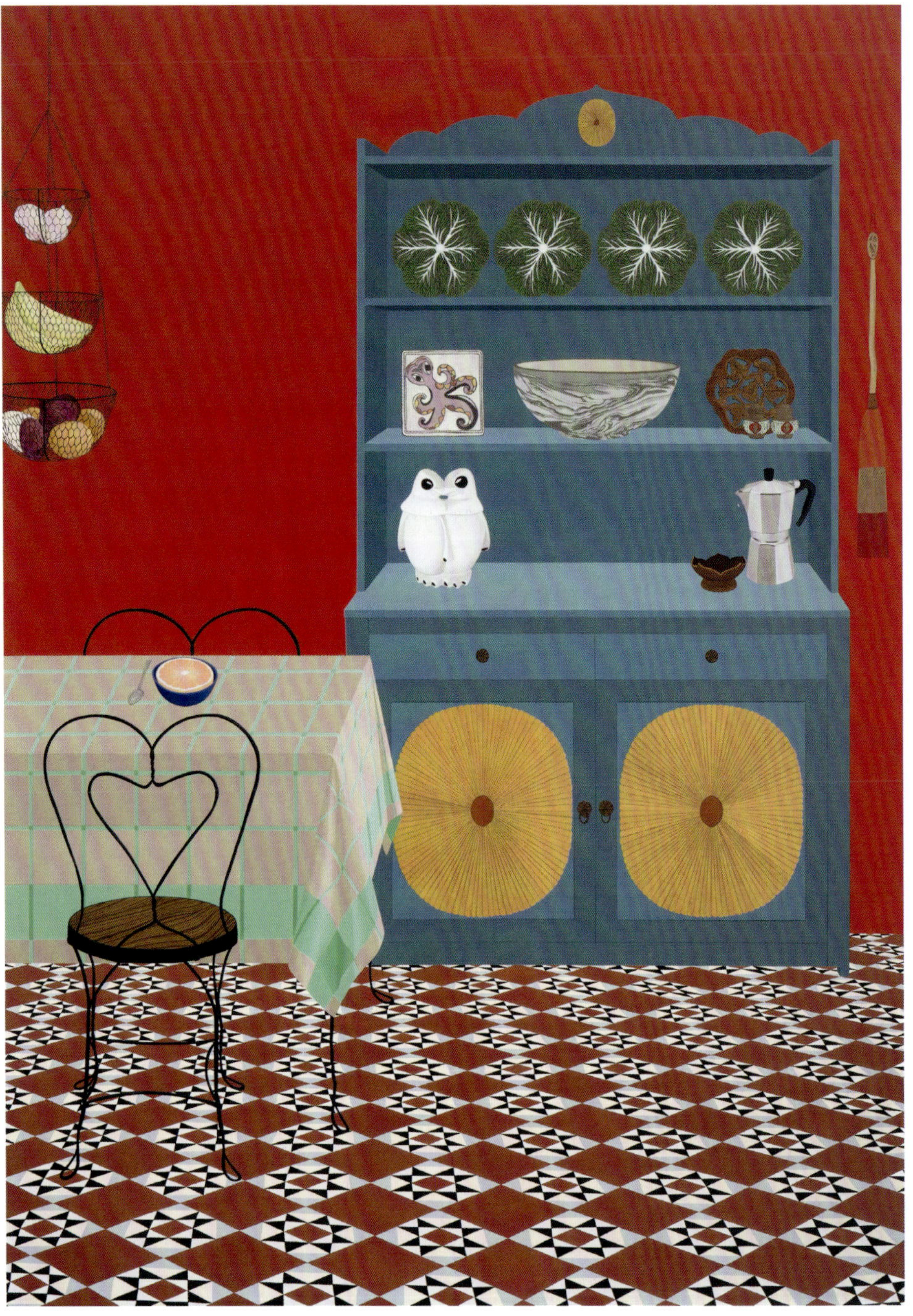

RED APARTMENT
2016, oil on canvas, 213.4 × 152.4 × 3.5 cm
(84 × 60 × 1 ⅜ in)

Becky Suss, born 1980, Philadelphia, USA.

Presenting domestic spaces and reimagined interiors from children's books on a monumental scale enables Suss to celebrate and elevate traditionally undervalued and formative spaces most closely associated with women and children. For inspiration the artist uses library archives, magazines, house museums, image databases and children's books, re-creating scenes and objects from the latter in a number of works. Suss first created interior scenes to immortalize her grandparents' demolished mid-century Long Island home. Initially depicting real spaces from memory, the artist added ubiquitous objects and decor her viewers could associate with, such as the Bialetti Moka seen in this work. In *Red Apartment* the crimson wall comes from Suss's family home and the Victorian tiled floor from a magazine photograph. This approach allows her to blur the boundaries between fact and fiction, the personal and the universal, and the present and the past. Suss's paintings are almost-lifesize spaces the viewer can imagine stepping into, though the flattened architecture, distorted perspectives and stylized textures and colours solicit a psychological-emotional response as much as a purely aesthetic or physical encounter.

VIVIAN SUTER

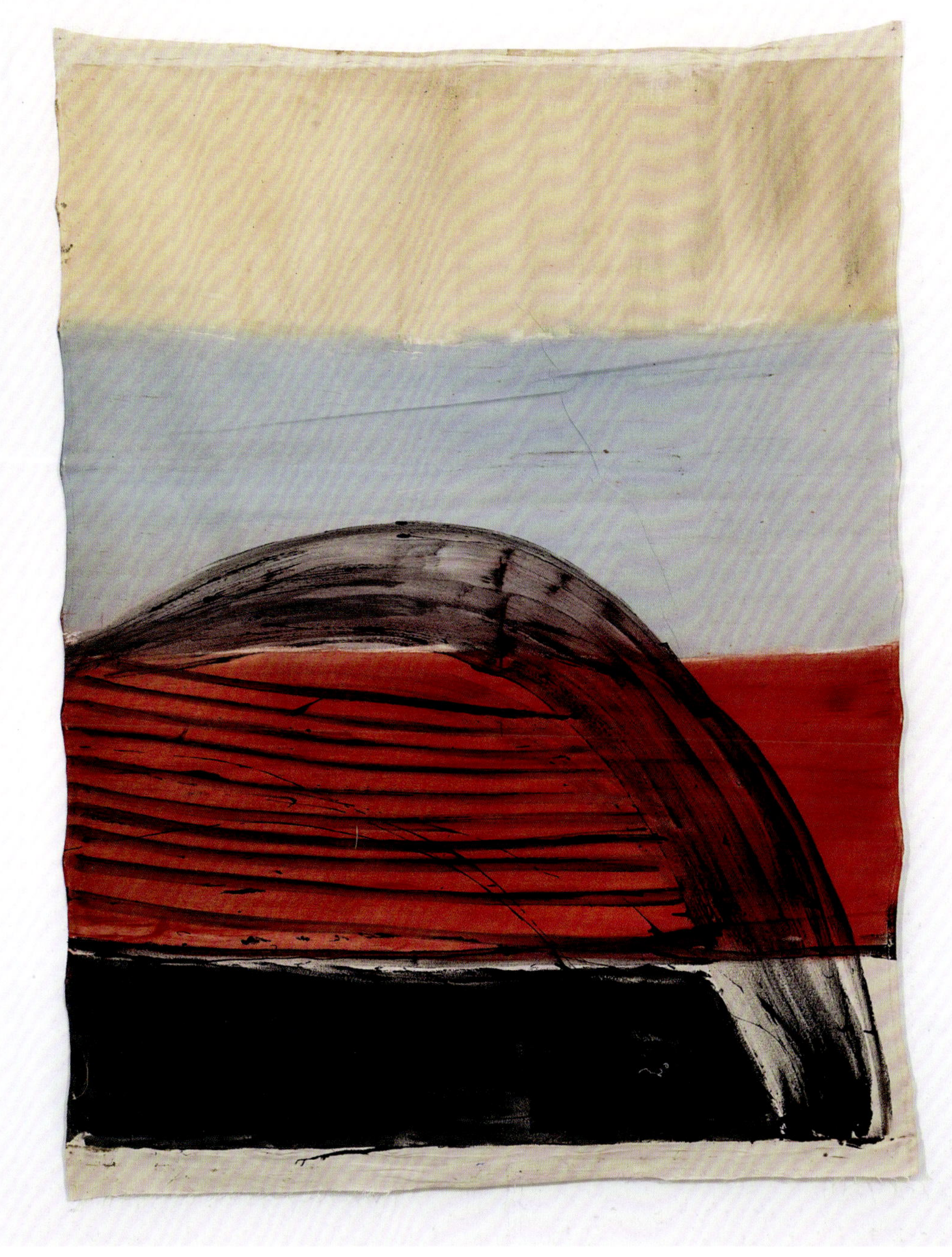

UNTITLED
date unknown, mixed media on canvas,
241.3 × 233.7 cm (95 × 92 in)

Vivian Suter, born 1949, Buenos Aires, Argentina.

Suter was born in Argentina but grew up in Basel, Switzerland, and enjoyed precocious success in her youth, with her first solo show at the age of twenty-two. After deciding that she disliked the socializing needed to build a career, she moved to Guatemala in 1983; she was only 'rediscovered' in 2011 for a group exhibition at Kunsthalle Basel. Suter lives and works in Guatemala's Panajachel rainforest, on the slopes of a volcano beside Lake Atitlán. Inevitably, the environment plays an important part in her work. After a mudslide in 2005 ruined the contents of her studio, Suter decided to work with nature instead of against it, and her abstract paintings since then exhibit not just her own designs but the random imprints of raindrops, leaves, twigs, mud and mildew. This work is characteristic of her painting process: Suter works outside on stretched canvas, mixing housepaint with rainwater, mud and fish glue, mark-making with heavy impasto brushstrokes; the painting is then left out in the wind and rain before being removed from the stretcher and hung on a drying rack. In installation, dozens of canvases are hung throughout the exhibition space, layered atop each other on the floors and walls, creating an immersive environment for visitors to inhabit.

MARY SWANZY

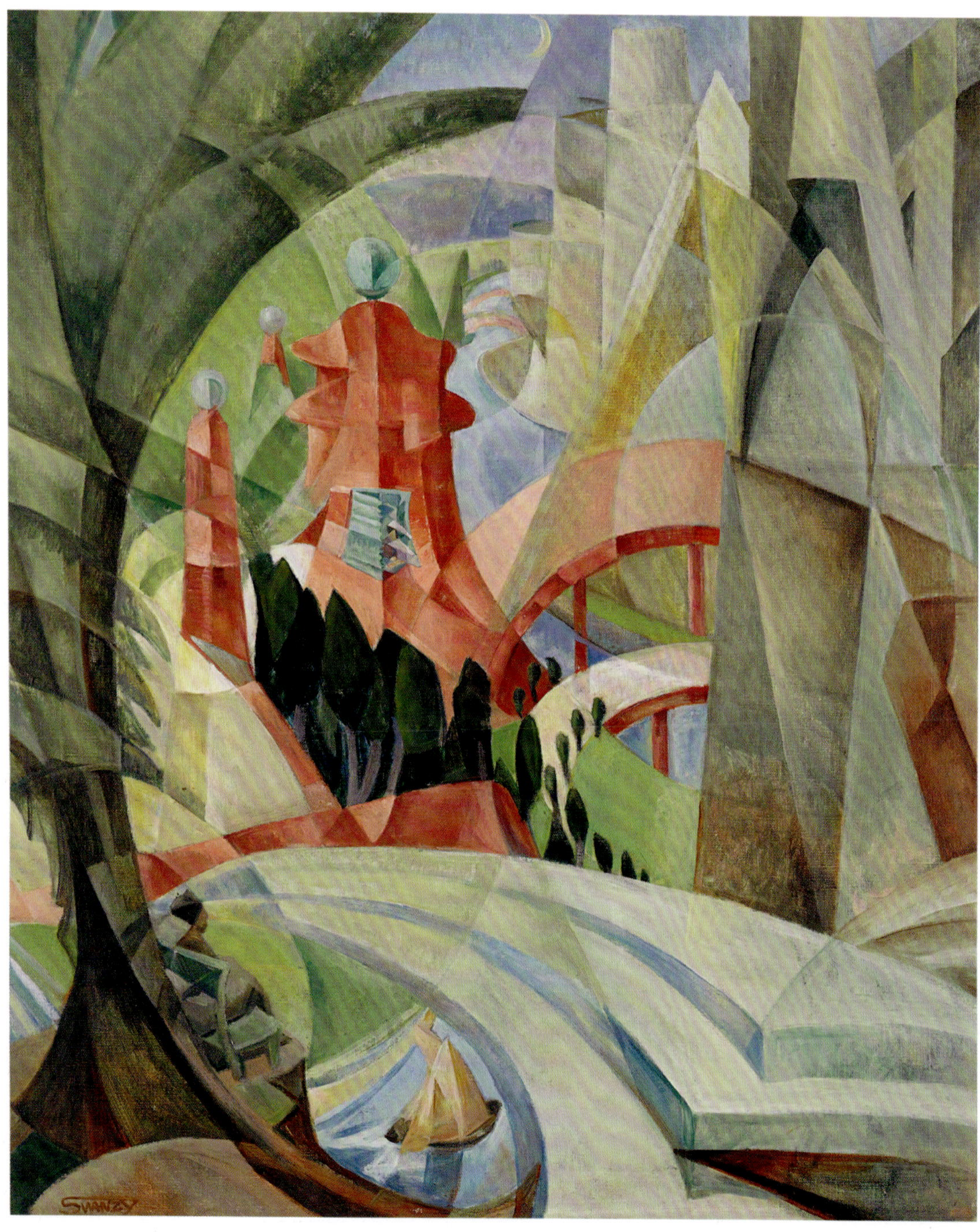

CUBIST LANDSCAPE WITH RED PAGODA AND BRIDGE
*c.*1925–30, oil on canvas, 76 × 63.5 cm (29 ⅞ × 25 in)

Mary Swanzy, born 1882, Dublin, Ireland. Died 1978, London, UK.

Swanzy's privileged Anglo-Irish upbringing enabled her to study in France and Germany and to travel widely. At Dublin's Metropolitan School of Art, she had studied with landscape painter Mary Manning (1853–1930), mastering academic realism at a young age. Encouraged by Manning to further her training in Paris, Swanzy attended the progressive Académie Colarossi and encountered Pablo Picasso's (1881–1973) early works at Gertrude Stein's famous home-gallery. Financially independent upon the death of her parents, Swanzy made the uncommon decision to travel extensively, producing her most recognizable body of work in the 1920s in Hawaii and Samoa. Her style in this period combines the fragmented planes of Cubism with the high-value colours of Orphism and Fauvism. Small figures in repose in this prismatic landscape foretell the artist's return to Surrealist-style figuration later in her career. Despite early high-profile exhibitions in Paris, Swanzy's later spiritual-mystical works were criticized by male contemporaries. In a 1977 interview with RTE Radio, Swanzy said, 'If I had been born Henry instead of Mary, my life would have been very different,' highlighting how gender inequity impacted her career and the reception of her work.

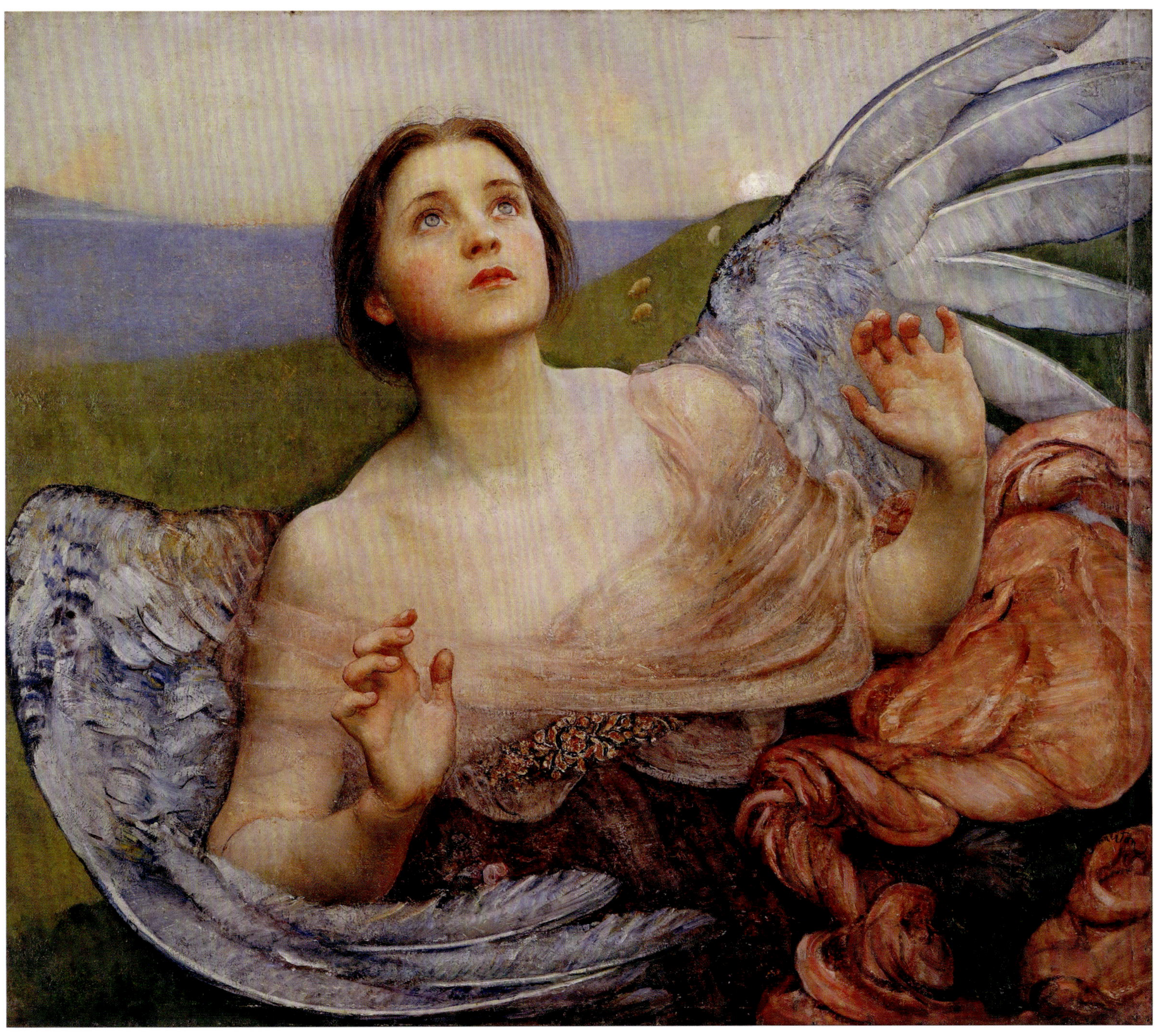

THE SENSE OF SIGHT
1895, oil on canvas, 87.3 × 101 cm (34 ⅜ × 39 ¾ in), Walker Art Gallery, Liverpool, UK

Annie Swynnerton, born 1844, Kersal, Manchester, UK. Died 1933, Hayling Island, Hampshire, UK.

A prolific artist as well as an active advocate of women's right to vote, Swynnerton completed hundreds of paintings, with many more unfinished canvases found posthumously. Having studied at Manchester School of Art, she travelled to Rome then Paris to continue her education. Returning to her native city, in 1879 she co-founded the Manchester Society of Women Painters with Isabel Dacre (1844–1933). Alongside commissioned portraits, Swynnerton become known for her Symbolist works, which drew comparisons to contemporaries George Frederic Watts (1817–1904) and Edward Burne-Jones (1833–98). In 1922, with the endorsement of John Singer Sargent (1856–1925), who had supported and collected her work, she became the first woman to be elected to the Royal Academy of Arts. Swynnerton was noted for her daring representations of the nude and while this winged figure is clothed with translucent cloth, the painting clearly demonstrates the artist's technical skill in rendering skin, human anatomy and reflected light, creating an image that suggests that sight can be spiritual as well as purely visual.

SARAH SZE

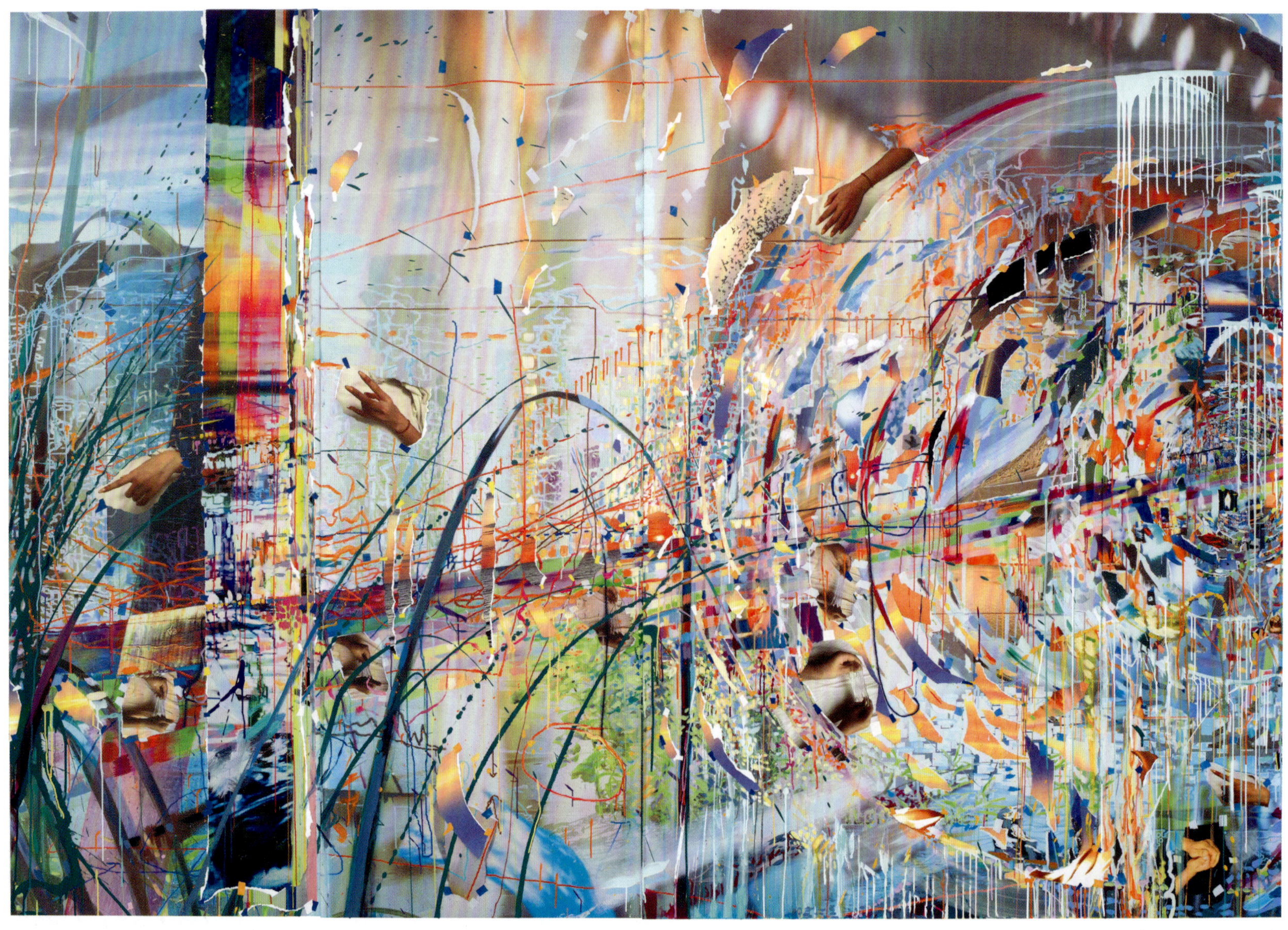

BLADE OF GRASS
2021, oil, acrylic, archival paper, acrylic polymers, ink, Dibond, aluminium and wood, 213.4 × 310.4 × 7.6 cm (84 × 122 ¼ × 3 in)

Sarah Sze, born 1969, Boston, USA.

First gaining art-world recognition in the late 1990s, Sze is best known for her sculptures and installations, in which she assembles constellations of images, everyday materials and screens into intricate immersive environments that consider how the proliferation of objects and images impacts contemporary visual culture. The United States representative at the 53rd Venice Biennale in 2013, Sze graduated with a BFA from Yale University in 1991 and an MFA from the School of Visual Arts, New York, in 1997, initially training in painting and architecture. Since 2018 she has focused renewed attention on a painting practice that furthers the themes and investigations of her sculptural works. Sze's paintings layer a wealth of painted, collaged and printed elements into beguiling, semi-abstract frames that appear as portals into past, future and alternative realities. She often repeats the same image – photographs of hands, a flock of birds or rural American highways, as seen in this work – between her canvases, each time reappearing in slightly altered form, manifesting how images morph, evolve and degrade over space and time. With paint applied in daubs, drips, sweeping brushstrokes and frenetic forking channels, these dynamic landscape paintings expand traditional definitions of the medium.

CLAIRE TABOURET

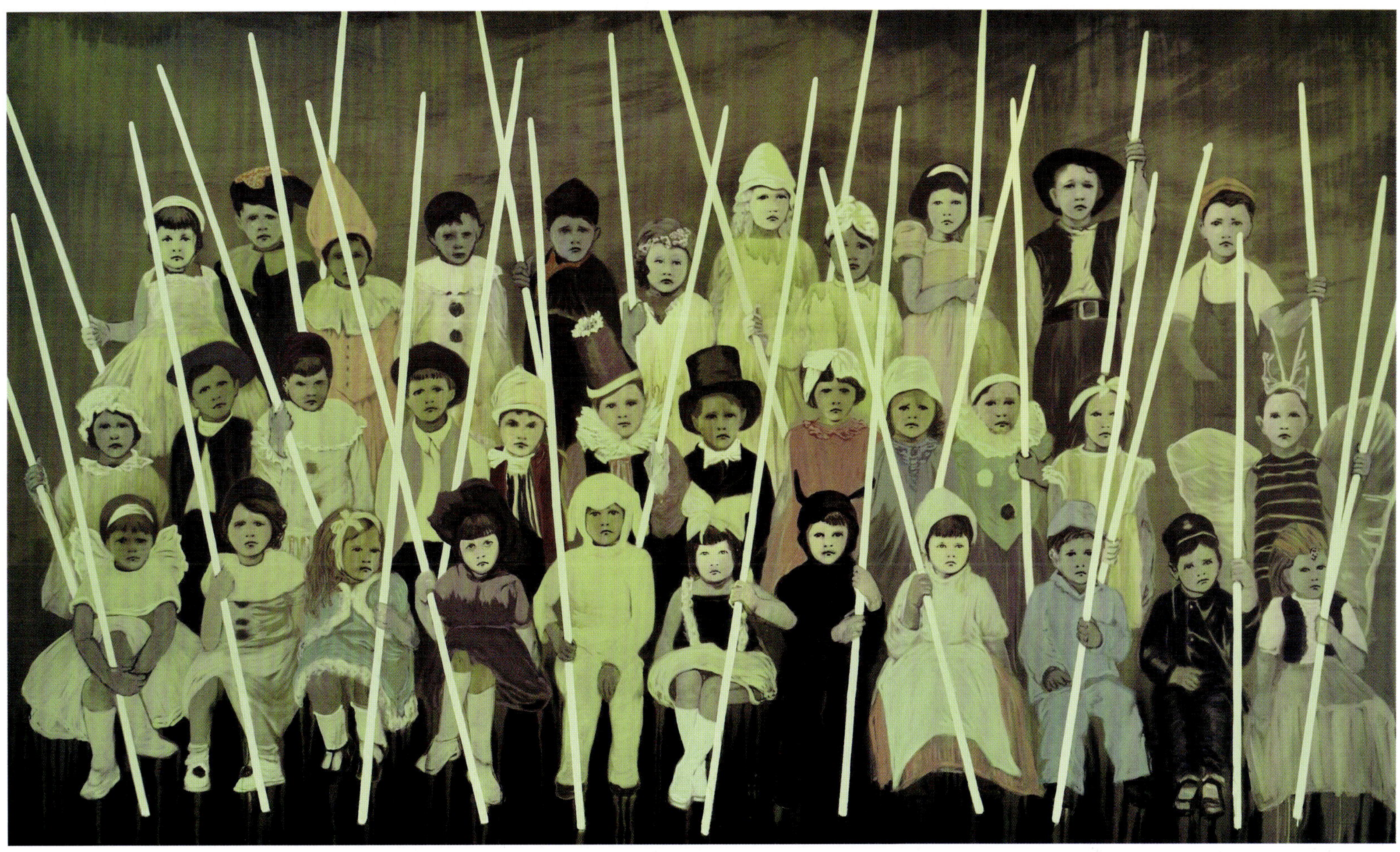

LES VEILLEURS (THE WATCHMEN)
2014, acrylic on canvas, 230 × 400 cm
(90½ × 157½ in)

Claire Tabouret, born 1981, Pertuis, Provence-Alpes-Côte d'Azur, France.

Tabouret has drawn acclaim for her disquieting, theatrical canvases, which are often coated with a fluorescent layer of pigment that bathes them in an eerie light. Trained at the École Nationale Supérieure des Beaux-Arts in Paris, her figurative art practice includes sculpture in a variety of materials as well as paintings on both canvas and paper, all of which are connected by subject matter – primarily representations of children and youth. Using found archival photographs or imagery culled from the internet, Tabouret imbues scenes of familiar childhood activities or snapshot portraits with an otherworldly atmosphere by stripping away reassuring contextual details. In *The Watchmen* the children are lined up in rows as if for a school photograph, wearing fancy dress costumes. While in other circumstances these Pierrots, Snow Whites and bumble bees might appear cute, their whitened, mask-like faces and stern expressions disrupt our expectations of childish innocence. Moreover, they all brandish luminous staffs with menace, an eerie, green glow settling over a group who are, as the title suggests, keeping watch.

SOPHIE TAEUBER-ARP

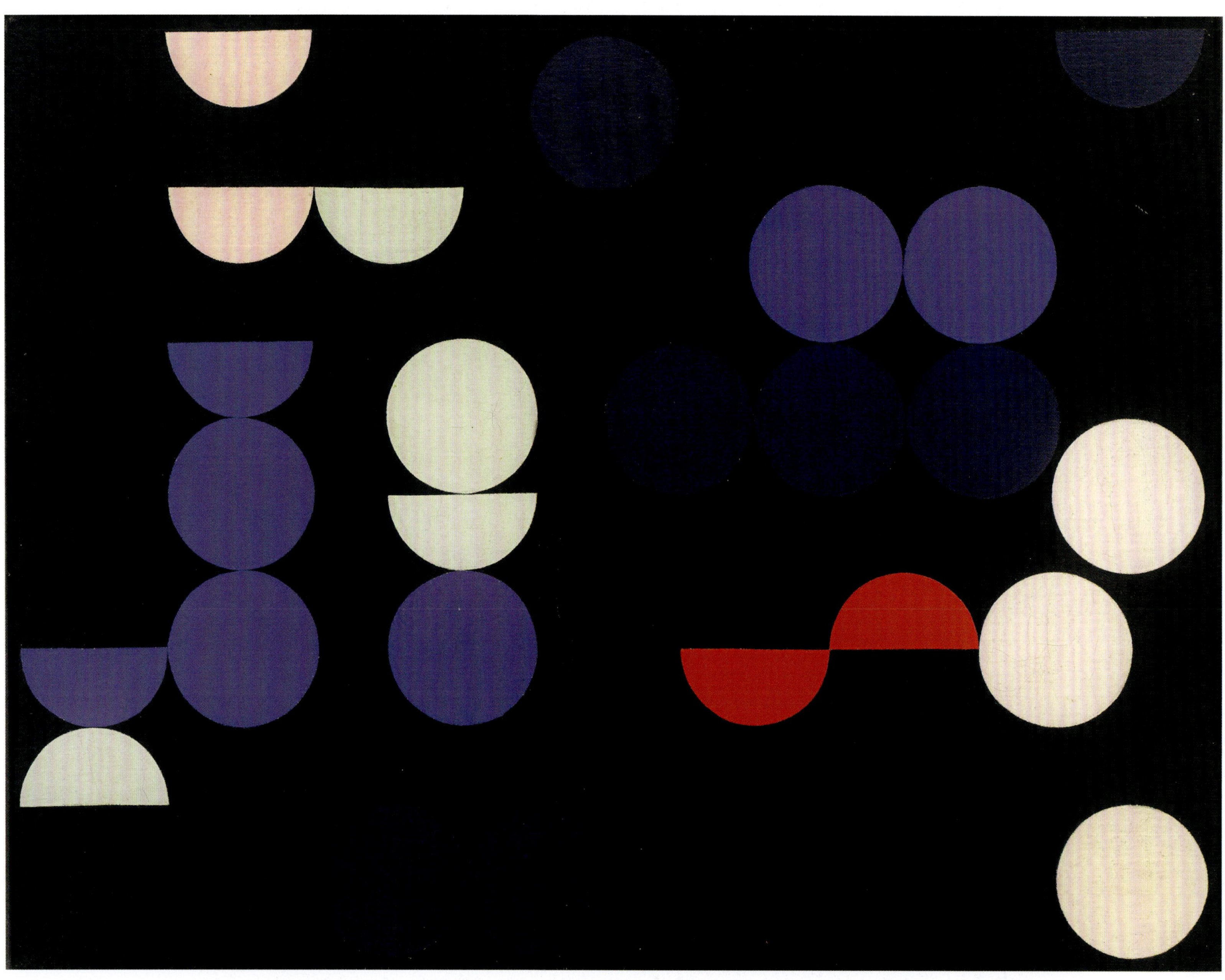

ANIMATED CIRCLE PICTURE
1935, oil on canvas, support: 50.5 × 65.1 cm (19 ⅞ × 25 ⅝ in), Albright-Knox Art Gallery, Buffalo, New York, USA

Sophie Taeuber-Arp, born 1889, Davos, Switzerland. Died 1943, Zurich, Switzerland.

A leading figure of the Dada movement, Taeuber-Arp was a multifaceted artist, working in painting, sculpture, marionette puppetry, textiles and costumes, dance, interior design and a number of other fine and applied arts methods. Her exploration of elemental colours, shapes and patterns across all mediums is exemplary of modernist non-objective abstraction in the early twentieth century, yet her work sought fusion with – rather than retreat from – the chaos and texture of modern life. Born in Davos, she trained in Germany before returning to Switzerland to join the vibrant artistic community in Zurich, where she met her husband and collaborator, Jean (Hans) Arp (1886–1966). The pair created immersive, absurdist performances at the Cabaret Voltaire that exemplified the spirit of Dada – a movement that responded to the violence and instability of interwar Europe with an embrace of irrationality and unleashed creativity. The influence of De Stijl and Bauhaus principles can be felt in her later works, as in *Animated Circle Picture* – a refined study of colour, form and geometric rhythm in painting.

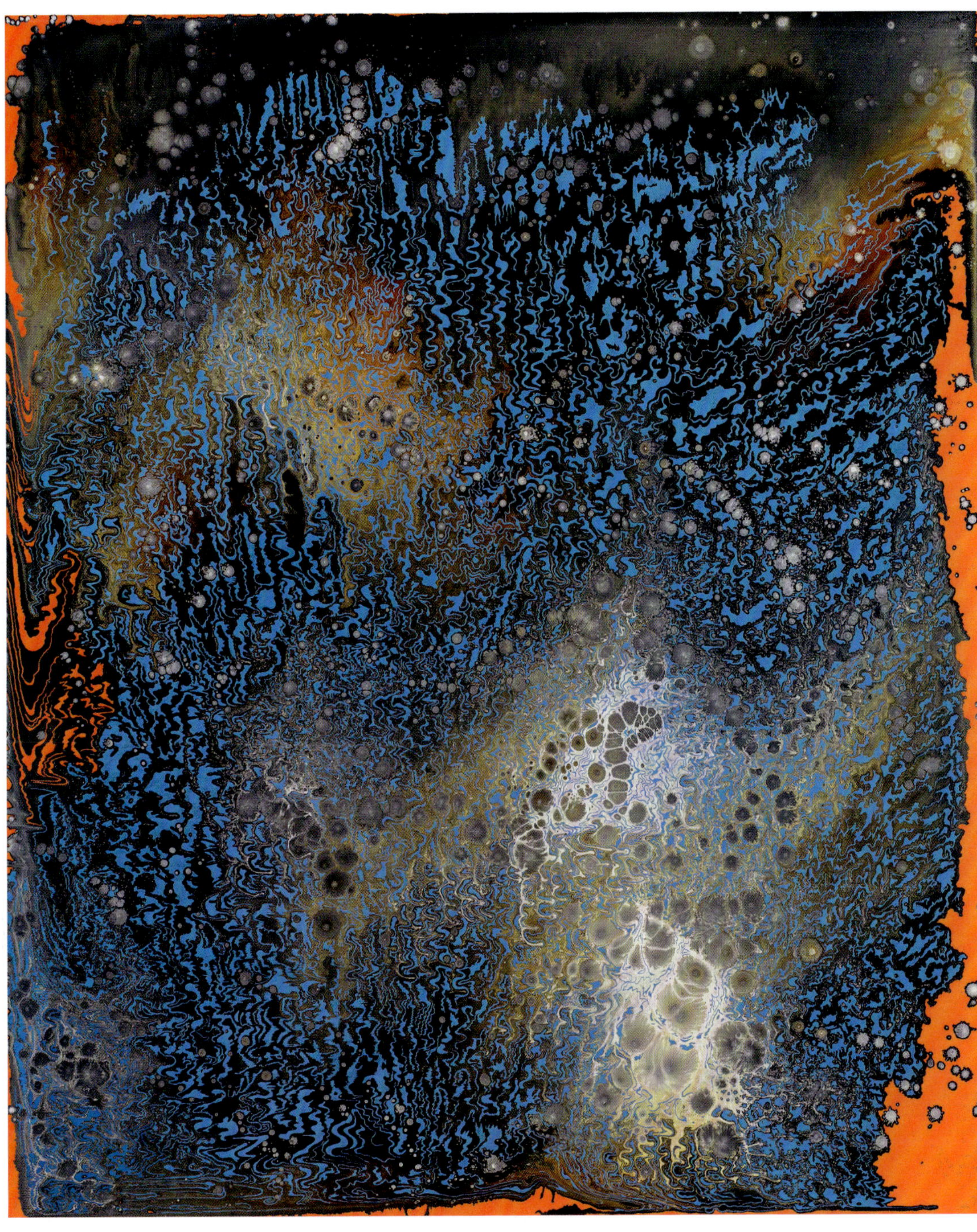

SURFACING (BLUE WITH ORANGE EDGE)
2021, acrylic on linen, 137.2 × 114.3 cm (54 × 45 in)

Barbara Takenaga, born 1949, North Platte, Nebraska, USA.

Evoking botany, cell structures, aquatic life and cosmologies, the seductive and disorienting surfaces of Takenaga's paintings read as kaleidoscopic cartographies electrified by colour. The result of scrupulous free-hand painting, the artist's works are galactic landscapes rife with atmospheric swathes of colour and repeating shapes, lines and dots. A professor emerita of art at Williams College in Massachusetts, Takenaga sources techniques and features from Japanese printmaking, Op art and Tantric art. The artist developed an interest in the kinship between poetry and the visual arts during her undergraduate studies in the early 1970s. Her works develop line by line and dot by dot as she paints from improvisation and instinct, and through painstaking repetition, acute differences evolve that cause optical fluctuations of space. Moving radially throughout the canvas, Takenaga's colours and forms distort the viewer's sense of proximity: whether the painting is a zoomed-in image of an organism or a telescopic capture of space is ultimately unimportant. Instead, her paintings insist on the aesthetic value of colours and a pleasurable visual experience for the viewer, the result of which is at once meditative and psychedelic.

DOROTHEA TANNING

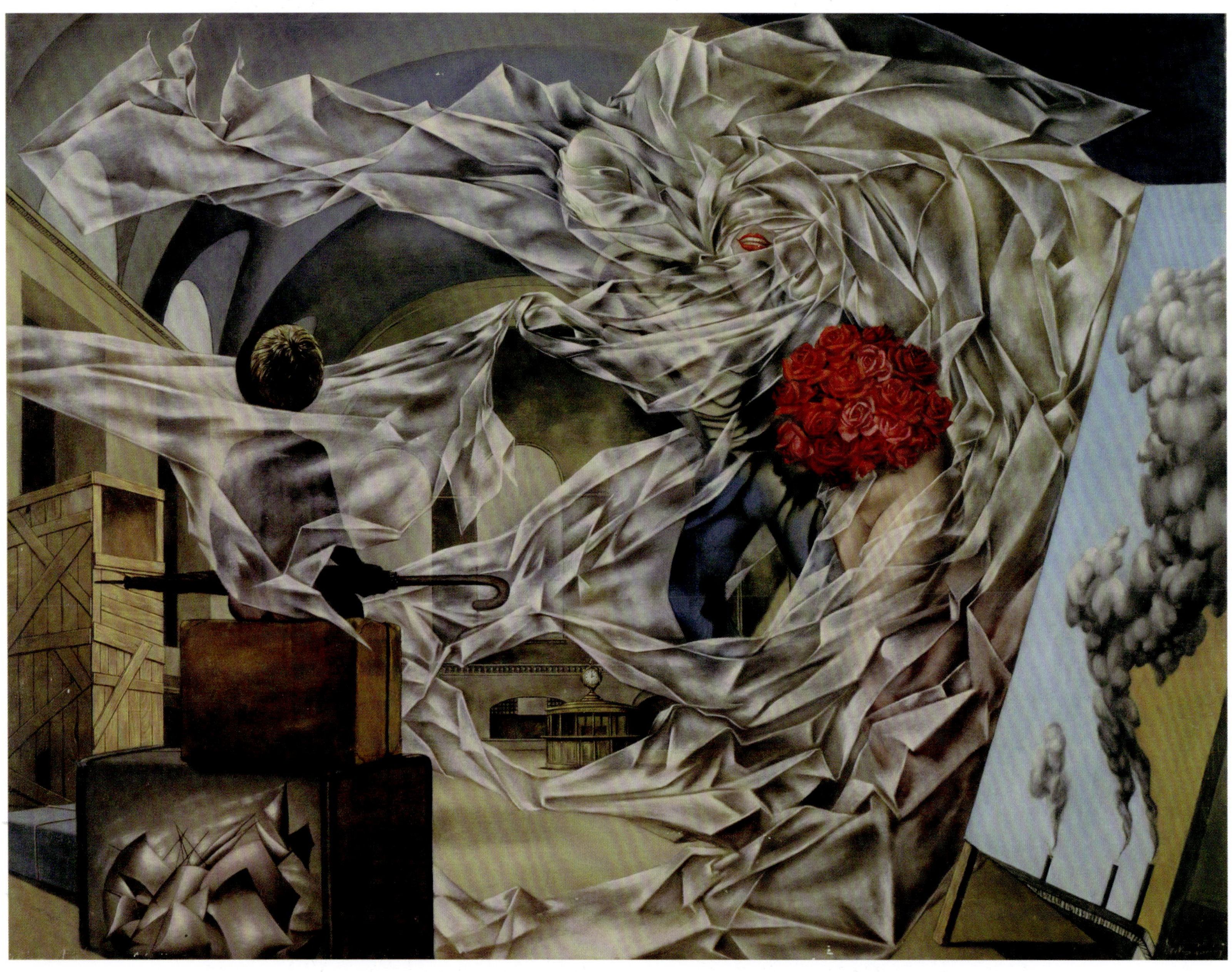

UN TABLEAU TRÈS HEUREUX (A VERY HAPPY PICTURE)
1947, oil on canvas, 91.1 × 122 cm (35 ⅞ × 48 in), Musée National d'Art Moderne, Centre Pompidou, Paris, France

Dorothea Tanning, born 1910, Galesburg, Illinois, USA. Died 2012, New York, USA.

After briefly attending the Chicago Academy of Fine Art, Tanning moved to New York in 1935. Prompted by a visit to the exhibition 'Fantastic Art, Dada, Surrealism' at the Museum of Modern Art the following year, she began to align herself with Surrealism, which she described in her 2001 memoir as a 'limitless expanse of POSSIBILITY'. During her travels in France, Tanning was introduced to German painter Max Ernst (1891–1976) and in 1946, they married and moved to Sedona, Arizona, where they would keep a house throughout the 1950s despite a move to France in 1949. The haunting strangeness of this work belies the optimism of its title. Translucent cloth unravels in impossibly undulating, jagged folds that enwrap a nude woman with smiling red lips and a bouquet of red roses – with the outline of a man next to her and another seated figure with a piercing umbrella. Here, Tanning plumbs the unconscious mind to rework indoor space into a hallucinatory dreamscape, with undertones of sexual fantasy and anxiety. Tanning would later turn to a more abstractionist mode in the 1960s, followed by experiments in soft sculpture in the 1970s.

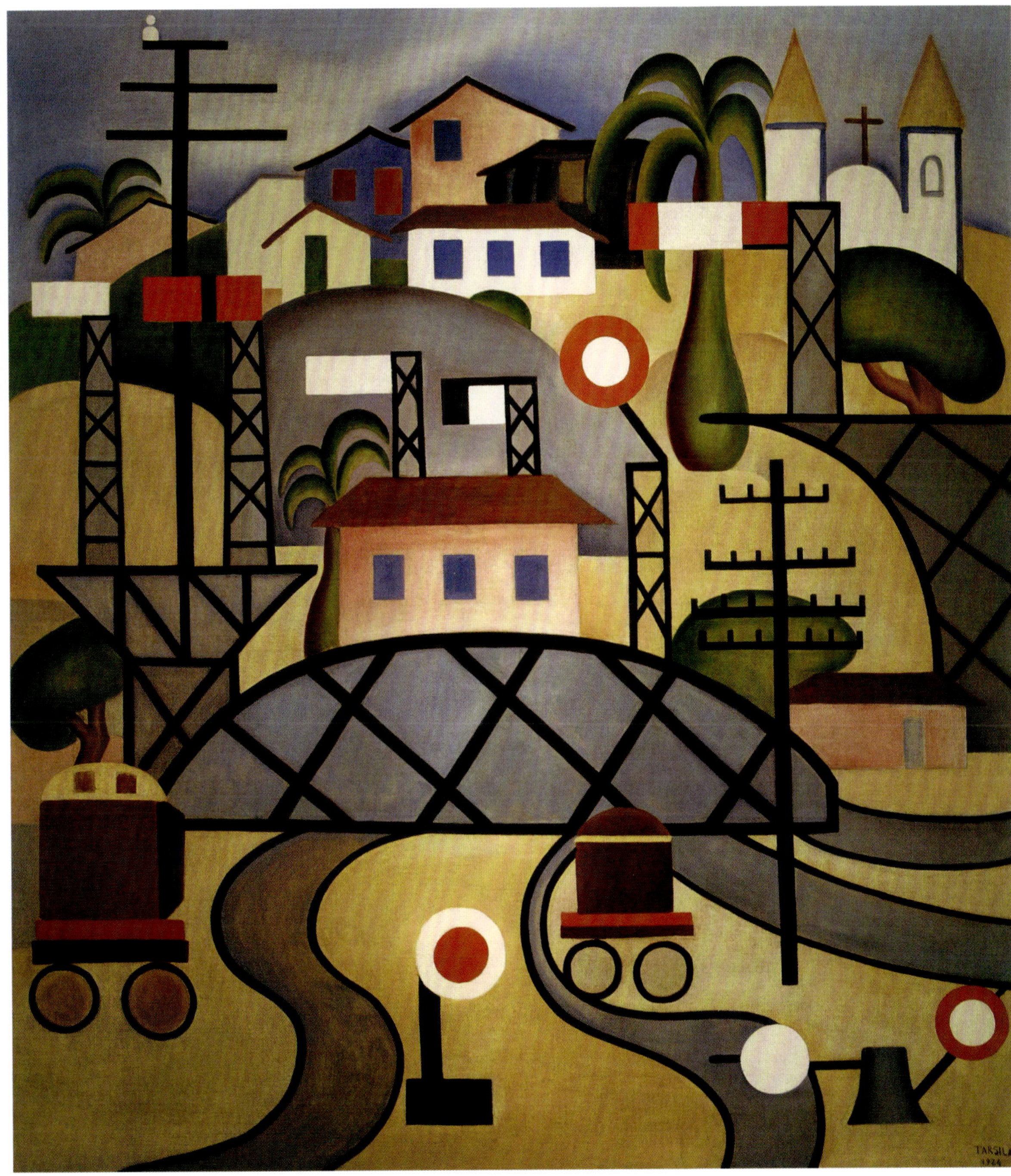

ESTRADA DE FERRO CENTRAL DO BRASIL (CENTRAL RAILWAY OF BRAZIL)
1924, oil on canvas, 142 × 126.8 cm (55 ⅞ × 49 ⅞ in), Museu de Arte Contemporânea da Universidade de São Paulo, Brazil

Tarsila, born 1886, Capivari, São Paulo, Brazil. Died 1973, São Paulo, Brazil.

Tarsila do Amaral, also known simply as Tarsila, is one of the definitive figures of modernist painting in Brazil. Raised in São Paulo, she studied painting privately and in 1920 moved to Paris to attend the Académie Julian. In 1922 she returned to her home city, where she became one of two painters in the Grupo dos Cinco (Group of Five, the other three members being writers), who were instrumental in defining Brazilian modernism in the 1920s. Although widely celebrated in her native Brazil, Tarsila gained little recognition abroad in her lifetime; a major retrospective at the Museum of Modern Art, New York, came in 2018. Tarsila's style synthesized the lush landscapes, vivid colours and vibrant life she observed in travels throughout her homeland with the exaggerated forms and perspectives found in European Surrealism. An example of Tarsila's pioneering modernist vision, *Central Railway of Brazil* depicts a train station in a small town in the state of Minas Gerais. Organic curves of coconut trees and vegetation are juxtaposed with the rigid geometric lines of telegraph poles and railways, reconciling symbols of the rural past and the industrial future and embodying Tarsila's search for a sincere expression of a new Brazilian aesthetic.

ANNA DOROTHEA THERBUSCH

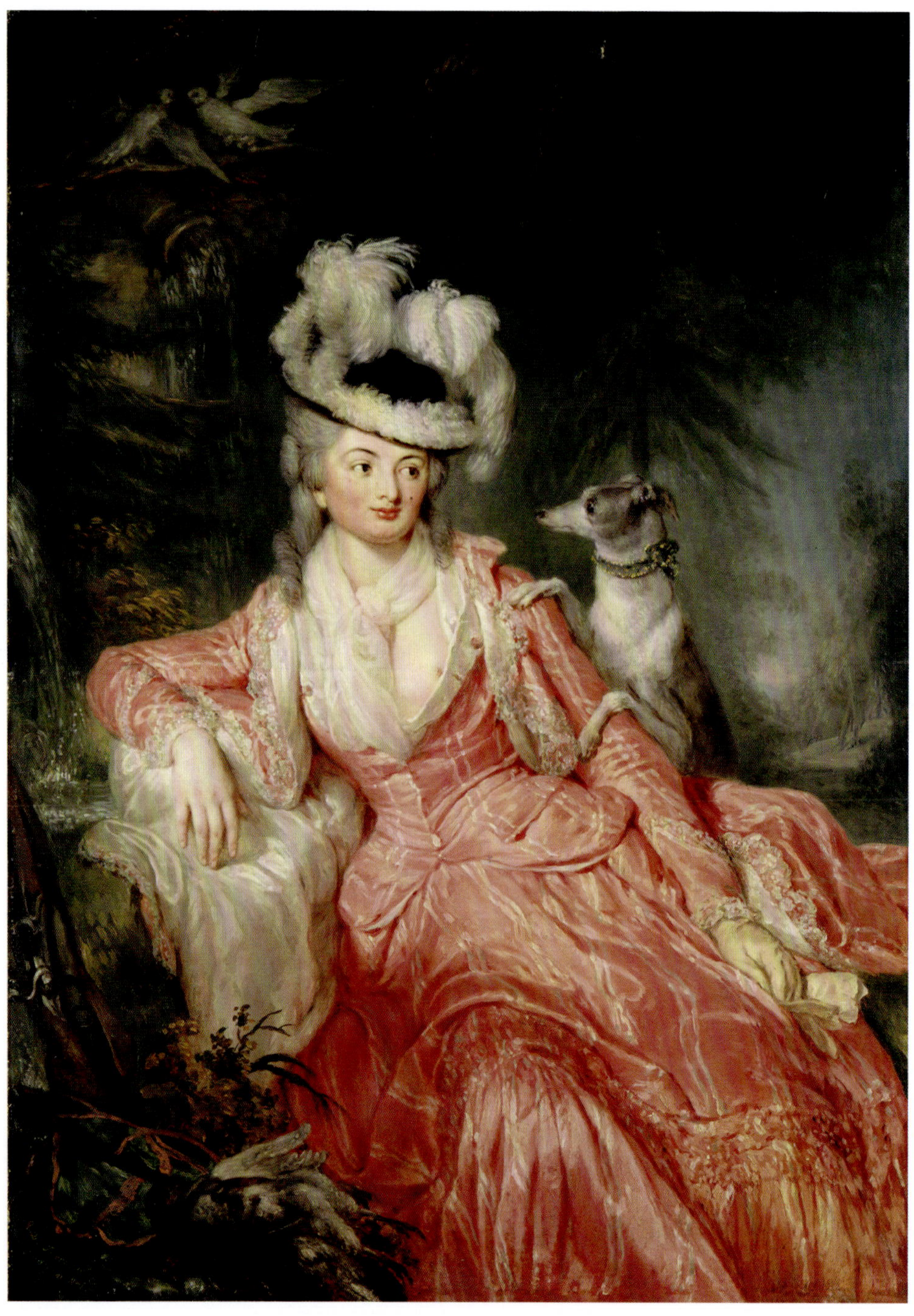

WILHELMINE ENCKE, COUNTESS OF LICHTENAU
1776, oil on canvas, 143 × 103 cm (56¼ × 40½ in), Schloss Sanssouci, Potsdam, Germany

Anna Dorothea Therbusch, born 1721, Berlin, Germany. Died 1782, Berlin.

Therbusch was one of the most important Rococo painters of the eighteenth century, who by the time of her death had completed over two hundred canvases. Although she received early tuition in portrait painting from her father – the Prussian court painter Georg Lisiewski (1674–1750) – she did not begin her professional career until her early forties, after having raised a family and helped run an inn with her husband. After a succession of courtly patrons, she became one of the few women painters to be granted membership to the Académie Royale de Peinture et de Sculpture in Paris, as well as academies in Stuttgart and Vienna. Returning to Berlin in 1773, Therbusch established a successful portrait studio, painting notable members of the German-speaking aristocracy, including commissions for Catherine II of Russia (Catherine the Great) and Frederick II of Prussia (Frederick the Great), whose palace she decorated with mythological scenes. In this portrait, Frederick's mistress, Wilhelmine Encke, poses in a pink gown, long-sleeved jacket and feathered hat, her corset lifting her breasts so that they are bared to the viewer.

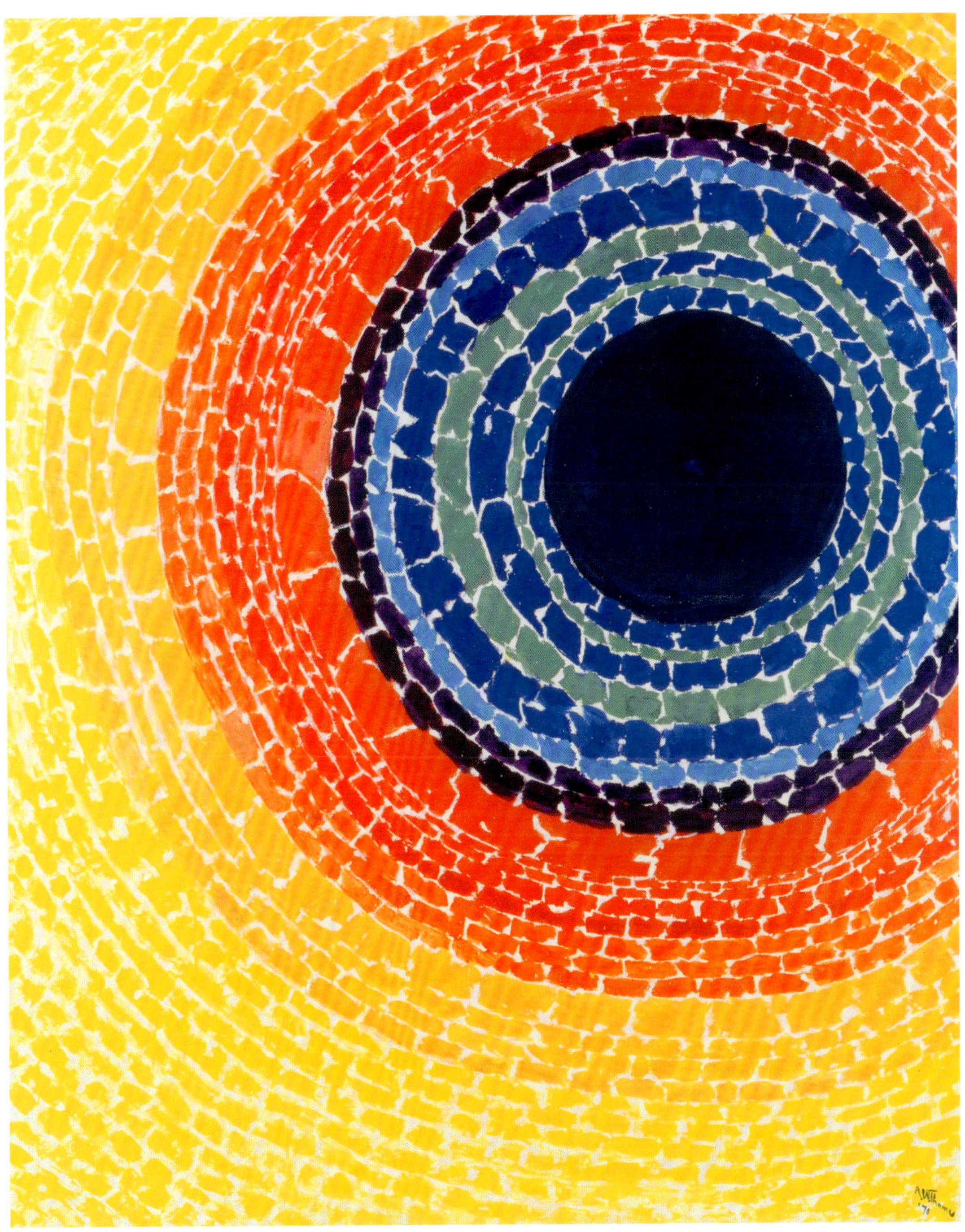

THE ECLIPSE
1970, acrylic on canvas, 126.5 × 57.5 cm (62 × 49 ¾ in), Smithsonian American Art Museum, Washington DC, USA

Alma Thomas, born 1891, Columbus, Georgia, USA. Died 1978, Washington DC, USA.

Now celebrated as one of the foremost American painters working in Colour Field abstraction in the late twentieth century, Thomas was in her seventies when she retired from a decades-long career as a junior high school art teacher and pursued a professional artistic practice full-time. Thomas was the first graduate of the fine art department at Howard University, Washington DC, in 1924 and would later receive a master's degree in art from Columbia University, New York. While she had trained in a realist, academic style, she would become known for her abstract, jewel-toned compositions, characterized by accentuated arcs and brilliant mosaics of daubed paint. Begun in the late 1960s when the artist was in her seventies, these works were inspired by her observations of the interplay of light and colour in nature, as well as qualities of rhythm and repetition found in music, and they often draw their titles from solar, celestial and planetary phenomena. *The Eclipse*, for instance, features a dark blue orb surrounded by radiating daubs of brilliant warm hues, exuding a sense of optimism sparked by the first moon landing and humankind's exploration of the cosmic frontier.

MICKALENE THOMAS

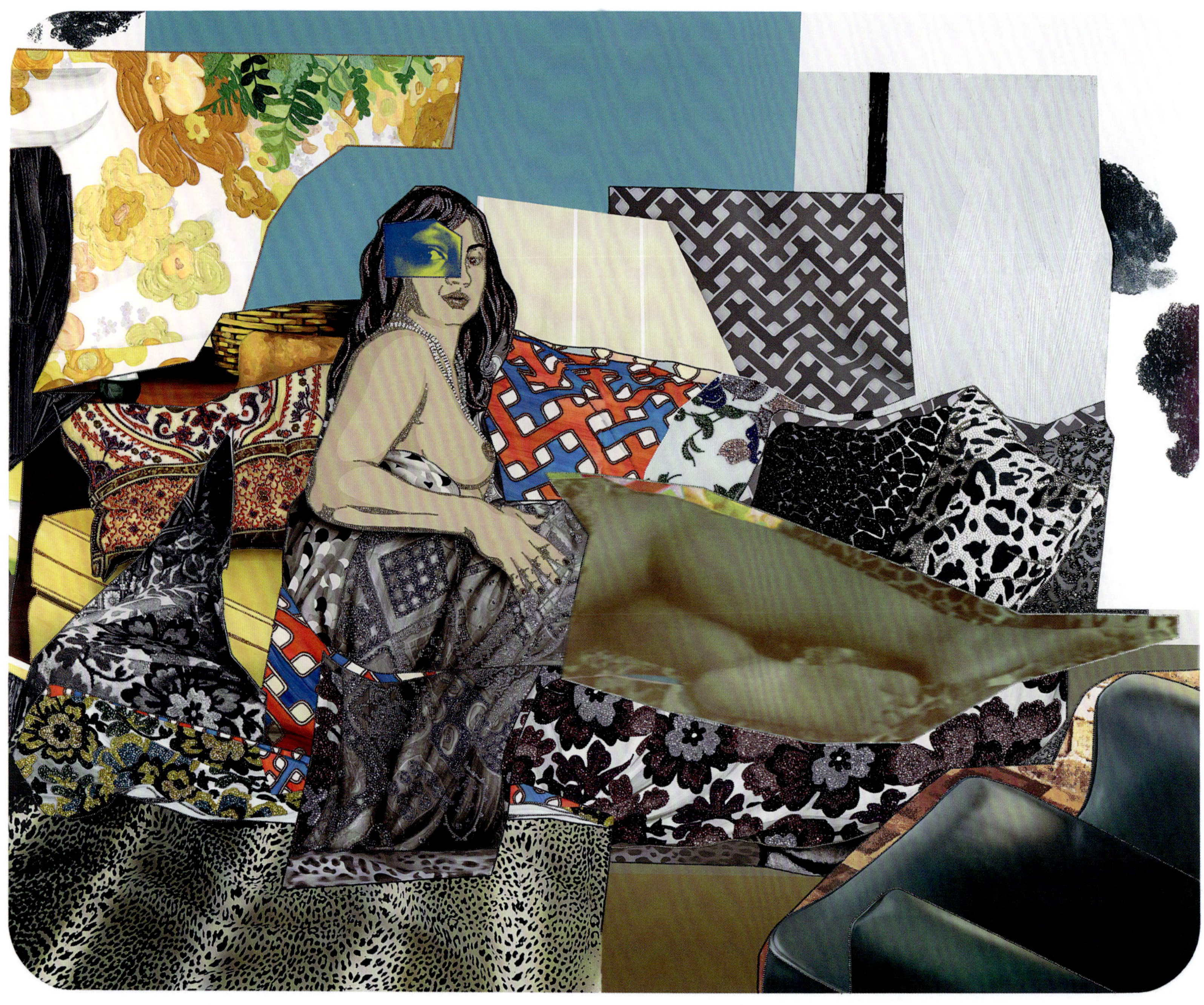

SHINIQUE: NOW I KNOW
2015, rhinestones, acrylic and oil on wood panel, 243.8 × 304.8 cm (96 × 120 in)

Mickalene Thomas, born 1971, Camden, New Jersey, USA.

Spanning painting, photography, collage, video and immersive installations, Thomas's art practice consistently centres and celebrates the Black female figure, constructing novel ways of visualizing bodies and spaces informed by the history of African American culture and aesthetics. With influences including nineteenth-century French painting, West African studio photography, 1970s interiors and her own autobiography, her work articulates a complex vision of beauty, empowerment and self-image rooted in gender and race. Her paintings are often based on her own photographs and collages, translating the patchwork of layered materials into expansive paintings on wood panel containing a variety of textures and applications of pigment. In *Shinique: Now I Know*, the figure – adopting the pose of Jean-Auguste-Dominique Ingres's *Grande Odalisque* (1814) – is fragmented into sections both painted and screen-printed, surrounded by sumptuous textiles of clashing patterns rendered in both colour and black and white. From the impastoed paint of the wallpaper to the rhinestone-bedecked pillows and creases of Shinique's flesh, the painting exemplifies Thomas's technique-driven practice that luxuriates in the haptic qualities of her materials.

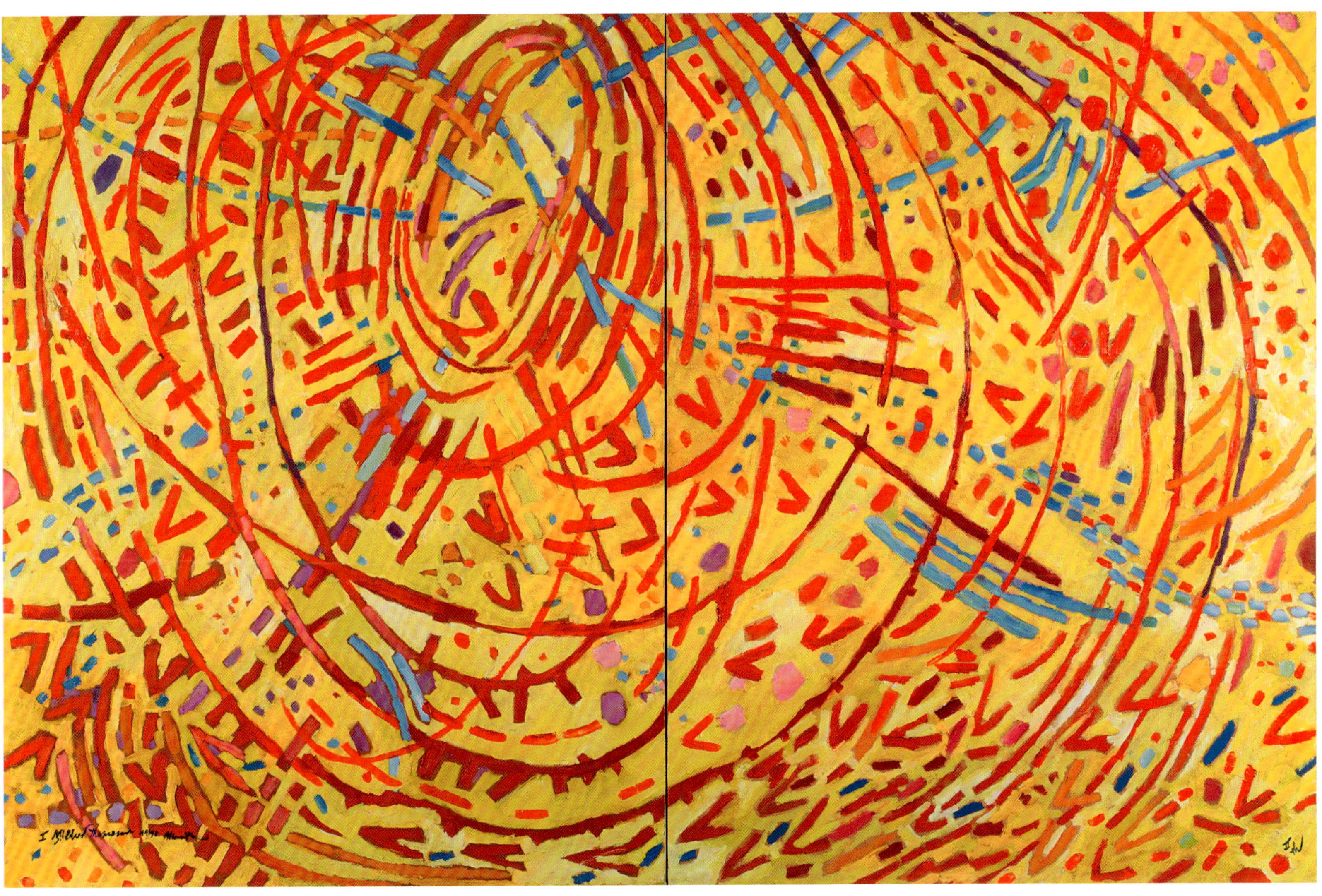

MAGNETIC FIELDS
1991, oil on canvas, 156.8 × 242.6 cm (61 ¾ × 95 ½ in), Cummer Museum of Art & Gardens, Jacksonville, Florida, USA

Mildred Thompson, born 1936, Jacksonville, Florida, USA. Died 2003, Atlanta, USA.

Endowed with a restlessly curious mind, Thompson developed a vibrant practice encompassing painting, sculpture and printmaking, along with careers as a writer and educator. Like many Black women abstractionists, she was overlooked for many years, in part due to her failure to engage with figuration and identity issues, favouring an aesthetic that transcended these expectations. Thompson studied art at Howard University in Washington DC under the influential art historian James A. Porter, graduating in 1957. Encountering racial and gender discrimination in America, she moved to Germany in the 1960s, where she lived until 1975 and developed her 'wood pictures' – geometric assemblages made of found wood. Thompson took inspiration from a range of subjects from philosophy and music to spiritualism and quantum physics, regarding her work as a 'personal interpretation of the universe', as posthumously quoted in a 2009 exhibition catalogue. *Magnetic Fields* is one of a series of sensory paintings she created in the 1990s that express invisible cosmic forces through vivid colour and dynamic mark-making. Energetic red spirals vibrate outwards as dashes of blue, purple and orange shoot across a hot yellow background, creating an electrifying, rhythmic symphony.

BETTY TOMPKINS

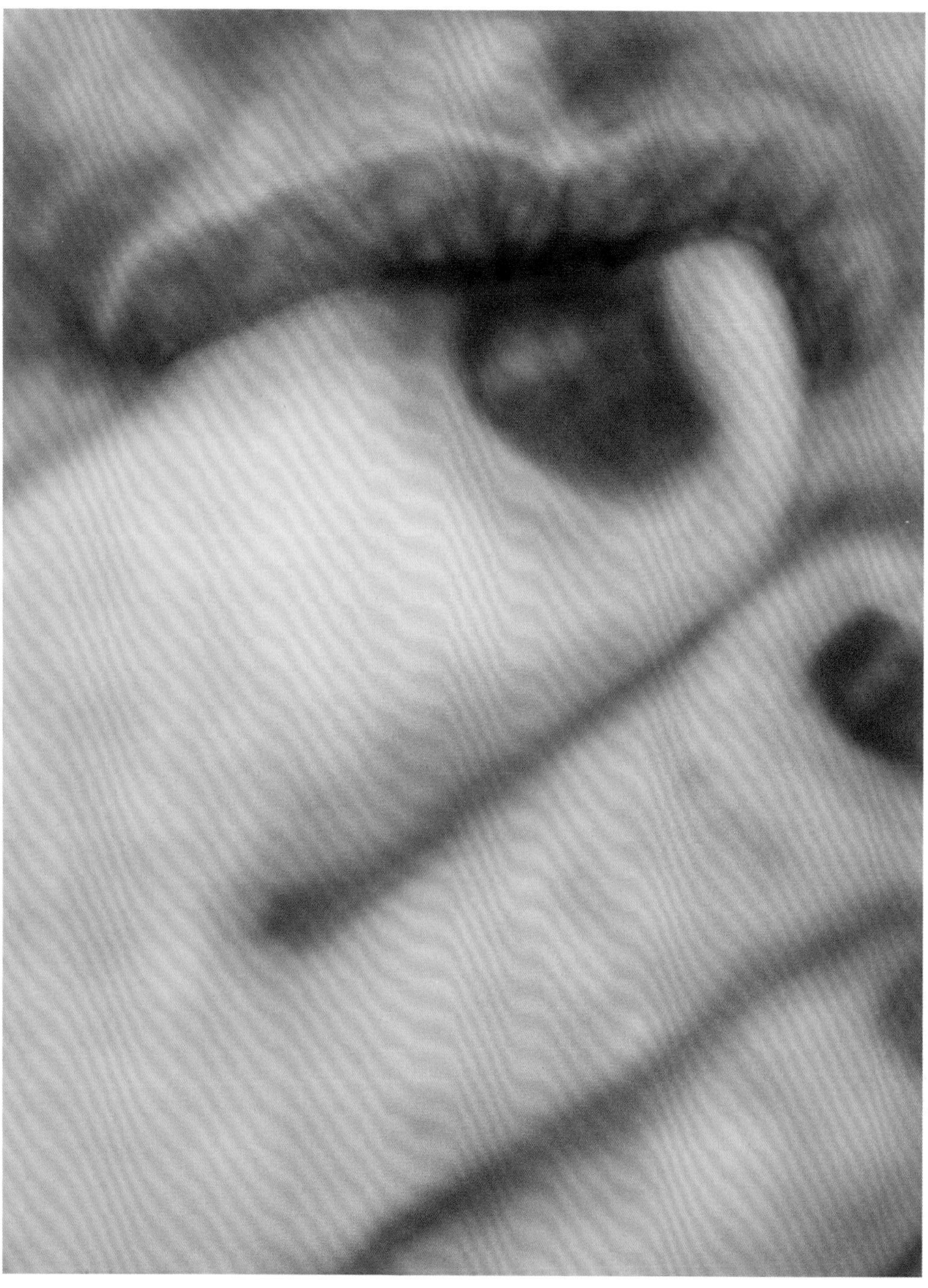

SEX PAINTING #7
2020, acrylic on canvas, 101.6 × 76.2 cm
(40 × 30 in)

Betty Tompkins, born 1945, Washington DC, USA.

Appropriating and reworking images from across visual culture, Tompkins's work represents a touchstone in the modern history of feminist art. Soon after moving to New York in the late 1960s, the artist became interested in her then-husband's collection of pornography, and in 1969 began a series of monumental photorealistic paintings of close-up couplings called the 'Fuck Paintings'. Created with airbrush, the black-and-white works' explicit imagery led French customs officials in 1973 to refuse their entry to the country for an exhibition at the Centre Pompidou in Paris. Tompkins's work received little critical appreciation in the years that followed, until 2002 when she had a solo show at Mitchell Algus Gallery in New York to great acclaim, the art world having caught up to her incisive exploration of the dynamics of sex and gender. Her practice has since included paintings and photographs of women made by men, onto which she scrawls pink text ranging from women's testimonies of abuse to prominent men's public apologies in response to sexual harassment. *Sex Painting #7* exemplifies Tompkins's favoured aesthetic, here displaying a puckered mouth wrapped around painted toes.

CHARLEY TOOROP

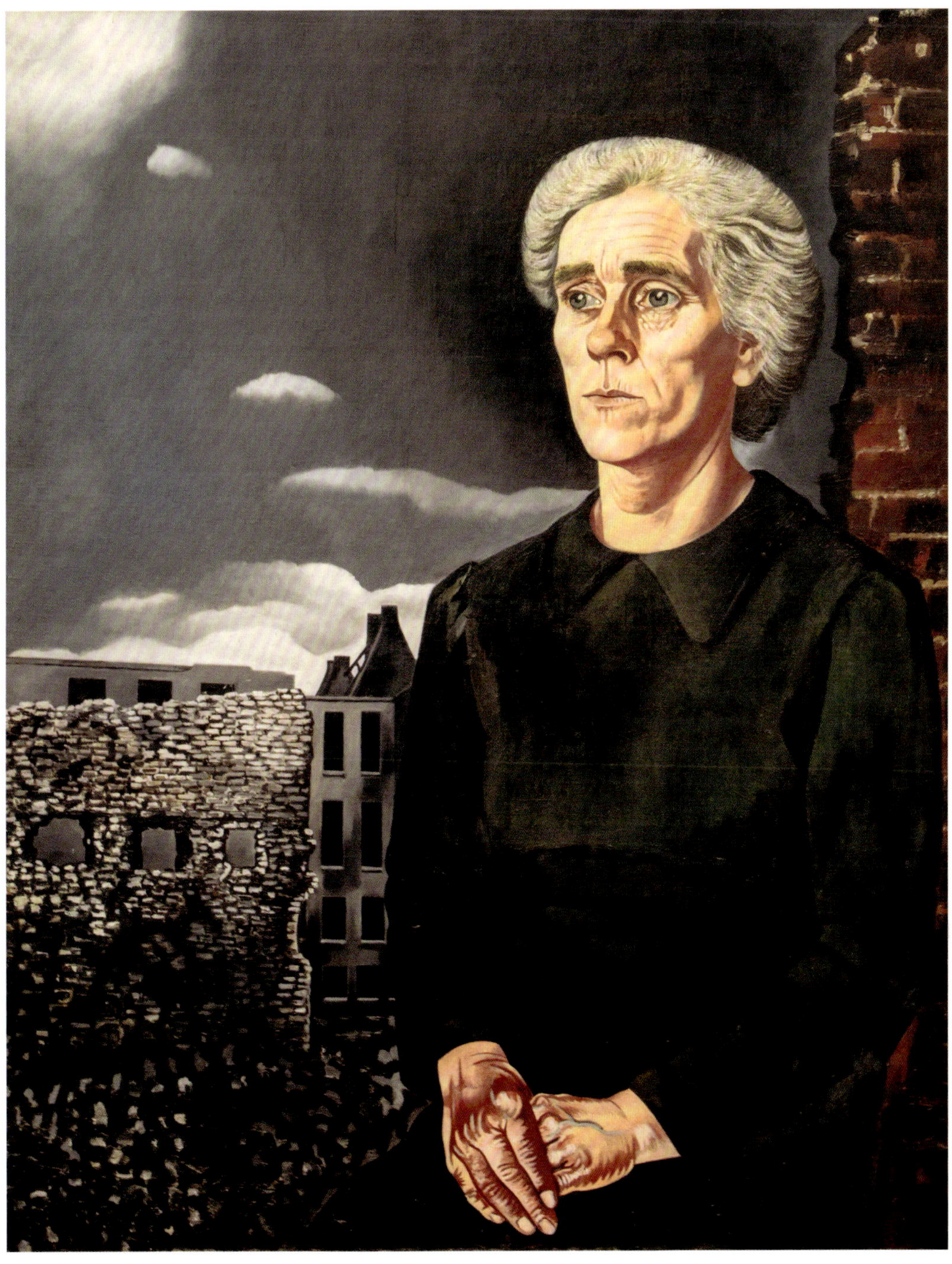

ARBEIDERSVROUW (WORKING-CLASS WOMAN)
1943, oil on canvas, 168.5 × 136.5 × 5 cm (66 ⅜ × 53 ¾ × 2 in), Stedelijk Museum, Amsterdam, Netherlands

Charley Toorop, born 1891, Katwijk aan Zee, Netherlands. Died 1955, Bergen, Netherlands.

The daughter of famous Symbolist artist Jan Toorop (1858–1928), Charley Toorop dabbled in various artistic movements before developing her own highly personal painterly style. She had no formal art education, having initially trained as a musician, but thanks to her father's career she was well connected in the cultural scene – Piet Mondrian (1872–1944), for example, was a lifelong friend. Begun in 1909, Toorop's early works were influenced by her father's interest in Luminism and the more widespread trends of Cubism and Expressionism, which led to her involvement in the Dutch Bergen School. By the 1920s, she had committed to her sober brand of realist painting – primarily portraits and self-portraits, in which the subject's wide-eyed gaze nearly always confronts the viewer, as well as occasional landscapes and still lifes. Although based in Bergen for most of her career, Toorop regularly travelled around Europe seeking commissions for portraits. During the Nazi occupation of the Netherlands, she was active in the resistance – her experiences of wartime devastation are reflected in paintings such as *Working-Class Woman*, a sombre portrait of Toorop's housekeeper, Johanna 'Jansje' Punt, depicted against the backdrop of a bombed-out Rotterdam.

TOYEN

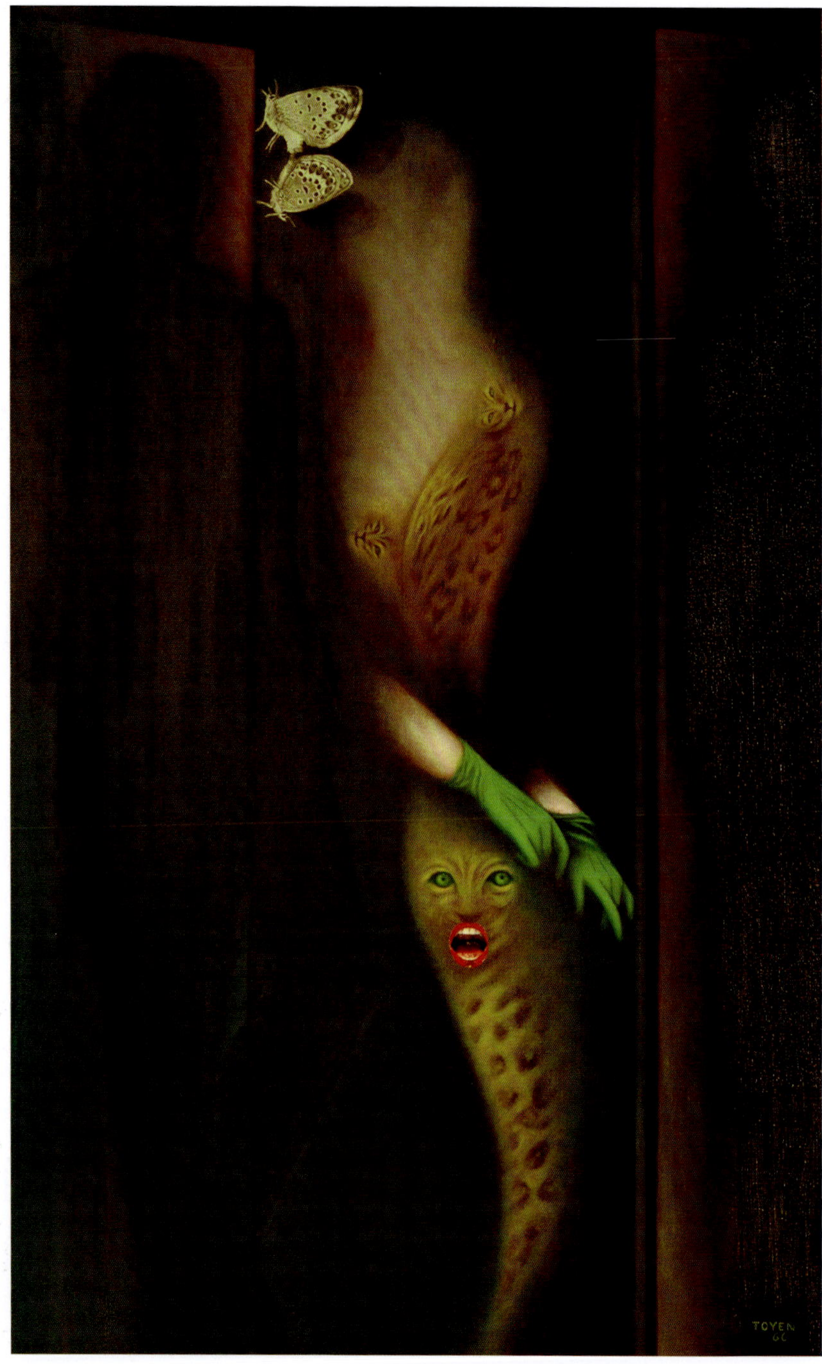

LE PARAVENT (THE SCREEN)
1966, oil and collage on canvas, 116 × 73 cm (45 ⅝ × 28 ¾ in), Musée d'Art Moderne de Paris, France

Toyen, born 1902, Prague, Czech Republic. Died 1980, Paris, France.

Toyen (born Marie Čermínová) adopted this pseudonym (which was possibly inspired by the French *citoyen*, 'citizen') in order to renounce gender – the artist identified with Czech masculine pronouns and dressed in men's clothing. Toyen studied at the Academy of Arts, Architecture and Design in Prague before moving to Paris with writer and artist Jindřich Štyrský (1899–1942) in 1925. Together they developed Artificialism, a form of abstract painting intended to arouse an emotional response beyond the visual. Toyen's interest in the erotic flourished in 1920s Paris, illustrating many of Štyrský's publications, including phallocentric drawings for his translation of the Marquis de Sade's *Justine* (originally published in 1791). Having returned to Prague, Toyen, along with Štyrský and others, co-founded the Czech wing of the Surrealist movement in 1934. Toyen's works contain an anguished quality, with canvases depicting enigmatic objects, wisps of smoke and hallucinatory imagery. *The Screen* features an eroticized woman with the faces of snarling felines at her genitals, breast and shoulder – one with piercing green eyes and the open mouth of a femme fatale – the figure ominously surrounded by male shadows on the screens that enclose her.

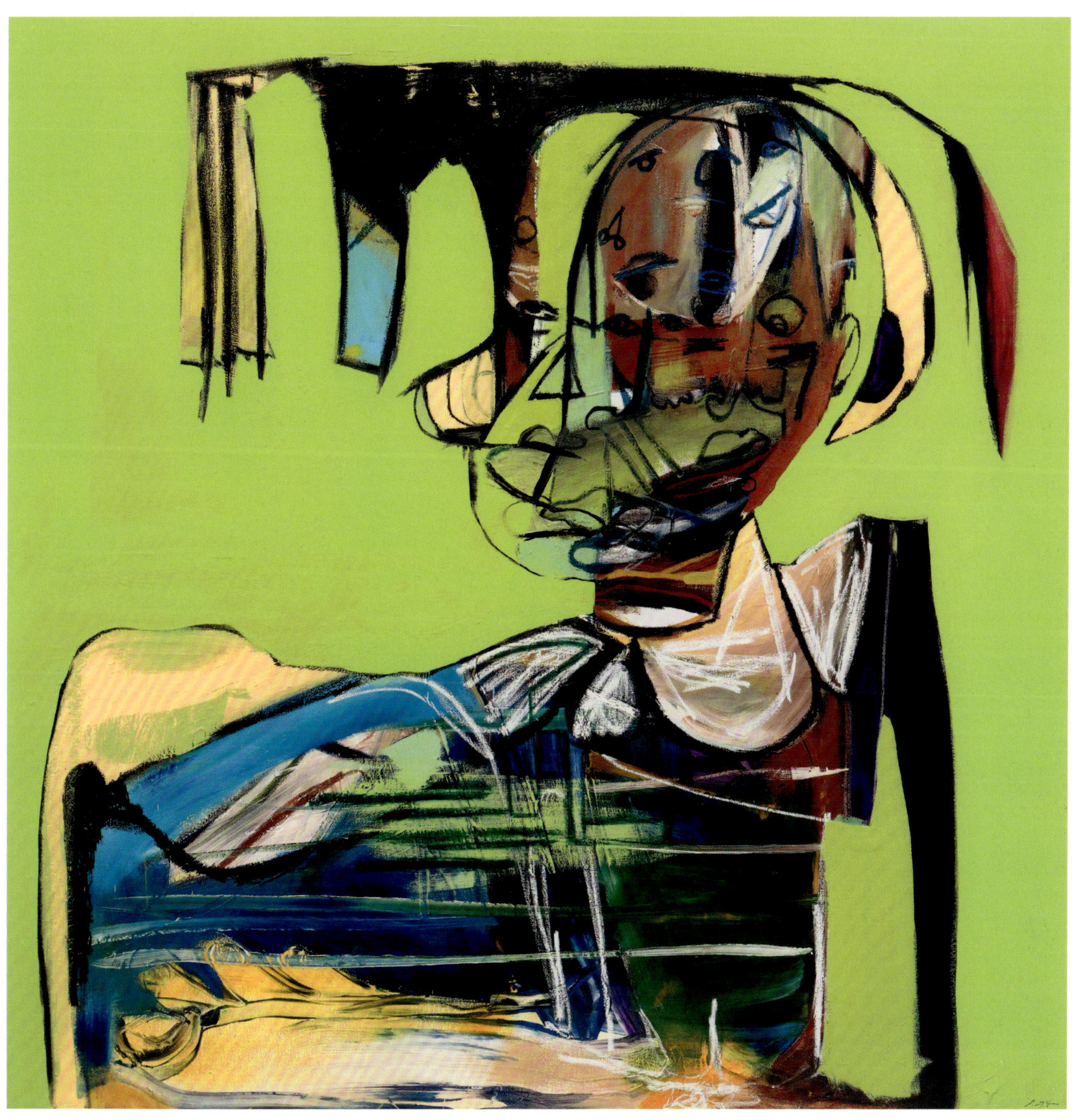

BEARER OF GOOD NEWS
2020, acrylic, oil sticks, spray paint, Yeshua, 182.9 × 182.9 × 6.4 cm (72 × 72 × 2½ in), collection of Sandra and Giancarlo Bonollo

Genesis Tramaine, born 1983, New York, USA.

Tramaine's mixed-media portraits channel her Christian faith. Her works, focusing on the depiction of Black American subjects and biblical allegories, have been compared to Art Brut and Expressionism. Using saturated colours – often with single-colour backdrops ranging from delicate pastels to deep reds and blues – and bold gestures, Tramaine's figurative works incorporate abstract mark-making, distortion, exaggeration and multiplication of features. In many of her works, Tramaine lists as her media spiritual materials such as 'the holy spirit', 'Yahweh' (Hebrew for God) or 'Yeshua' (Hebrew for Jesus). She sees herself as a vessel for divine transmission, preparing for each painting session with intensive prayer. As a Black woman, Tramaine's work also seeks to undo white, patriarchal depictions of religious visions. The energetic composition in *Bearer of Good News*, for example, features a young female figure sprawled against a lime-green background. As Tramaine explained to *Artsy* in June 2020, 'I have never met a Black girl that wasn't a bearer of good news' – the work thus celebrates the resilience of young Black women against societal forces that try to suppress their presence.

SUZANNE VALADON

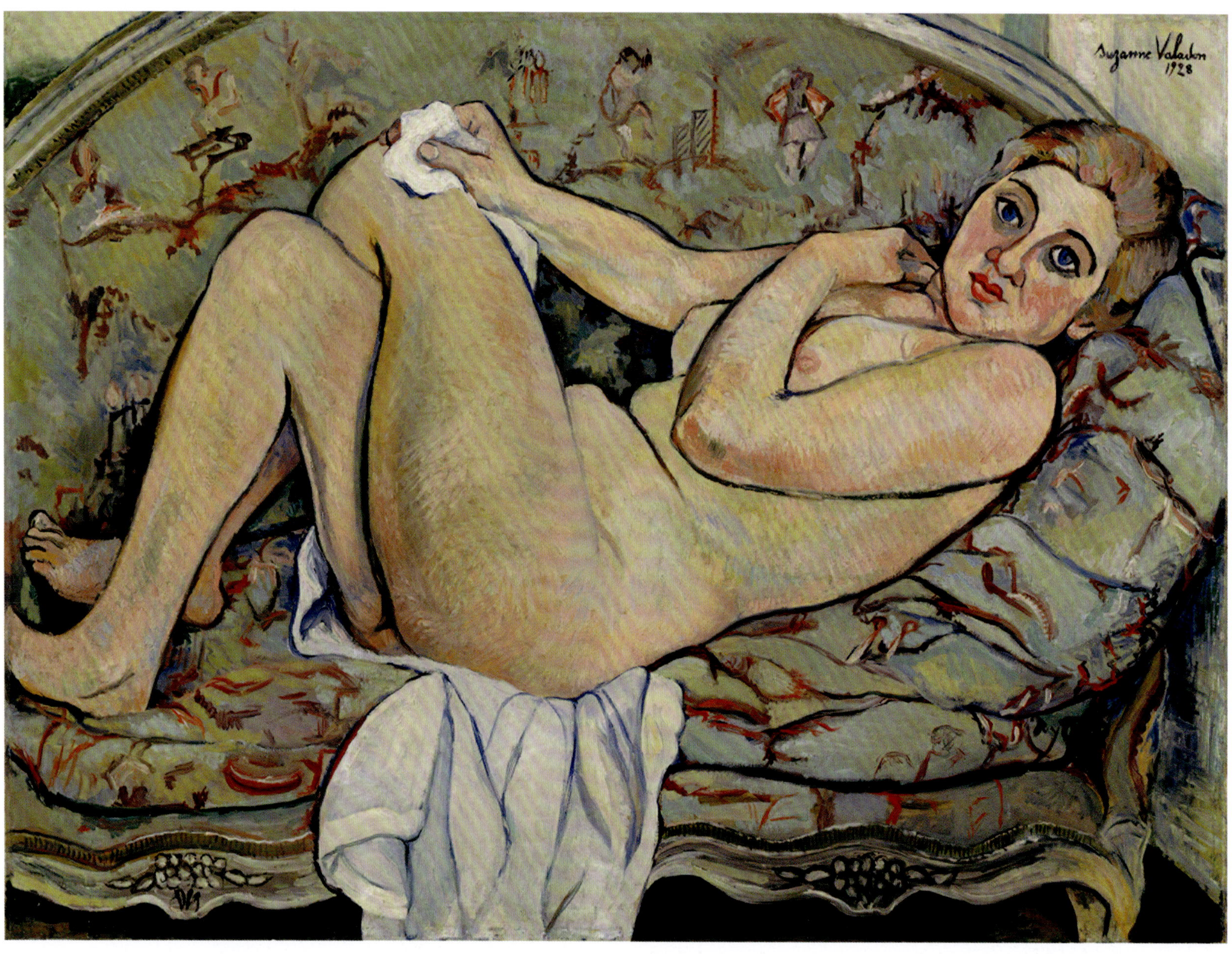

RECLINING NUDE
1928, oil on canvas (lined), 60 × 80.6 cm (23 ⅝ × 31 ¾ in), Metropolitan Museum of Art, New York, USA

Suzanne Valadon, born 1865, Bessines-sur-Gartempe, Nouvelle-Aquitaine, France. Died 1938, Paris, France.

A rebellious, independent spirit, Valadon hoped to become a circus performer but was prevented by an injury. Coming from an impoverished background, she began modelling at fifteen for artists including Pierre-Auguste Renoir (1841–1919) and Henri de Toulouse-Lautrec (1864–1901). By observing their techniques, she taught herself to draw. Edgar Degas (1834–1917), a close friend, bought her work and taught her soft-ground etching. From 1896 she painted full-time and exhibited regularly at prestigious salons. Her style evokes the Post-Impressionists, using strong black outlines along with greens, yellows, peaches and whites to convey skin tones. Valadon is noted for her unidealized interpretations of conventional art-historical tropes such as the reclining nude. This work subverts the tradition of the odalisque – instead of being sprawled on display for men's delectation, Valadon's nude covers her breasts and crosses her legs away from the viewer. She is awkwardly curled up, positioned at the front of the picture plane, and looks directly out of the canvas with an expression more akin to indifference than seduction.

ADRIANA VAREJÃO

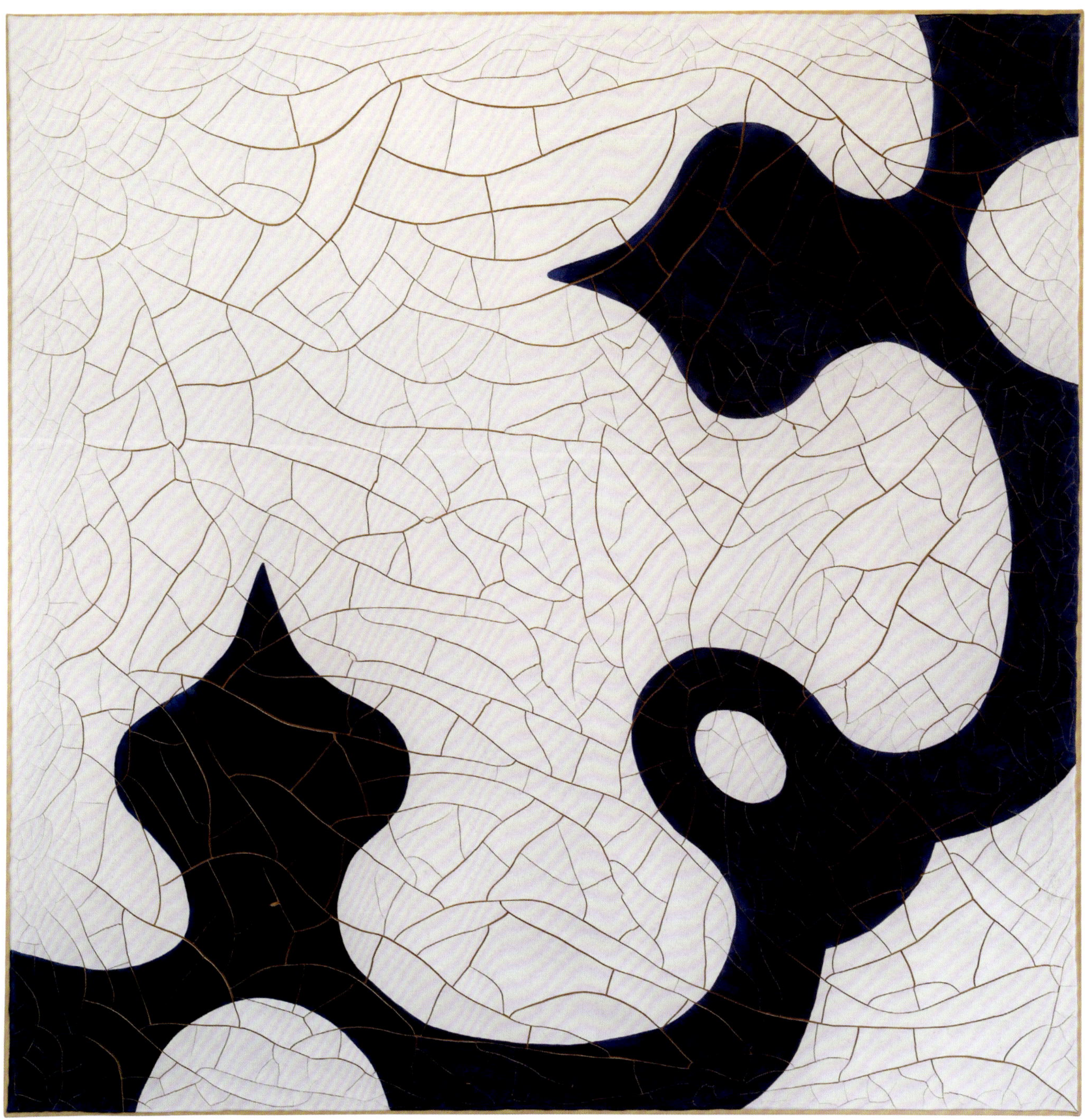

MOORISH ARABESQUE
2020, oil and plaster on canvas, 180 × 180 × 4 cm (70 ⅞ × 70 ⅞ × 1 ⅝ in)

Adriana Varejão, born 1964, Rio de Janeiro, Brazil.

One of Brazil's foremost contemporary artists, Varejão uses Baroque tactics of simulation, juxtaposition and parody to reflect on the complex cultural and political histories of her country. Tiles have been a recurring motif in her work since the early 1990s, when she employed *azulejos* – glazed terracotta tiles of Arab origin used in Portuguese art since the Middle Ages – as a motif for cultural pluralism in Brazil. Varejão has said that her works are often metaphors for 'themes dealing with rupture and discontinuity. Everything is contaminated.' The fissured effect in Varejão's tile paintings is achieved when a dense layer of gesso applied to the surface dries and cracks over time, alluding to the qualities of ancient ceramics and imparting a sense of instability. *Moorish Arabesque* belongs to a series entitled 'Talavera', which explores the Talavera *poblana* pottery tradition, brought to Mexico through Spanish colonialism where it evolved under the influence of Indigenous artisans. In Varejão's process, the motifs of this local craft tradition shift identity, conflating Indigenous histories with the dynamics of international modernism. Thus, this series evokes one of Varejão's persistent themes: to uncover and promote the overlooked links between ancient and modern cultures and histories, often erased through colonialism.

REMEDIOS VARO

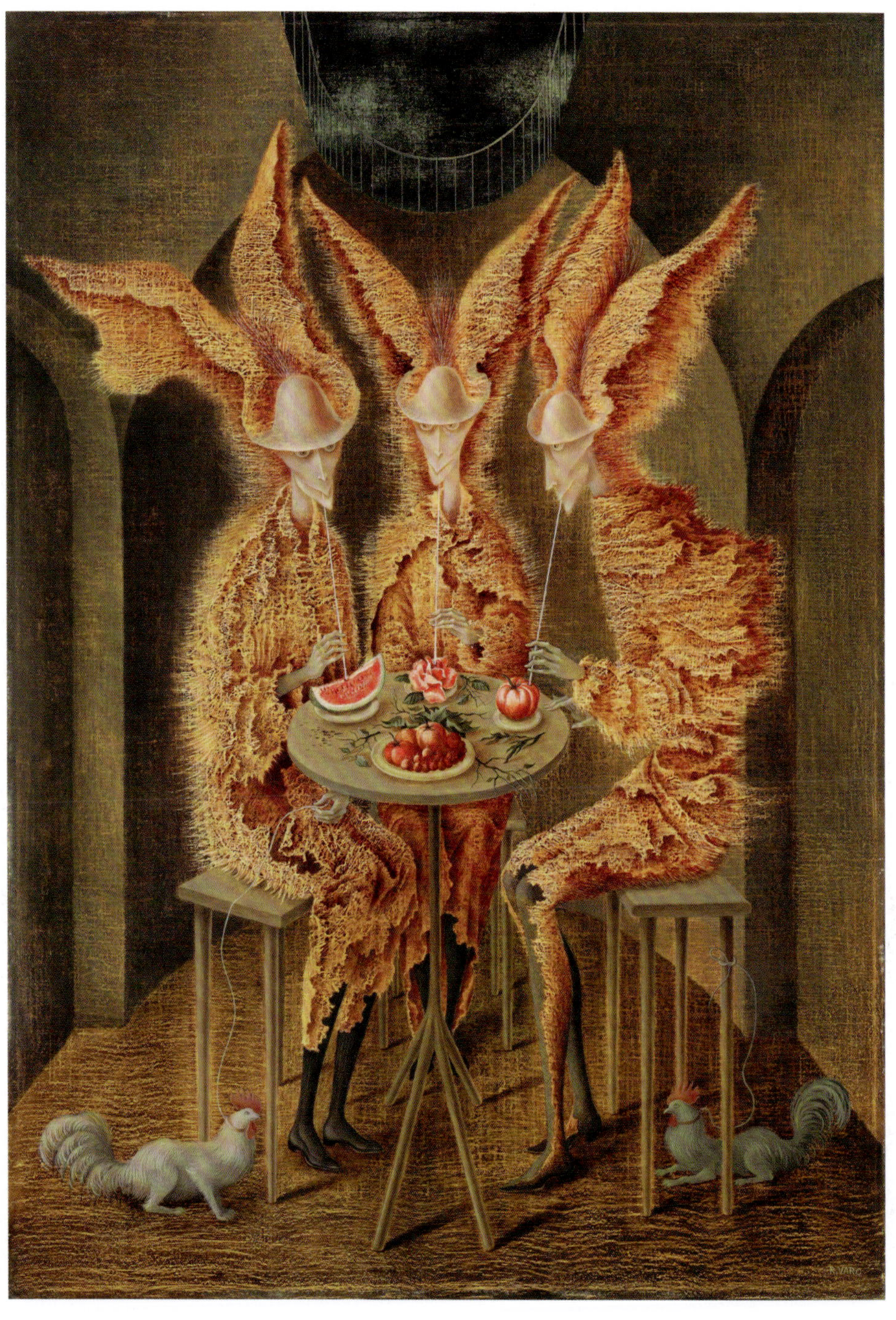

VAMPIROS VEGETARIANOS (VEGETARIAN VAMPIRES)
1962, oil on canvas, 85.7 × 60.3 cm (33 ¾ × 23 ¾ in)

Remedios Varo, born 1908, Anglès, Girona, Spain. Died 1963, Mexico City, Mexico.

Meticulously rendered, Varo's paintings combine the architectural harmony of the Renaissance with the Surrealist exploration of the irrational and the mystical. Varo rebelled against the academic and religious formalism into which her parents indoctrinated her, absconding to Paris in the 1930s. In 1938, she participated in the International Surrealist Exhibition organized by André Breton (1896–1966), though she would eventually distance herself from the male artists who dominated the movement. Varo deployed Surrealist techniques including decalcomania, a process of transferring ink from one surface to another, and *fumage*, wherein a candle flame leaves behind a sooty residue on fresh paint, but only in controlled settings where she could determine the operational outcomes – an approach antithetical to the Surrealist orthodoxy of automatism. By 1941, Varo had settled in Mexico to escape the advent of Fascism in Europe. Made one year before her death, *Vegetarian Vampires* is emblematic of Varo's technical prowess. Three androgynous, ghostly figures with electric wings surround a small round table inhaling blood-red juices through long straws. This scene, like Varo's best-known works, is consumed by an enigmatic aura added to by the two roosters with canine bodies tethered to leashes held by the skeletal beings.

MARIA HELENA VIEIRA DA SILVA

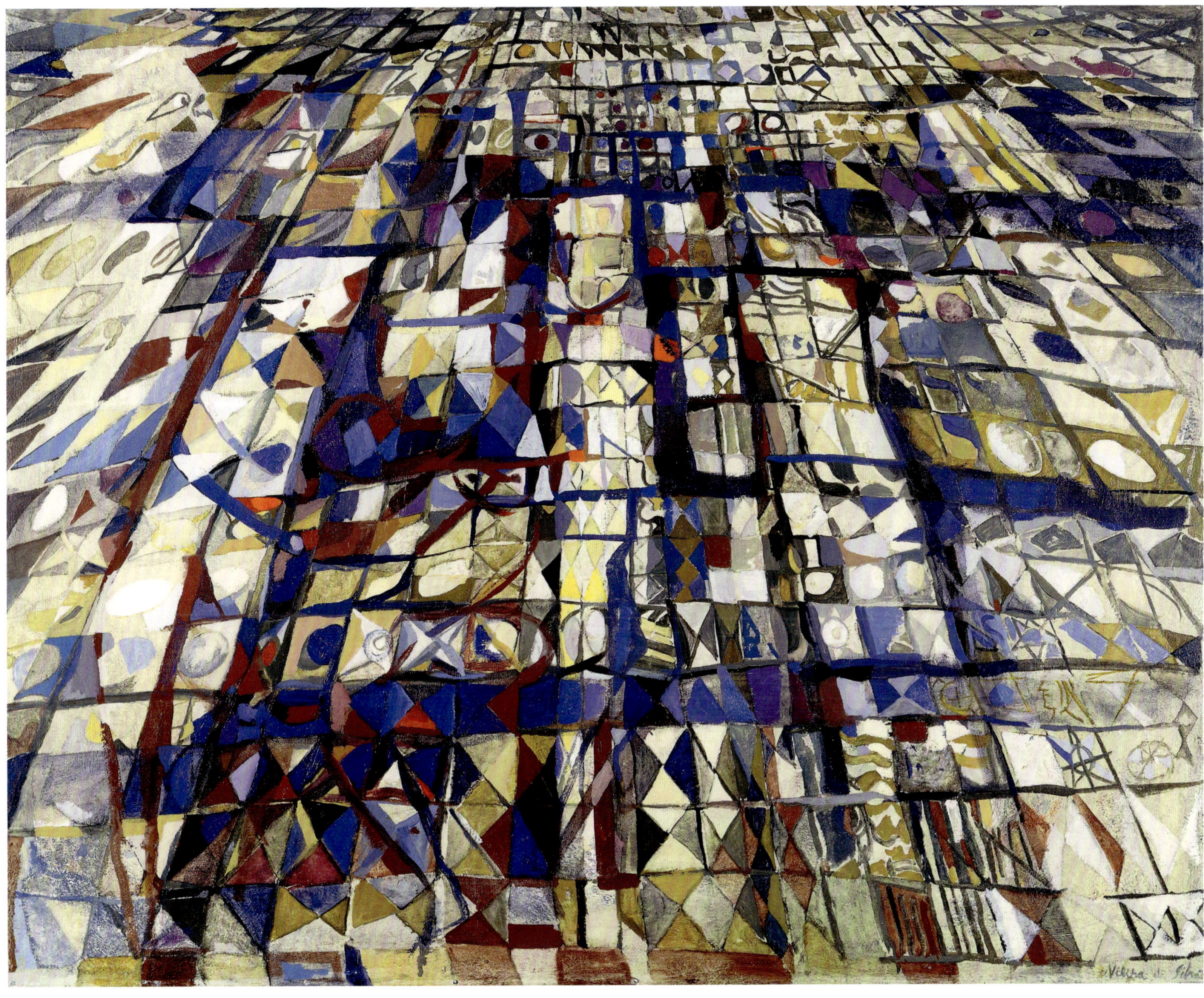

LES CARREAUX DE DELFT (DELFT TILES)
1948, oil on panel, 73 × 92 cm (28 ¾ × 36 ¼ in)

Maria Helena Vieira da Silva, born 1908, Lisbon, Portugal. Died 1992, Paris, France.

Creator of compositionally complex paintings, with dense pattern formations that often appear entirely abstract, Vieira da Silva's works have a sense of rhythm and movement that nevertheless creates pictorial depth and space. As the daughter of a Portuguese diplomat, she travelled widely as a child, soaking up diverse influences. Studying from the age of eleven at Lisbon's Academia Nacional de Belas-Artes, she worked in painting, sculpture and engraving under the tutelage of Fernand Léger (1881–1955), Antoine Bourdelle (1861–1929) and Stanley William Hayter (1901–88), respectively. Upon moving to Paris in 1928, she focused on painting, exploring perspective and the structures underpinning it. Thick impasto canvases of small rectangles defined her work of the 1930s and 1940s, including this painting, which references the colour palette and designs of ceramic tiles from Delft in the Netherlands. Vieira da Silva's compositions of the 1950s appear to evoke the damaged environment post-war, while in the 1960s and 1970s she expanded her practice, exploring tapestry and making eight stained-glass windows for the church of Saint-Jacques de Reims, France. Aside from a period in Portugal during the Second World War, Vieira da Silva lived mainly in Paris and was awarded the Légion d'Honneur in 1979.

ÉLISABETH VIGÉE-LEBRUN

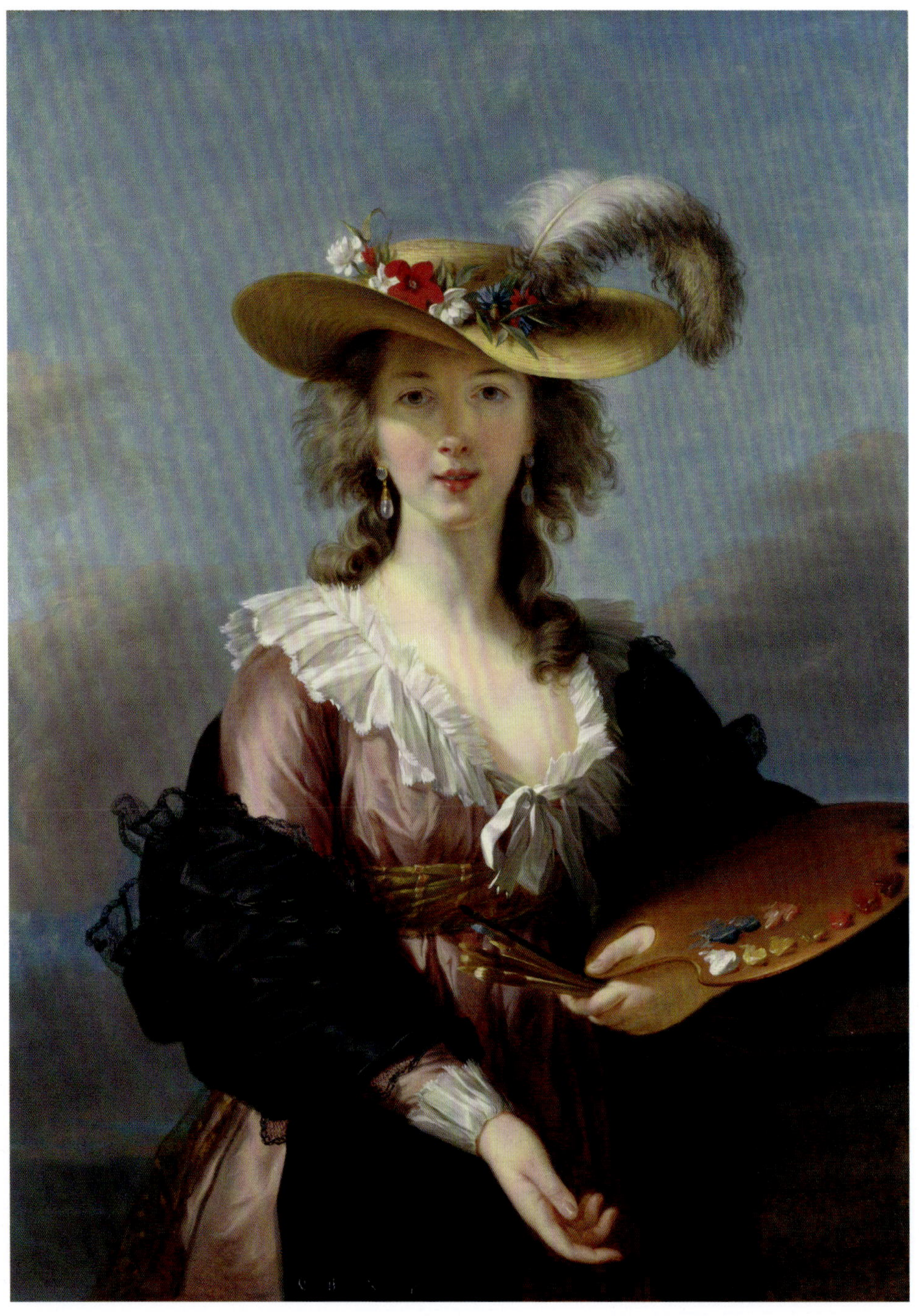

SELF PORTRAIT IN A STRAW HAT
1782, oil on canvas, 97.8 × 70.5 cm (38 ½ × 27 ¾ in), National Gallery, London, UK

Élisabeth Vigée-Lebrun, born 1755, Paris, France. Died 1842, Paris.

Today perhaps best remembered for her portraits of Marie Antoinette and her children, Vigée-Lebrun enjoyed a vertiginous rise to international artistic celebrity during the final years of pre-Revolutionary France. At the young age of nineteen, Vigée-Lebrun joined the Académie de Saint-Luc in Paris, and at twenty-eight she was admitted to France's prestigious Académie Royale de Peinture et de Sculpture, at a time when only four women were permitted among its members. Having become a high-profile painter of the monarchy, in 1789 she fled France and the Revolution to live in exile in Italy. She continued painting portraits, later pursuing commissions across Europe before eventually returning to France in 1809. Vigée-Lebrun made a number of self-portraits, sometimes picturing herself embracing her young daughter, Julie, who was born in 1780. In this *Self Portrait in a Straw Hat*, made at the height of her success, Vigée-Lebrun adopts the commanding posture of a great painter, palette and brushes held demonstratively in hand. Such a depiction seems to make the claim – radical in its moment – that a woman could be both a mother and a professional artist.

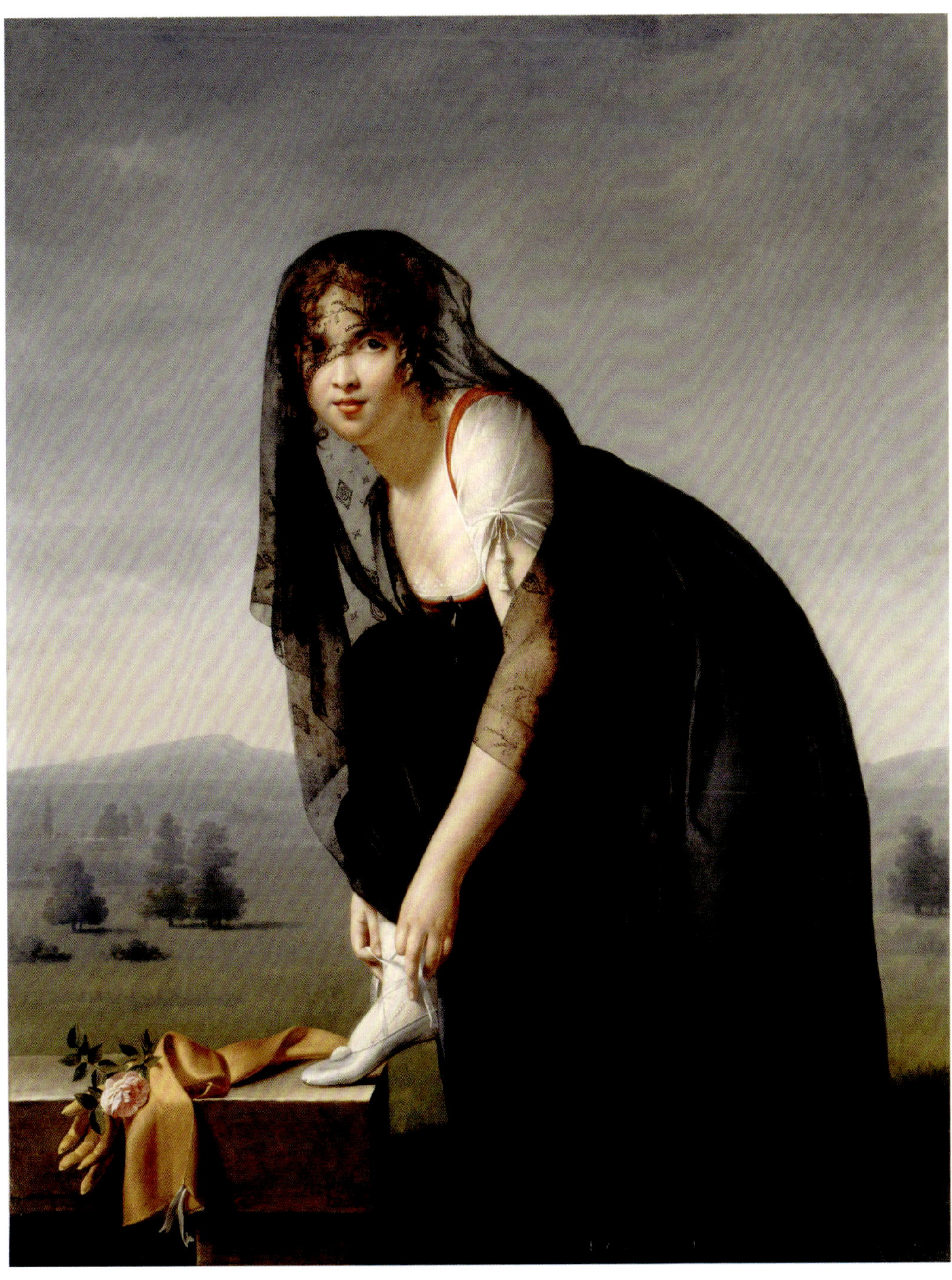

PORTRAIT PRÉSUMÉ DE MADAME SOUSTRAS LAÇANT SON CHAUSSON (PRESUMED PORTRAIT OF MADAME SOUSTRAS LACING HER SLIPPER)
1802, oil on canvas, 146 × 114 cm (57 ½ × 44 ⅞ in), Musée du Louvre, Paris, France

Marie-Denise Villers, born 1774, Paris, France. Died 1821, Paris.

Born into an artistic family – her older sister was painter Marie-Victoire Lemoine (p.177) – Villers first exhibited at the Paris Salon in 1799, where she won a *prix d'encouragement*. She had married Maximilien Villers (1760–1836), an architecture and painting student of Neo-Classical painter Anne Louis Girodet-Trioson (1767–1824), in 1794; unusually for the time, he supported her artistic career, and both took advantage of the new opportunities for patronage in the wake of the French Revolution. Villers was also a student of Girodet, who was himself a pupil of the pre-eminent Neo-Classical painter Jacques-Louis David (1748–1825). Villers's paintings have a history of attributions to that artist: her famous *Young Woman Drawing* (1801) was long attributed to David, and it was not until 1995 that the work's authorship was convincingly assigned to Villers. In this presumed portrait of Madame Soustras, exhibited at the Salon in 1802, Villers depicts a fashionable bourgeois woman wearing a black gown and lace mantilla as she ties the ribbons of her white slipper. Placed in the extreme foreground of the painting, the subject gazes out of the canvas, directly confronting the viewer.

MERRILL WAGNER

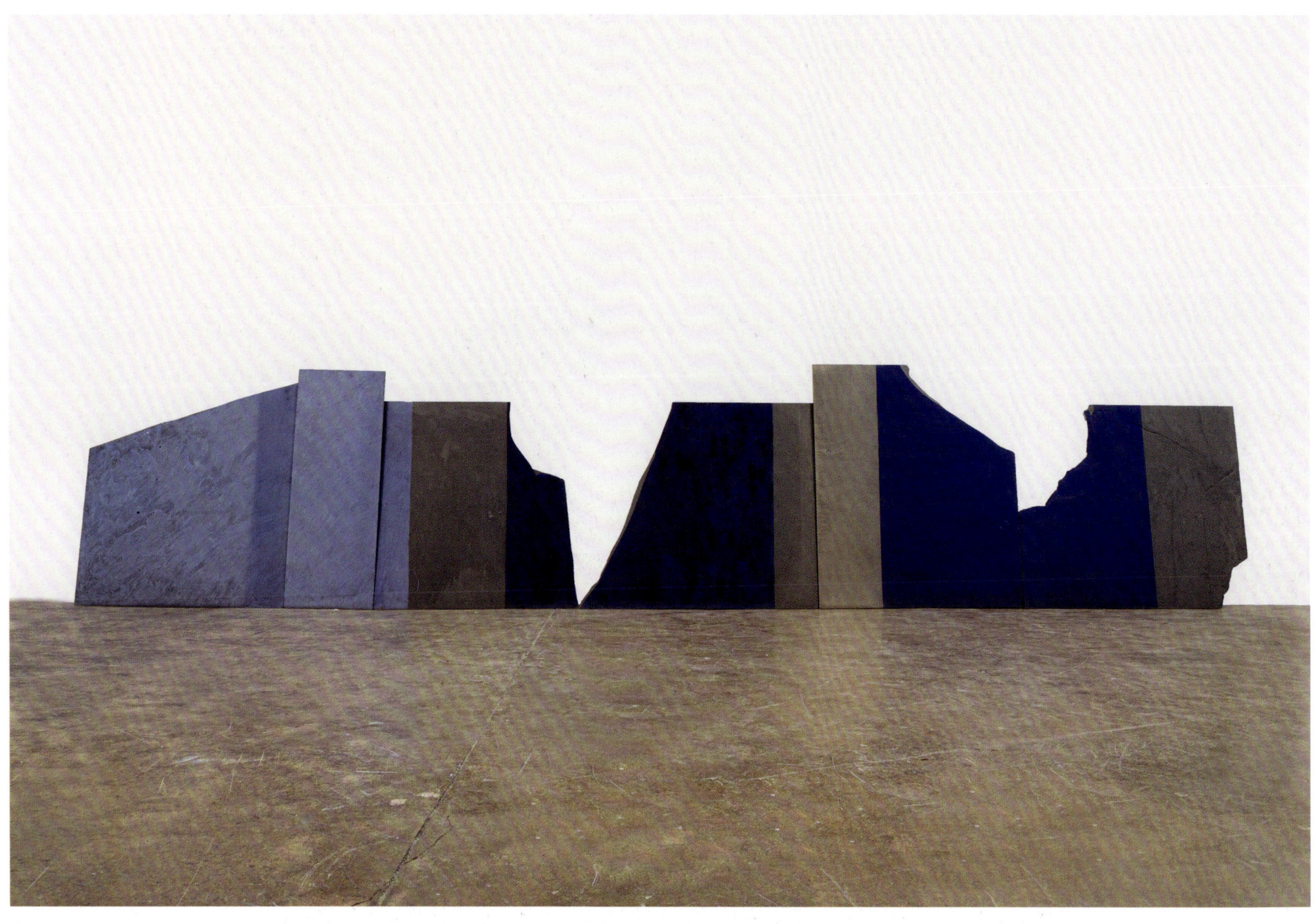

GORGES
1986, casein, oil, and acrylic on slate blackboard fragments in 6 parts, 127 × 609.6 cm (50 × 240 in)

Merrill Wagner, born 1935, Tacoma, Washington, USA.

Growing up in the Pacific Northwest fostered Wagner's deep connection with the land and the art of landscape. After graduating from Sarah Lawrence College in Yonkers, she moved to New York City, where she studied for several years with the American painter Edwin Dickinson (1891–1978). Her early work of the 1960s consisted of colourful and contrasting abstract paintings on large canvases. Wagner pursued her interest in the processes and potential of painting, introducing sculptural and spatial qualities into works whose assertive planes of colour remained in tune with the Minimalism and hard-edged abstraction of the time. Eva Hesse's (1936–70) work with unconventional materials was an inspiration to Wagner, who began experimenting in the early 1970s with painting on surfaces such as steel, stone and slate, producing works that blur traditional boundaries that separate painting from sculpture, relief and installation. These materials – as seen in this work, in which slate blackboard fragments are painted in tones of blue and grey – naturally offer unusual textures, inherent geometric patterns and marks, and introduce elements of chance into her work.

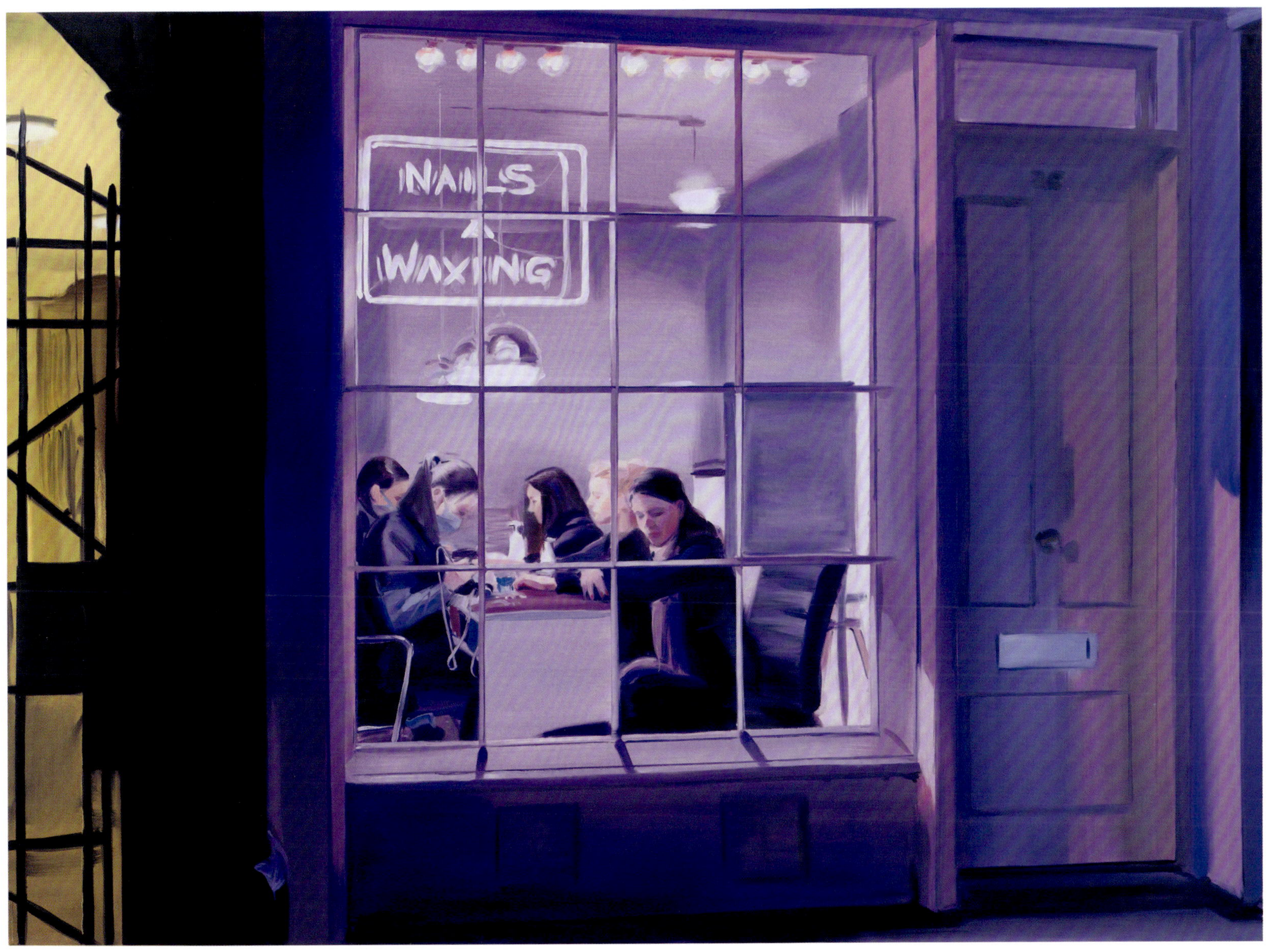

FILING
2018, oil on linen, 195 × 270 cm (76 ¾ × 106 ¼ in)

Caroline Walker, born 1982, Dunfermline, Scotland, UK.

Walker's paintings focus on the lives of women and the societal conditions that inform how and where they live and work. Walker's early paintings began with staged scenes created with props, costumes and hired models, from which she developed compositions that drew on but unsettled attitudes and assumptions about gender, particularly its intersections with socio-economic status. Since 2016, Walker has taken a more documentary approach, depicting the lives of women at work in the home or the primarily female-dominated professions of hospitality, cleaning and retail. Often shadowing and taking hundreds of photographs of her subjects, Walker then sketches and develops compositions on canvas. The viewer encounters the women in Walker's large-scale paintings sometimes intimately, sometimes voyeuristically, often as subjects seemingly unaware of being looked at, as with *Filing*, in which a neon purple glow settles on a night-time scene of women in a nail salon. These compositional strategies ground Walker's tender, psychologically charged scenes, which draw attention to how women's labour – often overlooked, rendered invisible and undervalued – can be represented and seen.

WANG ZHIBO

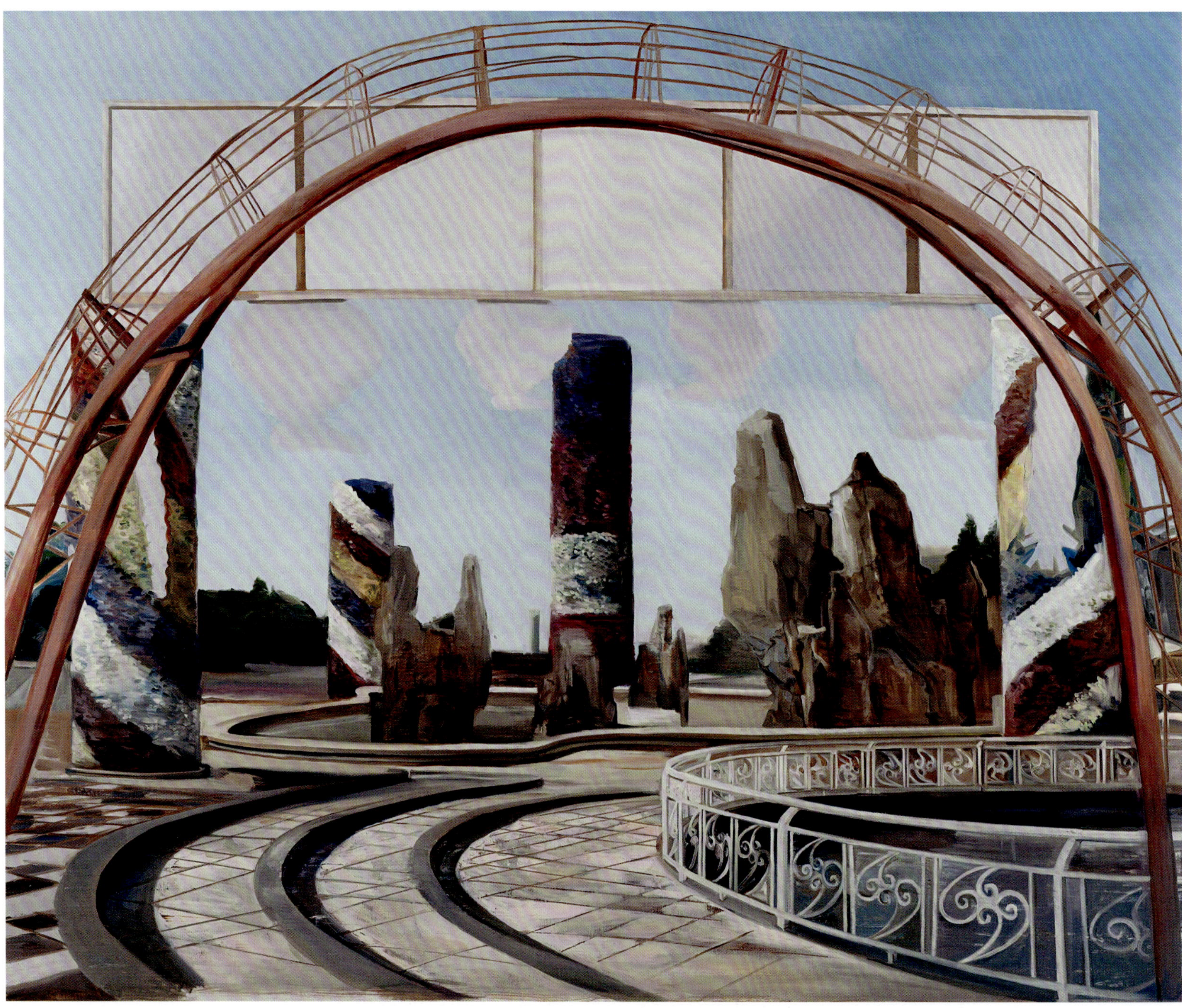

UNTITLED (FESTIVAL)
2012, oil on canvas, 147 × 180 cm (57 7/8 × 70 7/8 in), private collection

Wang Zhibo, born 1981, Wenzhou, Zhejiang Province, China.

Wang was part of China's 'Post-80s' generation of artists, a reference to the decade when they were born and signifying the era's cultural changes, including a shift away from overtly political subject matter in art. Utilizing a traditional style of representational painting, Wang depicts enigmatic, ambiguous and haunting scenes both interior and exterior, natural and manmade, that reflect on China's modernity. After graduating from Hangzhou's China Academy of Art Oil Painting Department in 2008, Wang was awarded the prestigious national Luo Zhongli Scholarship. Since then, she has honed an approach that conflates reality and illusion and muddles time and space, to create paintings whose composite locations are generic yet familiar. Her paintings can be seen through the lens of Surrealism and, at times, echo the empty urban spaces of Giorgio de Chirico's (1888–1978) 'metaphysical pictures'. In *Untitled (Festival)* a broad spectrum of architectural elements comes together: seemingly ancient rocks, brightly coloured, striped pillars, a paved path bordered by elaborate metalwork, the reverse of a sign hoarding and what might be the framework for a rollercoaster ride. The image bears the hallmarks of a festive theme park, a typical construction of modern-day China, yet one eerily devoid of visitors.

LAURA WHEELER WARING

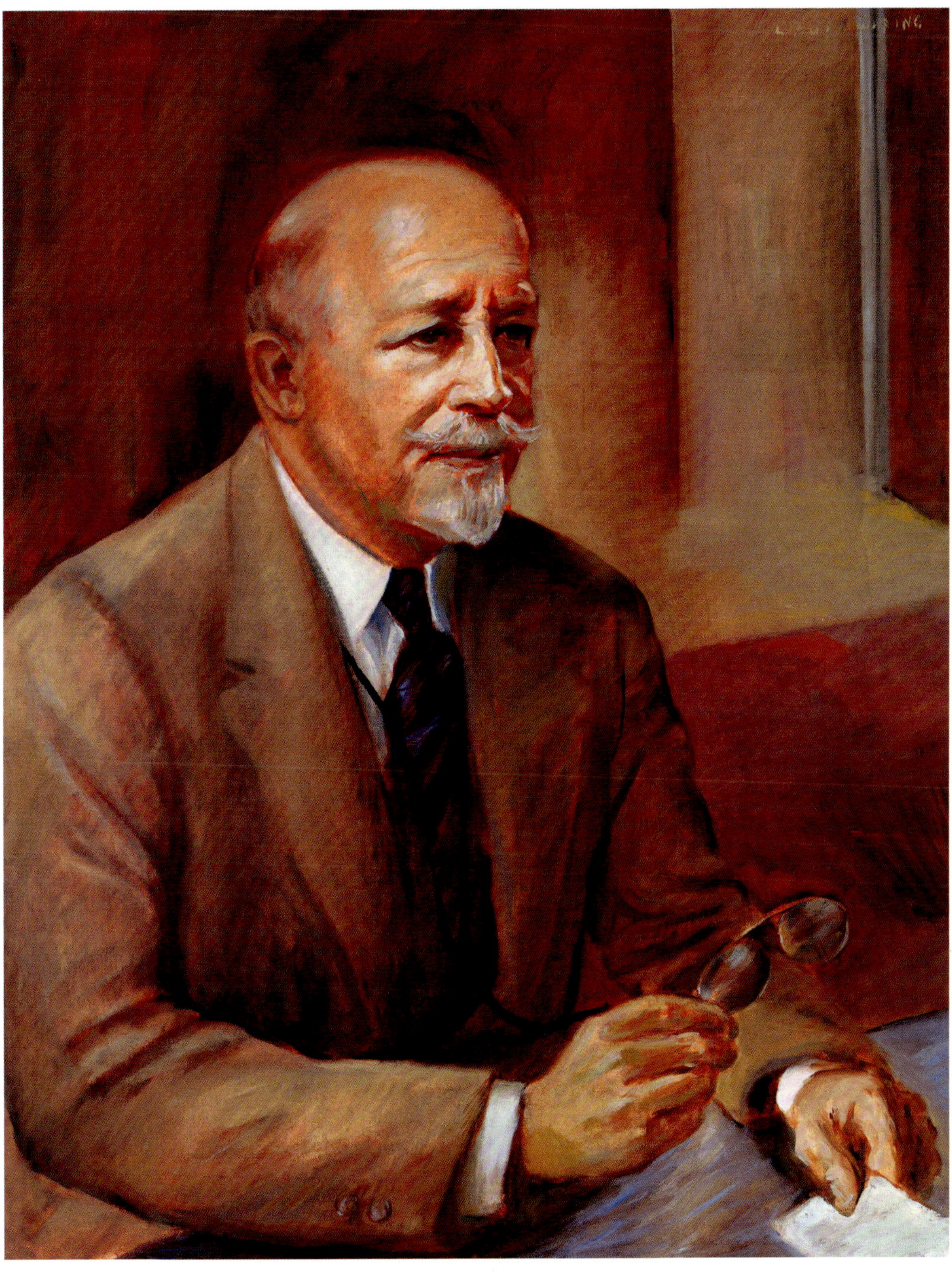

W. E. B. DU BOIS
before 1948, oil on canvas, 81.9 × 63.5 cm (32 ¼ × 25 in), National Portrait Gallery, Smithsonian Institution, Washington DC, USA

Laura Wheeler Waring, born 1887, Hartford, Connecticut, USA. Died 1948, Philadelphia, USA.

Waring was a portraitist, well known for sensitive depictions of Black Americans. She studied at the Pennsylvania Academy of Fine Arts, through which she was awarded a scholarship that enabled her to travel to Paris in 1914. In the 1920s, Waring returned twice more to the French city, where she joined a community of prominent Black artists, writers and intellectuals who also composed her social circle in the United States. Waring shared a deep commitment to civil rights with a number of her friends and used her realistic portraits of Black individuals to champion not only her subjects but her race more broadly. Her conviction that art could promote interracial understanding was also held by the Harmon Foundation (a funding programme that supported African American creativity), which in 1943 commissioned her, along with Betsy Graves Reyneau (1888–1964), to paint a series of significant Black Americans, among them her close friend W. E. B. Du Bois, a sociologist, historian and civil rights activist. From 1944 to 1954, the series toured the United States as part of a travelling exhibition in the hope that showcasing visual documentation of the subjects' contributions to American society would counteract racism.

SAIRA WASIM

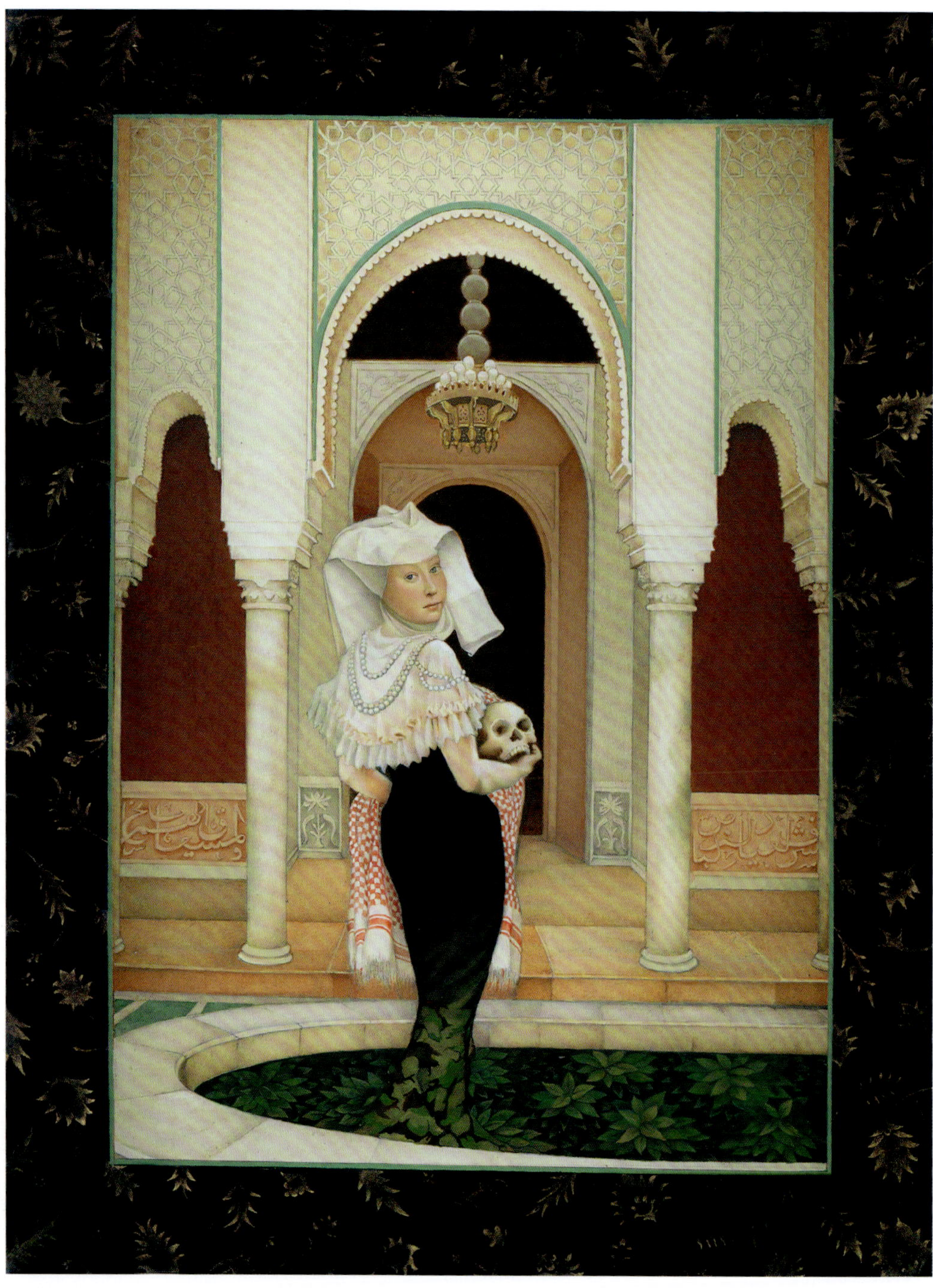

72 VIRGINS TO DIE FOR
2015, gouache and ink on wasli paper, 35 × 27 cm (13 ¾ × 10 ⅝ in), Jamil Collection, Denmark

Saira Wasim, born 1975, Lahore, Pakistan.

Wasim is known for her uncanny reworking of miniature styles of painting. Equated with Mughal royal tastes, the training in this art is an extensive process requiring considerable time studying with specialized teachers, preparing handmade *wasli* paper (smoothed and treated to deter insects) and making fine brushes, some from single hairs. Wasim's studies at the National College of Arts in Lahore introduced her to the form that she appropriates to explore contemporary world politics. Within each small frame, Wasim creates allegories of post-9/11 global politics using the delicate technique to achieve micro detail that encourages close scrutiny. In this painting garlanded by ornate borders, a femme fatale emerges from a pool of water dressed in an amalgamation of clothes that combines a white Flemish Renaissance headpiece with a close-fitting ball dress that seems to transform to army camouflage at its base, grasping a skull and keffiyeh that allude to the phenomenon of suicide bombing. The title of the work refers to a belief that Muslim martyrdom is rewarded by access to seventy-two companions and an abundance of sexual pleasures; the woman embodies this vision of paradise and the life that is said to lie beyond death.

ALISON WATT

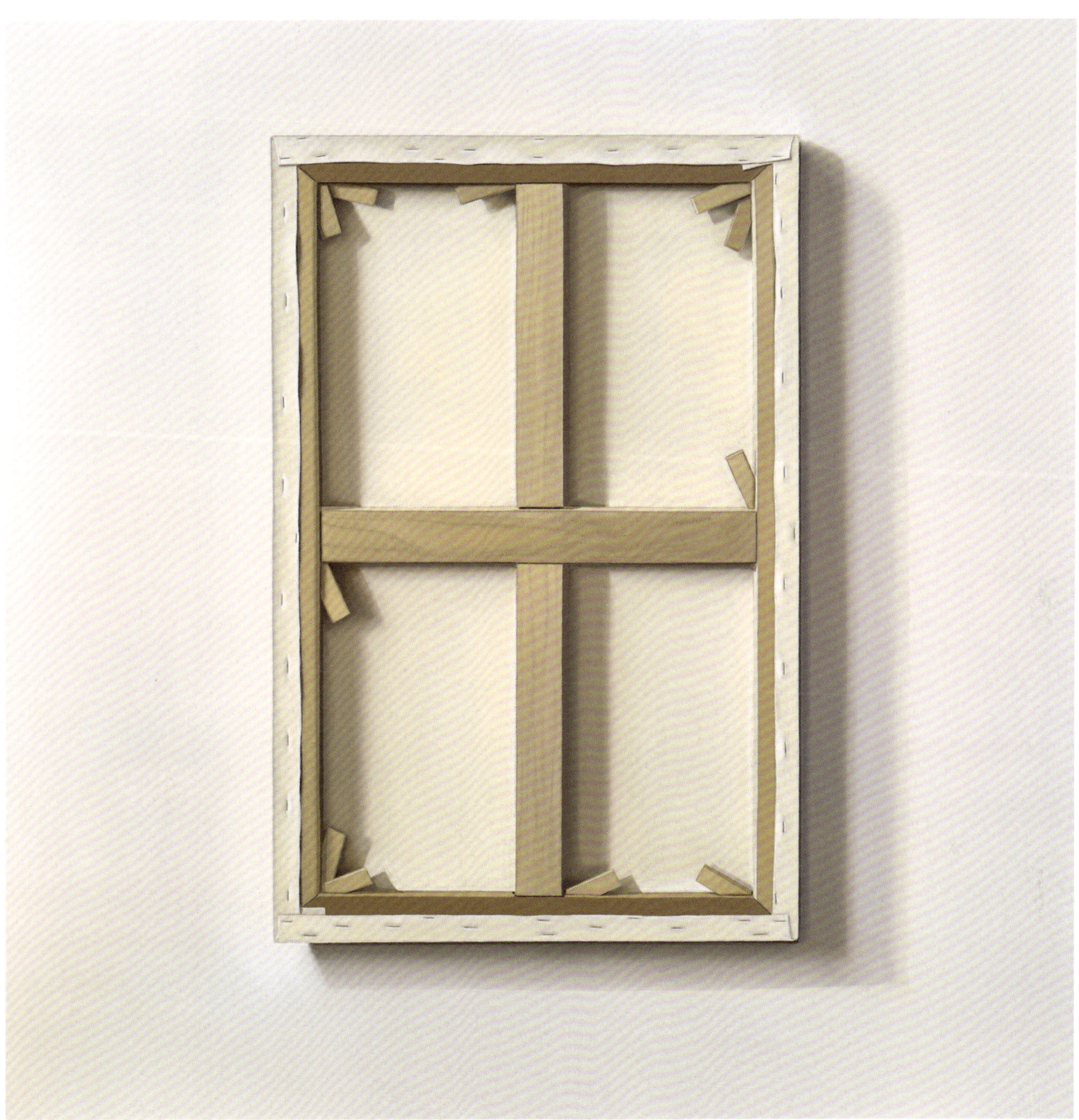

REVERSED CANVAS
2017, oil on canvas, 152.4 × 152.4 cm (60 × 60 in)

Alison Watt, born 1965, Greenock, Scotland, UK.

Watt's career was launched in 1987 when, while still a student at Glasgow School of Art, she won the annual portrait award at the National Portrait Gallery, London, which brought with it a commission to paint the Queen Mother. For the following decade she was primarily focused on portraiture – especially the female nude – until her 1997 solo exhibition 'Fold' at the Fruitmarket Gallery, Edinburgh, revealed a new body of work focused solely on details of fabric and drapery. From here, Watt moved away from portraits entirely, depicting close-ups of folds and tucks of cloth, which, as she explained in a 2016 interview with *AnOther Magazine*, she finds 'very evocative and suggestive of the human presence'. Alongside numerous variations on this theme, Watt made a series of trompe l'oeil paintings in the same spare palette: a hanging rectangular sheet of white cloth; a blank piece of paper quartered by crisp folds; a coiled loop of cable; and the reverse of a painter's canvas, stapled taut onto a wooden stretcher with corners neatly folded and wedges holding the whole form rigid. The work serves as a reminder that a painting is more than just the surface image but a three-dimensional physical object in itself.

MICHAELINA WAUTIER

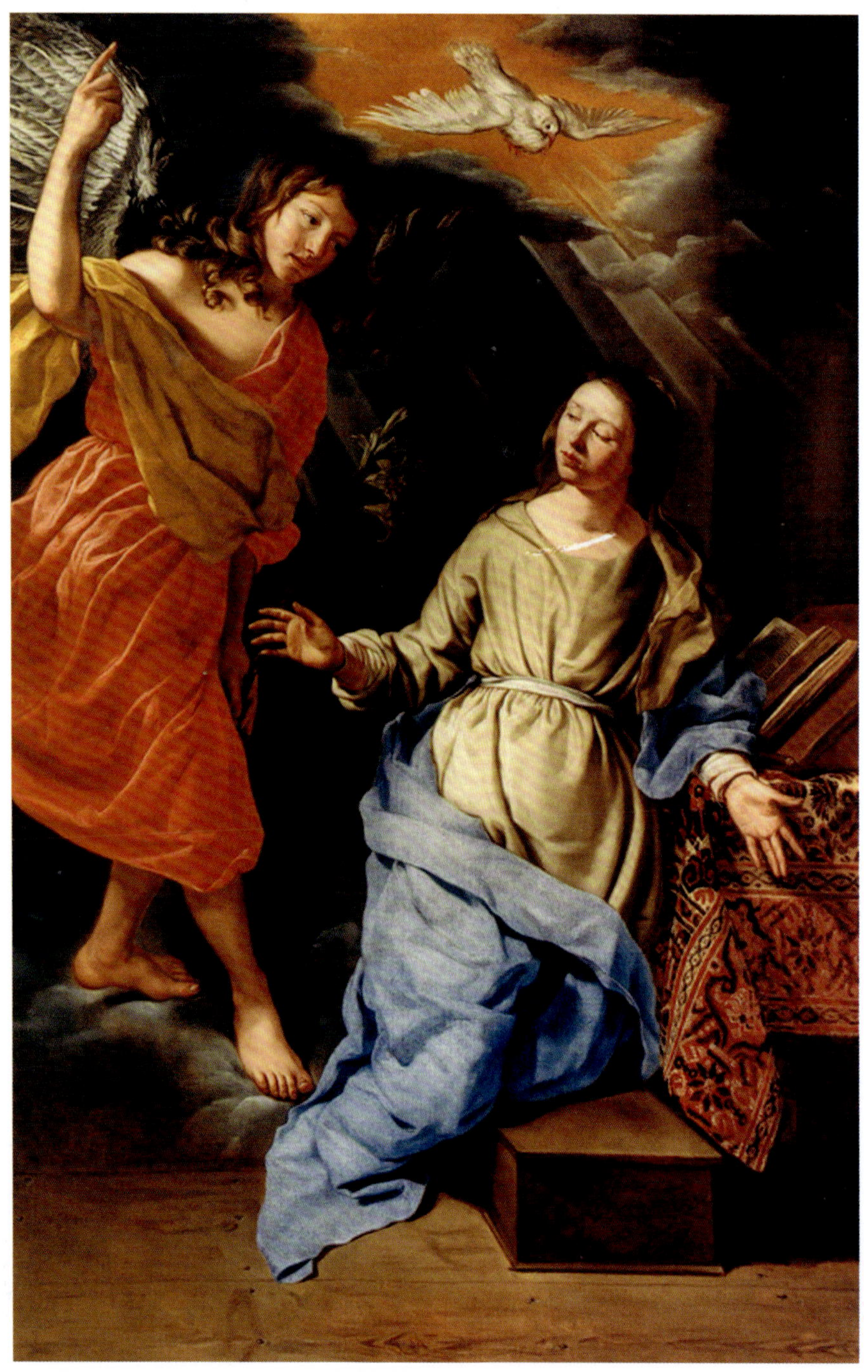

THE ANNUNCIATION
1659, oil on canvas, 200 × 134 cm (78 ¾ × 52 ¾ in), Musée du Domaine Royal de Marly, Marly-le-Roi, France

Michaelina Wautier, born 1617/18, Mons, Belgium. Died 1689, Brussels, Belgium.

Unusually for a woman artist working in the Baroque period, Wautier painted scenes that went beyond floral still lifes, composing sumptuous images of nude bodies, both male and female, at a time when women were banned from life drawing. Though little is documented about her life, Wautier probably began painting later in life, around the age of thirty-nine, and lived and shared a studio in Brussels with her brother, Charles Wautier (active 1652–60). The references to allegory and classical mythology in her oeuvre indicate her education and upper-class status. *The Annunciation* is her last-known painting. The work was incorrectly attributed to the French court painter Pierre Bedeau (*c.* 1647–1707) for centuries, with Wautier's signature only discovered on the canvas in 1983. The finely painted details, such as the wrinkled and draped robes, and the stylized use of chiaroscuro signify Wautier's knowledge and interest in the work of Italian painter Caravaggio (1571–1610). Largely forgotten for several centuries, Wautier was finally introduced to a wide public in 2018 with a retrospective exhibition in Antwerp, Belgium.

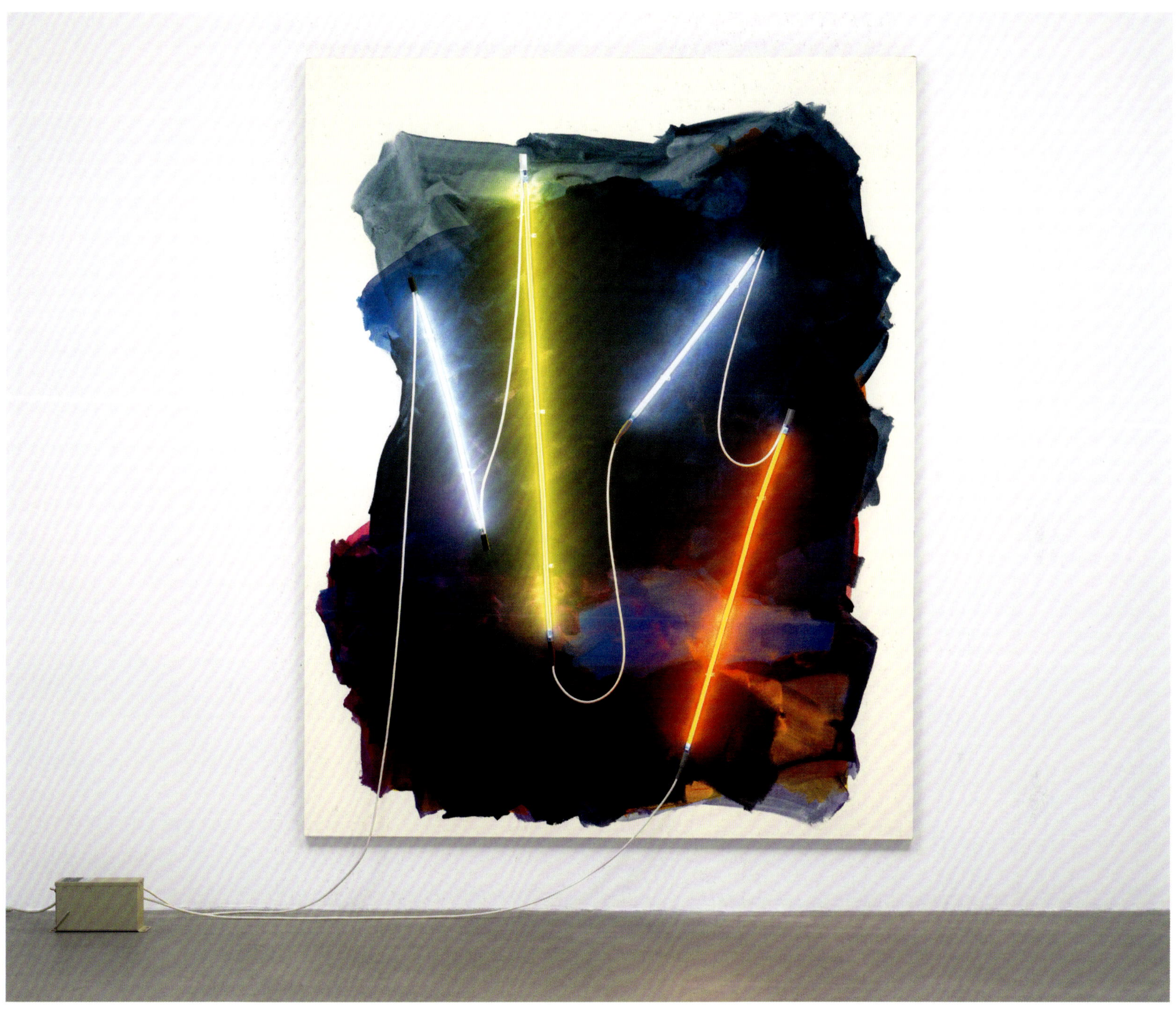

CONEY ISLAND II
2012, Flashe and neon on linen, 261.6 × 210.8 cm (103 × 83 in), Museum of Modern Art, New York, USA

Mary Weatherford, born 1963, Ojai, California, USA.

After graduating from Princeton University in 1984, Weatherford spent the years following in New York, where she attended the Whitney Museum of American Art's Independent Study Program. Her move back to her home state of California in 1999 heralded a new expressiveness in response to her natural surroundings. Drawing on the lexicon of Colour Field painting and Abstract Expressionism, Weatherford uses highly pigmented, liquid latex emulsion on linen, working rhythmically on the floor to build up depth and texture in her atmospheric scapes. In 2012, after approaching themes of the sublime from different angles – including target paintings and canvases that incorporated objects such as seashells, sponges and starfish – Weatherford began experimenting with attaching neon light to her canvases. Inspired by old signage in California's Central Valley, she began activating her paintings through the use of neon glass tubes with their thread-like wires left dangling. In this painting, Weatherford conjures the joyful gaudiness of Coney Island with neon strips that bleed into the layered ground of velvety indigos and purples. While her titles root her works in a specific place, they transcend a purely visual evocation, alluding to sounds, smells, rhythms and memories she has experienced.

MARIANNE VON WEREFKIN

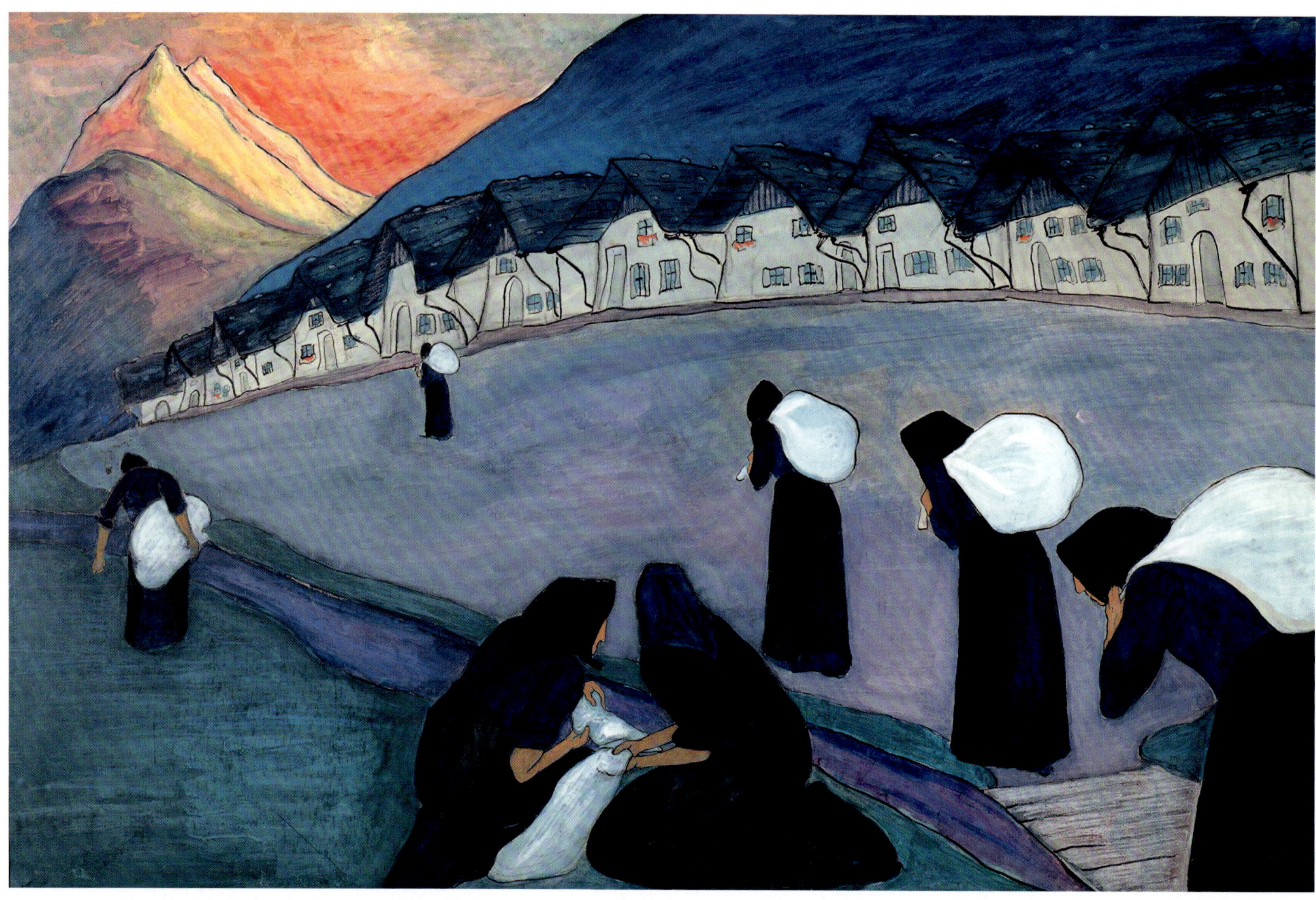

BLACK WOMEN
1910, gouache on cardboard, 53 × 81 cm (20 ⅞ × 31 ⅞ in), Sprengel Museum, Hanover, Germany

Marianne von Werefkin, born 1860, Tula, Russia. Died 1938, Ascona, Switzerland.

Born to an affluent military family at a time when women were not admitted to Russian art schools, Werefkin was a private student of esteemed realist painter Ilya Repin (1844–1930). She established herself as a capable portraitist in the 1880s and was dubbed the 'Russian Rembrandt' for her finesse with oils. After moving to Munich with her partner, Expressionist painter Alexej von Jawlensky (1864–1941), she withdrew from art for several years, allowing him to advance his own painting career. Returning to painting in 1906, she developed a radically different style influenced by Expressionist painters such as Emil Nolde (1867–1956) and Edvard Munch (1863–1944). Forsaking oils, she worked in watercolour and gouache, creating atmospheric, spiritually charged paintings. *Black Women* typifies her new direction, contrasting darkly dressed washerwomen with a vivid mountain sunset. Werefkin painted it in the Bavarian town of Murnau am Staffelsee, where she lived with Gabriele Münter (p.214) and Wassily Kandinsky (1866–1944), founding members of Der Blaue Reiter (The Blue Rider) group of artists, which she joined in 1913.

ROBIN F. WILLIAMS

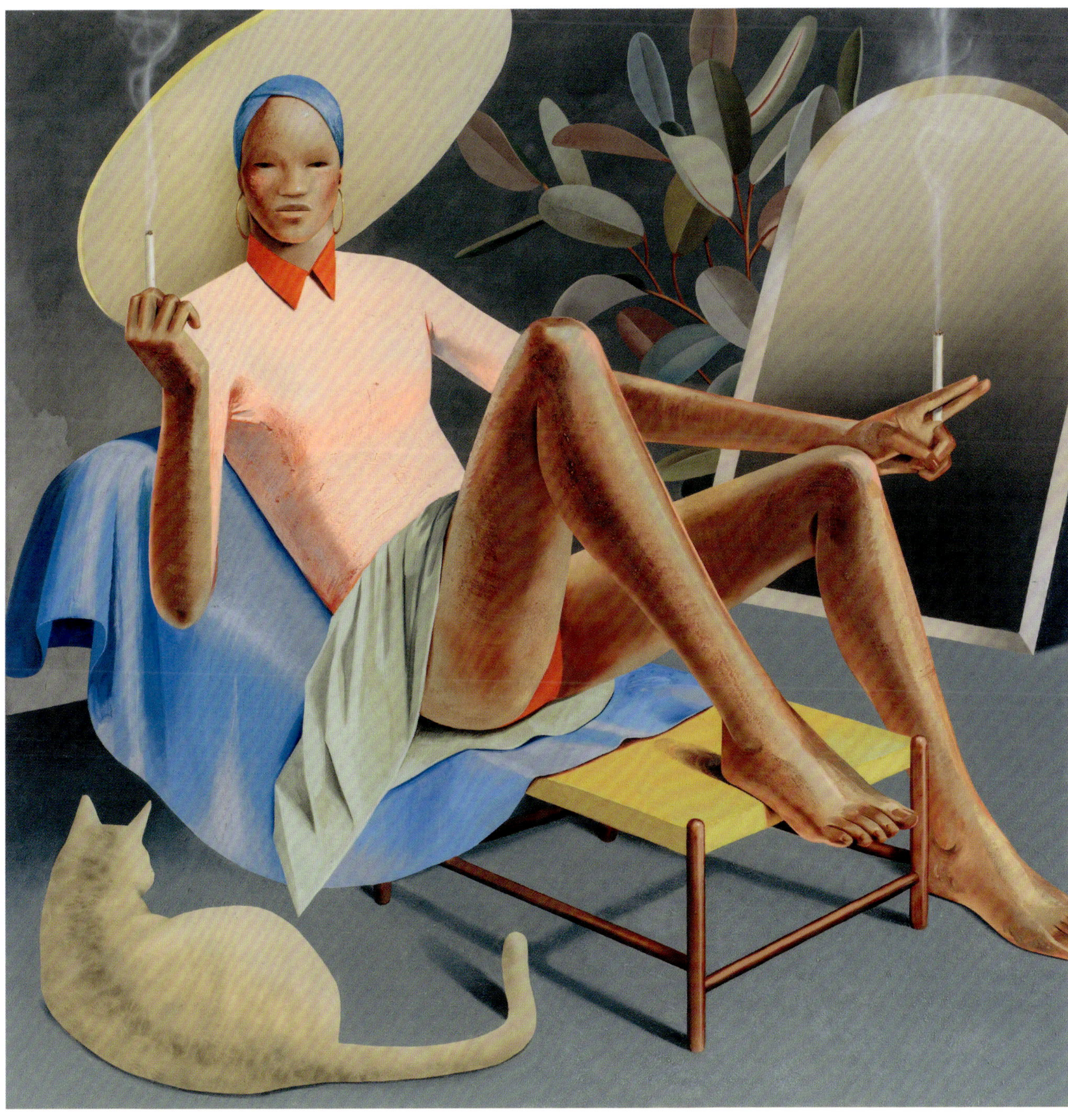

YOUR GOOD TASTE IS SHOWING
2017, acrylic, airbrush and oil on canvas,
182.9 × 182.9 cm (72 × 72 in)

Robin F. Williams, born 1984, Columbus, Ohio, USA.

Known for her sleek, monumental paintings of stylized female figures, Williams tackles the socialization, performance and representation of gender and sexuality in contemporary American culture. While undeniably contemporary in their airbrushed, marbled surfaces, cinematic stylization and coolly understated palette of pastels, greys and neon hues, Williams's works often make compositional reference to art-historical masterworks, both quoting and subverting archetypal representations of female subjects. *Your Good Taste is Showing* centres a modelesque sunbather donning an elegant sunhat who holds two lit cigarettes, strategically placed so that one of them appears to give the viewer the middle finger. The painting takes its inspiration from a 1970s advertisement of a Black model selling cigarettes that referenced Johannes Vermeer's *Girl with a Pearl Earring* (*c.*1665), which Williams combined with a reference to Balthus's *Girl with Cat* (1937). Reclining on an incongruously sized lounge chair (one far too short for her lithe physique), the subject exposes a portion of her underwear, reclaiming the desire Balthus's painting objectified and disavowing the class structures built on whiteness (or proximity to whiteness) that define 'good taste'.

CHLOE WISE

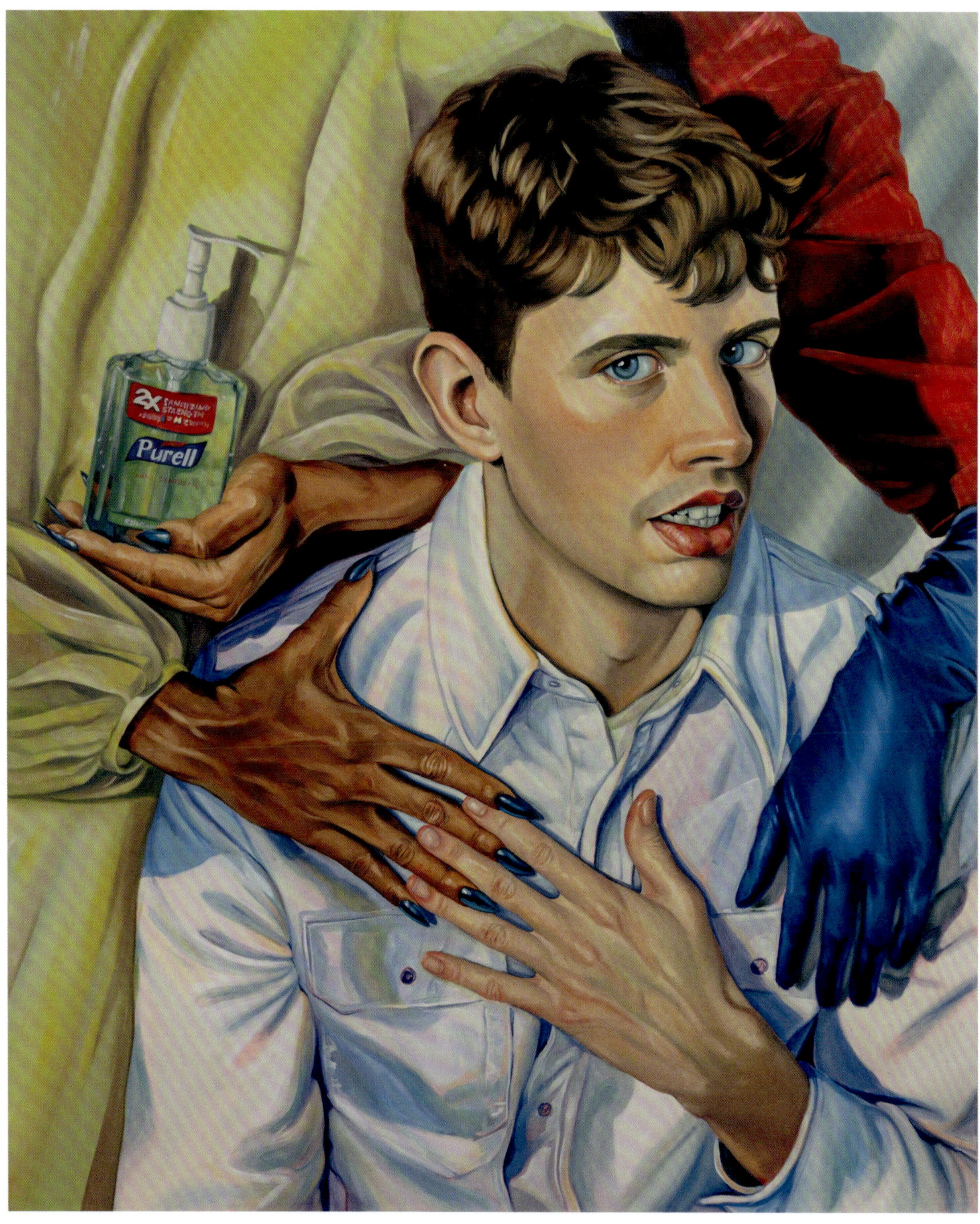

TORMENTEDLY UNTAINTED
2019, oil on linen, 183 × 152.5 cm (72 × 60 in), collection of Jessica Iclisoy

Chloe Wise, born 1990, Montreal, Canada.

Friends, models and muses populate the large-scale canvases of Wise, whose bright and youthful compositions contain subtle undertones of social critique. Based in New York, Wise has experienced a swift ascendance within an art world that is deeply intertwined with the spheres of haute design, celebrity and social media – her faux-couture 'Bagel Bag', worn by an actress friend in 2014, became a viral sensation and fuelled immediate public interest in her studio practice. Working in painting, sculpture, film and installation, Wise offers wry commentary on millennial culture, consumerism, body image and Instagram self-fashioning, often producing self-portraits or figural tableaux whose editorial staging recalls both Baroque masterworks and magazine advertisements. *Tormentedly Untainted* hints at the complexities of today's social contracts. The painting focuses on a Caravaggesque model who locks eyes with the viewer as his fingers gently graze those of two unseen figures. Their kitchen gloves and hand sanitizer – intentionally displayed like a sponsored product placement – suggest a sense of hesitation or unspoken boundaries and, perhaps, anticipate the sort of global health crisis that would spawn a frenzy for these items just a year later.

ISSY WOOD

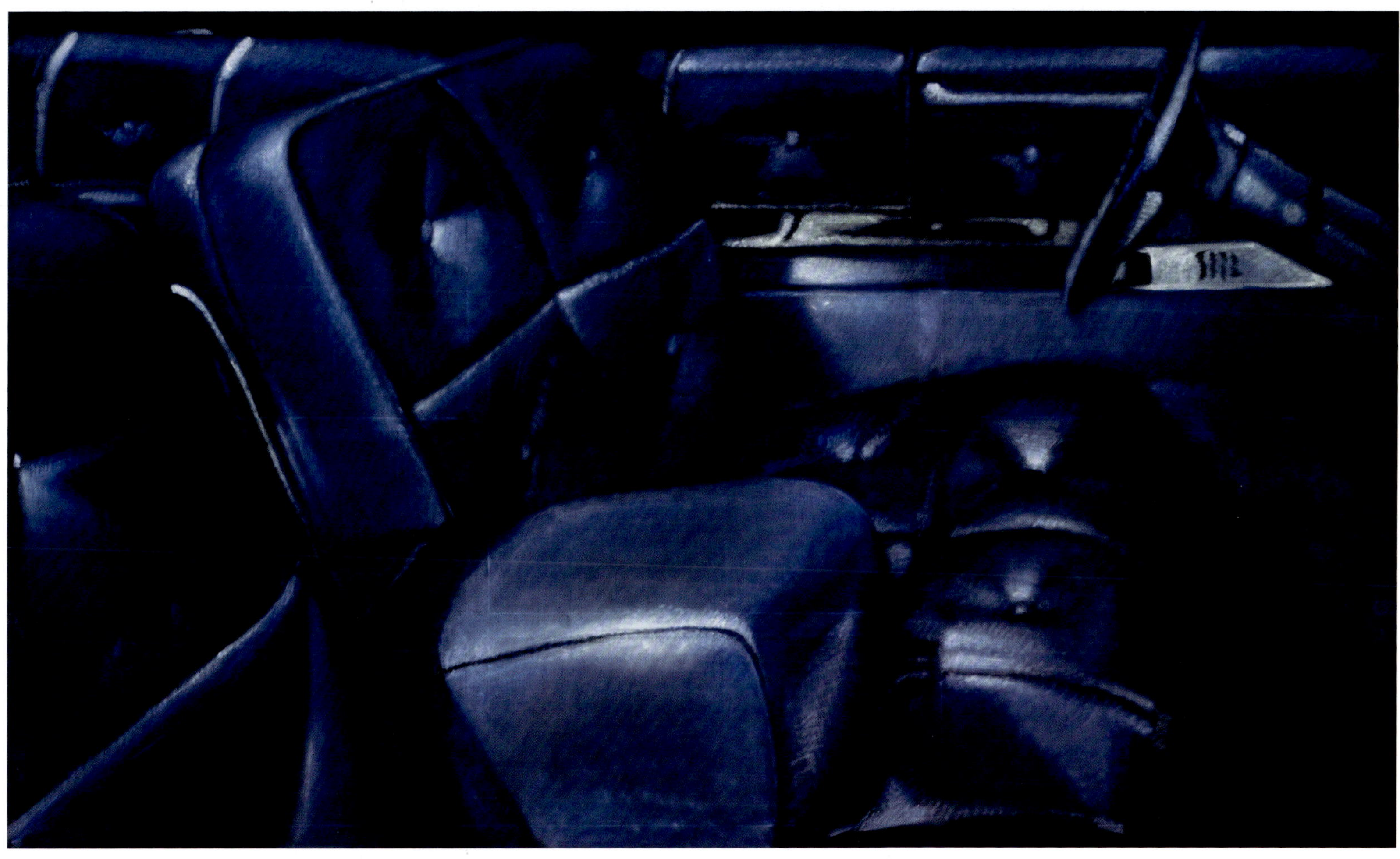

CAR INTERIOR / GO, DADDY 1
2019, oil on velvet, 170.5 × 290.5 × 4 cm
(67 ⅛ × 114 ⅜ × 1 ⅝ in)

Issy Wood, born 1993, Durham, North Carolina, USA.

A writer, musician and artist, Wood's varied practice deploys wry humour to address the heavier themes of contemporary life – alienation, apathy and excess – without resorting to earnest social critique. In a 2019 *Garage* interview, Wood jokingly described herself as a 'medieval Millennial'; she maintains some painterly traditions, while leaving signs of subversion – visual clues that reflect her own identity. Rendered in a realist manner, the artist's works often capture artifice, ranging from synthetic fabrics to antiques and outmoded technologies – subtle signifiers of transient consumerism awash with a lingering sense of malaise. Wood's paintings estrange the familiar, cropping and zooming in on everyday scenes to transform them into sites of ominous anxiety. Wood takes the same approach in her writing, which flits between prose and everyday observations of millennial life, a theme that also crosses over into her music. By applying oil paint to velvet, as seen in the glossy textures of *Car interior / go, Daddy 1*, Wood expands the material parameters and possibilities of the medium of painting, contributing a cloying texture that adds to the painting's sense of claustrophobic unease.

CLARE WOODS

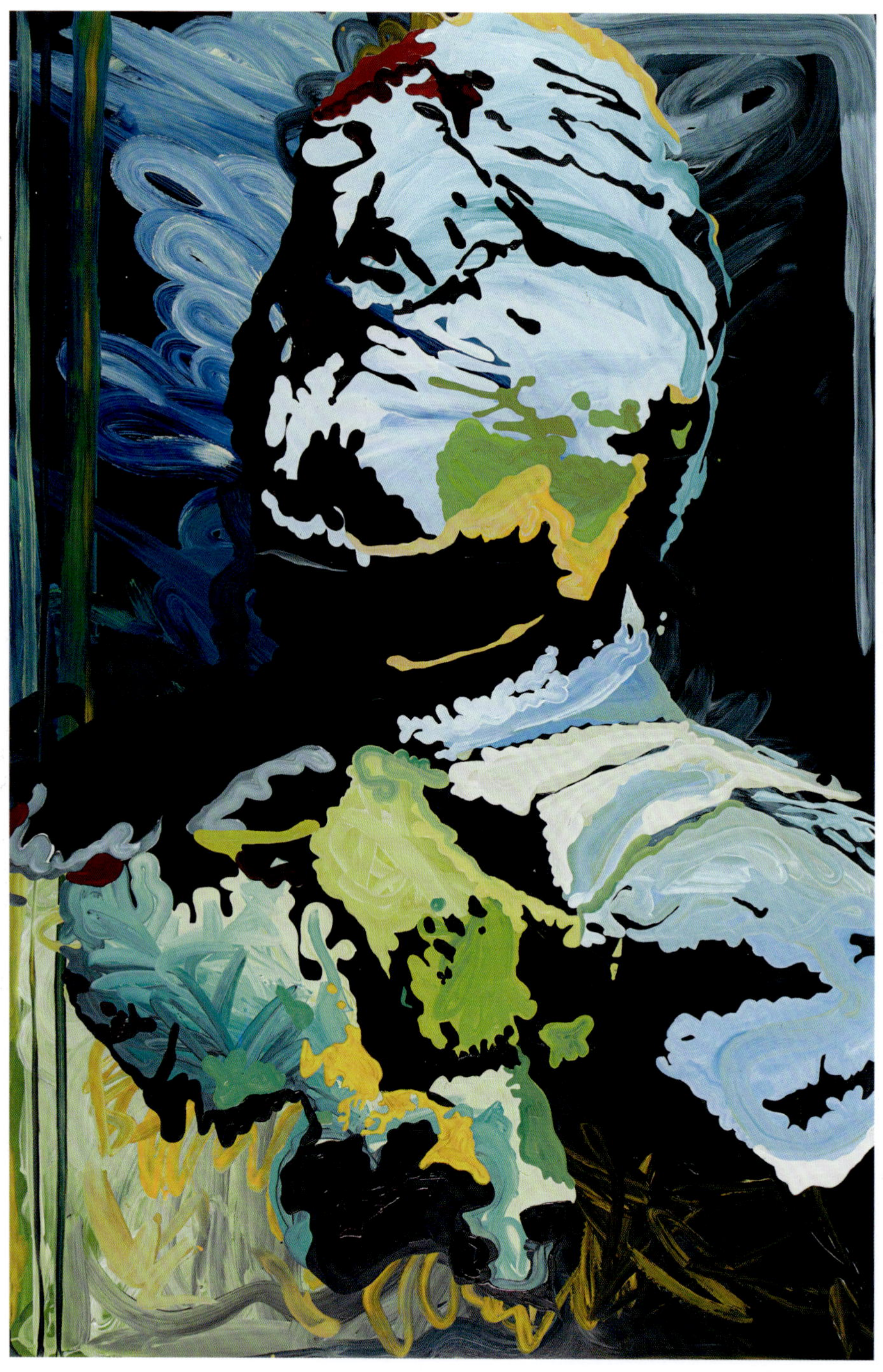

THE REPEATER
2014, oil on aluminium, 254 × 168 cm (100 × 66 in)

Clare Woods, born 1972, Southampton, UK.

Trained as a sculptor, Woods extends her considerations of how objects exist in space to her large-scale paintings. Preferring the smooth finish of aluminium sheeting to canvas, she works in oil and resin, pairing loose brush marks and sharp-edged shapes to describe unsettling scenes. Vulnerability and life's fragility are central to the artist's thematic enquiries, with flowers, landscapes and bodies her recurring motifs. 'The works are about being human, about being alive,' Woods said in a 2018 conversation with curator Anneka French. Using photographs as pictorial prompts, Woods crops them to the degree that they are rendered nearly illegible in the resulting painting, often cultivating a sense of claustrophobia. *The Repeater* echoes sculptor Eduardo Paolozzi's *Shattered Head* (1956), a bronze bust that evokes the post-war European psyche. Copied from a black-and-white photograph of the sculpture and repeated in paint, Paolozzi's faceless figure is depicted with hues and shapes unfamiliar to its original form. In this gesture of abstracted appropriation, Woods lends an idiosyncratic frame to the sculptured form, expressing how it exists as an object – not in reality but in her own imaginings.

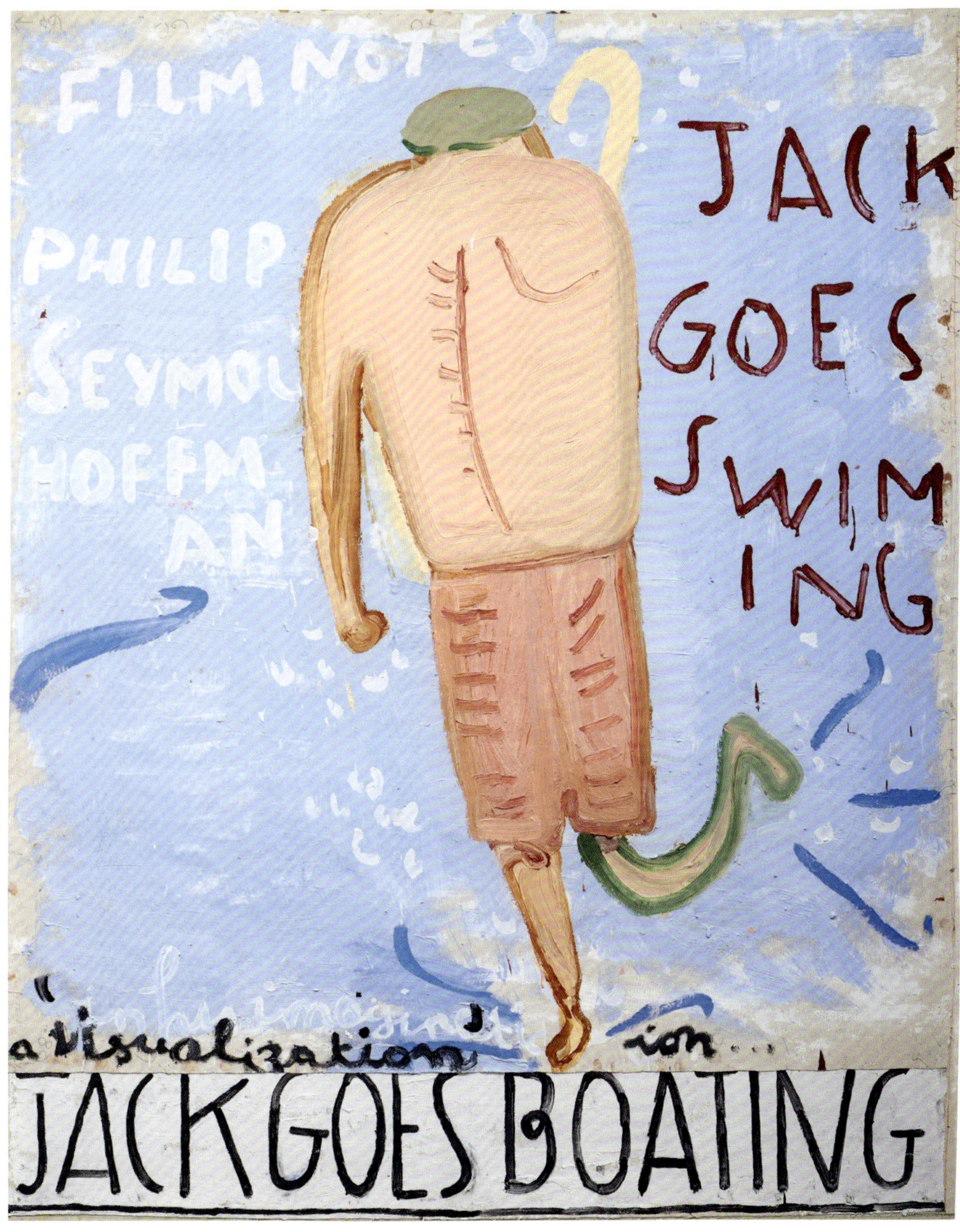

JACK GOES SWIMMING (JACK)
2013, oil on canvas, 207 × 168 cm (81 ½ × 66 ⅛ in)

Rose Wylie, born 1934, Hythe, Kent, UK.

Wylie is acclaimed for her large-scale paintings, which combine cartoonish depictions of people, animals and objects with snippets of hand-scrawled text, but success came to her relatively late in life. After meeting her husband, painter and writer Roy Oxlade (1929–2014), at art school in the 1950s, Wylie stopped painting to focus on raising their young family. She returned to her studies in 1979, graduating with an MA from London's Royal College of Art two years later. Her first solo exhibition was held at Trinity Arts Centre in Kent in 1985. Wylie creates her compositions from memory, beginning with drawings inspired by everything from quotidian encounters to scenes from films or paintings. She then translates these into thickly outlined and brightly coloured forms, rendered in bold brushstrokes, on panels of unstretched and unprimed canvas. Wylie often creates works in series: *Jack Goes Swimming (Jack)* is from 'Film Notes', a series of annotated paintings that distil moments from movies as she remembers them – in this case, a scene from the 2010 drama *Jack Goes Boating*, which starred Philip Seymour Hoffman.

LYNETTE YIADOM-BOAKYE

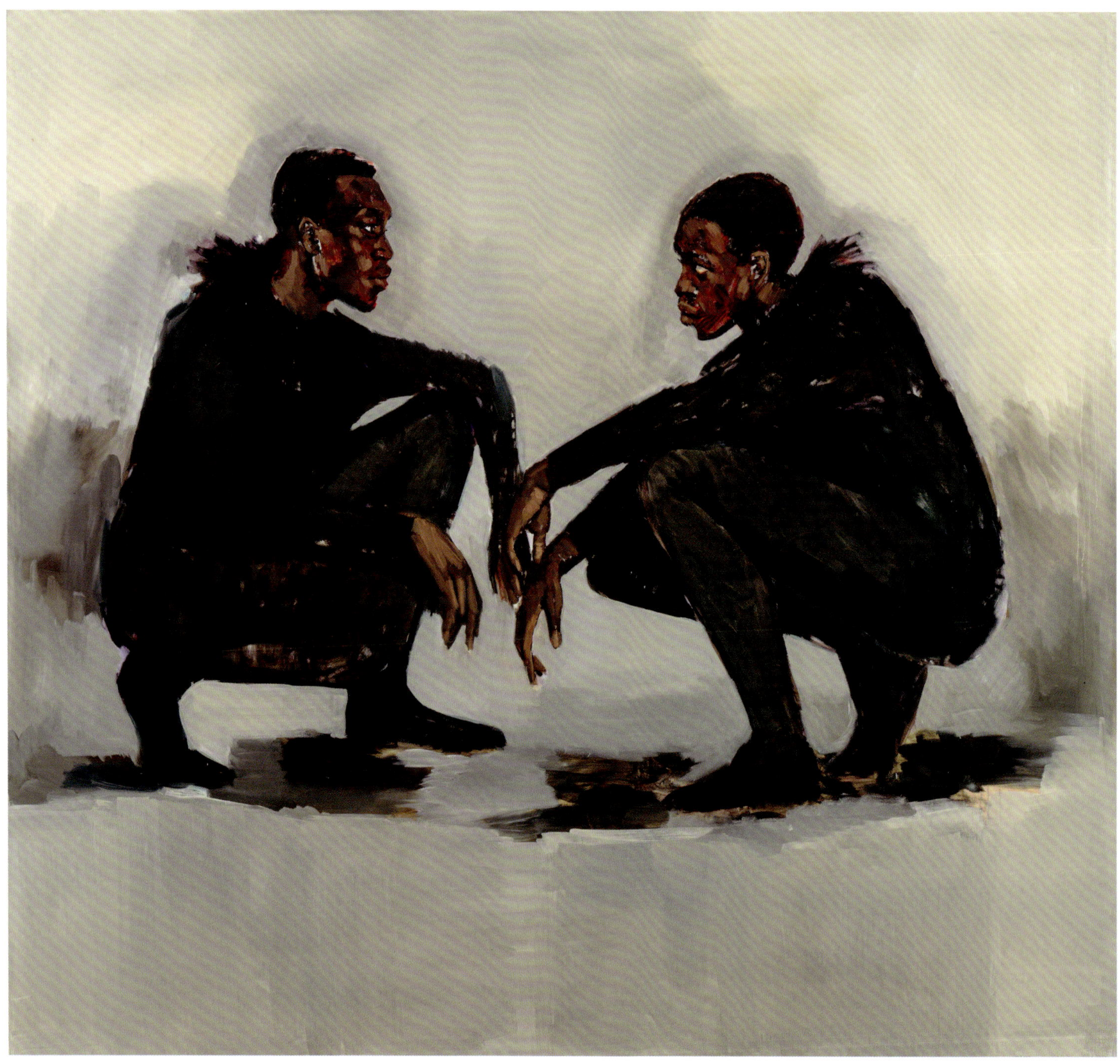

NO NEED OF SPEECH
2018, oil on canvas, 230 × 247.5 cm (90½ × 97½ in), Carnegie Museum of Art, Pittsburgh, USA

Lynette Yiadom-Boakye, born 1977, London, UK.

A British painter of Ghanaian heritage, Yiadom-Boakye has revitalized the genre of figurative painting through her timeless portraits of imagined Black subjects. Pictured within nondescript interiors – marked with loose brushwork in a palette of neutral and jewel-toned hues – the figures that populate Yiadom-Boakye's canvases are based on memories, found images and observations, and are often represented in states of creativity or contemplation. In *No Need of Speech*, two figures – dressed head-to-toe in black leotards accented with Elizabethan-style ruffs – crouch low to the floor and lock eyes across the canvas, delicately grazing one another's hands. The title may allude to the knowing silence of intimacy, whether between siblings, friends or partners, but also perhaps to the artist's eschewal of the expectation that her paintings should 'speak for' Blackness, as it has so often been defined from without. 'Blackness has never been other to me,' she asserted in an online feature for Tate's website. 'I've never liked being told who I am, how I should speak, what to think and how to think it. I've never needed telling.'

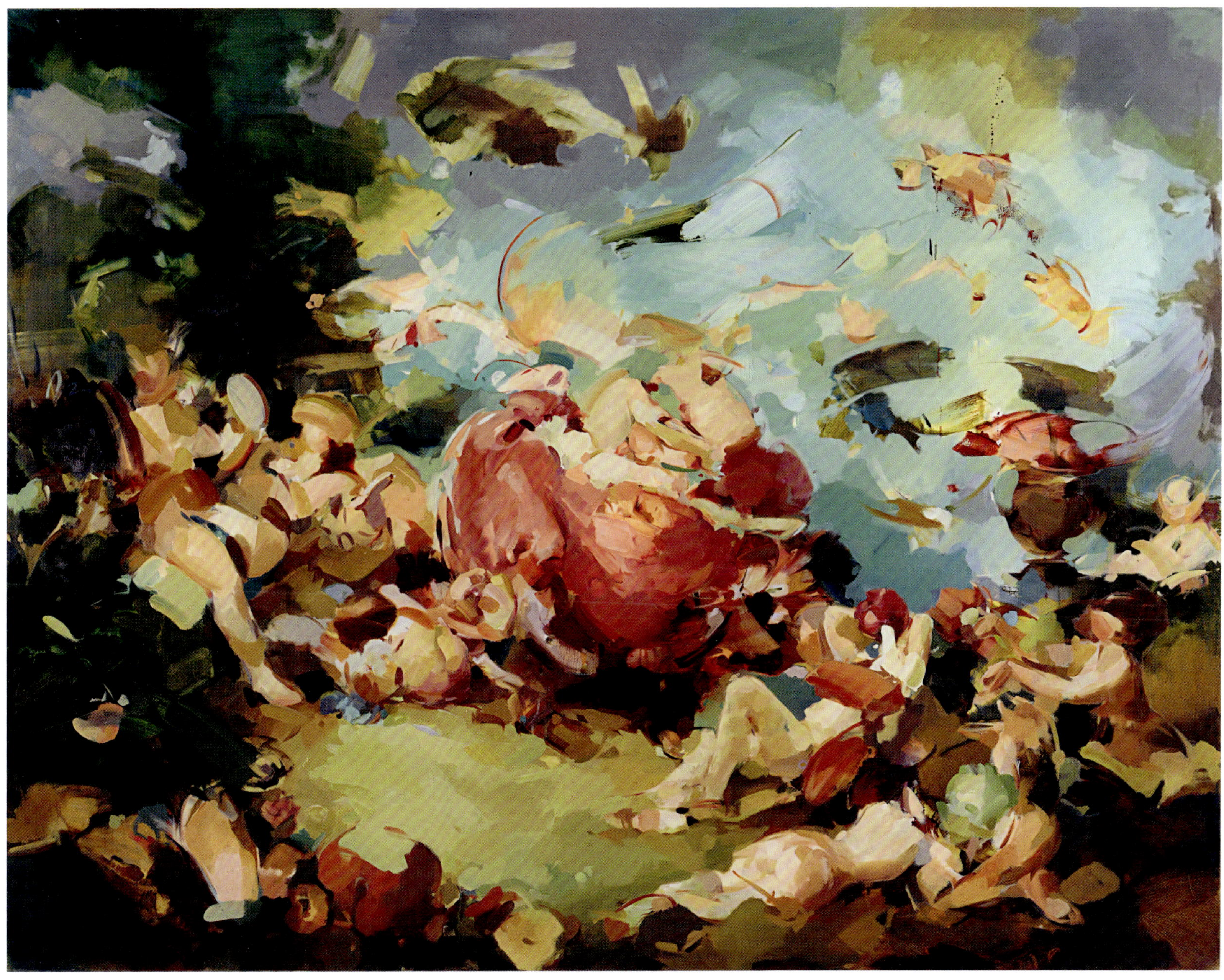

I'LL HAVE WHAT SHE'S HAVING
2020, oil on linen, 169.5 × 220 cm (66 ¾ × 86 ⅝ in)

Flora Yukhnovich, born 1990, Norwich, UK.

Since her first solo show in London in 2017, Yukhnovich has become known for her monumental paintings offering a contemporary take on highlights of Rococo art, from the *fête galante* paintings of French artists François Boucher (1703–70) and Jean-Honoré Fragonard (1732–1806) to the religious scenes of Venetian painter Giovanni Battista Tiepolo (1696–1770). Yukhnovich originally studied portraiture at the Heatherley School of Fine Art in London, before completing an MA in Fine Art at the City & Guilds of London Art School. This early grounding in techniques of figuration informs her interest in the way corporeality can be expressed through paint. She begins with small oil studies before working them up into large canvases composed of gestural brushstrokes that invoke the twentieth-century language of Abstract Expressionism and bear titles with pop-cultural references, such as *I'll Have What She's Having*. With its blur of loosely defined naked female forms in a forest-like setting, this painting edges the scene into abstraction – an approach that for Yukhnovich is a way to disrupt the male gaze predominant in Rococo and other periods of historical painting.

LISA YUSKAVAGE

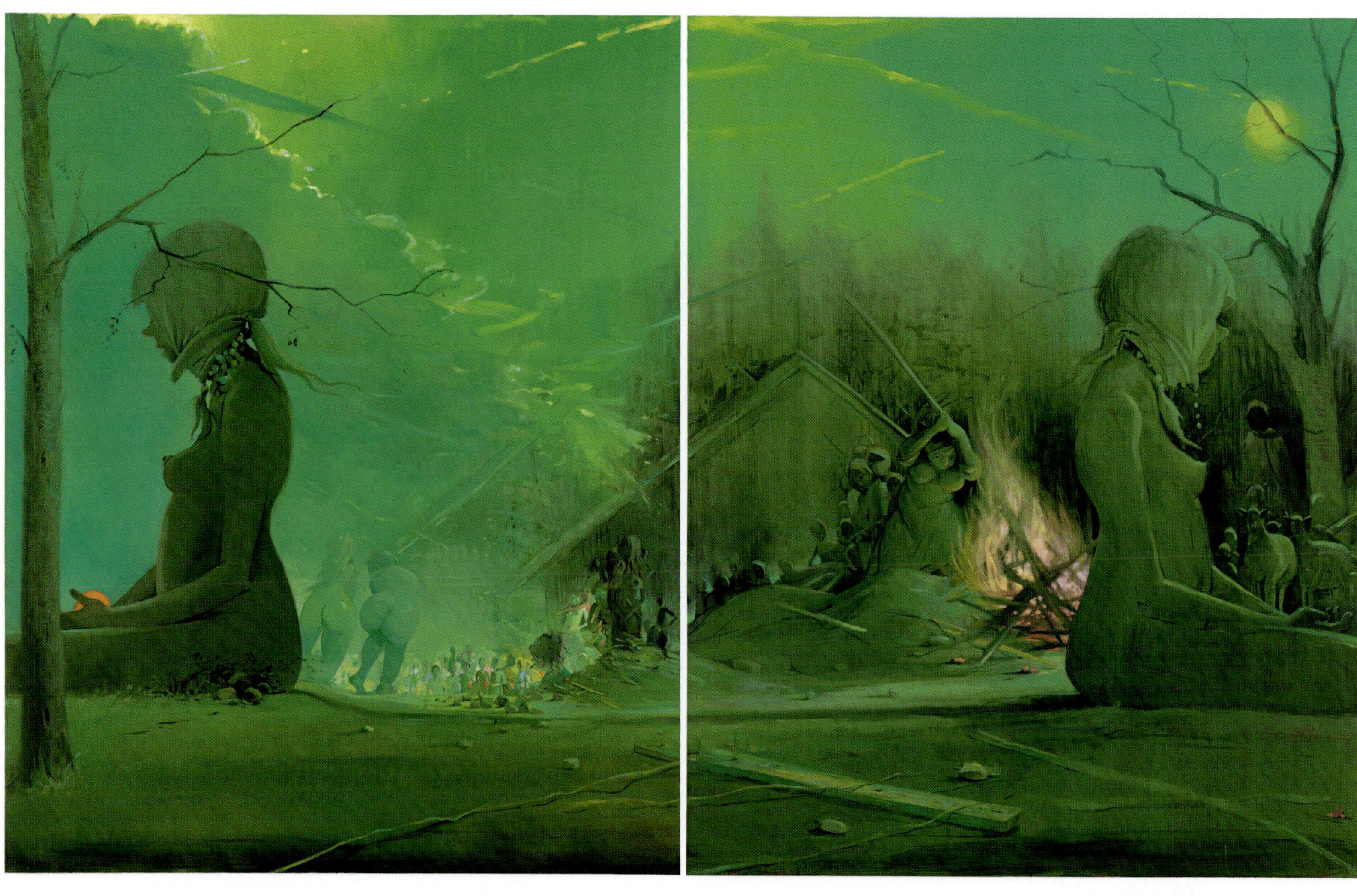

BONFIRE
2013–15, oil on linen, 2 panels,
each: 208.3 × 168.9 × 3.8 cm (82 × 66½ × 1½ in),
overall: 208.3 × 337.8 × 3.8 cm (82 × 133 × 1½ in),
Metropolitan Museum of Art, New York, USA

Lisa Yuskavage, born 1962, Philadelphia, USA.

Raised in a working-class family in Philadelphia, Yuskavage studied at Yale School of Art and emerged onto the art scene in the 1990s, part of a generation of American painters concerned with disrupting the figurative painting genre. Yuskavage became best known for her fantastical and hypersexualized nude female subjects, often employing ancient techniques (learnt from her study of Old Master painters) but basing her subjects on contemporary pop imagery. Her women are often objectified to an almost grotesque degree, which has been interpreted by some as a critique of the treatment of women's bodies, and by others as misogyny. In *Bonfire*, the nude female figures are both erotic and violent, active subjects and passive objects – trademarks of her practice. The eerie diptych also demonstrates Yuskavage's ongoing exploration into the formal possibilities of paintings, in particular the evocative power of colour, as seen in the striking emerald hues that create a misty, apocalyptic atmosphere. As is often the case in Yuskavage's works, the narrative is open-ended, and no one in the painting directly acknowledges the viewer's gaze, harnessing the pervasive power of ambiguity.

FAHRELNISSA ZEID

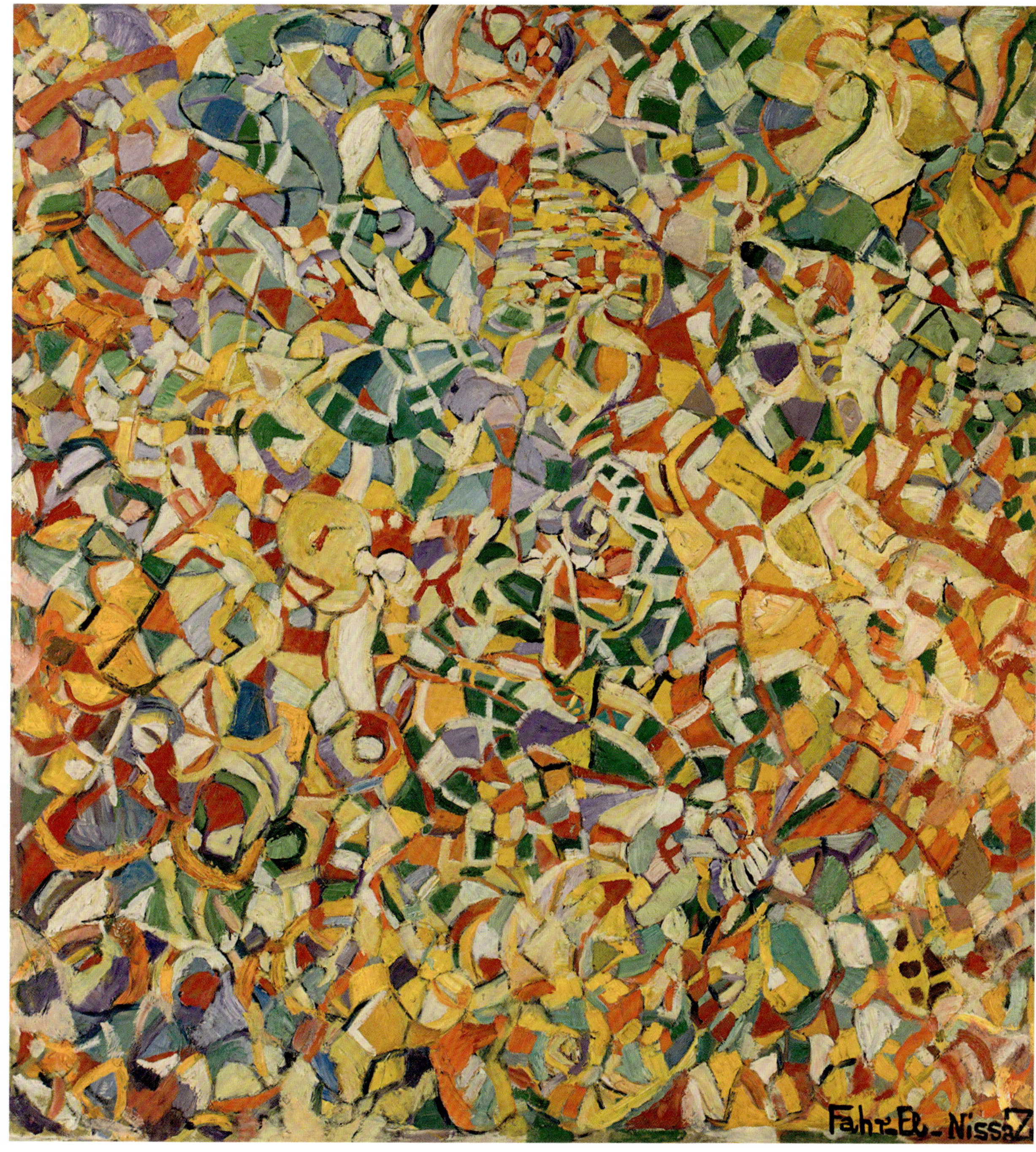

COMPOSITION
date unknown, oil on canvas, 188 × 175 cm (74 × 66 7/8 in), Musée d'Art Moderne de Paris, France

Fahrelnissa Zeid, born 1901, Istanbul, Turkey. Died 1991, Amman, Jordan.

The 1914 establishment of the Academy of Fine Arts for Women in Istanbul offered Zeid the chance to pursue a professional arts education, one previously only available to men. After completing her training there, Zeid spent an influential year in Paris in 1928 studying under the Cubist painter Roger Bissière (1886–1964) and soon rejected academic figuration to turn to pure abstraction, joining the avant-garde D Grubu (D Group) collective on her return to Turkey. In 1946 she moved to London with her second husband, an Iraqi royal who served as ambassador to Britain. She became embedded in the European post-war art world and was the first woman to have a solo exhibition at London's prestigious Institute of Contemporary Arts in 1954. *Composition* is an example of the large-scale kaleidoscopic paintings for which she was celebrated. Following the 1958 coup that saw her spouse's entire family assassinated, she was forced to leave the Iraqi embassy, and for the next twenty years would live between the UK, France and Italy. In 1975 she permanently relocated to Amman, Jordan, where she established a studio and an informal school for young women painters.

MARGUERITE ZORACH

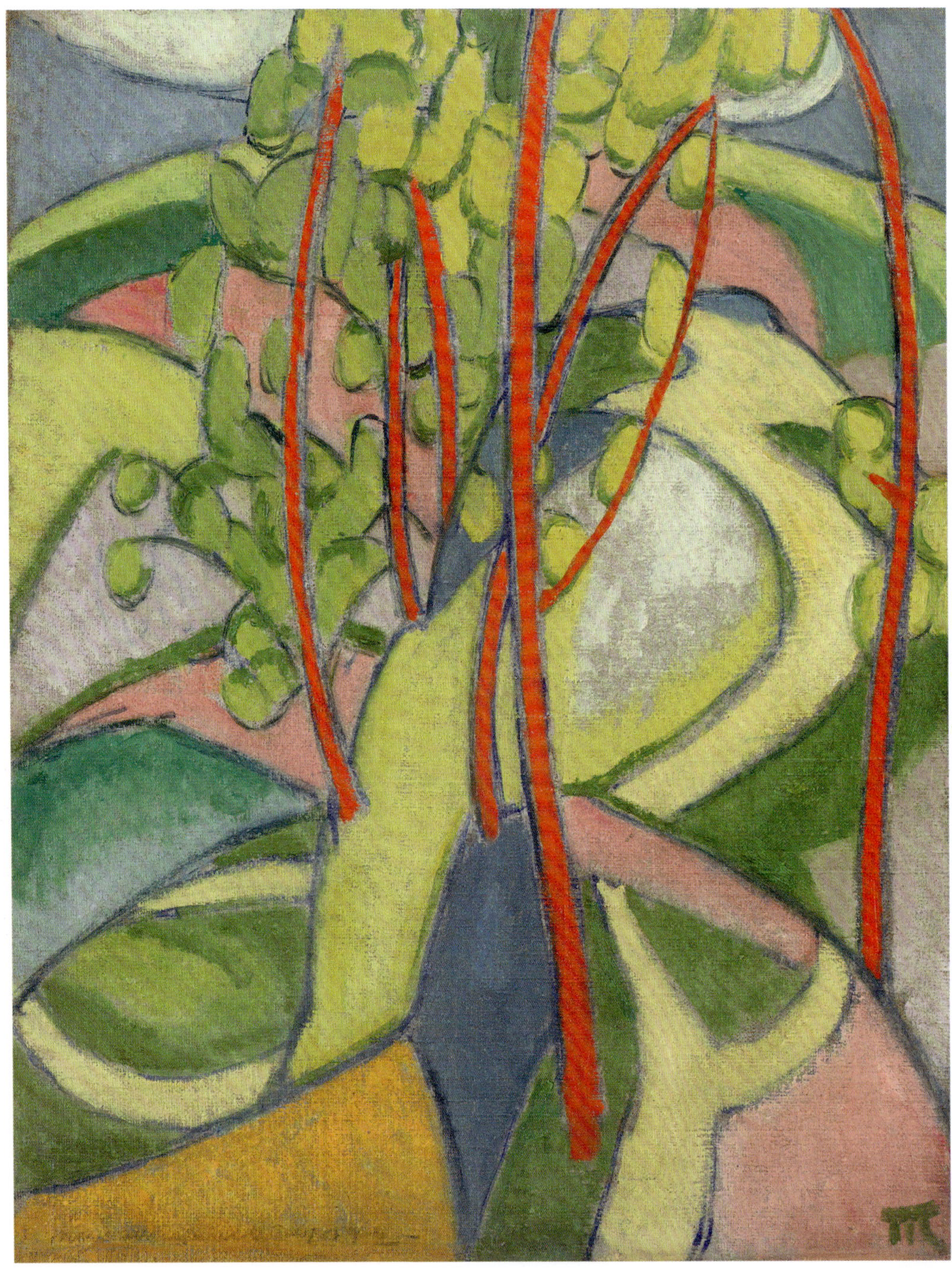

LANDSCAPE (RECTO)
c. 1911–12, oil on canvas, 59.1 × 48.9 cm (23 ¼ × 19 ¼ in), Art Institute of Chicago, USA

Marguerite Zorach, born 1887, Santa Rosa, California, USA. Died 1968, Brooklyn, USA.

An early exponent of modernism in America, Zorach gave a New England sensibility to European Post-Impressionism. Enrolling at Stanford University in 1908, Zorach moved to Paris shortly after, where she met her husband-to-be, American painter and sculptor William Zorach (1887–1966). The pair returned to the United States having absorbed Fauvism's bright hues and Cubism's compositions, and together continued to pursue modernism's emotive potentials. 'An art intent on expressing the inner spirit of persons and things will inevitably stray from the outer conventions of colour and form,' she said in a 1912 *Los Angeles Times* article. Both artists participated in the seminal Armory Show (1913) and later the more selective Forum Exhibition of Modern American Painters (1916), at which Zorach was the sole woman artist. Shortly after, she turned to embroidery and batik, finding in textiles a medium to further explore modernism's moods in parallel to her paintings. With its sensual lines and pastel palette, *Landscape* offers a Fauvist reimagining of a hillside scene, its rhythmic forms and shallow depth all but abstracting the trees and clouds. The painting's bold, blue outlines are characteristic of many of Zorach's early works.

PORTIA ZVAVAHERA

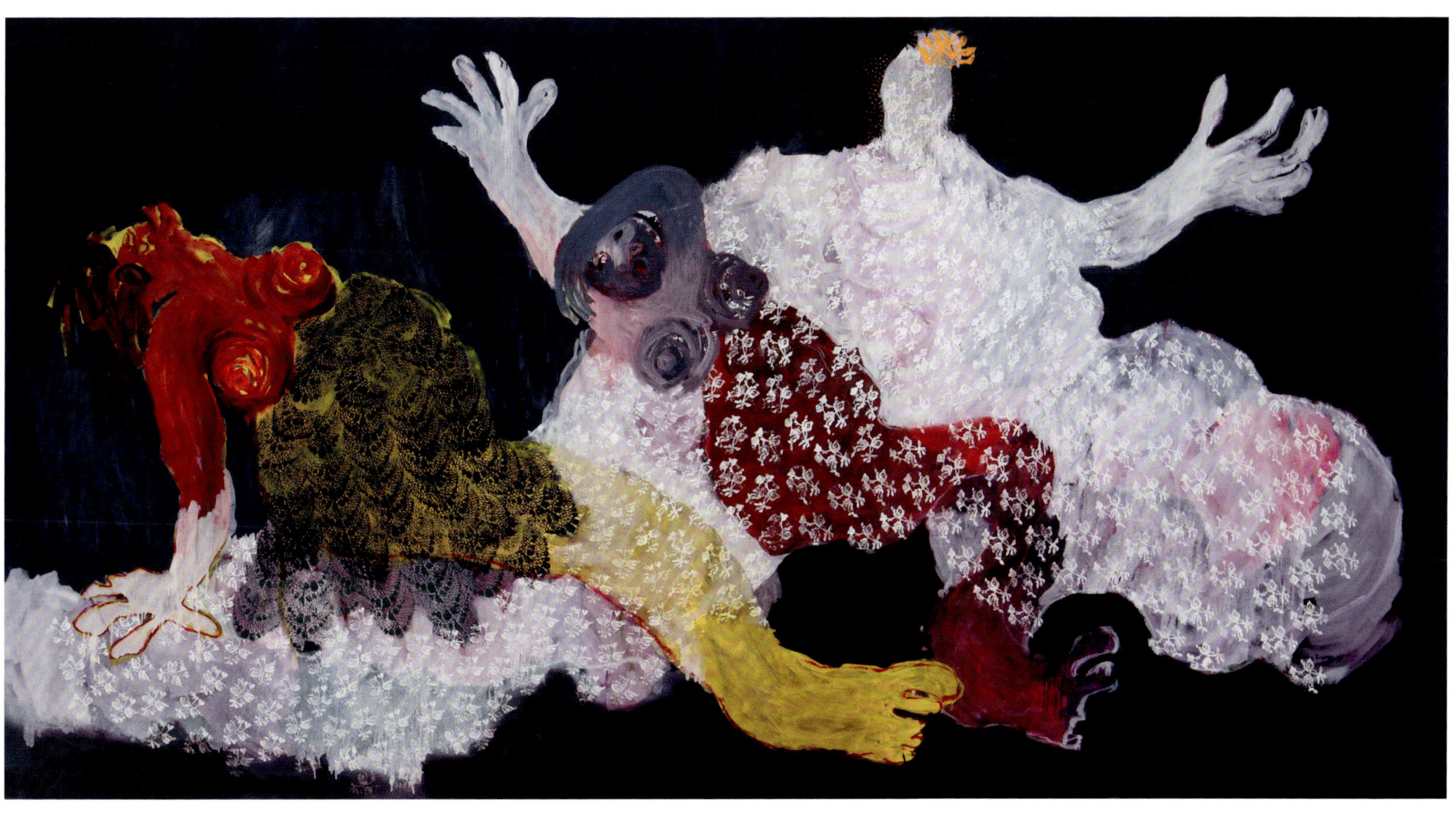

EMBRACED AND PROTECTED IN YOU
2016, oil-based printing ink and oil bar on canvas, 210 × 400 cm (82 ⅝ × 157 ½ in), collection of Wendy Fisher

Portia Zvavahera, born 1985, Harare, Zimbabwe.

The sources of Zvavahera's works lie in her dreams, prayers and rituals, often dealing with deep-rooted personal themes connected to longing, pain, loss and family. She has described her artistic process as cathartic, a way to manifest and elucidate these visions and address difficult moments, such as being separated from her family or coping with her mother's illness. Zvavahera's dazzling, layered compositions are created using oil bars, brushes and batik printmaking techniques – in which inks are applied directly to the surface of the canvas, employing beeswax as a stencil. Combining gestural figuration and abstract patterns, her vibrant visual language draws on traditions found in Zimbabwean art. Her work was part of the Zimbabwean Pavilion at the 55th Venice Biennale in 2013, three years after her solo exhibition at the National Gallery of Zimbabwe. *Embraced and Protected in You* depicts three exaggerated female forms: the large looming white figure is both menacing and protective, offering a cascading, intricate lace veil towards two other figures who seem struck, as if submitting to an indomitable force, heads thrust back. A dreamlike narrative emerges from the painting, evoking the strange workings of the subconscious mind.

GLOSSARY

OF ART TERMS, STYLES AND MOVEMENTS

ABJECT ART / ABJECTION

Art that explores transgressive themes and challenges notions of propriety, cleanliness and idealization, especially in relation to the human body and its functions. Used widely from the early 1990s onwards, it has particular currency for **feminist artists** as female bodily forms and functions are seen to have been 'abjected' by **patriarchal values**.

Cecily Brown (b. 1969)
Miriam Cahn (b. 1949)
Joy Labinjo (b. 1994)
Tala Madani (b. 1981)
Christina Quarles (b. 1985)
Dana Schutz (b. 1976)

ABSTRACT ART / ABSTRACTION

A composition that is not concerned with representing the world. Abstraction can be seen across many cultures and all times, though 'abstract art' strictly applied relates to **Western** painting and sculpture beginning at the turn of the twentieth century. See also **Minimalism** and **hard-edged painting**.

Tomma Abts (b. 1967)
Carla Accardi (1924–2014)
Hilma af Klint (1862–1944)
Huguette Caland (1931–2019)
Saloua Raouda Choucair (1916–2017)
Grace Crowley (1890–1979)
Katherine S. Dreier (1877–1952)
Tanya Goel (b. 1985)
Mary Heilmann (b. 1940)
Loie Hollowell (b. 1983)
Yukie Ishikawa (b. 1961)
Julie Mehretu (b. 1970)
Beatriz Milhazes (b. 1960)
Howardena Pindell (b. 1943)
Hilla Rebay (1890–1967)
Seundja Rhee (1918–2009)
Hedda Sterne (1910–2011)
Mildred Thompson (1936–2003)
Fahrelnissa Zeid (1901–91)

ABSTRACT EXPRESSIONISM

Painting movement that began in New York and flourished in the 1940s and 1950s. Although their styles and techniques varied, these artists used **abstraction** to externalize emotions, allowing the subconscious to express itself on the canvas. Hugely influential on the course of painting, variations on Abstract Expressionism occurred within and beyond the United States in the decades that followed. See also **Tachism**, **Colour Field** and **Neo-Expressionism**.

Mary Abbott (1921–2019)
Elaine de Kooning (1918–89)
Helen Frankenthaler (1928–2011)
Grace Hartigan (1922–2008)
Lee Krasner (1908–84)
Joan Mitchell (1925–92)
Janet Sobel (1893–1968)

ACADEMIC PAINTING

Term for a painting approach (in terms of style or subject matter) that conforms to the aesthetics and values of the mainstream art establishment – the **art academy** – in a given country.

ACRYLIC PAINT

Synthetic paint first available in the late 1940s as house paint, artists' acrylics combine some of the properties of **oil paint** and **watercolour**; acrylics can be diluted with water but are water-resistant when dry. They can be used to create a variety of effects from a thin wash to thick brushwork. Eileen Agar (1899–1991) was among the first painters to adopt acrylic in preference to oil paint, as seen in *Musical Garden (Spiky)* (1952, p. 25).

Souad Abdelrasoul (b. 1974)
Eileen Agar (1899–1991)
Tracey Emin (b. 1963)
Helen Frankenthaler (1928–2011)
Joyce Kozloff (b. 1942)
Yayoi Kusama (b. 1929)
Beatriz Milhazes (b. 1960)
Ad Minoliti (b. 1980)
Barbara Takenaga (b. 1949)

AIRBRUSH

Tool and method of paint application using a canister of compressed air to produce a fine spray that gives a smooth, consistent surface. Invented in the nineteenth century, it was initially popular with commercial artists and illustrators due to the high degree of precision and realism it can render. It was first used in a fine art context by **Pop artists** seeking to replicate the aesthetic of advertisements in their work. See also **spray paint**.

Judy Chicago (b. 1939)
Audrey Flack (b. 1931)
Avery Singer (b. 1987)
Betty Tompkins (b. 1945)
Robin F. Williams (b. 1984)

ALLEGORY / ALLEGORICAL ART

The subject of an allegorical artwork represents meanings beyond the literal elements depicted within it. Allegory offers the opportunity to represent intangible or complex concepts and values (love, virtue, justice, suffering, etc.) and has been used widely throughout many forms of art. Within the **hierarchy of art genres**, allegorical art falls within **history painting**, and from the late seventeenth century onwards was considered the highest form of history painting, above religious, mythological, historical and literary subjects.

Romaine Brooks (1874–1970)
Frida Kahlo (1907–54)
Angelica Kauffman (1741–1807)
Elisabetta Sirani (1638–65)
Saira Wasim (b. 1975)
Michaelina Wautier (1617/18–89)

ANIMAL PAINTING

Some of the earliest-known paintings in existence, namely prehistoric cave paintings that date from as far as 44,000 years ago, are representations of animals, yet the term 'animal painter' did not come into usage in **Western art** until the eighteenth century. It describes artists who make animals the primary subject of their work, rather than their being secondary to human figures or the landscape. As well as straightforward depictions, many animals and birds are encoded with symbolic meanings – so their inclusion in paintings may also be **allegorical**. Animals of all kinds, both real and imaginary, occupy a particularly prominent place in the arts of East Asia; in the Yuan dynasty (1271–1368) in China, for example, the phoenix, long associated with good fortune, when paired with a dragon became a symbol of happy marriage.

Rosa Bonheur (1822–99)
Jessie Arms Botke (1883–1971)
Gladys Mgudlandlu (1917–79)
Susan Rothenberg (1945–2020)

APPROPRIATION

The artistic practice of intentionally recycling or borrowing imagery from another context – from high art to popular culture – for inclusion in new work. With roots in ready-made, the term gained currency in 1980s North America, and continues to be a strategy for artists today.

Dotty Attie (b. 1938)
Genieve Figgis (b. 1972)
Ewa Juszkiewicz (b. 1984)
Emily Mae Smith (b. 1979)
Betty Tompkins (b. 1945)
Clare Woods (b. 1972)
Flora Yukhnovich (b. 1990)

AQUACRYL

Hybrid paint produced by Swiss manufacturer Lascaux that is water soluble and combines the performance of **acrylic paint** with the transparency and lightness of **watercolour**.

Shirazeh Houshiary (b. 1955)

ART ACADEMY

Established in Europe during the **Renaissance** and becoming more widespread by the seventeenth century, art academies were artist-run organizations that sought to professionalize and promote art through formal training and public **Salon** exhibitions. In **Western art**, the French Académie Royale de Peinture et de Sculpture (founded in Paris in 1648, and renamed Académie des Beaux-Arts after the French Revolution) and the Royal Academy of Arts (founded in London in 1768) were particularly central to the way in which art was taught, produced, exhibited and critically endorsed. Women artists were initially entirely excluded from becoming full members (and barred access to life drawing classes; see **the nude**), and even after they were admitted remained small in numbers, with gender parity still not yet achieved.

Angelica Kauffman (1741–1807)
Laura Knight (1877–1970)
Adélaïde Labille-Guiard (1749–1803)
Mary Moser (1744–1819)

ART AND LIBERTY

Active from 1938 to 1948, this Egyptian movement embraced principles of **Surrealism** and blended them with **modernist** art-making. In addition to organizing five group exhibitions, this artist group pushed back against Egyptian nationalism and the rise of fascism across Europe, a stance embodied by the name of their manifesto, *Vive L'Art Dégénéré!* (*Long Live* ***Degenerate Art!***), wherein they embraced the derogatory term that Nazi Germany applied to modern art.

Inji Efflatoun (1924–89)

ART BRUT

See **outsider art**.

ART DECO

A style from the 1920s and 1930s primarily used in furniture, decorative arts and architecture. Noted by its geometric character, it was a reaction against the organic forms of Art Nouveau and connected instead with the fragmented shapes of **Cubism**.

Gluck (1895–1978)
Tamara de Lempicka (1898–1980)

ART INFORMEL

French term meaning art 'without form'. In the 1950s, Art Informel artists were looking for a new way to create images without adopting the recognizable forms of **Cubism** and **Expressionism**. Their aim was to abandon both geometric and **figurative** forms and to discover a new artistic language, and their invented shapes and methods often came about by improvisation. The term is a broad label rather than a coherent school. See also **Tachism**.

AVANT-GARDE

Term used to describe a movement or work that is experimental, innovative and challenges the current predominant style. It comes from the French phrase meaning 'advance guard' and was first used in relation to art in 1825. While originally connected with **modernism**, the term continues to be applicable today.

AUTOMATISM

Automatic painting and drawing, in which the hand is allowed to move at random across the surface, was developed by the **Surrealists** as a means of expressing the subconscious. In applying chance and the accidental to mark-making, the process of producing art is freed from rational control.

Sylvia Fein (b. 1919)

BAROQUE

Principal European art style of the seventeenth and early eighteenth centuries. Beginning in Italy, it has been suggested that the Baroque style was born out of the Counter-Reformation, and was at first a form of propaganda for the Catholic Church. Baroque art was intended to address the senses directly and to influence the intellect through emotion rather than through reason. Decorative excess, dramatic movement and spectacle characterize the style.

Artemisia Gentileschi (1593–*c.* 1653)
Louise Moillon (1610–96)
Josefa de Óbidos (*c.* 1630–84)
Elisabetta Sirani (1638–65)
Michaelina Wautier (1617/18–89)

BAUHAUS

School of art, design and architecture established in Weimar Germany in 1919 by the architect Walter Gropius. Its roots lay in nineteenth- and early-twentieth-century attempts to re-establish the connection between design and manufacture, and it reinstated the idea of workshop training in preference to the **art academy**. Its disciplined, functional style widely influenced European and American architecture and design.

Ida Kerkovius (1879–1970)
Sophie Taeuber-Arp (1889–1943)

BIENNIAL

A large-scale exhibition held every two years, usually linked to a specific city or location. The most important (and oldest) is the

Venice Biennale (since 1895) but other influential biennials occur worldwide, including São Paulo (since 1951), Istanbul (since 1987), Sydney (since 1973), Sharjah (since 1993) and at the Whitney Museum of American Art, New York (annual from 1932, then biennial since 1973).

BINDER
General name for the substances that hold the particles of **pigment** together in paint. The main ingredient in paint, the binder is what keeps the pigment in place after the paint dries. **Oil paint** traditionally uses linseed oil. **Acrylic** mediums generally include a synthetic binder designed to form a film after water has evaporated. **Watercolour** uses gum arabic, a hardened tree sap.

BIOMORPHIC
Images or forms that are abstract yet evocative of natural, living things, including the human body or plants. The word came into art usage in the 1930s in relation to certain **Surrealist** artworks.

Hilma af Klint (1862–1944)
Rita Kernn-Larsen (1904–98)
Agnes Pelton (1881–1961)

BLACK ARTS MOVEMENT
An African American–led ideological movement beginning in the 1960s in which artists, writers and intellectuals united to create a distinctly Black aesthetic that centralized Black life and culture in literature and visual art. It has been called the 'aesthetic and spiritual sister of the Black Power'. Parallels have been drawn with the earlier **Harlem Renaissance**, although this lacked many of the radical political stances of the Black Arts Movement. An affiliated group, 'Where We At' Black Women Artists, was formed in New York in 1971. See also **Spiral**.

Emma Amos (1937–2020)
Loïs Mailou Jones (1905–98)
Dindga McCannon (b. 1947)
Faith Ringgold (b. 1930)

BLAUE REITER, DER
German for 'The Blue Rider', a loose group of **Expressionist** artists active from 1911 to 1918. The group had no unifying style, but its members were linked by the desire to explore their own emotions and consciousness and to promote the spiritual element of art.

Gabriele Münter (1877–1962)
Marianne von Werefkin (1860–1938)

BLK ART GROUP / BRITISH BLACK ARTS MOVEMENT
The BLK Art Group was formed in 1982 by artists from the British African-Caribbean community based in and around the West Midlands. The group was instrumental in the formation of a broader British Black Arts Movement, which highlighted issues of race, gender and the politics of representation and empowered Black artists by providing visibility through exhibitions and events.

Lubaina Himid (b. 1954)
Claudette Johnson (b. 1959)

CANON OF ART HISTORY
Artists and artworks featured in written art histories and museum collections are deemed to be 'canonical' because of their innovative approach or enduring influence. While the mainstream art-historical canon has been heavily critiqued since the late twentieth century for propagating wider power relations, in particular for its lack of racial and gender diversity, the canon of art history is still a valid starting point for learning about art of the past.

CANVAS
Plain-woven fabric, traditionally made of hemp but now usually cotton- or linen-based, that has been widely used as a surface for painting in the **Western** tradition since the **Renaissance**. Replacing wood panels and **fresco**, canvas had the advantage of portability, being lightweight and easily rolled, which enabled large-format paintings to be produced in one location and easily moved to another. Canvas is typically stretched across a wooden frame called a stretcher in order to create a rigid, flat plane and often painted with a primer such as **gesso** to create a smooth surface for the application of paint.

Angela de la Cruz (b. 1965)
Alison Watt (b. 1965)

CASEIN PAINT
A fast-drying, water-soluble medium derived from milk protein. It dries to a matt finish and can be used to create a variety of effects from the rich opaques of **oil paint** to thin **watercolour** washes. Casein is one of the most durable known art mediums; since the residue of a milk-based ochrepaint was found in 2015 on a 49,000-year-old stone tool in the Sibudu cave of northern KwaZulu-Natal, South Africa, casein is also believed to be humankind's oldest paint formulation.

Carla Accardi (1924–2014)
Nilima Sheikh (b. 1945)
Merrill Wagner (b. 1935)

CHIAROSCURO
Term used in drawing and painting that describes the utilization of light and shadow to produce an illusion of depth, from the Italian for 'light-dark'. The technique was developed during the **Renaissance**, and Italian and Dutch artists used it to create works full of exaggerated light and shadow. See also **Baroque**.

Artemisia Gentileschi (1593–*c.*1653)
Giulia Lama (1681–1747)
Judith Leyster (1609–60)
Louise Moillon (1610–96)

CHICAGO IMAGISTS
A loose group of **figurative** artists associated with the School of the Art Institute of Chicago in the late 1960s, who exhibited at the city's Hyde Park Art Center. Their work was known for its vibrant colours and bold lines, and depicted the human body in distorted, grotesque and stylized ways that led to comparisons with **Surrealism**. There are three distinct groups, which are often bundled together as Imagists: the Monster Roster, the Hairy Who and the Chicago Imagists.

Gladys Nilsson (b. 1940)
Christina Ramberg (1946–95)

CLASSICAL
Term used to suggest a continuation of style or approach that can be traced directly to the civilizations of ancient Greece and Rome. See also **Neo-Classicism**.

Angelica Kauffman (1741–1807)
Jesse Mockrin (b. 1981)

COLLAGE
Term for the technique, and the resulting work, in which materials such as pieces of paper or cloth are pasted onto another surface. It comes from the French word *coller* (to stick).

Njideka Akunyili Crosby (b. 1983)
Jay DeFeo (1929–89)
Rosalyn Drexler (b. 1926)
Ida Ekblad (b. 1980)
Kudzanai-Violet Hwami (b. 1993)
Loïs Mailou Jones (1905–98)
Shannon T. Lewis (b. 1981)
Tschabalala Self (b. 1990)
Jaune Quick-to-See Smith (b. 1940)
Sarah Sze (b. 1969)
Mickalene Thomas (b. 1971)
Toyen (1902–80)

COLOUR FIELD PAINTING
Emerging in the United States in the 1940s and 1950s, Colour Field paintings are characterized by expanses of intense and saturated colour. Artists set themselves apart from **Abstract Expressionism** by emphasizing the use of colour rather than gesture as the principal means of expression and by eliminating the emotional, mythic or spiritual elements from their work.

Helen Frankenthaler (1928–2011)
Alma Thomas (1891–1978)

CONCEPTUAL ART / CONCEPTUALISM
Broad term applied to art produced from the mid-1960s onwards in which artists eliminate or radically reduce emphasis on the aesthetic and material concerns in favour of the idea behind the work, thus elevating conception above execution.

Irma Blank (b. 1934)
Sarah Morris (b. 1967)
Pat Steir (b. 1940)

CONSTRUCTIVISM
Movement that began in Russia in the early 1920s and spread to other parts of Europe, remaining important throughout the mid-twentieth century. Inspired by the Bolshevik Revolution of 1917, Constructivists sought to break free from artistic conventions, experimenting with new forms of sculpture and modern technology, including kinetic art and practical design.

Alexandra Exter (1882–1949)
Marlow Moss (1889–1958)
Liubov Popova (1889–1924)

CONTEMPORARY ART
Loose term that at its most literal refers to art of the present day yet is also applied to art of the recent past that is considered innovative or **avant-garde**. The starting date for contemporary art is widely debated; however, many art historians consider the late 1960s to mark the end of **modernism** and the start of the contemporary.

CRYSTALIST GROUP
Breaking away from Sudan's Khartoum School and its principles of nationalist syncretism, the Crystalist Group was co-founded by Kamala Ibrahim Ishag as a **conceptual art** movement. With the publication of its manifesto in 1976, the group employed the image of a crystal for its transparency and its duality of interior/exterior growth, mirroring its members' anti-essentialist and anti-object beliefs that led to conceptual and performative artworks.

Kamala Ibrahim Ishag (b. 1937)

CUBISM
Artistic movement based in France from the late 1900s to the early 1920s. The style is characterized by the fracturing of images, the simplification of form to its essential elements and the use of unnatural and multiple perspectives.

Alice Bailly (1872–1938)
Maria Blanchard (1881–1932)
Grace Crowley (1890–1979)
Alexandra Exter (1882–1949)
Françoise Gilot (b. 1921)
Marie Laurencin (1883–1956)
Mary Swanzy (1882–1978)

DADA
Founded in Zurich in 1916, Dada was an anti-rational art movement formed in response to the horrors of the First World War. Rejecting artistic conventions, the Dadaists used performance, irony and humour to subvert societal norms and shock the establishment. Many independent Dada groups were later set up in other European and American cities, and the movement was a strong force throughout the 1920s, as well as influencing later generations.

Sophie Taeuber-Arp (1889–1943)

DEGENERATE ART
English translation of the German *entartete Kunst*, a label applied by Adolf Hitler's National Socialist regime in the 1930s to virtually all modern art, for being un-German in nature. Thousands of paintings were removed from museums, artists whose work did not meet with the Party's approval were subjected to sanctions, and an exhibition of 'degenerate' works was put on display in Munich in 1937 for propaganda purposes.

Anita Rée (1885–1933)
Erna Rosenstein (1913–2004)

DIASPORA / DIASPORIC ARTISTS
In relation to art, this term is used for artists who (or whose forebears) have migrated from one part of the world to another, including forcibly or under duress. Through their art they may express diverse experiences of multiple cultures and identities, often challenging the ideas and structures of dominant ideologies and expressing alternative perspectives and narratives. See also **identity politics**.

Lubaina Himid (b. 1954)
Loïs Mailou Jones (1905–98)
Wangari Mathenge (b. 1973)
Cassi Namoda (b. 1988)
Amrita Sher-Gil (1913–41)

DUTCH GOLDEN AGE
A period in the history of the Netherlands, roughly spanning the seventeenth century, in which Dutch trade, science, military and art were among the most acclaimed in the **Western** world. Dutch Golden Age painting followed many of the stylistic tendencies of **Baroque** art but was the leader in developing **still life**, **landscape** and **genre painting** – with newly wealthy middle-class patrons driving the popularity of such pictorial subjects. The term has been challenged by scholars who believe that it does not fairly represent those who were exploited during the era in which the Netherlands was at the forefront of scientific discovery and artistic achievement, specifically in relation to the colonial history of the country.

Judith Leyster (1609–60)
Clara Peeters (*c.*1594–*c.*1659)
Rachel Ruysch (1664–1750)

EDO PERIOD

From 1615 to 1868, Japan was ruled by the Tokugawa shogunate from its capital, Edo (modern Tokyo). A time of self-imposed near isolation from both **Western** and Chinese influences, it was a period of internal stability, when Japanese arts such as haiku poetry, kabuki theatre and **ukiyo-e** prints all flourished.

Ike Gyokuran (1727–84)
Katsushika Ōi (*c.* 1800–*c.* 1866)
Kiyohara Yukinobu (1643–82)

ENAMEL PAINT

Ready-mixed oil-based paint originally used domestically or commercially to provide a tough coat on outdoor surfaces or other surfaces subject to hard wear, including those used in marine or architectural constructions. It is also used by hobbyists for painting scale-model kits and toys. In 1897 Ripolin became the first commercially available brand of enamel paint, and the name became so synonymous with enamel paints that by 1907 it had entered the French dictionary.

Farah Atassi (b. 1981)
Gillian Ayres (1930–2018)
Inka Essenhigh (b. 1969)
Rachel Feinstein (b. 1971)
Marilyn Minter (b. 1948)
Janet Sobel (1893–1968)

ENCAUSTIC

From the Greek meaning 'burning in', encaustic painting involves the use of pigments mixed with hot, liquid wax, usually on prepared wood. Most famously used in Roman period funerary portraits found in Egypt, the technique enjoyed a revival among some painters from the mid-twentieth century onwards.

EXPRESSIONISM

International art style that flourished as a movement from 1905 until the 1920s, particularly in Germany and Scandinavia. Its practitioners sought to move away from pure representation in an attempt to externalize the human condition. Influenced by other art movements, and reacting against **Impressionism**, Expressionism used distortion, bold colours and abstract lines to convey spiritual and emotional messages. See also **Der Blaue Reiter** and **Neo-Expressionism**.

Paula Modersohn-Becker (1876–1907)
Gabriele Münter (1877–1962)
Hélène Schjerfbeck (1862–1946)
Irma Stern (1894–1966)
Marianne von Werefkin (1860–1938)

FAUVISM

French avant-garde movement of the early twentieth century that acted as a forerunner to **Expressionism** and **abstract art**. Taking its name from the French *fauve* (wild beast), Fauvism is characterized by loose, spontaneous compositions and the use of strong, often unrealistic colours, frequently laid on straight from the paint tube with broad, rough brushstrokes. While the movement itself only lasted a few years (1905–8) it was stylistically influential, in part because of the number of international artists spending time in Paris during this period.

Alice Bailly (1872–1938)
Emily Carr (1871–1945)
Mary Swanzy (1882–1978)
Georgette Chen (1906–93)
Marguerite Zorach (1887–1968)

FEMINIST ART

Feminism rejects the notion that a heterosexual, white, male view of the world is a universal one and seeks equality. The term 'feminist art' emerged in the 1960s as part of second-wave feminism but has roots in women artists' fight for increased visibility since the early twentieth century. In a move away from male-dominated traditions of painting and conventional sculpture (carved marble and cast bronze), feminist artists often utilized the materials and processes of crafts, as well as film, video, body art, performance, installation and **Conceptual art**. By changing the rules of how art is made and perceived, feminism questions the way in which women are represented by male artists. Feminist theorists and art historians have also challenged the orthodoxies of the mainstream **canon of art history** and initiated research into overlooked women artists. Artists today continue to make and advance feminist work, incorporating intersecting issues including race, class and gender fluidity.

Dotty Attie (b. 1938)
Judith Bernstein (b. 1942)
Judy Chicago (b. 1939)
Caroline Coon (b. 1945)
Hayv Kahraman (b. 1981)
Marilyn Minter (b. 1948)
Joan Semmel (b. 1932)
Sylvia Sleigh (1916–2010)
Betty Tompkins (b. 1945)

FIGURATIVE ART

Art that depicts the world around us, whether with truthful accuracy or deliberate distortion. Figurative art is typically associated with paintings and sculptures of human or animal forms, although it can be used in a more general sense where art is derived from real object sources. The term 'representational art' is often used synonymously, and **abstract art** is its opposite. See also **the nude**, **Realism** and **portraiture**.

Njideka Akunyili Crosby (b. 1983)
Marlene Dumas (b. 1953)
Gwen John (1876–1939)
Claudette Johnson (b. 1959)
Maria Lassnig (1919–2014)
Margherita Manzelli (b. 1968)
Jennifer Packer (b. 1984)
Paula Rego (b. 1935)
Jenny Saville (b. 1970)
Gazbia Sirry (1925–2021)
Florine Stettheimer (1871–1944)
Rose Wylie (b. 1934)
Lynette Yiadom-Boakye (b. 1977)

FLASHE

A high-pigment, water-diluted paint developed by the French art supplies brand Lefranc Bourgeois in the 1950s. It was initially intended for stage scenery painting but soon adopted by fine artists. Using a vinyl emulsion **binder**, the paint is more supple and flexible than **acrylic** but equally quick-drying. It adheres without requiring any primer (such as **gesso**), and leaves a smooth, flat, matt finish, without visible brush marks.

Laura Owens (b. 1970)
Susan Rothenberg (1945–2020)
Tschabalala Self (b. 1990)
Mary Weatherford (b. 1963)

FOLK ART

A broad term used to define art produced outside the professionally sanctioned sphere of artistic production, often created using materials and techniques that are traditional within a particular community.

Doris Lee (1905–83)
Anna ('Grandma') Moses (1860–1961)

FOUND OBJECT / IMAGE

Originating from the French *objet trouvé*, the term describes undisguised, but often modified, objects or images that are not normally considered art because they already have a non-art identity or function. A 'found' material may form part of a larger assemblage, be displayed on its own as a ready-made, or provide source material for an artwork. Featuring widely in **Dada**, **Surrealism** and **Pop art**, found objects and images are also commonly used in **contemporary art**.

Kudzanai-Violet Hwami (b. 1993)
Joy Labinjo (b. 1994)
Lorna Simpson (b. 1960)
Jaune Quick-to-See Smith (b. 1940)
Claire Tabouret (b. 1981)
Lynette Yiadom-Boakye (b. 1977)

FRESCO

Wall-painting technique that dates back to at least the fourth millennium BCE, in which water-based pigments are applied to wet lime plaster or combined with a binder such as egg white or glue and applied to dry plaster.

Ella Kruglyanskaya (b. 1978)

FUTURISM

Italian-centred art movement that started in 1908 and continued until the late 1920s. It glorified the dynamism of the newly mechanized world and rejected the veneration of past art, particularly the weighty tradition of Italian art. Variations of Futurism in other countries included Vorticism (UK) and Rayonism (Russia).

Barbara (1915–2002)
Benedetta (1897–1977)
Alexandra Exter (1882–1949)
Natalia Goncharova (1881–1962)
Liubov Popova (1889–1924)

GAZE, THE

The concept of 'the gaze' within art-historical discourse developed in parallel with **postmodern** philosophy and social theory in the 1960s. Within feminist theory, in particular, it relates to gendered looking: how men look at women (as represented within artworks, or as external viewers of women as subjects in art) and how women look at themselves and other women. A key text regarding the male gaze is 'Visual Pleasure and Narrative Cinema' (1975) by Laura Mulvey, in which she argues that perspectives in visual media are often built from an assumed viewpoint of a heterosexual male, whereas women are viewed through this lens. Many women artists have made works that deliberately mock or subvert the male gaze, drawing attention to unconscious biases and changing the ways in which women are represented.

Dotty Attie (b. 1938)
Lisa Brice (b. 1968)
Mary Cassatt (1844–1926)
Laura Knight (1877–1970)
Elke Silvia Krystufek (b. 1970)
Jessie Makinson (b. 1985)
Wangari Mathenge (b. 1973)
Robin F. Williams (b. 1984)

GENRE PAINTING

Term used to characterize art that takes scenes from everyday life as its subject matter, depicted in a realistic manner. This use of the phrase became established only in the eighteenth century, following the broader, and still current, use of genre to mean a specific category of art, such as the genre of **landscape** or genre of **still life**. See also **hierarchy of art genres**.

Harriet Backer (1845–1932)
Lotte Laserstein (1898–1993)
Marie-Victoire Lemoine (1754–1820)
Judith Leyster (1609–60)
Hilary Pecis (b. 1979)
Hélène Schjerfbeck (1862–1946)
Amy Sillman (b. 1955)
Becky Suss (b. 1980)

GESSO

White preparatory ground made of gypsum or chalk that is pulverized into a fine powder and mixed with glue and can be brushed onto wood panels, **canvas**, plaster or stone to create a smooth surface for painting. Some **contemporary artists** have foregrounded the material properties of gesso in their paintings.

Prabhavathi Meppayil (b. 1965)
Adriana Varejão (b. 1964)

GOUACHE

Opaque **watercolour**, also known as body colour. The **pigments** are bound together with glue; lighter tones are achieved by adding white. Gouache differs from transparent watercolour, the tone of which is lightened by adding water. The thick texture of gouache can produce the same effects as **oil paint**, but it dries lighter than it appears during application.

Gladys Mgudlandlu (1917–79)
Charlotte Salomon (1917–43)
Marianne von Werefkin (1860–1938)

GRUPO DOS CINCO (GROUP OF FIVE)

Influential group of five Brazilian painters, poets and writers who worked together in the 1920s. Reacting against the conservative artistic establishment, they led the development of Brazilian **modernism**, which sought to synthesize European styles and ideas with those indigenous to their native country, to create something uniquely Brazilian.

Tarsila (1886–1973)

GUILD

An association of people with related interests, such as goldsmiths, glassmakers, stonemasons or artists, who oversee the production and trade of their particular area. Guilds flourished in medieval Europe and often wielded considerable political and economic power. Many sixteenth-century painters, artists and craftsmen, for example, joined the Guild of St Luke, which educated apprentices and guaranteed quality.

Judith Leyster (1609–60)

HARD-EDGED PAINTING

Term coined in 1959 by Californian critic Jules Langster, to describe the work of **abstract** painters (especially on the West Coast of the United States) whose art was in contrast with the more gestural forms of **Abstract Expressionism**. Such painters often use monochromatic fields of colour to reinforce the flatness of the **picture plane** and adopt an impersonal approach to paint application.

Jo Baer (b. 1929)
Beverly Fishman (b. 1955)
Carmen Herrera (1915–2022)
Tess Jaray (b. 1937)
Lee Lozano (1930–99)
Dóra Maurer (b. 1937)
Sarah Morris (b. 1967)
Zilia Sánchez (b. 1926)
Miriam Schapiro (1923–2015)

HARLEM RENAISSANCE
African American intellectual and artistic movement of the 1920s and 1930s, centred in the Harlem neighbourhood of New York City and considered one of the most significant cultural eras in American history. Across literature and the visual and performing arts, the figures associated with the movement explored Black identity and celebrated Black culture and history. See also **Black Arts Movement**.

Loïs Mailou Jones (1905–98)

HIERARCHY OF ART GENRES
Term used in **Western art** history from the **Renaissance** onwards, by which time painting had come to be considered as the highest form of art. Formulated in Italy in the sixteenth century, the order of importance was: **history painting**; **portraiture**; **genre painting**; **landscape painting**; **animal painting**; **still life**. The rationale behind this hierarchy was a distinction between pictures with an intellectual intention to represent a universal essence of humankind, and those that merely sought to copy the appearance of things in the world. The hierarchy of genres was also accompanied by a hierarchy of formats, whereby the highest subjects were presented on large canvases, and still lifes were expected to be small in format. The hierarchy of art genres was later codified by European **art academies**, such as the French Académie Royale de Peinture et de Sculpture. It continued to dominate until the late nineteenth century, when artists associated with **Realism** and **Impressionism** sought to rebel against the rules of the art academy. The dominance of **abstract** painting from the early twentieth century onwards saw the hierarchy of art genres largely abandoned.

HISTORY PAINTING
Term introduced in the seventeenth century to describe painting that depicts the historical events of the past as well as scenes from Classical mythology and the Bible. Historically, history painting usually embodied some interpretation of life or conveyed a moral or intellectual message.

Maggi Hambling (b. 1945)
Lubaina Himid (b. 1954)
Angelica Kauffman (1741–1807)
Plautilla Nelli (1524–88)
Sabine Moritz (b. 1969)
Michaelina Wautier (1617/18–89)

HYPERREALISM
Term coined in the early 1970s to describe highly realistic art that is founded on the principles of **Photorealism** yet takes it further. Hyperrealist painters also use photographic images as source material, but create more definitive and detailed renderings, often evoking narrative elements, political values or emotive aspects.

Ellen Altfest (b. 1970)
Audrey Flack (b. 1931)
Marilyn Minter (b. 1948)
Chloe Wise (b. 1990)

IDENTITY POLITICS
Emerging from the 1960s Black civil rights movement, second-wave feminism and LGBT liberation, the term describes a cultural movement that gained prominence in Europe and the United States in the mid-1980s. Identity politics raises questions about repression, inequality and injustice, often focusing on the experiences of marginalized groups, past and present. In more recent years, 'intersectionality' – the idea that gender, race, sexual orientation, age, religion, etc. do not exist separately, but form an interwoven complex that defines an individual's lived experience – has expanded how identity politics are understood and represented in art.

Pacita Abad (1946–2004)
Kudzanai-Violet Hwami (b. 1993)
Claudette Johnson (b. 1959)
Hayv Kahraman (b. 1981)
Shannon T. Lewis (b. 1981)
Tala Madani (b. 1981)

IMPASTO
Acrylic or **oil paint** that is thickly applied to the **canvas** or panel so that it stands in relief and retains the marks of the brush or palette knife. The impasto technique is used by artists to evoke emotion, create drama through texture, or emphasize their experience with the materiality of paint.

Nadia Ayari (b. 1981)
Jadé Fadojutimi (b. 1993)
Genieve Figgis (b. 1972)
Liang Yuanwei (b. 1977)
Dana Schutz (b. 1976)
Arpita Singh (b. 1937)
Vivian Suter (b. 1949)
Maria Helena Vieira da Silva (1908–92)

IMPRESSIONISM
Art movement dating from about 1860 to 1900, which began in France. The term was initially used derisively after the first exhibition of independent artists in Paris in 1874, when critics seized on *Impression, Sunrise* by Claude Monet (1840–1926) as exemplifying the unfinished nature of the paintings; by 1877 artists themselves had adopted the term for their exhibition. Typically, Impressionist artworks depict **landscapes** or **genre** scenes of daily life, with special attention paid to the effects of light, atmosphere or movement. See also **Post-Impressionism** and ***plein air***.

Jessie Arms Botke (1883–1971)
Marie Bracquemond (1840–1916)
Mary Cassatt (1844–1926)
Berthe Morisot (1841–95)

INDIGENOUS ART
Broad term for art that addresses ethnic identity in relation to the native peoples of a given country, prior to its colonization. While some Indigenous artists make work that continues long-standing cultural traditions (40,000 years in the case of some Australian Aboriginal art practices), others make work that directly references the historic or contemporary plight of Indigenous peoples. See also **postcolonial art**.

Emily Kame Kngwarreye (*c.* 1910–96)
Esther Mahlangu (b. 1935)
Yukultji Napangati (b. *c.* 1971)
Jaune Quick-to-See Smith (b. 1940)

INSTALLATION ART
Originally used to describe the process of positioning works in the gallery setting, installation has also come to denote a distinct kind of art. Installation art describes works comprising individual elements within a defined space that is viewed as a single work. It can be made from one or several materials, including non-tangible media such as sound and light. Some installation art is ephemeral and exists only temporarily. Some is created for a particular location, with those that cannot be relocated elsewhere being referred to as 'site-specific'.

Katharina Grosse (b. 1961)
Lisa Milroy (b. 1959)
Vivian Suter (b. 1949)

KANŌ SCHOOL
One of the most famous schools of Japanese painting, Kanō was the dominant style from the late fifteenth century until the Meiji period (1868–1912), though its influence continued beyond. Inspired by Chinese ink painting and its landscape-focused subject matter, the Kanō school was noted for its incorporation of Chinese painting styles that emphasize strong brushwork with the bold colours and patterns of Japanese styles.

Kiyohara Yukinobu (1643–82)
Uemura Shōen (1875–1949)

LANDSCAPE PAINTING
Depictions of natural scenery, usually in wide view, such as mountains, countryside, forests and – in its broadest definition – sea, sky and even cityscapes. Representing the landscape is a long tradition in the history of both **Western** and East Asian painting in particular. In European art, pure landscape painting was prominent in **Romanticism**, **Impressionism** and **Post-Impressionism**, although detailed landscapes can be seen in the background of paintings from Giotto (d. 1337) onwards. Landscape painting is regarded as the highest form of Chinese painting where it is one of the oldest continuous artistic traditions in the world. See also **literati painting**.

Etel Adnan (1925–2021)
Anna-Eva Bergman (1909–87)
Grace Cossington Smith (1892–1984)
Cui Jie (b. 1983)
Eguchi Ayane (b. 1985)
Inka Essenhigh (b. 1969)
Jane Freilicher (1924–2014)
Sandra Gamarra (b. 1972)
Jennifer Guidi (b. 1972)
Shara Hughes (b. 1981)
Sanam Khatibi (b. 1979)
Karen Kilimnik (b. 1955)
Lalan (1921–95)
Louisa Matthíasdóttir (1917–2000)
Joan Mitchell (1925–92)
Georgia O'Keeffe (1887–1986)
Maria Serebriakova (b. 1965)
Mary Swanzy (1882–1978)
Sarah Sze (b. 1969)
Marguerite Zorach (1887–1968)

LIGHT AND SPACE MOVEMENT
Style that developed in the 1960s on the West Coast of the United States in parallel with **Minimalism** in New York. While both were characterized by industrial materials and a **hard-edged**, geometric aesthetic, Light and Space artists experimented with newer technologies and materials including polyester resins, cast acrylic, and neon and argon lights. Their works also embraced the concept of the **sublime** as an all-encompassing, timeless and transcendental, aesthetic experience.

Mary Corse (b. 1945)

LITERATI PAINTING
Style of Chinese ink painting that was practised by scholars, in contrast to the academic style of court painters. Literati painters were intellectuals who made ink paintings, sometimes with minimal colour, that merged painting with poetry and calligraphy. Mastery of the brush was understood as an expression of the spirit, and an impressionistic approach to landscape was more important than a realistic depiction of the scene.

Lalan (1921–95)
Ma Shouzhen (1548–1604)

METAPHYSICAL PAINTING
Strictly speaking, a term that refers to the Italian Pittura Metafisica, an early-twentieth-century art movement that depicted dreamlike visions of places – particularly urban public piazzas – with unexpected juxtapositions of objects and sharp contrasts of light and shadow. While the movement itself was short-lived (1911–20), it was highly influential on **Surrealism**. The term still continues to be used to describe art that encompasses an eerie atmosphere and unusual combinations of subjects within a single composition.

Hulda Guzmán (b. 1984)
Agnes Pelton (1881–1961)
Kay Sage (1898–1963)
Wang Zhibo (b. 1981)

MEXICAN RENAISSANCE
Resurgent movement in Mexican art that lasted from about 1920 to 1950. Triggered by the Mexican Revolution of 1910–20 and its socialist-inspired ideas, artists developed a new nationalistic style that included religious and pre-Columbian iconography and subjects in traditional Mexican dress. See also **mural painting**.

María Izquierdo (1902–55)
Frida Kahlo (1907–54)

MINIATURE PAINTING
In **Western** art history, miniature painting stemmed from the traditions of illuminated manuscripts – in which religious texts were decorated with elaborate motifs and illustrations – and metalwork portraits on medals. Miniaturists from the sixteenth century onwards painted highly detailed, small-scale portraits that were intended to be portable and sometimes inlaid into jewellery (such as lockets) or keepsake boxes (such as snuff boxes). Traditions of miniature painting – either for book illustrations or single works to be kept in albums – also existed in Persian art from the thirteenth century on, and in Mughal painting of North India between the sixteenth and nineteenth centuries. See also **Neo-Miniaturism**.

Sarah Biffin (1784–1850)
Mary Roberts (d. 1761)

MINIMALISM
Art movement beginning in the 1960s that can be seen as an extreme form of **abstract art**. Works are made of simple geometric configurations with serial, repeating elements and sculptural pieces incorporate modern materials. Minimalist art is concerned mainly with purity and perfection of form rather than representing the external world. See also **Post-Minimalism**.

Jo Baer (b. 1929)
Mary Corse (b. 1945)
Jennifer Guidi (b. 1972)
Carmen Herrera (1915–2022)
Beverly Fishman (b. 1955)
Agnes Martin (1912–2004)
Prabhavathi Meppayil (b. 1965)

MODERNISM
More of a paradigm than a style, modernism is a celebration of the new and a rejection of traditions of the past. The term encompasses an array of avant-garde movements in art, design and architecture from the mid-nineteenth to the mid-twentieth century (including **Impressionism**, **Precisionism**, **Constructivism**, **Dada**, **Cubism**, and **Expressionism**), with artists seeking to visually represent modern life. By the late 1960s, modernism was displaced as the

dominant cultural ideology by **postmodernism**, which deliberately sought to react against the principles and aesthetics of modernism. More recently, modernism has been revived as a stylistic motif resonant of an utopian ideology.

Hilma af Klint (1862–1944)
Etel Adnan (1925–2021)
Kamala Ibrahim Ishag (b. 1937)
Bertina Lopes (1924–2012)
Marlow Moss (1889–1958)
Saloua Raouda Choucair (1916–2017)
Arpita Singh (b. 1937)
Tarsila (1886–1973)

MURAL PAINTING

Murals are artworks directly applied to walls or ceilings, often at large-scale. The term is used in relation to site-specific mosaics as well as a number of forms of painting (from **fresco** and **tempera** to **spray-painted** graffiti art). Mural paintings have existed in art history since the earliest times (prehistoric cave art can be seen as a form of mural painting) and certain art-historical movements are especially associated with mural painting, such as the muralists of the **Mexican Renaissance** and the **Ndebele painting** of South Africa.

NDEBELE PAINTING

Style of **mural painting** undertaken by the Southern Ndebele people of South Africa since the mid-eighteenth century when grass huts were replaced by mud buildings. Houses were decorated externally with colourful, geometric motifs that are rich in symbolism and based on the patterns that were already used in beadwork. Ndebele house painting is predominantly practised by women, with the tradition being passed from generation to generation within families.

Esther Mahlangu (b. 1935)

NEO-CLASSICISM

Predominant artistic style in Europe and North America between 1750 and 1830. The revival of **Classical** (Greek and Roman) styles was based on a new and unprecedented understanding of the art and architecture of these ancient civilizations as a result of the discovery of Pompeii and Herculaneum in southern Italy. Neo-Classical art emphasized calm simplicity and noble grandeur, in reaction to the preceding **Rococo** movement.

Marie-Gabrielle Capet (1761–1818)
Angelica Kauffman (1741–1807)
Élisabeth Vigée-Lebrun (1755–1842)
Marie-Denise Villers (1744–1821)

NEO-EXPRESSIONISM

An international revival of **Expressionism** that came about as a reaction against **Conceptual art** and **Minimalism**, which had dominated art during the 1970s. While the term is often associated with a particular group of male painters who dominated the art market of the 1980s, the term can be more generally applied to **figurative art** from the late twentieth century onwards that is characterized by loose brushstrokes, the expressive use of colour and an emphasis on more personal subjects.

Cecily Brown (b. 1969)
Marlene Dumas (b. 1953)
Nicole Eisenman (b. 1965)
Genieve Figgis (b. 1972)
Shara Hughes (b. 1981)
Jacqueline de Jong (b. 1939)
Maria Lassnig (1919–2014)
Elizabeth Murray (1940–2007)
Paula Rego (b. 1935)
Susan Rothenberg (1945–2020)
Amy Sillman (b. 1955)
Genesis Tramaine (b. 1983)

NEO-MINIATURISM

Art movement with origins in Pakistan that seeks to revive the traditional techniques of Mughal-era **miniature painting**, while addressing subjects and themes that reflect modern-day concerns, including socio-political issues. Many artists in this group emerged from the National College of Arts, Lahore, and they typically paint on handmade, acid-free *wasli* paper, which was originally devised in tenth-century India.

Shahzia Sikander (b. 1969)
Saira Wasim (b. 1975)

NEUE SACHLICHKEIT

A strand within **Expressionism** that reflected the cynicism pervading Germany after the First World War. It translates as 'New Objectivity', and artists of this group tended to put greater emphasis on social criticism and political comment than did other Expressionist artists, who dealt with more subjective and emotional themes.

Jeanne Mammen (1890–1976)
Anita Rée (1885–1933)

NEW INK PAINTING MOVEMENT

Founded by Hong Kong–based artist Lui Shou-Kwan (1919–75), the movement sought to combine aspects of **Western** contemporary painting (particularly **Abstract Expressionism**) with the ancient arts of Chinese calligraphy, **landscape** and **literati painting**. While the style embraces representational, semi-abstract and abstract compositions, the unifying concern is that the work represents the individuality and spirit of its creator.

Irene Chou (1924–2011)

NIHONGA PAINTING

A Japanese style of painting of the Meiji period (1868–1912) based on styles that evolved over more than a thousand years. It emphasizes natural materials that require considerable determination to use – particularly the use of *washi* paper or silk as painting surfaces – rather than those used in **Western**-style painting (known in Japan as *yōga*).

NUDE, THE

In literal terms, the nude is the unclothed human figure as a subject in art. However, the nude is differentiated from the naked body in terms of the artist's intention, meaning and symbolism, which are usually rooted in the dominant cultural ideology in which an artist is operating. The nude in art has often represented the idealized human form (as perceived by a particular culture), or is used as a means of reflecting societal attitudes regarding sexuality, social structure or gender. The female nude has had a particular place in certain strands of art history – from its role as a symbol of fertility from the Upper Palaeolithic period onwards to the trope of the 'reclining nude' in **Western art** since the **Renaissance**. For Western women artists, representing the nude was made complicated after the professional route into art moved from the artist workshop to the **art academy**. Women were barred from direct study of the human figure – the life class – in art academies until the end of the nineteenth century. This in turn created barriers to their painting the subjects at the top of the **hierarchy of art genres**, which depended on skill in depicting the human form. A consideration of the nude, especially the female nude, has been a central focus in feminist art history and for many **feminist artists** who have sought to make works that both critiqued and overturned traditional representations of the nude. Discourse around the female nude is closely connected to the concept of **the gaze**.

Lisa Brice (b. 1968)
Cecily Brown (b. 1969)
Luchita Hurtado (1920–2020)
Laura Knight (1877–1970)
Giulia Lama (1681–1747)
Dindga McCannon (b. 1947)
Pan Yuliang (1895–1977)
Joan Semmel (b. 1932)
Jenna Gribbon (b. 1978)
Mickalene Thomas (b. 1971)
Suzanne Valadon (1865–1938)
Lisa Yuskavage (b. 1962)

OEUVRE

French word used to describe the body of work produced over the course of an artist's career.

OIL PAINT

Pigment bound together with an oil medium, usually linseed oil. Oil paint has the advantage of being slow to dry and thus reworkable. The origins of oil painting date to at least the seventh century, when artists used oil (probably extracted from walnuts or poppies) to decorate the ancient cave complex in Bamiyan, Afghanistan. In Europe, oil as a painting medium is recorded from the eleventh century; however, easel painting with oil stems directly from fifteenth-century **tempera** painting techniques. Improvements in the refining of linseed oil and the availability of volatile solvents after 1400 coincided with a need for a medium other than pure egg-yolk tempera to meet the changing requirements of **Renaissance** artists. Oil paints and varnishes were initially used to glaze tempera panels before being used as a medium in their own right. The majority of paintings in this book were made using oil paint, with some artists also depicting the paint itself, laid out on the **palette**.

Sofonisba Anguissola (*c.*1532–1625)
Marie-Gabrielle Capet (1761–1818)
Angelica Kauffman (1741–1807)
Marie-Victoire Lemoine (1754–1820)

OIL STICK

Also known as oil bars and pigment sticks, oil sticks are oil paint in stick form. They are composed of pigment, a drying oil (usually linseed or safflower oil) and a small amount of wax to allow the paint to be moulded into a portable cylindrical bar. Designed to be held in the hand, they are used to apply colour directly to a surface in light, crayon-like lines or thick, painterly marks.

Christine Ay Tjoe (b. 1973)
Jadé Fadojutimi (b. 1993)
Genesis Tramaine (b. 1983)
Portia Zvavahera (b. 1985)

OLD MASTERS

Umbrella term for recognized European artists, mostly painters, working between the **Renaissance** and the start of the nineteenth century. It does not refer to a specific art-historical style or movement and encompasses art that is **Baroque, Dutch Golden Age, Rococo, Neo-Classical**, etc. First-generation feminist art historians noted that the term 'Old Master' is inherently gender-biased and exclusive of women artists, as emphasized in the title of a 1981 book by Griselda Pollock and Rozsika Parker, *Old Mistresses: Women, Art and Ideology*. More recently, the term moved on to be considered less gender-specific and applied equally to art by women artists, simply to differentiate historic from modern or **contemporary artists**.

OP ART

Abbreviation for 'optical art', the term is used to describe art that uses illusions or produces effects caused by the limits of human vision. In the 1960s there was an Op art movement, characterized by paintings that appear to move and flicker.

Tomma Abts (b. 1967)
Rana Begum (b. 1977)
Bridget Riley (b. 1931)

OUTSIDER ART

Encompassing work produced beyond the professional art world by makers who have had little or no contact with art institutions. It was originally used as the English-language version of Art Brut – a term coined in the late 1940s by French artist Jean Dubuffet (1901–85) to describe his collection of artworks made in unusual contexts, including by psychiatric patients or recluses, whom he felt were able to create more authentic, spontaneous forms of expression than the art exhibited in museums and galleries. By the 1980s, the term began to be used more broadly to encompass a greater range of vernacular art. See also **folk art**.

Carol Rama (1918–2015)
Séraphine de Senlis (1864–1942)
Mary T. Smith (1905–95)

PALETTE

A rigid, flat surface on which a painter arranges and mixes paint. The word has also come to mean the range of colours that are used by an artist generally or in a specific work.

PAPUNYA TULA ABORIGINAL PAINTING

Papunya Tula is an Australian artist cooperative formed in 1972 in Papunya, Northern Territory. Owned and operated by Aboriginal artists, the group developed the Western Desert Art Movement, which drew on **Indigenous art** traditions of image-making that normally only occurred as impermanent body or sand art for ceremonial purposes. It is credited with bringing contemporary Aboriginal art to wider international attention.

Yukultji Napangati (b. *c.*1971)

PATRIARCHY / PATRIARCHAL VALUES

A patriarchy is a social system of male domination that can exist in both public and private spheres. Patriarchies are sustained with a set of ideas – a patriarchal ideology – that acts to explain and justify this dominance by attributing it to inherent natural differences between men and women. Feminist theorists have written extensively about patriarchy as a primary cause of gender inequality.

PATTERN AND DECORATION

American art movement of the mid-1970s to early 1980s that was led by female artists who felt that the **abstract art** that dominated the twentieth century, and in particular **Minimalism** and **Conceptual art**, had marginalized work that did not fit into the **canon of art history**. Pattern and Decoration sought to revive an interest in patterning – typically more aligned with craft – and reposition it as fine art.

Joyce Kozloff (b. 1942)
Miriam Schapiro (1923–2015)

PERSPECTIVE
Method of suggesting spatial recession on a flat surface, from the Latin *perspicere*, meaning 'to see through'. In the early fifteenth century, Filippo Brunelleschi (1377–1446) made public his geometric system of linear perspective for representing the illusion of three dimensions on a two-dimensional **picture plane**. Another approach is aerial perspective, in which atmospheric conditions (moisture and humidity) are suggested by blurring forms as they recede in space.

PHOTOREALISM
Term for art that encompasses painting, drawing and other graphic media, in which the artist attempts to reproduce an image as realistically as a photograph. Photorealism emerged as an art movement in Europe and the United States in the 1960s. It was positioned in opposition to **Abstract Expressionism** and **Minimalism**, which were the dominant art styles of the time. See also **hyperrealism**.

Ellen Altfest (b. 1970)
Helene Appel (b. 1976)
Marilyn Minter (b. 1948)
Ishbel Myerscough (b. 1968)
Sylvia Sleigh (1916–2010)
Betty Tompkins (b. 1945)

PICTURE PLANE
Term describing the physical surface of a painting on which the picture is presented. This is the case both in **figurative** painting, where the picture plane often creates an illusion of depth through the use of perspective, and in **abstract** painting, where the artwork is still contained on the front of the three-dimensional painted object.

PIGMENT
Particles of a colour, which are insoluble in water (soluble colours are called dyes). Historically, pigments were made by grinding earth, rocks or minerals, and both pigments and grinding equipment have been found in caves in Zambia dating from 350,000 years ago. The earliest-known pigment is ochre, which is made from iron oxide. Today, many pigments for artists' paints are synthetically produced, although some particular colours still rely on natural materials, such as true ultramarine, which is made from the blue semi-precious stone lapis lazuli. Some painters also experiment with creating their own pigments.

Tanya Goel (b. 1985)
Shahzia Sikander (b. 1969)

PLEIN AIR
French phrase to describe working outdoors. It became significant in European painting of the second half of the nineteenth century due to the invention of paint tubes, which enabled pre-mixed colours to be easily stored and carried. This allowed artists to create finished paintings outside, rather than just preparatory sketches that then needed to be completed in the studio. Artists involved with movements including **Realism** and **Impressionism** were noted for painting *en plein air*, with the latter, in particular, aiming to represent the direct experience of changing natural light and environmental conditions on their canvases.

Jessie Arms Botke (1883–1971)
Marie Bracquemond (1840–1916)
Joan Eardley (1921–63)
Berthe Morisot (1841–95)

POINTILLIST ART
Post-Impressionist style in which small dots or strokes of paint are applied separately to the canvas, allowing colours to mix in the viewer's eye, in order to achieve greater luminosity.

POLITICAL ART
Broad term to describe art where the maker's intention is to highlight or critique political, social or ideological systems in the wider world, particularly in relation to issues of power, economics, inequality and injustice. See also **feminist art** and **identity politics**.

Pacita Abad (1946–2004)
Shiva Ahmadi (b. 1975)
Sybil Atteck (1911–75)
Judith Bernstein (b. 1942)
Caroline Coon (b. 1945)
Inji Efflatoun (1924–89)
Beatriz González (b. 1932)
Leila Nseir (b. 1941)
Faith Ringgold (b. 1930)

POP ART
Abbreviation for 'popular art', the term is used to describe a movement that began in the late 1950s and flourished until the 1970s, independently but simultaneously in Europe and the United States. It included artists working in a variety of different styles whose subject matter embraced and celebrated popular commercial culture, including advertising, photography, comics and the entertainment industry.

Evelyne Axell (1935–72)
Gina Beavers (b. 1974)
Pauline Boty (1938–66)
Rosalyn Drexler (b. 1926)

PORTRAITURE
One of the oldest genres of art, going back to ancient Egypt, portraiture was one of art's primary functions before photography. Portraits are a means of documenting a person's physical appearance, but they are often also intended to represent non-physical aspects of the sitter, such as their values, wealth, taste and intellect. In contrast to **figurative art**, in which a human subject may be anonymous or generic, in order to represent an idea, in portraiture, the sitter is a specific individual who is usually named – many portraits are created on commission. As well as capturing others, artists often create self-portraits, taking themselves as the subject, sometimes repeatedly throughout their artistic careers.

Sofonisba Anguissola (*c.*1532–1625)
Rita Angus (1908–70)
Mary Beale (1633–99)
Vanessa Bell (1879–1961)
Joan Carlile (*c.*1603–79)
Jordan Casteel (b. 1989)
Chen Ke (b. 1978)
Elaine de Kooning (1918–89)
Lavinia Fontana (1552–1614)
Fede Galizia (*c.*1578–*c.*1630)
Catharina van Hemessen (1528–*c.*1588)
Chantal Joffe (b. 1969)
Gwen John (1876–1939)
Frida Kahlo (1907–1954)
Laura Knight (1877–1970)
Elke Silvia Krystufek (b. 1970)
Marie Laurencin (1883–1956)
Ishbel Myerscough (b. 1968)
Alice Neel (1900–84)
Aliza Nisenbaum (b. 1977)
Celia Paul (b. 1959)
Elizabeth Peyton (b. 1965)
Mary Roberts (d. 1761)
Amy Sherald (b. 1971)
Sylvia Sleigh (1916–2010)
Irma Stern (1894–1966)
Florine Stettheimer (1871–1944)
Anna Dorothea Therbusch (1721–82)
Laura Wheeler Waring (1887–1948)

POSTCOLONIAL ART
Art that analyses and exposes the legacies of colonial rule and the many consequences – short and long term – for those colonized and exploited. Issues relating to race, ethnicity and cultural and national identity are central themes. See also **disapora** and **identity politics**.

Njideka Akunyili Crosby (b. 1983)
Lubaina Himid (b. 1954)
Wangeri Mathenge (b. 1973)
Gazbia Sirry (1925–2021)
Jaune Quick-To-See Smith (b. 1940)
Adriana Varejão (b. 1964)

POST-IMPRESSIONISM
Broad movement that includes artists with many different styles, all reacting against the naturalism of **Impressionism**. After the last Impressionist exhibition in 1886, Post-Impressionist artists started to emphasize abstract qualities and symbolic subjects over the naturalistic depiction of light and colour. Post-Impressionism continued to be influential, including outside Europe, well into the twentieth century.

Emily Carr (1871–1945)
Grace Cossington Smith (1892–1984)
Suzanne Valadon (1865–1938)
Marguerite Zorach (1887–1968)

POST-MINIMALISM
Term used since the early 1970s to describe art that is influenced by, and develops further, the aesthetics and ideas of **Minimalism**. Often using non-typical art materials, artists employ themes found in Minimalism, such as the grid and seriality, but with a human element that contrasts the hard forms and lack of external references of pure Minimalism.

Irma Blank (b. 1934)
Harmony Hammond (b. 1944)

POSTMODERNISM
As well as pushing some aspects of **modernism** to the extreme, postmodernism saw the return of elements of **Classical** styles. Characteristics of postmodernism include a refusal to recognize any single definition of art, a blurring of the boundaries between fine art and popular culture, and frequent use of **appropriation**.

Jennifer Bartlett (b. 1941)
Nathalie Du Pasquier (b. 1957)

PRECISIONISM
The first indigenous modern art movement in the United States and an early American contribution to the rise of **modernism**. Painters associated with Precisionism reduced their compositions to simple, geometrical shapes, with clear outlines, minimal detail and smooth handling of surfaces. Showing the influence of photography and European **Futurism**, subjects were often drawn from urban life and the American landscape.

Elsie Driggs (1898–1992)
Georgia O'Keeffe (1887–1986)

QUEER ART
Term used for art that represents issues relating to queerness – an inclusive term that encompasses identities including gay, lesbian, bisexual, gender non-conforming, transgender and intersex. The term evolved out of the gender and **identity politics** of the 1980s and refers to art that takes alternative sexualities as its subject. It can also refer to historic works made at a time when sexual fluidity was considered deviant.

Nina Chanel Abney (b. 1982)
Nicole Eisenman (b. 1965)
Jenna Gribbon (b. 1978)
Harmony Hammond (b. 1944)
Fiza Khatri (b. 1992)
Ad Minoliti (b. 1980)
Zilia Sánchez (b. 1926)

RAYONISM
See **Futurism**.

REALISM
Art movement that began in the mid-nineteenth century and aimed to produce naturalistic works depicting everyday life, and in particular the lives of ordinary people, not just the elite classes. Realism is also used as a more generic term to refer to art that is visually true to life, such as in **Photorealism**. See also **Socialist Realism**.

Marie Bashkirtseff (1858–84)
Rosa Bonheur (1822–99)
Lotte Laserstein (1898–1993)
Elizabeth Nourse (1859–1938)
Zinaida Serebriakova (1884–1967)

REGIONALISM
American painting movement of the 1930s and 1940s that depicted everyday life, both rural and urban. Paintings were intended to be accessible to a wide audience.

Doris Lee (1905–83)

RELIEF PAINTING
Relief is a term more commonly applied to sculpture to describe works in which sculpted elements are raised from a flat plane and often presented wall hung. The same principle of a raised surface applies to relief paintings, where instead of being flat, elements project into the space in front of the **picture plane** so that, seen from an oblique angle, they are revealed as three-dimensional. Relief may be described as 'high relief', meaning the projection is substantial, or 'bas-relief', from the Italian *bassorilievo*, meaning 'low to the surface'.

Gina Beavers (b. 1974)
Jay DeFeo (1929–89)
Loie Hollowell (b. 1983)
Marlow Moss (1889–1958)
Zilia Sánchez (b. 1926)

RENAISSANCE
Word used generally to describe periods in which there is renewed artistic or cultural vigour, often inspired by the past. Specifically, it also refers to the period between the fourteenth and seventeenth centuries, starting in Italy and spreading across Europe, during which there was a revival of learning based on Classical literary sources. The use of **perspective** and other techniques was developed in painting, and increasing realism was expressed in sculpture; **Classical** art served as inspiration. The Early Renaissance spans the fifteenth century, the High Renaissance dates to the first quarter of the sixteenth century and was confined mainly to Italy, and the Late Renaissance followed after *c.*1525. See also **Mexican Renaissance** and **Harlem Renaissance**.

Sofonisba Anguissola (*c.*1532–1625)
Lavinia Fontana (1552–1614)
Catharina van Hemessen (1528–*c.*1588)
Barbara Longhi (1552–1638)
Plautilla Nelli (1524–88)
Lucrezia Quistelli (1541–94)
Marietta Robusti (*c.*1550/60–90)

ROCOCO
Ostentatious decorative style that became very popular in France, southern Germany and Austria in the eighteenth century. Rococo architecture, interiors, furniture and objects were characterized by asymmetry and the playful use of organic forms. Motifs such as shells, leaves and cherubs were particularly prominent. Rococo was lighter in tone than both the more monumental **Baroque** style from which it stemmed and the more formal **Neo-Classicism** that succeeded it.

Anna Dorothea Therbusch (1721–82)

ROMANTIC PAINTING
Romanticism was an artistic, musical, literary and intellectual movement that began in Europe towards the end of the eighteenth century. Prioritizing the imagination, emotion and individualism over reason and order, it is often considered as a reaction to the urbanization of the Industrial Revolution, the values of the Enlightenment and the scientific rationalization of nature. In art history, Romanticism is positioned in opposition to **Neo-Classicism**.

SALON
Originally the name of the official art exhibitions organized by the French **art academy** from 1725 onwards. Inclusion in Salons was at the discretion of academies. In the late nineteenth century there was a rise of alternative, unofficial Salons to accommodate more experimental work than the conservative establishment would allow. 'Salon' became adopted as a more generic term for mixed art exhibitions. See also **academic painting**.

SOCIAL REALISM
Term used for work produced by painters (and other creatives), that aims to draw attention to the socio-political realities of the working class as a means to critique the power structures behind these conditions.

Prunella Clough (1919–99)
Joan Eardley (1921–63)
Doris Lee (1905–83)
Hung Liu (1948–2021)
Dod Procter (1890–1972)
Charley Toorop (1891–1955)
Caroline Walker (b. 1982)

SOCIALIST REALISM
Term used to describe a style of painting and sculpture in which the rule of the proletariat is idealized and celebrated. It was made the official style of the USSR from 1934 – artists who worked in other styles risked imprisonment – until the death of Joseph Stalin. It later became the officially sanctioned style in China.

Zinaida Serebriakova (1884–1967)

SPIRAL
African American artist collective founded in 1963 and based in New York. The group aimed to address how Black artists should respond to the changing political and cultural landscape of America in the context of the civil rights movement. The group had only one woman member, and their only exhibition (while formally united as an alliance), titled 'First Group Showing: Works in Black and White', took place in summer 1965 at the space on Christopher Street where they met weekly.

Emma Amos (1937–2020)

SPRAY PAINT
Paint that comes in a sealed, pressurized container and is released in an aerosol spray when an integrated valve button is pressed. It was originally designed in the mid-twentieth century for industrial purposes to apply thin coatings of paint to metal surfaces such as cars or radiators. Its permanence and efficacy on most surfaces, as well as the portability of spray paint cans, has made it popular as a medium for graffiti, and it is particularly effective when used with stencils due to its quick-drying nature and the smooth, consistent coat it applies.

Nina Chanel Abney (b. 1982)
Katherine Bernhardt (b. 1975)
Judy Chicago (b. 1939)
Katharina Grosse (b. 1961)
Howardena Pindell (b. 1943)
Miriam Schapiro (1923–2015)
Genesis Tramaine (b. 1983)

STILL LIFE
A composition that depicts (mostly) inanimate subject matter, typically everyday objects. Arrangements of flowers and/or fruits and other foods are particularly popular subjects. Still life emerged as a distinct genre in **Western art** history in the **Dutch Golden Age**. Although it occupied the lowest position in the **hierarchy of art genres**, it has remained popular with art buyers who appreciate the technical skill that can be demonstrated through representations of familiar objects.

Ellen Altfest (b. 1970)
Farah Atassi (b. 1981)
Gillian Carnegie (b. 1971)
Georgette Chen (1906–93)
Audrey Flack (b. 1931)
Jane Freilicher (1924–2014)
Giovanna Garzoni (1600–70)
Josephine Joy (1869–1948)
Fiza Khatri (b. 1992)
Louise Moillon (1610–96)
Mary Moser (1744–1819)
GaHee Park (b. 1985)
Clara Peeters (*c.* 1594–*c.* 1659)
Rachel Ruysch (1664–1750)
Paula Siebra (b. 1998)

SUBLIME
In art, the sublime refers to a quality of greatness or grandeur that inspires awe and wonder. From the mid-eighteenth century it became a deliberate artistic effect, in which the artist aimed to evoke the strongest emotion possible in the mind of the viewer, particularly in relation to depictions of landscapes and nature.

Anna-Eva Bergman (1909–87)
Mary Weatherford (b. 1963)

SURREALISM
Artistic and literary movement prominent from the 1920s onwards – with continued influence today – which sought to explore the unconscious mind. Surrealists produced fantastical, disturbing and sometimes humorous works of art, using many styles and media, including **found objects** and **hyperrealistic** painting and manipulated photography. It was especially influential in France, Britain, Mexico and South America.

Gertrude Abercrombie (1909–77)
Eileen Agar (1899–1991)
Leonora Carrington (1917–2011)
Ithell Colquhoun (1906–88)
Leonor Fini (1907–96)
Rita Kernn-Larsen (1904–98)
Kay Sage (1898–1963)
Dorothea Tanning (1910–2012)
Toyen (1902–80)
Remedios Varo (1908–63)

SYMBOLISM
Literary and artistic movement of the 1880s and 1890s that aimed to explore the psyche, using objects symbolically to express underlying ideas and emotions. Reacting against the growing dominance of **Impressionism** and **Realism**, Symbolists aimed to reconcile matter and spirit through a language of signs and hidden meanings.

Annie Swynnerton (1844–1933)

TACHISM
European reaction to **Abstract Expressionism** in the United States; part of the **Art Informel** movement. This style of intuitive, improvisatory, non-geometric **abstract art** developed during the 1940s and 1950s and takes its name from the French *tache*, meaning 'spot' or 'splash'.

Gillian Ayres (1930–2018)

TEMPERA
Deriving from the verb 'to temper' – meaning to bring to a desired consistency – tempera describes a type of paint in which **pigments** were tempered with a water-miscible **binder** prior to applying them to a surface, in contrast with **fresco**, in which coloured pigments are applied without a binder. Tempera is an old art medium, dating back to at least ancient Egypt. It was traditionally made using fresh egg yolks, which creates the most durable form of the medium – little affected by temperature or humidity changes – but other emulsions can be made using **casein** and/or **oils**, and many artists developed their own specific recipes for tempera paint. Tempera is fast-drying, and though it dries to a lighter shade, its colour intensity can be restored with a layer of wax or varnish.

Sylvia Fein (b. 1919)
Giovanna Garzoni (1600–70)

TROMPE L'OEIL
French term meaning to 'deceive the eye', used to describe a painting designed to create the illusion that depicted objects exist in three dimensions, rather than being merely two-dimensional representations.

Helene Appel (b. 1976)
Louise Giovanelli (b. 1993)
Tess Jaray (b. 1937)
Laura Owens (b. 1970)
Avery Singer (b. 1987)
Alison Watt (b. 1965)

TURNER PRIZE
High-profile annual British art prize awarded since 1984 by the Tate Gallery, London. Presented to an artist born or based in Britain, originally only artists under fifty were eligible, until the upper age limit was lifted in 2017. In its first thirty years, just six of the winners were women artists.

UKIYO-E
Genre of Japanese art that flourished from the seventeenth to nineteenth centuries. Its artists produced woodblock prints and paintings of subjects such as actors, courtesans, scenes from history and folklore, landscape, nature and erotica.

Katsushika Ōi (*c.* 1800–*c.* 1866)

UNCANNY
Art evoking strange or anxious feelings, especially when created by familiar objects in unusual contexts. See also **Surrealism**.

Biserka Baretić (b. 1933)
Sascha Braunig (b. 1983)
Julie Curtiss (b. 1982)
Margherita Manzelli (b. 1968)
Jill Mulleady (b. 1980)
Claire Tabouret (b. 1981)
Issy Wood (b. 1993)

VENICE BIENNALE
The world's oldest **biennial** art exhibition that remains one of the most important platforms for the presentation and viewing of global **contemporary art**. It broadly comprises two main strands: a group exhibition held in the Arsenale and Central Pavilion of the Giardini, directed by a different invited curator for each edition; and national pavilions, for which countries select their own representative artist(s). For artists, the opportunity to exhibit work at the Venice Biennale, and particularly to represent their country, is considered a career milestone and major endorsement of their art.

WATERCOLOUR
Pigment bound by a water-soluble medium such as gum arabic. May be diluted with water to the point of transparency and applied to paper in a soft wash of colour. Areas of unpainted paper are often left exposed to create highlights, and washes may be applied one over another to achieve gradations of tone. Watercolour is an ancient form of painting, and in Chinese, Korean and Japanese art traditions it has been the dominant medium, used on silk as well as paper.

Shiva Ahmadi (b. 1975)
Sarah Biffin (1784–1850)
Gladys Nilsson (b. 1940)
Mary Roberts (d. 1761)
Uemura Shōen (1875–1949)

WESTERN ART
Term originally used to describe art from Europe and the United States, but now also used more generally for art from elsewhere that has stylistic or conceptual roots in European traditions and the **canon of art history**.

YOUNG BRITISH ARTISTS (YBAS)
A loose group of London-based artists active in the late 1980s and 1990s who became prominent figures in both the international art world and the British press at a young age. Many had studied at Goldsmiths College, were collected by Charles Saatchi or had work in the 1997 'Sensation' exhibition at the Royal Academy of Arts. While different in style and subject, their work was united by an openness to materials and processes and was often associated with controversy in the media.

Jenny Saville (b. 1970)
Fiona Rae (b. 1963)

INDEX

Page numbers in *italics* refer to the illustrations

PICTURE CREDITS

We would like to thank all those who gave their permission to reproduce the listed material. Every effort has been made to secure all permissions prior to publication. Phaidon apologizes for any inadvertent errors or omissions. If notified, the publisher will endeavour to correct these at the earliest opportunity.

All images © the artists. p.9a: Harley 4431, f.290 © British Library Board. All Rights Reserved / Bridgeman Images. p.9b: akg-images. p.11a: Royal MS 16 G V f.68v © British Library Board. All Rights Reserved / Bridgeman Images. p.13a: Copyright © Guerrilla Girls, courtesy guerrillagirls.com. p.13b: Museo di Capodimonte, Naples, Campania, Italy / Bridgeman Images. p.15: akg-images. p.16: Courtesy of Pacita Abad Art Estate. Photo: Max McClure. p.17: Courtesy Estate of Mary Lee Abbot. Photo courtesy McCormick Gallery, LLC, Chicago. p.18: Courtesy the artist and Circle Art Gallery, Nairobi. p.19: Gift of Powell and Barbara Bridges, 2009.59. Art Institute of Chicago. © 2021. The Art Institute of Chicago / Art Resource, NY / Scala, Florence. p.20: © Nina Chanel Abney. Courtesy of the artist and Jack Shainman Gallery, New York. p.21: Courtesy of the artist & greengrassi, London. Photo: Marcus J. Leith. p.22: © DACS 2022. © 2021. DeAgostini Picture Library / Scala, Florence. p.23: © Estate of Etel Adnan. Courtesy Galerie Lelong & Co. Photo: © 2022 RMN-Grand Palais / Dist. Photo SCALA, Florence p.24: IanDagnall Computing / Alamy Stock Photo. p.25: © Estate of Eileen Agar. All rights reserved 2021 / Bridgeman Images. p.26: © Shiva Ahmadi. p.27: © Njideka Akunyili Crosby. Courtesy the artist, Victoria Miro, and David Zwirner. Photo: Anders Sune Berg. p.28: © Ellen Altfest. Photo © Todd-White Art Photography. Courtesy White Cube. p.29: © Emma Amos. Courtesy of Ryan Lee Gallery, New York. p.30: Courtesy the artist, Galleri Magnus Karlsson, Stephen Friedman Gallery and David Zwirner. Photo: Johann Bergenholtz. p.31: akg-images. p.32: © The Estate of Rita Angus. p.33: © Helene Appel 2022. Image courtesy the artist and James Cohan, New York. p.34: Courtesy of the artist and Almine Rech. Photo: Melissa Castro Duarte. p.35: © Sybil Atteck Family Estate, and the Sybil Atteck Biography Project. Photo © 101artgallery.com. p.36: Courtesy of Dotty Attie and P.P.O.W., New York. p.37: Copyright ADAGP, Paris / DACS, London 2022. Courtesy Serge Goisse. p.38: Courtesy the artist and Taymour Grahne Projects. Photo: onwhitewall.com. p.39: © The Estate of the artist. Courtesy Marlborough London. p.40: © the artist. Photo: Kitmin Lee © White Cube. p.41: Nasjonalmuseet / Børre Høstland p.42: © Jo Baer. Courtesy Pace Gallery. Photo: Christine Ann Jones. p.43: akg-images. p.44: Photo: www.futurismo.org digital collection. p.45: © the artist. Photo: David Gazarov. p.46: © Jennifer Bartlett. Courtesy Locks Gallery, Philadelphia, Marianne Boesky Gallery, New York and Aspen, Paula Cooper Gallery, New York, and The Jennifer Bartlett 2013 Trust. p.47: Photo © Stefano Baldini / Bridgeman Images. p.48: Courtesy the artist and Marianne Boesky Gallery, New York and Aspen. © Gina Beavers. Photo: Charles Benton. p.49: Courtesy the artist and Parasol Unit. Photo: Stephen White. p.50: © Estate of Vanessa Bell. All rights reserved, DACS 2022. Photo © Christie's Images / Bridgeman Images. p.51: Album / Alamy Stock Photo. p.52: © Anna-Eva Bergman / ADAGP, Paris and DACS, London 2022. Courtesy Fondation Hartung Bergman, Antibes / Galerie Poggi, Paris. p.53: © Katherine Bernhardt. Courtesy the artist, David Zwirner, and Canada. p.54: Courtesy the artist and Kasmin, New York. p.55: Photo: © Sotheby's. p.56: Photo: © Sotheby's / Bridgeman Images. p.57: Courtesy the artist and P420, Bologna. Photo: Carlo Favero. p.58: © 2022. Photo Scala, Florence / bpk, Bildagentur fuer Kunst, Kultur und Geschichte, Berlin. p.59: © 2021. Christie's Images, London / Scala, Florence. p.60: Courtesy of the Pauline Boty Estate. Photo © Tate. p.61: Erich Lessing / akg-images. p.62: Courtesy the artist and Office Baroque. Photo: Isabelle Arthuis. p.63: © Lisa Brice. Courtesy the artist and Salon 94, New York. p.64: Photo © 2021. Smithsonian American Art Museum / Art Resource / Scala, Florence. p.65: © Cecily Brown. Courtesy Gagosian. Photo: Rob McKeever. p.66: Courtesy the artist. Photo: Serge Hasenboehler. p.67: Art Jameel Fund, 2020, The Metropolitan Museum of Art, New York. Courtesy Huguette Caland Estate. p.68: © 2022. Photo Scala, Florence / bpk, Bildagentur fuer Kunst, Kultur und Geschichte, Berlin. p.69: The Picture Art Collection / Alamy Stock Photo. p.70: © Gillian Carnegie. p.71: © Art Gallery of Ontario, purchase, 1937 / Bridgeman Images. p.72: © Estate of Leonora Carrington / ARS, NY and DACS, London 2022. © Sainsbury Centre for Visual Arts / Robert and Lisa Sainsbury Collection / Bridgeman Images. p.73: © 2021. Museum of Fine Arts, Boston. All rights reserved / Scala, Florence. p.74: © Jordan Casteel. Courtesy of Casey Kaplan, New York. p.75: Gift of the artist's estate. Collection of National Gallery Singapore. p.76: Courtesy of the artist and Perrotin. Photo: YANG Hao. p.77: © Judy Chicago. ARS, NY and DACS, London 2022. Photo courtesy of Judy Chicago / Art Resource, NY. p.78: Photo: courtesy Sotheby's. p.79: © Saloua Raouda Choucair Foundation. p.80: © Estate of Prunella Clough. All Rights Reserved, DACS 2022. © Arts Council Collection / Bridgeman Images. p.81: © Israel Museum, Jerusalem / Vera & Arturo Schwarz Collection of Dada and Surrealist Art / Bridgeman Images. p.82: © Caroline Coon. All rights reserved, DACS / Artimage 2022. p.83: © Mary Corse. Courtesy the artist and Kayne Griffin, Los Angeles. Photo: © 2022. Museum Associates / LACMA / Art Resource NY / Scala, Florence. p.84: © Art Gallery of South Australia / Ivor Francis Bequest Fund / Bridgeman Images. p.85: © Artist's Estate. Photo: © National Gallery of Australia, Canberra / Purchased 1959 / Bridgeman Images. p.86: Courtesy the artist and Pilar Corrias, London; Antenna Space, Shanghai. p.87: © the artist. Photo © Charles Benton. Courtesy White Cube. p.88: © The Jay DeFeo Foundation / DACS 2022. © 2021. Digital Image Museum Associates / LACMA / Art Resource NY / Scala, Florence. p.89: National Portrait Gallery, Smithsonian Institution. © Elaine de Kooning Trust / Edek Trust. p.90: © Angela de la Cruz. Courtesy Lisson Gallery. p.91: Abby Aldrich Rockefeller Fund, Museum of Modern Art, New York © 2021. Digital image, The Museum of Modern Art, New York / Scala, Florence p.92: © 2022 Rosalyn Drexler / ARS, NY and DACS, London 2022. Courtesy Garth Greenan Gallery, New York. p.93: Whitney Museum of American Art, New York; gift of Gertrude Vanderbilt Whitney. © Estate of Elsie Driggs. Photo: © 2021. Digital image Whitney Museum of American Art / Licensed by Scala p.94: © Marlene Dumas. Photo: Peter Cox, Eindhoven. p.95: Courtesy the artist and Galerie Greta Meert. p.96: © Estate of Joan Eardley. All Rights Reserved, DACS 2022. © National Galleries of Scotland / Bridgeman Images. p.97: Image courtesy Barjeel Art Foundation, Sharjah. Courtesy Safarkhan Art Gallery and Hassan Galal El Din. p.98: © Eguchi Ayane. Courtesy of Mizuma Art Gallery. p.99: © Nicole Eisenman. Courtesy the artist and Anton Kern Gallery, New York. p.100: Courtesy the artist and Kunsthalle Zürich, Switzerland. Photo: Marc Asekhame. Courtesy of Christen Sveaas and Kistefos AS. p.101: © Tracey Emin. All rights reserved, DACS / Artimage 2022 p.102: Courtesy the artist and Miles McEnery Gallery, New York. p.103: © 2021. Digital image, The Museum of Modern Art, New York / Scala, Florence. p.104: The Baltimore Museum of Art: Gift of Eva Chow, Los Angeles, BMA 2020.82. © Jadé Fadojutimi. Photo: Mitro Hood. p.105: © Sylvia Fein. p.106: © Rachel Feinstein. Courtesy Gagosian. Photo: Rob McKeever. p.107: Courtesy the artist and Half Gallery. p.108: © ADAGP, Paris and DACS, London 2022. © 2021. Christie's Images, London / Scala, Florence. p.109: Courtesy the artist and GAVLAK Los Angeles | Palm Beach. p.110: © 2021, Audrey Flack. Photo courtesy Louis K. Meisel Gallery. p.111: Album / Alamy Stock Photo p.112: Purchased with funds from the Friends of the Whitney Museum of American Art. © Helen Frankenthaler Foundation, Inc. / ARS, NY and DACS, London 2022. p.113: Kathryn E. Hurd Fund, 1995. © 2022. Image copyright The Metropolitan Museum of Art / Art Resource / Scala, Florence. p.114: © Veneranda Biblioteca Ambrosiana / Mondadori Portfolio / Bridgeman Images. p.115: Courtesy the artist. Photo: Felipe Brendt. p.116: The J. Paul Getty Museum. p.117: © 2021. The Museum of Fine Arts Budapest / Scala, Florence. p.118: Photo: courtesy of Sotheby's, Inc. © 2013. p.119: © Louise Giovanelli. Courtesy the artist and GRIMM Amsterdam / New York. Photo: Sonia Mangiapane. p.120: © The Gluck Estate. All rights reserved, DACS 2022. © 2021. Christie's Images, London / Scala, Florence. p.121: Courtesy the artist and Nature Morte, New Delhi. p.122: © UPRAVIS / DACS 2022. © Israel Museum, Jerusalem / Sam and Alaya Zacks Collection / Bridgeman Images. p.123: Courtesy the artist, Galería Casas Riegner, Bogotá, and Galerie Peter Kilchmann, Zurich. Photo: Sebastian Schaub. p.124: Courtesy the artist, MASSIMODECARLO and Fredericks & Freiser, NY. Photo: Todd-White Art Photography. p.125: © 2022 Katharina Grosse and VG Bild-Kunst, Bonn. © DACS 2022. Photo: Mitro Hood, courtesy of The Baltimore Museum of Art and Gagosian. p.126: Courtesy the artist, David Kordansky Gallery, Gagosian, and MASSIMODECARLO. p.127: Collection SFMOMA, gift of Liana Kadisha Cohn and Shaun Maguire Cohn. Courtesy of the artist and Alexander Berggruen, NY. Photo: Dario Lasagni p.128: Mary Griggs Burke Collection, Gift of the Mary and Jackson Burke Foundation, 2015 / The Metropolitan Museum of Art. p.129: © Maggi Hambling / Bridgeman Images. p.130: © Harmony Hammond / VAGA at ARS, NY and DACS, London 2022. Courtesy Alexander Gray Associates, New York. p.131: © Grace Hartigan Estate. © 2021. Digital image, The Museum of Modern Art, New York / Scala, Florence. p.132: © Mary Heilmann. Courtesy the artist, 303 Gallery, New York, and Hauser & Wirth. Photo: Christopher Burke. p.133: The Bowes Museum, County Durham, thebowesmuseum.org.uk. p.134: © Carmen Herrera. Courtesy Lisson Gallery. p.135: © Lubaina Himid. Image courtesy the artist and Hollybush Gardens, London. Photo: Andy Keate. p.136: © Loie Hollowell. Courtesy Pace Gallery. Photo: Melissa Goodwin. p.137: © Shirazeh Houshiary. Courtesy Lisson Gallery. p.138: © Shara Hughes. Courtesy of the artist, Pilar Corrias, London, David Kordansky Gallery, Los Angeles and New York, and Galerie Eva Presenhuber, Zurich / New York. p.139: © The Estate of Luchita Hurtado. Courtesy the Estate of Luchita Hurtado and Hauser & Wirth. Photo: Jeff McLane. p.140: © Kudzanai-Violet Hwami. Courtesy the artist and Victoria Miro. p.141: © Kamala Ishag. Image courtesy of Barjeel Art Foundation, Sharjah. p.142: © Yukie Ishikawa, Courtesy the artist and Blum & Poe, Los Angeles / New York / Tokyo. p.143: © DACS 2022. Photo Schalkwijk / Art Resource / Scala, Florence. p.144: p.145: © Chantal Joffe. Courtesy the artist and Victoria Miro. p.146: Leeds Museums and Galleries, UK / Bridgeman Images. p.147: © Claudette Johnson. Courtesy the artist and Hollybush Gardens, London, and Tate. p.148: Courtesy Lois Mailou Jones Pierre-Noel Trust. © 2021. Photo Smithsonian American Art Museum / Art Resource / Scala, Florence. p.149: Courtesy Pippy Houldsworth Gallery, London. © Jacqueline de Jong 2021. Photo: Gert Jan van Rooij. p.150: © 2021. Photo Smithsonian American Art Museum / Art Resource / Scala, Florence. p.151: Courtesy the artist and Almine Rech. Photo: Melissa Castro Duarte. p.152: © Banco de México Diego Rivera Frida Kahlo Museums Trust, Mexico, D.F. / DACS 2022. Harry Ransom Center, Texas. © 2021. Album / Scala, Florence. p.153: © Hayv Kahraman.

Courtesy the artist and Jack Shainman Gallery, New York. p.154: Kelvin Smith Fund / Cleveland Museum of Art. p.155: Album / Alamy Stock Photo. p.156: © DACS 2022. Bridgeman Images. p.157: © DACS 2022. © Israel Museum, Jerusalem / Vera & Arturo Schwarz Collection of Dada and Surrealist Art / Bridgeman Images. p.158: Courtesy of Sanam Khatibi and P.P.O.W, New York. p.159: Courtesy the artist, Fiza Khatri. p.160: Aishti Foundation, Beirut, Lebanon. Courtesy the artist, Galerie Eva Presenhuber Zurich / New York and Sprueth Magers. p.161: Mary Griggs Burke Collection, Gift of the Mary and Jackson Burke Foundation / Minneapolis Institute of Art. p.162: National Gallery of Victoria, Melbourne / Purchased by the National Gallery Women's Association to mark the directorship of Dr Timothy Potts, 1998 / Bridgeman Images. © Emily Kame Kngwarreye / Copyright Agency. Licensed by DACS 2022. p.163: Reproduced with permission of The Estate of Dame Laura Knight DBE RA 2021. All Rights Reserved / Bridgeman Images. p.164: Courtesy the artist and DC Moore Gallery, New York. p.165: © Indianapolis Museum of Art / Gift of the Herron Museum Alliance / Bridgeman Images. © The Pollock-Krasner Foundation ARS, NY and DACS, London 2022. p.166: Courtesy the artist and Bortolami, New York. p.167: Courtesy the artist and W&K–Wienerroither & Kohlbacher, Vienna. p.168: © Yayoi Kusama. Courtesy the artist, Ota Fine Arts and Victoria Miro. p.169: Gift of Julia A. Berwind, 1953 / The Metropolitan Museum of Art. p.170: Courtesy of the artist, Tiwani Contemporary and BALTIC Centre for Contemporary Art, Gateshead. Photo: Rob Harris. p.171: © Lalan Estate. © 2022. RMN-Grand Palais / Dist. Photo SCALA, Florence. p.172: Photo: courtesy Sotheby's, Inc. © 2019. p.173: © DACS 2022. Photo: Roman Maerz. bpk, Bildagentur fuer Kunst, Kultur und Geschichte, Berlin. © 2021. Photo Scala, Florence. p.174: © Maria Lassnig Foundation / Bildrecht Vienna, DACS London 2022. Photo: Stefan Altenburger Photography Zurich. p.175: © Fondation Foujita / ADAGP, Paris and DACS, London 2022. Musee National d'Art Moderne – Centre Pompidou, Paris. © 2021. RMN-Grand Palais / Dist. Photo SCALA, Florence. Photo: Jean-Claude Planchet. p.176: © Estate of Doris Lee,. Courtesy D. Wigmore Fine Art, Inc. p.177: Gift of Mrs. Thorneycroft Ryle, 1957 / The Metropolitan Museum of Art p.178: © Tamara de Lempicka Estate, LCC / DACS 2022. Photo © Christie's Images / Bridgeman Images. p.179: Courtesy Mariane Ibrahim. © Fabrice Gousset. p.180: Mauritshuis, The Hague. p.181: Courtesy the artist and White Rabbit Collection. p.182: Collection SFMOMA. Purchase through a gift of Nelcy Tarics. © Estate of Hung Liu. Photo: San Francisco Museum of Modern Art / Bridgeman Images. p.183: © Archivio Bertina Lopes (Maputo / Lisbona / Roma)–Roma Centro Mostre. Courtesy Richard Saltoun Gallery. p.184: © The Estate of Lee Lozano. Courtesy the Estate and Hauser & Wirth. p.185: Freer Gallery of Art, Smithsonian Institution / Gift of Charles Lang Freer / Bridgeman Images. p.186: © Tala Madani. Courtesy of the artist, Pilar Corrias, London and David Kordansky Gallery, Los Angeles and New York. Photo: Lee Thompson. p.187: Courtesy Esther Mahlangu and The Melrose Gallery. p.188: Courtesy the artist and Lyles & King, New York. Photo: Nick Paton. p.189: © DACS 2022. akg-images. p.190: Courtesy the artist and Lehmann Maupin, New York, Hong Kong, Seoul and London. Photo: Roberto Marossi p.191: © Agnes Martin Foundation, New York / DACS. © 2022. The Solomon R. Guggenheim Foundation / Art Resource, NY / Scala, Florence. p.192: Courtesy Pippy Houldsworth Gallery. © Wangari Mathenge 2021. Photo: Brian Griffin. p.193: © Estate of Louisa Matthiasdottir. Courtesy Tibor de Nagy Gallery, New York. p.194: © the artist. Photo: © White Cube (George Darrell) p.195: Courtesy the artist and Fridman Gallery, New York. p.196: © Julie Mehretu. Courtesy White Cube. Photo © Tom Powel. p.197: © Prabhavathi Meppayil. Courtesy Pace Gallery. Photo: Damian Griffiths. p.198: Strauss & Co. Photo: James Fox. p.199: © Beatriz Milhazes. Photo: © White Cube (Vincent Tsang) p.200: © Lisa Milroy. Photo: FXP Photography. p.201: Courtesy the artist and Peres Projects. p.202: © Marilyn Minter. Courtesy the artist and Salon 94, New York. p.203: Saint Louis Art Museum, Funds given by the Shoenberg Foundation, Inc. 86:1993a,b; © Estate of Joan Mitchell. p.204: Courtesy of the artist and Nathalie Karg Gallery. p.205: © Detroit Institute of Arts / Gift of Robert H. Tannahill / Bridgeman Images. p.206: RMN-Grand Palais / Dist. Photo SCALA, Florence. Photo: Jean-Gilles Berizzi. Paris, Louvre © 2021. p.207: © 2021. Photo Scala, Florence. p.208: © Sabine Moritz. Courtesy the artist, Pilar Corrias, London, and Marian Goodman Gallery, New York. p.209: © Sarah Morris. p.210: © Fitzwilliam Museum / Bridgeman Images. p.211: Wintermann Collection of American Art, gift of Mr. and Mrs. David R. Wintermann. Kallir Research Institute. © Grandma Moses Properties Co / Bridgeman Images. p.212: Photo: © Tate p.213: © Jill Mulleady. Courtesy the artist and Gladstone Gallery. p.214: © DACS 2022. © San Diego Museum of Art / Gift from the Estate of Vance E. Kondon and Liesbeth Giesberger / Bridgeman Images. p.215: © The Murray-Holman Family Trust / Artists Rights Society (ARS), New York / DACS 2022. © 2021. Digital image, The Museum of Modern Art, New York / Scala, Florence. p.216: © Ishbel Myerscough. Courtesy of Flowers Gallery. p.217: © Cassi Namoda. Courtesy the artist, François Ghebaly Gallery, and Pippy Houldsworth Gallery, London. Photo: Mark Blower. p.218: © Yukultji Napangati. Courtesy the artist and Salon 94, New York. p.219: Museum of Fine Arts, Boston / Seth K. Sweetser Fund. © The Estate of Alice Neel. Courtesy the artist's estate, David Zwirner, New York / London and Victoria Miro, London / Venice. pp.220–21: Rabatti & Domingie / akg-images. p.222: Courtesy the artist and Garth Greenan Gallery, New York. p.223: © Aliza Nisenbaum. Courtesy the artist and Anton Kern Gallery, New York. p.224: Cincinnati Art Museum / Gift of Harley I. Procter / Bridgeman Images. p.225: Courtesy the artist and Barjeel Art Foundation, Sharjah. p.226: MPortfolio / Electa / akg-images. p.227: © Georgia O'Keeffe Museum / DACS 2022. © 2021. The Art Institute of Chicago / Art Resource, NY / Scala, Florence. p.228: © Laura Owens. Courtesy the artist, Sadie Coles HQ, London, and Galerie Gisela Capitain, Cologne. p.229: Courtesy the artist, Sikkema Jenkins & Co., New York, and Corvi-Mora, London. p.230: © 2021. RMN-Grand Palais / Dist. Photo SCALA, Florence. p.231: Courtesy the artist and Perrotin. Photo: Guillaume Ziccarelli. p.232: © Celia Paul. Courtesy the artist and Victoria Miro. p.233: Courtesy the artist, Rachel Uffner Gallery and Timothy Taylor Gallery. Photo: Ed Mumford. p.234: Photo © Fine Art Images / Bridgeman Images. p.235: Peter Palladino / The Agnes Pelton Society / Bridgeman Images. p.236: © Elizabeth Peyton. Courtesy Sadie Coles HQ, London. p.237: Courtesy the artist and Garth Greenan Gallery, New York. Photo: © 2022. Digital image Whitney Museum of American Art / Licensed by Scala. p.238: The Riklis Collection of McCrory Corporation 1059.1983. © 2021. Digital image, The Museum of Modern Art, New York / Scala, Florence p.239: © Tate. p.240: © Christina Quarles. Courtesy the artist, Hauser & Wirth and Pilar Corrias, London. p.241: © Fiona Rae. All Rights Reserved, DACS / Artimage 2022. Photo: Antony Makinson and Prudence Cuming Associates Ltd. p.242: © Archivio Carol Rama, Torino. Photo: Elisabeth Bernstein. p.243: © The Estate of Christina Ramberg. Photo © 2021. Digital image Whitney Museum of American Art / Licensed by Scala. p.244: The Hilla Rebay Collection © 2021. The Solomon R. Guggenheim Foundation / Art Resource, NY / Scala, Florence. p.245: Bridgeman Images p.246: © Paula Rego. Courtesy the artist and Victoria Miro. p.247: © ADAGP, Paris and DACS, London 2022. Photo: courtesy Sotheby's. p.248: © Bridget Riley 2021. All rights reserved. p.249: © Faith Ringgold / ARS, NY and DACS, London, Courtesy ACA Galleries, New York 2022. p.250: Purchase, Dale T. Johnson Fund and Jan and Warren Adelson Gift, 2007 / The Metropolitan Museum of Art p.251: © 2021. Image Copyright Museo Nacional del Prado © Photo MNP / Scala, Florence p.252: © The Estate of Erna Rosenstein / Adam Sandauer. Courtesy Hauser & Wirth and Foksal Gallery Foundation. Moderna Museet Collection. Photo: Thomas Barratt. p.253: © ARS, NY and DACS, London 2022. Photo © Christie's Images / Bridgeman Images. p.254: Photo: Jens Mohr / Hallwyl Museum, Stockholm p.255: © Estate of Kay Sage / DACS, London and ARS, NY, 2022. © 2021. Princeton University Art Museum / Art Resource NY / Scala, Florence. Photo: Bruce M. White. p.256: The Picture Art Collection / Alamy Stock Photo. p.257: © Zilia Sánchez. Courtesy Galerie Lelong & Co., New York. p.258: © Jenny Saville. All rights reserved, DACS 2022. Courtesy Gagosian. p.259: © Estate of Miriam Schapiro / ARS, NY and DACS, London 2022. p.260: Heritage Images / Fine Art Images / akg-images. p.261: © Dana Schutz. Courtesy the artist, David Zwirner and Thomas Dane Gallery. Photo: Ben Westoby. p.262: © Tschabalala Self. Courtesy the artist, Pilar Corrias, London and Galerie Eva Presenhuber, Zurich / New York. p.263: © ARS, NY and DACS, London 2022. Courtesy Alexander Gray Associates, New York. © 2021 Joan Semmel / Artists Rights Society (ARS), New York. p.264: Bridgeman Images. p.265: © the artist. p.266: © ADAGP, Paris and DACS, London 2022. Album / Alamy Stock Photo. p.267: Courtesy the artist and Chemould Prescott Road. Photo: Anil Rane. p.268: © Amy Sherald. Courtesy the artist and Hauser & Wirth. Photo: Joseph Hyde. p.269: Photo: courtesy Sotheby's. p.270: Historic Collection / Alamy Stock Photo. p.271: Courtesy the artist and Mendes Wood DM São Paulo, Brussels, New York. Photo: Kristien Daem. p.272: © Shahzia Sikander. Courtesy the artist, Pilar Corrias, London, and Sean Kelly, New York. p.273: © Amy Sillman. Courtesy the artist and Gladstone Gallery, New York and Brussels. p.274: © Lorna Simpson. Courtesy the artist and Hauser & Wirth. Photo: James Wang. p.275: © Avery Singer. Courtesy the artist and Hauser & Wirth. Photo: Lance Brewer. p.276: Courtesy Arpita Singh & Vadehra Art Gallery. p.277: © 2021. Photo Josse / Scala, Florence. p.278: © Gazbia Sirry. Courtesy Azza Naguib, Gazbia Sirry Trustee. Image courtesy of Barjeel Art Foundation, Sharjah. p.279: Gift of the Estate of Sylvia Sleigh. Inv.n.:2016.234. Whitney Museum of American Art, New York. © 2021. Digital image Whitney Museum of American Art / Licensed by Scala. p.280: Courtesy the artist and Perrotin. Photo: Dario Lasagni. p.281: Courtesy the artist and Garth Greenan Gallery, New York. p.282: The Metropolitan Museum of Art, Gift of Souls Grown Deep Foundation from the William S. Arnett Collection, 2014. p.283: Courtesy the Estate of Janet Sobel. Digital image © 2021, The Museum of Modern Art, New York / Scala, Florence. Gift of the artist's family. p.284: Courtesy the artist and Lévy Gorvy. p.285: © The Irma Stern Trust, DACS 2022. Photo: courtesy Sotheby's. p.286: Arthur Hoppock Hearn Fund, 1953. 53.91. © 2021. The Metropolitan Museum of Art / Art Resource / Scala, Florence. © ARS, NY and DACS, London 2022. p.287: Album / akg-images. p.288: © Becky Suss. Courtesy the artist and Jack Shainman Gallery, New York. p.289: © Vivian Suter. Courtesy the artist and Gladstone Gallery. p.290: © The Artist's Estate. Photo: courtesy Sotheby's. p.291: Asar Studios / Alamy Stock Photo. p.292: p.293: Courtesy the artist, Almine Rech and Pinault Collection. Photo: Rebecca Fanuele p.294: Collection Albright-Knox Art Gallery, Buffalo, New York © 2021. Albright Knox Art Gallery / Art Resource, NY / Scala, Florence. p.295: Courtesy the artist and DC Moore Gallery, New York. p.296: Courtesy Centre Pompidou, MNAM-CCI. Musee National d'Art Moderne – Centre Pompidou, Paris. © 2021. RMN-Grand Palais / Dist. Photo SCALA, Florence. p.297: sfgp / Album / akg-images. p.298: Bridgeman Images. p.299: Gift of Alma W. Thomas. © 2021. Photo Smithsonian American Art Museum / Art Resource / Scala, Florence. p.300: Courtesy the artist. p.301: © The Estate of Mildred Thompson. Courtesy Galerie Lelong & Co., New York. p.302: Courtesy of Betty Tompkins, GAVLAK Los Angeles, and P.P.O.W., New York p.303: © DACS 2022. Jan Fritz / Alamy Stock Photo. p.304: © ADAGP, Paris and DACS, London 2022. akg-images. p.305: Courtesy of the Artist and Almine Rech. Photo: Melissa Castro Duarte. Sandra and Giancarlo Bonollo Collection p.306: © 2021. Image copyright The Metropolitan Museum of Art / Art Resource / Scala, Florence. Robert Lehman Collection, 1975. p.307: © Adriana Varejão. Courtesy Gagosian. Photo: Vicente de Mello. p.308: © Remedios Varo, DACS / VEGAP 2022. Photo © Christie's Images / Bridgeman Images. p.309: © ADAGP, Paris and DACS, London 2022. © 2021. Christie's Images, London / Scala, Florence. p.310: Antiquarian Images / Alamy Stock Photo. p.311: © 2021. RMN-Grand Palais / Dist. Photo SCALA, Florence. Photo: Jean-Gilles Berizzi. Paris, Louvre. p.312: © 2022 Merrill Wagner. Courtesy the artist and David Zwirner p.313: © Caroline Walker. Courtesy the artist and GRIMM Amsterdam / New York. Photo: Peter Mallet p.314: Courtesy the artist and Edouard Malingue Gallery. p.315: National Portrait Gallery, Smithsonian Institution: gift of Walter Waring in memory of his wife, Laura Wheeler Waring, through the Harmon Foundation. IanDagnall Computing / Alamy Stock Photo. p.316: Courtesy the artist. p.317: Courtesy the artist and Parafin, London. Photo: John McKenzie. p.318: The Picture Art Collection / Alamy Stock Photo. p.319: Collection of The Museum of Modern Art, New York. Fund for the Twenty-First Century. Courtesy of David Kordansky Gallery, Los Angeles and New York. Photo: Jonathan Muzikar. p.320: Luisa Ricciarini / Bridgeman Images. p.321: Courtesy Robin F. Williams and P.P.O.W., New York. p.322: Courtesy the artist and Almine Rech. Photo: Melissa Castro Duarte. p.323: © Issy Wood 2022. Courtesy the artist, Carlos / Ishikawa, London, and JTT, New York. Photo: Damian Griffiths. p.324: Courtesy Clare Woods and Buchmann Galerie. Photo: Studio Clare Woods. p.325: Courtesy Private Collection. Photo: Soon-Hak Kwon. p.326: © Lynette Yiadom-Boakye. Courtesy the artist and Jack Shainman Gallery, New York. Photo: Marcus Leith. p.327: © Flora Yukhnovich. Courtesy the artist and Victoria Miro. p.328: © Lisa Yuskavage. Courtesy the artist and David Zwirner. p.329: © 2021. RMN-Grand Palais / Dist. Photo SCALA, Florence. p.330: © 2021. The Art Institute of Chicago / Art Resource, NY / Scala, Florence. The Zorach Collection, LLC. p.331: © Portia Zvavahera. Courtesy of Stevenson Amsterdam / Cape Town / Johannesburg. Photo: Mario Todeschini.

WRITER BIOGRAPHIES

Rahel Aima is a writer, editor and critic from Dubai. She is the editor of *BXD: The Postwestern Review* and an associate editor at *Momus*.
pp.56, 202, 291, 329

Dr. Sheila Barker directs research on women artists at the Medici Archive Project. She has published books on Artemisia Gentileschi and Giovanna Garzoni.
pp.31, 114, 116, 220, 251

Lucienne Bestall is an arts writer and curatorial researcher based in Cape Town.
pp.47, 85, 104, 163, 273, 284, 285, 324, 330

Ian Bourland is an art historian at Georgetown University, Washington DC, and cultural critic for a range of leading publications.
pp.16, 46, 156, 184, 196

James Cahill is a writer and academic based in London. His is the author of the novel *Tiepolo Blue* (2022) and consultant editor/lead author of *Flying Too Close to the Sun* (2018).
p.236

Ellen Mara De Wachter is a writer based in London.
pp.21, 70, 75, 76, 81, 97, 98, 150, 160, 188, 233, 242, 272, 312

Louisa Elderton is a Berlin-based writer and Chief Editor of *Side Magazine* for Bergen Assembly 2022.
pp.67, 175, 218, 231, 241, 260, 271, 309

Philomena Epps is a writer and art critic living in London.
pp.18, 24, 82, 87, 179, 213, 279, 280, 318

Lydia Figes is Content Editor at Art UK. Her writing has appeared in *Dazed*, *AnOther Magazine*, *TANK*, *Elephant*, *BBC Arts* and *The Guardian*, among other publications.
pp.48, 62, 190, 223, 323

Diane Fortenberry is a Mississippi-born writer, editor and occasional archaeologist. She has published widely on Greek and Roman archaeology, art history, early travel and photography.
pp.58, 61, 89, 137, 155, 180, 189, 211, 214, 287, 289, 304, 311

Elizabeth Fullerton is a critic and writer for publications including *Art in America*, *The New York Times* and *The Guardian*, and author of *Artrage! The Story of the BritArt Revolution* (2016/2021).
pp.30, 43, 74, 105, 149, 169, 293, 301, 306, 319

Anna Furman is a Los Angeles–based writer. Her work has been published in *The New York Times*, *New York Magazine* and *The Guardian*.
pp.23, 134, 219

Helen Gørrill holds a PhD in contemporary painting research. She is the author of *Women Can't Paint* (2018) and lectures at Duncan of Jordanstone College of Art & Design, University of Dundee, Scotland.
pp.111, 120, 162, 224

Alison M. Gingeras is a curator and writer based in New York and Warsaw. She has served as curator at the Solomon R. Guggenheim Museum, New York; Centre Pompidou, Paris; and Palazzo Grassi, Venice. Gingeras currently serves as an adjunct curator at Dallas Contemporary and a guest curator at the Museum of Contemporary Art North Miami as well as the Museum of Modern Art in Warsaw, in addition to working independently.
Introductory essay, pp.9–18

PL Henderson is author of *Unravelling Women's Art* (2021), curator of @womensart1, a freelance writer and contributor to publications including *Great ~~Women~~ Artists* (2019).
pp.72, 244, 254, 266

Sarah Humphreville is a member of the curatorial department at the Whitney Museum of American Art in New York.
pp.54, 92, 165, 191, 227, 249, 259, 274, 315

Simon Hunegs is Project Editor at Phaidon Press based in New York.
pp.292, 300

Charlotte Jansen is an arts and culture journalist, author of *Girl on Girl* (2017) and *Photography Now* (2021) and host of the Dior Talks podcast series *The Female Gaze*.
pp.60, 63, 78, 96, 100, 102, 107, 133, 136, 144, 173, 176, 187, 210, 212, 247, 262, 283, 297, 307, 328, 331

Martha Kazungu is a Ugandan curator and art historian. She is founder of Njabala Foundation, which focuses on creating visibility of women artists.
pp.79, 122, 240, 286

Kelly Ma is an arts administrator based in Hong Kong and New York, where she organizes exhibitions and discussions to broaden historical narratives.
pp.40, 42, 171, 182, 207

Kathleen Madden is an independent writer and adjunct faculty at Christie's Education, Sotheby's Institute of Art and Barnard College, New York.
pp.28, 37, 93, 130

Henry Martin is author of *Agnes Martin: Pioneer, Painter, Icon* (2018), a Fulbright scholar and university lecturer.
pp.41, 44, 91, 112, 127, 142, 147, 153, 216, 288, 290

Marina Molarsky-Beck is an art historian, writer, curator and current PhD candidate at Yale University, New Haven, Connecticut, where she studies queer subjectivity in European modernism.
pp.19, 29, 65, 106, 124, 139, 195, 201, 250, 302, 310

Rebecca Morrill is Commissioning Editor (Art Surveys) at Phaidon Press based in London.
pp.39, 77, 117, 174, 186, 317

Maia Murphy is Senior Editor at Phaidon Press based in New York.
pp.52, 157

Yates Norton is a curator at the Roberts Institute of Art, London. He often works closely with his companion and collaborator, David Ruebain, on disability justice work.
pp.66, 101, 119, 138, 226, 313

Gabriella Nugent is an art historian and curator based in London.
pp.26, 80, 158, 198, 208, 234, 253, 256, 264, 296

Elizabeth O'Rourke is Editorial Assistant at Phaidon Press based in New York.
p.275

Sean O'Toole is a writer and editor based in Cape Town. He is the author of *Irma Stern: African in Europe – European in Africa* (2021).
pp.135, 152, 209, 215

Vanessa Peterson is a writer and associate editor at *frieze* magazine. She lives in London.
pp.94, 203, 229, 258, 268

Matt Price is a publisher, editor and writer based in London. He has authored two volumes of *The Anomie Review of Contemporary British Painting*.
pp.50, 51, 73, 123, 178

Michele Robecchi is Commissioning Editor, Contemporary Art, at Phaidon Press based in London.
pp.167, 183

Dr. Cleo Roberts-Komireddi writes on South and Southeast Asian art, hosts the podcast *Art Worlds* and is director at Edel Assanti, London.
pp.49, 108, 129, 238, 267, 277, 314, 316

Gabrielle Schwarz is an independent writer and editor living in London. She has contributed to publications including *Another Gaze*, *Apollo*, *Artforum*, *Outland* and *The Telegraph*.
pp.22, 25, 27, 69, 90, 118, 121, 143, 151, 154, 161, 168, 172, 185, 206, 237, 243, 252, 263, 276, 303, 325, 327

Molly Superfine is a doctoral candidate in the Department of Art History and Archaeology at Columbia University, New York.
pp.20, 45, 53, 59, 83, 110, 170, 205, 228, 235, 255, 269, 295, 308

David Trigg is a writer, critic and art historian based in Bristol, UK. He is the author of *Reading Art* (2018).
pp.32, 35, 36, 55, 68, 88, 109, 125, 126, 128, 140, 145, 159, 166, 177, 181, 200, 204, 222, 225, 230, 232, 239, 245, 246, 248, 257, 261, 265, 282, 298, 320

Wendy Vogel is a New York–based writer, educator and independent curator. She is a 2018 recipient of an Andy Warhol Foundation Arts Writers Grant.
pp.17, 33, 131, 141, 193, 197, 199, 305

Allison K. Young is Assistant Professor of Contemporary Art History at Louisiana State University. She specializes in postcolonial and contemporary art of the Global South.
pp.34, 38, 86, 95, 99, 115, 164, 192, 194, 217, 278, 281, 294, 299, 321, 322, 326

Dr. Orin Zahra is the assistant curator at the National Museum of Women in the Arts, Washington DC, examining gender and race in modern and contemporary art.
pp.57, 64, 71, 84, 103, 113, 132, 146, 148, 270

ACKNOWLEDGEMENTS

Thank you to all of the artists and their studios, artists' families and estates, representative galleries, museums, private collections, auction houses and other arts organizations who assisted this publication by providing images and arranging permissions.

We would especially like to acknowledge the following individuals who provided generous assistance, shared knowledge and expertise, and made helpful introductions and connections: Mage Abâtayguara-Örneberg, Bill Angus, Paul Arnett, Lara Asole, Keith Atteck, Paige Auerbach, Valentina Bandelloni, Mike Barnett, Jamie Bayard, Erin Beasley, Andrew Beccone, Stephen Behan, Frances Belsham, Jennifer Belt, Alex Bennett, Ella Blanchon, Maya Blumenberg-Taylor, Anne-Sophie Bocquier, Clara Bondis, Bea Bradley, Martin Brémond, Jennifer Carding, Kirsten Cave, Sinazo Chiya, Phil Clark, Edwige Cochois, Niamh Coghlan, Andrew Cole, Taber Colletti, Dominique Croshaw, Hazel Cuthbertson, Jacob Daugherty, Marie Denkens, Fariba Derakhshani, Clarice De Veyra, Jorien de Vries, Angelo Cacciola Donati, Susan Dunne, Rose Eastwood, Daisy Fornengo, Ilya Fridman, Rachel Garbade, Jack and Kristi Garrity, Andrea Glanninger-Leitner, Ross Godick, Emil Gombos, Kelly-Christina Grant, Susan Grogan, Megan Gross, Rosa Gubay, William Gustafsson, Molly Harrington, Sarah Haug, Nicola Hederich, Isabel Hildago, Grace Hong, Leanne Hong, Elisabeth Ivers, Danda Jaroljmek, Anastasija Jevtovic, Peter Kaiser, Sunaina Kewalramani, Sabeena Khosla, Sarah Kohn, Sydney Krantz, Adriana La Lime, Sophie Lambert, Laura Langeluddecke, Isla Macer Law, Breana Lee, Emily Lenz, Grace Leonhardt, Fiona Leung, Ella Liao, Rob Lloyd, Maya Lisewski, Efrain Lopez, Holly Lord, Kat Lowe, Holly MacGregor, Malyanah Manap, Elizabeth Mann, Erin Manns, Craig Mark, Maddy Martin, Tom McCormick, Quentin Metayer, Andrea Mihalovic, Charlie Minter, Weng Yee Mooi, Peter Nagy, Julie Niemi, Wade Nobile, Grady O'Connor, Milena Oldfield, Natalie Olesky-Piekarski, Miho Osada, Jamie Owen, Pietro Pantalani, Alessandro Pasotti, Michal Patchefsky, Mark Pereira, Javier Peres, Miriam Perez, Allyson Pinon, Princess Pratt, Ronja Primke, Evan Reiser, Kristin Rieber, Agata Rutkowska, Eleni Samantzopoulou, Christian Schmidt, Hala Schoukair, Michael Schultze, Vera Silvani, Catherine Song, Georgia Spickett-Jones, Rochelle Steiner, Diana Stephen, Fabian Strobel, Annie Stuart, Daphne Takahashi, Suheyla Takesh, Hui Min Teo, David Thompson, Poppy Trivedi, Kelsey Tyler, Felicitas von Woedtke, Audrey Warne, Matt Watkins, Alison White, Vince Wilcke, Caspar Williams, David Williams, Kara Winters, Natasha Woolliams, Pete Woronkowicz, Gladys Wu, Magali Wyns, Debby Yip and Juyoung Yoon.

Additional thanks go to Deborah Aaronson, Caitlin Arnell Argles, Sara Bader, Hilary Bird, Clive Burroughs, Stephen Clark, Keith Fox, Hélène Gallois-Montbrun, Julia Hasting, Tom Keyes, Violeta Mitrova, João Mota, Frankie Moutafis, Joanne Murray, Elizabeth O'Rourke, Michela Parkin, Michele Robecchi, Baptiste Roque-Genest, Tracey Smith, Elaine Ward and Jonathan Whale.

Phaidon Press Limited
2 Cooperage Yard
London E15 2QR

Phaidon Press Inc.
65 Bleecker Street
New York, NY 10012

phaidon.com

First published 2022

ISBN 978 1 83866 328 5

A CIP catalogue record of this book is available from the British Library and the Library of Congress.

Commissioning Editor: Rebecca Morrill
Project Editors: Simon Hunegs and Maia Murphy
Production Controller: Rebecca Price
Picture Researcher: Jennifer Veall
Art Direction: Astrid Stavro
Design: Alessandro Molent

Printed in China

All measurements are given height × width × depth unless otherwise specified.

Current place names are used throughout unless otherwise specified.

If this book contains inaccurate information or language that you feel we should improve or change, we would like to hear from you. Please email texts@phaidon.com.